Praise for *Madame Chiang Kai-shek:*

"Laura Tyson Li gives us Mayling Soong, not just Mme. Chiang Kai-shek . . . [and] helps us go beyond Madame's public face to reveal Mayling's private one. Here we find a transnational, postcolonial subject who sought, in her own way, to bridge the reigning binaries of the day: East vs. West, tradition vs. modernity, Confucianism vs. Christianity, masculinity vs. femininity. The story of Mayling Soong, in short, is a story of our times. We would do well to learn from her."
—L.H.M. Ling, Associate Professor of International Affairs, The New School, and author
of *Postcolonial International Relations: Conquest and Desire Between Asia and the West*

"Laura Tyson-Li has brought Mayling Soong back to life and back into the limelight. . . . [a] powerful and exciting book . . . beautifully crafted, well told, and fully fleshed-out . . . a balanced and nuanced portrait."—Murray A. Rubinstein, History Department, Baruch College/CUNY, and editor of *Taiwan: A New History*

"A riveting story, written with beautiful clarity and full of fresh information and startling anecdotes. Warm in her human sympathies yet stern in her criticisms, Laura Tyson Li presents an impeccably balanced portrayal of this weird compound of Joan of Arc and Marie Antoinette. . . . This is the story of the American China that never was."
—Philip Snow, author of *The Star Raft*

"Through the controversial life and turbulent times of Mayling Soong, China's original icon of 'New Womanhood,' Tyson Li explores the story of modern China's chaotic rise and compelling future. Breathtakingly researched and richly drawn, this is a fascinating portrait of one of contemporary history's most enduring and colorful boldfaced names."
—Jeff Yang, author of *Once Upon a Time in China*

"A well-balanced biography of one of the most powerful women in Chinese history . . . absorbing . . . While Tyson Li shows great admiration for Mayling's staunch opposition to Communism and her enviable oratory skills, which often saw her digging deep into the English language to use words even native English speakers found puzzling, she is also highly critical of her unwillingness to truly break free of her conservative shackles. This criticism is most pointed when Tyson Li examines the decadent lifestyle Mayling indulged in, which sharply countered that of her fellow countrymen—a factor that appears to have been frequently overlooked by those infatuated with the glamorous, charming woman. . . . An interesting and detailed account." —*Kirkus Reviews*

"To admirers, the wife of the Nationalist dictator of China and later Taiwan was a symbol of resistance to Communist tyranny; to detractors, she was a crafty 'Dragon Lady' or a quisling of American imperialism. In this absorbing biography, Tyson Li . . . manages a balanced portrait that situates Madame Chiang in an uneasy borderland between East and West. . . . Amply conveying her subject's charisma without falling under its spell, Tyson Li . . . offers a well-researched, fluently written assessment of the life and impact of one of the twentieth century's iconic figures." —*Publishers Weekly*

"Brings to life the little-known facts and dramatic dynamics of China's charmingly well-crafted and influential 'dragon lady.' " —*The Daily Record*

"It's surprising to note that this is the first biography of one of the most politically influential women of modern times, but *Madame Chiang Kai-shek: China's Eternal First Lady* remains the only title to provide the complete story of a woman who seized unofficial and official power during China's civil war. Her position against Chinese Communism and her diplomatic relations affected decades of Chinese-American relations, so this book is key to a thorough understanding of not just the woman, but Chinese politics and influences in particular." — *The Midwest Book Review*

"Petite, elegant, and mighty, Madame Chiang Kai-shek lived to be 105, but when she died in 2003, many Americans had no idea of how powerful a woman she was or of how much she suffered. . . . Li is the first to tell Madame Chiang's dramatic life story. . . . Sensational and indomitable, she infuriated Churchill; put Franklin Roosevelt on his guard; disappointed Eleanor Roosevelt with her narcissism, grandiosity, and insensitivity; and, Tyson Li theorizes, helped jump-start Washington's anti-Communist witch hunts. With access to newly opened files, fluent insights into China's convulsive transformation, and a phenomenal gift for elucidating intricate politics and complicated psyches, Li brilliantly analyzes a fearless and profoundly conflicted woman of extraordinary force." — *Booklist* (starred review)

"An amazing book. Madame Chiang Kai-shek is clearly one of the great characters of history, and Laura Tyson Li does her great justice, coloring her portrait with every hue imaginable. *Madame Chiang Kai-shek* is outstanding history, full of details that have eluded others, couched in a broad perspective that gives Madame more humanity, more uniqueness, and more depth than anything I have ever read. I am pretty familiar with Chinese history over the past century, but this book opened my eyes in many places. Bravo." — Seth Faison, author of *South of the Clouds*

"A fantastic book . . . it lets me really get to know more about this controversial and extraordinary woman. It exposes the historical and political insights into how her husband lost mainland China, and how she influenced American attitude toward Chinese communism. The book would also allow a Westerner to understand China and its government better." — Diana Lu, author of *Daughter of the Yellow River*

"Madame Chiang Kai-shek belongs with Eleanor Roosevelt and Eva Peron as three of the most politically influential women of the past century. In her comprehensive biography, Laura Tyson Li examines the extraordinary life of the Wellesley-educated Chinese aristocrat who married the Nationalist Party dictator of China. . . . Li presents both sides of this complicated woman." — *USA Today*

"Paints a picture of an intelligent, strong-willed, and single-minded woman who had a clear vision of what she wanted for her country. At a time when women even in the United States—one of the up-and-coming socially progressive nations in the world— clung to well-defined gender roles, Mayling defied tradition by becoming active in civic and social life in her native China." — *The Asian Reporter*

MADAME
CHIANG KAI-SHEK

MADAME
CHIANG KAI-SHEK

CHINA'S ETERNAL FIRST LADY

Laura Tyson Li

GROVE PRESS
NEW YORK

Published simultaneously in Canada
Printed in the United States of America

FIRST PAPERBACK EDITION

Library of Congress Cataloging-in-Publication Data

Tyson Li, Laura.
Madame Chiang Kai-shek : China's eternal first lady / Laura Tyson Li.
p. cm.
ISBN-10: 0-8021-4322-9
ISBN-13: 978-0-8021-4322-8
1. Chiang, Mayling Soong, 1898–2003   2. Presidents' spouses—China—
Biography.   I. Title.
DS777.488.C515L52 2006
95 .24'905092—dc21
[B]   2005058858

Map on p. xii by Brigadier General Frank Dorn, U.S.A. (Ret.), originally
from Barbara Tuchman, *Stilwell and the American Experience in China*.

Grove Press
an imprint of Grove/Atlantic, Inc.
841 Broadway
New York, NY 10003

Distributed by Publishers Group West

www.groveatlantic.com

07 08 09 10   10 9 8 7 6 5 4 3 2 1

For Richard and Sienna

Contents

Part III

Part IV

Acknowledgments

*Writing a book is an adventure. To begin with, it is a toy and an amuse-
ment; then it becomes a mistress, and then it becomes a master, and then
a tyrant. The last phase is that just as you are about to be reconciled to
your servitude, you kill the monster, and fling him out to the public.*
                                                        —Winston Churchill

Researching and writing this book has been not only an adventure, but an
odyssey. It has been an undertaking that could never have been accomplished without the help, generosity, and support, moral as much as material, of a great many people. Their names are legion—too many to be listed
here—but a few stand out.

Most of all I would like to thank Harold H. C. Han, founder and chairman of the Himalaya Foundation, for his courage. Mr. Han is that rare
combination—gentleman, scholar, and businessman. I am immensely
grateful for his belief in the project as well as for the foundation's generous
support—without which, it is safe to say, the book could not have been
written. I am also very grateful to Sunny Gong, Snow Li, Jack Shen, and
the staff at the Himalaya Foundation, which provided vital assistance during the research phase of the book.

I am greatly indebted to those who read part or all of the manuscript in
progress and offered encouragement, comments, corrections, and, on occasion, objections. In particular I wish to thank Wang Ke-wen, a scholar of
Republican Chinese history, who read and critiqued the draft with unstinting honesty and insight, and whose knowledge of facts and context contributed immeasurably to the book. I am very grateful to Seth Faison and
Murray Rubinstein, who read the entire manuscript and offered extremely
valuable comments and suggestions. I am also indebted to those who commented on sections of the manuscript: Donald Jordan, Fredrick Chien,
Sabrina Birner, Priscilla Roberts, Judith Evans, John Millus, David

Holmberg, Mavis Humes Baird, and Douglas Estella. Special thanks are due to Robert Reilly, who read early draft chapters and proofed the typeset galleys.

I have been privileged to work with talented researchers: Cecilia Andersson, Catherine Bellanca, Marc Bernstein, Kathy Best, Lisa Marie Borowski, Kevin Bower, Paul Brown, Ronald Brownlow, Virginia Buechele, Lan Bui, Anupreeta Das, Diane Fu, Stefanie Koch, Snow Li, Janet Liao, Bernard Scott Lucius, Glenda Lynch, Sean Malloy, Brian Miller, Greg Murphy, Janet Murphy, Jane Park, Katherine Prior, Hayet Sellami, Mr. Shen, Jill Snider, Tseng Yun-ching, Karen Tsui, Wang Chieh-ju, Wu Shih-chang, and Xu Youwei. Thank you all for your diligence.

I am grateful to patient and helpful archivists, especially (but by no means limited to) those at the following institutions: the Academia Historica; the Nationalist Party (Kuomintang) Archives; the Wellesley College Archives; the Hoover Archives; Wesleyan College; the Rare Book and Manuscript Library at Columbia University; the Library of Congress Manuscripts Division; and the New York Public Library. I would also like to thank Cecilia Koo Yan Zhuo-yun, Jiao Wei-cheng, and Nancy Chi at the Republic of China National Women's League, as well as Cynthia Yen, librarian at the *China News* (now *Taiwan News*), and Isabella Chen, librarian at the *China Post*.

I thank some of the many others who have variously offered ideas, materials, insight, inspiration, encouragement, and/or commiseration (in no particular order): Pamela Howard, Shih Chih-yu, Fredrick Chien, Wang Fong, Bo Yang, Chang Ping-nan, Larry Zuckerman, Peter Montagnon, Robert Thomson, Clara Chou, Betty Lin, Sandra and Chi-yu Li, Roxanne and Chi-hsien Li, Ren Nienzhen, Antonio Chiang, Eva Chou, Jeff Yang, Jay Taylor, Mei-fei Elrick and Malcolm Rosholt, Sabrina Birner, Ping Lu, Chou Wei-peng, Yang Shu-biao, Deborah Gage, Ulrick Gage, Nancy Zi Chiang, Israel Epstein, Tom Grunfeld, Stephen Endicott, Diane Allen, Craig Keating, Sue Hacker, John Cline Bassett Jr., Adele Argento, Edith Hay Wyckoff, Chow Lien-hwa, Chen Peng-jen, Wang Ziyin, Ann M. Jernigan, Mrs. Claude Flory, Hau Pei-tsun, Anna Chennault, John Chang (Chang Hsiao-yen), I-Cheng Loh, Feng Hu-hsiang, Chin Hsiao-yi, Lin Chien-yeh, Alice Chen, Wang Chi, Ann Maria Domingos, and Gen. Robert L. Scott.

Special thanks to the Writers Room and the Aubergine Café, for offering sanctuary while I drafted the manuscript. I would also like to thank

Elizabeth Dawson and Crystal Moh for cheerful help with inputting edits to the manuscript.

I am grateful to the many friends and acquaintances who generously let me stay in their homes while I was doing research in far-flung places, including Lee and Kathy Merkle-Raymond, Vaughn and Abby Chang, Scott and Betsy Tyson, Emmanuelle Lin, Vivian Makhmaltchi, Nancy Li, Berta and Andrew Joncus, Erik D'Amato, Joanne Omang and David Burnham, and Mandy Holton.

I would also like to add a special word of thanks to all the moms, friends, and relatives who babysat or offered playdates, sleepovers, or school pickups and drop-offs for our daughter Sienna while I labored to complete the manuscript: Kenneth and Regina Tyson, Roberta Tyson, Angela Bayer, Brenda Zlamany, Anita McDaniels, Mary Daalhuyzen, Jeffrey Li and Grace Sun, Janet Estella, Vivian Lee, Jeannie Conway, Vita Ose, and Betty Mei.

Last but not least, I would like to thank my husband, Richard Li, for his support and patience; my mother, Roberta Tyson, for inspiring in me an early interest in history; Morgan Entrekin, Grove/Atlantic's publisher, for staying the course; Margaret Stead for her bold and expert edits; Amy Hundley for her tactful shepherding; Tom Cherwin, for his careful copyediting; and my agent, Elizabeth Sheinkman, for her initial belief in the project and continuing support.

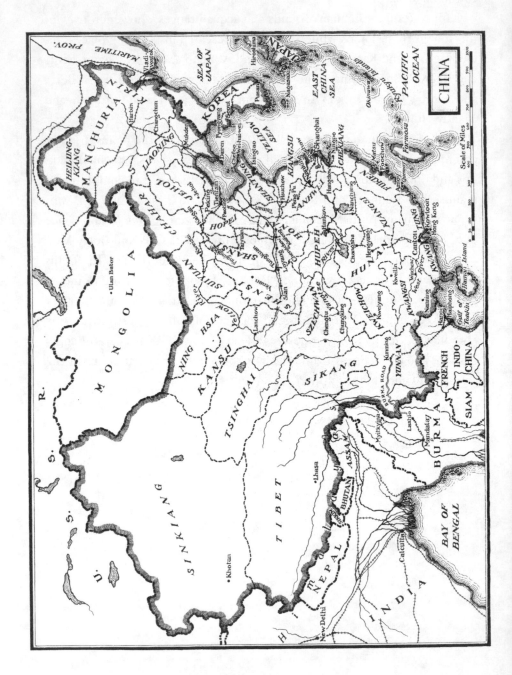

Notes on Chinese Romanization

In a historical work such as this, expressing Chinese personal and place-names in English is an endeavor fraught with dilemmas. Pronunciation variations among Chinese dialects and regions have historically contributed to inconsistent English spellings. Imperfect knowledge of Chinese, English, and/or of the various Romanization systems developed over the past century or so has led to a multiplicity of spellings, some sensible, some whimsical, and others perplexing.

As a rule, I have spelled personal names of key figures who were widely known in the West as they were spelled at the time, or as they themselves spelled them (if known). I have generally followed the Chinese custom of putting the surname first (as in Chiang Kai-shek), but not always (i.e., Mayling Soong, K. C. Wu). Similarly, I have spelled place-names that were well known to English-speaking readers in the manner they were spelled (apart from Peking/Peiping, which, so as not to overly tax the nonspecialist reader with historical explanations tangential to the main story, appears as "Beijing" throughout). The Nationalist Party (variously spelled Kuomintang or Guomindang) appears as "Kuomintang." Apart from these, for which a brief key is provided below, I have generally used the P.R.C.'s Pinyin Romanization system.

Former name spelling	Modern name Pinyin spelling
PLACES	
Burma	Myanmar
Canton	Guangzhou
Canton Province	Guangdong
Chungking	Chongqing
Formosa	Taiwan
Hangchow	Hangzhou

Hankow	Hankou (Wuhan)
Hongkew	Hongkou
Hsuchow	Xuzhou
Kuling	Guling (Lushan)
Mukden	Shenyang
Manchuria	Dongbei
Nanking	Nanjing
Peking (Peiping)	Beijing
Quemoy	Xiamen
Sian	Xi'an
Soochow (Suchow)	Suzhou
Taipei	Taibei
Tientsin	Tianjin
Tsingtao	Qingdao
Yangtze River	Yangzi River
Yenan	Yan'an

PEOPLE

Chiang Kai-shek	Jiang Jieshi
Sun Yat-sen	Sun Zhongshan
Mayling Soong	Song Meiling
Ching Ling Soong	Song Qingling
Eling Soong	Song Ailing
Chang Hsueh-liang	Zhang Xueliang
Chou En-lai	Zhou Enlai
K. C. Wu	Wu Guozhen
Chiang Ching-kuo	Jiang Jingguo
Wego Chiang	Jiang Weiguo
Wellington Koo	Gu Weijun
Lee Teng-hui	Li Denghui
Empress Dowager Tzu Hsi	Cixi Taihou
H. H. Kung	Kong Xiangxi

MADAME
CHIANG KAI-SHEK

Prologue

Her father, Charles Soong, was financier to the Chinese revolution; her mother sprang from one of China's most illustrious families. Her eldest sister, Eling, the Chinese said, loved money; middle sister Ching Ling loved China; and Mayling, the youngest, loved power. Her older brother, T. V., became one of China's richest men and served China as both financier and diplomat. Her two younger brothers prospered in business.

The life of Mayling Soong, the woman who would become Madame Chiang Kai-shek, was one in which public image and private reality often clashed. She was born comfortably, but obscurely, on the cusp of the nineteenth century and lived to see the twenty-first, a feat rare enough in itself. Buffeted by the fortunes of history, her life became inextricably entwined with the rise of modern China, and yet she lived much of it on the sidelines. Like many women of political renown before and since, the role she played on the world stage was landed through family ties and marriage, rather than purely by dint of her own efforts and merits. She saw herself in the traditional feminine role of supporting her husband in his work, yet she transcended her helpmeet status and took on a mantle of her own. At times she was successful in moving beyond the narrowly prescribed confines of conventional behavior and mores for a woman of her era, position, and social class, but her ingrained conservatism prevented her from truly breaking free of the fetters that compelled her to live within the bounds of convention.

Mayling's peculiar mettle was smelted in America and forged in Shanghai. The woman she became was a seamless alloy of Southern belle, New England bluestocking, and Chinese *tai-tai*, or matron. She was a bundle of contradictions: practicality and naivete, intellect and impulse, strength and weakness, romance and tragedy, all melded within her small and delicate frame. She was idealistic yet cynical, independent yet reliant, proud yet down-to-earth. She could be tolerant and yet righteous and rigid. She could be disarmingly warm yet disdainfully icy, spontaneous yet brittle, genuine yet disingenuous. She was famously plucky yet thin-skinned. Loyal to a fault, she was utterly blind to the flaws of those she loved. Possessed of tremendous élan, she was effervescent and exuded a magnetism that captivated even critics. She glowed with an incandescent energy and self-confidence that sometimes gave way to debilitating bouts of anxiety and despair.

Few figures in modern history have been more extravagantly exalted or more viciously condemned, and fewer still have experienced both extremes. In her final years her compatriots began to view her in a more favorable light. But in the West, where she had once been so celebrated, she died virtually unknown, her contribution to history relegated to a footnote. Hers was a life of much sorrow, with flashes of brilliance amid failed dreams, resplendence, and tragedy. Was her greatest tragedy—as she herself intimated in her twilight years—to have lived so long? For all her flaws, she was a woman of indomitable spirit, courage, and determination—and an ardent Chinese patriot—who helped shape China's relationship with the West, and in so doing the course of modern Chinese history.

PART I

Chapter One

Little Lantern

John Stuart Mill once wrote that no one could properly say what is natural to woman till she has been long enough emancipated to show her true instinct and character. . . . The same may be quite as truthfully predicated of the Chinaman.

—James Harrison Wilson, 1901

Mayling Soong was born in about 1898, at the cusp of the twentieth century, the fourth of six children and the youngest of three daughters in a family destined to play an extraordinary and unheralded role in the history of modern China. Her sister Eling was the eldest, followed by another sister, Ching Ling. Next came brother T. V., then Mayling. Brother T. L. would follow a year or so later, and youngest brother T. A. several years after that.

The milieu was Shanghai, that fabled "sink of iniquity" of the "Orient," where the "natives" lived in medieval ghettos in a colony built and run by foreigners in the image of the cities they came from. Nestled near the confluence of the Huangpu River and the East China Sea, Shanghai had been a foreign colony for nearly half a century. France controlled its French Concession and the International Settlement was administered by a council made up of nationals from several countries including England, Germany, and the United States. Vibrant, prosperous, and cosmopolitan, Shanghai's foreign enclaves were a world apart from the rest of China, which was virtually sealed off. The wealth and comfort of the Shanghai elite contrasted sharply with the abject poverty and suffering of hundreds of millions of ordinary Chinese across China and even in Shanghai, who lived as they had for millennia. Vast numbers of Chinese of all classes were addicted to opium. The weak and corrupt Qing dynasty imperial government in Beijing was powerless to stop the opium trade, which was orchestrated by British merchants with the profitable collusion of Qing officials. While Shanghai's foreign enclaves had all the luxuries of a "higher and a better civilization," in the words of one contemporary Western observer, its ancient walled Chinese city, with its "sordid multitudes," was "inconceivably squalid . . . and fills the foreign soul with a sentiment of unutterable disgust."

The Soong family did not live in the Chinese ghetto. Its sights and smells were as unfamiliar and deplorable to them as they were to Shanghai's well-heeled foreign residents. Neither did the Soongs live in the International Settlement or the French Concession, as did many Chinese of both low and high estate—the latter, by virtue of their wealth and social connections, being considered something akin to honorary foreigners. By 1896 Charles Soong had built a house for his growing family in the suburb of Hongkew, once known as the American Settlement. It was located on the north bank of the Soochow Creek, across from the International Settlement, the commercial heart of the city.

At the time Hongkew was far out in the country, and family friends thought Soong eccentric for choosing to live there. Eventually the area was overtaken by urban sprawl, but when Mayling was a girl the house was surrounded by green fields stretching for miles. Date palms grew in the garden and a stream ran beyond the wall that enclosed the front yard. The Soong children quickly learned to scale the wall and gadded about climbing trees and otherwise disturbing nearby farmers, whom the children's indulgent father mollified with coins rather than restrict his playful children to the garden.

Charles Soong had spent many years of his youth in America, where he studied theology at Vanderbilt University before returning to China as a missionary for the Methodist Church. When he built his own house it was a hybrid of traditional Chinese and American antebellum architectural styles. Amid the Chinese flourishes were occidental comforts to which he had grown accustomed during his sojourn in America, including running water, gas heating, and kerosene light. Behind the house was a large vegetable garden that Soong tended himself, shocking status-conscious acquaintances as further evidence of his American eccentricities.

In temperament, Charles Soong was extremely frank, outspoken, and impatient. He insisted on punctuality and did not hesitate to chastise those who possessed "Oriental" notions of time. His directness often offended people. Once he made a decision, he did not waver. His wife, Ni Guizhen, whom Charles called "Mamie," had similarly strong determination and convictions, but she possessed the virtue of patience and spoke only after careful consideration. The Soongs' aim was to make their children cultured, self-reliant, and useful. They were not sentimental parents and from an early age the Soong children were trained not to show emotion. Mayling grew up ashamed to admit fear and rarely wept.

Charles had a fine singing voice and taught his children hymns and other songs he had learned in the American South, including spirituals, Stephen Foster ballads, and, of course, that anthem of the South, "Dixie." His wife loved music too and was one of the first Chinese women to learn to play the piano. Eling, her father's favorite, showed the most talent, but the other siblings enjoyed singing too.

Despite a preference for things American, Soong wanted his children to have a semblance of a classical Chinese education. He engaged for them the same tutor who had coached him in the mysteries of the unfamiliar Shanghainese dialect, who also helped him to catch up on some of the Chinese schooling he had missed in his peripatetic boyhood. Like Soong, Dzau Tsz-zeh was a preacher returned from America, and was best known by his Anglicized name, C. K. "Charlie" Marshall. After fourteen years in America, Marshall had acquired a pronounced Deep South accent.

When Soong studied with Marshall, they resorted to English for explanations, as it was their common language. Soong hailed from the South China island of Hainan, where the dialect was unintelligible to the Shanghainese. Marshall's colorful trench English was a far cry from Soong's gentlemanly version, and irritated Soong so much that what were supposed to be Chinese lessons often became debating matches over the finer points of the English language. Once, Marshall lost his temper: "You, you upstart, you!" he cried. "Why you come pesterin' me wid dat Yankee talk. I bin talking English 'fo you was ever born. Now go 'way and leave me 'lone." Under Marshall's tutelage the Soong children learned the rudiments of Chinese characters and a smattering of the classics, but were spared the years of rigorous drills and rote learning to which students of traditional Chinese schools were typically subjected.

The children's spiritual education was of course not neglected. Mother
Soong was the guiding moral influence in the home and she became more
devout with each passing year. One of Mayling's earliest memories is of her
mother going to a special room on the third floor of the house to pray. She
would spend hours in prayer, often beginning before dawn. Whenever
Mayling or her siblings asked for advice about anything, she would say, "I
must ask God first." She could not be rushed into an answer. For Mother
Soong, this was not a perfunctory affair; it meant "waiting upon God until
she felt his leading." As a young woman Mayling thought her mother excessively pious.

The Soongs kept a Christian home in the best Southern Methodist tradition, veering toward puritanical. In addition to attending church services
and Sunday school each Sabbath, they held daily family devotions. Mayling
hated having to sit through long and tedious sermons while her friends
played, and subtly rebelled during Bible readings. "It must often have
grieved my beloved mother that I found family prayers tiresome and frequently found myself conveniently thirsty . . . so that I had to slip out of
the room," Mayling later wrote. The family's habits were also a model of
Christian propriety. There was no alcohol in the Soong household, and card
games and dancing were forbidden. On Sundays, no games whatsoever
were allowed.

Despite her early distaste for prayers and sermons, the religious environment in which Mayling was raised had a profound influence on her life and
her values. Similarly, her education set her apart from her peers. In an era
when Chinese parents bound the feet of their daughters, kept them cloistered at home, and, if the family was poor, sold them as slaves or even
abandoned them at birth, the Soongs were an anomaly. They were unusual
even among the Chinese elite of Shanghai in that they treated their daughters and sons the same, and made certain that the girls received the best
education available to women at the time. In this respect the family was
advanced even by the standards of the West, where "female education,"
apart from the domestic arts and perhaps a smattering of French, drawing,
and piano, was still a controversial notion.

In any event, traditional Chinese schools—which were at that time private, as there was no public school system—did not accept girls. The first
government-run girls' primary schools were not established until 1907. It

was the nineteenth-century foreign missionaries who had led the crusade for education of girls in China. Chinese generally held that anything more than a rudimentary education for girls was unnecessary and even unwise. But the foreign missionaries were convinced that educating native missionaries, women as well as men, was imperative not only for spreading the gospel, but for transforming the Chinese family and ultimately the nation. China's very salvation, they believed, hinged upon the elevation of women. "The degrading systems of the East are based mainly on the condition of women," argued Young John Allen, an American missionary known as the "great Mandarin of the Methodists" in nineteenth-century China.

As was true for the missionaries themselves, the very presence of mission schools for girls was subversive, even dangerous, for they threatened the patriarchal order upon which Chinese society and government were predicated. They posed a direct challenge to Confucianism, the all-encompassing moral, political, and family code of Chinese society and the justification for not only the scholar aristocracy but the imperial dynasty itself. The perpetuation of the Confucian hierarchy depended on the subservience of women, which in turn required that women remain ignorant. Paradoxically, although the mission schools reached just a tiny portion of the Chinese people, and converts to Christianity were still fewer, it would be difficult to overestimate their impact on the history of modern China. Although they failed miserably in achieving their goal—winning souls for Christ—they were in great measure responsible for many of the changes that China underwent in the late nineteenth and early twentieth centuries. The missionaries and their schools nurtured generations of Chinese patriots and reformers, fueling the rise of nationalism and ultimately helping to bring about the "great revolution."

Mayling's mother was among the first Chinese girls to receive an education, studying at a mission school until she married at the age of eighteen. There she cultivated a passion for learning as well as prayer. She excelled at mathematics, especially trigonometry. Such was her devotion to intellectual matters that she continued to study religion, mathematics, and language until the end of her life. She enjoyed puzzles and studied English, Chinese, and Japanese. Until the age of sixty she paid a scholar to hold stimulating discussions with her.

By the early twentieth century, Chinese reformers were arguing that the education of Chinese women was vital for building a strong and independent

China. The Soong girls were sent to Methodist-run McTyeire, the most fashionable girls' school in all Shanghai. Young John Allen founded McTyeire in 1892 to impart what was called the "gospel of gentility" to the fee-paying daughters of the Chinese elite. The school offered nontraditional female role models in its unmarried, well-educated, and strong-willed missionary teachers, who nonetheless were grooming their charges to be the "idealized vision of the good Christian wife, mother and helper" and a model for Chinese women. Mayling went when she was five, attending kindergarten and staying with Ching Ling in the dormitory. She was devoted to her big sister and often prepared tea for Ching Ling and her friends. Mayling appeared fearless, but after a time one of the teachers discovered that she was waking up at night in fits of trembling. She was experiencing nightmares and having trouble sleeping, and was sent back home to be tutored.

Mother Soong often dressed Mayling in her older brother T. V.'s castoff clothes. The little girl was so round that they nicknamed her "Little Lantern." During their childhood years Mayling developed deep affection for her eldest sister, Eling, who often defended and protected her against bullies. The feeling Mayling held for Eling bordered on hero worship and would endure throughout their lives. The two sisters were always the closest among all the Soong siblings. The older children in the neighborhood liked to tease and play tricks on Mayling. She begged them to let her join their games. One day they made her "it" in a game of hide-and-seek. She covered her eyes and attempted to count to a hundred. When she uncovered her eyes, not a child was to be found. When she realized they had abandoned her, she began to cry. Eling came to her rescue, comforting her and wiping her eyes. And so it would be always.

Chapter Two

Revelation to Revolution

They have borne the light of Western civilization into every nook and corner of the empire . . . The awakening of China may be traced in no small measure to the work of the missionaries.

—His Excellency Tuan Fang,
an emissary sent by the Empress Dowager Tzu Hsi
to study American institutions, 1906

T he story of Charles Jones Soong begins much like those of millions of other Chinese who over the last several centuries left China to seek their fortune, fanning out across the globe. But for a quirk of fate, he would have been just one among the multitude toiling away a lifetime unsung and largely unseen in the Chinese diaspora. Part Cinderella, part American dream, the story of the founder of China's fabled "Soong dynasty" inspired generations of churchgoing Americans and the dedicated China missionaries they supported with their nickels and dimes when the collection plate was passed around every Sunday in churches across America. It made them believe, passionately and absolutely, in the notion that China could and would become a Christian country, and that it was their spiritual and moral duty to lead a crusade for the souls of the Chinese people.

Charles Soong was born on Hainan, an island off the southern coast of China, in 1861. He was the second son of three and had one sister. His family lived in a tiny village called Guluyuan in Wenchang county. The family name was Han, not Soong, which he adopted later, together with the English name Charles. The Han family was of Hakka ancestry. In a country in which one's provincial background is paramount, the Hakka are the only Chinese without a geographical home base. The word "Hakka" literally means "guest families," and throughout Chinese history Hakka have migrated across China or overseas, forced to the margins of society and onto poorer lands. Speaking a distinct dialect, and by repute clannish, stubborn, and shrewd, they have been loosely compared with the gypsies and the Jews of Europe.

Chinese of Hakka blood have become leaders—among them Lee Kuan Yew, the founder of modern Singapore; China's late leader Deng Xiaoping; and Taiwan's former president Lee Teng-hui. The Hakka have historically been regarded with suspicion by authorities in China, as many revolts were fomented by disgruntled Hakka. The most notorious was the bloody Taiping Rebellion, launched in 1851 by Hong Xiuquan, a Christian convert who, after a period of tutelage under a Southern Baptist missionary from America, came to fancy himself the younger brother of Jesus Christ. Hong massed a million-strong army, captured a vast swath of south and central China, and declared the establishment of a new theocratic dynasty called the Heavenly Kingdom of Great Peace, with himself as absolute ruler, seated in Nanking. Imperial armies finally suppressed the rebellion in 1864, but only with European military assistance, and at the cost of over twenty million lives.

Soong was given the name Han Jiaozhun, but as was customary among the Chinese he had additional first names, in his case Jiashu and Yaoru. His father, Han Hongyi, was born in 1829. Soong's father owned a tiny plot 1.2 *mu* in size—just one-fifth of an acre. When not tilling his field, he worked on the docks at the nearby port of Qinglan, or made rope from coir, the fiber found in coconut husks. He died in 1893 at the age of sixty-four. Soong's mother is listed only by her surname, Wang, in Wenchang county records, and the year of her birth is not given. She told her children lively stories to entertain them while educating them in the ways of the world.

The Han family was poor but evidently had connections well beyond Hainan island, because as a boy Soong was sent to Java, now part of Indonesia, on the start of an extraordinary odyssey that ultimately brought him to America—and to Christianity. Legend holds that he was adopted, a practice then common in China, by an uncle with no sons. Wenchang county records say that his paternal uncle's wife was surnamed Soong, and that someone in her family adopted Charles. The "uncle," one of the first Chinese to settle in New England, ran a store selling Chinese goods in

Boston, and brought young Charles to America. As the Panama Canal had not yet been built, the journey took Charles around the southernmost tip of South America, where he saw penguins.

Charles began working in the store but before long his head was full of other notions. In 1879 he met some Chinese students who were part of a pioneering educational mission led by an 1854 graduate of Yale named Dr. Yung Wing, a Cantonese Christian convert who was the first Chinese graduate of an American university. China's humiliating defeat by Britain and France in two Opium Wars, compounded by the Qing government's reliance on foreign military aid to suppress the Taiping Rebellion, persuaded Qing officials that China must master Western military technology. Starting in 1872 some 120 Chinese boys lived with host families in New England towns while they studied English and scientific subjects. Among the supporters of Yung Wing and his mission were a Hartford minister, Reverend Joseph Twichell, and his close friend the celebrated author Mark Twain. The Chinese government canceled the Chinese Educational Mission in 1881, angered that students were becoming too Americanized. Many were converting to Christianity, playing baseball, and even dating American women.

But other factors were at work. Sino-American relations had taken an unpleasant turn. Anti-Chinese sentiment was fueling atrocities in the West and the Chinese government was aggrieved when several of the students were denied admission to West Point and Annapolis. A group of Americans led by Twain appealed to former president Ulysses S. Grant to help prevent the students from being sent home. Grant, who had visited China, willingly complied, but his intervention succeeded only in delaying the departure by about six months. However, the Chinese students had already made an indelible and favorable impression on the New Englanders among whom they lived. Their easy integration into American society challenged the prevailing anti-Chinese sentiments that pervaded the country at the time, particularly in the West. A handful of the students had become so attached to their new home that they chopped off their queues in defiance of the Manchu regime and refused to go back to China. For those who returned, the genie was out of the bottle. As the *New York Times* presciently observed on July 23, 1881, "China cannot borrow our learning, our science, and our material forms of industry without importing with them the virus of political rebellion."

Two of the students Soong met, Wen Bingzhong and Niu Shanzhou, were cousins from Shanghai. In America they styled themselves B. C. Wan and S. C. New. Wan lived in Amherst, Massachusetts, and attended the Worcester Institute of Technology. New lived in Springfield, Massachusetts, and later attended Phillips Exeter Academy in New Hampshire. Charles had never seen the likes of Wan and New, privileged scholarship students who seemingly had the world at their command. They sparked the ambition of the bright though modestly born young man. He began to chafe at the tedium of shopkeeping, and yearned to go to school.

One day in January 1879, he slipped away from the store and made his way to Boston Harbor. There he managed to stow away aboard the *Albert Gallatin,* a cutter in the U.S. Treasury's Revenue Service, the predecessor of the Coast Guard. He was found and brought before the commanding officer, Capt. Eric Gabrielson, who hailed from the Massachusetts whaling port of Nantucket. Soong was taken on as cabin boy. His name first appeared on the *Gallatin*'s muster roll on January 8, 1879, as "Sun." He was described as being sixteen years old and about five feet tall. He played with the captain's young nephew, Harry, and later sent him a photograph of himself inscribed on the back: "Charles J. Soon presented this to his little friend Harrie L. Wimpenney. Think of me when you play out the yard."

Despite his ties to Massachusetts, fate determined that Soong would become an adopted citizen of the Tar Heel State. The next spring, Captain Gabrielson was transferred to the command of the *Schuyler Colfax,* a revenue cutter based at Wilmington, North Carolina. Following Gabrielson, Soong left the *Gallatin* in June 1880 and reenlisted as cabin steward aboard the *Colfax* on the first of August under the name "C. A. Soon." Coast Guard records described him as eighteen years old and five feet, one inch tall. A stern disciplinarian and a God-fearing man, Gabrielson was impressed by Soong and wanted to help him get an education. He introduced the boy to Reverend Thomas Ricaud, minister of the Fifth Street Methodist Church in Wilmington. Soong attended a revival meeting led by Ricaud on October 31, 1880. He was so moved that he decided to be baptized.

Ricaud had himself been adopted by a childless uncle, and although born in Baltimore was raised in Mexico City. He served as interpreter for the port of Wilmington. The *Wilmington Star* of November 7, 1880, announced that on that morning a Chinese convert would be baptized, "probably being the first Celestial that has ever submitted to the ordinance of baptism in North Carolina." (In the West, China was commonly called the Celestial Empire—after the Manchu dynasty's Kingdom of Heaven—and its denizens Celestials.) Ricaud christened Soong "Charles Jones Soon" (Charles added the "g" later). After his conversion Soong gave a talk in which he expressed his desire to be educated and return to his own people as a missionary. In April 1881 he was honorably discharged from the *Colfax*. He did not have the means to attend school, so Ricaud tutored him. Charles took to calling him "Uncle Ricaud." Meanwhile he found a job at a Wilmington printer. Ricaud spoke to Dr. Braxton Craven, president of Methodist-run Trinity College, about enrolling Soong in the preparatory department. Trinity, which then had two hundred students and six faculty, later moved to Durham and was renamed Duke University.

Ricaud appealed to a wealthy North Carolina industrialist famous for his seemingly boundless generosity. When he heard about the bright Chinese boy, Julian S. Carr said: "Send him up, and we'll see that he gets an education." The son of a Chapel Hill merchant and a Civil War veteran, "General" Carr was an American original, a larger-than-life character who made his fortune manufacturing the celebrated Bull Durham smoking tobacco after the Civil War. He then diversified into banking, textiles, railways, hotels, electric and telephone services, newspapers, and Democratic politics. Carr's twin missions in life, apart from his business, were spreading the gospel according to the Southern Methodist Church and furthering the Reconstruction of his beloved South. He was the richest man in North Carolina and one of the South's most successful entrepreneurs.

In the winter of 1881 Ricaud took Soong on the first train ride of his life, from Wilmington to Durham, to meet Carr. By the 1880s the grand Protestant missionary endeavor that began in the latter half of the nineteenth century was nearing a fever pitch across America. Carr was quick to spot a likely-looking potential bearer of the word of God to far Cathay. "Listen, brethren, this missionary question is the burning question of the day, as far as the church is concerned," he once told fellow Methodists. "China is the key to the missionary situation. Bring China to Christ and the world is won." Soong charmed the ebullient General Carr. "He came to my house and lived there as a member of my family," Carr later said. "This was Soong, who is as a son to me." Landing Carr's support was a stroke of incredibly good luck. He became not just patron and mentor but also inspiration to the young Chinese man. In 1881 Soong wrote to his father that he was in a "great hurry to be educated so I can get back to China and tell you about the kindness of the friends in Durham and the grace of God."

The Protestant churches played a highly visible and powerful role in late-nineteenth-century American public life. The overseas missionary movement was widely discussed in the mainstream press and touched the lives of a great many Americans.

With its enormous population, China held the largest potential harvest of souls. "China was the lodestar, the great magnet that drew us all," observed Sherwood Eddy, the dynamic globetrotting evangelist and one of many prominent "missionary statesmen" of the late nineteenth and early twentieth centuries. The American Protestant missionary movement in China gained momentum in the mid-nineteenth century after the Qing court, under duress, concluded a series of unequal treaties with the foreign powers—Britain, France, America, Russia, and Germany—that allowed missionaries to preach freely throughout China, including the heretofore closed interior. The conquest of the American West was nearly complete but the pioneer ethos remained strong, and yearned for fresh opportunity. As Christianity became closely identified with American nationalism, the overseas missionary movement was viewed as but a natural extension of the notion of Manifest Destiny. "How can we better testify to our appreciation of [America's] free institutions than by laboring to plant them in foreign lands?" asked Reverend John Codman, a Massachusetts preacher, in the 1830s.

What began as an exercise in saving souls was soon transmogrified into a vastly more complex enterprise in which diplomatic, commercial, social, military, humanitarian, and ideological motives mingled, sometimes unbecomingly, with the divine. The emphasis shifted from saving souls to saving China. With a zeal befitting the original Crusaders, the dream of bringing China into the fold of Christendom became an American crusade that amounted to cultural and spiritual aggression. But evangelism was not the only goal of zealous American missionaries, who believed that benighted China could enjoy the benefits of the West's manifestly superior civilization only by remolding itself in America's image. Some argued that the Anglo-Saxon race had been "especially commissioned" with bringing Christianity and progress to backward peoples. Darwin's theories on survival of the fittest were abused to buttress this notion of "the white man's burden," as well as Americans' view of themselves as a "chosen people" in both a religious and a political sense.

The foundation of China's transformation would be mass conversion to Christianity, in tandem with abandonment of millennia of superstition, Confucianism, Buddhism, Taoism—"heathen" traditions and practices that, as Americans and the missionaries they supported saw it, kept China shackled in wretchedness. America was ascendant, and there was no reason for Americans to doubt their ability—indeed duty—to do well while doing good in the world. The foreign mission movement grew into a complex and unique form of "big business," comprised of large-scale multinational corporations with multimillion-dollar budgets whose chief export products were Christianity and American culture.

The missionaries carried with them an absolute faith in the moral and cultural superiority of American life and institutions. Once anchored in Christianity, they believed, China would adopt the hallowed American ideals of liberty, egalitarianism, and self-determination (promoters of this view invariably overlooked black slavery, the decimation of the American Indian, and women's disenfranchisement) and social progress, scientific advances, and prosperity would surely follow. In 1901, at the height of the China missionary fever, Mark Twain sounded a satirical cautionary note: "Leave them alone, they are plenty good enough just as they are," he wrote of the Chinese. "And besides, almost every convert runs a risk of catching our civilization. We ought to be careful . . . for, once civilized, China can never be uncivilized again."

Over time Americans came to regard China with a foggy mixture of paternalistic sentiment and altruism. It was not simply the tremendous investment of time, energy, and funds, but the peculiar emotional investment, as intense as it was naive, by Americans in the cause of uplifting China through Christianity that would inflame such national soul-searching, bitterness, and profound feelings of betrayal when that elusive dream met its inevitable and painful demise.

* * *

Soong entered Trinity in April 1881 as a preparatory student. He was the first Asian to attend the college, but not the first student of color: there were twelve Cherokee Indians in the preparatory department that same year. Trinity president Craven reported to the college's board of trustees that Soong "was doing very well in every way, studies closely and will be successful." Soong impressed the Durham Sunday school, through which Carr channeled his support, with his swift mastery of English and his hope of spreading the gospel in his native land. His greatest desire was to persuade his parents to throw down the "idols of heathenism" and embrace Christianity. He also impressed his classmates with his sociability and playful spirit.

A year later, the Board of Missions of the Southern Methodist Church decided Soong should continue his studies at Vanderbilt University's theological department. There he could receive the specialized training he needed for the life of the missionary preacher he would be on returning to his native China. Carr agreed to pay for his studies, and Soong headed for Nashville in the autumn of 1882. At Vanderbilt Soong studied English, mathematics, modern languages, theology, moral philosophy, and church history. He did not excel academically, but classmates appreciated his wit and admired his penmanship. He spent summers at the Carrs' house, where he knotted hammocks to sell. Carr, a staunch believer in the dictum that the Lord helps those who help themselves, encouraged him in this enterprise.

Soong was lucky to have landed on the East Coast, where "Celestials" were still something of a novelty and the strident anti-Chinese fervor prevailing in the West was less in evidence. There, agitators fearful of both competition from cheap labor and the supposed degrading moral influence of the Chinese stirred up antipathy toward them. Chinese were often physically abused or worse. "John Chinaman" was the most innocuous of the ethnic slurs as negative stereotypes abounded. Hostilities mounted to the point that in 1882, the year Soong enrolled at Vanderbilt, the U.S. Congress passed a Chinese Exclusion Act suspending all immigration from China. It also banned Chinese from becoming American citizens and forced those already in the U.S. to register.

In 1885 Soong graduated from Vanderbilt's theology department. He seized on a great new ambition—to study medicine and return to China as a medical missionary. Carr agreed to support his medical studies, but the powers-that-be of the Methodist Episcopal Church, South, had other plans. Bishop Holland N. McTyeire, chancellor of Vanderbilt University and head of the church's China mission, refused Soong's request to study medicine. McTyeire wanted him sent out on mission as soon as possible. He wrote Young J. Allen, Soong's future boss, in Shanghai: "We thought better that the Chinaman that is in him should not all be worked out before he labors among the Chinese. Already he has 'felt the easy chair'—& is not averse to the comforts of the higher civilization." McTyeire hoped that if Soong was a success, then other Chinese would be inspired to follow his example. "The destinies of many are bound up in his case," the bishop wrote Allen. Soong was ordained and appointed a missionary to China in late November 1885, waiving the usual two-year waiting period. He arrived in Shanghai on January 13, 1886.

Given the generous treatment he had received in the U.S., Soong was in for a rude shock. Filled with excitement, homesickness, and romantic notions of returning to his native land to preach the gospel, he was wholly unprepared for the chilly reception he received, not only from foreigners but from his own people. He was equally ill-prepared for the culture shock he faced returning "home" and for the privations of missionary life. Although he had experienced relatively little racial prejudice in America, in China he found himself in the worst possible predicament. His long sojourn in America had rendered him virtually foreign—and thus despised—in the eyes of his countrymen. Foreigners disdainfully regarded him as a second-rate "Chinaman" who had been stripped of his Chinese-ness.

This was particularly true of Young J. Allen. Before arriving Soong had been praised as the "brightest and best educated Chinaman you ever saw," but Allen, superintendent of the Southern Methodist mission in Shanghai, was unimpressed and complained about Soong, sight unseen, to Bishop McTyeire. Among Soong's deficiencies Allen listed the fact that he did not speak the dialects of the Shanghai area. "Soon never will become a Chinese scholar, at best will only be a *denationalized* Chinaman, discontented and unhappy unless he is located and paid far beyond his deserts." Soong later wrote wistfully of his mixed feelings to a friend in North Carolina: "Yes, I am walking once more on the land that gave me birth, but it is far from being a homelike place to me. I felt more homelike in America than I do in China."

Allen was the son of a wealthy Georgia cotton planter and a graduate of Atlanta's Emory University who came to China in 1860 and remained until his death in 1907. Most missionaries labored among the poor, who made up 90 percent of the population, but Allen eschewed the unlettered and unwashed masses in favor of the literati. He passionately believed in the educational approach to missionary work and had little taste for conventional evangelizing. He was convinced the salvation of China would be achieved not by old-fashioned preaching but through, as he phrased it, an "intellectual approach, that is by attacking the Chinese mind through a combination of science and the Biblical message." Science, Allen discovered, was particularly effective in "uprooting and destroying faith in their own theories of the world and nature." He had an enterprising bent and with the help of scholars wrote, translated, and published prolifically in classical Chinese, the stylized written language inaccessible to ordinary Chinese. His newspaper, *Wanguo Gongbao (Review of the Times)* was a Christian publication targeting a general audience. Its influence extended up to the emperor, who awarded Allen the rank of magistrate, a rare honor for a foreigner. Allen even adopted the elitist air of a Chinese official and invited no Chinese but the intelligentsia to his home—which excluded Soong.

Soong's early missionary experiences were not calculated to inspire confidence. To begin with, the church had not provided him with funds sufficient to last the journey across the Pacific. Then, upon arrival in China, he was unceremoniously demoted from the status of "missionary" to that of "native preacher"—in contemporary terms, he was made a "local" employee, which held much lower status and salary, rather than the "expatriate" employee he had been led to believe he would be, on a par with white missionary preachers. Worse, he was forced to comply with the laws of Manchu-run China, which decreed that all male subjects must don the long, flowing Chinese dress and wear their hair braided in a queue with the forehead shaven high. He resented having to trade his three-piece suit for the melon-peel cap and traditional gown. Especially loathsome was the queue, a potent symbol of Manchu domination. "He hated very much to have to become a Chinaman again in matter of dress, food, etc., but there was no help for it," Allen wrote. "He is terribly spoiled and will no doubt fret a good deal before he finally settles down. Indeed should he become utterly disquieted I should not be surprised—for he is naturally of a restless unquiet temperament." To Soong Allen wrote, "A great work is before you—measure up to it and you will accomplish great results." As it turned out, a "great work" *was* before Soong, although perhaps not of the sort that Allen had envisioned.

Allen initially placed Soong in Soochow, near Shanghai, to study the local dialect before being sent out to preach. His starting salary was fifteen U.S. dollars per month. Disgruntled, Soong went over Allen's head and wrote directly to the mission board asking for a raise, which was declined, and complaining of a lack of funds to cover traveling and living expenses. Soong resented Allen for ignoring "my privileges and equality which I am entitled to," and considered applying for a transfer to Japan.

Soong did eventually resign himself to his circumstances, and nearly a year later, he was sent to Kunshan, a walled city near Shanghai. There he served as a circuit preacher and teacher in a school for converts and their children. Perhaps spurred by the loneliness of his post in Kunshan, Soong's thoughts turned to female companionship, something he missed from his school days in America. Chinese mores were exceedingly strict and women were not permitted to associate with men. Incredibly, he ran into S. C. New, one of the Chinese students on imperial scholarship he had met briefly in Boston nearly a decade earlier. New introduced Soong to his eighteen-year-old sister-in-law, Miss Ni Guizhen. Not only was Miss Ni a member of one of China's most illustrious families, she was a Christian. Born June 3, 1869, Guizhen was the second daughter and her parents' favorite. Unusually for a Chinese woman, she was educated. She had recently graduated from a mission school for girls, and spoke English, albeit hesitatingly. Equally rare among well-bred young ladies, her feet were not bound. Deemed ugly by prevailing standards of beauty, her big feet were of little import to Soong, who had spent too much time among independent-minded American womenfolk to be enamored of crippled feet.

Blue-blooded Miss Ni traced her ancestral line back to Xu Guangqi, an eminent scholar who lived from 1562 to 1633. A prime minister during the Ming dynasty, Xu was converted to Catholicism in 1601 by the Italian Jesuit Matteo Ricci, under whose tutelage he pioneered in bringing European learning to China. Xu translated Euclid's geometry and other European works on trigonometry, hydraulics, firearms, astronomy, and geography. Miss Ni's mother (Mayling's maternal grandmother) was raised in the Xu family home in a western suburb of Shanghai called Xujiahui—"the Xu family gathering place." She married the family tutor, Ni Yunshan, and adopted his Episcopalian faith.

Soong's friend, New, acted as matchmaker, a tradition that worked to Soong's benefit. His humble origins and direct American ways were compounded by his still shaky grasp of Shanghai dialect and manners. New obtained the approval of Miss Ni's parents and Soong and she were married in the summer of 1887. The wedding was attended by the great and the good of Shanghai society and was accompanied by a suitably lavish dowry. Soong had vaulted into China's aristocracy.

Although the anger Soong initially felt upon his return to China had long since subsided, the underlying reasons for his dissatisfaction remained. Chief among these was pay. Evidently Allen never did raise Soong's salary, even after Soong married and started a family, even though it was within his power to do so. The discrimination in pay between native preachers and American missionaries still deeply rankled. In 1890 Soong asked to be "located," which meant ceasing to be an itinerant preacher, a request likely prompted by the birth of his eldest daughter, Eling, that year. He was appointed a part-time minister in Shanghai. By 1892 he had left the mission entirely to simultaneously pursue several careers, each with seemingly equal energy, enthusiasm, and success.

To supplement his income Soong taught English and was so popular a teacher that his services were sought after at schools across Shanghai. He was active in the Moore Memorial Church and helped found the Chinese YMCA. He also became an agent for the American Bible Society and sold Chinese-language Bibles through a network of native colporteurs. The ink he got on his fingers in North Carolina apparently never quite wore off, because in 1896 he founded a publishing company called the Commercial Press. He began printing Bibles and religious tracts, and branched into textbooks of Western learning, then in high demand. Seeing entrepreneurial opportunity in China's need to industrialize, he became one of the first agents importing manufacturing equipment and other machinery from overseas. He learned how to install and run the equipment. In this connection he became acquainted with leading Shanghai industrialists and was named a senior manager at a flour-milling company.

But of all his endeavors, that of the greatest portent was his work in support of the revolutionary Sun Yat-sen. Soong had relinquished his youthful dream of saving China through the word of God, but he plunged himself into a new vision of redeeming his troubled country through revolution. In 1892 he met the frustrated young Cantonese doctor who dreamed of revolution and the modernization of his homeland. Like Soong, Sun had "tasted Western ink," in his case in a Hawaiian mission school. Both men were Christian, and both had Hakka blood. Both were Cantonese, Hainan then being part of Canton province, and they spoke a similar dialect. And both had a burning desire to remold China. Sun believed that Triads, or secret societies, of south China had enormous influence but lacked intellectual leadership. He sought to unite and harness the power of these guilds and fraternal organizations, many of whom were already opposed to the Manchu dynasty, to carry out the revolution.

Sun persuaded Soong to join a secret society he founded around 1894 called the Revive China Society. The group's aim was to "revitalize" China by overthrowing China's Manchu rulers and establishing a republican form of government. After the group launched a failed revolt against the Qing dynasty in Canton in 1895, Sun spent most of his time in exile drumming up financial support for his revolutionary activities from overseas Chinese. Soong, the preacher-turned-entrepreneur, became one of Sun's closest confidants and supporters. By 1905, Sun had begun to formulate his political philosophy, the Three Principles of the People, drawing inspiration from the Gettysburg Address. Lincoln's "government of the people, by the people, for the people" closely corresponded to Sun's principles of *minzu*—people's nationalism, or freedom from foreign domination; *minquan*—people's power, meaning democracy; and *minsheng*—people's livelihood, sometimes interpreted as socialism. Over time he honed these into a coherent set of guiding principles he believed were the key to rescuing China from foreign domination and backwardness. Sun envisioned China's regeneration as taking place under a strong central government that would lead the country into modernity and democracy in stages. Initially there would be an interim period of "political tutelage"—enlightened dictatorship—

during which the people would be educated in the institutions of democracy. Only after that would the country be ready to advance to the next developmental stage and become a fully fledged democratic state.

For years Soong worked day and night at the revolutionary cause, secretly serving as Sun's right-hand man—treasurer, secretary, host, friend, and benefactor. Soong's printing press churned out not only Bibles and missionary tracts but revolutionary pamphlets. Sun and his associates often stayed at the Soong home and the revolutionists held secret meetings there. Even Mrs. Soong did not know the nature of the highly dangerous work her husband and Dr. Sun were doing.

Chapter Three

America's Moon
Is Rounder

Now is the time for the West to implant its ideals in the Orient, in such fashion as to minimize the chance of a dreadful future clash between two radically different and hostile civilizations.
— President Theodore Roosevelt, 1908

From the earliest days, the relationship between America and China has been colored by sentiment and riven by conflicting emotions. At the turn of the twentieth century, when Mayling Soong was a girl, Americans and Chinese viewed each other with a jumble of seemingly contradictory images, emotions, and motives. Some Americans inveighed against the "Yellow Peril," while many others, despite discomfort, disease, and danger, dedicated—and often lost—their lives ministering to the body, mind, and soul of the "heathen Chinee." For their part, many Chinese despised Americans as "foreign devils," resented their self-righteous proselytizing, and feared their military might. Still, many Chinese admired America's achievements in science and medicine, the democratic ideals upon which the United States was founded, and its spirit of civic duty and community service. Then, as perhaps now, the dissonance resulting from the deeply ambivalent views each side held of the other was irreconcilable.

Emblematic is China's name for America. China is called the Middle Country—*Zhong Guo*—but America is *Mei Guo*, Beautiful Country. Dating from the nineteenth century, the name reflects an irresistible attraction to all things Western, especially American. It was an attraction fueled by disillusionment with the weak Qing court and China's repeated humiliating defeats by the Western powers. It also grew out of a sense of shared ideals and aspirations among Chinese intellectuals, who looked westward for inspiration in their quest for the modernization of China. Such was the desire to emulate the West, and the belief that America was more advanced in nearly every way, that the Chinese often said: "The moon is rounder in America."

Charles Soong was a Chinese patriot, but he believed an American education was best for his children. The girls went to the McTyeire School for Girls, named for Bishop McTyeire, where both teachers and textbooks were imported from America. Mayling's older brother T. V. and her next younger brother, T. L., attended high school at Shanghai's St. John's University, founded by the Episcopal Church, once the most acclaimed university in China. One morning in May 1903, Soong called on an old Vanderbilt classmate-turned-missionary, William Burke, at his Shanghai parsonage. Soong wanted to send Eling to Wesleyan Female College in Macon, Georgia. Wesleyan was a Southern Methodist institution chartered in 1836, the first college in the world for women. Eling was only thirteen, but she spoke good English, and college entrance requirements were less stringent then. Burke wrote to the president of the college, DuPont Guerry, who responded positively and even offered to let Eling stay with his family until she felt ready to live in the dormitory.

Most Chinese believed it more prudent to save for a dowry than to send a girl to college, let alone send her abroad to study. But the Soongs wanted to educate their daughters so they would be equipped to work for the betterment of China, and China had no women's college. En route to America in 1904, Eling was detained for three weeks by immigration officers in San Francisco. She was released only after the Board of Missions of the Methodist Church pulled strings in Washington. For the first year at Wesleyan Eling studied as a subfreshman and lived with the Guerrys. She was liked by her fellow students and had no trouble getting used to college life. Soon she abandoned her pigtail for the more fashionable pompadour. A photo in the *Atlanta Constitution* of September 10, 1905, shows her looking every inch the American schoolgirl, clad in a blowsy Gibson-girl dress with her hair piled high beneath a wide bonnet.

As a pioneer among the Soong children in studying abroad, Eling honed the tough and manipulative personality for which she later became known. Her character and nerve were on full display when she met President Theodore Roosevelt in January 1906 with her uncle B. C. Wan, who had been dispatched on an imperial inspection tour of the American education system. Eling had not forgotten her treatment at San Francisco. "Why should a Chinese girl be kept out of a country if it is so free?" she angrily demanded of Roosevelt. "We would never treat visitors to China like that. America is supposed to be the Land of Liberty!" Roosevelt apologized, but privately he regarded the Chinese as an "immoral, degraded and worthless race."

In 1907 it was time for Ching Ling to go to Wesleyan. To her parents' consternation, little Mayling insisted on going along too. She was far too young to attend college, but she brandished a promise her parents had once made when she was ill—that if she took her medicine, she could have any wish she desired. Ching Ling and Mayling embarked from Shanghai in mid-1907 in the company of B. C. Wan, who was leading a group of students to America. Mayling was evidently influenced by her father's hopes that one of his children might become a physician. On the Pacific crossing, a young Englishwoman on her way home from Shanghai chatted on deck with the exuberant Mayling. "And what do you want to be when you grow up?" she asked. The nine-year-old replied: "I want to be a doctor." Taken aback by such progressive ambitions in a little Chinese girl, the Englishwoman said: "A doctor! Oh, my dear, I shouldn't think you would like that, you know. You would have to cut off people's legs, did you know that?" Surprised, Mayling pondered a minute before replying: "Then I don't want to be a doctor. It would be too dirty."

Mayling and Ching Ling went to study at a small private boarding school in Summit, New Jersey. The school was run by Clara Barton Potwin, a kind and energetic woman whose father had taught some of the first Chinese students to come to America. She had lived and traveled in the Far East. The sisters enrolled in the fall of 1907 and stayed for a year. An old photograph shows Potwin and some of her students, four of them Chinese, sitting on the front steps of the house in which they studied and lived. Mayling is perched on the railing of the stoop dressed in a dark sailor suit with white piping and a giant bow tied on the top of her head. Her manner exudes confidence. Ching Ling, who went by her English name Rosamonde, is sitting farther back on the steps, partly in shadow, shyly smiling at the camera.

Mayling often played at the Summit home of Dorothy Jaegels, a fellow student. She loved to ride in the Jaegelses' pony cart. The sisters "became

Americanized so fast we hardly remembered they were Chinese," Jaegels recalled. They soon replaced their Chinese outfits with American dresses and learned to speak English "apparently overnight." Mayling was as irrepressible as Ching Ling was reserved. The children played tag and hide-and-seek, but Mayling's favorite was blindman's buff. This game made her terribly excited and she would "dart about like a small tornado."

Louise Revere Morris, the librarian at Summit's public library, recalled Ching Ling as a shy, pretty girl and a prodigious reader who chose books "far beyond the taste of the average girl of her age." Mayling's literary tastes ranged from Peter Rabbit to Dickens, but for the most part she loved to drop by the library to see what Morris was doing. Determined to have Morris's undivided attention, Mayling would check to see no one else was there before making her entrance.

After school ended, Mayling went to New Hampshire for the summer of 1908. She stayed in the town of Meredith, where she attended a private summer school on the shore of Lake Winnipesaukee. "Yesterday I nearly drowned," she wrote a friend. "A Philadelphia girl caught me by the arm, but please don't tell anybody for I am greatly ashamed." Mayling enjoyed collecting stones and lakeside shells with a newfound friend, eleven-year-old Frances Moulton. She and Frances picked berries and cherries together, and roomed next to each other, knocking on each other's wall.

At summer's end, Mayling and Ching Ling headed south to Wesleyan to join Eling in Macon. They registered for classes on September 5, 1908. Following her confident signature in the matriculation book, Mayling wrote in her age as ten, while Ching Ling listed fifteen and Eling, who was beginning her senior year, eighteen. Mayling's registration was in name only; Ching Ling was placed in what was called the subfreshman class. As Eling had been, the girls were taken under the wing of the Guerrys.

A private tutor, Margie Burks, was engaged to teach Mayling, because as a Chinese girl she could not be admitted to public schools. Burks's mother, Mrs. M. M. Burks, was a professor of English at Wesleyan. A dowager-like woman, Mrs. Burks helped shape the impressionable minds of generations of Wesleyan students, and Mayling was no exception. She took the little girl in hand and became her surrogate mother. She attended to Mayling's attire as well as her education, taking her shopping for dresses, shoes, and hats. Mrs. Burks believed in the old-fashioned virtues of nobility, singleness of purpose, and duty to those less fortunate, and seldom missed an opportunity to impress these principles upon her charges. Those who knew Mrs. Burks found Mayling's later idealism to be reminiscent of her teachings.

Macon was a well-heeled town in the heart of the Old South whose charming antebellum architecture survived the Civil War. Antebellum attitudes were equally enduring. Mayling too became imbued with the spirit of the Confederacy. Once during a summertime visit up north, she was assigned by a teacher to describe the Union general William Tecumseh Sherman's infamous march to the sea that burned Atlanta to the ground. She wrote: "Pardon me, I am a southerner, and that subject is very painful to me. May I omit it?"

Mayling was an eager, saucy, precocious—and on occasion precious—child. She was very lively and often into mischief. While her older sisters struggled to acquire American mannerisms and figures of speech, Mayling adopted them effortlessly. Already she was known to make liberal use of the quick and clever tongue for which she would later become famous. Often she could extricate herself from awkward situations with a few words, delivered with a deftness that belied her foreign origins. Cosmetics were regarded as slightly vulgar at straitlaced Wesleyan, and once Mayling was seen with a touch of color on her cheeks and lips. "Why, Mayling, I believe your face is painted!" an older girl said accusingly. Mayling shot back: "Yes—China-painted." Her sisters feared that her lively tongue might get her into trouble, for she was often heard commenting freely on the strangeness of Americans. "She will never learn to watch her tongue," Ching Ling said.

After Eling graduated in 1909, the three sisters visited the home of Eling's classmate Blanche Moss in the tiny northeast Georgia town of Demorest in the foothills of the Blue Ridge Mountains. Demorest had been founded as a utopian experiment in Christian living. Drinking, smoking, and dancing were banned. Eling stayed three weeks before heading back to Shanghai, but Mayling and Ching Ling remained for the summer, as due to the altitude the temperature was much cooler than in sultry Macon. The three sisters were an exotic sight. One Saturday they donned their brilliantly colored Chinese silk dresses and created a stir by strolling down the main street, where bearded mountain men and farmers gathered to sell chestnuts, chickens, and other goods.

Mayling liked Demorest so much that she decided to stay on when Ching Ling went back to Wesleyan. That school year, 1909–10, she attended Piedmont College, a small Congregationalist-backed institution in town, where she received special tutoring in English. College records show that she finished with a 93.7 percent average in her studies, which included reading, spelling, grammar, the Bible, physiology, arithmetic, and serving. This last was a domestic science course intended to "prepare young ladies to take that initiative which modern society expects of the cultured hostess."

One of Mayling's schoolmates at Piedmont, Genevieve Fisher, remembered her as "always smiling" and always at the head of her class. Mayling "didn't mind a bit" when people teased her about being Chinese. Ironically, it was in America that she first came into contact with those less fortunate than she. It amazed her that many of her fellow eighth-grade students were grown men and women who came from far away in the hills. Many had taught primary school for years to save enough money to attend Piedmont. "All these people were greatly interested in me, and, for my part, I began to get an insight into the lives of those who had to struggle for a living and for even the means to acquire an elementary education," she later wrote. "My contact with these people as a girl influenced my interest in the lot of those who were not born with a silver spoon in their mouths."

All three sisters returned to Wesleyan in the fall of 1910 to find the college had a new president. William Ainsworth was a minister and a leading Prohibitionist campaigner who went on to head the Southern Methodist Church. The residence of this austere Georgian Methodist became a second home to Mayling. She lived in the college dormitory but spent much time at the Ainsworths' apartment. She quickly became inseparable from the Ainsworths' daughter Eloise, who was two years younger than she. They raced through the halls of the college and climbed the fig trees on the back lawn.

Mayling's mischievous streak would often have gotten her into trouble were it not for her quick sense of humor. Neither was she averse to flights of melodrama. One day Mayling was pouting over a quarrel she'd had with Eloise. Supposedly they had already made up, but Mayling was still making a show of being put out. "Because Eloise was so afraid her friend was hurt, I decided to speak to Mayling about the beauty of forgiveness,"

Mrs. Ainsworth recalled. "I asked her if she wasn't ashamed to show such an ugly spirit; but her reply, accompanied by a slight twinkle in her eyes, came back quickly, 'Why, no, Mrs. Ainsworth, I rather enjoy it.'"

Mayling was called a brilliant student, but her intense curiosity was at times unrelenting. Her mathematics teacher had difficulty persuading her to accept basic algebraic principles. She insisted on knowing the reason for everything. She did not have to struggle to get good marks, but she thought prayer would not hurt. One day soon after she began freshman year, she sneaked in to visit Eloise, who was sick in bed. Mrs. Ainsworth came in to find Eloise crawling back under the covers, and demanded an explanation. "Mayling just came in, and she's so worried because today she takes her first college exams, so we got down on our knees and prayed to the Lord to let her pass." A fellow student recalled Mayling as a "tempestuous" music pupil. She would often say to her long-suffering piano teacher, "I do not wish to play this piece," and toss it on top of the piano, pulling out a composition she liked better. A friend remembered that Mayling had journalistic ambitions and was very bright but a little snooty, once shunning a Chinese girl by saying she was not of her class.

As the youngsters on campus, Mayling and Eloise took a great interest in what the older girls were doing. They looked up to them and felt deeply miffed at being left out of their activities. "The big girls had secrets. How we wanted to know what they were talking about!" Mayling recalled. "But they would never tell us; they would say, 'Run away now, children.'" The two loved to eavesdrop as the college girls entertained their dates, peeking through the blinds of the parlors where these chaste assignations took place. They would rush back giggling to Mrs. Ainsworth to tell all they'd seen. "Two more romantic little souls could not be found, and they were as excited as anyone when one of the girls became engaged," Mrs. Ainsworth recalled.

Not to be outdone by the big girls, Mayling hit upon a plan. Not long after she began to study Latin, she organized a club consisting of herself, Eloise, and Marjorie Gugel, whose aunt worked in the college administration. Inspired by the college sororities, they dubbed the club the "Tri-Puellates," fashioned after the Latin word "triumvirate"—although its membership soon exceeded the founding trio. It had strict rules, including one that members were required to chew gum during business meetings. The chief business of the club was eating, and to this end the college dietitian was accepted as an honorary member, so she could supply free goodies.

The Tri-Puellates published a newsletter containing bits of gossip about the older girls. Mayling was literary editor, and Eloise and Marjorie shared duties of art editor and reporter. A typical society column might begin: "Of all the girls on this campus, none is so pretty as Betty Brown" or "Dorothy Dell is the cleverest girl in the whole school." Written on ordinary school exercise paper, five copies were sold each day at five cents each. The hardest part was deciding how to spend the profits—would it be ice cream, salted peanuts, or Hershey bars? "It must have been priceless," Mayling wrote later, "because there was one character who appeared every day called 'Madame Telle Storie,' dealing with beauty aids and advice to the lovelorn, comments on campus gossip, and had what I fondly imagined a decided *Tatler* and *Spectator* slant." Sadly, no copies have survived. Marjorie recalled Mayling as "so full of pep, vivacious, and always grand company."

Never one to be timid, Mayling was not embarrassed by people's curiosity about her because she was Chinese. When she entered the freshman class in the fall of 1912, she was elected sergeant-at-arms, carrying the banner and leading the cheering. The college yearbook for 1913 listed Mayling as a member of the tennis club and the Billy Crows, a club whose members met at the "crow's nest," a platform around an old oak tree, and ate licorice. The club flower was the black tulip. The Wesleyan girls often went to College Hill Pharmacy—known as "the Pharm"—for ice cream sodas.

At Wesleyan Mayling began to cultivate the great confidence and pride for which she would later become famous. She was convinced she had made much faster progress during the years of special tutoring than she would have attending classes. She was a quick learner and prided herself on her intellectual abilities, claiming to have read all of the works of Dickens by the time she was ten. She discovered a taste for long words and tried them out on her older sisters. "I've just met the most atter*ac*tive girl," she told Eling one day. "Oh, she's simply *fanisating*."

After Ching Ling graduated in 1913, Mayling went north to be near her brother T. V., who was then attending Harvard. She would enter nearby Wellesley College in the autumn. "Good bye, Macon, Georgia!" she said as the train left the station. "When we see you again—if we do—we will be old and doddering, with our great lives behind us."

Charles Soong, meanwhile, was playing an instrumental role in the political upheavals taking place in China. After a series of failed revolts, the revolution of 1911 finally toppled the moribund Manchu dynasty. Sun Yat-sen was hailed as the George Washington of China for his role as the inspiration behind the revolution, although he was out of the country when it began. He quickly returned and, soon after, the Republic of China was established with Sun as provisional president. But he proved unable to maintain power, and in 1912 he reluctantly yielded his post to Yuan Shikai, a former prime minister of the Manchu government, who established a military dictatorship. China subsequently sank into a prolonged period of warlordism and political chaos, during which Sun Yat-sen was sidelined from power and prospects for the realization of his dreams appeared grim.

Chapter Four

College Days

The Higher Education of Women is one of the great world battle cries for freedom; for right against might. It is the cry of the oppressed slave. It is the assertion of absolute equality. . . . Wellesley College desires to take the foremost place in the mighty struggle. All our plans are in outspoken opposition to the customs and prejudices of the public. Therefore, we expect every one of you to be, in the noblest sense, reformers.
   —Henry Fowle Durant, founder of Wellesley College

When Miss Mayling Olive Soong set foot upon Wellesley's leafy campus in the late summer of 1913, she was fifteen years old, a precocious age for Wellesley. Although she had completed the freshman year at Wesleyan, she was made to start again as a freshman. She was a short, stocky figure clad in American clothes with no pretensions to style. Classmates recalled that she was so American that at first she refused to admit she was Chinese. "I am Southern," Mayling would declare in the soft, languorous tones of Georgia. The self-described "hot confederate" was unimpressed by her first visit to campus. She marched into the office of the college registrar and sniffed: "Well, I reckon I shan't stay 'round here much longer."

The chill of the climate was matched by the cool reserve of the New England temperament. Mayling carried with her, at least at the outset, a measure of the inferiority complex felt by the people of the south toward their richer and technologically superior northern conquerors. As a Chinese girl who would be seen as somehow representative of her race, she felt doubly pressured to prove herself at Wellesley. But her irrepressible self-confidence, coupled with her early family training that emotions must be kept hidden, carried her through.

By the time Mayling arrived at Wellesley, the college on the shores of Lake Waban had lost some of the crusading spirit of its founders. The noble and romantic ideal of the dame schoolmistress carrying the "three R's" and the Christian message to the Western frontier had been diluted by bourgeois aspirations, even as the frontier itself had disappeared. The college motto was *Non Ministrari sed Ministrare*—"Not to be ministered unto, but to minister to." An old joke held that it meant "not to be ministers, but ministers' wives." An alumna observed ironically decades later that Wellesley students were not groomed to be the "heroines of their own lives" but rather "first ladies in the lives of big men." This was perhaps unfair, but it was true that Mayling would emerge feeling trapped between her Wellesley training as an independent and intelligent woman on one side and society's narrow expectations for women on the other.

Wellesley did not then have dormitory space to house the freshman class, so Mayling and her classmates boarded with families in the village of Wellesley. After classes she would return to the Porters' house at 6 Cross Street, mount a stool in the living room, and make speeches to Mrs. Porter. In the process she often lost her balance, and a slipper too, as she tried to stay upright on the wobbly makeshift soapbox. In her sophomore year Mayling moved onto campus and lived in Wood Cottage.

Trying to find her place at Wellesley, Mayling joined gatherings of the Southern Club occasionally and drawled with fellow Southerners—even though the drawl was used by teachers as an example of how *not* to enunciate. The soft "y'all" and "I reckon" somehow survived four years of college in New England, but her accent became more clipped. She had many lovely Chinese gowns, but she rarely wore them in public. Instead she wore the sensible middies, skirts, and sturdy clodhopper shoes that were in vogue at Wellesley, though often sporting a flash of silken color on her blouse or jacket.

Undergraduate mores and tastes were in flux. In 1913 the senior class held its first prom, with gentlemen guests and dancing. Bobbed hair and cubist art were coming into vogue; nonetheless Wellesley students still toted fancywork bags and tatted during lectures, to the annoyance of professors. But storm clouds lowered over innocent coed pursuits. Europe was in turmoil, and by August of 1914 the continent was engulfed in war. As Mayling began her sophomore year, spirited debates over the women's

suffrage movement gave way to sober discussions of war, peace, and preparedness. The pacifist movement was strong. Wellesley students were
exposed to both sides of the European conflict through lectures, and students raised funds for both German and Belgian relief efforts.

Mayling was a determined and intellectually curious student. "She kept
up an awful thinking about everything," observed Anne Kimball Tuell, one
of her professors. "She was always questioning, asking the nature of ideas,
rushing in one day to ask a definition of literature, the next day for a definition of religion." She pondered moral matters and was a stickler for truth.
At that time students did not pursue a defined major; instead the college
required them to specialize in two departments, plus take courses in a
variety of other fields. Mayling chose to concentrate on English literature
and philosophy. "She was easily bright at her work, wrote and spoke a finer
English than that of the average student, an English as idiomatic as any
of ours," wrote Tuell, one of her closest confidantes and mentors at
Wellesley. "[But] Mayling was not by any means a profound grind." She
took French and music—theory as well as violin and piano classes—
throughout college. She also took courses in astronomy, history, botany,
English composition, biblical history, and elocution.

The required course in Old Testament history made a particularly lasting impression on the girl from China, who felt that the Bible was part of
America's cultural foundation. "Perhaps I, as a foreigner, could see more
clearly than my schoolmates how closely the make-up of the country had
followed the principles of Christianity," she later recalled. "I connected
God's abundant blessing of America, whatever its foibles and sins, with the
keeping of the Lord's teaching."

Mayling's closest friend at Wellesley was Emma DeLong Mills, with
whom she would remain in close contact until Mills's death in 1987.
Mayling was "much admired, not for her beauty in those days, but there
was a fire about her and a genuineness"—something "strong and honest
and aspiring and individual" in her that appealed to people, Tuell wrote.
A fellow alumna who lived in Wood Cottage with Mayling recalled that she
had a "certain pride, the charm of culture." It seemed she always looked
at Americans with a "feeling of quiet amusement." Her later much-
vaunted wit and charm were then less in evidence, perhaps because among
friends, Mayling did not feel the need to perform. "We all liked her in the

house, and took her for granted as one of ourselves, quite forgetting any foreignness in her," wrote Tuell, who notwithstanding affectionately called her "my heathen Chinee," which Mayling accepted in good humor.

She was not entirely sweetness and light, however, and even as a teenager began to show a dark side to her temperament that would periodically manifest itself throughout her life. "She was often in her mood sober and sombre," Tuell noted, and on occasion could be "really moody and quite willing to show when she was bored." Her bursts of feverish activity were punctuated by spells of lethargy and idleness so pronounced that friends worried about her. "She would work good and hard for a while, and then suddenly she would refuse to do anything, work or play," her friend Helen Hull remembered. "No one could budge her. We thought she was lazy, or sulking, but she just brushed us off. Then suddenly she was flying around again." Mayling recalled these episodes as "fits" during which she would shut herself in her room for a week or ten days and stay up to the early hours of the morning reading. When she fell into those moods she was "cross as a bear," even "churlish," to her friends, she later wrote.

In her junior year Mayling was selected to join Tau Zeta Epsilon, one of six Wellesley societies open to upperclassmen. Known to Wellesley students then and now as "Tizzie," the society was dedicated to the "cultivation and dissemination of an artistic spirit, leading to a closer observation of Nature." Mayling was not especially athletic but played tennis and joined the class basketball team clad in ladies' sporting attire of the day— middy and bloomers. She once stayed at the home of a friend after classes let out for the summer. To retrieve the mail each day one had to ride a bicycle. One late afternoon Mayling came in, dirty, tired, and disheveled. "Where in the world have you been?" her astonished host asked. "I thought it was my turn to get the mail, and here it is," Mayling replied. "But you don't know how to ride a bicycle," the host pointed out. "I do now," Mayling replied.

Early in her college career, it troubled Mayling's friends that she seemed to feel so little ethnic pride, for she had told them she was "expected by her people to bring back to them the best that she had culled from American civilization." She appeared to them so thoroughly American in dress, manners, and thought that they found it difficult to imagine her returning to her native land. But during the early part of her sophomore year, she underwent a subtle transformation. None of her friends could pinpoint exactly when or why the change took place, but she started to talk less of America and her American acquaintances and more of China and her family connections. She began to articulate a "zealous desire to return to her native land and to put to use her Western education and training." She expressed sadness that China's contributions to civilization had been overlooked by the West and regretted that she knew so little of her native country. The ambition, spirit of leadership, and keen sense of mission in life that would later place her on the world stage were beginning to emerge.

Mayling's preoccupation with China was intensified by turbulence both in her homeland and in her family. While she was safely tucked away in the wooded hills of Wellesley, her parents shuttled between exile in Japan, where they had fled with Sun Yat-sen in the summer of 1913 following a failed armed revolt led by Sun against the dictator Yuan Shikai, and visits to Shanghai. After graduation from Wesleyan in 1913, Ching Ling joined her parents in Tokyo to help them and Dr. Sun plan for a new revolution. Charles Soong handled Sun's finances, and Eling served as Sun's secretary. Sun was married and had three grown children, but also courted Eling and was said to have bought her a fur coat with donations from revolutionary supporters. Her parents were appalled by the idea of Sun marrying their eldest daughter and instead she married Kung Hsiang-hsi, scion of a well-to-do North China family who was serving as secretary of the Chinese YMCA in Tokyo.

When Eling left Sun's service in September 1913, Ching Ling stepped into her shoes. It was not long before romance bloomed between the shy, beautiful girl barely out of her teens and the failed revolutionary more than twice her age. By November 1913, the idealistic young lady was clearly smitten: "I can help China and I can also help Dr. Sun. He needs me," she wrote Mayling, the only family member in whom she confided about the romance. Soon after, she and her parents returned to live in Shanghai, but she secretly kept in contact with Sun, who remained in Tokyo.

By early 1915 Charles Soong's health was deteriorating and he canceled plans to travel to America to visit Mayling and T. V. He consulted a renowned specialist at the Imperial University of Tokyo and was diagnosed with Bright's disease. Also known as nephritis, or chronic kidney disease, the debilitating condition gave him frequent headaches and left him nearly blind in the right eye.

Soon after, in March 1915, Sun sought a divorce from his village wife so he could marry Ching Ling. By June, her parents had learned of the lovers' intention to marry and, horrified, forbid it. Ching Ling defiantly vowed she would marry Dr. Sun or no man at all. Her distressed parents locked her in her bedroom in an attempt to prevent what they viewed as an abhorrent match. Undaunted, she managed to escape to Japan in October, and she and Sun were married in Tokyo on October 25, 1915.

A great furor ensued. Her parents followed her to Tokyo on the next steamship and wept and pleaded with Ching Ling to give up the marriage. Soong even appealed to the Japanese government to nullify the marriage, arguing that Ching Ling was underage and had been forced into the scandalous union, to no avail. Throughout the controversy over Ching Ling's elopement, Mayling staunchly supported her sister in the face of her parents' wrath. The elder Soongs eventually resigned themselves to the marriage and gave the newlyweds traditional wedding gifts, but Soong later confided to his missionary friend William Burke: "Bill, I was never so hurt in my life. My own daughter and my best friend."

Mayling was much sought after in the circle of Chinese students at Harvard and other nearby colleges. Her brother T. V. often visited with good-looking young men who were keenly interested in Mayling but whose interest was not reciprocated. "There always seemed to be some nice Chinese boy or other on the doorstep of Wood," a friend noted. After her parents' consternation at Ching Ling's elopement, Mayling became worried that her parents would try to force her to accept an arranged marriage on her return home. It was perhaps such fears that prompted her to become engaged to Peter Li, a Harvard student from China's Jiangsu province. Nothing more is known of the engagement, which was soon broken off. It must have been made in an uncharacteristic fit of youthful rebellion, because for all her curiosity, independence, and high spirits, Mayling was disinclined to challenge authority, particularly that of her family, of which she was very proud. At college she was especially close to T. V., who after graduation from Harvard in 1915 went to Columbia University in New York City to study finance. She called him "Brother" and always sought his advice and permission if she wanted to do anything out of the ordinary.

As the return to China drew near, Mayling began to fear that her Chinese had deteriorated. The looming return was a challenge to which she looked forward with both longing and trepidation. She feared the difficulties she would face in a world whose cultural standards she had grown away from, and confided to a friend, "The only thing oriental about me is my face."

Just months before Mayling's graduation, the U.S. finally entered the European conflict. The declaration of war on April 6, 1917, precipitated a handful of war weddings among Wellesley students. Eighty seniors signed up for a first aid course. Students knitted khaki sweaters and socks for soldiers, prepared "soldiers' boxes," and "adopted" French war orphans. The class yearbook, *Legenda 1917*, was dedicated to the ancient Greek deity Hera, "who guided the Argonauts through many devious wanderings. . . . For each of us has a golden fleece to seek, and a wild sea to sail over, ere we reach it, and dragons to fight ere it be ours." The mythological allusion held true perhaps more for Mayling than for her classmates.

The thirty-ninth annual commencement ceremony was held on Tuesday, June 19, 1917. Mayling O. Soong was one of thirty-three Durant scholars, recipients of the highest academic honor conferred by the college. At the senior class supper, newly minted graduates toasted the Class of 1917 as they marched forth to "enlighten the world," a mission Mayling evidently took to heart. Graduates debated such topics as "On How to be Reasonable, Though Women" and "As Missionaries." They sang the alma mater. Then the Class of 1917 and Mayling Soong, a determined round-faced girl of about nineteen, stepped out from the cocoon of Wellesley into a world at war.

Chapter Five
Belle of Shanghai

The profession of marriage is the one most important profession for every woman, and one not to be subordinated by any other profession or inspiration.

—Mayling Soong

After graduation from Wellesley Mayling took a train to Vancouver, where she boarded a steamship bound for China. Leaving her friends, especially Emma Mills, and the world she had known so long was wrenching, and as the train pulled out of New York's Grand Central Station she broke down and wept. She was acutely aware she was embarking on a new life in a world she barely knew but in which she already assumed she would play a significant role. "If ever I have any influence," she wrote Mills after seeing a trainload of Chinese laborers en route to France, "I shall see to it that no coolies are being shipped out, for China needs all her own men to develop the mines." It was an extraordinarily bold, even presumptuous, statement for a nineteen-year-old girl, and presaged the magisterial figure she would one day become.

When she set foot once again on the land of her birth on July 20, 1917, she confronted challenges in adjusting to a culture and values that clashed with those she had absorbed during ten years in America. She left Wellesley brimming with dreams and lofty ideals but neither practical skills nor concrete plans, apart from grand but vague aspirations of bettering China and the assumption she would marry. Infused with a tremendous sense of both entitlement and noblesse oblige, she felt an intense but as yet inchoate ambition. Her return to China marked the beginning of a decade of transformation and the discovery of her life's mission, as well as a lifelong struggle to find her identity on the cusp of East and West.

Like her father before her, Mayling carried back to China not only the language, manners, and mores of the people among whom she had sojourned, but an unshakable belief in the quintessentially American notions that one can shape one's own fate and that one has a moral obligation to better the fate of others. In the China to which she returned in the summer of 1917, these were radical beliefs, and they would not translate well across the vastness of the Pacific Ocean. During her time in America, she had constructed in her mind an image of what China ought to be, an image that could not be reconciled with what it then was. When her absolute certainties inevitably collided with the ageless inconstancies of China, she would cling to them all the more tightly.

Shanghai was the most prosperous, exotic, and freewheeling city in the Far East, immortalized in American popular imagination by such songs as Irving Berlin's "From Here to Shanghai," recorded by Al Jolson in 1917. "If God lets Shanghai endure, he owes an apology to Sodom and Gomorrah," one missionary said. One could buy French dresses and American shoes and books, go to Italian opera, and have one's hair done in a permanent wave using the latest technology. One could shop for the latest fashions on Nanking Road by day and listen to that new and decadent American music called jazz by night. Turbaned Sikh policemen directed traffic on bustling streets, broad and well-paved. Tree-lined residential boulevards boasted fine mansions on spacious lawns set behind high iron fences. The majestic Bund, with its bright lights and Western-style buildings, bordered the waterfront, where straw-sandal-clad coolies carried trunks on the jetty. But there was a vast gulf between the opulent lifestyle of the city's foreign inhabitants and its Chinese elite, and the abject poverty and misery in which most of the port city's Chinese population lived.

Shanghai society was an unlikely melange of businessmen, diplomats, missionaries, revolutionaries, socialites, poets, refugees, ronin, gangsters, and fortune-seekers. There were White Russians fleeing the Bolshevik revolution; there were the scions of great merchant dynasties such as the Kadoories, the Sassoons, and the Hardoons, descendants of Baghdadi Jews who had built extensive trading networks spanning the Far East. There were missionaries of every stripe laboring to save Chinese souls. There were also compradors, Chinese power brokers who acted as intermediaries between Chinese and foreign businesses. A Portuguese term meaning "buyer," the comprador was an institution in the treaty port cities—an indispensable trading partner for foreigners who spoke no Chinese. The Chinese gentry disdained the comprador as the uneducated "head servant of servants," and said that to the comprador, even the foreigner's fart smelled fragrant, but they envied his powerful and lucrative position. Generations of compradors facilitated trade between China and the West while adopting elements of the lifestyle and mores of the foreigners with whom they worked. The compradors became a class unto themselves, a hybrid peculiar to China's semicolonial treaty ports. It was with the comprador class that the Soong family was most closely identified.

Mayling moved into her parents' house at 491 Avenue Joffre in the exclusive enclave of the French Concession, the Soongs having given up their country house in Hongkew. The European-style residence held sixteen large rooms, not counting kitchen and baths. It was set in a beautiful garden and had an extensive lawn for playing tennis and croquet. The servants' quarters, Mayling boasted to Emma Mills, were better than the dorm rooms at Wellesley. She and her brother T. V. shared the entire third floor.

Mayling took on the task of managing her two younger brothers, whose behavior and poor academic showing distressed their parents. T. L., eighteen, was a year younger than Mayling, and T. A. was ten. "I have complete control over the boys," she wrote Mills. "I have whipped the younger one several times, & they are both afraid of me." To her mother's delight, she began teaching Sunday school to a class of boys, and grew especially fond of a chubby fourteen-year-old who called her "Sir." Another early challenge was taking charge of the household. "We have five maids and seven men servants. Let me tell you it is no joke!" She was frustrated by the fact that when she became angry at the servants, she lost all ability to speak Chinese and was forced to ring for the butler to interpret.

Her difficulties in communicating in her native tongue prompted her parents to insist that she study Chinese, for only if she knew the language could she do anything for China. Although she spoke the Shanghai dialect, she could not read or write Chinese well. She was invited by many Shanghai schools to teach but turned down all offers in favor of engaging an old-fashioned scholar to tutor her several hours a day in the classics and calligraphy. She memorized her lessons in the traditional way of schoolchildren, chanting them aloud while rocking the body rhythmically. The tutor was "terribly strict, and expects me to accomplish the 'almost impossible,'" she wrote Mills. She persevered in her studies for many years, later translating Chinese folk tales and stories from history. Several were published in an American magazine called *The Freeman.* She studied the stories of the French writer Guy de Maupassant to help her in translating "vulgar" Chinese novels. These she had difficulty reading, as they were written in classical Chinese, but given their explicit content she found it too "embarrassing" to ask her male tutor for explanations.

Living at home after ten years away proved an adjustment. "It seems very queer to have a family," Mayling wrote Mills. She found it hard to remember she was not free to "do and think what I please." Initially she had little time to reflect because she immediately plunged into the family's active social life, in addition to devoting herself to her studies and piano lessons twice a week. She went to many dinners, teas, and other affairs and her family often entertained at home. At such functions she was invariably quizzed on the "ways and manners of the 'foreign devils' among whom I have been residing the last ten years," she wrote Mills, using a Chinese colloquialism for Westerners. "I wonder if that is the reason I feel so 'divilish' since I came home!"

In the afternoons she practiced the piano, tutored T. A., and attended committee meetings on raising funds for famine victims or the Red Cross. In the evenings the Soongs took a drive in the family Buick, or went to the movies or theatre. She compared the music in Chinese theatrical performances to the banging of chafing dish lids at a Wellesley temperance speech she once attended. Her family chided her for lacking appreciation for Chinese music. "I have not yet assimilated the things . . . Oriental," she confessed. She complained that the various currencies in circulation made shopping confusing, as many shops accepted only one currency. "The Oriental mind, you see, is complicated," she wrote Mills. "When I first came home, I got cheated right and left, and I do not doubt that even now I am at a disadvantage."

Adjustment to life in their native land, even in worldly Shanghai, was particularly difficult for Mayling and her brother T. V., because of all the Soong children they were the most Westernized. Their impatient and demanding temperaments brought them into conflict with the imperfection, be it the result of inexperience or fatalistic lassitude, that they encountered in China. A visitor at the Soong house recalled seeing Mayling ring the bell for a servant and ask her to clean a dusty table, exclaiming, "These servants simply don't know how to clean a room." She then watched as the servant tried to do the task but finally in exasperation snatched the cloth and briskly finished herself. "I suppose most people would say I'm losing face by doing this," she said. "But I can't stop to think of those things." She dismissed her maid, she claimed, because she could execute her own orders in less time than it took to explain them. "All the years in democratic America have had their effect on me," she claimed rather unconvincingly in a letter to Mills.

American practices, of a sort, prevailed in the Soong home on October 10, 1917, the seventh anniversary of the uprising that led to the establishment of the Chinese republic under the leadership of Sun Yat-sen. As it was China's National Day, Mayling and T. V. begged their mother to give the servants the day off. Mother Soong humored them, and the family dressed in their oldest clothes and ventured into Shanghai's biggest market to do their own grocery shopping. "We *actually* bought our vegetables etc from the stands," gushed Mayling, thrilled by the novelty of the mundane expedition. "You can well imagine what my aristocratic mother thought of the whole business!" Back at home the entire family descended on the kitchen—normally the express preserve of the servants. Each member made a dish; Mayling's contribution was fudge. After lunch the children wanted to go to the horse races but decided against it, as their parents, pillars of the church, would have been aghast.

While conventional notions of class went unchallenged, race was another story. T. V. and Mayling were friends with an American newspaperman named George Sokolsky, who broke a social taboo by marrying a woman of mixed Caribbean-Chinese blood. Interracial liaisons in the concubine tradition were quietly tolerated, but intermarriage was viewed with horror by Chinese and foreigners alike. Foreigners believed it damaged the prestige of the white man in the Far East, and those who did marry Chinese were said to have "gone native," a grievous social offense. T. V. belonged to a group of male students returned from studies overseas called the "Flip Flap Club," who together with Sokolsky organized the first dance in Shanghai where Chinese and Westerners danced together. The event was the talk of the town.

The China to which Mayling returned after her prolonged absence was a land in great social and political ferment, and Shanghai was at the heart of it. Ancient mores were fast becoming obsolete, at least among students and the intelligentsia. There was an unslakable thirst among China's young urban elite for the fresh ideas and knowledge offered by the West. Many Western works of literature and thought, from Darwin to Shakespeare, from Tolstoy to Marx, were translated into vernacular Chinese, making them accessible to a wide readership for the first time. On the heels of the Russian Revolution, some young people were attracted to the ideals of communism.

The right of women to assume an equal place in China's traditionally male-dominated society was one of the many radical notions gaining currency. One work that struck a particular chord in the imagination of impressionable young Chinese intellectuals was the Norwegian playwright Henrik Ibsen's play *A Doll's House.* Young women as well as men were inspired by Nora's rejection of a loveless marriage and middle-class convention to defy their patriarchal families for a life of independence and true love. Some experimented with "free love"; others refused to submit to arranged marriages or abandoned such marriages for unions based on love. For generations "Nora" was a code word for women's liberation. Although change was slow to trickle down to the vast majority of oppressed and illiterate rural Chinese women, among whom foot-binding remained widespread despite a ban as early as 1902, the seeds had been sown.

Marriage was a prospect that occupied much of Mayling's interest and attention after her return to China, but one she viewed with anxiety and ambivalence. She poured out her feelings in letters to Mills. As the youngest daughter of the respected and well-to-do Soong family and the sister-in-law of Sun Yat-sen, she was much sought after. Suitors both Chinese and foreign flocked to the Soong house. A frequent caller was "H. K.," whom she knew from America and whose father ran the Jiangnan Arsenal, an important Chinese arms and munitions manufacturing complex. There was a "Mr. Yang." There was a Frenchman she had met aboard ship en route from the U.S. and with whom she spoke entirely in French, as she proudly boasted to Mills, and a Swiss man too. "I like them: but that's all," she wrote Mills, confiding she had already "lost my head" over a Dutch architect, "Mr. Van Eiveigh," she'd met onboard ship returning to China. "He asked me to marry him, and the family here is greatly wrought up!" she wrote.

"The way the family scorns him because he is a foreigner would make you think that he is a Barbarian!" For all their modern ways, the Soong family was, in fact, extremely traditional in outlook.

Mayling's older sisters were eager to throw her a grand coming-out party in the autumn of 1917, but she was not interested, as she had "met my fate"—the Dutchman—although her parents disapproved. "Since I cannot marry someone I really care for, I shall not marry for anything else except fame or money," she declared to Mills, affecting a precociously world-weary tone. "I know you think that I am mercenary, but . . . now all men are alike to me."

Soon the novelty of household responsibilities, suitors, and social engagements started to wear thin. Mayling began to chafe at the strictures placed on her as a young unmarried daughter of privilege in Shanghai. She was not permitted to leave the house without one of her sisters or her mother. She had never been so strictly chaperoned. She missed her Wellesley friends and the "semi-intellectual confabs" she used to have with Mills. "I just feel my mental powers getting more and more dulled every day," she lamented. "I must make an effort to be intelligent and to keep up interest, and not be worried because I see a speck of dust on the mantelpiece!" She eagerly awaited Mills's letters and subscribed to several American magazines, including the *Atlantic* and the *Saturday Evening Post*.

Mayling began to yearn for "real" work and a career, but apart from teaching and factory work, "respectable" jobs for women in Shanghai at that time were virtually nonexistent. Indeed, large numbers of young women who flocked to China's largest and most cosmopolitan city with dreams of an independent life in a bohemian idyll found themselves forced to make ends meet by resorting to the city's ubiquitous sexual services industry in one or another of its myriad permutations. For a young woman of Mayling's social background to break with family and class to become a Chinese George Eliot or Marie Curie, for instance, was an extremely daunting prospect, not least economically, and one that Mayling was unwilling to contemplate. Yet she was intermittently miserable as she was. "The life I am leading now will end up in marriage only," she lamented despairingly to Mills. She dreaded becoming a burden to her brothers if she did not marry, yet feared she would "degenerate mentally" if she did. Her married sisters were putting their heads together to make her a "grande alliance," arguing that if she did not marry while she was young, what would she do later? At one point Mayling lost her temper and shut herself in her room, threatening to return to America if the subject was raised again. She longed to talk to a man "as a human being, and not as a girl," she wrote Mills. "We certainly were mere infants at college! I haven't gotten to be a woman yet; but I am in that initiating stage of development called 'teething.'"

Mayling's fit of pique over her sisters' attempts at matchmaking did not last long. Ching Ling visited Shanghai in November 1917 and introduced her to Trinidad-born Eugene Chen, owner-editor of the English-language *Peking Gazette* and a close associate of Sun Yat-sen. Chen's paper was suppressed shortly afterward and he took refuge in Shanghai, where he subsequently founded the *Shanghai Gazette*—and courted Mayling, a wife and children notwithstanding. "He is very clever, and brilliant, but horribly egotistic and vain," she wrote Mills. "He is coming to call on me this week, and I hope I won't be rude."

In the autumn of 1917 Mayling was invited to join the National Film Censoring Committee of China. The best among the weekly screenings were Pathé and Victoria pictures, she wrote Mills; the others had "too much mushy love-making, and rolling of eyes." She met a typical missionary lady who decried movies because she felt spiritually aggrieved after seeing one and vowed never to go again. Mayling said she thought movies were "all right." The missionary retorted, "Would you like to be found there if Jesus Christ were to come to the world then?" Mayling repressed a desire to say, "Sure . . . provided that it was a screamingly funny one!" and made a face once the missionary's back was turned.

Mayling's film-censoring duties led to an experience emblematic of the alienation she would always feel in her native country. Somehow eluding chaperons, one evening in late autumn she set out alone for a censorship committee meeting and found herself lost in a Shanghai slum. As she frantically hunted for the address, the streets darkened and she stumbled into a maze of "dark narrow filthy alleyways." She grew terribly cold and was "scared to death," she later wrote Mills. She was afraid to take a rickshaw because she could not understand the dialect spoken by the rickshaw coolies, who looked so "menacing." Just as she was becoming desperate a Western man passed by in a carriage. She hailed him. He was greatly surprised to find an upper-class Chinese girl wandering about that part of town alone at that hour, and to her enormous relief he took her in his carriage. After hunting for an hour he found the address, dropped her off, and promised to come back for her later. "It seems very funny that I should find the greatest comfort in the English language in China," Mayling mused. It would not be the last time that she would look to a Western man to be rescued in time of extremity.

That autumn Mayling's high-strung temperament began to affect her health. In October she submitted to "hypodermic treatment" for a stubborn two-month case of "acne" after painful steam and massage treatments as well as Chinese medicine had failed. She was so distressed by the affliction that she "cried out of pure nervousness." Her mother would only let her out of the house "much bepowdered, and then only at night," she wrote Mills. "I am seized with such unreasonable and unreasoning fits of temper that sometimes I think I am going insane." By mid-December she was so desperately bored at home she decided to ignore the offending pimples and venture out anyway.

The death of an uncle soon after plunged her into despondency. "Dada, I don't know what is the matter with me—I feel so terribly moody and lonesome,—as though I were the sole surviving mortal in the world!" she wrote Mills in January 1918, using her nickname, with its connotation of "father," for her friend. "I wish you were here with me,—and let me just have a one-big hula hula cry!" She felt life was futile and empty. Although marriage was preferable to the "awful loneliness" of existence she so dreaded, "The average conversation between an average man and his wife would drive me to distraction," she wrote. She also worried about the responsibilities of raising children, especially if the husband lacked resources. But if one married for wealth alone, she fretted, should the fortune be lost there would not be even a "particle of affection to keep up one's courage!" She was toying with a proposal from a "Millionaire"; her relatives thought her a "fool" not to accept. But since returning to China her eyes had been opened to the value of self-respect as well as money, she asserted, concluding: "I shall never marry without money; at the same time equally certain am I that I shall never marry for money."

That winter, in early 1918, Charles Soong fell seriously ill with the Bright's disease that had troubled him for several years. He did his best to entertain Julian Carr, his old patron from North Carolina, who visited Shanghai in February on a junket to the Far East, but he was bedridden soon after. His eyesight was failing and Mayling spent much time reading aloud to him and nursing him. He was irritable and she had difficulty keeping him from eating foods forbidden by the doctors. She massaged him every night with olive oil, as his skin had become dry as parchment. In March he was hospitalized.

During her father's illness Mayling was again plunged into emotional turmoil. "I have such a hot temper that it needs great effort to control myself," she wrote Mills. By April 1918 her weight had fallen to 107 pounds from 130 at Wellesley and her family spoke of "sending her off to recuperate." Her father's illness was not the only source of her discontent; she struggled with her own demons. Money would never make her happy, she wrote Mills. "I lie awake nights thinking that I am getting no where," she lamented. She was equally upset that her hopes of marrying Mr. Van Eiveigh, the Dutch architect, had been thoroughly quashed. He wished to visit her and she had an "awful row" with her family because they refused to let him come. "They are afraid I am going to marry him if he comes, and who knows but they are right," she wrote Mills. "I feel like burying my head in the pillows on your couch, and cry[ing]."

Mayling felt frustrated and hemmed in by the norms of society and family, but preferred to conform rather than rebel and risk condemnation. As she saw it there were only two avenues open to her in China—she could either live by conventional mores or flout them entirely and be branded a "New Woman," an epithet she viewed as deeply unsavory. "As I am anxious that the 'Returned Student' class should not be confused with 'The New Woman' class, which really is quite shocking in their inability to distinguish . . . license from liberty," she wrote Mills, "I am bound to observe and to respect the old conventions which irritating as they are, at least bar women from actions questionable not only in themselves but in their influence," she wrote. "Ergo—drat them all!"

Mother Soong brought Charles home from the hospital, arguing that only God could cure him. She refused to let him be "sweated to throw off the poison," as the doctors had insisted. She belonged to the Apostolic Mission Faith, which did not believe in medicine, and mission people stayed in the house, constantly praying for Charles. "I believe in prayer, but I also believe in medicine," Mayling wrote Mills in exasperation. "I am going almost crazy with the tension and mother's refusal to follow the doctor's directions." She was exhausted from staying up nights tending her father— her mother refused to hire a nurse because she believed it was against the will of God.

Charles Soong died on May 3, 1918, with his family at his side. The funeral was simple and, as he desired, no notice appeared in newspapers. The family buried him in Shanghai's new International Cemetery, which they liked so much that they bought a plot big enough for the whole family. Mayling and her mother went into mourning and dressed in black. Soon after the family moved to a smaller house on Seymour Road in Shanghai's International Settlement. The new house was finished in teak and had a large wood-burning fireplace and a roof garden. There was a greenhouse where Mayling wanted the gardener to cultivate roses for flower shows. Her mother gave Mayling free rein in renovating, asking only for a small quiet chamber for her to use as a prayer room.

After her family's decisive rejection of the Dutchman, Mayling fell in love again—this time with a married man whose wife had been forced on him by his parents after he returned from America some years earlier. But unlike many of her contemporaries, she could not bring herself to defy tradition. "You know how my family feels towards divorce, and besides there is nothing the matter with his wife except that he does not care for her," Mayling wrote Mills. "Of course neither one of us would do what is not honorable— Only we both care more than words can tell,—and oh, it is terrible to care so much. . . . He said that he would go through hell to be free. But everything is hopeless." She vowed: "If I ever marry, it will not be for love."

Protestations to the contrary, Mayling did not abandon all hope of romantic love in matrimony, but it was true that after a year in the bosom of her family her views on the institution had shifted significantly. She now regarded marriage not only as a means to secure her future, but more critically as a means to realize her ambition. This was evident in her consideration of a proposal from an industrialist fifteen years her senior. "He understands that I do not love him, and in all probability I never shall," she wrote Mills in June 1918. "I like & respect him; he is a man of great executive ability, and very quiet and unassuming. . . . He is very wealthy too, and told me that if I marry him, I can help him with the social work of his many hundreds of laborers in his factories. We could do great things in educational and social improvements. . . . Just fancy, a school, a gymnasium, a recreation center for the factory hands, and trained social workers to instill ideas of decency, democracy, and humanity into the minds of these men and women. And I am to help in this great work!" She could not give him her love, she wrote Mills, but she could try to be a "thoughtful comrade." Evidently she turned him down, for nothing more was heard of the proposal.

In the summer of 1918, while Emma worked as a wartime "farmerette," Mayling played lawn tennis, gave dinners and card parties, and busied the servants. She was also increasingly active in social work. She volunteered at the Shanghai YWCA, serving on a social committee and starting an English conversation club. "I rather like the work . . . for it makes me more interested in all sorts of people," she wrote Mills. She worked in a neighborhood school for poor girls that her mother had started years earlier. She joined a club for returned students and wrote an article about American women's colleges that was reprinted in the *Shanghai Gazette.*

Encouraged by the response, she thought of writing articles on reforming certain Shanghai "evils." "So much misery everywhere!" she wrote Mills. "Sometimes when I look at the dirty, ragged swarming humanity in our slums, I feel the sense of utter futility in hoping for a great and a new China, and the sense of my own smallness." She considered working for some charitable organization. "I do hate nasty smells and dirty sights," she wrote. "But I suppose somebody has to see the dirt if it is ever going to be cleaned up." She vowed to spend her second year back in China studying Shanghai's social needs. "Maybe in time the Municipal Council here will awaken to the fact that while 9/10 of the population here are Chinese, the council has done little to improve the living conditions of those most in need," she wrote.

But just as it seemed she was beginning to forge a role for herself, Mayling sank into a bout of dissatisfaction. She yearned for "mental exercise" and felt surrounded with "every deadening force possible," she wrote Mills. The committees she served on were "nihil," she complained. "They are superficial and the members meet more to observe each other's clothes than to discuss means of improvement." She longed for "<u>hard</u>, real, live, amount-to-something, worthwhile work . . . that will make me damnably uncomfortable physically [and] too tired to care what kind of bed I shall be sleeping on." Her restless mood coincided with an attack of "paint poison"—perhaps the first appearance of hives, an affliction that would plague her for many decades. For weeks her skin broke out in little blisters that itched agonizingly. She attributed it to a type of varnish used to paint her brother's room, but her mother insisted the outbreak was "retribution" for having refused to go to church revival meetings with her. Mayling hoped that as compensation for her misery her mother would buy her a set of beautiful lynx furs they had seen at La Maison Parisienne, a dress shop.

Hardly had she gotten over the "paint poison" when the family Buick hit a child while Mayling was being driven by the chauffeur. She was immediately swamped by a terrifying throng of the "lower classes," she later wrote Mills. The mother howled; Mayling tried to take the bleeding child to the hospital but the Buick ran out of gas and the chauffeur vanished. She hailed a man in a Ford, left the child at the hospital, and finally returned home a "nervous wreck." Her mother dreaded publicity and seemed more worried that the house would be surrounded by "low-class detectives" than over the fate of the child. It emerged that the child had been only slightly injured, but Mayling developed a 105-degree fever and yelled deliriously not to have the car run over her. Doctors were summoned and pronounced her "scared." A police officer tried to interview her but could make no sense of her feverish answers.

Once recovered, Mayling went north to Tianjin, a treaty port city southeast of Beijing, to visit her sister Eling. She amused her niece and nephew and went to the theatre, the movies, or the opera each night. She visited Beijing, where she saw family friends who lived in "palaces" and visited the Great Wall and the Ming Tombs. On November 11, 1918, the Great War ended, precipitating a world economic boom in which Shanghai prospered. Mayling returned home from the north and soon began "chasing up" foreign bankers for a YWCA fund-raising campaign. "I go to the managers of the Banks personally and look them in the eye, and literally the money rolls in!" she wrote Mills excitedly. "I never say the same things to two men; I first size them up to see which of my arguments would most likely appeal to him, and then I strike while the iron is hot!" Some she plied with the social responsibility argument; others responded to a "commercial" appeal in which she argued it was in their interest to help China's young women. She stressed to them she was a volunteer and received nothing but "the satisfaction of knowing that I am trying to work for the betterment of China."

Mayling was clearly exhilarated by the challenge. "I am liking this job!" she exulted to Mills. Few among the sixty campaign workers were willing to "brave the lion's jaws" by calling on businessmen. She took a spinster YWCA secretary along on calls as chaperon but did all the talking because the appeal was more effective coming from a Chinese girl than from a foreigner. She insisted on wearing her best clothes. "Nothing gives one more confidence than the feeling that she has on a becoming hat, plenty of powder to keep the shine off the nose, and sumptuous furs," she wrote. "To be well dressed means that a larger contribution will be assured, for the men would be ashamed to give any sum too small to buy my shoes with at least! I never ask for money as charity: I always give the men the privilege of contributing to something which would in time benefit them, for a better China socially means a greater China commercially." In large measure due to Mayling's efforts, the campaign was a great success.

Next, she organized a Returned Students Bible Conference, the subject of which was the responsibility of Chinese women educated abroad to help progress and reform in China and their duties to the church. China, in Mayling's view, was not the only entity in need of reform. Her pastor preached the "rottenest sermons" and was "unsanctimoniously lazy," she wrote Mills. "But as our family is the oldest in that church and Mother is considered the backbone, I am going to try to reform him by giving him some books to read which might give him new ideas for his sermons."

Mayling rarely discussed politics in her letters to Mills, initially because of wartime censorship, but she was growing increasingly aware of China's political situation, as filtered through the lens of her family. Her early views, naive and unformed as they were, shed much light on the stands she would later take. She was distressed by China's chaotic political circumstances and wished she knew history well enough, she wrote Mills, to write for influential newspapers what she so strongly felt. "Chinese politics is impossible. . . . One never knows when one's head is going to be the next to be chopped off," she wrote Mills. At the same time she worried that editors would print any article she might write only because they thought "Doesn't she write well for a Chinese girl," which would be an insult to her pride.

At the time China had an internationally recognized government in Beijing and a rival government in Canton, initially established by Mayling's brother-in-law Sun Yat-sen, on September 1, 1917, upon his return from exile in Japan with Ching Ling. Not long after, Sun was forced out of office and he and his wife left for Shanghai. The two governments were jockeying for power, with each other and with a constellation of regional warlords across the country. Mayling fretted that amid the political chaos the country was doing nothing to aid the Allies or to secure its position in the world. "What our government really ought to do (in my humble opinion) is to work whole-heartedly for democracy, since we have already cast our lot in with those nations who are avowedly anti-autocratic," she wrote Mills in March 1919. She was convinced that a strong military was critical to securing China's future, and knew that China's weak armies lacked good military specialists. Since the U.S. had previously granted China military loans, she theorized confidently, if China asked for "a few generals to start training camps over here" Washington would agree to supply them. She worried that China would have no voice at the 1919 Versailles peace conference because she lacked a strong military to enforce her demands as an independent nation. She did not believe "Might is Right" but appreciated that might inspired fear in nations "whose ambitions are greater than their conscience," she wrote Mills.

In early June 1919 Mayling wrote Mills a long and passionate letter about a patriotic student movement in China that sprang into being in outrage over the terms of the Treaty of Versailles. Article 156 of the treaty, which was signed by Chinese representatives from the Beijing government, transferred German concessions in the treaty port city of Qingdao, Shandong province, to Japan rather than returning sovereign rights to China. This injustice, felt as a national humiliation, touched off what became known as the May Fourth movement, an "intellectual revolution" characterized by an awakening of patriotism, opposition to foreign domination, and a belief in the need for cultural reforms. The May Fourth movement profoundly influenced a generation of Chinese and was the genesis of communism in China. The movement was a cry by young intellectuals for changes in the country's political system, education system, language, and society that would overturn hundreds if not thousands of years of rigidity and inertia. It soon broadened into a campaign to modernize China through intellectual and social reforms, especially the Western concepts of science and democracy.

The demonstrations began in Beijing and spread to Shanghai, leading to widespread boycotts of Japanese goods. Mayling hoped the movement would continue but initially doubted the students' resolve. "I feel that this boycott movement is effective only in so far as it leads to a constructive program," she wrote Mills. She feared Japan would hold a grudge against China for the boycotts and would ultimately make China pay. "And if we are not ready to face them when the day of reckoning comes, we will get the worst of it," she wrote. It was widely believed the Japanese had bribed Beijing officials to agree to the Qingdao clause at Versailles, and now those same officials were opposing the boycott and arresting students. "My heart bleeds for the poor students, and I hope those who are so rotten, so damn greedy and inhuman as to sell their country Will Go To Hell," she railed in a letter to Mills. "It is bad enough to hate men of another nation, but to feel perfectly helpless with rage against the very men who by all laws of decency and humanity should be patriotic is Hell."

Mayling's next letter was full of praise for the student leaders of the movement and brimming with pride and hope for China's future. She and a group of women returned students had rather belatedly joined the movement. Under popular pressure the Beijing government accepted the resignation of the "traitors"—i.e., officials responsible for the terms of the Versailles treaty—and freed imprisoned students. "Even I who have so much faith in the ultimate outcome of China's salvation, was surprised at the wholeheartedness of the people," she exulted. "Every Japanese thinks we are a cold blooded people, incapable of united thought or action. We certainly have shown them something. Before this movement, the Japanese behaved with the most remarkable hauteur and superiority. You ought to see the way they slink around the corners now."

By the spring of 1919 Mayling seemed to have shed her ambivalence toward marriage, although she was not ready to take that step. When she received a borderline "hysterical" letter from Mills, she thought she discerned the source of her friend's discontent. "I think women . . . feel a distinct lack, as though they have been cheated out of life, if they do not marry," she wrote to Mills. "And what has one to look forward to if one does not have children?" Mayling had not taken her own counsel because, she asserted, "I was a damn fool enough to have fallen in love with a man I could not marry without giving sorrow to many people," she wrote, apparently referring to the married man. "Sometimes . . . I am tempted to chuck over everything and marry him." She admonished her friend: "The profession of marriage is the one most important profession for every woman, and one not to be subordinated by any other profession or inspiration." As for the raw material, the most successful men, she mused prophetically, were not "geniuses" but those who had "such ultimate faith in their own selves that invariably they hypnotize others to that belief as well as themselves."

Mayling consoled Mills after her friend recounted a "beastly unpleasant" incident with a man. She advised her friend to "ignore the question of sex entirely" when dealing with men. "Love is partly sexual in its composition and there is nothing disgusting about it if you consider it in conjunction with the other elements which make up love," she wrote confidently, although it was unlikely her knowledge of the subject extended beyond the academic. "Physical love is like certain parts of Bach's or Beethoven's works, which if considered by themselves are discords but which if combined with the parts [with which] the authors mean to have them considered, they become harmonious and beautiful." The man who had looked at Mills so "disgustingly" was "a brute and an animal," but not all men were like that, Mayling assured her.

In July 1919 Shanghai was abuzz with rumors that Mayling was engaged to various men. Her scandalized mother barred her from seeing men for a month and Mayling thought of getting engaged "out of revenge." In truth, she wrote Mills, "I am dreadfully bored, outrageously so. I have even had teas unchaperoned a couple of times, just because . . . I feel so wretchedly oppressed. The funny part is I do not care a snap about any of the men. . . . I think if one does not love, the next best thing is to be loved, don't you?"

Her sister Eling, now living in Shanghai, delivered her third child in August 1919. She was called Jeanette May, the "May" after her aunt Mayling. That autumn Mayling was elected vice president of the American College Women's Club of Shanghai. Eling was president of the

McTyeire Sorority, the city's largest association for Chinese women. In between helping care for her nieces and nephew, Mayling was constantly busy with teas, dinners, and outings to the theatre. "My circle of friends in Shanghai is really getting to be almost too huge for me to be able to keep up with," she wrote Mills. "The funny thing is that when I do have a moment to myself now, I am so awfully restless that I cannot sit still." In an indication of her popularity, a photograph of Mayling clad in Wellesley cap and gown ran in the May 12, 1920, *Shanghai Gazette*. The caption was "Charming Type of the Chinese 'Returned Student.'"

In the early fall of 1919 Mayling begged her mother to let her leave home and do real, satisfying work. She had been disappointed when earlier that year her family had refused to let her take a nursing course. Volunteer work was makeshift; she did not feel she was accomplishing anything. She was offered a position on a newspaper but feared her family's wrath should she accept. "The Celestials can not get into their nutty domes that a girl can be decent morally if she works with men," she wrote Mills in exasperation. "Damn it all, I think that if I had my way, I could amount to something, but hampered with a respectable family whom everyone knows about, it is impossible for me to go out driving with a perfectly decent man without chaperons." She was irritated by suitors and yearned to be finished with all that "tommyrot."

In 1920 Mayling briefly considered returning to America to study medicine. Her mother was utterly opposed, not least because her youngest daughter would be away for six years. Mayling's health could not stand the stress of a doctor's life, her mother argued, and she could be just as useful to China in some other career. Her mother was so good to her and relied on her so much that Mayling "hated" to think of leaving her, she wrote Mills. Since returning to China she had enjoyed the home life that she missed during her adolescence. "I think I am beginning to be a little less individualistic . . . and understand 'family feeling' more than I ever did." But she wanted to become a doctor because "I <u>want</u> a career in preference to marriage, and . . . a doctor's life has sufficient varied <u>human</u> interests to be interesting, and to keep me in <u>active</u> touch with humanity. Barring matrimony, and teaching, there is nothing open to women in China,—nothing open to <u>me</u> without trespassing upon the traditions of the family." She could not possibly go into business, as it would provoke great amounts of

gossip and resulting "annoyances." Social service work was "too theoretical" and "amateurish," with much "gabbing" but few practical results. Her
mother said Mayling was "chasing the Blue Bird of Happiness."

Mayling advised Mills that a lesson she had learned since coming home
was that "friends are very nice, <u>but</u> remember when you . . . really get to a
hard fix, the <u>family</u> is the one that will stand by you." She had lately had
infected tonsils removed and was "on the verge of a nervous breakdown" as
a result of the operation, she said, due to her "exceedingly nervous temperament." Nerves notwithstanding, she was by this time acting president of the
American College Club and a board member of the YWCA, and had accepted
an invitation to join the board of directors of the Margaret Williamson Hospital in Shanghai. She was secretary of two other organizations and chairman
of several committees. She was exhausted but "I like to be active, and I love
to see things hum," she wrote. "I have no patience with a namby-pamby sort
of existence. Ergo—I am not married yet!"

In February 1921 Mayling visited her sister Ching Ling in Canton. Since
their marriage in late 1915, Ching Ling and her husband, Sun Yat-sen, had
struggled without success to restore Sun to the helm of the Chinese republic. To his great frustration, Sun had been sidelined from power since 1912
and forced to live in exile abroad for much of the period until 1917, when the
couple returned to China, living in Shanghai and Canton. Sun was subsequently forced out of the Canton government and they settled in a house
given to them by friends at 29 Rue Molière in Shanghai's French Concession. There Sun revived his long-dormant Geming Dang, or Revolutionary
Party, and in 1919 changed its name to Kuomintang, or "Nationalist Party."
In 1920 Sun and Ching Ling returned to Canton, where Sun was elected
"President of China," although his government's effective sovereignty initially did not extend beyond Guangdong province, and later only to neigh-
boring Guangxi province.

Mayling stayed at Ching Ling's home on Guanyin Mountain, named for
its famous Goddess of Mercy Temple. The house was surrounded by armed
guards. Just below were the barracks of five thousand of Sun Yat-sen's soldiers. Mayling heard bugle calls all day and could see the troops drilling on
the marching grounds. Ching Ling took her to the city's famous sites,
which meant much unaccustomed climbing on rocky paths in French heels
under the blazing sun. At first the change of scene agreed with her, but

soon Mayling fell into an introspective mood. She felt she had accomplished nothing worthwhile in the four years since graduation; had she stayed in America she could have been a medical doctor by now. "If I really had something in me," she wrote Mills despondently, "I could have overcome all the obstacles . . . left the comfortable homeside, and gone into the interior and done some work 'on my own.'"

As it was, that "vibrant joy" was missing from her life. She wondered what was wrong with her and thought of becoming a nun or marrying to "just drift along, and keep myself from thinking." But since returning home she had come to know men thoroughly, she claimed. "If they have not already had liaisons, they will," she wrote Mills. "I have seen so many instances of this; men whom I thought were absolutely reliable. . . . The continual dread overhanging the average married woman is intolerable for me to even contemplate. Especially at this time in China where the standard of morality is so different from that of America." She had hoped the change of scene would improve her mental state, but "I cannot seem to get away from myself," she wrote. She stayed in Canton three months, despite several "frantic" telegrams from her mother begging her to return.

Finally, in May 1921, her brother T. V. "dragged" her home via Hong Kong. There she met a "Mr. Birnie" at a friend's house the night before sailing for Shanghai. On the three-day journey they became "very good friends" and despite not having seen the family in months she spent the day of their arrival with him. "We had a beautiful time together, and I am *so glad* I was so rash for once in my life," she wrote Mills. Her family was mortified and accused Mayling of "picking him up" onboard ship. She liked him better, perhaps, than any other man she had ever met, she wrote, but the matter could go no further than friendship. "Our family is so conservative and puffed up with family pride over keeping 'pure' the family blood that they would rather see me dead than marry a foreigner."

Despite being the envy of friends and family, Mayling wrestled with existential angst. She had failed to find relief from "emptiness" and "boredom" in social service, self-improvement, or "butterflying." Now she was trying something new—faith in God. She was not a religious person, she insisted: "I am too darned independent and pert to be meek or humble or submissive." But Eling, whom Mayling called "the most brilliant mind in the family," had in difficulty turned to God after previously dismissing any talk of religion as "old woman's nonsense." Mayling had earlier decided that Eling had "intentionally drugged her mind, psychologically" and would become furiously irritated whenever the subject arose. Now, however, she realized her sister was right: The only way to conquer this "lassitude of mind" was to "commune with God." She insisted to Mills she had not gone crazy or, worse, turned into a "goody-goody"; in fact she was savoring a cigarette on the verandah as she wrote. Mayling again invited her friend to visit China. Mills came in early 1922 and stayed for several years.

In addition to writing a great deal for Eugene Chen's *Shanghai Gazette*, Mayling took an interest in labor reform and visited silk filatures, both foreign and Chinese-owned, in the city's International Settlement. In these factories she saw child workers, many barely past infancy and ill with tuberculosis, standing by steaming basins overflowing with boiling water plucking silk fibers from boiled cocoons. They worked twelve to fourteen hours a day. Mayling was horrified by the squalor and the dangerous conditions prevalent in the firetraps that served as factories, which often doubled as living quarters. Mothers worked at machines with their babies lying in the aisles. She attacked the sweatshop system and launched a campaign to rid Shanghai of child labor. The effort led to her appointment on the Shanghai Municipal Council as a member of a child labor commission. She was the first Chinese, and the first woman, to hold the post, her maiden appearance on the political stage.

In 1922 she half-jokingly remarked that to justify her existence she would have to live in "reflected glory," but unlike most of her peers, Mayling remained single for a full decade after her return from America. Among her many suitors was a serious love interest, the handsome Liu Jiwen from Guangdong province. Liu had studied at the College of Law and Political Economy in Japan from 1915 to 1917, when he returned to China to work for Sun Yat-sen. In 1924 Liu traveled to England to study at the London School of Economics and at Cambridge and returned to China in 1926. Little is known of their romance, but it is thought they were once engaged. When asked years later if this were true, Liu appeared embarrassed and avoided a direct answer, saying only that Mayling had introduced him to his wife.

* * *

In an attempt to corral more provinces under his control, Sun led his army on a Northern Expedition that promptly collapsed due to lack of funds and arms. On June 16, 1922, an armed revolt by a disgruntled former subordinate forced Sun and Ching Ling to flee Canton. Ching Ling made her way to Shanghai, but Sun camped onboard a Chinese gunboat near Canton for nearly two months, waiting in vain for foreign help or a revolt among the troops that had taken over the city. Eventually he abandoned hope and went to live with his wife in Shanghai. Remaining faithfully by the doctor's side through the ordeal was a young protégé named Chiang Kai-shek.

Chapter Six
Man in Uniform

Here was my opportunity. With my husband, I would work ceaselessly to make China strong.

—Mayling Soong

When Chiang Kai-shek first encountered Mayling Soong in late 1922, he was just a junior military aide to Sun Yat-sen, and by no means the most stable or promising among Sun's protégés. But he was exceptionally aggressive, resourceful, and brimming with ambition. By the time he embarked on his courtship of Mayling in 1926, Chiang had shaken off a checkered past, conquered inner demons, and seized the mantle of the late Dr. Sun to become the strongman of the Kuomintang and the Canton government.

The future Nationalist Chinese leader was born in 1887 in the hamlet of Xikou in Fenghua county, Zhejiang province. The son of a salt merchant who died young, Chiang witnessed his widowed mother struggle to make ends meet. In 1902, when Chiang was fifteen, she arranged a blind marriage to a woman four years his senior named Mao Fumei, a union that eventually produced a son, Chiang Ching-kuo. After a traditional Chinese education and a stint in a military academy, Chiang cut off his queue—that hated symbol of Manchu domination—to protest the Qing regime and went to military school in Japan, where he joined Sun Yat-sen's Revolutionary Alliance.

Chiang's temperament was evident from an early age. His boyhood tutor described him as "wild and ungovernable . . . one would think he had two different personalities." He entered adulthood harboring a deep sense of persecution and alienation that rendered him emotionally unstable. He was impulsive, impatient, and ill-tempered, and manifested symptoms of psychosomatic dysfunction. He was prone to volcanic displays of emotion, wild accusations, and fears of abandonment. He spent much of his early adulthood in an intense, prolonged internal struggle to tame his temperament.

Chiang returned to Shanghai shortly after the Chinese Revolution broke out in Wuhan on October 10, 1911, to command a brigade of three thousand men, but soon after inexplicably "abandoned himself to a life of intense dissipation," according to a fellow revolutionary. "He would disappear for months from headquarters in the houses of sing-song girls [a euphemism for prostitutes] and for some reason or other he acquired a fiery, uncompromising temper which weighed very tryingly on his friends." In late 1911 he assassinated a political rival of Chen Qimei, his patron, and subsequently fled to Japan to avoid arrest by Shanghai police. After returning to China a year later, having long neglected his arranged marriage, he acquired a secondary wife, or concubine. Her name was Yao Zhicheng, and as an indication of her relatively high status, she came to be known as Madame Yao.

Chiang was greatly disillusioned by the political chaos that followed the 1911 revolution. He took part in attempts to overthrow the dictator Yuan Shikai, to whom Sun Yat-sen was compelled to concede the presidency in 1912. After Chen Qimei was assassinated in 1915, Chiang spent several years in search of another patron, which he needed to launch a military career. Meanwhile he made a living in the Shanghai underworld, working for the Green Gang (Qing Bang), a secret society and racketeering organization that exerted pervasive influence in the port city. The Green Gang had played a role in the 1911 revolution and many of Chiang's contemporaries, including Sun Yat-sen, had secret society ties. Chiang found a new patron in Zhang Jingjiang, a benefactor of Sun Yat-sen who had spent many years in Paris making a fortune in Chinese curios, silk, and tea. The crippled merchant, seen as the "brains" of Sun's movement, introduced Chiang to Sun. In 1918 Chiang became Sun's military adviser, with an interlude as a commodities broker in Shanghai, a scheme launched by Sun to raise funds.

In 1919 Chiang met a slim, pretty young girl at the curio merchant's Shanghai home. Thirteen-year-old Chen Jieru, known as Jennie, was the merchant's goddaughter. She came from a conservative, well-to-do family that owned a paper business, but her father had recently died. She was well educated and had studied some English. Despite repeated rebuffs, Chiang pursued her doggedly.

Chiang's temperament and conduct exasperated Sun Yat-sen. "You have a fiery temper, and your hatred of mediocrity is too excessive," Sun admonished Chiang in an October 1920 letter. "You should sacrifice your ideals a little and try to compromise." Chiang was painfully aware of his problematic personality. He once called himself "unsuitable for society" and said he ought to live alone in the mountains. To fellow revolutionaries he wrote, "Everybody says I am given to lust, but they do not know that this is a thing of last resort, in a state of utter depression." To his friend and revolutionary comrade Dai Jitao he lamented his poor manners and lack of self-control, but blamed it on others who had "taken advantage" of him and made him suffer. He bemoaned the fact that while he had lifelong sworn brothers through his revolutionary and secret society ties, he had few companions or social acquaintances. Dai told Chiang he was incorrigible and added: "Whenever you are despondent and in a state of intoxication, you let your anger go unchecked."

In 1921 Chiang tried to remedy his defects through a daily routine of readings and meditations of his own devising. In this way, he hoped, "my nature will be purified." It was during that pivotal year that he became convinced he was China's man of destiny: "With an expansive and illumined mind, a firm and courageous spirit, I will cultivate a glorious stature so as to be illustrious throughout the world," he wrote.

Two years after meeting her Chiang was still pursuing Jennie Chen. According to her, at one point he lured her into a hotel room and attempted to seduce her. Later he threatened to chop off a finger as proof of his "undying love" for her. After his mother died in June 1921, he pledged to Jennie that she would be his only legal wife and secured formal separation agreements from both his first wife and his second, Madame Yao. Under pressure from her godfather, whom Chiang had enlisted as matchmaker, Jennie and her mother agreed to the match. On December 5, 1921, at Shanghai's Great Eastern Hotel, Chiang and Chen were married according to Chinese custom, with godfather Zhang, the curio merchant, officiating.

On honeymoon in Chiang's ancestral village, the newlyweds visited a Buddhist temple where they rummaged for fortunes from a bamboo drum.

Chiang's read, "The pine tree stretches its head to heaven." But Jennie's was less auspicious: "The sapling caught in a typhoon." The ill boded by the fortune soon made an appearance. Jennie wanted children, but shortly after her marriage, she later wrote, she suffered a bout of venereal disease that left her sterile. She threatened to divorce Chiang, but the contrite husband pledged to his distraught young bride that he would drink nothing but boiled water for the rest of his life. True to his word, he never again touched alcohol, coffee, or even tea. In any case, Jennie claimed, Chiang had been rendered infertile by the same malady. Her assertion cannot be verified, but it is true that despite several known liaisons and rumors of others, he fathered no children after Ching-kuo, who was born in 1909.

In 1923 Chiang wrote that after examining "past transgressions" he resolved to "practice meticulous self-control and amiability in my personal conduct." He subjected himself to intense self-criticism, tortured soul-searching, and rigorous self-cultivation to overcome his shortcomings and mold himself into the great figure he wanted to become. His efforts began to pay off when in August 1923, Sun Yat-sen dispatched Chiang, by now Sun's chief military adviser, to Moscow as head of a delegation to study military matters. Sun sought to unify China's defenseless "kaleidoscopic patchwork of warlord satrapies" into an integrated political system that could make China strong and independent, and key to that drive was to forge a strong army. After being snubbed by the U.S., Britain, and Japan, Sun Yat-sen in desperation turned to revolutionary Russia for assistance. The move inspired much controversy over whether Sun was turning socialist or even Communist. The truth was that although he admired Lenin and the Soviet government in some respects, Sun opposed Communism and his new friendship with Moscow was not so much ideologically motivated as opportunistic. As Chiang later said, "When a man is drowning and someone extends a hand, he will seize that hand no matter to whom it belongs." For his part, Soviet leader Vladimir Lenin seized the opportunity to use the Kuomintang's "national bourgeois revolution" as an unlikely instrument to bolshevize China—an interim strategy adopted until the nascent Chinese Communist party gained strength.

While Chiang was away in Moscow in the autumn of 1923, China's "Lafayette," as Sun called him, arrived in the person of Mikhail Borodin. Born a shtetl Jew in the Tsar's Pale, that part of Western Russia to which the tsars tried to confine their Jewish subjects, the multilingual Mikhail Markovich Gruzenberg—Borodin was his nom de guerre—was dispatched by the politburo to Canton in October 1923 to win China over to Marx. As Sun Yat-sen's top political adviser, the thirty-nine-year-old professional agent provocateur—who had advised Ataturk and Mexican agitators—soon wielded substantial power. Former officers in the Russian Imperial Army took up key posts in the Canton government's military. The secret service, as well as committees overseeing naval and military affairs, were influenced by Russians.

A onetime student of the New Testament, Borodin now believed passionately in the inevitability of class struggle and the eventual dominance of Marxist principles. "The Christian notion that human nature can be changed is a pipe dream," he argued. "The only way to make a capitalist unselfish is to liquidate him. You can only bring in the kingdom of God by force." The crowd that crucified Christ and saved Barabbas, the thief, the victim of the rich, was truly revolutionary, he argued. Although he spoke no Chinese and addressed mass rallies through an interpreter, Borodin was a skillful and audacious propagandist among troops, peasants, and intellectuals alike. His mission was to bring communism to the Chinese people, for if China was ever brought to Marx, the world would surely follow. Sun introduced Borodin into the salons of Canton's affluent Chinese, where he evangelized among the American-educated students about Sun's ideals and aspirations for China. In such intimate settings the charismatic and polished Marxist was highly effective. Sun praised Borodin's "genius for organization."

While in Moscow Chiang met senior Communist officials, including Leon Trotsky, principal architect of the Soviet army. The trip proved to be a turning point in Chiang's career, for shortly after his return to China in December he was appointed commandant of the planned Whampoa Military Academy. The appointment was announced at the first national congress of the Kuomintang in January 1924, which Mayling attended. Chiang was also present but was not a delegate. During the congress, Borodin—at Moscow's behest—brokered a partnership between the Kuomintang and the nascent Chinese Communist party in what became known as the United Front. As the nucleus of a modern army, Whampoa was critical to the Canton government's aspirations to unite China under a strong centralized government. Borodin and his Russian advisers designed the curriculum, and Zhou Enlai, a Communist, headed the political section. When Lenin died as the congress was under way, Sun saluted him with the words "You have shown us the path for the common struggle."

The Whampoa Military Academy was formally established in May 1924 on an island near Canton, and Chiang and his wife, Jennie, lived on the first floor. Aided by her good command of English, she became Chiang's personal secretary, as Ching Ling was for Sun Yat-sen. Chiang entrusted her with handling his ever-growing "secret" correspondence, the existence of which staff and even officers were unaware. At first, Chiang was a devoted and loving husband, who could even be playful and romantic. But as time went on his volatile temperament made life difficult. He was a "moody, tempestuous soul" whose depressive tendencies were evident. Every few months he would abruptly take to the mountains to hide away in a Buddhist retreat. He made little effort to control his terrible temper. He did not hesitate to publicly humiliate his soldiers or throw them into the brig for an unlaced shoe or a jacket with the top button undone. At home he was often sullen and grouchy, and flew into a rage at the least provocation. Married life became "a series of tantrums and shoutings," Jennie wrote.

By November 1924 Sun Yat-sen was gravely ill and as far as ever from achieving his dream of a unified, strong, and independent China. The country was like "the carcass of a horse in a land of vultures and jackals," one observer wrote. Sun died of cancer on March 12, 1925, in Beijing at the age of fifty-eight. He had asked to be embalmed and placed in a glass-topped casket like Lenin. The casket was ordered from Moscow, but his embalming was less than successful, and before long serious decomposition had occurred. The difficulties preserving his mortal remains notwithstanding, Sun proved to be more inspiring dead than alive. Although a perennial failure in life, in death he became an enduring symbol of selfless patriotism embraced by Chinese of all political leanings.

Hardly had Sun been laid to rest when Chiang sent an intermediary to his widow bearing a proposal of marriage, despite his already being married. The move could hardly have been better calculated to earn Ching Ling's enduring disgust.

Jennie took a motherly interest in Chiang's sons, Ching-kuo—who was just four years younger than she—and Wego, Chiang's adopted son. Wego, the result of an extramarital liaison between Chiang's friend Dai Jitao and a Japanese woman, had been raised by Madame Yao, Chiang's second wife. In 1924 Jennie Chen had adopted a baby and named her Chiang Yao-kuang, but Chiang never treated the girl as his child. Ching-kuo was terrified of his brusque and largely absent father, and Jennie took pity on the boy. She spoke to Chiang on Ching-kuo's behalf when he wished to study in Russia. Just fifteen years old, in October 1925 Ching-kuo left for Moscow, where he studied at Sun Yat-sen University for the Toilers of China, newly established by the Kremlin to groom—at Russian expense—an elite corps of Russian-speaking, Soviet-indoctrinated cadres to staff the Chinese Revolution. Ching-kuo and fellow students, including Deng Xiaoping, fresh from five years in Paris, studied Russian language and such subjects as infiltration of governments and fomenting peasant and labor movements. He became a fervent Trotskyite. Many future leaders of the Chinese Communist Party were drawn from the thousand-odd students of the school.

Lamenting China's seemingly insurmountable divisiveness, Sun Yat-sen once ruefully compared the Chinese people to a dish of sand. The country's inherent centrifugal tendencies were mirrored within the Kuomintang itself. This was not helped by the fact that Sun neglected to anoint a political heir before his demise. Bereft of its founder's "catalytic charisma," the Kuomintang threatened to disintegrate and the Canton government was in turmoil. Then in March 1926, Chiang, who had taken over from Sun as head of the armed forces, suddenly declared martial law and detained many Soviet advisers and Chinese Communists in what became known as the Zhongshan Gunboat Incident. The aim was to oust Wang Jingwei, one of Sun's closest associates and a contender to succeed Sun, from the party leadership. The Russians and Communists were released, but Wang was forced to flee Canton.

Thus by the spring of 1926 Chiang had snatched the top spot in the Kuomintang hierarchy and now held far more power than Sun ever had. The "Ningpo Napoleon," as detractors quickly dubbed him—in a dismissive reference to his Zhejiang province origins—controlled the government, party, and army of the South China province. Ironically, the foreign press labeled him the "Red General." He began styling himself "Generalissimo," a title Sun Yat-sen had used. A May 1926 Soviet report provided telling insight into Chiang's character. He was "conceited, self-loving, reserved and ambitious," a man with "some idea" of Western progress but who retained his Chinese prejudices. "By praising him in a delicate manner . . . much can be obtained from him: only one must never show one's self to be above or beneath him . . . [or] show that one wants to usurp even a particle of his power," the report read. Chiang was an "energetic executor" of plans, but despite dreams of prominence on the "stage of Chinese history," he was a mediocre military leader. He "easily becomes enthusiastic and then, just as easily crest-fallen . . . lacking the necessary coolness and firmness of character. His timidity in making definite decisions in military operations can perhaps be explained by his fear of making fatal mistakes, which would cause his down-fall, before he becomes powerful enough to afford making them." Chiang's subordinates vied among each other while sharing a "peculiar antipathy" toward him, tempered by awe. "It is difficult to foretell whether Chiang Kai-shek will turn [into] an ordinary Tuchun [warlord] and cease playing with left[ist] principles, or if he will go further in the same direction," the report concluded.

Whatever his shortcomings and ideological leanings, Chiang had emerged as a strong yet flexible centrist figure, the power broker most able to sustain the uneasy partnership between the Communists and Sun's fractious revo-lutionary movement. In early July 1926, Chiang formally launched from Canton what was called the Northern Expedition. The "expedition" was a northward march of his National armies to unify the country under the Na-tionalist (or Kuomintang) banner—a bid to succeed where Sun Yat-sen had failed several years earlier. Advised by the Russian general Vasily Blyukher, Chiang and his brown-uniformed National Revolutionary Army met with success. What little resistance Chiang encountered was readily bought off with "silver bullets"—cash, or promises thereof—or failing that, overcome by force. His forces grew en route as local armies were gathered under the wing of the National Revolutionary Army. The Northern Expedition loosely fol-lowed the route of the nineteenth-century Taiping rebels, who similarly began in weakness and gained strength as they went.

It is not clear when Chiang's courtship of Mayling, which by necessity of his marital status was sub rosa, began. At their first meeting, believed to have

been in early December 1922 during a Christian revival meeting held at Sun
Yat-sen's home on Rue Molière, Chiang was struck by the outspoken "New
Woman" and asked Sun to formally introduce him to her. But it appears that
romance did not bloom until at least 1926, when after a string of military victories in the Northern Expedition, the young upstart Canton general was attracting wide acclaim, and Eling Kung fastened upon him as a likely prospect
to which she could attach her family's star. "He was the only revolutionist in
China who could make the revolution stick," wrote the American journalist
George Sokolsky. "Mayling understood that earlier than anyone, except
possibly Madame Kung, who always picked Chiang Kai-shek for a winner."

Chiang was handsome in a rakish sort of way, despite a prematurely
balding pate and long lupine teeth. He typically wore either an army uniform or a flowing dark scholar's robe, and in winter affected a long black
wool Inverness cloak topped by an Al Capone–style slouch hat. He sported
a trimmed mustache above full lips and a strong squarish jaw. Above a receding hairline still grew the sparsest fringe of black hair, which he periodically shaved. His wide-eyed gaze pierced with startling intensity. He
smiled often but without humor.

One evening in the summer of 1926, according to Jennie Chen's memoir, Chiang came home agitated and "strutted the floor like a peacock."
Madame Kung had invited them to dinner. Jennie did not want to go, but
Chiang pleaded: "You must be sensible and realize how very important it
is for me to get closer to the Soong family." Although Chiang controlled the
Kuomintang and the Canton government, he had many enemies and his
position was vulnerable. Because the Soongs were related to the late leader
by marriage, an alliance with the Soongs would strengthen Chiang's political legitimacy.

When Jennie arrived at the Kung residence before Chiang, Madame Kung
introduced her to Mayling and other guests. The Soong sisters looked Jennie
over appraisingly. On returning from a tour of the garden, Jennie recounted,
she overheard laughter. "She's only a middle-class housewife!" said Eling.
"How can she ever qualify to be the wife of a budding leader?" Mayling replied sarcastically, "She makes a very good housewife for a Ningpo peasant."
The sisters questioned Jennie closely about life with Chiang and her relations with his former wives, and commented on Chiang's notorious temper.
"But a bad temper in a man is preferable to a man without a temper,"

Mayling declared. Chiang arrived and the party sat down to dinner. He was placed between Mayling and Eling, who continually praised her clever little sister.

Chiang succeeded in his goal of getting closer to the Soong family. Eling's nine-year-old son David joined the Nationalist general on the Northern Expedition as mascot, calling him "Uncle." The boy had his own uniform, and to appear fierce he drew thick black brows over his eyes in the manner of Chinese theatre. Chiang's forces moved north and by early October 1926 took the three cities on the Yangtze River collectively known as Wuhan. Seven hundred miles upriver from Shanghai, Wuhan was China's third-largest metropolis and a thriving industrial center and treaty port. Mayling telegraphed Chiang congratulating him on the capture of Wuhan and called him a hero. Chiang invited her and her family to visit Hankow to "see our Nationalist Party's new achievements." Addressing Chiang as "Big Brother," Mayling replied that she would visit when she had time.

By this time there were serious strains in the United Front. The tiny Chinese Communist party, which in January 1925 had by its own admission only a thousand members, had under orders from Moscow been cooperating, albeit uneasily, with the Nationalist government since 1924. Sun was happy to accept Soviet aid and Borodin's organizational talents, but not its ideology. He had steadfastly rejected Borodin's demands for land reform and insisted that the conditions for establishing communism or soviets did not exist in China.

In late 1926 the seat of the Soviet-backed Nationalist government was moved from Canton to Wuhan. Its leaders included Mayling's sister Madame Sun Yat-sen; T. V. Soong as finance minister; and Eugene Chen as foreign minister. The group also included Borodin, who with his commanding presence and booming voice was in effect running the Wuhan government while Chiang led the Northern Expedition down the lower Yangtze toward Shanghai. Mayling and her family were well acquainted with the swashbuckling Comintern agitator and his American wife, Fanya. A dashing figure with dark good looks, Borodin found himself infatuated with Mayling, his wife notwithstanding. Once a keen-eyed servant swiped from Borodin's quarters a piece of blotter paper on which he had written again and again, "Mayling Darling, Darling Mayling." When her sisters saw the telltale doodles, they teased Mayling. If Chiang heard of the matter, it is doubtful he found it amusing, given his own interest in the youngest Soong daughter.

In the winter of 1926–27, Mayling, together with her mother and sister Eling, spent three months in Wuhan visiting Ching Ling and T. V., who held senior posts in the Hankow government. There Mayling held a series of long conversations with the colorful and charismatic Marxist revolutionary, during which they debated the relative merits of communism and capitalism. Borodin had proselytized the likes of Claire Sheridan, a famous British artist and journalist and a cousin of Winston Churchill, as well as the internationally celebrated dancer Isadora Duncan, but Mayling was a challenge of a different sort. The talks took place in T. V. Soong's apartment in the Central Bank of China building, which once housed the tsarist Russo-Asiatic Bank, on the bund of the Yangtze River in Hankow's former Russian Concession. In those days, "communism" was a far cry from the fraught term it later became—in fact it was the fashionable new ideology— and Mayling approached the discussions in a spirit of intellectual curiosity, if not intellectual flirtation. She took notes on the dialogue, in which Eling and T. V. occasionally joined. The chain-smoking Bolshevik clearly made a deep impression, as half a century later Mayling's memory of him remained clear. She described him as tall and heavyset, with a "leonine head, with a shock of neatly coifed, long, slightly wavy dark brown mane that came down to the nape of his neck, with an unexaggerated but ample mustache." He spoke in a deep resonant baritone with an American accent and gave the impression, she wrote, of "great control and personal magnetism."

Borodin deployed his formidable charms in a bid to convert the preacher's daughter even as he decried the "dangerous" Christian concept of forgiveness as the "cursed despoiler" in the Communist vision of the world. He knew well Mayling's campaign to improve the working conditions of factory workers, particularly women and children, in Shanghai's International Concession. But labor reforms alone were "futile," he insisted, because in a democracy laws protecting workers could easily be overturned or nullified. The best and only permanent cure was communism, he contended. Borodin "sermonized" Mayling on how there was a dearth of the "right kind of revolutionary spirit and talent" in the world, and tried to persuade her that her talents would be far better spent awakening people to the "blessings of egalitarian Socialism." Mayling found the Marxist revolutionary himself exotic and attractive but his political and religious beliefs abhorrent. However, given her siblings' positions in the Wuhan government, and China's need for Soviet assistance, it is unlikely she directly challenged him.

It may be, however, that partly as a consequence of the talks with Borodin, Eling Kung, the family kingmaker, decided to jettison the Soviet-backed Wuhan government in favor of one more amenable to the Kung-Soong clan's interests. Already Eling's clout was attracting wide notice. In February 1927 the French consul in Canton, in a report to Paris, called her "*très intrigante*" and added, "She aspires to play a political role and is as involved as her husband in public affairs: she is the Vice Ministresse of Finance and also to a certain extent of Foreign Affairs." T. V. Soong was minister of finance of the Wuhan government and head of its central bank; H. H. Kung was minister of commerce and industry. At this critical juncture, Eling presented Chiang with a bargain. She would help to rally Shanghai financiers behind him, enabling him to regain uncontested power by routing the Communist-backed Hankow government, under three conditions: that he appoint T. V. Soong finance minister in the new Nanking government once it was established; that H. H. Kung be given the post of prime minister; and—the clincher—that Chiang marry her little sister Mayling.

This was an offer the ambitious general could not refuse. He broke the news to Jennie Chen by saying it would be a "political marriage" only, and asked her to "step aside" for five years so he could complete his great mission of unifying the country. For the salvation of China, would she make the sacrifice? She could go to America and study, and when she returned they would resume their life together, he assured her. On March 19, 1927, he wrote separate letters to Eling Kung and Mayling Soong, effectively confirming his earlier agreement to Eling's bargain. He asked Mayling to send him a recent photograph of herself so he could "look at you constantly." Presented with a fait accompli, an anguished Jennie immediately began packing her bags and returned to her mother's Shanghai home. On March 21 appeared the first mention of Mayling in Chiang's diary. "Today I am longing for Little Sister May very much," he wrote, in a manner that suggested the romance had been under way for some time.

The next day, March 22, Chiang's forces occupied Shanghai. He had secured foreign support by promising to safeguard the lives and property of foreigners in the port city. Wishing to avoid provoking foreign intervention, Chiang insisted his purpose was only to rid the country of warlords—the enemies from within, he believed, posed the greater threat. On March 24 he took Nanking. The weeks that followed constitute one of the most controversial and murky episodes in modern Chinese history.

Tensions between the Kuomintang and the Communists erupted into deadly clashes as unions rioted in Shanghai, Canton, and other cities. In Moscow, Marshal Joseph Stalin, who had succeeded Lenin, declared in early April that once Chiang was no longer useful he was to be discarded like a squeezed lemon—a remark that if it reached Chiang's ear might help explain what happened next. On April 12, with the backing of Shanghai's commercial and underworld powers, as well as a considerable portion of the Kuomintang, Chiang unleashed a bloodbath. In what was euphemistically couched as a "party purification," many thousands of striking labor activists and other suspected Communists were rounded up and executed, their bodies left to litter the streets of Shanghai, Canton, and Nanking. Thousands more were jailed during the period of "White Terror" that followed. In a fiery speech Chiang denounced both "Reds" and Russians. The purge is generally depicted as a betrayal of the unsuspecting Communists, but may have been a case of Chiang beating the Communists to the punch.

When news of the massacre reached Moscow, Ching-kuo denounced his father as his "enemy" and a "counter-revolutionary." He issued a statement in the Soviet press: "Down with Chiang Kai-shek. Down with the traitor!" In an open letter to Chiang, which ran in part in the Russian daily *Izvestia*, he wrote: "Revolution is the only thing I know, and I do not know you as my father any more." Ching-kuo's action was anathema to traditional Chinese thinking, in which parents are to be obeyed and revered at all costs, and must have infuriated his father. But Chiang made no public reaction to the statements and may have believed that his son made them under duress. Whether or not that was indeed the case, the door for Ching-kuo's return to China had slammed shut, leaving him in forced exile, effectively a hostage. That year he entered the Red Army and continued studies at the military academy in Leningrad.

After the breach with the Communist-led Kuomintang headquarters in Wuhan, Chiang declared the establishment of a "permanent" national government at Nanking, as Sun Yat-sen had wished. Stalin called for an armed Communist takeover of the National Revolution. Ching Ling, ensconced in Hankow, harshly condemned Chiang as a traitor to her late husband's revolution and a criminal against the people. Two years after she rejected his marriage proposal, he tried to woo her again—this time in a political sense. Madame Sun, who wore her widow's weeds like a thorny crown, was by this time the world's most celebrated woman revolutionary. She was hailed as "China's Joan of Arc" by breathless American journalists. Such was her moral stature as the living embodiment of the ideals of Sun Yat-sen that Chiang desperately desired her presence to lend ornamental legitimacy to his new regime. After briefly wavering, practical-minded T. V. Soong switched sides and went to Nanking as finance minister, but Ching Ling refused to budge, despite mounting family pressure. Mayling was even dispatched from Shanghai to try to persuade Ching Ling to leave Hankow, but returned without her famous sister. Chiang—characteristically—ordered her to come to Nanking, but he underestimated the resolve of the outwardly timid and retiring Madame Sun, whom Borodin once famously called "the only man in the whole left wing of the Kuomintang."

Borodin too remained in Hankow, locked in a power struggle with Chiang Kai-shek. In May he told a young American reporter, "Good God, girl! Do you think I'm wet nurse to this revolution?" He was frustrated, ill with malaria, and worried about his wife Fanya, who had been kidnapped by the Manchurian warlord Zhang Zuolin. Looking haggard and drawn, the veteran agitator said, "Our revolution in Russia was big, but nothing like this. We work blindly here. Then we lift the curtain and are frightened by the immensity of the scene." It was ridiculous to suggest that Soviet Russia was trying to communize China. "You can't communize ignorance," he insisted. In June Chiang put a price on Borodin's head and he fled to Russia in July, declaring: "The KMT, like all bourgeois parties, is a toilet, which, as often as you flush it, still stinks!"

Shifting his approach from bullying to cajoling, Chiang tried to entice Madame Sun with offers of a post in the Nanking government, but Ching Ling refused to be either a "traitor or a fence-sitter," electing instead to go into voluntary exile when she could have lived quietly in Shanghai's French Concession. Lest anyone doubt where her sympathies lay, she proceeded to Moscow in August. But before departing she ignored her family's pleas not to publicly criticize Chiang and attacked the "cancerous force of Chinese militarism." She accused Nationalist party leaders of doing "violence to Dr. Sun's ideas and ideals." Any so-called revolution not based on fundamental social change was "merely a change of government." The Kuomintang had ceased working for the welfare of the Chinese people, becoming instead "a parasite fattening on the present enslaving system." Revolution in China was inevitable, she concluded. "My disheartenment is only for the path into which some of those who had been leading the revolution have strayed."

In July Chiang's armies were decisively routed north of the Yangtze and forced to retreat to the south bank. By August his opposition within the Nationalist party was so vehement that on August 12 he staged a "retirement" as commander in chief of the National Revolutionary Army and retreated home to his "Summer White House" in Fenghua. Apparently taken to facilitate a party reunion, the "retirement" was to Chiang's advantage on several counts. Not only did it "enhance his greatness in the minds of both the masses and the troops," it starkly revealed Chiang's indispensability to the Nanking government, which squabbled in his absence.

Shortly before this political maneuver, Chiang visited Jennie Chen and presented her with steamship tickets to America. Jennie did not want to go into exile, but Chiang insisted, citing her departure abroad as one of Eling Kung's conditions. Jennie claimed that her mother made him swear before a shrine in her home that he would keep his promises to her. Holding three joss sticks, Chiang faced the shrine and said: "I promise to resume my marital relationship with Chieh-ju [Jieru] . . . within five years from today. Should I break my promise and fail to take her back, may the Great Buddha smite me . . . topple my government and banish me from China forever."

Jennie arrived in San Francisco on September 8. Fashionably attired and wearing a stylish short haircut, "Madame Chiang . . . speaks almost perfect English," reported the *San Francisco Chronicle*. This was her first visit to America, and she and her party were on a world tour, she told the press. Although retired, her husband was continuing to work for the nation, she said, comparing China's struggle for unity to that of the United States during and after the American Revolution. "When we need a friend we can always look toward our sister republic."

But while Jennie was fêted in San Francisco as "Madame Chiang Kai-shek," as she was known in China and abroad, Chiang was busily reinventing history. From Fenghua, he declared that the woman in question was not his wife and he did not know her; the report was "the work of political enemies." He had divorced his legal wife in 1921, he told foreign news reporters, and had recently "freed" two "concubines" in the belief that the practice of concubinage was undesirable, and he was now entirely without wife.

Scarcely had Jennie left for America when Shanghai began swirling with rumors that Chiang planned to marry Mayling Soong. Finally, on September 21, Mayling held a dinner party for her most intimate Chinese and foreign friends at which she confirmed the wedding plans. There would be no formal announcement as yet due to her family's objections to the match, she said. She hoped to obtain their consent but was determined to proceed regardless. "I sincerely love the great general," she told the gathering.

On September 23 Chiang arrived in Shanghai from his native village and that evening met Mayling for a long talk. "I am very excited by our mutual love and affection," he wrote in his diary that night. "This is a joy rarely found in life." On September 26 they were formally engaged.

On September 28 Chiang departed for Japan with Liu Jiwen, his chief secretary and Mayling's erstwhile suitor, to seek Mother Soong's blessing. He followed Mother Soong from Kobe to Kamakura, a seaside town on the outskirts of Tokyo. The family matriarch was deeply distressed at the thought of her youngest daughter marrying Chiang Kai-shek. Her dreams of a good match for Ching Ling had been dashed when she'd eloped with Sun Yat-sen, who was more than twice her age, married, and impecunious. Only the eldest daughter, Eling, had married well by the solidly bourgeois and aspiring standards of the Soong family. When Chiang's suit became known, Mother Soong refused to see him—this being the time-honored Chinese way of saying no.

For a God-fearing, conservative Chinese woman of good family such as Mother Soong, Chiang was possibly the most unsavory potential son-in-law imaginable. First, he was a soldier, an occupation that ranked low on the traditional Chinese social ladder. "Nails are not made of good iron nor soldiers of good men," went the old saying. Worse, Chiang already had three wives, although he tried to finesse this tricky matter by fashioning the last two "concubines." To add to his curriculum vitae, the Municipal Police of Shanghai's International Settlement still had no fewer than three outstanding warrants for his arrest: one for murder, another for armed robbery, and a third for an unspecified crime. In contrast to Mother Soong's patri-

cian origins, he did not come from a family of any particular merit. He was
not financially secure, and neither was he well educated. Next to the cosmopolitan Soongs he was uncouth and provincial. But most troubling to
Mother Soong was the fact that he was a Buddhist.

On October 2, Shanghai's leading daily newspaper, *Shen Bao,* ran a story
citing widespread rumors that the Soong family insisted Chiang meet several conditions for marriage into the family. These included that he provide proof of divorce from his first wife, that he travel abroad to widen his
horizons, and that Mayling control the family finances. That same day, as
if on cue, the paper carried another article quoting Chiang as claiming he'd
formally divorced his first wife, Mao Fumei, in 1921. The paper reprinted
a letter Chiang had ostensibly written to Mao's brother, dated April 3, 1921,
and published at that time in *Shen Bao,* stating his reasons for divorcing her.
For Chinese men, a public announcement was all that was required to effect
a divorce.

Mother Soong at last relented and agreed to meet the importunate
suitor. He apparently satisfied her as to the disposal of his other women.
As to religion, Chiang promised to study the Bible diligently but as a matter of principle could not convert to Christianity without understanding its
beliefs. His answer must have swayed Mother Soong, for *Shen Bao* reported
on October 6 that she had consented to the match. T. V. Soong loathed
Chiang and tried to prevent the marriage, but accepted it once his mother
acquiesced. He was quite close to Ching Ling and found the ideological
breach between her and the rest of the family extremely uncomfortable.
Chiang disliked T. V. in return, but superficially they cooperated. Their
mutual enmity was not due to politics but "chemistry." As the eldest surviving male and nominal head of the family, T. V. dutifully made arrangements for the wedding. Mayling's future husband returned to Shanghai
from Japan on November 10 to find his fiancée ill and confined to bed.

When Ching Ling learned of Mayling's intention to marry Chiang Kai-
shek she said she would rather see her sister dead than wed to such a man
and begged her to reconsider. She refused to return to China for the wedding, deriding it as a "marriage of opportunism on both sides, with no love
involved." Her evident disgust belied the strong similarities between
the marriages of the two sisters. During her school days, Ching Ling—a
romantic soul—had been greatly moved by the story of Joan of Arc, and

there may have been more to her opposition to the match than dislike of
Chiang Kai-shek. "Could it not be that Mayling, a sincere conservative, was
quite as convinced that she was marrying China's saviour as Ching Ling, a
sincere radical, was convinced of the same when she married Dr. Sun?"
asked Ching Ling's friend, the writer Edgar Snow. "Sibling rivalry between
the two 'first ladies' of China was always very strong." Mayling was likely
as driven to compete with her sister as much as she was inspired by her
example. As was her wont, Mayling no doubt set out to outshine her
sister—and usurp her role as China's Joan of Arc.

There was one sticking point: the Soongs insisted upon a Christian wedding ceremony by a Methodist minister. The Southern Methodist Church,
however, had decreed that there could be no marriage after divorce. The
Soongs argued that since Chiang's earlier marriage was not Christian, what
had not been joined together could not be put asunder, but such was the
distaste for the union of Chiang and Mayling that no ordained Methodist
minister could be persuaded to marry them. Bishop William Ainsworth,
newly installed head of the church's Far East missions, was in China at the
time. Mayling wanted her former surrogate father at Wesleyan College to
officiate, but he declined. Next she asked China's most prominent Methodist minister, Dr. Z. T. Kaung, a close friend of Mother Soong. He, too,
demurred. Finally a lay minister, Dr. David Yui, general secretary of the
Chinese YMCA, agreed to perform the ceremony. Just days in advance, it
was announced the wedding would take place on December 1, 1927. Fifteen hundred invitations were issued, each bearing T. V. Soong's personal
chop, or seal.

Chiang released an extraordinary statement, published in *Shen Bao* on
the wedding day. He portrayed the union as one fired not by passion but
by shared ideals. The marriage, he intimated, would breathe new life into
the moribund Chinese Revolution and usher in a period of social reform
and stability. Most surprising, in view of contemporary Chinese mores, he
depicted Mayling as determinedly pursuing him rather than the reverse.
"When I first saw Miss Soong, I felt she was my ideal wife, and she vowed
that if she could not win Chiang Kai-shek as her husband, she would rather
die a spinster," Chiang wrote. Husband and wife were equals in a modern
relationship, he implied. She was the inspiration behind his renewed revolutionary zeal, and together they would reconstruct China. "Miss Soong

and I have discussed the problems of China's revolution, and on this point we truly hold the same faith," he wrote. "It is our hope that our marriage can have some influence on the old society and make a contribution to the new society. Our wedding is more than a celebration of our happiness in marriage; it is a symbol of the reconstruction of Chinese society. . . . Therefore, our marriage today is the foundation of the Revolution."

Chiang's statement sparked wide comment, including a December 2, 1927, editorial in *Dagong Bao*, another Shanghai newspaper, ridiculing his attempt to link his marriage to the "Revolution." As with the union of Sun Yat-sen and Ching Ling Soong, charges of bigamy surrounded the marriage. Attempts were made to demonstrate that divorces had been secured beforehand with the consent of the previous wives. But the legality of those divorces was problematic, even in the lenient context of Chinese family law. That Chiang married Jennie Chen in a lawful ceremony was well known. Although second marriages were common during that era of social change, his decision to brazenly repudiate Chen, with Mayling's connivance, was widely seen as reprehensible. Anti-Christian Chinese bitterly scorned the couple as hypocrites who used religion to suit their own ends. Naturally the episode did nothing to enhance the image of Christianity in the eyes of the Chinese.

Ethical concerns notwithstanding, the wedding of the Nationalist generalissimo and Charles Soong's youngest daughter was the high point of Shanghai's social calendar that year. A small, private Christian wedding at the Soong home at 139 Seymour Road was followed by an elaborate Chinese-style ceremony at the Majestic Hotel, Shanghai's grandest hostelry. Cai Yuanpei, education minister in the Nanking government and former chancellor of the prestigious Beijing University, conducted the ceremony. Guests numbered at least thirteen hundred, several hundred of whom were foreigners, including Shanghai's entire diplomatic corps and a contingent of foreign military officers. Outside, thousands of Chinese crowded the streets in the hope of glimpsing the retired Generalissimo and his bride. Scores of plainclothes detectives, both Chinese and foreign, were on hand.

In the center of the dais stood a large and lifelike portrait of Dr. Sun Yat-sen, below crossed flags of the Kuomintang and the government. Cinema cameras ground furiously. Chiang wore morning coat and tails, striped pants, and wing collar, but he appeared uncomfortable in the unaccustomed attire.

Mayling held a bouquet of white and pink carnations and wore a beaded gown of silver and white georgette topped by a wreath of orange buds over a long flowing lace veil. A train of white charmeuse embroidered in silver was matched by silver shoes. Mayling's niece and nephew, Jeanette and Louis Kung, served as pages, wearing black velvet suits. The bride and groom bowed three times to the portrait of Sun Yat-sen. Under the brilliant glare of motion picture lights, the marriage certificate was read in Chinese, signed, and sealed. The bride and groom faced each other and bowed solemnly once. They then bowed to witnesses and guests. In accord with Chinese custom, the newlyweds did not kiss or embrace. Every aspect of the wedding was carefully orchestrated with an eye to publicity; a film of the proceedings was made and distributed to cinemas.

The newlyweds received thousands of gifts from across China, including hundreds of figures of Buddha and Guanyin, goddess of mercy. Mother Soong's Christian sensibilities were affronted by the pagan idols and she insisted that they be destroyed. So bride, groom, and mother set to work with hammers and shattered them all, except one particularly fine Buddha of green jade that Chiang managed to hide away, intending to place it in the tomb of his Buddhist ancestors one day.

Exactly why Mayling decided to marry Chiang remains something of a mystery. While her sister Eling may have orchestrated the match, it is certain that no one, not even Eling, could have persuaded Mayling to do something she did not wish to do. Chiang appealed to her because he was a "heroic figure," even though his prospects were uncertain. She was fired with "tremendous enthusiasm and patriotism—a passionate desire to do something for my country," she wrote later. "Here was my opportunity. With my husband, I would work ceaselessly to make China strong." It must be said, however, that not all of her equally patriotic contemporaries would have chosen to marry Chiang Kai-shek.

Twenty-year-old Jennie Chen, meanwhile, found herself in New York City, humiliated and outcast. Hysterical with grief, she tried to take her own life by leaping into the Hudson River but was stopped by a kind elderly man. Chiang, she claimed, offered no support.

PART II

Chapter Seven
The Generalissimo's Wife

I have the greatest blessings which any woman could have: the opportunity to lose myself in a great Will, and a husband who has the same faith that I have.

—Mayling Soong Chiang

The honeymoon lasted barely a week. In desperation, the Nanking government begged Chiang to resume his place as commander in chief of the Nationalist armies and continue the Northern Expedition to unify the country. No one, least of all Chiang Kai-shek, was surprised. In his absence the government had fallen into disarray amid internecine squabbling. This would not be the last time that Chiang would "retire" from public life, only to be called back when warring factions in the Kuomintang realized that much as they disliked him, he was the only figure in Chinese public life who could hold everyone together. With carefully staged reluctance, Chiang returned, insisting that he wished to resign once the goal of the Northern Expedition was accomplished. The Kuomintang leadership responded by giving him wider powers than before.

Chiang moved swiftly to consolidate his grasp on the revolutionary legacy of Sun Yat-sen, cemented by his marriage into the Soong family. After his forces defeated the Manchurian warlord Zhang Zuolin in June 1928, thus completing the Northern Expedition, Mayling and Chiang went to Beijing to attend a service in honor of the dead Nationalist leader. Keen to cultivate ties with the outside world while in the ancient northern capital, on July 21, 1928, the pair made an appearance at a weekly gathering of the leading lights of the city's foreign community. Beijing was abuzz with excitement and speculation at the sensational prospect of hosting a ruthless warlord at a civilized tea party. But in the flesh the Generalissimo was a disappointment. Appearing "frail and ascetic," with an "overly polite and timid" demeanor, he was outshone by his sparkling and vivacious American-educated bride. He was plainly in love, wrote a guest. "He glanced at her from time to time with obvious pride and affection, and occasionally furtively held her hand"—a display of affection shocking to the Chinese.

The fledgling Nationalist administration claimed to represent China, but in reality Chiang's Nanking government controlled less than one-tenth of China's territory and more than one-fifth of its population. Undaunted, Chiang embarked on an ambitious plan to lay the foundation for a unified, stable, and modern—if not democratic—state while attempting to expand the area under his government's effective control. His schemes, however, were beset with difficulties. From the start Chiang's army was forced to repel repeated challenges from regional warlords, and the Communists, driven underground in 1927, were regrouping in the countryside. After the Northern Expedition, Chiang embarked on a series of costly "bandit suppression" campaigns intended to exterminate the Communists. But perhaps the most critical threat to the Nanking government's future came from within. Soon after its hopeful beginnings it became clear that the 1927 purge and the reign of terror that followed had virtually bled the Kuomintang of idealists, reformers, and visionaries, leaving behind the selfish and corrupt careerists to run the government.

When the newlyweds first arrived in Nanking, the capital was a "sad mixture of ancient, crumbling glory and new raw ugliness." The fabled Purple Mountain overlooked "nothing but a little village with one so-called broad street . . . so narrow that if two motor cars were coming in opposite directions one of them had to back off on a side street until the other passed," Mayling wrote. Apart from missionary compounds the houses were "primitive, cold and uncomfortable." Chiang Kai-shek and his bride soon set about remaking Nanking into a city fit to be the capital of the nation they dreamed of building. Streets were widened, and an American architect was engaged to help China's best architects design new ministry buildings in a style that blended Chinese and modern elements. While the foreign ministry was under construction, the first couple were often seen strolling the site arm-in-arm. Apart from their official quarters at Nanking, Mayling's brother T. V., finance minister in the Nanking government, had purchased the newlyweds a house in Shanghai's French Concession in lieu of a dowry. Chiang dubbed the European-style villa *Ai Lu*—Love Cottage.

Life in the capital was difficult, especially given that all the wives of government officials opted to reside in Shanghai rather than face the privations of the capital. Chiang insisted Mayling attend official functions, and initially she found it trying to be the only woman. "The officials themselves were also very conscious of me as a woman," she wrote, "but later on I forgot about myself in my interest in helping my husband in his work, and they also began to regard me not as a woman but as one of themselves."

Chiang was a notoriously poor conversationalist and came to rely on Mayling to enliven social functions, particularly with foreigners. His idea of holding up his end of a conversation consisted of saying "Aunk, aunk," like a duck honking, which meant "Yes, yes." Government officials and foreign diplomats alike noticed that when Madame Chiang was absent, formal dinners with Chiang were stiff and awkward affairs during which a "painful silence" prevailed.

For a period after her marriage, Mayling mostly avoided the public eye and appeared only with her husband. But soon she grew restless and set to work. She led a fund-raising campaign for a thousand-bed military hospital. Then she turned her attention to the many young military officers without families, who lacked what she termed "wholesome companionship or amusement" after working hours. Chiang's former cadets from the Whampoa Military Academy often visited their home. She started a social club for army officers modeled on the YMCA and gave it the austere name of the Officers' Moral Endeavor Association. She recruited a friend, J. L. Huang, from the Shanghai YMCA to run the OMEA, whose aim was to "instill a new and creative spirit" and, as the name suggests, a high moral standard in the Chinese army. Many officers initially resisted, thinking the club a "new method of foreign propaganda and a hidden way of forcing them to become Christians," as Huang put it. Many officers did eventually join, but it is unclear how much moral impact the club had on Chiang's soldiers.

Mayling's next project was to establish schools for the children of "revolutionary heroes," the orphans of Chiang's soldiers. "These children, I thought, would be the most valuable material if they were molded right as they all had revolutionary blood in their veins," she wrote. She was appalled by typical

Chinese foundling homes, which she called "dark, dirty, pestiferous holes." The idea of educating soldiers' children was a new concept in a land in which soldiers were traditionally held in low esteem and universal education was but a distant dream. Although the officer corps was drawn from the gentry class, recruits came from the poorest families and often joined because they were hungry or conscripted. Along with her husband, Mayling sought to make the military an honorable and respected profession, as it was in the West. She felt that the least the government could do to keep up troop morale was to provide for the offspring of fallen soldiers. She was, however, partisan in her charity—orphans of soldiers who died fighting for Chiang's rivals, including the Communists, were not welcome.

Drawing on her early educational experience in America, Mayling sought to create utopian Chinese schools for these orphans, where students would not only be taught the "three R's" but also instilled with moral and civic values by teachers who served in loco parentis. It was as though she thought that since she could not save all of China's countless impoverished children, she would compensate by creating a tiny island of perfection in an ocean of ignorance and poverty. She chose the thousand-acre site for the two schools—one for boys and one for girls—for its scenic beauty. Located near Sun Yat-sen's mausoleum and the Ming Tombs at the foot of Purple Mountain, the modern new buildings were spacious and well furnished. Architecturally and educationally, the schools were on a par with some of the better American private schools. In China they were a unique and astonishing privilege. There were playgrounds, a swimming pool, a gymnasium, model classrooms, and dormitories. They were intended as a training ground for the future elite of China. Mayling hand-picked the teachers.

The children played sports—unheard of in China before the missionaries. The boys grew vegetables and flowers for use by the school and sold the remainder. Mayling imported ten milk cows from America and started a dairy. Girls were trained in sewing and crafts and sold their products. The students were instilled with a consciousness of their future as "pillars and reformers of Chinese society." They called Mayling "Mama" and followed her around when she visited.

Along with their undeniably positive attributes, the schools had a quasi-military aspect. Students were confined to campus, not even returning to family for vacations lest their characters be tainted by contact with the outside world. Boys and girls gave teachers the military salute. Discipline and regimentation were de rigueur. The schools were a mild version of the Hitler Jugend and Mussolini's Fascist Youth, with an ethos comprising a puzzling mixture of Chinese, American, Christian, and fascist thinking—in short, very much a product of Mayling's own curious blend of experience.

Mayling's interests were not confined to social work. From 1929 to 1932, she served as an appointed member of the Nanking government's parliament, one of three women in the lawmaking body. The country's archaic legal system needed updating, and characteristically she armed herself for the task by reading up on legal philosophy. She was particularly attracted to Ulpian's definition of the science of law as "the knowledge of things human and divine, the science of the just and the unjust."

Sun Yat-sen believed that women should have rights equal to men, a principle spelled out at the first National Congress of the Kuomintang in 1924. Despite her husband's reluctance and her own shyness, Mayling publicly spoke out for women's rights. She pushed the parliament to enact a civil code designed to protect married women. Under the new law a husband who took a concubine could be charged with bigamy. Daughters were entitled to share inheritance equally with sons, and the offspring of concubines could not inherit. Minimum ages were set for betrothal and marriage, which could be undertaken only with the agreement of both parties. In practice, however, the law had little impact. Mayling used her position to recommend capable women to positions of prominence in the legislature, the Kuomintang, and elsewhere. She fought to rid China of the hated extraterritoriality laws, under which Chinese citizens living in Shanghai and other treaty ports were tried under the laws of the various foreign countries operating the concessions.

Gradually Mayling became her husband's chief adviser and translator, as the only foreign language he spoke was Japanese, and poorly at that. She started to teach him English, to make him less dependent on her help. One day he tried out his English on the British minister to China, Sir Miles Lampson. "Kiss me, Lampson," Chiang said. It emerged to the chagrin of both that he had meant to say "Good morning," but had gotten confused. He never again attempted to speak English to foreigners, but foreign visitors were convinced that he understood most of what was said while pretending not to.

Mayling entertained visitors constantly and sat in on meetings with her husband, and as time passed she gained confidence, clout, and a reputation for getting things done. "Take that up with Madame" soon became a byword in the capital as she shouldered more and more of the burden of filtering problems, requests, and contacts with the outside world for the Generalissimo. She interpreted for him at meetings with foreigners, and she handled much of his foreign correspondence. She kept him abreast of foreign affairs by reading him articles from her favorite American magazines. She became his muse, his eyes, his ears, often his voice, and above all his most loyal champion.

She often accompanied Chiang on campaign, serving as his aide-de-camp. "My place is at the front," she said. Before marriage her few excursions outside Shanghai had been limited to treaty port cities. Of the vast hinterland of China, where the overwhelming majority of her four hundred million countrymen lived, she had no knowledge whatsoever. She had never lived in a "purely Chinese" environment, she wrote, nor faced so many physical discomforts, which she mitigated by bringing curtains and flower pots to brighten the thatched mud huts, railway stations, or tents in which she and Chiang stayed. "Whatever material comforts we have to forgo . . . we do not mind because we have each other and our work," she wrote a friend.

The rigors of the battlefront did not prevent her from traveling with a sixty-strong entourage including her American nurse, a secretary, her maid, manservants, and bodyguards. She traveled by air, automobile, rail, foot, rickshaw, litter, and sampan. As well as acting as her husband's secretary, she directed soldiers' relief efforts and organized local women to comfort the wounded. She talked to the women, asking them about their daily lives and troubles. She filed news dispatches and essays for Shanghai and American newspapers from behind the front lines. Keenly aware of their propaganda value, she wrote long letters to American friends, who often sent them on to newspapers.

In one missive she recounted a brush with danger in "bandit"—Communist—territory. In the dead of night she heard shooting. She threw on her clothes and grabbed her revolver. "I had only two things on my mind," she wrote. "First, the papers giving information of our troop movements and positions must not fall into enemy hands; second, should I find myself about to be taken captive, I must shoot myself, for death would be clean, honorable and preferable, since women who have been captured by the communist-bandits suffered untold brutalities and indignities." It emerged that the incident resulted from confusion among different groups of Nationalist troops. Mayling, whether out of naivete or bravado, seemed blithely unconcerned, for her husband had told her that "since we are fighting for the country, Heaven will protect us. And should we be killed, what more glorious than to die in action?"

During the early years of her marriage, Mayling appeared to be blissfully happy and fulfilled. On New Year's Eve in 1934, she and Chiang took a walk in the mountains of Fukien, where Chiang was on campaign. They came across a plum tree in full bloom, a sign of good luck. The Generalissimo picked a few branches of the white blossoms, and after they returned to camp he presented them to her. "I think from this perhaps you will understand why I am so willing to share life with him," she wrote a friend. "He has the courage of a soldier and the sensitiveness of a poet!" Despite dangers and worries, she and her husband had an "inexplicable security and sureness in our hearts," she wrote. "I am far happier than I have ever been . . . because I am not living on the surface, but reaching towards something that is beyond myself. I thank God many times that I have the greatest blessings which any woman could have: the opportunity to lose myself in a great Will, and a husband who has the same faith that I have." But there was one sorrow she found too great to mention. The subject of children had been a painful one ever since she had a miscarriage in late August 1929. Chiang avoided raising the topic and rarely mentioned it in his diary.

After the completion of the Northern Expedition in 1929, Chiang had declared that the period of "political tutelage," the interim stage of Sun Yat-sen's three phases of democratic development, had begun. In reality, however, more rather than less power was concentrated in the hands of Chiang Kai-shek over time. This fact did not go unnoticed at home or abroad, despite a vigorous publicity campaign aimed at portraying China as moving toward democracy. Through letters to American friends, essays, and articles, Mayling bravely—or brazenly—strived to create the image of a benevolent, forward-thinking and Western-oriented government that was working toward bringing China into the modern world.

In fact the government was virtually overwhelmed by the enormity of the country's problems. When the Nanking government was launched in 1927, China was a nation in name only. There existed no effective and nationally functioning administrative, legal, judicial, financial, monetary, or taxation systems—in other words, none of the architecture of a modern state. Where such systems existed they were a patchwork. The power of taxation lay in the hands of the provincial authorities, leaving the Nanking government with limited financial resources. The practical difficulties in administering such a vast land, with some four hundred million mostly impoverished and illiterate inhabitants and desperately inadequate public infrastructure, were staggering. Constant military challenges from within and the threat of Japanese militarism through the late 1920s and into the 1930s served only to exacerbate problems. Famine and natural disasters were devastating. A great flood in the summer of 1931 inundated an area the size of Britain across the Yangtze River Valley, leaving 14 million refugees and killing 3.7 million people in the flooding and subsequent disease and starvation.

Chiang's "bandit suppression" campaigns failed to wipe out the Communists, although the Nationalists succeeded in executing the first wife of Communist leader Mao Zedong in 1930. Chiang did manage to drive the Communists out of southern and central China in 1934, when they began their famous "Long March" northwestward to their future stronghold in Yenan. There had been visible improvement in the urban centers of East China, but Nanking's failure to extend the benefits of modernization to the peasantry had left the countryside a powderkeg. Given its limited resources and corrupt, ineffective bureaucracy, it was inevitable that the government's effectiveness in raising the quality of life for all Chinese would be negligible. Perhaps more surprising is that the Nanking government accomplished as much as it did, for despite the odds it had made considerable progress in putting together the framework of a modern state. Mayling and Chiang were acutely aware of the challenges. "Were it not for the fact that my husband and I realize that this is the inevitable transition stage between China's emerging from a self-contained feudalist nation to a modern democracy, we would indeed feel hopeless," she wrote an American friend.

Some Chinese critics blamed the government's woes on its "Eurasian" nature, a reference to the many foreign advisers and Western-educated Chinese in its ranks. Rising patriotic sentiment was accompanied by heightened antiforeign feeling. A generation of intellectuals whose mettle was forged in the May Fourth movement of 1919 sought inspiration from the West, absorbing Western ideas and values while rejecting Western influence in China. Many had liberal if not leftist leanings, and were filled with disillusionment and yearnings for a strong and modern China. As the Nanking government centralized its power in the early 1930s, it tightened censorship and restricted intellectual freedoms. In the midst of civil war, any form of dissent, especially of a Communist flavor, was severely repressed, and a sort of "reign of terror" existed on some university campuses, with occasional raids, expulsions, and arrests. Espousal of communism was a capital offense and often no proof was required. In one incident, six young writers were forced to dig their own graves and then buried alive—an ancient punishment. "That is our Christian Generalissimo—burying our best young people alive," said Ching Ling, who had friends among those killed.

In 1930, Chiang defeated a challenge from two northern warlords, Feng Yuxiang and Yan Xishan, with the aid of Young Marshal Zhang Xueliang. In May 1931, Chiang's rivals in the Kuomintang, led by Wang Jingwei and Sun Yat-sen's son Sun Fo, set up a short-lived separatist government in Canton. While Communists, warlords, and factions besieged the Nationalist government from within, Japan was crouching to pounce from without. Following years of tentative forays, Japan invaded Manchuria in 1931 in a first step toward the realization of a Greater East Asian Co-Prosperity Sphere, Japan's answer to the nineteenth-century American doctrine of Manifest Destiny. Under the scheme, which in Japan took on the flavor of a national mission to achieve world power, China would be exploited as a boundless source of raw materials and labor to feed the surging Japanese military and industrial machine. Despite China's nominal unification under the Kuomintang in the late 1920s, Japan continued to regard China as a mere "geographical expression" rather than a nation.

The first step in Tokyo's grand plan was to annex the three northeastern provinces collectively known as Manchuria. *Dongbei*, or Northeast, as the region is called by the Chinese, is a vast land the size of France and Germany combined, rich in agricultural and mineral resources. Soy, wheat, sorghum, and rice were produced in abundance and most of China's heavy industry was in Dongbei as well.

Mayling and Manchurian leader Zhang Xueliang, known as the Young Marshal, were old friends. Zhang was as unlike Chiang Kai-shek as anyone could be. Where Chiang was stiff, socially inept, and bad at foreign languages, the Young Marshal was personable, humorous, and spoke reasonably good English. Chiang was an avowed Christian and ascetic in his personal habits; Zhang enjoyed tennis and golf as well as gambling, drink, and women. He was an opium addict to boot. When he took command of Manchuria at the age of thirty, he was widely regarded as a wastrel playboy. Few—least of all the Japanese—believed he would live up to the record of his bandit-turned-warlord father, assassinated by the Japanese on July 4, 1928. The Old Marshal, Zhang Zuolin, had been a formidable character reputed to drink tiger's blood and keep a large harem of white as well as Chinese women.

But the Young Marshal showed unexpected verve and, ignoring Japanese warnings, he pledged loyalty to the Nationalist Chinese government in Nanking shortly after. The size of his Manchurian forces made him de facto second-in-command of China's military. In 1930 he further annoyed Japan by expanding his territory and working in concert with Chiang Kai-shek to keep rival warlords at bay. But on September 18, 1931, zealous Japanese army officers stationed in Manchuria sparked a confrontation with Chinese forces in the city of Mukden, the Young Marshal's stronghold. At that critical juncture, Zhang was desperately ill with "typhoid"—in fact because of his opium habit—in a Beijing hospital. From his sickbed, he ordered his troops not to resist. Manchuria quickly fell to the Japanese, who subsequently established a puppet state called Manchukuo and installed twenty-five-year-old Pu Yi, "last emperor" of the Qing dynasty, as nominal head. Hoping for international intervention, the Nanking government referred the matter to the League of Nations, but no action was taken. The episode was a humiliation to China and to the Young Marshal, who came under attack for having lost his homeland.

Horrified, Mayling pressed China's case through diplomatic channels, but was told by Western representatives that their countries were not "international policemen." The loss of Manchuria to Japan ignited public anger and prompted boycotts of Japanese goods. The Nanking government faced great pressure to repel the invader, but Chiang Kai-shek believed his straw-sandaled forces were woefully unprepared to face Japan's advanced military might in an all-out confrontation.

If China went to war with Japan now, he reasoned, the result would be defeat. Chiang felt that the only way to survive was to delay the inevitable as long as possible. The Communists, Mayling later contended, under the "cloak of patriotism, whipped up and took advantage of the innocent zeal of our youthful students to agitate for immediate hostility against the Japanese warlords." Chiang's "bamboo" strategy of bending but not breaking under the strain of Japanese encroachment into China was deeply unpopular, and the sense of disillusionment among the country's intellectuals was keen.

In the early years of her marriage Mayling emerged from shy bride to full political partner of Chiang Kai-shek. "She sits alongside the Generalissimo and tells him what to do, and he does it," wrote Clarence E. Gauss, an American diplomat in Nanking. "She issues instructions and they are obeyed. . . . She has developed a tremendous influence." The many awed journalists who visited her were amazed by her energy and efficiency. The Wellesley alumnae magazine proudly reported that "the bound feet of the Celestial maiden have been replaced forever by the Wellesley stride."

But political adviser and aide-de-camp were not the only roles that Mayling played vis-à-vis her husband; she also became his spiritual mentor. Before they married Chiang had promised Mother Soong that he would study the Bible, and he did so in earnest. Mayling tutored him using notes from her biblical history course at Wellesley. It was three years before he was ready to convert. He made the decision when at one point his forces were fighting a challenge from warlord Feng Yuxiang. Chiang found himself surrounded. Trapped and desperate, he entered a small country church and prayed to God for deliverance, vowing that if he were rescued he would acknowledge Jesus Christ as his Lord. His prayers were answered in the form of a heavy snowstorm, which slowed the enemy advance long enough for reinforcements to arrive from Nanking. Despite heavy losses, Chiang emerged victorious in the face of certain defeat. He asked to be baptized, saying, "I feel the need of a God such as Jesus Christ." The service was performed on October 23, 1930, at Mother Soong's home by Reverend Z. T. Kaung, pastor of the Young J. Allen Memorial Church.

While America's faithful rejoiced in Chiang's conversion as a sign that China was being won to Christ, many observers were skeptical. "There's Methodism in his madness," cynics quipped. The *New York Herald Tribune*, then America's leading daily, suggested Chiang might be a "rice Christian"—one who converted for food rather than spiritual motives—who had converted in the hope of enlisting American backing in his campaign against the Communists and other enemies. Ironically, Chiang's Northern Expedition had been aided by propaganda denouncing all things Christian—churches, hospitals, and schools—as imperialistic.

Due to censorship the Chinese newspapers did not report the baptism, but the English-language as well as foreign press did. The news quickly spread in China, where it was greeted with astonishment, and much intense speculation as to his motives ensued in both Chinese and foreign circles. Christians jubilantly compared his conversion to that of the Roman emperor Constantine, while others derided it as a political ploy. Nanking officials maintained a discreet public silence on the matter, but in private vented indignation. Anti-Christian and antireligious propaganda was prevalent, and opposition to missionary presence had risen to such an extent that all mission schools had lately been compelled either to offer theretofore compulsory religious courses as electives or to drop them from the curriculum entirely. So unpopular was Christianity that despite hundreds of years of evangelism, Chinese Christians numbered less than half a million out of China's some four hundred million people. In this context, Chiang's decision to convert was either foolhardy or courageous, but in any event it could hardly have been one that he undertook lightly or merely for public consumption, as critics charged. To the contrary, Chiang was possessed of a fervor that few but the converted can muster. He did not proselytize, but for the rest of his life he would turn to the Bible and the life of Jesus to inspire, justify, and sustain himself in carrying out what he regarded as his life's mission—China's salvation and rebirth.

Of the depth of Chiang's religious feeling there could be little doubt. However, his interpretation of Christianity gives pause. Ching Ling voiced the cynicism of many when she said: "If he is a Christian, then I am not." Already he showed signs of his trademark messianic—even megalomaniac—zeal. Conversion infused his overweening ambition with divine purpose: he would be the Christ of China. He would lead his country out of foreign oppression and weakness, and the end would justify every means. "So long as the task of national salvation is not accomplished, I shall be responsible for the distress and sufferings of the people," Chiang declared. Mayling embraced his hubris as divine mission and saw her role as his anointed helpmate.

Although she called her husband a greater Christian than herself, Mayling too was becoming more religious. The trend intensified when her mother fell seriously ill not long after Chiang's baptism. The prospect of losing her mother frightened her, for she had always felt that whatever might happen, she could rely on her mother to "pray me through." She would have to learn to pray for herself, as her mother had long insisted she must. One day as her mother lay ill, they spoke of the looming Japanese threat to China. Mayling suddenly burst out, "Mother, you are so powerful in prayer, why don't you pray to God to destroy Japan in an earthquake so that she can no longer harm China?" Mother Soong remained silent for a time before replying: "Don't ask me to pray to God to do anything that is unworthy even of you, a mortal. Vengeance is mine, saith the Lord. It certainly isn't yours." Her words made a lasting impression on Mayling.

During this time Mayling had the first of what she called spiritual experiences. One night she took a room in the Shanghai sanatorium next to her ailing mother. Chiang took the next room. Mayling dreamed that a strange man with a brutal face appeared outside her door with a revolver in each hand. She screamed in her sleep so loudly that she woke her husband. The next night they stayed at their residence in the French Concession. She dreamed that she stood with her mother behind the house and sprinkled a circle of flour on the lawn. In the circle appeared an apparition dressed in white, looking like Guanyin, the goddess of mercy, but with a face of evil. It said, "I know everything and will tell you anything. Ask me what you want to know." But Mayling's mother cast a glance of warning, and Mayling replied: "Before I ask you a question, tell me whether you are God or the devil?"

The specter shrieked and melted away, and Mayling awoke screaming. Chiang, also suffering from bad dreams, clapped for his bodyguard. Oddly, two men appeared instead of the usual one on duty, but he thought little of it. Mayling remembered the jade Buddha they had received as a wedding gift, the one that escaped her mother's hammers. Disturbed by the dreams, they fetched the idol from the attic, broke it, and threw it away.

The third night Mayling dreamed of two men creeping toward the door of her bedroom. Again she awoke screaming, only to find her husband's bed empty. She found him outside talking with Shanghai police officers, who had arrived in time to foil a Communist plot to assassinate them both. Two bodyguards had tried to carry out the attack the two previous nights but were deterred by Mayling's screams. She was convinced their lives had been saved by "Divine Providence."

Mother Soong died in July 1931. The *North-China Daily News* called her the "Mother-in-law of the country," as two of her sons-in-law had headed the Chinese government. Ching Ling returned from self-imposed exile in Europe to attend the funeral. Mayling was plunged into the "blackness" of despair and felt compelled to turn to her mother's god for the first time. Already disheartened by the famine, floods, foreign invaders, and internal warfare that besieged China, after her mother's death a "terrible depression settled on me—spiritual despair, bleakness, desolation." She was overwhelmed by feelings of inadequacy and hopelessness. "To try to do anything for the country seemed like trying to put out a great conflagration with a cup of water," she wrote. Even life itself seemed futile. "What if we do achieve a strong, unified country?" she thought, but never said to her husband. "In the sum total of things what does it amount to?" Behind the existential angst lay the melancholy that plagued her for much of her life.

Chapter Eight

New Life

Outward beauty is a manifestation and forerunner of inward and spiritual beauty. To the West this idea may seem fantastic, but to us it appears natural. Which one of us would appear in the ancestral hall in untidy dress? . . . If dirt and carelessness are . . . an insult to the dead, are they not equally an outrage to the living?

—Mayling Soong Chiang

After a few short years in power, the Kuomintang saw its popular support begin to erode. Growing discontent was directed at China's leaders personally. On July 23, 1931, T. V. Soong narrowly missed being killed by Communist assassins shouting, "Down with the Soong dynasty!" Whatever confidence had once been placed in the Nanking regime was waning quickly.

Despite nominal success in unifying the country under the Nationalist flag, Chiang and Mayling realized that the "Revolution" would fail were it not underpinned by something stronger than patriotism. Bereft of his charismatic presence, Sun Yat-sen's Three Principles of the People hardly sufficed as a governing philosophy. Sun's writings were vague, contradictory, and offered no blueprint for concrete organization and action. They offered still less in the way of common appeal, and the Communists were rising to fill the gap.

Mayling's ambition, outspokenness, and visibility made her a convenient scapegoat and an obvious target for criticism, some of which was not unwarranted. Women in power have always aroused mistrust and fear in China, and she was no exception. She was likened to Yang Guifei (719–56 A.D.), the most famous beauty of Chinese history, whose tragic love story was a favorite theme of poets. Yang was a concubine who, according to legend, so captivated the emperor Xuan Zong that he neglected matters of state. She adopted An Lushan, a Moslem Turkish general, as her son. But a power struggle between An and Yang's younger brother over control of the government led An to attempt a coup in 755. Angry imperial guards forced the emperor to order the execution of Yang Guifei and her brother as they tried to flee the capital. The emperor soon abdicated.

Less charitably, Mayling was compared to the Empress Dowager Tzu Hsi, infamous for her selfish folly. In 1928 Chiang's troops had looted the tombs of Qing dynasty emperor Chien Lung and the Empress Dowager. It subsequently became conventional wisdom that many precious jewels buried with the bodies ended up in the hands of the Chiang family and that Madame Chiang had used Tzu Hsi's pearls to decorate her shoes. Apocryphal or not, the tale reflected the intense dislike for her. A newspaper editorial claimed that in the bazaars of Beijing it was commonly said, "If Mei-ling were at the bottom of the Yangtze, China would suffer less." Frustrated visitors complained that one could never see Chiang Kai-shek alone because "that woman" always sat in on meetings, leaving her open to blame for many of Chiang's unpopular decisions. Others were blamed on the Soong family, now referred to in sinister tones as the "royal family" or the "Soong dynasty."

As ever, Chiang's most vocal critic was his sister-in-law Ching Ling. In early 1929 the Soong family dispatched Mayling's younger brother T. L. to Berlin in a bid to persuade Ching Ling to return to China for a ceremony commemorating the removal of Sun Yat-sen's remains from Beijing to an immense, newly constructed mausoleum on Purple Mountain in Nanking. Then in March the Kuomintang reelected Ching Ling, in absentia, to the party's leadership committee. She was furious at Chiang Kai-shek's repeated attempts to co-opt her prestige to suit his own ends but reluctantly agreed to return for the event. Before embarking for China in May, she issued a typically blunt declaration stating her refusal to have anything to do with the current Nanking regime. When T. L. objected, she tartly replied: "The Soong family was made for China, not China for the Soong family."

After Japan snatched Manchuria as the Nationalist government stood by helplessly, public anguish mounted. The disillusionment was complete when in early 1932 Nanking's valiant but doomed defense of Shanghai ended in bitter defeat after a prolonged and bloody siege as the Japanese occupied the Chinese section of the city in retaliation for anti-Japanese boycotts. "It is now undeniable that the Kuomintang . . . has lost its position as the country's revolutionary party," Ching Ling declared in a fresh public salvo against Chiang Kai-shek. "Those in the Central Government have made their friends happy but the people miserable." The party, she charged, was now miserably corrupt and doomed to extinction. Chiang himself declared in 1932, "The Chinese revolution has failed." The decadence and corruption in party and government had by this time become blatant. Officials flew to Shanghai on the weekends and built palatial homes in Nanking. As salaries were not high, it was self-evident that "inappropriate methods" were used to support that lifestyle. Dynastic rule was long gone but the ancient ethos of *shengguan facai*—using official position for self-enrichment—was flourishing as Nanking officials became the new capitalists. Chiang's arbitrary and sporadic attempts to combat the pervasive corruption were more a device to control subordinates than a genuine effort to abolish it, despite his criticism of the practice.

By 1933 it was clear to Chiang and Mayling that something had to be done to revitalize the revolution. Since the toppling of the Confucian state in 1911 China had been in search of a unifying ideology to replace it. The greatest need of Chinese society, argued Chiang, was an "integrating force" like that provided by churches and civic organizations in America and England and by the ruling party in Germany and Japan, and what he termed the "Christian spirit of service." He and his wife looked abroad for inspiration—to Germany's Nazism, to Mussolini's *Vita Nuova*, to Roosevelt's New Deal, and even to their archenemy, the Soviet Union, and its five-year plans. These ideologies appeared to be infusing those nations, struggling with the effects of the First World War and the Great Depression, with fresh energy, enthusiasm, and hope.

But the depth of China's problems called for something more profound. What China needed, the first couple decided, was nothing less than a program of spiritual enlightenment. The moral regeneration of the people, as they envisioned it, was to be accomplished by purging the country of unhealthy and unhygienic habits of mind and body. Carried out on an individual as well as a national level, they genuinely if naively believed, such a program would bring about a renaissance in Chinese morale and morality and make the public more responsive to the needs of the nation. "It has become obvious that mere accumulation of wealth is not sufficient to enable China to resume her position as a great nation," Mayling wrote in the American magazine *Forum* in 1935. "There must be also revival of the spirit, since spiritual values transcend mere material riches."

The scheme Mayling and Chiang devised was launched in February 1934 as the New Life Movement, a curious East-West ideological fusion of neo-Confucian precepts, thinly disguised New Testament Christianity, YMCA-style social activism, elements of Bushido—the samurai code—and European fascism, along with a generous dose of New England Puritanism. The movement was riddled with inherent ironies and contradictions, the most profound of these being its simultaneously revolutionary yet conservative theoretical basis. In the inaugural speech Chiang Kai-shek attributed China's inability to achieve equality with other nations to the inferiority of "knowledge and morality" of her citizens. He decried the "unbearable filthiness," "hedonism," and "laziness" of the Chinese people, who, he said, led a "barbaric" and "irrational" life little better than that of animals. In application the movement teetered between Boy Scoutism at best and police-state fascism at worst. While superficially antiforeign— shop signs in foreign languages were banned—the New Life Movement was at heart a quixotic effort to infuse a medieval, superstitious, and largely illiterate people with the moral, civic, and sanitary sensibilities that had ostensibly made the twentieth-century West, and Japan, so powerful.

Although not billed as such, New Life was also in part intended to counter the Communists' success in generating popular support in Jiangxi province. Mayling tacitly admitted this when she later dubiously claimed, "We are giving the people what the Communists promised but could not perform." After being driven out of the urban centers in the late 1920s under Nanking repression, the Communists had regrouped in the Jiangxi countryside, where in 1931 they established a Chinese Soviet Workers' and Peasants' Republic headed by Mao Zedong. Only after Chiang's fifth bloody "annihilation" campaign did he manage to dislodge the ninety thousand remaining Communists from Jiangxi, forcing them on their epic six-thousand-mile Long March to the northwestern province of Shaanxi. Although by the time they arrived a year later their number was reduced to a battle-hardened seven thousand, in adversity they became stronger than ever, to Chiang's ultimate chagrin.

The Chiangs invited missionaries to plan a comprehensive program of rural reconstruction in Jiangxi. The American Board of Foreign Missions lent Reverend George W. Shepherd, a New Zealand–born, Harvard-trained Congregationalist missionary with long experience in rural China, as chief adviser to the New Life Movement. When the Chiangs asked him to take the post in March 1936, he had a "strange feeling," but all doubts were dispelled when he attended a religious service with the Chinese leaders and saw their "spiritual hunger" as they "sang joyously the grand old hymns of the Christian Church." Shepherd asked himself, "What would Borodin do with a chance like this?" Sherwood Eddy, globetrotting YMCA activist and prominent evangelist, called the New Life Movement the "World's Greatest Evangelistic Opportunity." The Nanking regime had hired many foreign advisers, but Shepherd was the first to be given actual administrative authority in the government. Canadian James G. Endicott, another longtime China missionary, later succeeded Shepherd.

The movement had its origins, in part, in an evangelical movement called the Oxford Group, founded in Britain by a controversial but charismatic YMCA activist and preacher, Frank Buchman. Drawing its early adherents from the ranks of Oxford University, the eponymous group attracted skeptical comment as well as a considerable worldwide following in the 1920s and early 1930s. Later renamed Moral Re-Armament (MRA), its influence subsequently declined amid outcry after Buchman publicly praised Hitler in 1936, but not before the group had spawned one of the world's largest nonsectarian spiritual movements. For at the same time the New Life Movement was being formulated in China, a few Oxford Group members in Akron stumbled on the idea of applying Oxford Group principles to reform supposedly incurable drunks. They met with success, and soon after helped found Alcoholics Anonymous.

The Oxford Group had a following in China. Buchman had visited China in 1916 and had met many prominent Chinese, including Sun Yat-sen. Mayling was widely reported to be an adherent of the Oxford Group, an assertion she denied, albeit unconvincingly. In a 1937 interview with *Liberty* magazine she admitted to having studied the movement carefully, and said it had its "excellent points," but she balked at its practice of public confession. She neglected to mention, however, that she had translated Oxford Group literature into Chinese, which suggests a closer affinity. In any case, she and Chiang often sought counsel from the influential Reverend Logan H. Roots, Episcopal bishop of Hankow from 1904 to 1938, who with his sons was deeply involved in the Oxford Group. The balding bishop was a self-described "Christian revolutionary" whose Hankow home was dubbed the "Moscow-Heaven Axis" in tribute to the stream of leftist foreign visitors who stayed there. Radical houseguests notwithstanding, Mayling and the Generalissimo had been friendly with Roots for years and looked to him for spiritual guidance. With Roots's encouragement, the couple began the practice of early morning "quiet time" and meditation—an Oxford Group practice—during which the Generalissimo jotted down his thoughts on Christ in a book.

In the summer of 1933, Chiang and Mayling summoned Bishop Roots to their temporary home in Nanchang, the capital of Jiangxi province, where they were staying during Chiang's military campaign against his Communist rivals in the province. The bishop held frank talks and prayed with them. Not long after the meeting, Chiang turned over a large section of recovered territory in southern Jiangxi to missionary groups for reconstruction and launched the New Life Movement. Chiang intended to make Jiangxi a model province whose success would be emulated across the country.

As well as drawing on Christian teachings, the movement also aimed to bring about a revival of Confucian values. Two of the ancient "five virtues" of Confucius—*li* (correct behavior) and *yi* (justice)—were resurrected. To these were added *lian* (integrity) and *chi* (honor) to create New Life's "four virtues." Interestingly, love (benevolence), central to both Confucian and Christian traditions, was omitted.

Like the Oxford Group, New Life targeted the official, educated, and affluent classes in the belief that China's ills could be cured "by example and exhortation from above." This trickle-down philosophy of societal transformation neatly paralleled a Confucian belief: "The virtue of the gentleman is like wind; the virtue of the commoner is like grass. Let the wind blow over the grass and it is sure to bend."

Officially Mayling headed the women's division of the New Life Movement, but in practice she was its driving force, and it may well have been her brainchild, although she invariably credited her husband. Certainly its conception seems to reflect at least as much her thinking as Chiang's, and she threw herself into its execution. She and Chiang flew around the country, evangelizing the movement to Chinese and foreign missionaries alike. She formulated much of the movement's propaganda and often wrote the English versions herself. She wrote articles for American publications and gave interviews to foreign journalists extolling the movement's aims and achievements.

Within a couple of years, she virtually controlled the entire movement, which expanded to include educational and war work across China. Under Mayling's command alone there were four thousand salaried women and two hundred thousand "volunteers." She traveled frequently to direct her staff in the field and see local conditions firsthand. "I sometimes despair as I see the low level of living that is so prevalent among our country villages," Mayling admitted after visiting a rural district. "But . . . we must not despair. We will do more about it." She told a missionary group: "The regeneration of China is coming, no matter what happens." How prophetic that last remark would be, although not in the way she imagined.

The movement's motto, Mayling told Americans in a radio broadcast, was "salvation from within," which on a national level meant not isolationism but rather relying on native leadership while using modern technology. "We do not need outside political assistance as long as we draw upon the experience of our forefathers and use the means science has provided us." The New Life Movement, Mayling claimed to foreigners, was welcomed by the people "as water is craved by the famishing" and was spreading across the country "like wildfire." Overt references to Christianity were carefully excised from the New Life Movement's literature, but Mayling admitted that the cross had always been "in the background" of the movement. Its very name carries Christian undertones, with its obvious reference to the resurrection of Christ. The concept of "salvation from within" is clearly modeled on the Christian notion of changing the world by changing individuals.

Sublime as its ideals may have been, in execution the New Life Movement often bordered on ridiculous. Seeking to rid China of a bewildering panoply of societal ills, scores of rules were issued at the outset. Many of the strictures resembled the blue laws of colonial New England. Gambling, including the Chinese institution of mah-jongg, was banned, along with spitting, smoking cigarettes on the street, opium smoking, cabarets, dancing, drinking, and patronizing sing-song girls. Public display of affection was forbidden. Rudeness, vulgar manners, gaping and shuffling, bribery,

extortion and "squeeze"—corruption—were similarly targeted for aboli-
tion. Playing American jazz favorites such as "A Hot Time in the Old
Town Tonight" in funeral processions was banned. Men with hats askew
or buttons undone were stopped in the street by Boy Scouts and made to
straighten up. Women could not wear cosmetics, get permanent waves
or modern "bob" haircuts, or wear skirts above the knee. The mayor of
Beijing banned stockingless female legs. Western dresses were banned
for a time and squads of enforcers especially created to police New Life
regulations would stamp women wearing them with the Chinese characters
for "queer clothes." Mayling was forced to give up smoking her mentholated cigarettes—but only in public.

While some New Life innovations were farcical, others were eminently
sensible. To end the tradition of wasting money on elaborate weddings,
Mayling—ironically, in view of her own lavish ceremony—introduced the
practice of mass marriages, which stirred criticism but was a success. The
public was instructed in basic hygiene, as modern notions of sanitation
were largely nonexistent. Orders were issued that vegetables should be
washed before being eaten and that everyone must wash their hands and
face three times a day and bathe once a week. Modern sewer, water supply, and plumbing systems were installed in some cities. "Cleanliness
Weeks" were held in major cities. Sanitary brigades patrolled the streets of
major cities. Citizens armed with brooms swept streets and gutters. Missionaries and New Life workers went into the countryside and taught birth
control and infant care. Under Mayling's direction "housewives' leagues"
were formed. Girls were organized and trained in hygiene and civic duties.
Posters were displayed in schools showing neatly dressed children doing
physical exercises, taking baths, and brushing their teeth.

Sometimes enforcement was taken to extremes, and people who did not
follow New Life dictums were roughed up by morality patrols. In 1932
Chiang had founded a paramilitary organization popularly known as the
"Blue Shirts." Comprised of selected army officers fanatically loyal to
Chiang, the corps was modeled after Hitler's Brown Shirts and Mussolini's
Black Shirts. This fascist group, along with the police and the Boy Scouts,
acted as enforcers of New Life rules. Mayling acknowledged that some of
these New Life enforcers were "stupid, overzealous, dizzy with success,"
but insisted that the government did not condone their behavior.

One New Life champion enthused that the Chinese people were "happy and hopeful" because they had been given a "New Deal." Others, not least Chiang Kai-shek himself, took a more cautious view. "It is a gigantic task . . . to wipe out the backward conditions of society by a wild storm and to supply the community with vitality and the right spirit by a gentle breeze," he said, in an apparent reference to Confucius' gentlemanly wind blowing over the grass. And indeed, after an auspicious beginning the movement began to "bore rather than inspire" the public. Its earnest yet hypocritical and even offensive emphasis on apparently superficial concerns became the butt of scorn. An American professor lecturing at a Chinese college was surprised that students burst into laughter when he made a serious reference to the New Life Movement. It was an open secret that despite an official ban and New Life's avowed intention of stamping out the scourge of opium, its use was ubiquitous. In practice Chiang's cash-strapped Nationalist government took a "realistic view" of the situation and found it preferable to collect revenue from the opium trade rather than let it enrich the government's enemies.

The idea that China needed spiritual and moral improvement more than it needed improvement in the standard of living had many detractors, including Sun Yat-sen's widow. Ching Ling had nothing but scorn for the New Life Movement, which she dismissed as a "pedantic" exercise that "gives nothing to the people." She had no patience for the movement's neo-Confucian dogma, calling the teachings of Confucius feudalistic and patriarchal. Confucianism represented "autocracy, oppression and misery" and was antithetical to the concept of revolution. "We must cleanse the Chinese mentality and free it from the cobwebs of Confucian ideology which block our cultural development," she wrote. She used her exalted perch of virtuous widowhood to criticize Chiang Kai-shek as only she could, charging him with neglecting the most critical of her late husband's three principles: improving people's livelihood. "The aim of revolution is the material welfare of human beings," she argued. "If that is not reached then there has been no revolution."

The movement was ridiculed by intellectuals and liberals as "shallow and sentimental." It failed to address China's fundamental social and economic problems, said critics, who attributed to those associated with the movement "a certain mental vapidity." Mayling responded to this accusation by stating, "Some people have criticized the New Life Movement on the ground that, since there is not sufficient food for everyone in the land, it is useless to talk about or seek spiritual regeneration. We refute this argument by pointing out the very evident fact that, if everyone from the highest official to the lowest wheelbarrow coolie would conscientiously practice these principles in everyday life, there would be food for all." To those who sneered at the New Life Movement as "Boy Scout stuff," she quoted a Chinese saying: "If planning for one year, sow grain; for two years, plant trees; for a hundred years, grow men." Some critics also attributed sinister implications to the movement, comparing it with the social control experiments of Italy's *Vita Nuova*.

Mayling believed the New Life Movement to be the "biggest thing the Kuomintang has done." She proudly predicted that in twenty-five years the movement would make China "the greatest nation in the world." She told friend Fulton Oursler, editor of the influential *Liberty* magazine and an Oxford Group member: "With God's help we will drive out disease, famine, opium, ignorance—all these monsters that stand in [China's] way. . . . We will liberate four hundred million people for a new and better life. . . . All China is on the march." How brave, and yet grandiose, these words seem in retrospect. In reality, the real and lasting impact of the New Life Movement on Chinese society was limited. Albeit noble, its battle against the immemorial ills of Chinese life—gambling, opium, debauchery, poverty, begging, robbery, filth, corruption, and indifference to the public good— amounted to tilting at windmills. It lacked popular appeal and proved unable to assert itself by force. Ultimately, however, it failed due to its inherent contradictions. A mass movement that rejected popular initiative, New Life tried to imbue the public with a political consciousness while denying it a political voice. It was a social revolution whose goal was to suppress newly emerging forces calling for fundamental socioeconomic change. It tried to mobilize people in the service of the state but offered them nothing in return—not even a scapegoat to explain their misery. Instead, it blamed their predicament on themselves, in effect trying to shame them into modernity. Tragically, it intensified the alienation of intellectuals and liberals from the Nanking regime. Many "anguished patriots" turned to the Communists in rejection of New Life's Confucian underpinnings and what they saw as its banal and irrelevant concerns.

The movement did, however, give Mayling her own power base and a national platform. While she held the title of director-general, her right-hand man in running the movement was her protégé J. L. Huang, who also ran the OMEA, Officers' Moral Endeavor Association, a precursor of the movement. In addition, New Life propelled her into a formal role in China's public life, where she honed her public speaking skills and grew into her role as a powerful public figure in her own right rather than merely hovering in the shadow of her husband. The movement might have achieved more success had not war with Japan broken out in July 1937, just over three years after it was launched, at which point much of its focus was shifted to war work. But the basic problem with the New Life Movement was that unlike the Oxford Group or the YMCA, it was a paternalistic state-sponsored cult, designed to serve the state, rather than a grassroots movement. Whether of the civic, moral, or sanitary variety, virtue is difficult to instill by official edict.

Try as it might, the Kuomintang was no match for the Communists in cultivating grassroots appeal, and this was its Achilles' heel. Against enormous obstacles, the Generalissimo, his wife, and his government made great strides in constructing the rudiments of a modern state in the decade following the couple's marriage. They were much touted abroad, yet they were not particularly well liked in their own country, even within the ranks of the Kuomintang. Cynicism directed toward China's rulers also undermined the New Life Movement. "It is doubtful whether the personalities interested in the movement are sufficiently pure themselves to give the movement much prestige," dryly observed Nelson T. Johnson, the American minister to China.

As unelected leaders, the Chiangs may have found it unnecessary to ingratiate themselves with the public in the manner of elected political figures, or perhaps they were too busy. In any case they probably didn't know how. As in the New Life Movement, they invariably emphasized the duties of citizens, but paid scant attention to rights. They were distrusted, even loathed, by the intelligentsia, who bridled at their Christian pieties, chafed at limits on intellectual freedoms, and fumed at arrests and executions of government opponents. But intellectuals were a minority. The illiterate and politically unaware, who comprised some 80 percent of China's four hundred million people, were likely ignorant of the good that the Kuomintang had done but keenly aware that their lives were as miserable as they had been in 1911. The Chiangs did not rule China because they were loved, but because there was no better alternative—yet.

The Nanking government's critics were not confined to outsiders. Ching Ling had been the Nanking regime's most vocal critic for years. In the early 1930s she was joined by T. V. Soong. Mayling's eldest brother had served ably as finance minister in Chiang's government since 1927. The Harvard and Columbia–trained financier was able to put aside his intense dislike and mistrust of Chiang to lay the foundation for a solid and functioning financial, monetary, and taxation system in China. Along with an excellent practical grasp of finance and economics T. V. had a "very quick mind" and was "sincerely eager" to improve China's finances. He was lauded by merchants and financiers as the Alexander Hamilton of China for his success in modernizing China's monetary and banking system in the early days of the Nationalist government in Nanking.

However, Soong's unvarnished contempt for incompetence, corruption, and other ingrained cultural practices in his native land had made him highly unpopular in many quarters. His habit of surrounding himself with a corps of like-minded, overseas-educated Chinese and foreign experts, combined with his brusque, impatient temperament and American ways— he even preferred Western to Chinese food—did not help to endear him to many of his countrymen. He did not write his own papers or speeches; his material was written for him by staff, in English, for although he'd studied the Chinese classics he was more comfortable in English. To critics he countered that only Western methods could rescue China from the havoc wrought by two thousand years of Chinese methods.

The fault line within the Soong family was first exposed in 1927 when Chiang purged the Communists from the Kuomintang in a bloody coup and married Mayling. T. V. held no fixed ideological position vis-à-vis the Communists, but the split in the family was uncomfortable for him. In the years that followed he clashed repeatedly with his brother-in-law, behind closed doors vigorously attacking what he viewed as Chiang's unsound fiscal notions and excessive military expenditures at the expense of economic development. In 1931 Soong became head of a newly formed National Economic Council, which in cooperation with the League of

Nations began planning improvements in agriculture, infrastructure, and water conservation. But with 45 percent of the national budget going to defense, few resources were left to carry out his plans. After the Japanese annexed Manchuria in September 1931, relations with Chiang worsened due to T. V.'s support of Young Marshal Zhang Xueliang, the ousted Manchurian warlord who irritated Chiang with pleas to fight the Japanese first and the Communists later.

By 1933 the uneasy partnership between the brilliant, ambitious, and hardworking technocrat and his soldier brother-in-law was wearing thin. Part of the trouble was T. V.'s disdain and jealousy of Chiang, whom he regarded as his intellectual inferior. For his part, Chiang had always doubted Soong's loyalty. Soong took a great interest in aviation—helping bring a mission of retired American air officers to China—and by the early 1930s had built up the Salt Troops, which enforced the state monopoly on that vital commodity, into a well-trained and armed fighting force under his own control. Alarmed, Chiang saw him as a rival and feared a coup.

The final break came in October 1933 in a stormy meeting, when Chiang fired T. V. and replaced him with H. H. Kung. Soong had lately secured from Washington a $50 million loan from the Reconstruction Finance Corporation, pushed through by U.S. treasury secretary Henry Morgenthau Jr., who was sympathetic to China. Soong wanted to use the credit for economic development as it was intended, but Chiang wanted to use the funds to equip his army to fight the Communists. Soong believed that the best means to fight communism was economic progress. Chiang refused to let a lack of financial resources stand in the way of doing what he thought was militarily necessary. The meeting grew heated, with Soong becoming "sarcastic" on the subject of Chiang's anti-Communist campaign. Afterward Mayling flew to Shanghai, where she obtained T. V.'s resignation and brought it back to Chiang. Madame Kung, universally conceded to be the most brilliant, if not the most scrupulous, mind in the clan, engineered the switch. Mayling, who always followed the lead of her eldest sister, complied.

Sir Alexander Frederick Whyte, a British political adviser in the confidence of China's ruling clan, regarded this as unfortunate, and faulted Mayling for the breach. She had "failed in what should have been her greatest task, to be an unbreakable link between her husband and her brother," Whyte wrote in his diary on September 12, 1934.

Chiang's fears of T. V.'s ambitions were not unfounded. Less than a year after being ousted from the finance ministry, in September 1934, Mayling's brother told Whyte he believed the "tide was turning" against Chiang and that there were many factors that would be "nails in Chiang's coffin." Soong was convinced that his friends among Chiang's officers would join him in a breakaway and was "confident that his chance would come—[he] said there wasn't room in Nanking for him and C.K.S., and spoke of the time when the whole [government] would turn to him as leader. He believes his position already stronger. I was a little dismayed to find him so confident," Whyte observed, noting that he had advised Soong that it was no time to make a move against Chiang.

Mayling was "very much to blame" for Chiang's "blindness to the economic, agrarian, common-people aspect" of China's problems, believed Whyte. She gave an "impertinent snort" and smiled—but Chiang did not—when Whyte warned that Chiang needed to pursue a civil policy alongside the military policy. In September 1934 Chiang confidently told Whyte: "Communism as a menace will be finished this year."

H. H. Kung was an amiable man with a "feather-pillow head"—in the words of Whyte—who did not give Chiang trouble. If Chiang wanted cash for military adventures, Kung found a way to oblige him. In late April 1934, Mayling made the "astounding" statement to Minister Johnson that Chiang thought Kung to be the "best Minister of Finance China had ever had, for . . . he had already been able to build up a surplus." Were that true, it would have been attributable to years of work by T. V., not Kung's half year in the post. Mayling reported Kung as saying that balancing the budget was not necessary; China needed only to balance its trade. Whether she was being disingenuous or merely gullible is unclear, but math never was her strong suit.

Dubious fiscal policies aside, Kung's tenure in the finance ministry was already making itself felt in other ways. Johnson reported that by May 1934 a "whispering campaign" against Dr. Kung had begun in Nanking and Shanghai, alleging that through his wife, Kung was getting a "rake-off" on all government purchases. Whether or not there was any truth to the "nasty stories" circulating, "There is no doubt that under Kung there has been a let-up in the type of official discipline that T. V. Soong was endeavoring to establish," the American minister observed. This trend would ultimately prove disastrous to the reputation of Chiang Kai-shek's government and the Kuomintang. Some, it seemed, were more equal than others when it came to enforcing New Life's virtues.

Chapter Nine

Rescuing the Gimo

The Lord has created a new thing on the earth: a woman protects a man.

—The Bible, Jeremiah 31:22, RSV

Mayling first met "Young Marshal" Zhang Xueliang at a party in Shanghai in the early 1920s, before he took control of Manchuria. Zhang, about two years Mayling's junior and known as a wealthy playboy, may have wooed her briefly without success. In any case the two became friends, with Mayling taking on the role of wise elder sister to a lovable but errant younger brother. In 1929, soon after she married Chiang Kai-shek, she and her new husband met the Young Marshal at a tea in Beijing. Mayling greeted Zhang warmly by his private name, Hanqing, used only by family and intimate friends. Startled, Chiang demanded, "How do you know him?" Mayling replied smoothly, "I met him before I met you." It was no surprise that Mayling and Chiang Kai-shek were fond of Zhang Xueliang. At his best, he was handsome, personable, and well spoken. Dressed in a long blue Chinese gown, he resembled a *xiao sheng*, the traditional young man's role in Beijing opera. Mayling was the big sister he never had, and he regarded Chiang, some thirteen years his senior, as a father. Chiang in turn protected the Young Marshal, shouldering some of the blame for the fall of Manchuria in September 1931. He had high expectations for his young protégé, and was grooming him for greater things.

But over time Zhang's worsening narcotic problem became an embarrassment to Chiang's government, which—officially at least—had banned opium. "I smoked opium out of anger, and the pressure of leading an army," Zhang said later. A Chinese army doctor attempted to cure him of the habit by giving him morphine injections instead, with predictably infelicitous results. By 1933, Zhang was an ineffectual, dope-addled figure with so many needle punctures on his arms and shoulders that—as he himself later said—it was difficult to find a fresh spot of skin to shoot up. Zhang's loyal Australian adviser, William Henry Donald, had for years endeavored to persuade his recalcitrant charge—whom he called the "Young Fellow"—to give up his beloved vices of gambling, women, and the needle, and to exercise and take cures, but all of these efforts failed. Although Zhang did back Nanking during a 1929 warlord rebellion, by 1931 his increasingly exasperated adviser called him "a young man of no ambition whatever, rather resentful of the fact that he had responsibilities and that troublesome people should expect him to bestir himself in matters concerning China as a whole."

In early 1933 matters reached such a pass that Chiang relieved the Young Marshal of his command. In concert with Mayling and Chiang, Donald bundled Zhang into a German hospital in Shanghai and called in Dr. D. W. Miller Jr., a brusque Seventh-Day Adventist renowned for his "opium cure." As a condition for treatment, Dr. Miller insisted on absolute authority over the patient, above any order Zhang or his aides might issue. At one point during the weeklong ordeal the Young Marshal ordered the doctor's execution by firing squad. "This means we are making progress," was Dr. Miller's response. Zhang was successfully weaned off the drug and immediately dispatched on an extended European tour to reinforce his cure. He embarked in April 1933 with his wife and children; Donald; his Scottish financial adviser and boyhood friend, James C. Elder; a retinue of nurses and servants; and his secretary, Edith Zhao. He was particularly impressed by what he saw in Nazi Germany and in fascist Italy, where nationalism was on the rise under strong right-wing leaders. But this flirtation with fascism—and Italian aircraft—did not last. In any case, Zhang was not of an ideological bent.

The Young Marshal returned to China in January 1934 a changed man—healthy, fit, alert, and full of patriotic feeling. Mayling met with the newly recovered opium addict for a talk. She lectured him that his "great vitality, unless directed along right channels, would be dangerous for any man." She warned him to "consider deeply" any future step he might take. Chiang restored Zhang to second-in-command of Nanking's armies in 1934 and appointed him head of "bandit suppression"—Chiang-speak for Communist eradication—in the provinces of Henan, Hubei, and Anhui. The Young Marshal was soon put to the test. T. V. Soong, lately ejected as finance minister, urged Zhang to help him oust the Generalissimo, but Zhang refused to have anything to do with the scheme and reiterated his loyalty to Nanking.

Not long after his return to China, Zhang and Donald gave Chiang Kai-shek a stern lecture on what ailed China. "You are ignorant because no one dares to correct you," Donald said. "Goddam it, sir, you've all become insufferably stupid!" Mayling interpreted. Chiang blinked. Donald railed. The country was ridden with graft and opium; millions perished from disease, floods, famine, and civil war, he said. There was virtually no modern infrastructure or skilled administrators. "Above all, where is the decency and nobility for the common man?" he demanded. "China should be ashamed. . . . There is the staleness, the obeseness of wealth on the one hand—the hog wallow of poverty on the other. The rickshaw man and the wharf coolie are worse off than the horse and camel in many another land." Zhang offered an equally blistering denunciation. "You were wonderful," Mayling told Donald afterward. "Why don't you come work for us? We need a brain like yours." He replied, "I don't work for women. Why should I try to advise one of heaven's whimsies? They can't take it." She retorted she could, or she wouldn't have dared translate all he said. Zhang added, "She even put in your goddams."

"Don" was an enigmatic character who hailed from New South Wales and was a newspaperman to the bone. Like Chiang, he was a teetotaler, a rare breed in the journalistic profession in which guise he had arrived in China in 1903. Donald turned down an offer to be private secretary to the famed Wu Ting-fang, the Empress Dowager's foreign minister, to work with Sun Yat-sen. He knew the Soong children, who called him "Gran," even before they went to study in America. He helped draft Sun's Republican Manifesto, issued days after Sun's election as provisional president in 1912. Donald was a fount of information and opinions about China, which he did not hesitate to share with the many foreign visitors who passed through the country. The idiosyncratic Australian spent over four decades in his adopted country, but utterly refused to touch Chinese food—often toting a loaf of bread to official banquets—or learn the language.

Initially Donald split his time between Mayling and the Young Marshal. Along with helping to sort through the voluminous correspondence that crossed her desk, and drafting speeches and articles, he bombarded Mayling with stinging reports on China's infinite ills. In one missive he advised that salt taxes be enforced with a "big stick" and corruption be made a capital offense. "Shoot a lot of people soon and there would be a change," he wrote. "But start high up and not among the unhappy low salaried unfortunates." He proposed a New Mentality movement as a psychological complement to the New Life Movement. He agitated for a People's Economic Reconstruction movement. He prodded, he scolded, he cajoled, he goaded. Through these efforts, as well as anonymous editorials penned for the Chinese press, the prodigiously energetic Australian quickly became China's enfant terrible.

After working with Mayling for a few months he began to toy with leaving to write a memoir of his years in China, which he called "a jumble and a miserable business." But when she appeared one day with an armload of letters and said, "It's too much for me," he finally agreed to work full-time. Soon he was advising her and the Generalissimo on matters foreign as well as domestic. He took to calling Chiang "Gissimo" and Mayling "Missimo," short for "Madamissimo." The three became nearly inseparable, Donald even living in their house and taking meals with them. He screened nearly all visitors. He eschewed any official title, but his influence over Mayling and his role in creating propaganda for the Nanking government and building up Mayling in the eyes of the world were immeasurable. She soon took few steps and uttered few words in public without consulting him. He was one of the few people unrelated to her in whom she had absolute trust, and she used his companionship as "roughage for her Western wits" and as "a refuge from [Chiang's] tantrums." As he was the only person apart from her who did not fear to tell the unvarnished truth to the Generalissimo's face, he earned Chiang's confidence too. He did not, however, share the Chiangs' Christian piety, and maintained a healthy cynicism toward just about everything except Mayling, who in his eyes could do no wrong. As well as adviser, propagandist, and gadfly, Donald also played the role of court jester to China's rulers, as illustrated by a bit of doggerel entitled "The Patriot's Soliloquy" or "That Great God Face" that he dashed off for Mayling:

. . . They say that China's in distress,
That creditors upon us press,
That we must now reorganize
And follow foreign enterprise.
Pooh! Pooh! I say, that's a disgrace,
So I fight that, thus to save my face.

I have my job, my friends have power,
Rich gifts on them I always shower,
Reform to them means irksome work,
And work is what I always shirk,
Reforms aren't needed by our race,
So I'll grow nails and save my face.

. . . God in His wisdom suffers fools
To cut strange capers, act as tools,
For wicked people, plunged in crime
And some whose lives are lived in slime.
What puzzles me is his sweet grace
To silly fools who live for face.

Mayling may have appreciated Donald's forthright manner and views, but many Chinese in the Chiangs' inner circle did not. They felt threatened by and jealous of his proximity to power, though his real influence was limited. Donald's close ties with Mayling were seen by those inclined to criticize her as further evidence of her Western ways and alienation from her own people.

If Chiang Kai-shek was still holding out for foreign intervention to rescue China from the depredations of Japan, he was in the minority. Japan was growing bolder by the day in the absence of action by the League of Nations, and it had long been abundantly clear to most Chinese that China would have to fend for itself or be swallowed piecemeal by its rapacious neighbor. "I am sorry to see China under the control of Japan, or any other power, but if she lacks the strength to protect herself from aggression and exploitation, she cannot reasonably expect the other nations to do the job for her," Wall Street financier Thomas W. Lamont wrote Ambassador Johnson in 1936, summing up the American attitude. "Certainly America is not going to court trouble by any quixotic attempt to checkmate Japan in Asia." Many Westerners cynically believed that it served Western interests to have a strongman controlling China, and that Japan, as an Asian nation, was uniquely suited to the role.

Mayling privately agreed with Donald, who urged Chiang to drop his conciliatory policy and take a bolder line toward Japan, but in public she felt compelled to defend her husband's policies. Despite the blatant and growing Japanese menace, Chiang persisted in focusing Nationalist army efforts on quelling the Communists instead of repelling the Japanese, famously declaring that the Japanese were a disease of the skin, but the Communists were a disease of the heart. But by the mid-1930s the popular mood overwhelmingly favored resisting Japanese depredations. The Communists, students, most intellectuals, and segments of the military argued, "Better to be a smashed piece of jade than an unbroken tile." Still smarting from his disastrous defeat by the Japanese at Shanghai in 1932, the Generalissimo adamantly refused to discuss the matter and ignored or repressed calls for action. He faced a terrible dilemma. If he went head-to-head with the Japanese, China would be crushed. His strategy was to "trade space for time"—to postpone a showdown, and meanwhile modernize the military and unify the country so that when war came, China could put up an effective resistance.

In 1935 Chiang transferred the Young Marshal to head "bandit suppression" in the strategically important northwest. As he proceeded to China's old western capital of Xi'an to take up his post, Zhang was in "high spirits" because he thought he could easily wipe out the Communists, and thus recoup some of the loss of face he suffered in the Manchuria debacle. But things were not as he imagined. Over time the Young Marshal grew convinced that Chiang's policy was wrongheaded. His troops were heartsick over the loss of their homeland and had no appetite for killing fellow Chinese while the Japanese marched on their soil. Worse, Communist soldiers taunted Zhang's troops: "Why do you Chinese fight us, who are Chinese, to help a lot of worthless officers make money, to ride about in motorcars, get concubines, gamble and live a life of luxury?"

In April 1936 Zhang met Zhou Enlai, right-hand man of Communist leader Mao Zedong, for five hours of talks in an abandoned Catholic church in the Communist stronghold of Yenan. Handsome, charming, reasonable, persuasive, and fiercely committed to the Communist cause, Zhou was an accomplished diplomat who spoke fluent French thanks to a youthful sojourn in France. Zhou easily persuaded Zhang that "Chinese should not fight Chinese," at least not while the country was being devoured by Japan. "Inhuman is he who slays his own brother to feed the wolf," Zhou wrote Zhang, who burst into tears as he read the words. They soon reached a secret accord and Zhang ceased military operations against the "red bandits." He and his officers lodged a resolution before the Supreme Military Council in Nanking calling for war against Japan. Zhang also forged a secret alliance with a local militarist, Yang Hucheng, whose troops effectively controlled the city of Xi'an.

It was evident that tension was building in the northwest. Zhang's lack of progress in suppressing the "bandits" did not pass unnoticed in Nanking, and in the autumn of 1936 Chiang headed northwest to prod his recalcitrant general. While Chiang stayed in Luoyang, a city near Xi'an, Zhang tearfully implored him in a series of meetings to stop fighting the Communists and instead join forces in a united front against the Japanese. Outside his office, Chiang's aides could hear the Generalissimo mercilessly cursing Zhang, lecturing him that unification had to be completed first. Once Zhang joked upon emerging, "I got another scolding today."

Meanwhile, Mayling was quite ill and once again "on the verge of a nervous breakdown," ostensibly due to overwork and strain. Eling told Ambassador Johnson that Mayling was troubled by a problem with the "surface nerves, so that when she gets excited she breaks out in a rash which is very uncomfortable." Nonetheless, in late October she flew from Shanghai, where she was under treatment, to Luoyang to join her husband on his fiftieth birthday. H. H. Kung had a feeling "something was going to happen" and told Mayling she should persuade Chiang to return to Nanking with her. For the occasion patriotic overseas Chinese donated a hundred airplanes to the government, with funds to buy more. At the birthday celebration the Young Marshal again approached Chiang, but to no avail. Mayling came back without her husband.

The Young Marshal asked Chiang to go to Xi'an in person to mollify his disgruntled troops. Chiang agreed and in early December set up headquarters at a hot spring resort about ten miles out of the city. While soaking in the therapeutic baths of China's ancient emperors, Chiang made plans for a final mopping-up campaign against the "Reds," a feat he believed could be accomplished in a matter of weeks. Zhang made a last-ditch attempt to appeal to his commander in chief, pointing out that his soldiers had killed more innocent peasants than Communist bandits. Furthermore, his troops no longer had the heart to fight the Communists and were about to join them. Enraged, Chiang told Zhang to resign or be fired. The Young Marshal refused to give up his army while Japanese soldiers tramped on his father's grave. Tensions between the two generals had reached an impasse.

The final showdown came within days. Probably on Chiang's orders, on December 9 the Blue Shirts fired on Xi'an student demonstrators demanding war with Japan. Zhang was infuriated. He had given permission for the event, although he did try to dissuade the students from marching out to Chiang's headquarters. In the drama that was to unfold he took a page from Chinese history: A loyal Ming dynasty official had once tried to petition Emperor Ying Tsung first through words, then by tears. Failing those, he had resorted to force. Zhang concluded that snatching the obdurate Generalissimo was the only way to "stimulate his awakening," as he later explained it, and secure China's "salvation."

Shortly before dawn on December 12, Zhang, working in concert with Yang Hucheng, dispatched a contingent of men to the Generalissimo's headquarters at the Palace of Glorious Purity. As was his habit, Chiang was up before daybreak doing morning exercises in his pajamas in front of an open window. Suddenly a volley of gunshots rang out. His bodyguards engaged the rebels in a brief skirmish, giving Chiang time to throw on a bathrobe before fleeing but not enough time to put on shoes or insert his false teeth. He scaled the ten-foot-high compound wall and lowered himself by feel over the other side and let go, thinking there would be a similar drop to the ground. Instead he fell thirty feet into a moat. Despite sustaining a severe back injury in the fall, he managed to scramble up a rocky snow-covered hillside and hide in a cave. A few hours later he was found, shivering, toothless, and his bare feet bloody, and escorted to Xi'an, where the Young Marshal came to see him and greeted him respectfully, as subordinate to commanding officer.

Chiang did not return the courtesy. In excruciating pain from his injuries and doubtless terrified for his life, he raged and cursed at his captor. "Who are you, my subordinate or my enemy?" he demanded. "If my subordinate, you should obey my orders. If you are my enemy you should kill me without delay." The Young Marshal replied that his motives were revolutionary, not mutinous, and added that if "Your Excellency" would accept his "suggestions," then he would obey orders. He presented Chiang with a list of eight "points of national salvation." Chiang claimed Zhang then told him that China's future and the kidnapping should be "referred to the people for their verdict." If the people were sympathetic to Zhang, Chiang should "retire from office and let me do the work." If not, then the Generalissimo would be permitted to resume his duties as before, Zhang said. Chiang, however, was convinced his kidnapping was simply an old-fashioned coup d'état and not the desperate if virtuous patriotic act the Young Marshal claimed it to be. "Living, there will be no place to put your feet; dead, there will be no place to bury your bones," Chiang hissed through his gums. Little did he know that with this imprecation he cursed himself as well as his captor.

The central government was thrown into confusion by news of the Generalissimo's abduction, along with a few dozen bodyguards and officials, a number of whom were injured or killed. H. H. Kung received word of the kidnapping the same evening while he was entertaining a group of Japanese military officers and politicians at his Shanghai residence. He immediately notified Mayling. Visibly distraught, she hurried from her home in the French Concession to the Kung residence, where she found T. V. Soong and Donald. They all rushed to Nanking that night and called an emergency meeting of the Kuomintang inner circle at the Generalissimo's headquarters. It soon became clear that the Soong clan stood alone against the rest of the government in advocating a peaceful resolution to the crisis. To her dismay, Mayling found she was viewed only as a distressed wife "who could not be expected to be reasonable" under the circumstances. She realized that if there was to be any chance of a peaceful settlement she must assert her views forcefully and insist on a "sane line of action." Donald asserted that during the crisis she personified the "whole driving spirit in China" and "took complete command."

Chiang's inner circle hotly debated what should be done. Mayling wanted to go to Xi'an as emissary, and T. V. offered to go too. But war minister He Yingqin vehemently opposed negotiation, insisting the government should bomb Xi'an immediately and launch a punitive force. It was pointed out that Chiang might die as a result. "If he is killed that is too bad, but he is a soldier and he must take the chances of a soldier," the war minister replied. Horrified, Mayling was convinced He's "unhealthy obsession" with force was motivated by a desire to dispose of Chiang and seize power himself.

In arguing for talks, Mayling faced the taunt that she was merely a "woman pleading for the life of her husband." She countered: "If it is necessary that the Generalissimo should die for the good of the country, I would be the first to sacrifice him." She was troubled by feelings of guilt; if she had been with her husband as she usually was on his campaigns, somehow the crisis could have been prevented, or so she thought. Knowing the leading figures in the crisis as well as she did, she was convinced that she could bring about a resolution if only she could go to Xi'an. But the suggestion was met with "stern disapproval" from all sides. She might be taken hostage and tortured to force Chiang to submit to the kidnappers' demands, she was told. Moreover, the Generalissimo would be dead soon, if he was not already.

Finally it was decided to dispatch Donald to Xi'an on a reconnaissance mission. He was a friend of the Young Marshal's, and as a foreigner it was unlikely he would be harmed. When Donald arrived at Zhang's heavily guarded headquarters in Xi'an, he found Chiang showering his captor in a torrent of abuse while the Young Marshal stood silently at attention. Chiang then turned sullen and mute, refusing to speak or eat. Determined to make a revolutionary martyr of himself, he issued orders to the central government to bomb Xi'an, made out his will, and wrote a letter to Mayling asking her to look after his sons. Donald told him that the kidnappers' demands represented popular will; that China was in crisis and if Chiang would only be reasonable the country could be saved. Chiang appeared unmoved, but cried when he read a letter from his wife. He remained "stubborn as a mule" for several days, until Donald—by his own account—finally persuaded him that "a live ass is better than a dead lion." Whether Chiang would have agreed with this characterization of events is unknown, but he did take nourishment. He requested his Bible, which was given to him once the guards were persuaded it was suitable reading material.

On December 16 Donald telephoned Mayling from Luoyang while en route back to Nanking to say that the Generalissimo was well and in good spirits, but still refusing to discuss the kidnappers' demands. The greatest danger to Chiang's life, she replied, came from Nanking, not Xi'an. Despite her strenuous protests, the government pushed ahead with plans to bomb Xi'an and send in armed forces. The only reason bombing had not yet been carried out was that a blizzard had raged for much of the week following Chiang's arrest, preventing bombers from reaching the city.

Moscow publicly denied any connection with the coup. Kung asked Ching Ling to denounce the kidnapping and demand Chiang's release. The indomitable widow stoutly refused. "I would have done the same thing if I had been in his place," she retorted, referring to the Young Marshal. "Only I would have gone further!" But she recognized the threat to China's survival, and when Mayling asked her to bring a high-level Communist to Nanking, one was sent. Mayling was said to have begged for a guarantee of her husband's safety.

Once news of the abduction was widely known, Chiang Kai-shek's prestige soared. In the eyes of many Chinese at home and abroad, he was a symbol of the national unity for which China had struggled so long and sacrificed so much to achieve. Overnight, Zhang Xueliang became a symbol of the chaos and disunity that Chinese people felt had shamed them before the world. The public rallied behind Chiang, as did foreigners. In a telegram to Zhang the British ambassador called the kidnapping a treacherous "stab in the back." The Nanking government unleashed a barrage of propaganda depicting Zhang as the "supreme traitor of ten thousand years." He tried to send out a telegram to the press, foreign embassies, and elsewhere explaining his case, but Nanking had disrupted communication links with Xi'an. In the statement Zhang said he understood that though kidnapping the country's leader was indefensible, he wanted China to stop wasting money, lives, and property fighting incessant civil wars against the so-called bandits, who after all were "still Chinese despite their views

[and] who at worst aren't [a] menace to their country as are Japanese." He wanted China to defend itself but saw instead "suppression [of] public opinion . . . regarding this vitally important national question."

On December 17 Zhang sent his private plane to pick up Zhou Enlai and bring him to Xi'an. In 1924–25 Zhou had been Chiang Kai-shek's subordinate at Whampoa Military Academy, where Chiang was then commandant. Had they not forsworn religion, the Chinese Communists would have regarded the Xi'an crisis as a godsend. It was an unexpected opportunity that they exploited with tremendous skill and success, contributing to their eventual rise to power. By some accounts, they had been mortally wounded by a decade of purges and "bandit suppression" campaigns. Whether their demise was nigh, as Chiang claimed, is doubtful, but they had been marginalized. Chiang's abduction gave them the chance not only to get back in the game, but to do so on virtually equal footing with the Nationalists.

Zhou was keenly aware of Chiang's moral authority across the country, and was committed to a peaceful resolution to the imbroglio. Only by restoring Chiang to power could a united front between Nanking and the Communists be achieved and a course be set for war against Japan—the sine qua non for an ultimate Communist victory. Contrary to expectations, the Communists behaved magnanimously and graciously in Chiang's extremity. It was a brilliant performance at a critical juncture, one not lost on the Chinese public. As the ominous Chinese saying held, the hour of Chiang Kai-shek's dispatch was yet to come.

Chiang dreaded the visit of his former subordinate, on whose own head he had placed a bounty, and whose comrades he had persecuted mercilessly. To Chiang's surprise, Zhou greeted his captive enemy in a disarmingly friendly manner. But the central government had yet to send a suitable representative to negotiate for the Generalissimo's release, as per Zhang's request. Zhang again sent messages asking Mayling and Kung to come. Kung could not go, because he was acting head of state in Chiang's absence. Despite her husband's entreaties, Mayling desperately wanted to go, and she requested two American pilots. Because they were the only unmarried American fliers, Billy "Mac" McDonald and Sebie Biggs Smith volunteered for the hazardous mission. When they arrived in Nanking

Mayling came out in the snow to meet them. "It was obvious that she had been crying and was very upset," recounted Smith. Kung had refused to let her go. He believed Chiang was already dead and feared they might kill her too.

T. V. Soong was sent instead, as he was close to the Young Marshal and he was not in the government. He flew to Xi'an on December 19, and handed Chiang a note from Mayling: "Should T. V. fail to return to Nanking within three days, I will come to [Xi'an] to live and die with you." Chiang nearly cried on reading it. T. V. Soong returned on December 21, and the following morning Mayling finally flew to Xi'an accompanied by her maid; T. V.; Donald; Chiang's spy chief, Dai Li; and Gen. Jiang Dingwen. Passing through Luoyang en route, Mayling demanded commanders halt the bombing raids ordered by Nanking. Ironically, the planes being used were the ones given Chiang as a birthday present. In any event, pilots had merely flown from Luoyang and dumped their deadly cargo on open fields and reported they had bombed Xi'an.

En route to Xi'an, Mayling reflected on what attitude she should take with the kidnappers, knowing that the future of China and quite possibly her life and Chiang's depended on it. She decided that "even if they were rude, I should not lose my temper but talk to them as man to man and be as natural as I could." As they neared the ancient city she began to feel apprehensive. Before landing she handed Donald a revolver and instructed him to shoot her without hesitation if she were taken captive. On arrival Marshal Zhang, looking tired and embarrassed, boarded the plane. She greeted him warmly and asked him not to let his men search her luggage as she hated to have her things "messed up." He replied, "Madame, I would never dare do that." He offered to take her to her husband immediately, but she asked to have tea first, to show that she regarded him as a gentleman and expected to be treated in a civilized fashion.

When she appeared unannounced in Chiang's quarters he exclaimed, "Why have you come? You have walked into a tiger's lair." He looked at her as though seeing a ghost. He was "very much moved and wanted to cry," he later wrote. She remained calm, but felt a wave of anger toward his captors when she saw her injured husband lying helplessly in bed looking wan and ill. She gave him his spare set of false teeth. He showed her a biblical verse he had read that very morning: "The Lord has created a new thing on the earth: a woman protects a man." He became agitated recounting his capture, so she read him Psalms until he slept.

Mayling quietly told Zhang he had made a "bad mess of things" and had to find a way out. The contrite Young Marshal replied that none of this would have happened had she been there; when he had tried to discuss matters the Generalissimo would not listen and scolded him instead. Zhang was "too impatient and impulsive," Mayling said. "The Generalissimo only scolds people of whom he has high hopes." Not one to let pass an opportunity to proselytize, she told the irreligious Zhang if he really wanted to do something for the country he must "seek spiritual guidance."

Long hours of arguing and pleading ensued, relieved only by walks in the snow-covered compound that served as the Young Marshal's headquarters. Under the combined efforts of Mayling, Zhang, T. V., and Donald, Chiang eventually seemed to be persuaded Zhang's motives were honest and patriotic. He appeared to agree that the kidnappers' aims were desirable and he would take these matters up with the government on his return to Nanking. The snowstorms, he decided, were the hand of God intervening to give him time to ponder China's future.

On Christmas Eve talks continued far into the night, with no resolution. Mayling felt sad there was no Christmas tree, but Christmas morning Donald presented her with a typewriter and Chiang with a steamer rug—each attached to a golf sock in lieu of stockings. Kung, who knew Zhang had enjoyed Christmas and exchanging presents since boyhood even though he was not a Christian, sent him a telegram saying that he could give the country no better gift than releasing the Generalissimo. Finally, despite the Chinese proverb "One cannot send the tiger back to the mountain," Zhang allowed Chiang to leave on the afternoon of Christmas Day, with no firm commitment from Chiang that he would carry out his kidnappers' demands.

The terms of the settlement for Chiang's release remain a mystery. Yang Hucheng is thought to have opposed his release, and the Chinese Communists initially hoped Zhang would execute him. It is believed that Stalin ordered the Chinese Communists to release him, in the belief that he was critical to keep China viable as a counterweight against Japan. According to Donald, it was agreed that the Communists would be left alone; a subsidy would be paid to keep their troops quiet; and a commission would be set up to determine whether they were truly Communists or merely disgruntled citizens. Zhang's original eight demands were pared down to four—resist Japan, release political prisoners, reorganize the cabinet, and end the war against the Communists. The kidnappers were apparently promised little or no punishment. News reports claimed the Soongs dipped into their family fortune to pay a ransom, but in view of Zhang's own immense wealth this is unlikely. According to Zhou Enlai, all guarantees to the kidnappers were made by Mayling and her brother. "Most of the talk was through Madame Chiang and T. V. Soong," Zhou said. "Personally Chiang Kai-shek promised nothing directly."

On departing, Chiang recognized Zhang's loyalty and asked him to stay behind in his post, but—against Zhou's advice—Zhang insisted on returning to Nanking. "By nature I am crude and precipitate, and I have now committed the great crime of violating law and discipline as well as disrespecting you," Zhang wrote the Generalissimo. "Shamefacedly I have followed you to Nanking wishing to surrender myself with utter sincerity for reprimand and punishment." In a quixotic display of loyalty, he left with his erstwhile captive in a show of repentance for the loss of face he had caused his superior officer, and to prove he had kidnapped Chiang not for personal gain but for patriotic reasons. Many believed he was going to his death.

With the news of Chiang's release, rejoicing swept China and his prestige and popular support surged as never before. Wherever the news reached by radio, citizens held spontaneous celebrations and set off firecrackers. The mood of the country completely changed. War with Japan was now inevitable. When Chiang and Mayling arrived in Nanking on December 26, jubilant crowds thronged the airport. Chiang held a cabinet meeting at which he submitted a pro forma resignation, charging himself with "incompetence." The resignation was rejected and Chiang took a month's leave to recuperate from his injuries in his ancestral village.

What transpired next remains murky. Mayling urged Chiang to treat the "Young Fellow" magnanimously, saying he had not wanted money or territory, but had only wanted to sacrifice himself for China. Chiang ostensibly asked the Military Affairs Commission to give Zhang a "lenient punishment so as to encourage him to improve himself." But at the military tribunal, held on December 31, Zhang could not restrain himself from being excessively candid. "The only man I respect in Nanking is the Generalissimo," he said. "I despise all you people. If I get out of this I shall, even single-handed, start a revolution to kick you all out." Chiang and Mayling were "terribly upset" that he had publicly unburdened himself in such a manner. "Now I can't help him," Chiang was quoted as saying.

Zhang was sentenced to ten years in prison and stripped of civil rights for five years. Chiang petitioned for a pardon on the basis of Zhang's remorse, and it was generally believed in Nanking that Zhang would resume his duties. Oddly, he was granted a "special pardon" but ordered kept under strict surveillance. No mention was made of restoring his position and civil rights. In the months that followed, Zhang disappeared from view, and his status remained the subject of speculation. According to Donald, the Chiangs tried to convert him to Christianity. Mayling told Zhang that "although there was a lot of bad in him there was also a lot of good, and if he would give up women and become a Christian there may be some hope for him." Mayling understood him as only a close friend could, Zhang believed. Although her sympathy for Zhang was genuine, her husband's show of magnanimity toward his captor was not. "The only reason I'm still alive is because of Madame Chiang," Zhang said near the end of his life. "Chiang Kai-shek was going to have me shot."

The Xi'an incident—aptly termed a "perfect phantasmagoria" by a British diplomat—was a pivotal event in Chinese history, forcing the Chinese Nationalists and Communists into a marriage of necessity once again. Its peaceful resolution temporarily arrested civil war and made Japan's aims of Chinese conquest more difficult. But the second united front forged between the warring Chinese parties as a result of the Xi'an crisis was not the only union with cracks in it. In public Mayling and Chiang were the ideal modern couple of the day, comparable only to Franklin D. and Eleanor Roosevelt. Mayling was the feisty little woman to his gallant Generalissimo. But after the Xi'an crisis differences surfaced. In Xi'an Mayling and T. V. had agreed to Zhang's demands in order to free Chiang. Although Chiang publicly asserted that he had neither made concessions to nor negotiated with his captors, he had been a party to, or at least tacitly agreed with, the commitments that were made. In the weeks following his release, however, Chiang changed his tune, going back on the word of his wife. She privately threatened to leave him if he abandoned the agreements reached in Xi'an.

According to Donald, Mayling was outraged over her treatment by government ministers while Chiang's life had been in danger. She drafted a twenty-six-page account of her interactions with Nanking during Chiang's detention and threatened to publish it. A Chinese newspaper attacked Donald as a traitor to China and demanded his deportation. Mayling flew to his defense, and Chiang wrote a public letter asserting his confidence in him. But the New Life Movement had struck hard at vested interests, and Donald was suspected of having inspired many of the anticorruption reforms. As a result he had enemies, as did Mayling.

Mayling and Chiang wrote his-and-her accounts of the kidnapping, both of which were serialized in American newspapers and published in book form. A deluxe limited edition was published, printed in folio on handmade bamboo paper, with Chiang Kai-shek's calligraphy on a silk cover. These Mayling autographed and gave as gifts to contributors of $100 or more to her orphanages. The proceeds from foreign publication went to support the families of the Chiangs' bodyguards killed in the Xi'an incident. The *New York Times* opined: "Madame Chiang Kai-shek is not only a picturesque but a powerful figure in the turbulent drama of resurgent China" and her account of the kidnapping was a "thrilling and extraordinary tale." Her husband's narrative was, the *Times* declared charitably, a "singular blend of realism and fantasy," and his account of his interactions with Zhang bore the "air of a Platonic dialogue." Mayling resented the often sensationalistic coverage of the Xi'an crisis in the foreign press, which she said portrayed the episode as a "Gilbert and Sullivan comic opera." But she did not object to the adulation she received.

Madame Chiang emerged from Xi'an a heroine, but at the cost of having earned powerful enemies. Chen Li-fu, Chiang's longtime comrade, disputed her claim that a faction in Nanking wanted to kill Chiang and seize power. Chen, who was one of those she had criticized for advocating an attack on Xi'an, later claimed everyone was "sympathetic" toward her and had no "bad intentions." It was a "wonderful thing" for a woman to brave danger to save her husband, "but she cannot . . . take all the credit and discredit others," Chen said bitterly. "It is just as if someone receives a medal after war and by doing so claims that he represents the thousands of men killed in the war." Her book "hurt quite a lot of people," Chen said.

Mayling's role in resolving the Xi'an crisis lifted her standing in the eyes of her husband and in the eyes of the West, catapulting her onto the international stage. She also became the image of modern Chinese womanhood, emancipated, Christian, and at her husband's side, sharing in his struggles and helping him achieve his goals. She was built up into a larger-than-life heroic figure, especially in the American media. The *New York Times* wrote that she "at no time in her brilliant career showed more clearly her penetrating intelligence and the strength of her extraordinary personality than when she frustrated these evil machinations." The *Boston Post* proclaimed, "The real ruler of modern China is a woman—Madame Chiang Kai-shek. She dictates to the dictator."

Chapter Ten

Undeclared War

We will do our best and fight to the bitter end. We do not expect to win many battles, but we are convinced, nevertheless, that we will win the war.

—Mayling Soong Chiang

China had a long history of inviting foreign advisers to work for the government, from Jesuit scholars in the sixteenth century to British customs officials in the nineteenth to Russian political and military advisers under Sun Yat-sen's Canton government in the 1920s. Through the centuries the ranks of foreign advisers were filled by a motley crew of priests, adventurers, mavericks, merchants, mercenaries, missionaries, and the occasional éminence grise.

Chiang turned to Germany in 1928, exchanging antimony and tungsten for advice on how to modernize his armies to fight the Chinese Communists and eventually Japan. In 1933 he recruited Col.-Gen. Hans von Seeckt, venerated as the architect of the modern *Reichswehr*, Germany's army. He was succeeded in 1935 by the equally distinguished Gen. Alexander von Falkenhausen, who detested Hitler. But the most intriguing of the many German experts, and the one to whom Mayling grew closest, was Capt. Walther Stennes. Tall, attractive, and fearless, the Prussian was "every inch the blond, blue-eyed, toughly elegant, heel-clicking German officer." The former Berlin commander of Hitler's *Sturm Abteilung* (Storm Troops or SA), also known as the Brown Shirts, was persona non grata with *der Führer* thanks to having led a 1931 revolt. Stennes's wife, Hilde, helped him escape from a concentration camp and he fled to China in 1933, where Hitler cabled Berlin's ambassador in Nanking, "On no account start a row with that man Stennes."

Stennes knew Mayling had sought his appointment, but he was unprepared for the warmth of her greeting, her girlishness, and her "casual,
unaffected friendliness." Chiang charged Stennes with molding his three-
thousand-strong bodyguard into an elite force like the Prussian Guards
and commanding the presidential air transport squadron. Stennes called
Chiang "the greatest man I have ever known. Greater than Hitler? Yes,
every time!" He maintained that had he been present at Xi'an, the Young
Marshal would not have dared to kidnap the Generalissimo, but Chiang
had insisted on going without him. He termed his relations with the Chiangs
gemütlich—cozy—and found Mayling especially helpful. Once his favorite
interpreter mysteriously vanished. No one seemed to have any idea what
had become of him—it was as though he had never existed. Stennes turned
to Mayling. A week later the interpreter mysteriously reappeared at his
desk, looking pale and frightened. It emerged that he had overheard talk
of war and had written of it to his family. Chiang's agents intercepted the
letter and detained its author. Were it not for Stennes and Mayling he
would never have been heard from again.

China's armies were not alone in needing foreign expertise. The deficiencies of the fledgling air force were painfully exposed when the Japanese trounced Chinese forces at Shanghai in early 1932. Mayling took a
keen early interest in aviation. The air force was cobbled together with
pilots, instructors, mechanics, and engineers from Britain, Russia, Italy,
France, Germany, and the U.S., as well as aircraft from each country, leading to confusion, competition, and communication difficulties. The thirty
American mercenary pilots were told to keep their Chinese air force con-
tracts secret. So strong was isolationist sentiment in the U.S. that under
the Neutrality Act, the airmen risked being stripped of American citizenship if caught engaging in an act of war on behalf of the Nationalist Chinese government. But they often came under pressure to violate the act.
While ferrying cash to pay the salaries of Chinese troops, Thomas Taylor
was asked to fly munitions to resupply Nationalist troops fighting Communists in Yunnan province. He refused. Mayling pleaded that the Communists would behead American missionaries trapped in the area if he did not
transport the material, and he relented.

By late 1936 the Chinese air force was in chaos and rumored to be rife
with corruption. Apparently in the belief that he could trust no one else,

Chiang appointed his wife the first secretary-general of the Commission on Aeronautical Affairs. As head of China's air ministry Mayling was also commander in chief of the Chinese air force. Her job was to reorganize and clean up the ministry and the air force and, most critically, prepare it for the looming war with Japan—tasks that would have been daunting for the most experienced aviation administrator. Ironically, Mayling suffered terribly from airsickness in those days of unpressurized cabins and no oxygen, but that did not stop her from making countless cold, bumpy journeys across China.

Predictably, there was much jealousy among air force generals, who did not like taking orders from a woman. A woman with no military experience heading the air force, a plum job, was a slap in the face to ambitious career officers. She encountered much disapproval and passive resistance. The Russians threatened to stop sending planes if she remained in charge. Mayling was aware of her deficiencies. She read up on aviation and listened closely to American and European experts as they explained tactics, performance, and maintenance of various types of aircraft.

Technical matters, however, were the least of her challenges. For some time her sister, Madame Kung, was rumored to have been involved in corruption in the purchasing of aircraft and aviation equipment by the Chinese government, with the connivance of American suppliers. Mayling's strategy in this and other matters was to hire foreigners to investigate. No Chinese, she patronizingly concluded, could be entrusted with the task—they had too many vested interests, friends, and relatives and were burdened by Chinese notions of "face" and personal feelings. Despite suffering one of her "nervous breakdowns" in the spring of 1937 for which doctors ordered four months of rest, with Donald's help she launched a secret investigation. She appointed Wing Commander Garnet Malley, an Australian aviation adviser, to investigate on her behalf.

Malley discovered that the Chinese government was being defrauded with the collusion of both Chinese and foreign parties. The air ministry had attempted to deal with American aviation manufacturers directly but was forced to go through China-based agents. One agent, A. L. Patterson, had through bribery apparently cornered the Chinese market, to the annoyance of his American and European competitors. Patterson doubled as a representative of the U.S. Commerce Department, which brought his activities to the attention of U.S. authorities. The amount of "squeeze," meaning kickbacks or commission, Patterson was skimming was "almost unbelievable," Malley told American diplomats. To deceive the Chinese into paying extortionate prices, Patterson printed up catalogs purporting to be the original American catalogs, but listing prices several times higher. In one case he sold the Aeronautics Commission two hundred radio sets at quadruple the correct price—and they were not even suitable for use in military aircraft.

Mayling was fully aware of the situation and asked Malley for suggestions on how to stop the squeeze. All Chinese government procurement was funneled through the Central Trust, a government organization charged with effecting such purchases. The Central Trust had come under the influence of Madame Kung, and at her behest was refusing to give orders to any firm not represented by Patterson. Malley reported that General Zhou Zhirou, head of the air force and a West Point graduate, was Patterson's "boon companion and accomplice." This came as no surprise to American diplomats, as Zhou was reputed to be the agent of Madame Kung in collecting squeeze on aircraft purchases. When asked if Madame Chiang could take action that might expose her sister's alleged role, Malley told diplomats that she had ordered the investigation to be pursued to the bottom and that the matter of kickbacks in connection with aircraft purchases had been "the subject of a struggle" between the two sisters for some time. Malley doubted that H. H. Kung was involved in the corruption or was even aware it was taking place.

As part of her effort to reform the Chinese air force, she recruited an American aviator named Claire Lee Chennault as adviser. The Louisiana planter's son had been a country schoolteacher before joining the Army Air Corps, where he earned a reputation as a brilliant air combat tactician and acrobatic pilot that was equaled only by his reputation for not suffering fools gladly. Eventually he antagonized Air Corps brass and was shunted off as commander of the Flying Trapeze Army Air Show, an exhibition team of daredevil stunt fliers. In the eyes of admirers he was a singular character, salty, daring, and canny, with the air of a "gamecock of the wilderness." In military circles he was viewed as a maverick who challenged the army establishment with his unorthodox theories on the primacy of air combat. Nicknamed "Old Leatherface" for his craggy visage, he chain-smoked

Camel cigarettes and had chronic bronchitis. He was partially deaf due to flying in open cockpits without ear protection. His health problems and controversial theories had forced his retirement from the army, but did not stop him from flying.

Chennault agreed to work for the Chinese government, but there was one hitch: he was only a major in the Army Air Corps, and Mayling did not think that rank sounded impressive enough. She suggested he try to get promoted to at least colonel. Chennault finagled this by getting the governor of Louisiana to appoint him a "colonel" on his staff. Leaving a wife and eight children back in the States, Chennault arrived in China in June 1937 on a three-month assignment. He was utterly bowled over by Mayling from the first meeting. "She will always be a princess to me," he recorded in his diary that evening. On her orders he began an inspection tour of China's airports, after which he was to report to her on how to build a modern air force.

Chennault's mission was overtaken by events. Hardly had he unpacked his bags when long-simmering tensions between Japan and China finally ignited. On the night of July 7, 1937, Japanese soldiers attacked Chinese troops at Marco Polo Bridge on the outskirts of Beijing. The Chinese retaliated in a skirmish later seen as the first battle of the Second World War. The newly installed Japanese premier, Prince Konoye, ordered China to apologize for "illegal anti-Japanese actions." Mayling and Chiang received word of the hostilities at the summer capital in the mountain resort town of Kuling, where they then called a conference of Kuomintang leaders and the country's intellectual elite. Before descending from the mountain two weeks later, Chiang declared: "If we allow one more inch of our territory to be lost, we shall be guilty of an unpardonable crime against our race."

Capt. Royal Leonard, the Young Marshal's former pilot, flew Mayling and Chiang to Nanking, where they met with ambassadors of Western powers in the hopes of Western mediation in the conflict. Now that China was truly at war, Mayling's position as head of the Chinese air force was of critical importance. The air force was in pitiful condition, especially compared with that of the enemy. The Chinese were short of planes, pilots, weapons, training, experience, and everything else necessary for a modern fighting fleet. Chiang asked how many planes the air force had. When told there were eighty-seven serviceable planes, he "went through the roof." What had happened to the planes that had sup-

posedly been bought and the money that had been provided to do so? he
raved. He was told that the number of effective aircraft might be brought
to 120 if spare parts could be found. Within weeks that number was reduced to nineteen.

Chennault, Leonard, and the other American airmen hatched a scheme to
bomb Tokyo. The idea was promptly quashed by Chiang and Mayling, who
felt the government's very existence depended on friendly relations with the
U.S. and refused to risk losing American lives in such a blatant violation of
U.S. neutrality. Sino-American ties were soon put to the test. On August 14
inexperienced Chinese pilots accidentally dropped bombs on Shanghai's
International Settlement, killing 1,740 and wounding 1,873. Another international embarrassment occurred on August 30 when Chinese airmen mistakenly bombed the USS *President Hoover,* a Dollar Line vessel anchored at
the mouth of the Yangtze River among a group of Japanese transport ships
that were the intended target. One seaman was killed and much damage incurred. Mayling called Leonard into the Generalissimo's headquarters in
Nanking. She was dressed in slacks and looking like a schoolgirl, but her
manner was all business. She asked Leonard to take charge of aerial bombardment for the Chinese air force. Leonard protested he knew nothing
about bombardment—he was a pursuit pilot. "That doesn't matter," said
Mayling. "You are a good flier and you have a good head. We need your judgment. You can be trusted. That is what we want."

In typical fashion, the Generalissimo ordered that the pilot responsible
for the *Hoover* accident be executed. Chennault did not wish to see the
shaky morale of his Chinese pilots further undermined and with Mayling's
support delicately intervened. He and Leonard told the airmen that frank
admission of errors would yield leniency but excuses would be punished.
Chennault put the pilot at fault back in the air.

On August 28, 1937, the Japanese premier, Prince Konoye, declared that
Japan would beat China to her knees in three months. The Japanese were
not alone in the belief that the Chinese would soon knuckle under. At
Shanghai's famous Long Bar, foreign patrons predicted the war would be
over by Christmas. When Stennes said he thought the war could last two
or three years, the bar crowd roared with laughter and ordered another
round. "You Americans are damned fools," Stennes afterward told Leonard.
"Japan wants your blood even more than the blood of the British."

The day of Prince Konoye's statement Mayling inspected the damage in Shanghai's walled Chinese city after Japanese bomb raids killed two hundred and wounded twice that number. "China is not afraid," she stoutly told the foreign press. "Japan may be a fighting machine, but China has found her soul. China will defend her people and her rights." In a superior tone, *Time* magazine said of the Sino-Japanese conflict: "Much as a hill of ants are driven by their impulses to conquer another ant hill, the Japanese have gone forth to war." It was an undeclared war that the Japanese called the "China Incident."

Chennault persuaded Mayling and Chiang that with a relatively small but well-equipped air outfit manned by mercenary pilots, he could defeat the Japanese in China. He secretly recruited American fliers and in the autumn of 1937 organized the 14th Volunteer Bombardment Squadron with a dozen mercenary pilots. Some were veterans of the Spanish Civil War. The outfit was based in Hankow and along with a large Soviet contingent fought in combat for five months. It was disbanded in March 1938, but many of the pilots stayed on in China.

Mayling visited the front lines, chatting with soldiers and handing out cigarettes and sweets. She investigated the damage from every air raid and bandaged the wounded. In addition to her responsibilities as commander of the air force, she took the lead in organizing civilian support for the armed forces. She appealed to Chinese women to join in the war "according to their ability." A campaign to "Give one day to your country" was launched. Chinese were urged to contribute one day's pay to the nation, and collection boxes were placed in public places.

Mayling consulted with advisers and issued orders to air combat and defense units from the modest office she shared with her husband. She typed out commands on a portable typewriter, occasionally nibbling from a box of American chocolates. Behind her desk stood two Lewis machine guns from a Japanese plane shot down in an air raid over Nanking. A pastel likeness of Jesus Christ hung nearby. Foreign visitors were startled to see her issue orders from a "swivel chair on a tiger rug." She and Chiang often worked sixteen- or twenty-hour days.

With the advent of war Mayling and Donald turned their energies from reform to propaganda to stir worldwide sympathy. To this end, Mayling was made into a symbol of plucky China, fighting off the barbarian invader with bare fists. There was bitter resentment against the U.S. for its policies. Citing the Neutrality Act, Washington embargoed weapons sales to China but continued to feed Japan's war machine, selling oil, scrap iron, and munitions. Americans also bought Japanese goods such as silk stockings that provided Japan foreign exchange.

In the September 4, 1937, issue of *Liberty*, Mayling charged the Western democracies with "pathetic pusillanimity" following Japan's 1931 takeover of Manchuria. China had learned that "not only God, as Napoleon said, but everyone else, was on the side of the big battalions," she wrote. China asked not for favors but a "fair chance . . . so that we may, in time, catch up" with the advanced nations. A week later she addressed America via shortwave radio, entreating the nation to support China in the conflict or become "accessory to this mass murder." Japan intended to erect upon China's ashes a "continental Japanese empire," she argued, before conquering all Asia.

In the autumn of 1937 Chiang and Mayling moved into Donald's camouflaged bungalow for safety. The modest house doubled as cramped offices for them and their secretaries. There they worked and listened to Donald's powerful shortwave radio, which picked up stations around the world. Donald would take notes of newscasts and speeches and interpret them to Mayling and Chiang.

Polish-born journalist Ilona Ralf Sues's first impression of Mayling was that of a "princess confined in a secondhand furniture store," as her office was so crammed with her favorite chairs, cabinets, and couches one could hardly get to her small desk, which was blanketed with papers. Mayling had appointed Sues to clean house in the government's hopelessly corrupt and inefficient propaganda bureau. "You may blame everything on me—I am a foreign devil without obligations," declared Sues. She initially found Mayling a terrifyingly cold beauty, but was won over by her contagious enthusiasm for reform and was soon "ready to go through hellfire" for this "courageous, temperamental little lady."

Sues discovered that the information ministry had a foreign publicity department of sixty men, none of whom knew any foreign languages. As she pursued her mission Sues encountered from every quarter a "visible hostile stiffening" at the mention of Madame Chiang's name. Mayling was an idiosyncratic boss. Sues soon learned that the words "propaganda" and "retreat," as applied to Chinese troops, were forbidden and would send the First Lady into a rage. The words "publicity" and "strategic withdrawal" were the preferred terms. Garlic was taboo, as Sues discovered when Donald sent her home from the office one day because she had eaten a dish flavored with that ubiquitous staple of Chinese cuisine.

For public consumption Mayling was a First Lady of the World molded by Donald. But behind closed doors she could be selfish, petty, and capricious. Everyone except Donald trembled when she lost her temper. "She had admirers but no true friends," observed Sues. "She did not talk with people, she talked at them." The Madame demanded unquestioning loyalty from her staff and banished anyone who expressed opinions at variance with hers. But Sues nonetheless admired Madame for her "fighting heart of a lioness, courage, tenacity, and ruse."

In the end Mayling's whirlwind publicity reform effort was watered down. Initially the Generalissimo was furious after hearing of the conditions in the propaganda bureau and ordered it abolished. But he came under pressure and the foreign publicity men who knew no foreign languages were not summarily fired, as Mayling had demanded. They could not be dismissed because they were either party members or had important relatives who were. Soon after Mayling had another "nervous breakdown" and Donald told her staff she was "through with publicity." In the wake of the debacle, Sues found herself "dropped" by Mayling because she made the cardinal error of mentioning—albeit in a positive light—the First Lady's name in the presence of other foreigners.

Mayling spoke frequently to the Western press and in the autumn of 1937 wrote almost daily war dispatches for the Washington, D.C., *Evening Star*. Her vivid and heartfelt writing style, though perhaps not stellar journalism, appealed to readers, who increasingly sympathized with China's plight. On October 15 she described watching aerial dogfights during a Japanese bombing raid on Nanking. In another article she described inspecting three hundred soldiers, victims of mustard gas, being treated in the bombed-out ruins of the Central University. "All the old library tables were being used as beds and every bit of space was crammed with wounded," she wrote. "Their eyes were sorely inflamed, their bodies blistered and their feet and legs swollen. Most of them were coughing violently and having great difficulty to breathe."

In an article in the December 1937 issue of *Forum,* she decried the American ban on weapons sales to China and the refusal of the U.S. government to issue American military instructors passports. China felt it was being "struck in the face by the great republic whom we had been taught to look up to with respect and, indeed, to emulate," she wrote. The Chinese were particularly infuriated when the U.S. yielded to Japanese demands and unloaded airplanes for which the Chinese government had paid cash from American ships at San Diego. In her writings she repeatedly called for an embargo on U.S. sales of scrap iron and other raw materials of war to Japan, but to no avail.

Her articles precipitated a torrent of letters and telegrams from readers in America and around the world offering encouragement and advice on how to win the war. A groundswell of interest in and sympathy for China was fueled by *The Good Earth,* the film version of Pearl Buck's book having hit cinemas that year. Some readers were fascinated that Madame Chiang was playing such an active role in China's defense. Others wanted to help, including several American airwomen who offered their services as pilots. Christians told Mayling they were praying for China and the triumph of her "righteous cause." An admirer from Clinton, Connecticut, called Mayling a beautiful, "living Chinese goddess far greater than Joan of Arc." Others sent money for war relief. "We, in China, are left alone to oppose the murderous aggression of a power that already threatens civilization," Mayling wrote to thank Maude May Babcock of Salt Lake City for her $10 donation. "Every move to refrain from buying from, or selling to, the Japanese will help to lessen the power of that country to bring complete ruin to China."

As the battle for Shanghai progressed Mayling traveled frequently between Nanking and the port city, despite danger of Japanese attack. On October 23, 1937, she and Donald were en route to Shanghai to inspect wounded soldiers when their driver lost control of the automobile and it flipped. Mayling was thrown into a muddy ditch and knocked unconscious. Trying to shake her awake, Donald sang, "She flies through the air with the greatest of ease, this daring young girl who fights Japanese." He carried her to a nearby farmhouse, where she soon revived. "You can never say that I didn't pick you out of the gutter!" he joked. She insisted on continuing to Shanghai. "It hurts me to breathe," she said. She was found to have broken a rib and wrenched her back.

By mid-November Japanese forces had captured Shanghai after three months of fighting that took heavy casualties on both sides. In the wake of devastating waves of aerial bombing, the Japanese pressed on up the Yangtze River Valley toward the Nationalist Chinese capital. The Nanking government hurriedly evacuated to a provisional post in Wuhan, the old treaty port city six hundred miles up the Yangtze. Hundreds of thousands of residents followed by car or on foot. The Chiangs left Nanking by plane less than a week before Japanese troops breached the city's medieval walls on December 13.

Japanese forces showered Nanking with leaflets promising fair treatment of civilians. But war-drunk troops—with the apparent blessing of commanding officers—perpetrated a seven-week orgy of unimaginable brutality and depravity on the city's unarmed civilian population and defeated troops. Not only was there mass rape of women of all ages, but testimony of witnesses as well as photos documenting the savagery show that many women were horribly mutilated, babies bayoneted, and men beheaded en masse as an exercise in sword practice. Foreign diplomats and missionaries, along with German businessman John Rabe, sheltered as many Chinese as they could, but in the months that followed an estimated seventy to three hundred thousand Chinese, mostly civilians, were slaughtered during what became known as the Rape of Nanking. Mayling was horrified. Chiang Kai-shek subsequently lifted a ban on compulsory religion courses in China's mission schools, in appreciation of the foreign missionaries who courageously held their ground despite Japanese threats and abuse directed toward the missionaries themselves.

Time magazine named Chiang Kai-shek and Mayling "Man and Wife of the Year" for 1937, the first couple to be jointly awarded the honor. She was also the first woman so named, albeit not on her own. A painting of the couple on the cover of the January 3, 1938, issue of the magazine depicted him looking somber in a dark cloak and her looking relaxed in an open-collared Western blouse. A quote beneath read: "Any sacrifice should not be regarded as too costly." Wife of the Year was in bed with influenza, but Chiang told the *Time* reporter: "Tell America to have complete confidence in us. The tide of battle is turning and eventually victory will be ours!"

Americans, in their need to understand the world through the lens of their own country, called the industrial metropolis of Wuhan the "Chi-

Charles Soong as a student in America. *(Duke University Rare Book, Manuscript, and Special Collections Library)*

Mayling's parents, Charles and "Mamie" Soong, in Shanghai. *(Duke University Rare Book, Manuscript, and Special Collections Library)*

Soong family portrait, circa autumn 1917. Mayling stands at right behind her mother; her brother Tse-liang is standing behind her father. Seated on the floor from left to right are sister Eling (Madame H. H. Kung), brother Tse-wen, sister Ching Ling (Madame Sun Yat-sen), with Tse-an, the youngest, in front. *(Courtesy of Kuomintang Archives)*

Mayling Soong as a young girl, while she was a student in Georgia. *(Archives and Special Collections/Willet Memorial Library/Wesleyan College)*

Mayling with classmates at Wesleyan College in Macon, Georgia, circa 1913. *(Courtesy of Kuomintang Archives)*

Mayling Soong, as she appeared in the Wellesley College yearbook of 1917, the year she graduated from the college in the suburbs of Boston, Massachusetts. She was about nineteen years old. *(Wellesley College Archives)*

Chiang Kai-shek and Mayling Soong during their courtship. *(Granger Collection, New York)*

Liu Jiwen, who courted Mayling Soong while she lived in Shanghai during the 1920s. It is rumored that they were once engaged. *(Central News Agency, Taiwan)*

Jennie Chen, Chiang Kai-shek's third wife, whom he repudiated in 1927 to marry Mayling Soong. *(Brown Brothers, Sterling, PA)*

The Chiangs as they appeared in a wedding portrait, taken in December 1927. *(Wellesley College Archives, photo by Chung Hwa Studio)*

Mayling with her dog in the early 1930s. *(Courtesy of Kuomintang Archives)*

Chiang Kai-shek in cloak and fedora with "Young Marshal" Zhang Xueliang, circa 1930. In December 1936 Zhang kidnapped Chiang in Xi'an, calling for a united front with the Chinese communists to fight the Japanese invasion. *(Hulton Archive/Getty Images)*

Madame Chiang Kai-shek in Xi'an with her Australian advisor, William H. Donald, in 1936. *(Courtesy of Kuomintang Archives)*

A portrait of Madame Chiang Kai-shek taken by renowned photographer Yousuf Karsh, in June 1943. She is wearing her treasured Chinese Air Force "wings" pin. *(Yousuf Karsh/Camera Press/Retna Ltd.)*

General Claire Lee Chennault, head of the American air combat corps popularly known as the Flying Tigers, with the Chiangs in China. *(Courtesy of Kuomintang Archives)*

Madame Chiang greets Clare Boothe Luce, wife of *Time* and *Life* magazine publisher Henry Luce, in Burma in 1942. Boothe Luce was writing an article for *Life* on the war in the Far East. *(Imperial War Museum, London, JAR 1571)*

The three famous Soong sisters inspecting Chinese "warphans." *(Wellesley College Archives)*

The Chiangs meeting with Mahatma Gandhi in Calcutta in February 1942. *(Courtesy of Kuomintang Archives)*

Wendell Willkie greeting Madame Chiang in Chungking during his October 1942 "One World" tour. Willkie's press secretary, Gardner Cowles, claimed that she and the charismatic politician embarked on an affair in Chungking, an assertion Madame Chiang later vigorously contested. *(Courtesy of Kuomintang Archives)*

A chic Madame Chiang inspecting saluting "warphans," whose heads were routinely shaved on arrival at the orphanges to remove lice. *(Wellesley College Archives)*

cago" of China. Junketing journalists thronged the city. "History, grown weary of Shanghai, bored with Barcelona, has fixed her capricious interest on Hankow," wrote poet W. H. Auden, who visited with his friend, the writer Christopher Isherwood. They pronounced Mayling "vivacious rather than pretty, and possessed of an almost terrifying charm and poise." Her perfume was the "most delicious" they had ever smelt. "Please tell me, do poets like cake?" she asked. When they said they did, she replied: "Good. . . . I thought they preferred only spiritual food." She ate nothing and behind her mask she looked tired and unwell.

The American author John Gunther and his wife, Frances, also visited Hankow in 1938. Frances wondered on meeting Mayling: "Was this the face that launched a thousand ships?" John Gunther condescendingly likened Mayling to "the president of a really first-rate American woman's club." When he suggested that Hitler wanted a "digestive interval," Mayling demanded who would offer "international soda mints." Experts told Gunther that Mayling grasped military problems more quickly than her husband, but of the Communists she showed a "curious glib lack of comprehension."

In January 1938 Mayling flew to Hong Kong, ostensibly for rest and medical treatment. Speculation that she was involved in peace talks between China and Japan, or negotiating for a loan from Britain, were fueled by the fact that her sisters Eling and Ching Ling, brothers T. V. and T. L., and other Chinese officials were in the British crown colony at the time. She denied the rumor vigorously, if not entirely convincingly: "My visit has no political purpose or significance, nor is there any mystery about it," she told the press. In fact she was investigating corruption in aircraft purchases.

Mayling found that all the aircraft suppliers paid squeeze. She put all of them "in the dog house" and tried to secure sufficient evidence to have a few members of the air ministry shot. But in the end the Generalissimo refused to do a thorough housecleaning because it would have entirely gutted his air force, he said. He—and no doubt Mayling too—was reluctant to bring to light a scandal that would embarrass him and cast a pall over foreign aid that the country desperately needed as it struggled to resist the Japanese invasion. To build the Chinese air force the government had appealed to Chinese at home and overseas for patriotic contributions. Exasperated, Donald told Mayling to resign and get out of the "damned business. . . . If you don't, you'll be blamed for the entire mess someday."

On her return to Hankow in late February 1938 Mayling abruptly re-signed as head of China's air ministry. "I have simply been a cog in China's defense," she told the press. "I believe I have served my purpose. . . . After all, I am not a military expert." The greatest contribution she could now make to the nation, she claimed, was to devote herself to her husband. "The strain on the Generalissimo now is gigantic, almost superhuman," she said. She was given much of the credit for organizing and revitalizing China's air defenses. Some had held her responsible for the humiliating collapse of the country's air force early in the war, but in fact, though badly outnumbered and outgunned, it had proven itself a challenge to the Japa-nese air force.

It was true that she had lately been "feeling the strain of her intense war activities," as the press were told, and her back injury from the previ-ous October still troubled her. But the real reason she stepped down was graft, which she could neither eliminate nor expose. As punishment for his role, General Zhou was merely demoted a rung in the air force hierarchy, as was General Mao Bangchu, another senior air force official implicated in the corruption scandal. Mayling's sister Eling escaped unscathed, but her activities provided fresh grist for the rumor mill. For all Donald's efforts to depict Mayling as a courageous heroine battling China's evils, the portrayal is unconvincing, for it begs the question of why she tolerated her sister's corruption.

Although Mayling no longer held an official post, she continued to serve as liaison between Chennault and her husband. She meanwhile in-tensified her campaign to drum up international sympathy for China. Asked her views on China's future, she wrote: "Generally speaking, my views are unpalatable—sometimes unprintable." China wanted to follow the democratic path, but "What have the governments of the democra-cies done for us?" she asked. The chief problem was acquiring munitions and equipment. "When this war broke out . . . there was a feeling in China, and, indeed in the world, that the Japanese were . . . invincible," Mayling wrote. "All I can say is that we will do our best and fight to the bitter end. We do not expect to win many battles, but we are convinced, nevertheless, that we will win the war." She considered going to America, where she had been offered a very large fee for a lecture tour and would be received "like a queen." But she was repelled by the thought that her visit might be seen as a "begging expedition." Besides, "the Generalissimo does not want me to go, and I feel that I must stand by him in these critical days," she said in April 1938. Her workload was taking a toll on her health. She shared her husband's defect, an inability to delegate sufficiently.

But despite war and work she still managed to relax. In Hankow Mayling became friendly with Berkeley Gage, second secretary of the British embassy. Gage was a diplomat of the old school—he much preferred parties to composing dry dispatches. Life around Mayling in wartime could be "fun, as well as inspiring," he wrote. One day he and other foreign dignitaries, including the American ambassador and a brace of admirals, were invited to tea at the Generalissimo's headquarters. Mayling decided to give the party an impromptu cooking lesson. She herded the surprised dignitaries into the kitchen, made them don aprons, and set them to work on making a cake. Suddenly the air raid alert went off and Japanese bombs began falling nearby. Mayling paid not the slightest attention, but Gage was rattled and dropped the eggs. Suddenly he announced he had just received word that his younger son, Ulick, had been born in London; would Madame be his godmother? She agreed without hesitation, adding he would be her first godson. Thus was she "bombed into Godmaternity," as Gage put it.

That winter the German ambassador, Oskar Trautmann, made Chiang a peace offer on Tokyo's behalf, one of many such overtures. When tea was finished the diplomat duly delivered his prepared speech. After an awkward silence, he said, "Of course, I give you this message without any comment." Mayling said icily, "I should hope so." Then, quickly shifting gears, she asked the ambassador: "Tell me, how are your children?" Behind her public front of anti-Japanese defiance, however, Mayling and Chiang still hoped for foreign intervention and were engaging Tokyo in sub rosa peace talks. The fact that the talks were partially an attempt to distract Japan as well as to undercut Chiang's political rival, Wang Jingwei, did not mean they were not at least partly a genuine effort to end the war.

Mayling repeatedly sounded the alarm concerning Japanese aggression and intentions, but her Cassandra-like warnings fell on deaf ears. As early as November 1936 she had warned that Japan might one day attack the continental U.S. "If Japanese planes can bomb our cities with impunity," she wrote in a private letter published in 1937, "there is no reason why they should not, some day, push toward Hawaii, establish a base there and with California near at hand, invade your national territory." Imperial Japan's goal, she insisted, was Asian conquest followed by world domination. "Two decades after 'that war to end all wars,'" she wrote in 1938, "I see the wide world seething with excitement and expectation of another welter of blood and ruin."

From the Xi'an incident through the early stages of war with Japan, the Nanking regime enjoyed a honeymoon in public opinion. Chiang was hailed as a national hero and the only person who could rally the country to war. But the reprieve did not last. As the war progressed, the public grew disillusioned. Intellectuals were alienated by a thought control system. Naturally, the devastation and deprivations of war took a heavy toll, and faith in the government was critically undermined by discriminatory and corrupt military conscription policies, rising prices, government corruption, and conflict with the Communists behind the façade of the united front.

Government spending skyrocketed under the strain of war demands, but even before the war there had been no oversight of military spending. The Generalissimo "used the public purse as his own," according to Franklin Ho, a Nationalist official at the time. "Although he did not spend the money on himself personally, he often gave orders for public funds to be given to this or that person or project, without regard to budget or procedure." In late 1936, Ho recalled, as Finance Minister H. H. Kung was holding a meeting, an aide to Chiang called and asked Kung to send a sum of cash. "Look here, the Generalissimo wants money," Kung said jokingly to those present. "What can I do?" He directed the Central Bank to send the cash by special plane. Inevitably, the government turned to the printing press to finance the war, sending prices spiraling upward.

Among the wealthy urban residents of the capital, there was a blithe disregard of the war. Evans Carlson, a U.S. marine, was amazed at the young elite Chinese of Hankow. "They danced and played, gave elaborate cocktail and dinner parties, and were apparently oblivious of the fact that their countrymen were fighting for the nation's existence," he wrote. He asked Mayling why these people were not mobilized. "That is what the New Life Movement is supposed to do," she replied. Foreign cynics quipped: "These people are willing to fight—to the last drop of coolie blood."

* * *

During this period, in the spring of 1937, Mayling experienced a change in her family configuration. Chiang once supposedly said that if his eldest son Ching-kuo came back to China, he would arrest him immediately. But in a 1934 diary entry he wrote sadly of his "son gone away." In late 1936, as Stalin's "Great Terror" stalked Russia, Mayling asked Tsiang T'ing-fu, who was departing for Moscow as China's ambassador, to look into the possibility of Ching-kuo's return. Perhaps due to considerations of face, Chiang was unwilling or unable to take the initiative himself. Mayling may also have been motivated by the realization that it was by this time unlikely she would have children of her own.

Ching-kuo had lately applied for membership in the Communist party of the Soviet Union, evidently in the belief he would stay in Russia indefinitely. After denouncing his father in 1927, he was caught in political and personal exile. Father and son were incommunicado. Stalin took an interest in Ching-kuo and met with him more than once during his Soviet sojourn. After completing military studies, Ching-kuo worked at a factory in the industrial city of Sverdlovsk, interrupted by a nine-month stint as a laborer in Siberia. The Xi'an kidnapping and the rapprochement that ensued between Moscow and Nanking made Ching-kuo's repatriation possible sooner than anyone could have predicted. He returned to China in April 1937 after more than twelve years away, bringing his Russian wife, Faina, and their two-year-old son, Alan. Chiang refused to see him, to Ching-kuo's dismay. Not only was his Chinese rusty but he was out of touch with traditional Chinese notions of filial respect. One of Chiang's aides suggested Ching-kuo write a letter of apology to his father.

Only after receiving the letter did Chiang agree to see his prodigal "Red" son. They met at the presidential residence in Hangchow, along with Mayling and Faina. According to *Time*, Chiang said, "Welcome, my son!" and added, "Now you must meet your new mother." Ching-kuo retorted, "That is not my mother, and having paid my respects to you, father, I am going to my mother and your wife!" Another version holds that Ching-kuo merely addressed Mayling politely as "Mother," and as they said good-bye she slipped him an envelope of cash to buy clothes for himself and his family. Perhaps apocryphal, *Time*'s version nonetheless presaged the uneasy relationship that unfolded between "mother" and "son."

Not long before Ching-kuo's return, Chiang sent his adopted younger son to Munich in 1936 to attend the Kriegshochschule, a military academy. Wego was both ambassador and apprentice. Oddly, Chiang had never introduced him to Mayling, who, it was somewhat improbably later claimed, did not even know of his existence. In 1938, wearing a German uniform with the rank of sergeant officer-candidate, Wego rode into Austria in the *Anschluss*. In 1939 he went to the U.S. for a year, where he served as a consultant at Fort Knox. When Mayling finally met him in late 1940, she greeted him warmly and expressed sorrow that they had not met sooner.

After Ching-kuo's return, Chiang made him study the Chinese classics. During this period Ching-kuo made friends with the Young Marshal, who was living under house arrest in the mountains near Chiang's ancestral village. Before long, however, Ching-kuo was given major responsibilities. With his father he founded and ran the *Sanmin Zhuyi*—Three Principles—Youth Corps, a paramilitary organization modeled on the Hitler Youth. Chiang then appointed him an administrator in Jiangxi province, the former Communist soviet. Ching-kuo ruffled feathers while making a name for himself there as a crusader against vice and corruption. He had no use for his wealthy American-educated in-laws, and referred to H. H. Kung and T. V. Soong as "big bourgeoisie" until it was suggested that he refrain from doing so in the interest of tact. Ching-kuo cultivated a down-to-earth manner, in contrast to his father, whom he called "The Old Man" instead of "Generalissimo" to discourage his personal staff from leaping to attention at the mention of his father's name. He was distraught when his mother, Mao Fumei, was killed by a Japanese bomb in 1939.

Meanwhile, the Young Marshal's foreign friends were concerned. His adviser, Jimmy Elder, visited the U.S. to lobby influential Americans to try to improve Zhang's "unsatisfactory" situation. "A great deal of mystery exists in this country as to what has become of Zhang," Roy Howard, publisher of Scripps-Howard newspapers, wrote Donald, especially in view of the wide publicity given to the fact that the Generalissimo had ostensibly pardoned him for his role in the Xi'an kidnapping. Americans wondered whether that was "a lot of blather" and feared Zhang had vanished in the manner of Russian leaders who lost favor with Stalin. Donald confirmed that the Young Marshal was alive and well, but "under surveillance." He was living in the mountains with his lady friend Edith Zhao, his former secretary, studying Ming dynasty history. Donald thought of leaving China, he wrote Howard, but stayed to help Mayling and to "wait for a chance to get the Young Marshal out."

After a string of defeats, China trounced enemy forces in April 1938 at Taierzhuang. Japanese forces lost thirty thousand men in a brilliantly executed blow, proving that the Chinese, if properly trained, equipped, and led, could hold their own against the Japanese. In Hankow the public went wild with joy. Firecrackers resounded everywhere, people sang, and bands played. But Mayling and Chiang showed no sign of rejoicing. The Generalissimo looked "subdued, almost morose," Donald observed. "We must stop this," Chiang said. "This is no time for shouting. This war has hardly started. The people must be prevented from fooling themselves."

Not long after, in July 1938, Hitler recalled the German military mission to China. Germany had forged an alliance with Japan in November 1936 but continued to supply China munitions and technical assistance. Stennes was among those who refused to leave and he continued to work for the Chiangs. Von Falkenhausen departed with great reluctance, and only because he feared what Hitler might do to his family in Germany. "In those days it was not always easy to be both a good German and an honorable man," Stennes observed. The Nationalist government was left to fend for itself, with limited aid from Moscow, but Mayling remained defiant. She sent her Wellesley classmates silver spoons to show that "a spoon may be licked but China can't." On Christmas Eve 1938 came news that Japan had purchased another 150,000 tons of scrap iron from America. "That Christmas gift will come to the Chinese as a rain of explosives," Donald complained bitterly to Roy Howard.

Far outgunned by Japan, China's armies held the dubious distinction of having pioneered the "scorched earth" tactic to prevent the enemy from feeding off the land. Rather than capitulate, Chiang pursued a "magnetic" strategy, avoiding direct engagements while luring the Japanese deeper into Chinese territory. There they would become bogged down, overextended, and demoralized, he theorized, winning battles but ultimately losing the war. Indeed the Japanese found that the conquest of China was not the simple matter they had imagined. Their impossibly long supply and communication lines were frequently broken. They discovered that fighting the Chinese was like "trying to fight a jelly," as Donald put it.

Nonetheless, in little more than a year, Japan had killed two million Chinese, mostly civilians; overran the eastern half of the country, which contained most of China's wealth; cut off areas under Chinese control from access to the ocean; and either seized or destroyed much of China's industry and infrastructure. As Japan closed in on the provisional capital at Wuhan in October 1938, Chiang's "iron nerves" were giving Stennes great anxiety. Nationalist forces had already withdrawn and Japanese troops were entering the city, but Chiang refused to allow his plane to take off until the last possible moment.

Chapter Eleven

Chungking

Any medicine that does not make a man dizzy will not help him recover.
—Chinese proverb

By October 25, 1938, Japanese forces had occupied Wuhan. The provisional capital had lasted barely ten months. The Nationalist government moved again, to Chungking, the sleepy capital of Sichuan province, on the upper reaches of the Yangtze. Fourteen hundred miles from the sea, Chungking would be Chiang Kai-shek's hinterland redoubt for the duration of the war. Using every imaginable conveyance—from trucks to rickshaws, from sedan chairs to wheelbarrows—the Nationalist government and millions of refugees followed the ancient trading routes through mountains and gorges, moving factories, colleges, arsenals. Even the Jersey and Guernsey cows from Mayling's orphanages were marched to Chungking. Girded by mountains, Chungking straddled the confluence of the Yangtze and the Chialing Rivers. Steep stone staircases wound up hillsides to which old houses clung. In summer the city was a furnace; in winter it was shrouded in cold, damp fog. So rare was the sun, it was said, dogs barked when it appeared.

Hardly had they arrived when the Japanese began bombing the new provisional capital by air, attacking civilian and military targets alike in an effort to break Chinese morale. After air raids in early May 1939, whole swaths of the city were bombed flat or burned by incendiary bombs that turned the tightly packed wooden houses on stilts into raging infernos, killing thousands. Remains were still being dug from the embers a week later, as Mayling vividly described in a letter to Emma Mills:

Lines of coffins still stand in front of every heap of wreckage—big ornate coffins for the affluent, wooden boxes for the less fortunate. But the bombs have reduced rich and poor, wise and stupid, to one common level—pieces of burnt flesh which are extracted from the smoldering piles with tongs. Relatives and friends are still digging furiously. . . . Do what you can to make your people realize that this death and havoc come to us with the help of American gasoline and oil, and materials for bombs.

Like many others, this letter was published in American newspapers. Within months the people of Chungking had dug an underground network of dugouts and tunnels in the rock in which the entire city could hide during air raids. Chennault, who had moved his headquarters to Kunming, the capital of Yunnan province in the southwest, devised an elaborate air raid warning system extending across unoccupied China to give the public time to get to safety. Bombers would harass Chungking on clear days and moonlit nights for the next four years. Sometimes they came round the clock. Residents of the wartime capital became as accustomed to the "bombing season" as coastal dwellers were to the monsoon. The dugouts were airless, damp, and fetid with the stench of many humans living in close proximity. Between bombing waves Mayling would rush outside for fresh air. The humidity aggravated her skin condition and brought on rheumatic pains. To ward off misery, boredom, and sheer physical exhaustion during the many hours spent in the dugouts, she practiced conversational French with a Belgian priest, read, or played games with her secretary.

From remote Chungking, Mayling made constant pleas abroad for funds for food, clothing, and medical supplies. But it was not a role she relished. "I don't like this 'gimme something' business," she said. "Handouts are demoralizing and right now we need the highest morale." At her side, William Donald labored ceaselessly to foster the illusion of Mayling as a "tiny living statue in the midst of carnage" making a cry for help to the world. Through radio broadcasts, photographs, articles, and statements, Madame Chiang was molded into the frail yet valiant symbol of distressed China—a symbol calculated to arouse chivalrous sympathies in the West.

Mayling wrote in November 1940 a "Letter to Boys and Girls Across the Ocean," a plea for funds for China's "warphans" that was widely distributed in America. She described children playing by day and reliving the horror of war by night. "The shades of night stir children's memories," she wrote. "They live again through terrible things; they whimper or sob or cry for their fathers and their mothers, and for their homes they will see no more." On November 1, 1940, Mrs. Theodore Roosevelt and her husband, Col. Theodore Roosevelt Jr., son of the late president, hosted a "Bowl of Rice" dinner at New York's Waldorf-Astoria Hotel, one of many such events held across America, to raise funds for China relief efforts.

Wendell Willkie, Pearl S. Buck, the Luces, and other American luminaries led fund-raising campaigns for China—for its two million wounded, two million orphans, and fifty million refugees. "Ever since I was a little boy I have had a sentimental feeling about China," said Willkie, Roosevelt's Republican challenger in the 1940 presidential election, at a June 1941 event. "I think anybody who contributes to this cause contributes not only to the government in China, but is contributing greatly to the cause of their own country." Henry R. Luce, publisher of *Time* and *Life* magazines, told Americans in a national radio broadcast that the Japanese invasion had been "stopped cold in its tracks" by China's four-million-strong army. In 1941 Mayling donated a baby giant panda to the Bronx Zoo, saying she hoped the tiny creature would bring "as much joy to American children as American friendship has brought to our Chinese people."

Americans were sympathetic to China's plight and admired her courage, but their attention was fixed on the war in Europe. And though Washington denounced Japanese aggression and gave China relief aid, it continued to sell key war materials to Japan. Relief groups urged Mayling to come to America on a speaking tour, arguing she would be "worth ten divisions" to China if she did. Chiang refused to let her go, saying she was "worth twenty divisions" to him in China.

When Japan occupied China's eastern seaboard in 1938, the Nationalist government was cut off from supplies of arms, fuel, and other imported necessities. A new road was built from Kunming through the mountainous jungles to Burma. The Burma Road was built by hundreds of thousands of conscripted laborers—men, women, and children—many of whom died from accidents, disease, or malnutrition. Its 715-mile serpentine course was unoccupied China's only overland link to the outside world—and critical supplies—and was vulnerable to Japanese attack by air.

Despite Chennault's best efforts, China's tiny mercenary air force was no match for Japan. Chinese efforts to purchase aircraft from America were thwarted, and Chungking was virtually defenseless to aerial attack. In 1940 Chennault went to Washington seeking planes and pilots to counter the Japanese bombing. At the time China had just 37 fighter planes and 31 outdated Russian bombers, compared with Japan's fleet of 968 mostly new craft that were being utilized in China alone. America was building planes for Britain and could spare few for China, but Roosevelt sensed that war with Japan was coming. Circumventing the Neutrality Act, he secretly issued orders to sell China a hundred Curtiss P-40 fighters and to recruit American airmen to fight the Japanese in combat. Three squadrons of volunteer army, navy, and marine pilots were released from duty and arrived in China in the autumn of 1941.

Paul Frillmann, a Hankow-based Lutheran missionary from Illinois whom Chennault had recruited as chaplain, at first glance called the band of fliers "the most reprehensible bunch of people" he had ever seen. Officially called the American Volunteer Group (A.V.G.), these mercenary pilots became famous as the Flying Tigers, or *feihu dui* in Chinese. There is more than one story to account for the memorable moniker, but perhaps the most likely involves T. V. Soong. The outfit sought a distinctive symbol. The Chinese dragon was dismissed as too dated and the eagle as too American. Soong suggested the "flying tiger." The airmen objected that a tiger could not fly. But T. V. told them the Chinese saying "giving wings to the tiger," which meant endowing the most formidable creature with wings to create a "super-colossal" beast.

Mayling called them "my boys" or "American Knights of the Air." She was fond of giving them lengthy and patronizing "Sunday-school talks." Most of the men raved about her, but one cynic in the outfit grumbled, "I'd be ashamed to talk like this to a football team of twelve-year-olds. She treats us like we were nitwits." For all her stern lectures, Mayling was amused when several Tigers went backstage at a Chinese theatre intending to spirit away the lovely leading lady—only to promptly return "her" to the stage. No one had told them that in Chinese opera the female roles were played by men.

Chennault's base in Kunming was a hub of activity. His bungalow in the rice paddies boasted a large staff, including three servants called Gunboat,

Steamboat, and Showboat who lived in the garage with their wives and children. The chauffeur's small daughter rode in Chennault's car wherever he went. Wartime deprivations notwithstanding, Chennault's table never lacked Louisiana specialties, especially corn bread and ice cream. He had his house staff keep a vegetable garden to grow okra, sweet potatoes, and strawberries.

Chennault was circumspect and loyal to his Chinese employers, exercising patience and tact under working conditions that "would have driven most men to resign," in the words of the U.S. naval attaché, James M. McHugh. Chinese resentful of Chennault's position "opposed and obstructed him . . . to the point of complete exasperation." Mayling was his direct channel to Chiang Kai-shek. She made certain his concerns were brought to the Generalissimo and to the right people in Washington. Chennault refused to learn Chinese, arguing, "If I say the wrong thing, I can always blame it on the interpreter." But he did learn Chinese etiquette. "Your words alone make me feel greatly overpaid for my poor services to China," he wrote Mayling in thanks for praise she'd given him.

He sought her intervention on matters ranging from obtaining spare parts for his airplanes to raising the salaries of A.V.G. chauffeurs in order to deter theft of critical spare parts and gasoline. In late 1941, under pressure from officials jealous of Mayling's influential role, Chiang tried to remove her as the conduit between Chennault and himself. The American threatened to resign, arguing she was essential to the A.V.G.'s success. "Without you to back me up, I know I shall find it increasingly difficult to carry on my work," he wrote her. "I hope you will remember that I undertook my present duties relying on you to serve as liaison between me and the Generalissimo." Mayling continued as liaison.

From her perch in Hong Kong during the early years of the anti-Japanese war, Ching Ling too attacked the West for supplying war materials to Japan. Such attacks were not appreciated by Hong Kong's colonial authorities, but she was able to continue her relief and propaganda work. She remained at odds with her family, though she was not as isolated from them as widely believed. Despite tensions, and the fact that Ching Ling was kept under surveillance by Chiang's agents, the sisters still socialized and were occasionally seen together "laughing and chattering like schoolgirls." When Ching Ling visited Chungking in 1939, Mayling announced to a dinner guest unacquainted with Madame Sun: "I present my Red sister!" The entire party burst into laughter.

Ching Ling was painfully shy and hated public appearances. Like Mayling, she suffered from skin trouble and nervous complaints. Yet those who met her never failed to be won over, and she attracted a coterie of worshipful admirers. One American journalist called her a "childlike figure of enchanting delicacy." Writer Frances Gunther wrote: "There is a great woman! A deep wide warm wise woman, full of life—young people about her always deriving vitality and faith from her."

From the vantage point of time, the woman her friends called "Susie" looked back on her union with the revered Sun Yat-sen. "I didn't fall in love," she once admitted. "It was hero worship from afar. . . . I wanted to save China and Dr. Sun was the one man who could do it, so I wanted to help him." She reserved a certain "bitter laughter" for romantics who saw "love" in her marriage. "She was more of a daughter, an acolyte, an amenuensis [sic] . . . and carrying the weight of it ever since has been her cross," observed a friend. She believed her historical role took precedence over her personal life. She would never have remarried, for that would have undermined her moral authority to carry on the legacy of her late husband.

The years had also tempered Ching Ling's view of the Chinese Communists, and she now spoke of having "disagreements" with them. Her position on the Communists was "a little fuzzy and criss-crossed with curious contradictions," one acquaintance noted. Deeply ambivalent, she vacillated between unqualified support and a certain cynical mistrust, alluding to past "flip-flops [and] to the quality of their integrity . . . of which she does not have a very high opinion." She warned a friend, "They are capable of anything."

There was one person, however, of whom her opinion had not changed—her brother-in-law. She still held him in utter contempt and referred to him sarcastically as the Generalissimo. She could never forgive what she regarded as his "betrayal of the revolution" in 1927, nor her sister's betrayal in lending the Soong name to Chiang's acts. But she conceded that had it not been for Mayling, Chiang's excesses "might have been much worse." She distrusted all Chinese politicians, but distrusted Mao

Zedong "less than the others," she once said. H. H. Kung she dubbed "the Sage," mocking his claim to Confucian ancestry. Regarding her sister Eling's alleged financial wizardry, Ching Ling commented: "She's very clever. . . . She never gambles. She buys and sells only when she gets advance information from confederates in the ministry of finance about changes in government fiscal policy. It's a pity she can't do it for the people instead of against them."

In February 1940, Mayling went to Hong Kong for sinus treatment. She stayed with Eling at her house on the Peak, the colony's most exclusive residential district. Ching Ling moved in too, and for a few days political differences were forgotten as the sisters chatted and joked. One night they all dined together at the Hong Kong Hotel in a famous dinner seen as emblematic of renewed United Front vigor. When Mayling returned to wartorn Chungking in early April 1940, with both sisters in tow, Mayling's New Life adviser James Endicott was waiting at the top of the steps as the famous sisters were being carried up the cliff in sedan chairs. When Mayling saw him she waved her handkerchief and said proudly: "Hello, see what I have brought back." They embarked on a publicity blitz intended to quash rampant rumors that the United Front was under strain. Together they inspected factories, dugouts, hospitals, and orphanages. The three sisters made an unprecedented joint radio broadcast to the United States. Ching Ling even allowed herself to be photographed toasting her despised brother-in-law Chiang Kai-shek.

By early 1941 the Nationalists and Chinese Communists were in thinly veiled conflict again and, despite the Japanese threat in their midst, beginning to position themselves for eventual civil war. The Communists had profited from the United Front and Chiang's preoccupation with resisting the Japanese invasion to build up their strength in the north and northwest. Party membership jumped from forty thousand in 1937, when the United Front was forged, to eight hundred thousand in 1940 as Mao's forces skillfully recruited and organized behind enemy lines. On the orders of Stalin and the Comintern, the Chinese Communist party sharply moderated its rhetoric and tactics in order to make itself more palatable both in China and internationally. Instead of forcibly seizing property from large landholders and redistributing it to peasants, the Communists changed tack, implementing in areas under their control a program of systematic forced rent reduction, making it uneconomical for rich landlords to keep large landholdings. In this way the Communists generated much loyalty among the rural population.

The Nationalists were at a disadvantage, having experienced greater dislocation and disruption. As well, although the Communist forces had nominally joined the Nationalist forces as the Eighth Route Army, the burden of prosecuting the war fell to the Nationalists. Nationalist leaders were not blind to the improvement in Communist fortunes, and despite the United Front remained hostile and dismissive toward them. In 1939 British journalist Freda Utley interviewed Mayling in Chungking during an air raid. In the dugout, Mayling dropped her persona of gracious queen and spoke frankly of her difficulties and failures in "tackling a sea of troubles with patience and understanding, and without illusions." But Utley detected an "emotional bitterness" toward the Communists and an unwillingness to see their merits. When Utley remarked that the Communists were seen as China's least corrupt political group, Mayling retorted: "That's because they haven't got power yet." Despite the evident truth in the observation, her hatred for the Communists "obscured her political judgment which in other respects is so penetrating," Utley wrote. Similarly, her Christian beliefs "blind her to the shortcomings of those who share or appear to share them."

Mayling was also perhaps slow to see that some of those close to her were increasing her unpopularity and suspicions about her conduct. It was highly improbable that her relationship with Donald was anything but friendship. Still, after six years of devoted service to Mayling, by 1940 Donald saw his welcome wearing thin. He had many enemies who "had their knives out for him," so it was probably just a matter of time before he was forced to leave China. His position in the inner circle and his influence over Mayling made him a target of jealousy and mistrust. His attacks on corruption and incompetence in the government struck at powerful vested interests. He was also prone to exaggerating his not insubstantial influence. To hear him tell it, he was the "grandfather of the Chinese revolution" and the "pusher behind the pawns of every Chinese chess move," wrote Frances Gunther.

The legendary "Donald of China" did have an international reputation, and visitors ranging from tourists to diplomats to businessmen to military men to journalists were invariably told to "see Donald." Magazines wanted interviews and publishers begged him to write his memoirs of his years in China, offering lavish advances. He toyed with them, coyly refusing yet occasionally threatening to take off on his yacht, the *Mei-Hwa*, to write them. "Were I to attempt to write such a book it would not be believed," he wrote Col. Theodore Roosevelt Jr., publisher of Doubleday. "It would not do China any good, and it would debunk Dr. Sun Yat-sen. . . . I do not feel like going on a bedunking [sic] razzle just yet." Sun was not only an "impractical visionary, but the worst of it was that old boy could not keep his hands off women," Donald told another friend. He would, he concluded, simply write a manuscript and give it to Mayling for her collection.

Despite his idiosyncrasies, Donald was at this time one of the few people who could tell Chiang and Mayling unpleasant things and persuade them to listen to grievances. He once sternly said to a group of missionaries, "Now tell the Generalissimo and Madame to their faces the things you say behind their backs," and they did. But perhaps virtue was taken to a fault. Either he became all too eager to tell them exactly what was wrong, or they simply became less willing to hear it. Not least of his irritating virtues was sniffing out stories of alleged graft and speculation by the Kung family and bringing them to Mayling "like a dog carrying into the house a particularly malodorous bone." One such tale, concerning Eling Kung's exchange market activities, hit too close to home. Mayling pounced on him angrily: "Donald, you may criticize the government or anything in China, but there are some persons even you cannot criticize!" He looked at her silently for a moment before walking away.

Donald was not alone. Critics of the Chiang regime and the "Soong dynasty"—a moniker Mayling detested—were increasing. Journalist Vincent Sheean wrote a scathing attack in the *New York Herald Tribune* in November 1941. He told of a Chinese "Gestapo" that suppressed opposition; pro-Axis elements in the Chinese government; "unspeakable tortures"; "new concentration camps . . . being formed all the time"; profiteers; and people starving because they couldn't afford inflated prices. Lin Yutang, the best-selling writer, defended the Nationalist government, arguing that Sheean's article was the unfortunate result of the influence of a small group of "parlor Communists upon the highly idealistic mind of Mr. Sheean during his flying visit to Chungking." Sheean's assertion that repression in Nationalist China was "more cruel than anything yet developed in Europe" was overstated, wrote Lin, but it was true that an "antidote to the fulsome and misleading nonsense" pouring out about "Free China" was much needed.

With no help forthcoming from the democracies, pressures on the Nationalist regime to formally align itself with Germany and Italy were growing. The pro-Axis contingent in government, no friends of Donald, took umbrage when Mayling criticized the "inimical totalitarians" in a broadcast to America. Chiang wanted the phrase removed from her speech, and when Donald refused, Chiang called the Australian a "traitor" who would sacrifice the Chinese to British interests. Madame Kung was said to be incensed by Chiang's alleged pro-Axis leanings and threatened to have her husband resign. "I hope it is genuine for she could hardly render greater service to her country than to make [Kung] resign office," the British ambassador, Archibald Clark Kerr, dryly wrote London.

Donald, an Australian but also a British subject, grew increasingly harsh toward Germany and Hitler in the speeches he penned for the Generalissimo. The final straw came in the spring of 1940 when Chiang sent one back with a note: "I am not at war with Germany." Donald replied, "I am," and said good-bye to Mayling. That evening he caught a flight to Hong Kong. She was "genuinely upset" over his abrupt departure. She continued to consult him on her difficulties via letter, and as late as November 1940 still spoke of him as if he were merely away on holiday.

Captain Stennes's position was also becoming increasingly untenable by 1940. The presence of a German at the side of the Gimo—as Chiang was called—was regarded with suspicion by the Russians and the Americans. Many high-level Chinese, meanwhile, thought Hitler would win the war in Europe and feared that having a notorious anti-Nazi in their midst might prove embarrassing. Intriguingly, by this time Stennes had become an important secret agent for Soviet intelligence, providing information on German and Japanese military plans. It is unclear how his secret dual role may have affected his relations with Chiang Kai-shek and Mayling. Stennes complained to her and others that Chiang had begun paying less attention to his work and that he had been reduced to a "messenger boy handling the private mail box." Stennes left Chungking in early 1941 intending to go to America, but stopped in Japanese-controlled Shanghai instead, where he remained until the end of the war. There he remained in the service of Chiang Kai-shek while dodging direct orders from Hitler to local Gestapo agents that he be liquidated, and continuing his role as Soviet agent. He promised Mayling he would protect her belongings in the Chiangs' house in the French Concession. Through maneuverings and use of his senior Japanese officer contacts, Stennes managed to prevent confiscation of the house and its contents.

In 1940 Mayling wrote ten highly controversial articles for Chinese newspapers under the title *Resurgam*—Latin for "I shall rise again"—in hopes of shaking the Chinese people from the "slackness" she regarded as a "strangling national habit." The series was also printed in English for foreign readers. The aim was to "inspire all delinquents possessed of a sense of shame to reform or resign" and to "inspire all patriotic people blessed with integrity . . . with the will . . . to detect and overcome national shortcomings." She lashed out at her educated and affluent countrymen in unmincing terms.

In these articles, Mayling urged women to play a greater role in the war and in public life, calling for "national spiritual mobilization" and for service to country and to those less fortunate. She exhorted intellectuals and gentry to teach people to read and write and to talk to them about citizenship, patriotism, and responsibility to country, including sanitation. "Always it is a stinging disgrace to see our beautiful countryside littered with dirt and filth which is aesthetically repulsive and physically nauseating," she wrote. She called for the wiping out of what she termed a "creeping paralysis" dating back to the reign of the Manchus that prevented China from claiming the "international eminence and prosperity, which is rightly ours." The causes of this "criminal stagnation" were psychological, not political; China's backwardness and poverty were due to the twin evils of "self-seeking and stupidity," she asserted. "If we are worthy of our heritage we will boldly face the facts, unpalatable though they may be, and with genuine intellectual honesty admit the faults that are ours." She catalogued "Seven Deadly Sins," which she termed "cankerous growths," that had long prevented China's emergence as a first-class world power and delayed victory in the war. The notion of "face" was one of China's "supreme follies." Cliques were a "refuge for incompetents." She excoriated the "dead-wood" in the government as the "Grand Army of the Paid Unemployable."

Well intended though they may have been, the *Resurgam* articles were unpopular with many Chinese, who were appalled that she would air China's dirty laundry in public. The series was calculated to cause a stir, but Mayling did not anticipate the backlash it provoked. "The exposure of certain of our national weaknesses and foibles was not overwhelmingly enjoyed by some of my compatriots," she wrote, in rare understatement. "The fact that I branded as characteristically Chinese those vices not peculiar to us celestials, but common to humankind, seemed to them a further folly." To make matters worse, her approving husband had parts of the articles clipped and sent to people on whom he thought they would have a salutary effect. To mollify her critics, Mayling wrote a caustic article attacking the West for failing to rescue China. "We have been virtually abandoned, even victimized, by those in high authority whom we had been taught we could regard with unshaken confidence as our friends," she wrote in the December 21, 1940, issue of *Liberty*. China was being "strangled to death by an economic noose fashioned by Japan out of British appeasement, American profiteering, and French fear."

A Chinese saying holds that even the household dogs dislike whomever has been running the house for three years. By 1940 rice prices in Chungking were sky-high, but mention of the word "inflation" was taboo. Chiang Kai-shek seemed unable or unwilling to comprehend the inexorable economic laws underlying the behavior of the rice market. "He thought that by cutting off the heads of a few we could intimidate the populace at large to comply with government wishes," said Franklin L. Ho, an American-trained economist and senior Nationalist official during the 1930s and 1940s. So strongly did he believe that the rice market could be stabilized by force that Chiang did have a number of people, including the mayor of Chengdu, executed.

The Japanese invasion had cut the Nationalist government off from not only supplies but also the crucial tax revenues of the industrial eastern cities. This loss of revenue combined with rocketing military spending to set into motion an inflationary spiral; and rising prices, coupled with high military casualties, led to low popular morale. By the end of 1941 some 2.6 million Chinese soldiers had died, with untold numbers wounded. Chiang, however, attributed the low morale to a "whispering campaign . . . attacking the prestige of the government."

In early 1941 Roosevelt dispatched Lauchlin Currie, one of his closest aides, to China as his personal representative. Currie was one of a team of personal advisers dubbed by the press as Roosevelt's "Bright Young Men," a Harvard-trained economist who had helped to shape the New Deal. Currie spent three weeks in China, during which, an American diplomat grumbled, he "fell hard" for Mayling. Officially he was to advise on the inflation problem; unofficially he looked into China's military needs. A direct channel of communication between Chiang and Roosevelt was established, with Mayling as conduit on one end and Currie on the other. The purpose was to bypass the State Department, which neither leader trusted. Mayling was entrusted with a special code and personally drafted and decoded all messages between Currie and Chiang. Roosevelt subsequently dispatched Owen Lattimore, a renowned Sinologist, to Chungking in 1941 to serve as adviser to Chiang Kai-shek. Lattimore admired the Chiangs and they often sought his views.

Maj. James McHugh, naval attaché to the U.S. embassy and an intelligence officer, met Mayling and Chiang in April 1941, six weeks after Currie's visit. McHugh suggested Mayling visit America. She replied that her husband did not consider the timing "opportune." Laughing nervously, Chiang complained that no U.S. aid had been pledged to China despite the Currie visit. The U.S. was discussing billions in aid to Britain without question but was bargaining with China, Chiang said, showing signs of "disillusionment and despair," according to McHugh. Currie visited China again in 1942.

Over the years of war, Mayling had matured while losing none of her vivacity and looks. By the early 1940s, the woman hailed in America as an "almond-eyed Cleopatra" and the "power behind the throne" had "grown in dignity" since her marriage and exuded supreme confidence. She was invariably said to be more beautiful in person than in photographs. She wore a faint scent of perfume, a touch of lipstick, and long jet earrings, with her hair pulled back into a bun at the nape of her neck. Gone were the youthful bangs. She smoked mentholated cigarettes in a long ebony holder. She exuded an intense nervous energy and her charisma was such that visitors rarely failed to be impressed on meeting her. "Madame Chiang fairly radiated charm. . . . [She had] a mature graciousness born of an inward peace and consciousness of being an instrument of destiny, with the power to serve her people," enthused the famed U.S. Marine raider Evans F. Carlson, despite his sympathy for the Chinese Communists. The renowned Swedish explorer Sven Hedin called her "the greatest woman in the world."

Not everyone was quite so taken with Mayling. Despite her much-advertised good works, she was a "hard, shallow and selfish woman . . . but she can turn on the charm to melt the heart of the most hard-boiled foreigner," opined an American diplomat, John Carter Vincent. "But not so with her own countrymen. They don't trust her—but the Generalissimo does and that is what counts." For his part Chiang had aged considerably since taking control of the Nationalist party, but appeared to be as driven as ever; if anything, his famed "Olympian self-possession" had intensified. "His brilliant black eyes met mine with steady, almost relentless, gaze. Here was intelligence, loyalty and stubborn determination," observed Carlson, who served as military attaché in China.

James Endicott, Mayling's New Life Movement adviser, admired her prodigious capacity for work and her ability to maintain her spirits and humor despite the burdens of work and the suffering she was exposed to. His respect deepened when he saw she had no fear of making enemies of government officials if she wanted to promote her reformist agenda. But he felt it was a great mistake to involve the New Life Movement in politics. He protested when New Life schoolgirls were compelled to take an oath of allegiance to the Three People's Principles Youth Corps in a mass public ceremony before Chungking officials. Endicott objected the children were given no choice. Mayling countered they were not forced to take the oath. They had an angry exchange.

Endicott wrote a frank letter to Mayling protesting what he saw as a dangerous drift toward fascism within the government. She invited him to tell the Generalissimo himself. In a heated meeting, Endicott told Chiang that if he didn't base his policies on the needs of the people—which meant, among other things, instituting agrarian reform—then revolutionary forces would ultimately rise against him. Chiang replied that he had plans for land reform but could not carry them out "while there are so many Communists around to take advantage of it." Endicott ventured that there did not seem to be many Communists in Sichuan province, so why not try it there. "You are mistaken," Chiang replied. "There are Communists all around and I must deal with them first." Endicott asked, "How do you judge whether a person is Communist or not?" Chiang answered curtly, "Generally anyone who is in favor of land reform is a Communist!" Mayling flushed and appeared highly nervous, signaling that Chiang was extremely angry. Endicott quit his job advising the New Life Movement, but remained in China, working as a missionary. He believed in Mayling's liberalizing influence but felt the Kuomintang had "little more social conscience than a cholera germ." By the time he left China in 1947, he was backing the Communists.

In early 1941 the writer Martha Gellhorn and her new husband Ernest Hemingway, whom she called U. C. (Unwilling Companion), visited China. When the newlyweds lunched with the Chiangs, the Generalissimo neglected to wear his teeth. American embassy staff later assured them that for Chiang to receive them with his teeth out was a compliment of the highest order. Mayling and Chiang dismissed the Communists as a threat and as a fighting force, claiming that they were hindering, not helping, the war against Japan. "We are not trying to crush them," insisted Mayling. Gellhorn, who had difficulty stomaching China's misery, asked Mayling why lepers were not taken care of and were instead left to beg. Unlike Westerners, Mayling angrily lectured her guests, the Chinese were humane and civilized, and would never lock lepers away. "China had a great culture when your ancestors were living in trees and painting themselves blue," she fumed. Gellhorn was furious. She was not mollified by Mayling's gifts of a peasant straw hat and a jade brooch. Afterward, Hemingway laughed like a hyena. "I guess that'll teach you not to take on the Empress of China," he said. Gellhorn left convinced that the Chiangs cared nothing for China's "miserable hordes."

Mayling's testiness with Gellhorn was doubtless fueled by the stresses of living in Chungking, which were taking a toll on her health. By the summer of 1941, five or six bombing raids a day, combined with misery, fatigue, and tension caused by the extreme summer heat and humidity, were causing Mayling severe physical and emotional strain. She had bouts of malaria and dengue fever, and her skin condition was troubling her. By the third year of living half-underground in dank dugouts, she had succumbed to despair and "spiritual desolation," she wrote. "I knew that to dwell on what the enemy was doing to my country caused me such resentment and hate that mentally and physically I was like a top, winding ever more taut and which, when the momentum is spent, will surely fall."

Then she visited an orphanage for blind children and had an epiphany. "Though I hated the instinctive tendency in myself, I have always been repulsed by abnormality, whether mental or physical," she later wrote. "As I entered their school, the expressions on some of the faces of the children seemed unnervingly dull and apathetic. . . . I fought hard against an impulse to push them away and flee." Then she was struck by a sudden thought. "If I am so repulsed by physical blindness and defacement, how much more repulsed must God be by my spiritual blindness and ugliness?" With this realization, she claimed, she was able to let go of her hatred of Japan, and to "hate the evil in men, but not men themselves."

However, raw nerves were more in evidence than religious insights at a dinner with a visiting American dignitary in August 1941, when Mayling indulged in an impulsive outburst of criticism against the U.S. and Britain. She complained bitterly that after four years of fighting aggression, China had been ignored at a recent Roosevelt-Churchill meeting, and accused the Allies of appeasing Japan. The discussion became animated. The Generalissimo laughingly scolded her for being impolite to a guest. Mayling explained that her husband often reproved her for taking American friends to task over Washington's inaction vis-à-vis Japan, but insisted that "it was her nature and she was not a diplomat." The American observed in reply that "the squeaky wheel gets the grease." The Generalissimo laughed heartily when the expression was translated for him.

Mayling made an impassioned radio address to America on October 10, 1941. "We feel we have earned equality of status with the other democracies, but we do not want it granted to us in charity," she said, referring to China as a member of the antifascist camp. "We have an indispensable right to be consulted and to make our voice heard when others deliberate about Asia and the Pacific. We are the senior nation in the stand against aggression, therefore we ought not to be treated as a junior." The speech, warned American diplomat John Paton Davies, revealed the "psychological results" of U.S. policy. "It is evident that the Chinese feel that we have treated them in a cavalier fashion and that we have made them lose face, all of which has had a damaging effect upon their morale." Japan, meanwhile, continued its inexorable assault on China.

Then, suddenly, the equation in the Far East changed dramatically as Mayling's warnings of Japanese intentions proved true. On December 7, 1941, Japan bombed Pearl Harbor in a surprise attack intended to cripple U.S. naval power in the Pacific. The bombings killed 2,335 American servicemen and 68 civilians, and wounded 1,178. At last, the United States was compelled to enter the war raging in Europe and the Pacific.

Chapter Twelve
Little Sister's Easiest Conquest

India is like a beautiful woman who expects her admirers to give her everything she wants for nothing even if they ruin themselves and then if it turns out wrong, not resent being blamed for having done as asked.
—Victor Sassoon

The era of the Second World War was a cauldron of larger-than-life personalities fighting a common enemy while jostling to protect the interests of their own countries. These were titans with egos to match: Roosevelt, Churchill, Stalin—and the "Chiang Kai-sheks," as China's First Couple were collectively referred to. Within the Allied camp, debates raged over military and geopolitical strategy as well as ideology. There was debate over ground power versus airpower; debate over whether to conquer Japan or Germany first; and debate over whether China was vital to the Allied war effort and if so whether Chiang Kai-shek was the man to back. Was he the best hope, or was he a hopelessly inept and corrupt reactionary? There was also debate over the Chinese Communists. Were they real Communists and a threat to Asia and the world, or were they merely agrarian reformers and democrats under their "Red" skin who were the hope for China's future?

After Pearl Harbor and the American entry into the Second World War, tensions among the Allies heightened. The British regarded Americans as a "well-meaning but incurably meddlesome" people with a startling blend of "fierce dogmatism and . . . bland ignorance, freely confessed and . . . almost gloried in." In Washington there existed a "deeply rooted suspicion" of British designs in Asia. China was enormously fascinating to Roosevelt, whose mother's family, the Delanos, had made its fortune trading tea, silks, and opium with China. He had the idea that the Chinese might "someday get together and invade the Western world." He, like many Americans, feared that the old Yellow Peril myth might come true, in the form of a militant China rallying Asia against the West, and so wanted to bring China into the Western fold.

Chiang felt politically isolated, having borne the brunt of Japanese aggression for four years. He was apprehensive that even if the Allies won the war in Europe and the Pacific, China might still not win equal status and treatment. Japanese propaganda exploited these fears by insinuating that China was being used as a tool by the Allies rather than recognized as an ally in itself, and would be victimized if there was a peace. Chiang had asked repeatedly for more aircraft, munitions, and other military supplies, and soon after Pearl Harbor called for a formal alliance with the Allies. He also demanded Chinese participation in key Allied military meetings. These requests were politely rebuffed by both London and Washington.

Chiang and Mayling bitterly resented China's exclusion, which they saw as racial discrimination. Matters were not helped in the least when after Pearl Harbor, Field Marshal Sir Archibald Wavell arrived in Chungking for his first meeting with Chiang Kai-shek and told the press he had come to "sound the Chinaman's chest." On December 23, 1941, Mayling and aide Hollington Tong interpreted at meetings between Chiang and Wavell and U.S. generals from four in the afternoon until two the next morning. At one point, the Generalissimo launched into a "rancorous" tirade. "You and your people have no idea of how to fight the Japanese," he told Wavell. "Resisting the Japanese is not like suppressing colonial rebellions. . . . Fighting against them for many years, we Chinese are the ones who know how to do it. For this kind of job, you British are incompetent." Tong delivered a mild translation of Chiang's remarks. Mayling interrupted: "That is not exactly what the Generalissimo said." She proceeded to give her own version, which was even harsher than the original. Wavell listened politely. Britain had lost two prize battleships to the Japanese in the South China Sea in an attack days after that on Pearl Harbor and he was not in a strong position to object.

Into this cauldron of tensions the Chiang Kai-sheks jumped with all four feet, taking on Indian aspirations for independence as a pet crusade— a tack that could hardly have been better calculated to irritate the British. Jawaharlal Nehru had visited the Chiangs in 1939 and forged an enthusiastic friendship with China's leaders—especially Mayling, whose subsequent bubbly letters to the Indian leader had the air of a schoolgirl crush. After the fall of Hong Kong the Chiangs worried over India's military readiness should Japan strike the subcontinent. They feared Indians might regard an Asiatic colonial master as no worse than a European one, and possibly better. Only independence, the Chiangs concluded, could ignite India's fighting spirit. Buoyed by news in early February 1942 that the U.S. Congress had passed a half-billion-dollar aid package to China, they decided to visit India to warn of the danger of Japanese aggression and rally the Indian people for war.

British and colonial authorities were less than thrilled about the prospect of a state visit by the Chiang Kai-sheks, but decided to put the best possible face on the matter. The British government was painfully aware of the precipitous decline in imperial prestige wrought by the geopolitical changes of recent decades, and in particular by Britain's recent disastrous military reverses. Officials also recognized that Britain's position as a colonial power was fast becoming untenable. Britain was accepting Chinese military assistance in the war and had been driven to a grudging recognition of China as a partner, if not an equal.

British officials were also acutely aware of the irony inherent in asking Indians to fight for democracy when they were not free themselves. Mohandas Gandhi, the Indian nationalist leader, had called for a refusal to fight in "England's war" without first being granted independence. The viceroy, India's colonial ruler, the Marquess of Linlithgow, was fully cognizant of the delicacy of the visit. "To attempt to manage Chiang will, I feel sure, make him cross and suspicious, while if he makes his own plans and these go amiss, he will have only himself to blame," he wrote. "I think I can handle him well enough and I shall be surprised and disappointed if I don't send him home as pleased as Punch." Churchill was less optimistic and more suspicious. "We cannot possibly agree to a Head of Foreign State intervening as a kind of impartial arbiter between the representative of King Emperor and Messrs. Gandhi and Nehru," he declared. In no circumstances should Chiang be allowed to see Nehru or Gandhi before seeing the viceroy. "There could be no possibility of such a meeting remaining secret and nothing would be more likely to spread Pan-Asiatic *malaise* through all the bazaars of India."

Ambassador to China Archibald Clark Kerr argued it would be a "very grave mistake" to prevent Chiang from seeing "the recalcitrants" on whom Chiang believed he could use his personal influence to persuade them to throw their weight behind the war effort. One British official hoped Chiang would "size them up for the niggling impractical creatures they are."

The state banquet held at the viceroy's residence in honor of China's leaders on their arrival in early February was "beyond doubt one of the biggest things that has been given in New Delhi in a long, long time," noted an American diplomat. "Nobody can come near the English when they set out to achieve ceremonial perfection." The enormous viceregal palace was a monument to colonial splendor. Situated at the end of an immense tree-lined boulevard leading from India Gate, the complex was built from red sandstone. Reception rooms whose soaring ceilings depicted ancient moguls and rajahs looked through eighteen-foot windows onto terraces and vast manicured gardens.

The viceroy escorted Madame Chiang on his arm, followed by Lady Linlithgow on the arm of the Generalissimo. The six-foot-six Scot was resplendent in tails. Lady Linlithgow towered over Chiang, who wore his flowing black scholar's robe. There were eighty-five guests at the table. The Chiangs' visit was "dramatic and spectacular to an astonishing degree and of enormous news interest," the American diplomat wrote. The viceroy told guests "India's heart is one with China" and, quoting Confucius, said it was "delightful to have men of kindred spirit come . . . from afar." Chiang spoke of "spiritual bonds" between the two ancient cultures and quoted a Chinese proverb: "To have one look at things is a hundred times more satisfactory than hearsay."

Lord Linlithgow, evidently a shrewd judge of character, called Madame "an amusing study." She was a "typical product of the American 'Co-ed' system, complete with lipstick," he wrote. "She has a perfect command of the English language, and is never at a loss for the right word. I suspect that in the highly sophisticated upper layers of her mind, she is a typical American liberal whose enthusiasms are unimpaired by any restraining considerations of a practical kind. . . . But, underneath . . . I detect a caution and a conservatism which, in a fair fight, would prevail over the more flashy and spectacular elements of her nature." His first impression of Chiang was that he was "entirely Chinese in his mental furniture, and—while he evidently depends a great deal upon his wife for help and counsel—I should judge that he is accustomed in essentials to depend upon his own understanding of the business at hand." Neither Chiang nor his wife had the least notion of India's political situation, but the viceroy was fairly confident they had no desire to be mischievous.

The Chiangs stayed in a villa on the viceregal estate. Mayling brought pearls for Nehru's daughter, Indira, and for Nehru himself a Rolex watch, the hands of which would "mark the hours until our common victory shines upon us." On emerging from his first meeting with the Chiangs, Nehru was coy. "Certainly we discussed India," he told reporters, smiling broadly, and grandly declared: "I am India." He called Chiang not only a great Chinese but a great Asian and world figure. His charming and vital wife was a "star of hope" to the people of China. The visit, he said, cemented a "bond of friendship" between two ancient and great cultures whose combined population comprised half the world. China's plight held lessons for India, now struggling for its own independence. "The old world is crumbling before our eyes," he said.

Chiang urged the British to move quickly to give Indians power and urged Indian leaders to moderate demands for independence and cooperate with the British in fighting the common enemy. But neither side was willing to compromise, and in any case Chiang's sympathies lay entirely with the Congress party leaders. He believed the British government exaggerated sectarian differences in India. Although the Congress party had no Moslems, rajahs, or untouchables among its members, Chiang was nonetheless convinced that it represented Indian aspirations in the same way he believed the Kuomintang represented Chinese aspirations.

Nan Pandit, Nehru's sister, called Mayling "to all women of Asia a symbol of gracious womanhood, unflinching courage and firm determination" in the war. "We pray we may not falter even as the women of China have not faltered," Pandit said, adding: "We want to fight but we must fight for something. If we are to fight for liberty we must have liberty to fight." Mayling was presented with a sari. To a gathering of Indian women, she spoke of her work with women and orphans in the war with Japan. "I pray that you should never have to suffer what we have suffered in China," she said in an emotional unscripted address. "But if you are to escape this fate, you must be prepared to defend yourselves. . . . The

Japanese are already at your door. . . . They will say to you: 'We have
come to liberate you.' But that is a lie." She recounted the atrocities in
Nanking and elsewhere.

Mayling toured the Taj Mahal while Chiang visited Peshawar and inspected defenses at the Khyber Pass. The Taj was symbolic of a "spirit
even more beautiful than the building itself . . . this devotion of an emperor to his empress," Mayling said. Nehru, meanwhile, invited the Chinese delegation to a picnic on a beautiful rolling lawn. He removed his coat
and began turning somersaults. Daughter Indira was embarrassed and "disgusted" at his undignified behavior and demanded that he stop, but Nehru
was enjoying himself and ignored her. A senior Chinese official in the delegation felt Nehru needed moral support, so he stripped off his coat and
began to roll on the lawn himself.

The Chiangs proceeded to meet Gandhi. Originally they wished to see
the Mahatma at his village headquarters. But Churchill refused to allow
them to go to Wardha, which had become a place of political pilgrimage
and was regarded as rival headquarters of authority. Anthony Eden, the
foreign secretary, reminded Churchill it was "of the utmost importance" to
avoid offending the Chiangs, explaining, "If things do go wrong in Burma,
it will be most difficult to keep China in the war and Chiang Kai-shek
would be our only hope." Churchill retorted: "It would I am sure be a great
mistake for [Chiang] to travel many hundreds of miles across India to parley with Gandhi about whether the British Empire should come to an end
or not." The contretemps was settled by holding the meeting in Calcutta,
where, accompanied by Nehru, the Chiangs met the "Great Soul" at Birla
Park, the estate of an Indian industrialist. Gandhi wore his customary unbleached cotton robe. Mayling interpreted. He told Chiang he liked to
hear her "sweet voice while I listen to the unfolding of your thoughts." As
was his habit Gandhi abstained from lunch. The Birla women helped
Mayling don a handmade sari, complete with vermilion *tilak*—an auspicious
mark—on her forehead. She chatted with Gandhi for an hour before the
Generalissimo joined them after his nap. During the five-hour meeting
Gandhi spun cotton yarn with a *charka*, a handheld spinning wheel. He
then presented the yarn to Chiang and the wheel to Mayling as gifts.

The symbolism of the Chiangs' visit was not lost on the Indians. If Britain could treat China as an equal, why not India? But Gandhi was dubious.

"They will never voluntarily treat us Indians as equals," he said. "Why, they do not even admit your country to their talks."

On February 15, 1942, Japan captured Singapore, giving Chiang's message even greater urgency and credence. His hosts were deeply chagrined. The U.S. government began to share Chiang's alarm over India's military preparedness. But Chiang's entreaties had little effect. Chiang told Linlithgow that he had tried to persuade Nehru of the need for unity in the face of a common foe but had failed. He had hoped for better luck with Gandhi, but the Mahatma proved as immune to Chiang's blandishments as Nehru, whose attitude, wrote Linlithgow, had "not changed an atom and he is so obsessed by his blind hatred for us—or what he calls British Imperialism—that he is blind to the harm that he is doing his own countrymen. That is not the mark of a big man."

On departing in late February 1942, Chiang made a final appeal. "At this most critical moment in the history of civilization our two peoples should exert themselves to the utmost in the cause of freedom for all mankind," he argued. "For only in a free world could Chinese and Indian peoples obtain their freedom." He then called on Britain to give Indians political power so that they might find the "spiritual and material strength" to join in the war on their own behalf, not merely to aid the Allied nations. The *Hindustan Times* applauded Chiang's "courage" and urged Britain to accept his advice, but *The Dawn*, a Muslim daily, labeled him "Meddlesome Marshal." "It is unfortunate that the Marshal should have indulged in generalities without understanding the political situation in India," said Muslim leader Mohammad Ali Jinnah. "I am afraid he is saturated with the ideas of those who surrounded him most while he was in India."

The viceroy pronounced the visit a success but concluded Chiang "quite failed to understand the complexity of Indian politics, except that it is all a good deal harder than he had been led to believe." Madame was a "very clever and competent little lady, but, in my opinion, great only in courage and devotion," he wrote. "She and her husband hunt together and she is clearly invaluable to him. When they are on a big job she starts with the family trousers firmly fixed on her limbs, but by the final stage of any venture the Generalissimo is invariably discovered to have transferred the pants to his own person. The process is well worth watching." She was, he noted slyly, "not averse [to] a flirtation," and added that the "long lashes and good looks of Nehru" had made an impression on her.

Her interest was evident in a letter she wrote Nehru en route to China. "We shall leave nothing undone in assisting you to gain freedom and independence," she pledged. "Our hearts are drawn to you, and . . . the bonds of affection between you and us have been strengthened by our visit, and in more ways than one. When you are discouraged and weary, and I think you must be sometimes although you have that rare quality of childlike spontaneity and joy . . . remember that you are not alone in your struggle, for at all times we are with you in spirit." The Chinese leaders' visit had made a "deep impression" on the Indian people, Nehru replied, adding that destiny was bringing the two countries closer together. Gandhi later wrote Chiang that he could "never forget the five hours close contact I had with you and your noble wife in Calcutta. I had always felt drawn towards you in your fight for freedom." The Chiangs took up India's cause, barraging Roosevelt and Churchill with impassioned letters and cables. "You may count on us to press India's interest to the utmost," Mayling wrote Nehru. "We feel that India's and China's destinies are inextricably interwoven."

Following the Chiangs' visit, India became the training base for China's air force and infantry, its base of supply to its war fronts, and the most important geographical link between China and its allies. The Generalissimo was pleased at being briefed on military matters while in India, and was "gratified at being regarded as an equal, an ally and not as a 'backward boy,'" the Foreign Office reported. Chiang, however, grumbled that the British did not inform allies when they withdrew or surrendered and Mayling complained that British military strategy was super-secret.

Dismayed, the Chiangs had concluded that India was desperately ill-prepared, both psychologically and militarily, for war. If India fell, China would be in peril. Chiang informed Roosevelt and Churchill that if the Japanese attacked India they would be virtually unopposed. Mayling told the U.S. ambassador in Chungking that dominion status would not satisfy the Indians, since they had "neither racial affinity nor a common destiny" with Britain. She told Sir Horace Seymour, Britain's ambassador in Chungking, that she had hoped their visit would help galvanize both Indians and British into a sense of imminent danger, but they had failed. If Britain gave India immediate independence, she said, she knew confidentially the

Congress party was ready to "break with Gandhi and his doctrine of passive resistance."

Seymour warned the Foreign Office that criticism of British efforts in the Pacific war was "practically universal." There was a growing feeling that the war would greatly reduce or even end British and American influence in the Far East and that the New China stood poised to take their place as leader of Asia. British defeats in Hong Kong, Singapore, and elsewhere had resulted in a "feeling of superiority" that was making the Chinese intolerant of foreign advice in general and British advice in particular. "The Chinese have always been intolerant of foreign advice, but they have been willing to accept help provided they could use it in their own way while giving little or no help in return," sniffed a Foreign Office official. He added that the Chinese were "lucky enough to have two milch cows" in the U.S. and Britain.

Sino-British relations, already at a nadir, were not improved by the Chiangs' criticisms following a trip to the Burma front in mid-April 1942. Mayling sent Roosevelt aide Lauchlin Currie a blistering telegram to reinforce those her husband had sent to Churchill and Roosevelt:

> Situation there unspeakably dangerous with complete disorganization both front and rear, collapse civil administration, breakdown communications, population panicky resulting utmost confusion. . . . British seem hopeless helpless while Burmese people antagonistic and countryside honeycombed with fifth columnists. Wherever bombing occurred corpses men animals unremoved and exposed to hordes flies. With extreme heat prevailing I greatly fear cholera other epidemics for our troops now entering districts. . . . Generalissimo told [British General Harold Alexander] if such conditions obtained in China heads would have been chopped off.

She gleefully wrote Nehru that "the imp in me gloated shamelessly. . . . Alexander's face was a study in rich rainbow hues. It changed from green surprise to crimson anger, from choleric purple to baffled blue, and finally, from bilious resentment to embarrassed ashiness. I always told you the imp is incorrigible."

Lt. Gen. Joseph Stilwell, who had lately been sent to China as supreme allied commander of the China theatre of war, accompanied the Chiangs to Burma. Stilwell was "utterly disheartened," Mayling confided in a letter to Nehru. The Chinese troops were excellent, but the commanding officer simply ignored him. "Your people may be converts to non-violence but my people are past masters in the art of passive resistance," she continued. "I was worried, for Stilwell is not only a fine strategist but he also possesses a sound knowledge of Chinese psychology, and so if he thinks it impossible to work with our people, then no other American can either." She pushed for a new Chinese commander and used her "woman's touch" on him to good effect.

Minutes after the Chiangs departed Mandalay for Kunming their plane was spotted by the Japanese. "I felt headachy and feverish and couldn't reason logically," Mayling wrote, describing the incident to Nehru. "I did have a vague hope . . . that if the Island Dwarfs did catch us, my last earthly sensation would be adventurous exhilaration . . . [before] my descent to inferno. You see, I did not think that I rate Paradise; I am that modest!" She donned a parachute, a tricky maneuver in her Chinese dress. There were twenty people but only four parachutes. Mayling's maid did not have one and began to cry. Mayling told her that if they had to evacuate she should cling tightly to her and they would jump together, that the parachute was designed to carry 250 pounds and combined they weighed less. "Madame, if I die, I won't be missed, but you are needed by our people," the maid replied. "I would not think of risking your life to save mine." Soon after, the plane was escorted to safety by a squadron of fighters from Kunming.

The Burma campaign in the spring of 1942 met with utter failure, to Chinese dismay, forcing Allied forces into an infamous brutal retreat. The Japanese captured Burma in May and closed the Burma Road, unoccupied China's only link to the outside world and critical supplies. Chungking's survival was now dependent on supplies flown in from India over "the Hump," as pilots dubbed the massive and forbidding Himalayan mountains dividing the two continents. Bitter recriminations ensued. Stilwell blamed Chiang; Chiang blamed Stilwell; and they both blamed the British. Stilwell said Chiang was arbitrary and indecisive in battle, ordering troop movements and then reversing the orders. Chiang questioned the wisdom of Stilwell's having refused air transport out of Burma and personally leading troops in retreat on a three-week jungle trek. The feat earned "Vinegar Joe" a heroic reputation at home, but Chiang and Chennault argued that he should have spent the time reorganizing China's resistance. Obsessed with reopening the Burma Road, Stilwell began hoarding supplies for a fresh offensive, depriving Chennault and his tiny but formidable band of fighters of sufficient fuel and spare parts to keep planes in the air. As Chiang and Chennault saw it, the most successful Allied military force in Asia was being starved to the bone. They believed a ground campaign in the malarial Burmese jungle was a waste of time and resources that would be better spent on an air campaign.

Mayling complained to Currie that China was receiving neither respect nor her fair share of Lend-Lease supplies, war materials the U.S. had pledged to its Allies. "If China is really an ally then why has she not equal partnership on the Joint Staff?" She accused Britain of placing China "on a par with her Dominions." T. V. Soong, now China's foreign minister and based in Washington, wrote Roosevelt a plaintive letter terming China a "forlorn client." Despite the president's "generous enthusiasm" for China and recognition of China as one of the Allied powers, China ranked lowest priority for Lend-Lease supplies. When China's needs were considered, she was frequently not consulted. Since Pearl Harbor the British had repeatedly hijacked supplies intended for China by offloading them at Rangoon. Chiang accused the British of "double-crossing" and feared China would "just be a pawn in the game." Less than 10 percent of supplies pledged by Roosevelt had reached China. U.S. officials mollified the Chinese with vague promises but offered little of substance.

British officials deplored China's "critical carping" over British war efforts. "Where I suppose we fail and the Americans succeed is that while we both act mainly from motives of self interest the Americans generally manage to throw a rose-tinted fog of the most utter altruism over all their activities," a Foreign Office official sniffed. "The Chinese even seem to prefer a promise accompanied by fine sentiments to actual help not so accompanied. Certainly we must blow our trumpet more in future, now that trumpet-blowing is in fashion."

In late July 1942, amid rising tensions between Indian nationalist leaders and Britain, Chiang asked Roosevelt to step in as mediator between the Congress party and the British. Roosevelt's natural sympathies lay with self-determination for the Indian people, but he was unwilling to threaten the transatlantic alliance and the war effort by taking a firm stand. He replied to Chiang that he felt it unwise to intervene, but asked Chiang to keep in close touch with him, so as to reduce the risk of the Chinese taking action on their own initiative. Churchill was livid over China's meddling, which he termed "mischievous and ignorant."

On August 9, Gandhi and Nehru were arrested after demanding the British "quit India" immediately. In distress Chiang cabled Roosevelt, pleading for intervention on grounds the arrests would have a "disastrous effect" on the Allied war effort. The troubles in India were "unfortunate," Roosevelt replied, but the best course of action was to stand "in the position of friends who will gladly help if we are called upon by both sides." He rather naively compared communal differences in India to those among the thirteen American colonies before the American Revolution. He forwarded Chiang's message to Churchill. Churchill's swift and indignant reply pointed a finger at Mayling. "All Chiang's talk of congress leaders wishing us to quit in order that they may help the Allies is eye wash. . . . The style of his message prompts me to say *Cherchez la Femme.*"

Churchill bluntly informed Chiang that unless Gandhi got the Japanese to lend him an army to hold down the Muslims, "he and his friends would be speedily overthrown by the martial races" if the British withdrew. "I think the best rule to follow is not to interfere in each other's internal affairs," he wrote, noting Britain had abstained from commenting on differences between the Kuomintang and the Communists.

The Chiangs' efforts were not appreciated by all Indians. Sir Muhammad Zafrulla Khan, a Muslim jurist, was deeply suspicious of the Chiangs' interest in India's internal politics. He was convinced that the Chinese expected to take control of Indochina after the war, as well as Burma and parts of northern India. He believed the Chiangs wanted to install a "Chinese Raj" in India once the British were ousted, and aspired to dominate Asia. "What is it . . . that makes the claim of China to be ranked among the great nations irresistible and makes the same claim on behalf of India unacceptable?" he complained.

Mayling wrote a strongly worded critique of Allied policies for the *New York Times* that was calculated to win friends in neither Washington nor London. "With such dynamite as I served, the Bowl of Rice dinners [were] hard to dish up," she wrote Nehru with some glee. In the acerbic article she attacked an "arrogant belief in innate Western ascendancy . . . fostered by the treaty port Taipans . . . whose prejudiced knowledge of China was restricted to associations with their subservient Chinese compradors and the ignorant gossip gleaned in their club bars." She lambasted the Allies for swallowing for so long "insults, indignities and face-slapping" from Japan. She ridiculed Britain for its loss of Hong Kong and Singapore in quick succession. "The West must revise its ideas about the East," she concluded. "In the great world society that we are going to create, there must be no thought of superiors and inferiors." The great nations must take the "bitter medicine" of humility. She followed with an article in the *Atlantic Monthly* decrying the "ruthless and shameless exploitation of our country by the West in the past and the hard-dying illusion that the best way to win our hearts was to kick us in the ribs. Such asinine stupidities must never be repeated." She denounced racial discrimination in a June 1942 radio broadcast to the U.S. "The time has passed when we can determine a man's status by the color of his skin or the shape of his eyes," she declared.

The British government keenly resented Mayling's attacks on Britain. She was an "indiscreet and unfriendly woman," wrote one Foreign Office official. Another asked: "As a matter of interest, what right has she to be called Madame?" Another official pointed out that much as the Americans admired the Chinese, they did not accept China as an equal partner in the planning and prosecution of the war. The Chinese "have never even been able to make a motor-car for themselves, let alone a tank or a plane," he wrote. "Their claim to be one of the 'big four' in this war of machines and ships is pathetic." Churchill claimed he "liked and admired [the Chinese] as a race and pitied them for their endless misgovernment" but found the American view incomprehensible. "At Washington I had found the extraordinary significance of China in American minds, even at the top, strangely out of proportion."

Matters came to a head in late June 1942, when a promised force of B-24 heavy bombers en route to China was diverted to Khartoum for the British, who had just suffered a major setback against German forces in the Middle East. Stilwell was as frustrated as the Chiangs and equally as helpless to control the situation, but nonetheless the brunt of their anger fell on him. Every time Britain ran into trouble, China's share of supplies was diverted to the British, Mayling complained. "Such being the case there is no need for China to continue in the war," she raged, adding menacingly: "The Generalissimo wants a yes or no answer whether the Allies consider this theater necessary and will support it."

With nothing to lose, the Chiangs resorted to blackmail. Chiang presented Stilwell with "three demands"—three American divisions in China, five hundred combat planes, and five thousand tons of military supplies per month. If these demands were not satisfied Chiang would have to "make other arrangements," namely—according to Mayling—peace with Japan. She demanded that Stilwell endorse the demands, but he refused, saying he could not back an ultimatum to his own government. Mayling "started to bawl me out," wrote Stilwell. She was "mad as *hell*. She had snapped the whip and the stooge had not come across."

U.S. Ambassador Clarence Gauss dismissed the threat as "the type of bluff that Madame Chiang was capable of concocting and selling to the Generalissimo." Gauss and Stilwell concurred in the view that the Chinese had been "built up" in the U.S. to a point where Americans believed that China had been "fighting" the Japanese for five years and that the Generalissimo was a great leader and a world hero directing China's "energetic resistance" to Japan. "Looking at the cold facts in the face one could only dismiss this as 'rot,'" Gauss wrote.

Clare Boothe Luce extolled Mayling as the world's "greatest living woman" in the July 1942 issue of *Life* in an article that might have embarrassed even Mayling with its unabashed superlatives. She was, Luce wrote, one of the world's greatest wives and one of the world's best mothers—to Chinese "warphans." Luce compared her to Joan of Arc and Florence Nightingale. She was one of the world's most influential missionaries, one of its most famous bilinguists, and unequaled as a bridge between East and West. She was also one of the world's most skilled diplomats and statesmen. Not least, she was one of the world's most beautiful and charming women. In the last line, Luce incongruously observed that Madame Chiang, despite all her achievements, was "something of a tragic figure," a prescient hint that she might not always be so exalted.

The late summer of 1942 was perhaps the lowest point in the war. Setbacks plagued the Allies on all fronts. Roosevelt decided that a strong signal was needed to show that Americans were united behind the war effort.

He hit on the plan of sending Wendell Willkie, his unsuccessful opponent in the 1940 election, on a worldwide trip to reassure embattled nations that the U.S. was determined to win. Willkie remained enormously popular and Roosevelt figured his formidable political skills would work abroad as well as at home. He dispatched him on a whirlwind forty-nine-day, thirty-one-thousand-mile goodwill tour. Traveling aboard the *Gulliver*, a U.S. Army bomber, Willkie would see the war on three fronts—the Middle East, Europe, and Asia. "You are bound to hit it off magnificently," Clare Boothe Luce wrote Mayling ahead of Willkie's visit to China.

Willkie was a political maverick and self-described "free spirit" who reveled in his public image as an Indiana farmer and whose appeal extended from Main Street to Wall Street. At fifty, Willkie was a handsome, vigorous figure with an attractively tousled mane, a booming voice, and a homespun manner. The ebullient chain-smoking lawyer exuded boyish charm, vitality, and charisma. Gardner "Mike" Cowles, a Midwestern media magnate and founder of *Look* magazine, saw Willkie's "overwhelming magnetism" and backed him in the 1940 campaign, running advertisements calling him "another Lincoln."

Roosevelt, however, joked privately during the 1940 campaign that he was going to name his new Scottish terrier puppy Wendell Willkie because it wasn't housebroken yet, and Vice President Henry Wallace delicately termed Willkie "rambunctious." To his credit, Willkie found intelligent strong-willed women a challenge rather than a threat—no doubt due to his mother, the first woman ever admitted to the Indiana bar, and his grandmother, a Presbyterian minister. It was an open secret that Willkie and Irita Van Doren, the *New York Herald Tribune*'s influential books editor, were carrying on a long-running extramarital affair.

After a tête-à-tête with Stalin in Moscow, accompanied by large quantities of vodka, Willkie and his entourage made their way through Siberia to Chungking, where on October 2, 1942, he stepped off the *Gulliver* clad in a rumpled gray suit. He was unprepared for the throngs that turned out to welcome him. The Chiangs realized he could be the next president and gave him the red-carpet treatment. The Generalissimo hailed him as the highest-ranking American envoy to visit China since former president Ulysses S. Grant in 1879. The eleven miles of roads from airport to guesthouse were lined with people, many of them schoolchildren, barefoot and in rags, waving little paper American and Chinese flags and setting off firecrackers. Shanties were razed, beggars hustled away, and streets festooned with banners.

The envoy was "smothered" with parades, receptions, military reviews, and banquets, to keep Willkie "well insulated from pollution by Americans," Stilwell cynically wrote. "The idea is to get him so exhausted and keep him so torpid with food and drink that his faculties will be dulled and he'll be stuffed with the right doctrines." The strategy evidently succeeded, because Willkie soon declared: "I have fallen so much in love with the Chinese people that it is going to be difficult to carry out my fact-finding mission with the correct critical approach."

Willkie, it emerged, was in love not so much with the Chinese in general as with one in particular—none other than the Generalissimo's wife. He declared her the "most charming woman he ever met." From their first encounter, he was "under her spell." "There is little doubt," wrote diplomat John Paton Davies, "that Little Sister has accomplished one of her easiest conquests." She was equally besotted with him.

Chiang, however, was less taken with the American visitor. John Carter Vincent, an American diplomat present during meetings between Willkie and the Chiangs, called Willkie the sort of foreigner who "smelled like raw beef" to the Chinese nose. After he left the room Chiang ordered the windows thrown open to get rid of the odor. Willkie found the Generalissimo a "strangely quiet" scholarly figure who appeared "even bigger than his legendary reputation." Willkie was deeply impressed by Zhou Enlai, Mao Zedong's right-hand man, and urged the Kungs to invite the Communist leader to a dinner party, which they did. Willkie felt that "if all Chinese Communists are like [Zhou], their movement is more a national and agrarian awakening than an international or proletarian conspiracy."

Willkie was serenaded by a group of Mayling's "warphans" at a tea in his honor. "Madame Chiang and I are going to howl and howl for the right kind of world when this war is over so that all nations can be free and seek their own just aspirations," he declared when they had finished singing. Impulsively he grabbed a big cake from the table of honor and handed it to the children, kissing one of the girls while the guests applauded. Flustered, Mayling told guests she found Willkie a "very disturbing personality." She had prepared "a nice speech all ready to read to him and here he comes and shows he is not the sort of person for whom the speech was made," she said. "I will have to, therefore, speak from my heart because he is so spontaneous, so warm-hearted, so essentially human that anything written down could not express the welcome felt in our hearts for him."

Although during his visit Japanese planes advanced on Chungking before being deterred by fog, Willkie said there was "more danger of my being killed by the kindness of the Chinese than by enemy bullets." Mayling's stepson, Capt. Wego Chiang, led Willkie on an inspection tour of what were ostensibly the front lines near the Yellow River. But apart from a few Japanese shells lying about that exploded unexpectedly, Willkie saw no fire on what was in fact a "cold" battlefield used as a showplace for visiting journalists and dignitaries. To lend an aura of authenticity to the visit, the Generalissimo's younger son handed out as gifts to the guests Japanese cavalry swords and bottles of excellent French wine. These had been captured, he claimed, in a night raid across the river.

Willkie spent six days with the Chiangs, talking of everything from world politics to the mass production of automobiles. He was entertained by folk musicians and fed vanilla ice cream, a delicacy banned in Chungking after a spring cholera outbreak. The ban was lifted for Willkie's benefit, which made him and his traveling companions anxious. Willkie concluded that America had no better ally in East Asia than China and was therefore obliged to understand the Chinese and their problems. He politely glossed over the Chiang government's fascist tendencies as "centralized control," concluding, "You cannot present democracy to China on a silver platter next Tuesday." Photos of him with Mayling were splashed across American newspapers. With her encouragement Willkie used Chungking as a pulpit from which to lambaste imperialism. "The colonial days are past," he declared. "We believe this war must mean an end to the empire of nations over other nations." Churchill famously proclaimed soon after: "I have not become the King's first minister in order to preside over the liquidation of the British Empire." Still, Willkie's blast from Chungking prompted the U.S. and Britain to promise to end extraterritoriality in China.

At a dinner party in his honor held on the lawn of H. H. Kung's residence, Willkie sat between Mayling and Ching Ling. According to his account, as the dinner ended Mayling took him by the arm and said, "I want you to meet my other sister. She has neuralgia and couldn't come outdoors for the party." The abrupt vanishing of the two leading guests from the dinner party started tongues wagging. Willkie recounted afterward that they went inside and found Eling Kung, her arm in a sling. "The three of us talked and had such a good time we forgot about the hour and the people outdoors," he wrote. At about eleven in the evening, H. H. Kung came looking for them. He scolded Mayling and Willkie for deserting the party, which had long since broken up. Then the four of them "set out to solve the problems of the universe," embarking on a discussion of the "revolution of ideas that is sweeping the East."

In mid-October Chiang Kai-shek hosted a parting reception for Willkie in a vast hall with a cast of thousands. The Chiangs made a dramatic entrance and seated themselves on two thronelike chairs perched on a stage. After welcoming remarks the three formed a receiving line. An hour later Willkie summoned Gardner Cowles, who had accompanied him on the trip. He whispered that he and the Madame were going to sneak away and told Cowles to take his place and cover up for them. Cowles stood by the Generalissimo and distracted him with questions. Eventually Chiang departed. Cowles returned to the Soong house and poured himself a Scotch, a wartime luxury generously provided by Mayling.

According to Cowles, Willkie did not appear for dinner. Late that evening Chiang Kai-shek stormed into the house with three bodyguards carrying tommy guns. "Where's Willkie?" he demanded, barely restraining his rage. "I have absolutely no idea," Cowles replied. Chiang searched the house, looking under beds and opening closets, before departing. Alarmed, Cowles had visions of his friend standing before a firing squad. Willkie, buoyant and cocky, finally appeared at four in the morning and gave Cowles a play-by-play account of his alleged amorous conquest of the Madame. Willkie told Cowles "there was never anything like this before," and said it was the only time he had ever been in love. He finished by saying he had invited Mayling to fly back to Washington with him. Cowles exploded. "Wendell, you're just a goddam fool!"

Cowles agreed with Willkie that Madame Chiang was "one of the most beautiful, intelligent, and sexy women either one of us had ever met" and he understood the "tremendous attraction" between the two charismatic people. But the Chungking press corps was already gossiping about them. Cowles reminded Willkie that his wife and son would be meeting him at the airport in Washington and the presence of Madame Chiang would be embarrassing. He also reminded him that he wanted to run for president again in 1944. Willkie angrily stomped off to bed. The next day Cowles met Mayling at her secret apartment, where the alleged tryst had taken place, and told her she could not fly back with Willkie on the *Gulliver*. "Who says I can't?" she asked. "I do," replied Cowles. In a flash, Cowles claimed, she reached up and scratched his cheek with her fingernails.

Undaunted, Willkie publicly invited Mayling to visit the U.S. to "educate us about China and India." She would be the "perfect ambassador," he said. "She would find herself not only beloved, but immensely effective. We would listen to her as to no one else. With wit and charm, a generous and understanding heart, a gracious and beautiful manner and appearance, and a burning conviction, she is just what we need as a visitor."

Mayling wrote Clare Boothe Luce that both she and Chiang were very glad Willkie had come to visit. "He is all you led us to expect—and more," she gushed. "The effect he has had on the populace has been immense; they took him to their hearts at once. His popularity is due, of course, to his perfect naturalness and evident sincerity." She added, "I would so like to go to America with Mr. Willkie, but my husband does not want me to go right now. So you see, after all, I am not an emancipated woman—still tied to my husband's (I cannot say apron-strings so I must say) military belt."

As they were about to return to the U.S., Cowles and Willkie stopped to say good-bye to Madame Chiang at one of her charities, where she maintained offices. Willkie went in; the door closed. Cowles waited an hour and twenty minutes before the pair finally emerged. Madame accompanied them to the airfield. As Willkie was about to board the plane, she "jumped into his arms." He picked her up and gave her a "terrific soul kiss."

The December issue of *Look* carried an article decorously entitled "Wendell Willkie Calls on Madame Chiang Kai-shek." Willkie had this to say of Mayling: "In that ultimate test of charm—the breakfast table—she still measured up." When Willkie went to see Roosevelt after his One World trip, he had "obviously been drinking quite a bit." The president thought Willkie drank too heavily. Vice President Henry Wallace relayed to Roosevelt stories circulating about Willkie's Russian "ballerina" and "girls of Bagdad."

Willkie's visit to China was seized on as an opportunity to mount a campaign in Washington to replace Stilwell with Chennault, who promised that if he were given command in China he and his air corps would single-handedly end the Pacific war within a year. Chennault enjoyed the Chiangs' favor, while Stilwell was barely tolerated. The two American military men, equally colorful and driven, thoroughly despised one another and held fundamentally different views on how the war in China should be fought. Stilwell, the consummate West Point–trained army man, favored time-consuming conventional ground campaigns and had little understanding of or use for airpower. Chennault was keen to demonstrate his theories on the superiority of air combat to the military establishment, which viewed him as a maverick.

Hailed as a hero in China, Chennault encouraged the widely held notion in America that he and his Flying Tigers were all that stood between China and certain destruction by Japan. Air combat was exciting, glamorous, and romantic, peopled by dashing characters like Robert Lee Scott, whose best-selling memoir, *God Is My Co-Pilot*, was made into a popular feature film. Ground warfare was dirty, brutish, and boring. In the eyes of Chiang and Mayling, the loyal and uncomplaining Chennault could do no wrong, while the acerbic and uncompromising Stilwell fell increasingly out of favor. He vented his frustrations against the Chinese in general and "Peanut"—his nickname for Chiang Kai-shek—in particular in diaries and private letters that were often an unremitting torrent of vitriol. Gen. George C. Marshall dismissed Chennault's claims as nonsense. Chiang was told that "pepper was required more than molasses," a reference to Stilwell's notorious temperament. Stilwell stayed.

A Chinese precept is that the highest form of warfare is to defeat the enemy without fighting. The Chinese were war-weary, and after five years of resistance felt justified in their belief that the Allies should now do the fighting for them. Stilwell was appalled by the abysmal conditions in the Chinese army. Many recruits died from disease and malnutrition. Corruption and profiteering among officers was rampant. Training and medical care were miserable. Chiang was kept in what Stilwell termed "ignorance and fatuous complacency" by subordinates who were unwilling to tell him the facts for reasons of fear and face. But Stilwell told Chiang and Mayling the truth as he saw it. "It was like kicking an old lady in the stomach," the American general wrote on one occasion. But "NO ONE else dares to tell him, so it's up to me all the more." In a report, he recommended a complete overhaul of ground forces in order to replace quantity with quality and a purge of ineffective and corrupt commanders, failing which "the Army will continue to go downhill no matter how much materiel is supplied for it."

He left the report with Mayling, who after a brief glance exclaimed, "That's what the German advisers told him!" She was referring to Gen. Hans von Seeckt, who had made similar recommendations years earlier. Chiang did not bother to reply to the report and soon after resumed demands for planes and arms. When Stilwell called again for reorganization, Mayling said Chiang had to consider "certain influences," meaning intractable political rivalries with the fractious coalition of local warlords on whom he depended. On other occasions, however, Mayling took Stilwell's wishes up with Chiang and was instrumental in pushing them through.

Mayling served as message-bearer between her husband and Chennault, Stilwell, and T. V. Soong, and often among the latter three as well. She was Chennault's champion and a determined gadfly, because in her unofficial capacity she could speak bluntly in a way no one else could. When once she told Chennault he must communicate directly with Chiang, he threatened to resign. Without her involvement, others resentful of U.S. influence convinced Chiang to issue "unacceptable orders," Chennault wrote.

Mayling and her husband were thoroughly convinced of the correctness of Chennault's theory that the war could be won simply by boosting airpower. The theory was especially attractive because it appeared to reduce the need for distasteful ground operations. "If we destroy fifteen Nippon planes every day," Mayling wrote hopefully to Chennault, "soon there will be no more left." She and Chiang labored to persuade Roosevelt to supply China with the five-hundred-plane air force Chennault wanted and to expand the supply service over the Hump from India to maintain it. Stilwell, they believed, was standing in the way, either willfully or because his influence in Washington was insufficient. Mayling declared, "We're going to see that you are made a *full general*," as if that would solve the problem. "The hell they are," Stilwell groused in his diary.

Stilwell grew increasingly frustrated with Chiang, who often ignored his memoranda and requests for interviews. The American general concluded Chiang did not want a well-trained army because it could be used against him as well as the enemy, that he did not want to replace the corrupt incompetents who ran the army because they were loyal to him; that his real motive in demanding more and more military equipment despite China's inability to utilize it was to hoard it for use against the Communists. In short, he felt that Chiang was less interested in fighting the Japanese than in remaining in power. He was a "stubborn, ignorant, prejudiced, conceited despot who never hears the truth except from me," Stilwell grumbled. "He has no friends at all, only servants who are without exception ill at ease in his presence." His only true friend was his wife, but "she is very much afraid of him and she subsides at once when his anger flares up. She considers her job to be the fight to make China great" and if only she were the Generalissimo, "progress would be five times faster than it is."

PART III

Chapter Thirteen

Coming Home to America

In our national tendency to exalt the lowly and lower the exalted, our hearts may run away with our heads.
—*Boston Herald*, February 17, 1943

On a cold morning in mid-November 1942, an American bush pilot named C. N. Shelton waited at Chengtu airport for a secret VIP he had flown halfway around the world to fetch in Boeing's new four-engine 307 Stratoliner, dubbed the *Apache*. An ambulance accompanied by cars carrying numerous high-ranking Chinese officials including Chiang Kai-shek pulled up; the doors flew open and attendants gently lifted out a stretcher bearing Madame Chiang Kai-shek, bundled in blankets. The plane soon departed for the U.S. with her and her party, which included niece Jeanette Kung, adviser Owen Lattimore, secretary Pearl Chen, press secretary Hollington Tong, a doctor, and three servants.

The plane stopped in Agra, India, ostensibly so the Madame could recover from nervous indigestion, but she was reported to have visited the Taj Mahal by moonlight. The viceroy was furious that she had been "smuggled" through his domain by the U.S. government without his notification and deemed the act "discourteous in the highest degree." He feared opponents of British rule in India would make political capital of her blatant snub, or that she might claim the colonial authorities had not been willing to show her even basic courtesies. The Foreign Office felt he had a grievance, but was anxious to avoid giving the Americans the impression they were "worrying about any insult to our dignity." Ironically, on learning of her departure from China the British government extended her an invitation to visit Britain, to which she did not immediately respond. "How long do we have to wait for this woman to reply to an invitation she doesn't deserve?" groused Foreign Secretary Eden. "I hope she doesn't dangle indefinitely."

Shortly before she arrived in New York, the White House learned that Mayling had asked to see Harry Hopkins first. Hopkins was not only the president's most intimate adviser; he was also in charge of Lend-Lease. "You'd better watch your step," Roosevelt ribbed Hopkins, "or before you know it she will have you wound around her little finger. You know how she charmed Wendell Willkie and Lauch Currie. . . . We might even provide you with a bodyguard if you'd like one."

Mayling had left China seriously ill with a debilitating outbreak of urticaria, or hives, and it was feared she had stomach cancer too. She was utterly exhausted, was unable to sleep, and had intense abdominal pain. She had lost weight and could barely eat. "This state was unquestionably the product of prolonged fatigue and devastating emotional strain," wrote her renowned physician, Dr. Robert Loeb. Cancer was ruled out, but doctors discovered an intestinal parasite. She had severe sinus problems from a botched surgery. More seriously, she was apparently dependent on sedatives. Allergy tests failed to reveal the cause of her skin trouble, but it was exacerbated by fatigue and tension. She was given two weeks of intensive antiamebic therapy, followed by surgery and extensive dental work.

When Mayling landed in New York on November 27, 1942, Hopkins met her at Mitchel Field, a U.S. Army airbase on Long Island, and accompanied her directly to Presbyterian Hospital in upper Manhattan. On the ride she told Hopkins she had come only for medical treatment and rest, but in the same breath proceeded to discuss the war. She argued that the Allies should defeat Japan before Germany. Hopkins said he thought that "infeasible." She criticized Britain and America over the loss of Burma, and made it clear she did not like Stilwell and had the greatest admiration for Chennault.

On arriving at the hospital she checked in under the name "Madame Lin." At the request of the Secret Service men and FBI agents assigned to her, the entire twelfth floor of the hospital was reserved for her and her entourage. Eleanor Roosevelt visited Mayling in the hospital soon after her arrival and reported that she appeared nervous and could hardly bear to have anything touching her body. Mayling gave her a jade and rhinestone pin she said once belonged to her mother. Roosevelt cabled

Chiang, "Your wife is in good hands here and I am looking forward to seeing her soon." Willkie sent Mayling several bouquets of flowers and said he was "subject to her command."

Mayling's visit was supposed to be entirely incognito and subject to a news embargo, but rumors flew the moment she landed and her name soon surfaced in Drew Pearson's gossip column. On December 12, the St. Louis *Star-Times* ran a story quoting her reply, evidently made some time earlier, to the question of why she did not imitate Catherine the Great. "Because the Generalissimo is the head of his family and I assist him by helping my people through love and kindness," she said. "Catherine ruled her people through fear . . . and Catherine's husband was a nit-wit." Mayling was enraged by news reports of her arrival and tried to have the leak traced.

Journalist Frances Gunther was one of the lucky few summoned to visit the hospital, where she found Mayling sequestered in her room wearing a pink velvet bed jacket and coral earrings. The nails on her very pale slender hands were long and brightly lacquered, and she was perfectly made up and coiffed—the handiwork of daily visits by a beautician and a hairdresser. Mayling smiled in greeting but there was "an aftermath of . . . horror still in her eyes," Gunther noted. She had not been out at all except to go to the dentist and confided to Gunther that she could not sleep without "hypodermics." The two women commiserated over their mutual friend "poor Nehru." Mayling had not heard from him since he was last imprisoned; she had tried to send him a letter, but the viceroy had refused to allow it.

Pearl S. Buck visited Mayling on January 27 and found her "extremely low indeed," both physically and mentally. She was "very bitter and unhappy" that her husband had not been invited to the secret wartime summit at Casablanca that had concluded on January 24, where to China's consternation Roosevelt and Churchill decided the Allies would first win the war in Europe and then tackle Japan. She appeared "utterly discouraged," and was far from well. She was "still in a nervous state and was keeping very quiet, not even reading much, and eating very little," Buck reported. The enforced inactivity was necessary, doctors said, but did not suit her temperament and made her irritable.

After the U.S. government lifted the news embargo on her visit in mid-January, thousands of friends and well-wishers clamored to see her. The adulation she received even before making a public appearance was aston-ishing. Her mail quickly swelled to a thousand letters a day. Her nephew, David Kung, took leave from studies at Harvard to handle correspondence and public relations. No date had been set but as her anticipated visit to the White House neared, she received much advance billing. "She radiates a courage of spirit and a will to accomplish her convictions which fairly takes your breath away," wrote Anna Roosevelt Boettiger, the president's daughter. Eleanor Roosevelt was besieged with requests for introductions and autographed photographs of Madame Chiang. Walter White, head of the National Association for the Advancement of Colored People, sought to make common cause with her in the international struggle for racial equality. Eleanor conveyed White's request to Mayling and offered to join them in a meeting. But oddly, Mayling did not reply to repeated overtures from White, who felt snubbed.

By the time she emerged from the hospital in early February, public curiosity had reached a crescendo, fueled by the secrecy of her visit and the mystery of her illness. China was a gallant ally in the titanic struggle for democracy, a magical faraway land of infinitely noble poverty, peopled by legions of peasants along the lines of Paul Muni and Luise Rainer in *The Good Earth*. "Most Americans have always had a missionary complex about China," said a longtime American resident of China. "The Chinese are small and very attractive and exceptionally bright, so we think we should treat them like children. It's a great mistake." The attitude of most Ameri-cans toward China was "recklessly romantic; almost hopelessly so"—a love affair fueled by Hollywood, which was gripped by China fever. Tradi-tional American sympathy for the underdog found its full expression in admiration for plucky China. It was a period of "dreamy unreality" in Sino-American relations, during which the American public seemed prepared to accept "anything and everything good and wonderful that was said about the Chinese, their Generalissimo, the Generalissimo's wife and the heroic Chinese people."

Detective Charlie Chan had become a cultural icon, as was the pirate heroine Dragon Lady from Milton Caniff's enormously popular comic strip, "Terry and the Pirates." American pilot Terry Lee was often rescued by the Oriental vamp, an archetypal femme fatale loosely modeled on Ma-dame Chiang Kai-shek. She was alluring and delicate yet scheming and ruthless; she smoked cigarettes in a long holder and wore slinky black dresses slit high on the side. China was depicted as an exotic land of opium dens and dark cruelty. Caniff, a self-described "armchair Marco Polo," had never set foot in China—he gleaned fodder for his strip from the Encyclopedia Britannica and the New York Public Library. "Confucius say" gags such as "He who sit on electric chair get amps in pants" were extremely popular with comedians such as Jack Benny and Fred Allen. The ridiculing of China's most revered philosopher made Chinese-Americans indignant.

As images of China vacillated between magical and despicable, ridiculous and heroic, American attitudes were shifting from fear to admiration, and from condescension to sympathy. Until recently most Americans regarded the Chinese as "washee-washee agents, servants, coolies, and heathens whose rights and feelings nobody was bound to respect," wrote the *Boston Herald.* Now a mention of China or Chiang Kai-shek would spark a round of applause in Congress, as Roosevelt found during his January State of the Union address. But sounding a rare cautionary note in a sea of breathless praise, the paper warned: "The Chinese have fought so much better than we thought they could that now we are probably ascribing qualities . . . to them which they do not possess in abundance."

For her part, Mayling had deeply ambivalent feelings about America. She publicly supported the pleasant fiction that America was less imperialistic than other nations and was China's best friend, but her true feelings were more nuanced. She remained bitter that half a century earlier her father had been treated by American missionaries more like a servant than a colleague. She confided to her husband's adviser Owen Lattimore that she felt the American attitude toward her personally was racist and condescending and she resented it deeply. "Oh yes, she is clever, of course, but after all she is only a Chinese" was how she felt Americans saw her. This was why she insisted on top ceremonial protocol on her visit to the U.S.

During her hospital stay Mayling prepared a major speech she planned to give to the U.S. Congress when she visited Washington. Her doctors, however, insisted she needed two to four months of absolute rest, free from public responsibilities, in order to recover. She had a "vast amount of nervous vitality with which she wars against a lack of physical strength," wrote a friend. "Her doctors say she has a Mercedes engine on a Ford chassis." Now that remedial treatments were completed they wanted to treat her underlying "exhaustion," as they termed it, but she insisted on being discharged in early February. The doctors reluctantly agreed, but with orders to follow a strict regimen. She was to take "chloral," a habit-forming sedative, several times daily for insomnia; another medication for the urticaria; vitamin capsules; and aspirin. She was ordered to remain in bed until ten-thirty each day for at least several months and to rest at least one hour every afternoon. One day each week was to be devoted entirely to rest. She was to limit herself to five speeches during her stay in America; to avoid extemporaneous talks or "sharing" the platform; to attend at most one official dinner engagement or large reception a month; and to avoid reception lines. Stressful meetings were to be limited to a maximum of one a day. "The more time spent in driving and out doors walking, the better," Dr. Loeb wrote. He tried to enlist T. V. Soong in ensuring orders were followed. Soong replied he would "do my best" but warned that he might not succeed.

At Eleanor Roosevelt's invitation Mayling proceeded from the hospital to the Roosevelt home in Hyde Park, New York, for six days. She thanked Eleanor for the "beautifully serene and quiet visit. . . . I feel myself getting stronger by the minute." She then went to Washington by train with Jeanette and David Kung. On the afternoon of February 17 she arrived at Union Station, where she was met by Roosevelt, Eleanor, and Fala, the president's Scottish terrier. Wearing a mink coat and a red-trimmed black Chinese dress, she greeted the first couple with a bouquet of red roses. The hour of her arrival had been kept secret, but crowds awaited.

At the White House, Eleanor assigned the "Large Pink Room" to Mayling; the "Little Pink Room" to Jeanette; the Monroe Room for Madame's sitting room; and the Yellow Room to David. Two nurses in the entourage stayed at the Chinese embassy. Mayling's favorite niece, then twenty-three but appearing much younger, was a "tomboy" who had tried to join the Chinese air force and fight the Japanese. Her father, H. H. Kung, did not approve. "I think a girl should be a girl," he later said. Jeanette created much consternation for the White House valets by wearing boys' clothes. Confusing her with her brother, they unpacked her bags in his room, to her great annoyance. When Roosevelt first saw Jeanette, he greeted her as "my boy." Hopkins scribbled a note saying: "This is Miss Kung." Roosevelt tried to cover up by saying he always called all young things "my boy."

That very evening Mayling raised with Roosevelt the subject of sending badly needed war materials to China. He listened attentively and agreed with her but said the problem was that the U.S. government was obligated to supply her other allies as well as her own troops. He promised to study China's case and consult with army supply officers. Meanwhile, he told Mayling he appreciated China's "tying down" huge numbers of Japanese troops and equipment so they could not be deployed elsewhere. She persisted, demanding that the president use his position to immediately send those crucial supplies to China. "At this point the President only smiled and did not make any promise to Madame Chiang," according to Currie. She also pushed for Chennault's appointment to major general with his own command, the Fourteenth Air Force. The conversation was cordial but fell far short of her hopes. Afterward she spoke with Eleanor Roosevelt, who sympathized with her position and responsibility as far as her mission to the U.S. was concerned, but said she was powerless to persuade her husband to carry out Madame Chiang's demands.

The next day, February 18, Mayling was to make her debut before the American public with an address to Congress. Her months spent hidden from public view had whetted curiosity. Questions swirled over the motives behind her visit. Reports of her frail health added sympathy to the drama. The national exercise in hero worship reached a fever pitch; there was a tremendous and inexplicable thirst to simply ogle her. But the buildup did not begin to explain the meteoric effect her appearance before Congress would have. She was the first Asian and the first private citizen ever to address the Congress and only the second woman, the first being Queen Wilhelmina of the Netherlands the previous August. She was acutely aware that she was up against not only negative American stereotypes of Chinese, but also negative views of women, and she knew full well that she was carrying the banner not only of her race but also of her sex. She knew she would be judged by the American public and the world as much on her appearance as on what she had to say, and she did her utmost to meet the challenge on both fronts. She was under tremendous pressure to turn in a spectacular performance.

The day was cold and clear. Admirers, many of them women, crowded outside for over an hour to await her arrival. A thousand policemen, detectives, and Secret Service men swarmed the Capitol, preventing anyone without a coveted ticket from entering. Across the country people stopped to tune in by radio. Inside, the air was electric with anticipation. Generally foreign dignitaries addressed a joint session of both houses, but such was the demand—especially from congressional wives—to see Madame Chiang that she had to speak to the House and the Senate separately.

Eleanor Roosevelt accompanied her into the Senate shortly after noon. In those pretelevision days, press and radio reporters captured for their eager audience every visual detail of events. As she walked to the rostrum, senators caught glimpses of "well-turned, beautifully flashing legs" when the split sides of her red-lined dress opened to the knee as she walked. She wore a dainty sequined turban; a slim black Chinese dress, severe yet alluring with a high collar and embellished with the bejeweled wings of her Chinese air force pin; jade earrings; and a jade ring. Her appearance had the senators "completely boggle-eyed." She removed the turban, flashed a dazzling smile, and gave a brief off-the-cuff talk full of homespun color. She told of an American airman forced to bail out of his plane over China. He knew only one word of Chinese, the Chinese name for America, *Meiguo* —"beautiful country"—so he shouted it to villagers running toward him. They welcomed him "like a long-lost brother." This airman later told Madame Chiang he felt like he had come home. She declared, "Coming here today, I feel that I am also coming home." She added:

> If the Chinese people could speak to you in their own tongue, or if you could understand our tongue, they would tell you that . . . fundamentally we are fighting for the same cause, that we have identity of ideals. . . . I assure you that our people are willing and eager to cooperate with you in the realization of these ideals . . . for ourselves, for our children, for our children's children, and for all of mankind.

Next she headed to the House to deliver her prepared address, leaving her audience with an "overpowering sense that here they were in the presence of one of the world's greatest personalities." The House was packed, with many wives sitting on the steps, as Mayling made a dramatic entrance, her four-inch heels failing to prevent her diminutive frame from being dwarfed by the cluster of tall men protectively surrounding her as she walked down the center aisle. Congressmen held their small daughters on their knees. A congressional chaplain opened the proceedings with a prayer "using terms about Madame which would have been excessive if applied to the Madonna," noted a skeptical British observer. Texas Congressman Sam Rayburn introduced her as "one of the outstanding women of all the earth" and "helpmate and co-worker of one of the outstanding figures of the world." A battery of red-hot blinding klieg lights glared from the press galleries, where flashbulbs burst in a frenzy and news cameras ground furiously. She leaned over and whispered to Rayburn, who then asked that the lights be dimmed, as they were making it difficult for Madame to read her speech. There was a long silence and the lights persisted. She smiled angelically as shouts of "Lights out!" rose from the floor, but the cameramen stalled. She held her ground. Irritated, Rayburn ordered loudly that the lights be extinguished. This time they were.

Diminutive and erect, clenching a white silk handkerchief in her right hand and tracing the lines of her speech with red-lacquered fingernails, Mayling spoke slowly, in soft, clear tones imbued with "tremendous vitality." Her English was flawlessly American, a pleasing mix of "Georgia softness and Massachusetts cultivation," resonant yet gentle, neither Southern drawl nor Yankee twang. She had an extraordinary mastery of drama and timing, beginning a sentence in a low tone, then working up to an emotional crescendo, only to drop her voice at exactly the right moment before raising it again forcefully to drive home her point.

The audience was entranced by her exotic looks, which contrasted with her utterly American manner of speaking. She was intensely—almost pruriently—scrutinized. One newspaper called her "China's lissome Joan of Arc." The inordinate fascination with her looks was due in part to the traditional view of women as decorative objects; in part to wartime sartorial solemnity, which left people hungry for visual appeal; and in part to the unfortunate contrast between the dainty, attractive, glamorous Madame Chiang and the large, frumpy, and decidedly plain American First Lady. But it must be attributed also to the extreme curiosity of the mostly male audience—reporters included—about her as a mysterious and exotic Asian female. She projected the image of a tiny woman, frail yet valiant, being rescued by tall, strong, chivalrous male senators. China was the damsel in distress and America the knight in shining armor. It was a calculated strategy. Mayling was supremely confident. She was aware of the power of her looks and her message, and of the effect she had on men as well as women. She knew her audience; she knew her part. And she played them both to perfection.

Her speech was in fact a sharp criticism of American policy cloaked as an homage to American culture and values. It was replete with obscure allusions intended to show off her knowledge of Western learning, and both subtle and not-so-subtle jabs at Allied war strategy. "It takes little effort to watch the other fellow carry the load," she told her audience, quoting a Chinese proverb. The House burst into frequent applause, but it was her assertion that Hitler's defeat was of secondary importance to the defeat of Japan, which "in her occupied areas today has greater resources at her command than Germany," that had the greatest impact. Listeners jumped to their feet, whistling and cheering.

This reasoning attracted a great deal of sympathy, especially on the West Coast, where Pearl Harbor loomed closer in geography as well as in the popular imagination. Not all of the sympathy her words evoked stemmed from rational or well-intentioned motives. In a mass effort driven by resurgent fears of the "Yellow Peril," some 120,000 Japanese-Americans throughout the western states, most of whom were American citizens, were being rounded up, stripped of their property, and transported to what were euphemistically termed "internment camps" for the duration of the war. Such was the climate of suspicion, hatred, and fear at the time that few Americans questioned this tragedy, one of the blackest hours in U.S. history.

Mayling knew she was competing directly with Churchill for U.S. sympathy and largesse. She knew she was at a disadvantage. No matter how strong American sympathy might be for the Chinese underdog, feeling for the plight of European Allies ran far deeper due to ties of kinship, culture, race, and shared history. American priorities lay with Europe, and she knew it. So she attempted to position China in the American imagination as not merely a military ally but a "spiritual ally" as well.

Her attack on American policy was cleverly camouflaged by a carefully worded appeal to Americans' deepest emotional need as a nation: to be admired, emulated, and—most of all—needed by weak, oppressed, and ostensibly less civilized peoples. To fit the bill, she had to portray China as not merely pathetic and downtrodden, but heroic, and the Chinese people as an enormous wellspring of American values, if only they were given the opportunity. She appealed to Americans' ingrained perception of themselves as a people with a unique sense of justice, altruism, and values. Her reasoning was subtle but persuasive. In effect she argued that not only were the lives of the Chinese at stake, but by extension American values— and thus America itself. Common ideals, she argued, were "the strongest possible solvent of racial dissimilarities."

The essence of her argument was that Chinese and American values were one and the same. Was she not living proof of this? Of course, the culture and values of China and America were vastly dissimilar. But the truth was that Madame Chiang desperately wanted China to be "Americanized," for reasons as much personal as political. She needed to forge common cause where none existed between America and China because she needed to justify before her people her own strange mix of American and Chinese. She needed to redeem herself in the eyes of Chinese who despised her for who she was and scorned her failed efforts to reform China and to remake it in the image of America. She needed to show the Chinese that they had much in common with America, whether they knew it or not, or liked it or not. Because of her very Americanness—so despised—she could serve as a bridge between the two societies and help rescue China from the clutches of Japan.

Americans saw China through the lens of their own history. In the American mind, China's 1911 revolution was equated with the American Revolution of 1776, and the wisdom of America's founding fathers and its democratic ideals were shared by China. China's efforts to unite the country against a common enemy were inspired by the same motives—to establish a nation based on the values of equality and liberty. The war against Japan was in pursuit of freedom and democracy. This was of course fantasy at best, but Mayling's own persona—a refreshing antidote to the familiar stereotype of coolies and laundrymen—planted illusions of great progress and promise. "We white Americans are the best friends the Chinese have," opined the *News* of Burlington, Vermont.

Mayling's debut was a heart-melting sensation. Observers said she outshone the Olympian Churchill, famed for his oratorical prowess, who had conquered Congress soon after Pearl Harbor. She dazzled with her "emerald phrases" and "pearly beauty," gushed *Life* reporter Frank McNaughton. Grizzled congressmen were putty in her hands. When she finished, the crowd in the House and galleries leapt to its feet, cheering and whistling amid thunderous applause. They struggled for words to express their amazement. One said, "By God, after hearing her, I feel like enlisting in the Chinese Army. She is something to worship." Connecticut Congresswoman Clare Boothe Luce said Madame Chiang spoke "in a brilliant parable. . . . She is too proud to beg us for what is China's right and too gracious to reproach us for what we have failed to do." Representative Edith Nourse Rogers, a Republican congresswoman from Massachusetts, said, "It thrilled the hearts of all of us to glimpse the very soul of China."

One newsman was unimpressed. "It was too, too Wellesley, with graceful modulations of the feminine order—and a bit femininely shrill when she got worked up," he wrote. For some, her thinking was obscured by her extraordinary mastery of English. "It sounds swell," said one listener tuning in by radio, "but what's she talking about?" U.S. military analysts regarded her speech as the emotional and illogical product of a feminine mind. The Combined Chiefs of Staff were alarmed that she might bring about a fundamental change in war strategy, but Roosevelt stuck to the "Germany first" principle.

Scattered critics aside, however, all America was "pixillated" by Madame Chiang, as a Foreign Office official wryly observed. She appeared on the March 1 cover of *Time.* Sympathy for China swept the country "like a tidal wave," wrote one columnist. Pity for China's ancient but weak civilization was reinforced by Mayling's femininity—too helpless to be a threat, but exotic enough to be intriguing, a perfect focus for America's rescue complex.

On February 19, the day after her congressional speech, Mayling held a joint press conference with the president and Eleanor Roosevelt in the president's executive office. By the time the spectacle was over, she had conquered the hearts of even the most calloused and cynical of Washington's newshawks. "Churchill was but a memory and the Roosevelts, *père et mère*, looked like a couple of bumps on a log," one newsman who witnessed the event recounted gleefully. "Mme. Chiang had outcharmed the master charmer of the American body politic. So deftly did the little lady choose her words that Roosevelt didn't know until it was all over what had hit him. It was at once a rapier thrust and a bat in the teeth."

Eleanor's brood of "women correspondents" debated whether Madame Chiang's bracelet was amber, and was the color of the First Lady's dress pink or rose? When the doors of the executive office opened there was jostling and shouting as the White House press corps swarmed in. "Wouldn't it be too bad if some of the little ladies were trampled to death," some men were heard to say. Three armchairs were placed before the window, with Madame Chiang in the center. The president, in blue suit and navy tie, sat smoking calmly to Mayling's left and Eleanor sat to her right. "Tiny little Mme. Chiang, in black silk with blue embroidered flowers, looking like an exquisite Chinese doll, sat perilously on the edge of the President's big swivel chair," a Time-Life reporter wrote. "The little Madame was apparently in danger of rocking about, for when she sat back in the chair at the end of the conference, her feet in doll-size open-toed, very American pumps, swung several inches clear of the floor. . . . Mrs. Roosevelt steadied the chair with her left hand throughout the conference."

Roosevelt introduced the press to Madame, adding that after nearly a thousand press conferences, "I think we rather like each other." He wished that he and the press "knew half as much about China as Madame Chiang knows about us." For well over a century, the people of China "have been, in thought and objective, closer to us Americans than almost any other people in the world—the same great ideals." With a civilization thousands of years older that that of America, China had lately become "one of the great democracies of the world," he said.

Mayling said she had been to battlefronts across China and never felt any fear of Japanese swords, but as "the pen is mightier than the sword," she did not know whether to be afraid or not at the sight of "all those pencils flashing across the pages." She felt she was among friends and they would not "heckle" her with "catch" questions.

The press asked her how best the American people could help China. Roosevelt beat her to the punch: "I can answer that: with more munitions. We are all for it. That is unanimous." She responded amid laughter, "The President is right." She was asked to comment on criticism that China was not fully utilizing its manpower. "We are using as much manpower as there are munitions to be used," she replied. "We can't fight with bare hands. . . . Although we have fought with nothing but swords in hand-to-hand combat." She praised the American Volunteer Group not only for helping protect China from indiscriminate bombing but for making the Chinese "feel that America is really heart and soul with us" in the fight against aggression. China had trained pilots but lacked munitions, planes, and the gasoline to fly them. "But the President has solved so many difficult questions, he has come through so many great crises with flying colors, that I feel I can safely leave that answer to him," she said. The press laughed.

Roosevelt responded with a lengthy analysis of the geographical and technical problems preventing more planes and fuel from being delivered to China. He ended with: "If I were a member of the Chinese government, I would say, 'But when?' . . . and I say that as a member of the American Government too. Just as fast as the Lord will let us, with the best brains that we can bring to bear on it." A pressman asked whether the president was willing to be quoted:

> The President: No, I wouldn't. A lot of people wouldn't like to have the name of the Lord taken in vain. (laughter)
>
> Mayling was asked how she thought aid could be stepped up.
>
> Madame Chiang: The President just said that "as soon as the Lord will let us." He didn't want that to be quoted. Well, I might say—add on to that, "The Lord helps those who help themselves."
>
> Q: Madame Chiang, do you object to being quoted directly about the Lord?
>
> Madame Chiang: I think I shall follow the President exactly.
>
> Q: Do you care to extend your remarks, Mr. President? (laughter)
>
> Q: (aside) Wonderful!
>
> Q: (aside) How about it?
>
> The President: Well, have you got anything to ask me, because we have got to get along pretty soon.

The master charmer was not used to being upstaged and was obviously rattled, much to the amusement of the White House press corps.

Soon after, the Chinese embassy threw a cocktail party for Mayling at the Shoreham Hotel. Three thousand people were invited, but so many more wanted invitations that the embassy ran a newspaper advertisement saying no more would be issued. The receiving line was so long it took forty-five minutes to reach "the presence," sniffed a British guest, and when they did arrive guests were warned not to speak to her. She smiled mechanically, looking quite ill. "What the Americans would have said if the British Embassy had put on a party like that does not bear contemplation; it was another proof that the Chinese can get away with anything in Washington."

For Madame Chiang's visit, Eleanor Roosevelt brought back from retirement former "Number One White House Maid" Maggie Rogers. It was widely reported that Madame Chiang eschewed White House linens and "demanded" silk sheets instead, but in fact she brought her own because she was allergic to both wool and cotton. Rogers's daughter, Lillian Rogers Parks, who also worked at the White House, had the job of attaching Madame's sheets to the White House's blankets to make a coverlet. She had to crawl around on the floor basting by hand the coverlet to the blanket with six-inch borders and mitered corners. The complicated operation had to be repeated each day because the sheets were removed and laundered daily. Her labors were the subject of much lively comment among White House staff, some of which found its way into the press. Madame gave Parks a "handsome" tip of $15, Parks recounted in a memoir.

During her two-week stay at the White House, Mayling took a nap each afternoon and ate most of her meals in her rooms. Roosevelt invited her to dine with him each day if she felt well enough, but she rarely answered before late afternoon and often changed her mind even when she did accept. Even so, on February 25 Dr. Robert Loeb cabled T. V. Soong that he was "profoundly disturbed" his orders were being ignored and warned that Mayling's activities might result in "serious relapse." He sternly demanded Soong to curtail her schedule. "We did not consider your sister cured upon discharge from the hospital and explained to Madame and her family that the next months must be primarily devoted to convalescence," Loeb wrote.

The Kung children were visibly annoyed by White House rules and gave the impression that they felt their hosts and most Americans "thought all Chinese were laundrymen and looked down on them," Eleanor Roosevelt wrote. "It seemed at times that they had chips on their shoulders, and did not want to be really friendly." Jeanette tried to impress a guest by telling him she was the seventy-sixth lineal descendant of Confucius. Nonplussed, the visitor remarked: "I did not know that China had a Newport set." One day, Grace Tully of the White House staff was taken aback to hear a loud clapping of hands coming from Madame's rooms. "This goes on all day," an usher told her. "That Chinese crowd has run us ragged. They think they're in China calling the coolies."

During Mayling's stay at the White House, Eleanor Roosevelt was amused by the reactions of the men with whom Mayling came into contact. "They found her charming, intelligent and fascinating, but they were all a little afraid of her, because she could be a cool-headed statesman when she was fighting for something she deemed necessary to China and to her husband's regime; the little velvet hand and the low gentle voice disguised a determination that could be as hard as steel." Mrs. Roosevelt was surprised by a "casualness about cruelty" that emerged in Mayling's conversations. "I had painted for Franklin such a sweet, gentle and pathetic figure that, as he came to recognize the other side of the lady, it gave him keen pleasure to tease me about my lack of perception," Eleanor wrote. At dinner one day Roosevelt asked Mayling, "What would you do in China with a labor leader like John Lewis?" Lewis was giving the president trouble. "She never said a word, but the beautiful, small hand came up very quietly and slid across her throat— a most expressive gesture." Roosevelt looked at Eleanor. "Well, what about your gentle and sweet character?" he said later. Mayling afterward recounted the story to a Wellesley friend quite differently: "I was so nonplussed when the President turned to me and said, 'What would you do in your country?' that I just threw up my hands, because I didn't know."

During conversations with Roosevelt, Mayling raised again the issues of financial and military aid and China's rightful place in the United Nations. They discussed her views on a postwar world: Manchuria, Taiwan, and the Ryukyu islands should be restored to Chinese sovereignty; pending full independence Korea should be placed under a temporary joint trusteeship of the U.S. and China; Hong Kong should be made a free port under Chinese sovereignty. But for all Roosevelt's apparent receptiveness, Madame Chiang was acutely aware that her mission had been unsuccessful.

Near the end of her stay in the White House, Mayling spoke with Hopkins again. While she claimed her talks with Roosevelt had gone well, Hopkins sensed that she was not entirely happy with her visit. She insisted on getting planes for the new Fourteenth Air Force. "We do not want promises that are not fulfilled," she told Hopkins. "The President has told me the planes will get there and he must not let me down with the Generalissimo." She proposed that the Allies should immediately begin talks, led by Roosevelt, on postwar affairs. At Chiang's request, she urged Hopkins to visit China. Hopkins demurred. She appeared "tired and a little dispirited." She saw Roosevelt for an hour and a half the following afternoon, after which he told Hopkins he had "learned nothing new but had given her every chance to tell her story."

Before she'd arrived in Washington, Roosevelt told Lord Halifax, the British ambassador, that he was "scared stiff" of her. After her visit Roosevelt viewed Madame Chiang with a measure of distrust, and "always had his fingers crossed" concerning her. He had, perhaps, met his match. Roosevelt was all breezy charm, while Mayling's charm had an edge to it. Although they differed in style, both were masters of the hidden agenda. The president had a "feminine" mind, according to his vice president Wallace. "He could very successfully go in two directions at almost the same time. By feminine I mean proceeding by a process of intuition and indirection. I'd say he had a golden heart, but I wouldn't want to be in business with him."

Mayling returned to New York at the end of February 1943. Thousands thronged the majestic old Pennsylvania Station to glimpse her. Fifty thousand turned out at City Hall Plaza for the mayor's reception, and she was given a tumultuous welcome in Chinatown. She took up residence at the Waldorf-Astoria Hotel and soon held a press conference. Smiling, pleasant, quick, and ready with the bon mot, she deftly parried queries. Had she invited Mrs. Roosevelt to visit China? She laughed and opened her arms wide, answering that she invited everybody to visit China. Would she stop in Britain on her way back to China? The Japanese would be glad to know her route home, she pointed out. One reporter asked her views regarding the colonies, but Mayling skirted the trap by replying that the wisest men in the world had not been able to solve that problem and she was not very wise at all.

While she stayed at the Waldorf-Astoria, Willkie spent much time with her and often sent flowers. He took the liberty of sending her two more bouquets in the name of the two pressmen, Gardner Cowles and Joseph

Barnes, who had accompanied him on the One World trip. "When I got a note of thanks this morning," he wrote Barnes, "I was fearful that you, with your complete honesty, might write to disclaim having sent the flowers when you receive a letter of thanks. It is hell to have to worry about the transparent honesty of a friend."

One day Cowles was summoned to appear the same evening at a black-tie dinner with the Madame in her suite. At great inconvenience, he managed to obtain the necessary permits—needed due to wartime travel restrictions—to travel to New York from Washington on short notice and arrived suitably attired. Mayling appeared exquisitely dressed for what Cowles belatedly realized would be a tête-à-tête. After the meal Mayling got straight to the point. Her marriage to Chiang, she told Cowles, was purely one of convenience, arranged by her mother. They had scarcely known one another beforehand and on their wedding night the Generalissimo informed her that he did not believe in sexual relations apart from procreation, and as he already had a son he was not interested in having more children. Therefore, there would be no sex between them. Cowles found the disclosures dubious, but said nothing. She then told Cowles it was his duty to dedicate himself to Willkie's 1944 presidential campaign, and promised to cover all expenses. "You know, Mike, if Wendell could be elected, then he and I would rule the world," she said. "I would rule the Orient and Wendell would rule the Western world." Cowles was so "mesmerized" by one of the world's most formidable women that he did not immediately dismiss her outlandish proposal.

On March 2, Mayling made a speech at Madison Square Garden. Oddly, she did not appear at a banquet in her honor, attended by a constellation of luminaries, before the speech. Henry Luce, the host, dispatched an emissary to her suite and was told Madame was indisposed. When she appeared for the speech, she told Willkie, also present, that she was nervous. He replied that no one ever made a good speech unless they were nearly paralyzed with fright before beginning. She entered the hall escorted by an honor guard of Flying Tigers as the "Star-Spangled Banner" and the Chinese national anthem were played. Sharing the stage were dignitaries including John D. Rockefeller Jr., Fiorello La Guardia, and governors of nine states. Willkie presented Madame Chiang, saying that he had met many wartime leaders but she was "the most fascinating of them all." The huge and enthusiastic crowd roared with approval as he called her "an avenging angel" and a "soldier unafraid in the fight for justice." Emblazoned on the backdrop behind her was a huge red Chinese character—*kai,* the ideogram for victory. She wore a long black dress with gold trim, green earrings, and black gloves. *Time* magazine said she looked more like "next month's *Vogue*" than the avenging angel of 422 million people.

In addressing the capacity crowd, Mayling said she was touched by the many thousands of letters and telegrams of goodwill she had received from Americans. "In July 1937 Prince Konoye said, 'We shall bring China cringing to her knees in three months,'" she declared. "How many three months have elapsed since he said that?" She was proud of China's contribution to the "titanic fight for a free and just world." The Axis powers respected nothing but brute force, she said. She spoke of the United Nations and the shape of the postwar world and called for an end to recrimination and hatred. Appealing to the churchgoers in the audience, she called for a spirit of forgiveness: "The teachings of Christ radiate ideas for the elevation of souls and intellectual capacities far above the common passions of hate and degradation. . . . He taught us to hate the evil in men, but not men themselves." Madame Chiang's speech could be included in any "college textbook on politics, ethics, literature, the art of discourse and speech," the renowned poet Carl Sandburg enthused in his newspaper column. "She is a marvel at timing her pauses and making each word count. . . . Yet she doesn't know how she does it any more than Ty Cobb knew which one of his eleven ways of sliding into second he was using."

On March 4, Dr. Loeb sternly implored David Kung to see to it that his aunt's activities were "radically and consistently" curtailed for the rest of her visit in America. "If the present pace is continued, serious collapse is, in my opinion, certain," he warned. "I am deeply concerned by the fact that Madame is growing progressively more tense and nervous, and is having again to increase the sedatives necessary to obtain her much-needed sleep. . . . She is losing weight and is progressively more exhausted."

Ignoring Dr. Loeb's warning, she shortly afterward addressed the Chinese community in New York. She said that not so long ago her people were referred to as "Chinamen" instead of "Chinese." In a maternal fashion, she admonished her audience to continue exhibiting the good behavior that had ostensibly earned this change in attitude. She was pleased by the greater respect accorded Chinese living in America, but had found that discrimination still existed against them, not only in the form of the Chinese exclusion laws, but also in many local real estate zoning regulations and social practices. The tremendous acclaim she was now receiving did nothing to make her forget that as a child in Macon, Georgia, she had to be tutored in the home of her hosts, the Ainsworths, because as a Chinese girl she was not admitted to the local public schools.

Soon after she set off for Boston, where she was to visit Wellesley, her alma mater. Thousands awaited as she arrived by special train in a raging sleet storm. Roosevelt's armored car drove straight up to her Pullman car to bring her from South Station to Wellesley. Wellesley's president, Mildred McAfee, apologized for the weather, but Mayling said she liked it because it was the New England weather she remembered, and Wellesley was "loveliest under the snow." Town and gown eagerly anticipated her visit and the Chinese flag flew over the village of Wellesley. Mayling demanded to stop in front of the house on Cross Street where she lived as a freshman.

The many former classmates who came to see Mayling despite gasoline rationing were as excited and nervous as schoolgirls about to have an audience with the Queen of England. They had heard her broadcasts, read her letters and articles, and raised funds for her seventy-five thousand "warphans" and for the Mayling Soong Foundation at Wellesley. "Like a butterfly out of a cocoon," one observer marveled. "I wonder sometimes whether it is the same person!" said another. A gray-haired matron retorted ruefully, "She may wonder the same thing when she sees us!" A third, grown ample, said, "Of course, marriage does a great deal for any woman!" as if that explained Mayling's metamorphosis from plump coed into svelte international stateswoman.

They were not disappointed. Madame Chiang appeared, slender and beautiful, in a long black gown, mink coat, and matching muff. She sparkled—literally and figuratively. "My dress is studded with rhinestones and they cost a dollar a dozen," she explained. When she spied her former professor Annie K. Tuell, she exclaimed, "You're wearing the same hat as in 1917!" She called to old friends, "Carrie, come here, I want to see you! Is that you, Jeanie? . . . Mary, you're fatter." Her professors said they would never have known her. "It is because I was fat then," Mayling reassured them. At a tea, classmates sat on the floor gazing up at her with adoration and excitement as she perched on the edge of the divan by the fire, gaily holding court. Her classmates burst into a spontaneous rendition of the alma mater. During a visit to T.Z.E., her sorority, Mayling wanted to know the names of all the new members and where they came from. At one point she lit a cigarette. "Of course, you infants are too young for this," she said, and impishly asked her classmates, "Will I corrupt their morals?"

For her Wellesley speech, Mayling wore the color of her alma mater, a clinging sheath of shimmering velvet blue with blue sequins, matched by sapphire and diamond earrings. As she began the tears welled up and she bit her lip as hard as she could so the physical pain would keep the emotions in check. Tears sprang to the eyes of those who watched her, even McAfee and the Secret Service men. Suddenly, she swayed and clutched the lectern, her face drained of color, on the verge of collapse. Her nurse held smelling salts under her nose to revive her. There was a long quiet moment during which it appeared uncertain whether she would be able to carry on, as she struggled to keep from fainting.

"Strong emotions often render one inarticulate" was how she finally opened her speech, which was broadcast live on national radio. She praised the achievements of women in American education and society, lauding the "pioneers" of the women's movement. In China, a woman's position had been previously measured by the social, economic, and political position of her husband, but "the Chinese woman of today stands on her own feet and is acknowledged for what she is." She overestimated the vocabularies of even Wellesley students when she warned: "Indehiscence and mawkish maunder will not equip us for our battle through life. . . . Yet within these very portals is the cenote of learning." Some newspapers mistakenly printed "keynote" instead of "cenote," which is an underground reservoir.

She did not believe in stooping to conquer. The recondite allusions sent newspaper reporters scurrying for their dictionaries and encyclopedias. Even her former English composition professor, Elizabeth Manwaring, was stumped by "obtund" (to dullen). When David Kung was asked why she used such obscure words in her speeches, he replied that those were the words that most exactly expressed what she meant to say, and she expected Americans to know what they meant. "It is Madame's conviction," he said, "that those critics underestimate the intelligence of the masses."

The next day she incited a national fashion furor when she appeared for a campus stroll wearing dark blue slacks, comfortable walking shoes, and a long beaver coat, topped by a stylish blue wool cap with her Chinese air force wings pinned on it. Flanked by Lieutenant Commander McAfee and fedora-wearing burly Secret Service men scurrying to keep up with her brisk pace, Wellesley's most distinguished daughter confidently strode the snow-covered campus. McAfee, who was on leave from the navy for the occasion, wore a navy-blue uniform with skirt. "Her slacks have ruined our anti-slacks campaign," McAfee ruefully acknowledged afterward. Mayling quipped: "I was always told that Britannia ruled the waves, but now I know Wellesley rules the WAVEs."

"It is safe to say no other woman, and few men, made so profound an impression on the hearts and minds of the American people of this generation as has the gallant little First Lady of China," asserted the *Boston Post*. The paper compared her to Churchill during the Nazi bombing of 1940 and President Roosevelt in 1933, when the American economy was on the brink of collapse. A columnist joked, "If Madame is a product of Chinese beauty parlors, the Chinese in America are just wasting their time in the restaurant business." Her fan mail was running at over two thousand letters a day. One of Mayling's favorites was from the young children of an Austin, Minnesota, school, who wrote: "We think you are the most beautiful woman in the world."

The question of whether Mayling would visit Britain at the end of her U.S. tour was still hanging in the balance. His Majesty the king was unwilling to offer to host Madame Chiang at Buckingham Palace until she had accepted the invitation to visit Britain. Mayling's national, personal, and ethnic pride would not allow her to accept the invitation without advance guarantee that she would be accorded the same treatment as the American First Lady—in other words, be received by the palace. Neither side would give ground. The Foreign Office was anxious for her to visit Britain, for the benefit of Britain's relations with the U.S. as much as its ties with China. Much of the anti-British feeling in the U.S. on colonial questions had been stirred up by the Chinese, and if Madame Chiang could be mollified this agitation might cease.

Sir Horace Seymour, Britain's ambassador to China, believed that if Madame Chiang visited Britain and the visit were "well-staged," it would have "valuable results." Foreign Office mandarins debated raising the matter yet again with the obdurate palace. The king had made it "quite clear that he need not conform" to the model adopted on Eleanor Roosevelt's visit, during which she was a guest of the king and stayed with the royal family. The palace cited the technicality that Madame Chiang was not in fact the wife of a titular head of state—Chiang Kai-shek held a number of titles, but president was not among them. "The Americans are pathological about China, and keenly suspicious of any possible unfriendliness towards her on the part of others," Foreign Secretary Anthony Eden pleaded in a letter to the palace. "'I don't care if he wears a crown, he can't go kickin' my dawg aroun'' would be their reaction to any fancied slight to the Gallant Chinese Ally." The domestic repercussions would be no less troublesome, Eden noted. "No ordinary English man or woman will ever be made to understand that it wasn't wrong to treat Madame Chiang Kai-shek less well than Mrs. Roosevelt. Of the two, I should think the former is the more popular."

The king finally agreed that he would host Madame at either Buckingham Palace or Windsor Castle. But no reply was received from Madame Chiang. In March the Foreign Office complained about "laying the Palace at the feet of this tiresome woman," but recognized that the value of a visit outweighed considerations of royal dignity. "Admittedly her unexpected bad manners have put us in an awkward position vis-à-vis the Palace," wrote one official. "But in any case we should not allow Madame's discourtesy to deter us from trying to get her over here: once here she should . . . be handsomely treated, however distasteful the heaping of such coals of fire may be." Oxford proposed to confer an honorary degree if she visited Britain, and the Royal College of Surgeons elected her an honorary fellow in absentia, a rare honor. By May she had yet to respond to the invitation, pleading doctors' orders.

Chapter Fourteen

Backfire

There are a terrible lot of lies going around the world, and the worst of it is half of them are true.

—Winston Churchill

In China, there was a groundswell of pleasure and pride over Madame Chiang's warm reception in America. Spirits were buoyed, and confidence in her ability to get what China wanted, and expectations that she would, were high—whether it was aid for China, repeal of extraterritoriality in China and the Chinese exclusion laws in America, or recognition of China's "rightful position" among the United Nations. But in America, the tide began to turn. Something in the American psyche lent itself to building up idols, but once they were erected, an undercurrent surged beneath the hero worship that threatened to tear them down.

As Madame Chiang's speaking tour reached a crescendo, John S. Service, an American diplomat stationed in China, visited Washington. There he was asked to brief Roosevelt aide Lauchlin Currie on Chinese affairs. The son of China missionaries, Service spoke Chinese and had traveled extensively through China. In conversation with Currie he was extremely pessimistic and critical about the Kuomintang and praised the achievements of the Communists. Service was no Communist, but Currie, a secret Soviet agent, appeared keenly interested and indicated that he agreed with Service's views. He gave Service the impression that "the man across the street"—the White House was opposite Currie's offices—felt the same way. Roosevelt knew Edgar Snow, author of *Red Star Over China*, well, and was a friend of Evans Carlson, the marine colonel who sympathized with the Chinese Communists and wrote a book about his experiences with the Eighth Route Army, the name assigned to the Red Army when it joined the Nationalist armies in fighting the Japanese after the formation of the second United Front.

Currie expressed concern that Madame Chiang's visit was creating a "terrific furor" of propaganda favorable to the Kuomintang. He told Service something had to be done to "build a backfire" against all this publicity. Madame Chiang was going over Roosevelt's head and appealing directly to Congress, attacking the Allied strategy to defeat Germany first and Japan second. Currie arranged for Service to meet with renowned political columnist Drew Pearson in a little bar in the basement of the Hay-Adams Hotel. Pearson's nationally syndicated column, "Washington Merry-Go-Round," was a tremendously influential force in American journalism, largely because people fed him information. They met several times. Pearson had been to China and was a "hell of a good newspaperman," said Service, but he was "not terribly fussy or meticulous about details. Almost anything you gave to Drew would somehow get a little changed or garbled." Pearson's column grew increasingly acerbic on the subject of China.

Currie asked Service to talk to others as well, and to spread the word that the picture in China was not as rosy as depicted in the press. He also asked Service to send him letters and reports from China, as he felt that he was not being kept informed by the State Department. It was quite true that neither Madame Chiang nor her husband's government was all they portrayed themselves to be; nonetheless, it seems odd that Currie sought to undermine her image and that of the Chinese government, America's ally in the war, even as Roosevelt—publicly at least—sought to elevate China's standing in the world. Whether Currie's secret campaign to undermine Madame Chiang Kai-shek and the Chinese government was ordered by Moscow, arose of his own initiative, or was even undertaken at Roosevelt's behest is unclear, but he began to track Mayling's activities and collect information on her finances. On May 26, 1943, he noted that according to his source, checks totaling $370,000—funds Madame Chiang had collected on her tour for China relief efforts—had been turned over to her nephew, David Kung, who deposited them into his personal account in the U.S. On June 10, Currie's source told him that funds transferred to Madame Chiang's U.S. account to date amounted to $800,000.

The FBI had also been gathering information on her and her family since her arrival in America. The Soong family was "the most influential in all China and practically has a 'death grip' on that country," FBI director John Edgar Hoover, citing a "confidential source of unknown reliability," wrote in a January 15, 1943, memorandum. "The Soongs have been depicted as 'money mad' and their desire to secure additional funds appears to prompt their every move." The family was engaged in a "giant conspiracy" to divert Lend-Lease supplies into their own hands and earn huge profits. It was also alleged, Hoover wrote, that Madame Chiang was not the legal wife of the Generalissimo, who was married to a "very venerable woman who never appears in public." The Soong organization was said to be "very closely knit and ruthlessly operated. . . . Anyone 'getting out of hand' is either bought off or exterminated." The "double-dealing and double-crossing" activities of the Soong family were "notorious" in China. Madame Kung, the "brains" behind the group, was an "evil and clever" woman who directed the family from behind the scenes; T. V. Soong executed her ideas. "So closely welded is the Soong organization that everything happening in China must clear through at least one member of the family," Hoover wrote. Madame Kung's activities, which included hiring assassins, were well known among Chinese officials. "The fury of these officials resulting from the Soong manipulations is said to be equaled only by their contempt for the laxity by which the Americans have allowed themselves to be hoodwinked," Hoover wrote. Madame Chiang's purpose in coming to the U.S., informants contended, was not to seek medical treatment but to devise some means of moving funds that had been siphoned off from American aid back to China. Hoover related much other hearsay and vague tales, some of which were later recanted by the informants, or found to be inaccurate.

Another FBI report noted that the Japanese had announced over Hong Kong radio that T. V. Soong had $70 million in accounts at New York banks, Madame Kung had $80 million, and Madame Chiang had $150 million. The report cautioned, however, that Japanese sources "could be expected to mislead the public." Other informants told congressional sources that the Kungs, Soongs, and Chiangs had some $2 billion "hidden away for their own personal use."

Some of the allegations began to seep into the American press, but they were largely spread through gossip. Although supporters argued that Madame Chiang and her husband were the victims of a planned slander campaign, there was enough truth to some of the charges to lend credence to all of them. She was accused of being snobbish, extravagant, and living lavishly while her people starved. Much was made of reports that White House linens were not good enough for her. In fact, when her skin condition flared up, blotches of red welts broke out over much of her body, causing terrible itching. She could sleep only after applying oily lotions or treatments prescribed by doctors—in one case a black liquid coal tar was applied to the welt and coated with boric powder. "The reason I did not like to use other people's sheets was because the medication sometimes rubbed off and would cause a stain which is difficult to remove by ordinary washing," Mayling later explained to a friend. She used silk, produced in China, because linen and cotton aggravated her skin condition. To Americans, however, the idea of sleeping in silk sheets was the height of extravagance, particularly with wartime rationing in effect. After imports from Japan were cut off by the war, silk was commandeered to make parachutes, forcing millions of American women to do without stockings, as nylon stockings, a recent innovation, were not yet widely available.

Just as Mayling's American conquest by charm was in full swing, *Time* published a story about a terrible famine in Henan province in the magazine's March 22 issue. Correspondent Theodore H. White described "dogs eating human bodies by the roads, peasants seeking dead human flesh under the cover of darkness, endless deserted villages, beggars swarming at every gate, babies abandoned to cry and die on every highway." There were some three million refugees; five million were expected to die before the next harvest. White blamed the Chinese army for the catastrophe, saying it had collected a grain tax from farmers despite crop failures. The Chinese government, he charged, compounded the tragedy by failing to send food relief in time. Somehow the article reached New York uncensored, and astonishingly, Henry Luce let it run nearly untouched. Mayling was livid. She confronted Luce and demanded he fire White. The press baron refused. Currie's "backfire" had been ignited.

White left the Henan famine traumatized and depressed. In part as a result of what he witnessed in Henan, and in part based on years of close observation, the influential writer turned unrelentingly critical of the Nationalist Chinese government. He also reversed his position on Madame Chiang. "It would be impossible to exaggerate her loveliness," he had written in 1941. "No photograph does her justice because her beauty—aside from perfection of feature, a complexion that puts cosmetics to shame, and about the best figure in Free China—is electric, incandescent and internal. She is the spiritual engine of the New Life Movement . . . and she organizes most of the women's welfare work, the care of orphans . . . and general repairs of the human wreckage of war." But later he called her "a beautiful, tart and brittle woman, more American than Chinese, and mistress of every level of the American language from the verses of the hymnal to the most sophisticated bitchery. . . . Always stunning in her gowns, [she] could be as coy and kittenish as a college co-ed, or as commanding and petty as a dormitory house mother."

U.S. intelligence gathered stories circulating among Chinese in New York and Washington of Mayling's "extravagant purchases of forty pairs of shoes, $45,000 worth of furs." The behavior of the "Kung brats," especially Jeanette Kung, at the White House had damaged China's prestige in elite circles in the U.S. Many Chinese complained about the way Mayling's tour was being handled by the "Kunglets," who kept Dr. Wellington Koo, the Chinese ambassador, waiting three days to be allowed into "the Presence." Rumors grew rampant, but no one was willing to tell Mayling about the gathering storm. It was rumored that the U.S. government footed the bill for her prolonged hospital stay and other expenses related to her visit. The U.S. Treasury discovered $867,000 of American aid funds, evidently the relief checks that Madame Chiang was collecting on her tour, tucked away in the private bank accounts of members of her entourage. Pearl Chen, Madame's English-language secretary, told FBI agents that Madame "doesn't care a darn" for her husband except insofar as he helped her own position. She regarded him as a "great man," took pride in his achievements and her own role in helping to build him up as a national leader, but she did not love him.

Madame engaged the wife of C. T. Feng, Chinese consul general at San Francisco, as her official shopper during her trip. Mrs. Feng, a childhood friend, shopped for silks and woolens and other items at Saks Fifth Avenue, Bergdorf, and McCutcheon. During the three months she stayed with Mayling, she could not make any engagement in advance, a fact her acquaintances could not comprehend. One asked, "Why don't you stand on your own legs?"

Some Chinese embassy staff assigned to Madame Chiang resented her treatment of them. They were kept on round-the-clock duty. Even when there was absolutely nothing to do, she'd insist they remain outside her suite in case she needed them. They questioned the lavish entertainment bills and other expenses of her tour, especially at a time when people in China were starving. They faulted David Kung's "stupidity and bungling," terming him a "nitwit." They criticized Madame Chiang for prolonging her stay because it had greatly eroded the tremendous goodwill she had garnered in the early days of her visit.

Tensions were high within her entourage, and members often bickered. David Kung acted as majordomo but lacked the requisite public relations skills. Jeanette Kung competed with him for control, resulting in contradictory orders being given by the siblings. Blame for the confusion fell on press secretary Hollington Tong, who played "second fiddle" to Mayling's beloved niece and nephew.

Unaware of the growing tide of feeling against her, among both her own entourage and the American people, Mayling set off for Chicago in late March. Her five-car special train was met at Chicago's Union Station by a crowd of two thousand, held back with difficulty by police. As she stepped onto the platform, a spontaneous cheer erupted from the enthusiastic throng. At a packed press conference, she told reporters she felt "high, wide and handsome." Her easy use of American slang sparked laughter. Asked if she would see British foreign secretary Anthony Eden, then visiting the U.S., she replied she would be glad to meet him if they crossed paths. Did she know of Eden's postwar plans? He had not consulted her, she observed, drawing more laughs. When asked, she declared that China's most pressing need was "planes, planes and more planes." The only question that stumped her momentarily was one from a *Chicago Defender* reporter asking if she had any message for America's "Negroes." She paused and appeared puzzled. "Why should anyone differentiate," she asked, "between Negro newspapers and others? All are Americans who are born and reared in this country, aren't they? Isn't the United States a cauldron of races and peoples?"

Soon afterward she spoke to thousands in Chicago's Chinatown, and accepted a check for $65,587 collected from Chinese in Chicago, Detroit, Cleveland, and Milwaukee. When Anita McCormick Blaine, heiress to the McCormick reaper fortune, gave Mayling $100,000 of International

Harvester Company preferred stock certificates, Madame Chiang tearfully said she would use the income for her "warphans."

On March 22, Mayling was to address the people of Chicago at a rally in Chicago Stadium. On the eve of her speech, Churchill made a radio address in which he bluntly dismissed Mayling's call for the Allies to defeat Japan before Germany. He had resolved, Churchill said, not to tell "fairy tales." The war in Asia would be prosecuted with the aim of recovering lost imperial territories from the Japanese. This was a swipe at Roosevelt as well as Mayling, both fervent critics of colonialism. Adding sting to the message, he pointedly neglected to mention China as an ally or partner in postwar plans, promising only in a patronizing manner that China would be "rescued" from Japan. Churchill's slight toward China doubtless ended any thought Mayling may have entertained of visiting Britain.

Before the Chicago speech ten-year-old Abigail Ann Oleson of Downers Grove gave Madame Chiang a doll, handmade by her mother, for the children of China, saying "children in those bombed cities want their dollies." She also gave Madame a sockful of pennies collected from her schoolmates. The rally at Chicago Stadium, attended by twenty-three thousand people, resembled a revival meeting more than a political event. After the playing of the American and Chinese national anthems, the "Battle Hymn of the Republic" and "Swing Low Sweet Chariot" were sung. The Metropolitan Church Choir sang "Anchors Aweigh" and the "Marine Hymn," and these were followed by the Chinese Children's Rhythm Band and Tchaikovsky's Symphony No. 4 in F Minor. Speeches were made by the Chicago mayor, Illinois governor, and national chairman of United China Relief, and then, finally, Madame Chiang.

In her address, Mayling compared American isolationists to those who built the Great Wall of China. She gave Americans a lesson in their own history, from the Mayflower to the Thirteen Colonies, attempting to draw parallels between the two countries she called home, even comparing presidents Abraham Lincoln and Andrew Jackson to Chinese emperors who rose from peasant stock. "Though our two countries have widely varied . . . histories, cultures, and traditions, both recognize the inherent ability of the individual . . . to help mold the destiny of a nation."

In a hastily inserted riposte to Churchill's speech, she declared: "Today there are peoples and nations who are yet bent on trampling underfoot the inalienable rights and dignity of men. They have not the eyes to see that . . . in the wake of bursting bombs, there is a vision of a new world—a world founded on practiced justice and equality for all mankind." The purpose of the Atlantic Charter "was not to tantalize the sorely tried and staunch peoples, fighting against violence," but to create a better world based upon universal principles. She depicted China as yearning to be a part of the family of nations. The Chinese were fighting to help build the "mosaic of world civilization." The audience came to its feet at her impassioned finale, in which she told a Confucian fable on the meaning of faith. At her request the extraordinary spectacle closed with the hymn "Onward Christian Soldiers."

Mayling went directly to her special train, then set off to carry her gospel to the West Coast. At a brief dawn stop in rural Utah, seemingly all the local residents turned out to meet her. Madame Chiang was asleep in her compartment, but her maid emerged on the steps. A pack of some fifty children saw the maid and ran toward her, shouting, "There she is!" The woman knew no English, and simply smiled and nodded. Neither she nor the thrilled children knew that she was standing in for China's First Lady. At another stop the stationmaster's wife appeared with cookies at three in the morning. Secret Service men examined them for explosives or poison before Mayling served them with tea to the reporters traveling with her.

As she headed west her receptions became grander and grander, as each city tried to outdo the last. In San Francisco she was escorted into the city on a navy ship with Coast Guard cutters flanking it and a fire ship throwing out water displays. Tens of thousands of residents lined the streets. She made two addresses, one for the general public and one to Chinese residents. She met with unions of longshoremen, shipyard workers, and railroad workers. As Dr. Loeb had warned, her health was deteriorating under the strain; she suffered a fresh attack of hives, and tried at one point to cancel her engagements. The local Chinese community put up "a hell of a fight" to get her to go to Chinatown, and in the end she went.

The showmanship reached a pinnacle of extravagance—fittingly—in Los Angeles, where Mayling's train arrived at the start of April. Movie mogul David O. Selznick and his wife, Irene, were friendly with Henry Luce and his wife, Clare. Luce, national chairman of United China Relief, had named

Selznick the organization's Hollywood chairman. For Madame Chiang's visit, nothing less than a grand extravaganza of suitable majesty would do for the acclaimed producer of the epic film *Gone With the Wind*. The small, dark, fiery, and photogenic Madame Chiang was reminiscent of Scarlett O'Hara, and a leading lady ideally suited to Selznick, who felt the drama of history through the lives of heroines. Working day and night, he threw himself into preparations.

On April 4, 1943, under blue California skies, the Hollywood Bowl was packed with a capacity crowd of over thirty thousand for the star-studded pageant that was to unfold—the grand finale of Madame Chiang's tour. Like most Selznick productions, the event started late and ran slow. Squadrons of bombers flew overhead. Actress Mary Pickford presented Mayling with flowers. The national anthems of the two countries were played. The Methodist bishop of California led the invocation. A symphonic narrative of China specially composed for the occasion was played. "These hands—a woman's hands—have helped to shape a nation's destiny," narrated actor Walter Huston. "This heart—a woman's heart—whispers a simple woman's hope, and all the world must pause and heed." If listeners' patience was not tried by this point, surely it was by the time Madame Chiang had finished her forty-five-minute speech, the longest and most impassioned of her tour.

She recited painful memories of six years of war: a young boy twitching with the excruciating pain of a stomach wound, clutching at her coat and begging for water; the "nightmare" of running the hopelessly out-gunned Chinese air force; the heartbreak of sending inexperienced cadets up in the air, knowing many would not return. She related in grisly detail the Rape of Nanking. Japanese troops "molested our women and rounded up all able-bodied men, tied them together like animals, forced them to dig their own graves and finally kicked them in and buried them alive." She lashed out at skeptics of China's "magnetic strategy," the intention of which was to "make the enemy pay, and pay dearly, for every inch of land they wrested from us so that in time we would wear them out. . . . What other people in the modern world has endured the agonies of war for so long and so bravely, held so tenaciously and so staunchly to the defense of principles as the Chinese people?"

Chinese and American flags bedecked the city. Children skipped school to see her. As Madame Chiang's motorcade passed by, hundreds of women, overcome by emotion, cried and dabbed their eyes with handkerchiefs. She was fêted by Hollywood's great and good, including Orson Welles, Marlene Dietrich—who hovered at her side—Joan Bennett, Luise Rainer, Anna May Wong, Gary Cooper, and Fred Astaire. In a meeting with studio chiefs, she urged them to portray China more realistically in their films. The plea evidently fell on some deaf ears, for Jack Warner of Warner Bros. Studio opened a speech at a Chinese war relief dinner in Madame Chiang's honor by quipping, "Hey, you guys reminded me! I gotta get my laundry!" Selznick and wife Irene treated her to a private showing of the movie he had made of the Hollywood Bowl extravaganza. He later sent her 182,000 multivitamin tablets for Chinese children.

But beneath the adulation an undercurrent of criticism continued to grow. Although Mayling was showered with praise, there was also growing cynicism and resentment. This was in part caused by her misjudgment of American wartime sensibility. Her much-publicized wardrobe, complete with jewels and fur coats, compounded by the reports of her silk sheets, large entourage, and royal demeanor, did not jibe with Americans' love of public figures who appeared to be homespun everymen, however false that impression might be. Snide comments about Mayling began to appear in print, and a constant source of criticism stemmed from the fact that in behavior and dress she did not reflect the poverty to which she pleaded. Her reputation was not improved by the fact that during her tour she often received lady callers in bed, propped up by embroidered silk pillows, wearing a quilted silk jacket and with a Chinese quilt over her lap. Men she received lying on a chaise lounge or divan in her suite.

Eleanor Roosevelt later wrote that Madame Chiang was "mystified" at how the First Lady could travel with only her secretary, "Tommy" Thompson, while Mayling needed dozens of staff. "She asked Tommy who packed our bags, and Tommy said she packed hers and I packed mine." Mayling then asked who answered the telephone, and Tommy replied that whoever was nearer the phone did and that often Eleanor pretended to be Tommy. Who took care of correspondence and the clothes? she wondered. The mail they did jointly and if a dress needed pressing, the hotel did it. But what was most incomprehensible to Mayling was how Mrs. Roosevelt could travel without security.

Two books by the Chinese first couple were published in America in

April 1943. His was *All We Are and All We Have*—a biblical reference—a collection of his wartime speeches. The author was "a soldier with a scholar's mind and a philosopher's heart," the *New York Times Book Review* enthused, adding that "every American" should read the book. Madame Chiang's volume of speeches and writings, *We Chinese Women*, was described by the same reviewer as reflecting the "gentle, amiable soul of a woman . . . decisive and dynamic." The author was "an ardent feminist," a stateswoman, and "one of the world's most outstanding women," the reviewer wrote breathlessly. "She cherishes her ideals and her principles and her love of mankind. She represents the liberal thinking of all countries. She and the Generalissimo combine to make the perfect couple." If Chiang's speeches had been as widely read as *Mein Kampf,* the reviewer ventured implausibly, world events "might have taken a different turn."

Meanwhile another book by Chiang, *China's Destiny,* had recently become a best-seller in China. Largely ghostwritten by associates, the book was soon branded "China's *Mein Kampf.*" The Chinese Communists denounced it as "comprador-feudalist fascism." The U.S. State Department was concerned at the book's violently anti-Western slant and the fact that it claimed as China's rightful territory a vast swath of the Far East. Beginning with a history of China's victimization under foreign—largely British—oppression, the book proceeded to examine how China would fulfill her destiny as a great world power. A chapter was devoted to the Three People's Principles Youth Corps, Chiang's answer to the Hitler Youth. In China the book became a textbook in schools and colleges. Due to its unapologetically antiforeign and irredentist rhetoric, the State Department banned its publication in the U.S.

Another controversial book appeared in the U.S. at the same time. Madame Wellington Koo, the pampered and enormously wealthy wife of the Chinese ambassador to Britain, wrote a tell-all memoir whose publication was abruptly canceled due to State Department pressure, but four hundred review copies had already been sent out. Blithely oblivious to the bloodshed and suffering of her countrymen, let alone around the globe, the author made much about her fabulous life of wealth and privilege. Mayling was livid and demanded that her husband call his ambassador in Britain to account. The Chinese government spent a small fortune buying up all copies that could be found, but the damage had been done.

Willkie's book *One World* was published in early April 1943, reportedly with the editorial assistance of his mistress, Irita Van Doren. Based on his trip, it was a manifesto for postwar America. With its homespun appeal—and glowing portrayal of Madame Chiang—the book received enthusiastic reviews and was wildly successful, eventually selling three million copies. Twentieth Century–Fox bought the movie rights and enlisted Spencer Tracy to play Willkie, but no film was made. Soon after the book's publication it appeared that Mayling fell out with Willkie, for on April 19 he sent her a cryptic one-line cable: "The gospel according to Hoyle prescribes that angels don't throw cards and the[y] should pay their debts." Its admonishing tone suggests that she may have lost her temper with him over something. She later privately told Roosevelt that Willkie was a "perpetual adolescent." Nothing more was heard of her bizarre proposal to Cowles. Churchill later said that Willkie reminded him of a "Newfoundland dog rushing into the water, coming out again, shaking himself, jumping up on the ladies and putting his paws on their shoulders, wagging his tail and sweeping all the dishes off the table at the same time."

On concluding her cross-country tour in mid-April, Mayling returned to New York and retreated to her sister Madame Kung's house on the Hudson, in the Riverdale section of the Bronx. From there, to the annoyance of Britain, she made a statement in which she called on the "Four Great Powers"—as she called the Allies—to form a postwar council that would "impartially administer former colonies that might need a transitional period between subjugation and freedom." Adding insult to injury, she called for Nehru to be freed, in order that he might throw India's political weight behind the Allied cause, because he was a man with "world vision." But Gandhi, also in prison, was "somewhat cloudy in his thinking and had no world vision because he was overcome by his restricted obsession for India's freedom regardless of world conditions," she said. Viceroy Linlithgow was outraged and demanded a formal protest to Chungking and the extraction of a promise of no more "mischievous statements" on Indian affairs. Eden suggested that Madame Chiang be reminded that Britain had scrupulously avoided public criticism of the "deplorable internal dissension" between the Nationalists and Communists in China that were undermining efforts against the common enemy. The reaction among Indians was no less heated. T. V. Soong forwarded to Mayling comments likening the idea of the U.S. intervening in India with Britain interfering between white and "colored" people in the U.S. Soong smoothed matters over by instructing Chinese diplomats in India to say that Madame Chiang was a "devoted friend" of the Indian people and they should not be taken in by "willful distortions" of her remarks.

Chiang and Mayling had enjoyed tremendous support in China and around the world in the early years of war with Japan, but by 1943 patience was wearing thin as the unpleasant realities of Chiang's rule were revealed. Gradually the Chinese Communists began to co-opt the underdog role and the Nationalists began to be viewed as oppressors. Supporters of the Nationalists believed that this change in world opinion was the result of an insidious international vilification campaign that had been mounted against Chiang, his wife, and his government, orchestrated by Moscow with the collusion of supposedly gullible Western liberals. According to this theory, eager American and British scribes helped to recast the Chinese Communists in the Western imagination as kind and gentle "agrarian reformers"— China's true democrats—while the Nationalists were beginning to be depicted as incompetent and thuggish despots. Chiang strenuously attempted to refute the former perception, which was by then beginning to gain wide currency. "The Chinese Communists are not socialists or liberal democrats as they have been said to be by their propagandists in Britain and America," he said. "It must be understood that all this kind of talk is designed to befuddle a credulous world."

The Trident Conference, held in Washington in May 1943, was the most important parley of top Allied command in the war to date. During Trident meetings, differences over strategy in the Far East were aired. Chiang sent Stilwell as his representative, instructing him to impress upon Roosevelt and Marshall the seriousness of the situation in China, and press once more for planes and war materials. Unfortunately Stilwell did not make a good impression on Roosevelt, and Chennault did not win many converts to his scheme for Japanese conquest by air. General Marshall asked Mayling to "help Stilwell," hinting that if Stilwell was forced to leave China, so would American aid. At the conference, Stilwell complained bitterly to Roosevelt about what he viewed as the poor quality of Chinese leadership, calling the Generalissimo a "vacillating tricky undependable old scoundrel who never keeps his word." Chennault countered with his view that Chiang was one of the world's greatest leaders and had never broken a commitment to him.

Roosevelt remained determined to keep China in the war at any cost. At Trident he ordered Marshall and the Joint Chiefs to give China's air defenses high priority. Supplies over the Hump were to be boosted to 7,000 tons a month, of which Chennault would get 4,750 tons and Stilwell 2,250. Stilwell was disgusted and believed Roosevelt had been taken in by Chiang. Marshall and the new chief of the U.S. Army Air Forces, Gen. Henry Arnold, were convinced that the technical challenges of airlifting huge quantities of supplies over the Himalayas to landlocked China were prohibitive, and moreover did not wish to increase Chennault's supplies at Stilwell's expense. Roosevelt was loath to anger the War Department, but neither did he wish to disappoint Chiang Kai-shek, so he came up with a typically crafty Rooseveltian solution. He met with Madame Chiang and offered her a "gold brick" he hoped she could peddle to her husband—namely, none of the aid requested by Chiang and Chennault, but planes for the Chinese air force instead.

Sibling rivalry between Mayling and her brother T. V. was nearing a fever pitch. Throughout her time in the U.S., Madame Chiang had been laboring to persuade Hopkins and the president that she and she alone had the ear of the Generalissimo and that all communications should be channeled through her, not her brother, the foreign minister. After Roosevelt made his counteroffer, Mayling strode triumphantly into Soong's opulent V Street offices at China Defense Supplies—the company he had set up to administer China's allotment of Lend-Lease supplies—and trumpeted, "I have won for China; I have got the Generalissimo everything he wants!" T. V. Soong quickly drew her into his office, where they remained closeted for an hour. She stalked out angry and chagrined. Soong's staff begged him to ask Chiang to veto the deal his wife had struck with Roosevelt. Soong, who still feared Chiang, was acutely aware that the situation was fraught with danger and at one point even shed tears. If Chiang contradicted his wife before the American president it would be felt as a blow to Chiang's prestige, incur Mayling's wrath, and spark speculation that Soong was attempting to advance his own position at the expense of his little sister's. Ultimately, he did contact Chiang, who cabled Roosevelt to the effect that his wife was not authorized to negotiate on his behalf and that he stood by his request of increased supplies over the Hump as well as more fighter planes and bombers for Chennault's American Volunteer Group. Roosevelt agreed.

On May 20, 1943, T. V. Soong joined the president, Churchill, who was visiting Washington, British ambassador Lord Halifax, and others in a meeting of the Pacific War Council. Roosevelt said that measures were being taken to triple air cargo over the Hump to enable Chennault to increase his forces. Churchill said he was prepared to send three squadrons of pursuit planes. Churchill complained that Chinese troops were mobilized for action against Tibet, provoking in "that independent country a very great alarm." Soong reminded the prime minister of treaties with Great Britain in which Tibet was acknowledged to fall under Chinese sovereignty. Halifax interjected to ask if he didn't mean "suzerainty." Soong asserted that Tibet was a part of the Chinese Republic, a religious hierarchy and not an independent country. Churchill said, "We ourselves are not interested in Tibet; it is a bleak, forbidding country. We are only anxious that energies not be dissipated; they should be concentrated against the common enemy."

As to the war, Churchill said: "We must recognize that Burma is very difficult jungle country. The Japanese are better fitted to withstand the hardships of these conditions than white troops." Soong replied that it would be "catastrophic" for China if it were found that Britain had reneged on the Casablanca commitment to recapture Burma. Churchill replied, "There was no commitment." Soong grew heated and insisted that the accord was presented as definite and that a conference was subsequently held in Calcutta to discuss details. Churchill replied: "These were only plans; there was no decision." Soong later conceded that, where China's vital interests were concerned, "it may be that I do not control my language," but added that the "promised relief of China should be honored." Roosevelt conceded to Soong that Churchill "really was provocative yesterday." Churchill subsequently proposed a limited operation in North Burma, but Chiang insisted on an offensive that would tackle the entire country. On May 25 Roosevelt told Soong he had been "working on this . . . proposal for the last two nights sitting with Winston until 2:30 a.m. but finally I convinced him and got him committed."

*   *   *

Even as Mayling basked in the glory of what she later recalled as "the days of great China consciousness," during which her country was "swamped" with praise, "some much deserved, [some] undeserved," she reminded herself that the "stress of emotions and of great tension in times of war lent an atmosphere of unreality and artificiality that saturated all, their demands of epic proportions because of their suspected and real transiency, and therefore more cruel or generous as the mood of the moment dictated." The mood was beginning to shift.

Pearl S. Buck was another influential figure who was growing disillusioned with the Nationalist regime. She warned Henry Luce in late March 1943—soon after White's article about the Henan famine ran in *Time*—that she was "fearful that certain dark possibilities now looming in China will materialize and cause undue disillusionment and pessimism about China over here." She offered an article on China to *Life* magazine. Luce agonized over whether to publish Buck's article. In a memo to senior staff, he indulged in some uncharacteristic soul-searching: "I do not want to be found guilty of having misled the American people—bringing their friendship for China to the 'verge of sentimentality' which will 'inevitably end in disillusionment'. . . . But there is a very real question whether Pearl's article would not do much more harm than good." He eventually decided to run the piece.

In her article, Buck called for increased aid to China but pulled no punches in describing the current situation there. Freedom of speech was stifled by a conservative and corrupt bureaucracy. Chiang Kai-shek was still respected as the nation's leader, but a question mark hung over how effectively he would be able to deal with the country's "evils" and bring about democracy. "We are in the process of throwing away a nation of people who could and would save democracy with us but who, if we do not help them, will be compelled to lose it because they are being lost themselves," Buck concluded.

By the time Buck's article was published on May 10, 1943, patience with Mayling was wearing thin in the White House. This was not helped by a contretemps between her and Churchill that arose during his visit to Washington. Churchill was the scion of an aristocratic British family whose mother was an American beauty, the former Jeanette Jerome, whose father was once editor of the *New York Times*. The cigar-smoking British prime minister was a man of phenomenal energy and brilliance. He was also an unabashed racist. "To the President, China means four hundred million people who are going to count in the world of tomorrow, but Winston thinks only of the color of their skin," Churchill's personal physician, Lord Moran, wrote. "It is when he talks of India or China that you remember he is a Victorian." When Roosevelt once argued that it was better to be friends than enemies with China, Moran recalled, Churchill listened in silence, but afterward privately spoke scornfully of "little yellow men."

Churchill asked to see Madame Chiang in Washington, where he was staying as Roosevelt's guest at the White House. Mayling pleaded indisposition and invited him to come to New York to see her. Churchill in turn pleaded pressing business in the capital, which prevented him from going to New York. In an attempt to resolve the impasse, Roosevelt invited Mayling to dine with him and Churchill at the White House, but she balked. T. V. Soong begged his recalcitrant sister to make the trip to Washington to meet Churchill. On May 18 Soong saw the president, who again inquired if Mayling would attend the luncheon. "My dear Sister," Soong wrote, "These are fateful days for China and for the Chinese people. Therefore I feel Chiang Kai-shek is right in urging that you see Churchill during his present trip. Churchill really is physically unable to come to New York, and the President's idea of giving a luncheon for you both is an excellent way out." He continued, "The part you have played and are still called upon to play in moulding Chinese relations with the Western world is a matter of historic record. In this critical time in our history it is most important that we keep on friendly relations with the British and you could make a real contribution now. Affectionately yours." But Mayling ignored her brother's plea. On May 21 Churchill wrote Anthony Eden:

> Madame Chiang Kai-shek who has taken a floor at the Ritz [in fact it was a suite at the Waldorf-Astoria] in New York is a problem here. The President invited her to luncheon for today Friday as she had expressed a desire to meet me. The lady gives herself royal airs and considers herself co-ruler of China and in consequence she replied that it was necessary for me to go and see her.

I very much regret pressure of serious business here has and will prevent my undertaking the journey to New York. The President could not understand why she should consider an invitation from himself as Head of the State as in any way derogatory. Mr. T. V. Soong considers she is behaving like a spoilt child. Apparently she demanded to be present at the military discussions and is much offended with her husband for telegraphing that Soong alone would speak for China. The Soong family oligarchy is a strange arrangement. Madame Chiang is always accompanied by an extremely masculine niece dressed as a boy. She is considered to have long outstayed her welcome here.

Frances Gunther dined with Mayling at her suite in the Waldorf Towers on May 23. Mayling told Gunther she was exhausted. For the first time in her life she had drank whiskey straight, and it made her feel "queer." She swore Gunther to secrecy and told her conspiratorially that Churchill had asked to see her and she had refused, once again. She told him he could come to New York if he wished to see her. She insisted she "would not kow-tow." She looked healthier than she had when Gunther had seen her in January, but still showed "great strain in her eyes," and still could not sleep without pills, she told Gunther. After some discussion of their feelings for Nehru and their husbands, Mayling told Gunther she had learned that "One went through everything alone [in life]—Therefore to live [one had] to have one's own self-respect—Not to try to please others or to sell out."

Churchill and Roosevelt lunched without Mayling the next day, May 24, in the president's study. The prime minister launched into one of his favorite themes—joint citizenship between the British Empire and the United States—recalled Vice President Henry Wallace:

[Churchill] said the Anglo-Saxons were superior and they should not be apologetic about it. . . . He himself was half-American and he felt he was called on as a result to serve the function of uniting the two great Anglo-Saxon civilizations in order to confer the benefit of freedom on the rest of the world. I suggested it might be a good plan to bring in the Latin American nations so that the citizens of the New World and the British Empire could all travel freely without passports. Churchill did not like this. He said if we took all the colors on the painter's palette and mixed them up together we'd get just a smudgy grayish brown.

Mayling's behavior subsequently grew increasingly odd and incomprehensible. On June 2, she failed to appear at a two-thousand-head dinner in her honor hosted by the *Churchman,* America's most important religious journal—even though she was staying at the Waldorf Hotel where the event was being held. "Let's hope she keeps it up," penned one Foreign Office mandarin sourly. Another noted, "Disillusionment about China and Mme Chiang is spreading in the U.S. . . . . Her presence there has more 'nuisance value' than propaganda value." In conversation with Congressman Walter Judd Roosevelt called her China's "prima donna" and said it would be best if she returned to China soon so that "these irritations might subside."

In mid-June she visited Ottawa, where she mystified Canadian parliamentarians with an obscure discourse on the roots of democracy and statements such as "Ochlocracy . . . is but the inchoate rococo of mob rule bred in febrile emotions and unrestraint." Germany, she said, was ruled by a "demoniac Mephistopheles nurturing persecution and miasmic hate." But she was greeted enthusiastically and left with checks for aid to China collected by the Red Cross. She next proceeded to Georgia. Her train arrived a half hour late when she stopped in Atlanta en route to Macon to receive an honorary degree from Wesleyan College. She posed for photographers while a navy musician played "Dixie" on an accordion. "I feel as if I am coming back to my home state," she told a large crowd that had turned out to greet her, including Governor and Mrs. J. G. Arnall. "Forgive me for being late, but you know it is an old Southern custom."

Twelve hundred Wesleyan alumnae and thousands of VIPs from across the state—not to mention some six hundred military police from nearby army camps, reinforcements of police detectives, plainclothesmen, and Secret Service men—descended on Macon to get a glimpse of the famous guest. The college had been spruced up to look its best for Mayling's visit. She delivered the final address of her American tour, broadcast nationwide.

She was lauded as a "living symbol of the courageous spirit of the new China" and a "world Christian leader."

"I feel that in coming back to Wesleyan, I am just coming back to the old folks at home," she declared, adding that she wished her sisters could be there too. She praised their efforts in the war and their work in organizing Chinese women. "Whenever we three sisters are able to meet, we sit and chat about our Southern friends whom we feel to be almost members of our own family," she told her audience, which included her childhood tutors, mentors, and friends. "What an influence their lives had in the direction of our education, and what good they wrought for the world." Octavia "Tava" Domingos, a student and Wesleyan president Strickland's daughter, presented flowers to Mayling, who kissed them as she accepted the bouquet. Domingos later said, "No, you can't clean this dress! That's where Madame Chiang touched it!"

In June David Kung received funds from Mayling to open an office in New York to handle her correspondence and perform other work following her imminent return to China. Initially Kung—branded a "scatterbrain" by a Chinese diplomat—planned to open a posh office in the Time-Life Building in Rockefeller Center, but lacking the necessary funds he scaled the plan down to a small office and put a friend in charge while he finished his studies at Harvard. Kung asked an American woman working on Madame's staff during her tour to be secretary in the new office. She refused, she told FBI agents, because "I hate his guts and so does everybody else." Jeanette Kung, she said, had made advances toward her and was an "insufferable pig." The Kung children tested the patience of even the long-suffering Hollington Tong, one of Chiang's most loyal officials. Tong was "fed up" with the trip and Chinese politics and was considering resigning from government service. He was especially tired of being pushed around, brushed off, and insulted by the Kungs.

In late June 1943, shortly before her return to China, Mayling met with Roosevelt. He told her that Formosa, called Taiwan by the Chinese, and the Pescadores off the east coast of China would be returned to China after the war but that the U.S. should have a base there, subject to Chinese approval. Not until the eve of her departure did the Chinese ambassador formally inform the British government that she would not travel to Britain. Mayling later expressed regret that she had been unable to visit England due to doctors' advice.

Mayling's return on July 4, 1943, in time for the sixth anniversary of the beginning of war against Japan, was to be an inauspicious homecoming. She was airsick on the trip home via Natal, South Africa, and India. "The weather was rough as the devil and she was in a pretty bad way. She didn't say a word the entire trip," said one of the American pilots after the fifteen-thousand-mile journey. While they were flying home over Japanese-occupied Burma, her plane had an encounter that "nearly left us guests of the Japanese imperial government," she later told reporters. In bad weather, the pilot tried to get a radio bearing on an airfield in the vicinity. He got signals from what appeared to be an American base in Assam, India, and began to head in that direction, but became suspicious and headed elsewhere. They later learned the signals were coming from a field in Burma occupied by the Japanese.

Mayling's travel plans were kept so secret that even her husband knew only the date, and not the location, of her arrival. He flew to Chengdu, expecting to meet her at the airport there, but she had landed at Chungking. Shortly after takeoff, his plane nearly collided in midair with his wife's, which was approaching for landing. Unaware that she was in the plane, he proceeded to Chengdu, where he learned that she had landed at Chungking. He was furious that he had not been informed of her schedule, which had apparently been kept secret for security reasons. He ordered his pilot to return immediately to Chungking. The pilot approached the airfield at Chungking from the downriver side and landed downwind without circling —in violation of regulations—no doubt because Chiang had ordered him to hurry. At the same time, another plane belonging to the Commission on Aeronautical Affairs, piloted by the commission's best pilot, came in for a landing in the proper direction, against the wind. Just before touching down, the commission's pilot spotted the other plane coming directly toward him and was able to swiftly pull up in the air again to avoid a head-on collision. He was carrying on the commission's plane Chiang's son, Ching-kuo, who was coming from Guilin for a family reunion.

Mayling, meanwhile, was stranded at Chungking airport with no one to greet her but two American airfield attendants who pulled up to the plane in a station wagon. Jeanette Kung hopped down from the plane and said, "Where the hell is everybody?" She helped Mayling, by now in tears, into the car. Then she grabbed the American mechanic driving the car by the arm, yanked him out, took the wheel herself, and drove away.

The Generalissimo was livid. The next day he summoned General Zhou Zhirou, by now head of the commission, and Colonel Wang, managing director of China National Aviation Corporation, a Sino-American joint venture airline, although CNAC had nothing to do with the incidents. Chiang severely chastised Wang, who had no prior knowledge of the mishaps, said he ought to be shot, and threatened to call in his guards. Finally Chiang decided to have Wang arrested and court-martialed instead—a certain death sentence. A Massachusetts Institute of Technology graduate, Wang was seen as honest and efficient, and was perhaps China's best aeronautical engineer. While awaiting arrest, he sat in his office reading the entry on the Magna Carta from the Encyclopedia Britannica, in particular the article stating that no free man may be detained without the lawful judgment of his peers. Mayling intervened and with H. H. and Madame Kung finally prevailed on Chiang to rescind the arrest order. Wang's punishment was commuted to a "great demerit" and he was forced to resign.

Soon after, Mayling's arrival scene was reenacted with pomp and circumstance in front of movie cameras. News of the death of Lin Sen, China's nominal president, had been kept secret pending her return so a triumphal celebration could be held for her, as according to Chinese etiquette such a reception would have been exceedingly bad form in light of the respected Lin's death. After an appropriate interval, Lin's death was announced, although he had in fact departed this world weeks before Mayling's return.

Mayling told reporters she was given an "enormous spiritual lift" by the "spontaneous goodwill" she encountered from Americans, but in truth she had overstayed her welcome, and her prolonged visit to America may have done more harm than good.

Chapter Fifteen

In the Shadow of the Pyramids

American public disillusionment in regard to China, if and when it occurs, may be so great that it may becloud China's virtues in the minds of China's friends.

—American diplomat, 1943

After Madame Chiang's return to China in July 1943 the correspondents who saw her found her with something of an anti-American bias, because she had not obtained from the U.S. government all that she wanted. Her frustration, and the feeling that she had failed in her mission, was heightened by a barrage of articles in the American media criticizing China—even if much of the criticism was not unjustified. She was upset by Pearl Buck's *Life* magazine article, which was in fact quite muted. Hardly had Mayling returned to China when Hanson Baldwin, a respected *New York Times* military analyst, wrote an influential article stating that the Chinese were magnifying Sino-Japanese skirmishes into large battles.

Madame Chiang was subsequently deeply agitated by an article by Nathaniel Peffer in the *New York Times Magazine* critical of China in general and herself in particular. Other negative articles by T. A. Bisson in the influential journal of the Institute of Pacific Relations and *Far Eastern Survey* were followed by another Baldwin article in the August issue of *Reader's Digest*, entitled "Too Much Wishful Thinking About China," which raised the old argument that China was "not a nation but a geographical expression." China's military leaders were merely warlords in new clothing, Baldwin argued, and China could not be counted on militarily. Whether Baldwin's and Bisson's status as secret Soviet agents had any bearing on their views is unclear, given that other analysts who did not have Soviet or

Communist ties expressed similar views. In any event their articles were widely read and had repercussions in China and in the U.S.

Mayling poured out her bitterness to T. V. Soong, who remained in Washington, in a letter complaining that the Tenth Air Force, headquartered in New Delhi, was holding up China-bound personnel, equipment, and supplies desperately needed by Chennault's Fourteenth Air Force. She demanded an end to China's "subservience" to the Tenth Air Force and insisted that an independent air command be established. The telegram was so harsh that Chiang initially had it canceled at the time of dispatch.

Mayling maintained contact with Willkie after she returned to China, but the tone of her letters was formal. "I shall never forget the delightful chats we had together while you were in the United States and also your little lectures," he wrote her in August 1943. "[One] of these days when the stresses of the present have passed, I shall give you equally good lectures in return. Seriously, I think you know how much I am concerned for you yourself personally and your cause." Willkie made a run for the presidency in 1944, withdrawing after a crushing defeat in the Wisconsin primary. Roosevelt asked him to join the Democratic ticket as his vice presidential running mate, but Willkie turned down the offer. Shortly before the election, he died of a heart attack, at age fifty-two. "I did not know Mr. Willkie well or for long but recall him as a man of great sincerity," Mayling later wrote, praising him for his "worldwide vision" and "qualities of a great statesman."

In October 1943 an Allied meeting was to be held in Chungking as Admiral Lord Louis Mountbatten, who as head of Combined Operations had overseen the British Commandos, took over as supreme Allied commander for Southeast Asia. Arriving in Chungking ahead of the meetings, Mountbatten immediately embarked on an all-fronts charm offensive to woo Madame Chiang's crucial support. Mayling told the polo-playing British admiral that she made up her mind quickly about people and had made up her mind to be his friend. Mountbatten scored points with the Generalissimo too, by telling him that he had come "straight on to Chungking without even waiting to set up my staff in Delhi, because I felt it was essential for so young and comparatively inexperienced an officer as myself to seek the advice of so renowned a soldier at the earliest possible moment." Chiang took this "very well," Mountbatten reported.

Chiang had meanwhile grown ever more annoyed with Stilwell, and in the autumn of 1943 had asked T. V. Soong to press Washington for the prickly general's recall. Stilwell had taken to calling Chiang "Peanut"—and worse—behind his back. Already angered by the fact that the war in China had been relegated to a distant second after the war in Europe in the minds of Allied command, Chiang felt further humiliated by the fact that he was not trusted enough by Roosevelt to be given unambiguous authority in his own country. Soong initiated a campaign at his end, but unknown to him Mayling and Eling started one of their own in Chungking, aimed at keeping the acid-tongued general widely known as "Vinegar Joe." Mayling reminded her husband that Marshall had threatened to cut off aid to China if Chiang could not get along with Stilwell. The sisters wooed the unsuspecting Stilwell mercilessly, inviting him to teas, boosting his ego, and generally trying to win him over so that he would be more cooperative with China's war aims. Mayling commiserated with Stilwell over the difficulties they both had in handling the Generalissimo. After a particularly strenuous effort to persuade her obstinate husband of something, Mayling reported despairingly to Stilwell: "I've prayed with him; I've done everything but murder him."

The sisters' campaign was an unqualified success. Soon Stilwell was eating from the hands of the "two intelligent dames," calling them "May" and "Ella" and terming them his "fellow co-conspirators." He nicknamed Mayling "Snow White" and thought she should be made China's minister of war. Stilwell did not realize the sisters had a hidden agenda. According to Joseph Alsop, an aide to Chennault and an intimate observer of the elaborate pantomime, their plan was for Stilwell to undermine T. V. Soong in the eyes of the Generalissimo and to thereby boost the fortunes of H. H. Kung. When Chiang wavered, the sisters seized the offensive. Stilwell was told that he could be restored into Chiang's good graces if he would only be humble and admit his errors. On October 17 Stilwell saw Chiang and "put on the act." Chiang lectured him on the duties of a subordinate to his commanding officer, and chastised him for treating the Chinese arrogantly. "This was all balderdash, but I listened politely," Stilwell wrote in his diary.

On the eve of the Allied meeting Soong returned to Chungking triumphant, bearing a promise extracted with great effort from the White House that Stilwell would be recalled if Chiang so requested. But on the morning of October 18, Chiang informed Soong that he had changed his mind. Soong lost his temper and gave the Generalissimo a severe tongue-lashing. Infuriated, Chiang shattered a teacup and threatened to have Soong shot. Soong returned from the confrontation "in a state of serious emotional collapse" and burst into tears as Alsop tried to console him. T. V. retained his job as foreign minister, but under virtual house arrest. Soong's capable protégé, Pei Tsu-yi, was replaced as head of the Bank of China by H. H. Kung, and the economy began to deteriorate as a result. Wherever Soong went he was followed by a detachment of gun-toting "goons." Soong once said of Madame Kung, who was behind the machinations: "If elder sister had been a man, the Generalissimo would have been dead, and she would have been ruling China fifteen years ago."

Shortly after the Allied meeting, Churchill sent a personal representative to be based in Chungking in an effort to improve acrimonious Sino-British relations. Gen. Sir Adrian Carton de Wiart was a Brussels-born, Oxford-educated soldier-turned-diplomat who had fought in the Boer War and the First World War. Tall, with an eye patch and an armless sleeve fastened to his side, the much-decorated Carton de Wiart's military exploits were legendary. He was the ideal man to patch up ties with the Generalissimo.

Carton de Wiart quickly sized up the American commander. "Stilwell is most friendly, but I cannot somehow feel sure of him," he wrote Mountbatten. "He abuses the Chinese wholeheartedly from the Generalissimo downwards, says he is nothing but a coolie, and should be treated as such. . . . It is ridiculous to think that one can treat a man who has risen to the position the Generalissimo has, as if he were a coolie." He concluded Stilwell could not be trusted. "On the surface he is all honey, underneath a particularly vile form of vinegar," he wrote Churchill's chief of staff.

In late November 1943 Mayling accompanied her husband to Cairo for a wartime summit with Roosevelt and Churchill. "Uncle Joe," as Roosevelt called Stalin, would be dealt with later in Teheran. As Russia had not declared war against Japan, it was too awkward to bring the Chinese and Soviet leaders together at Cairo. Before departing for the Middle East,

Mayling suffered bouts of dysentery and influenza and developed iritis in her left eye, hampering her vision.

The Cairo summit came at a critical point in the war. Roosevelt feared a Chinese military collapse, but was determined to keep China in the war, holding the Japanese at bay at least until the war in Europe could be won. Tensions among the Allies were running high and competition for war materials was intense. All parties were anxious to protect and promote their own interests. Roosevelt's self-appointed role at the conference was to be "peacemaker."

The Chiangs were invited, as almost an afterthought, to the conference by the Nile at Roosevelt's insistence and over Churchill's vehement opposition. By this time Chiang was fast losing cachet, but Roosevelt needed the world to continue to see him as a great statesman and China as a major power, not least to play off a fractious Russia—and perhaps to keep the British in line. Chiang and Mayling believed that as China had been fighting fascist aggression the longest among the Allies, it was entitled to be treated as one of the so-called "Big Four" world powers. Chiang continued to trust Roosevelt's good intentions toward China, and his ability to make them come true. Despite China's presence, however, Churchill regarded Cairo as an Anglo-American meeting and Teheran as a meeting of the "three major Powers."

The conference was conducted in utmost secrecy with high security and a total ban on the press. The visiting heads of state were ensconced in luxurious villas in the Kasserine woods, a wealthy Cairo enclave. The meetings were held in the Mena House Hotel near the Pyramids. The entire area was surrounded by a tight cordon and bristled with troops and antiaircraft guns. Eight squadrons of British planes patrolled the skies.

Roosevelt landed at Cairo on the morning of November 22, 1943, to find both Chiang and Churchill waiting for him. To Churchill's dismay, the president wanted to meet with Chiang alone before meeting with the British. With Mayling interpreting, Roosevelt stressed the need to work out a postwar settlement between China and the Soviets and indicated that he assumed China would join in the occupation of Japan following the war. But in focusing on maintaining American control over the Pacific, he refused any discussion of a supreme Allied commander in that theatre.

On November 23 the conference opened with Mountbatten, backed by Marshall, Stilwell, and Admiral Ernest J. King, U.S. Navy chief, pleading the case for an operation to retake Burma. This was agreed upon in principle. The next day, the subject of Chinese participation in the Burma campaign was explored. Chiang was absent from the meeting without explanation. The Chinese demanded more air transports and supplies for the Burma operation. Marshall refused. When a Chinese general protested that supplies had been promised and China had "rights," Marshall lost his patience. "Now let me get this straight. . . . I thought these were American planes, and American personnel, and American material." The session ended inconclusively due to Chiang's absence in what was derided by one participant as "a ghastly waste of time."

At another meeting at which the Chinese were not present, Stilwell bluntly said the two greatest obstacles to prosecution of Allied strategy in China were the "medieval machinery of the [Chinese] War Ministry and the incompetence of the high command." Apart from this he thought the outlook was good, and he praised the junior officers. Marshall privately advised Stilwell to leave China because he had been "mistreated so" by the Chinese, but Stilwell wanted to stay. "Then stop your outrageous talking," Marshall ordered. Stilwell said he hadn't called Chiang "Peanut" openly. Marshall retorted, "My God, you have never lied. Don't now." Marshall did not know his protégé was writing far worse things to his wife.

Mayling's participation as the fourth "man" at the Cairo confab was unprecedented and viewed with disfavor in some quarters, particularly by the British. L. S. Amery, secretary of state for India and Burma, sarcastically referred to the Cairo conference as "the meeting of the [three] All-Highest (plus the feminine Super All-Highest)." Although she was not officially a delegate, she joined nearly all important discussions. As well as acting as her husband's interpreter, she frequently spoke for him. "If you allow me," she would break in, "I shall put before you the Generalissimo's real thoughts." She even joined in official portraits of the conference participants, and sat beside the three Allied leaders, as though she were one of them. "Little Lady at Big Conference" ran a *New York Mirror* headline.

When the British prime minister and Madame Chiang finally met, Churchill said, "You think I'm a terrible old man, don't you?" She replied, "I really don't know. You believe in colonialism and I don't." After a long talk he said: "Now tell me what do you think of me?" She replied: "I think your bark is worse than your bite." He was impressed by Chiang's "calm, reserved, and efficient" demeanor and found Madame a "remarkable and charming" personality. Mayling liked Churchill for his frankness, although she did not always agree with him. When he took her to task about her refusal of His Majesty's invitation to visit Britain, saying she should learn more about England as it was a very old country, she tartly retorted that he should visit China because it was an "even older country."

Mayling's eyes troubled her in Cairo, and she consulted the best eye specialists in the Middle East, but none could help. During the summit she had another attack of hives, so severe that she could not sleep. Although she had brought her own doctor with her, she asked Churchill's physician, Lord Moran, to examine her. When he finished she asked what was wrong with her. He replied, "Nothing," and said her health would improve only when "the strain of your life is relaxed." She told Moran he was one of the few honest doctors she had met.

During the Cairo talks the U.S. Congress passed the long-debated and long-awaited repeal of all Chinese exclusion laws. The bill was transported to a waiting plane after it went through the Senate to rush it to Cairo, where Roosevelt signed it as Madame Chiang looked on. With the right to become U.S. citizens and own property, the ghettoized bachelor society of Chinese in America would begin to shift to a community of families that would assimilate into the broader culture.

Churchill later complained that Chiang's presence undermined the conference. "The talks of the British and American Staffs were sadly distracted by the Chinese story, which was lengthy, complicated and minor," he wrote. "Moreover . . . the President, who took an exaggerated view of the Indian-Chinese sphere, was soon closeted in long conferences with the Generalissimo. All hope of persuading Chiang and his wife to go and see the Pyramids and enjoy themselves till we returned from Teheran fell to the ground, with the result that Chinese business occupied first instead of last place at Cairo."

Before departing, Chiang and Mayling asked Roosevelt for a $1 billion loan. Roosevelt declined. The Chiangs also demanded that Roosevelt furnish arms and equipment for ninety army divisions. He made a "flat promise" to equip thirty divisions immediately and another sixty later, without consulting the Joint Chiefs of Staff. Hopkins later commented to Roosevelt that he had promised them a great deal.

Stilwell met privately afterward with Roosevelt and reported that the president showed "considerable impatience with the procrastination and constant demands" of the Chinese, and that Roosevelt even went so far as to say that it "might be necessary to replace [Chiang] with a more active leader." Stilwell instructed his aide, Brig. Gen. Frank Dorn, to prepare a plan for the assassination of Chiang Kai-shek, with an airtight guarantee that no American agency or individual could be blamed. Stilwell would not reveal who ordered the plan, saying merely it "comes from the very top." Dorn prepared a plan but never heard anything further on the subject.

As Roosevelt had promised Mayling, the Allied leaders agreed at Cairo that the island of Formosa (Taiwan), would be handed over to Chiang Kai-shek and his government after the war. Although nothing more than a simple declaration of intent, the accord was to have profound and unexpected consequences for the future of Sino-American relations—and the island. The Cairo Declaration seemed innocuous but represented a victory for Chiang. It reflected Roosevelt's conviction of the value of a friendly, democratic, and prosperous China, blossoming into world-powerhood under the motherly wing of the United States. Roosevelt showed a draft of the Cairo Declaration to the Chinese first, making it awkward for a skeptical Churchill to push for changes.

Ironically, while the declaration called for the return of territories, including Manchuria and Formosa, to China, British hopes for a similar pledge to restore its colonies after the war were firmly quashed. Churchill's refusal to dismantle the British Empire strengthened Roosevelt's conviction that China must play an important role in the postwar world. He viewed colonialism as a dangerous anachronism, and assumed America would play a leading role in Asia, with China as junior partner. The president was suspicious of British designs in the Far East and had secretly "worked out an arrangement whereby he hoped to get the British out of Hong Kong," according to Vice President Wallace.

Despite his apparent coup at Cairo, Chiang was "filled with anxiety and apprehension." Churchill, he believed, was an incorrigible imperialist and did not want to see Manchuria, Formosa, and the Pescadores restored to China; neither did he wish the Cairo Declaration to call for Korean independence, lest it give India, Malaysia, and other British territories encouragement. Chiang was disappointed he did not get the billion-dollar loan, but he was mollified by the promise of a major offensive to recover Burma—a promise that would be unceremoniously retracted at Teheran just days later.

The Chiangs departed for China and Roosevelt and Churchill flew to Teheran, where Stalin spoke disparagingly of China and opposed her elevation to great-power status. He secretly pledged to join the war against Japan once Germany was defeated, but only on condition that tsarist privileges in Manchuria be restored to Russia after the war. Chiang was not consulted. The outcome of the Cairo-Teheran talks was that Buccaneer—the Southeast Asian offensive agreed on at Cairo—was called off in favor of Overlord—a major invasion of northern France—and other European initiatives. Although the organization of the postwar world was left vague, there was general agreement that there should be cooperation among the self-appointed "policemen." The concept of what was to become the United Nations was sketched out.

On arrival in Chungking Mayling took to her bed, so run-down that she was once again in danger of a "complete nervous breakdown." Nonetheless, at her husband's instruction, she summoned the energy to write Roosevelt to tell him that the effect on Chinese morale of the Cairo Declaration was "electric" and to praise him for his leadership and the "magnificent spirit permeating all that you are undertaking for the good of humanity." She reminded Roosevelt of his pledge to "speak to the Treasury" about $200 million in gold bars to stabilize the Chinese currency.

Mayling's appeal did not achieve the desired result, so in January 1944 Chiang renewed his call for a $1 billion loan. If it was not forthcoming, he threatened, China might be forced to stop contributing financially or militarily to the American war effort in China, and the U.S. would have to cover the expense of maintaining its forces in China at the official exchange rate of 20 Chinese dollars to the greenback. At that time a U.S. dollar bought 330 Chinese dollars on the black market. The cost of building airfields and feeding American troops at the official rate would be astronomical. "Tell them to go jump in the Yangtze River," Treasury Secretary Henry Morgenthau fumed to assistant secretary Harry Dexter White. "I am not going up on the Hill and ask the bastards for anything. [The Chinese] are just a bunch of crooks, and I won't go up and ask for one nickel." Morgenthau suggested that if the U.S. needed Chinese currency to build the airfields, funds could be raised by selling gold on China's black market.

Mayling's deteriorating health kept her from matters of state. In February 1944 she went to Kunming, hoping the dry climate and warm springs would "relieve me of the torture of sleepless nights" brought on by severe hives. After "two miserable weeks of agony" she discovered that the springs contained arsenic and went home. The doctors attributed her problem to nerves. "They are trying to find the root of the trouble, but so far have been unsuccessful," she wrote Eleanor Roosevelt. "I hope they will succeed soon because the irritation is far worse than any pain. I am terribly run down." In April her doctors told her the only hope of a cure was a complete rest, as the problem was caused by a "bad blood condition" brought on by "nervous strain." She had been taking injections sent by her doctors in New York, but they did not help.

The pressures on Mayling were enormous. Her pride was injured by a cascade of what she considered to be smears and attacks in the foreign press. She became hypersensitive to the remotest hint of criticism. Hardly had she returned from Cairo when a lively tell-all book by Ilona Ralf Sues, who had worked for her in the late 1930s, was published in America to great acclaim. Sues's book, *Shark's Fins and Millet,* described Mayling as a "sparkling political cocktail—radical by nature, Christian by education, capitalist by circumstances, pseudo-democrat by conviction, and temperamentally a dictator." Sues wrote: "Democracy to her is not the inalienable right of the people, but a candy which the government may in time dole out as a reward for good behavior."

Then an article appeared in the *Boston Post* under the headline "First Lady of China Too Chic." Madame Chiang's role as champion of "Free China" was obscured by her fashionable clothes and jewels, it argued. She was widely acclaimed for her appearance, but it was a double-edged sword. The popular illusion of Madame Chiang ministering to the wounded and orphans in war-torn China was shattered by her "priceless" sable coats and a "king's ransom" of diamonds and jade, the article said.

An article in the *New Republic,* reprinted in the British socialist weekly *Tribune,* attacked corruption and weakness in the Chinese government and described planeloads of cash arriving while soldiers and schoolteachers starved. Mayling and Chiang were bewildered by the torrent of critical accounts. "What exactly is wrong with China that Americans do not like?" Chiang asked his inner circle. At an early April 1944 cabinet meeting H. H. Kung and T. V. Soong exchanged words. Kung said much of the criticism concerned economic and financial matters and was aimed at him. He felt China was unfairly singled out. Soong countered that much of the criticism was true, including charges of political factionalism, a lack of democracy, weak economic controls, and a lackluster war effort. If the Chinese embassy objected to every article it would create a bad impression, given America's tradition of press freedom, he argued.

The Chinese leadership would have been chagrined to learn it was getting even rougher treatment at the hands of Allied diplomats than in the foreign press. In a report to Washington, Solomon Adler, U.S. Treasury representative in Chungking, lampooned a book called *Chinese Economic Theory*, published under Chiang's name but penned by a member of what Adler sarcastically referred to as Chiang's "brain trust." The book was an irresistible target. It elaborated on what it termed Chinese economics, drawn from scattered references in the Chinese classics.

There was perhaps another reason for Mayling's nervous state of mind. By this time, it was obvious that Chiang was endeavoring to build up his eldest son, Ching-kuo, to a position of prominence. After Ching-kuo returned from Russia in 1937, Chiang had appointed him administrator of a district in Jiangxi province that had been devastated by intense fighting as the Communists embarked on their legendary Long March. He was given a lavish rehabilitation budget and told to create a model district. The experiment's success, due in part to its ample budget, earned Ching-kuo a reputation for administration. But despite his ability, he was suspect in the eyes of many Chinese officials, compounded by the fact his wife was Russian.

Chiang's in-laws viewed Ching-kuo's advancement with disfavor. During Mayling's extended visit to America, Chiang had grown closer to his son. Outwardly relations between stepmother and stepson were cordial, but there was no real warmth. His presence was an unwelcome reminder of Chiang's first wife. Moreover, Ching-kuo let Wego Chiang's Japanese mother stay at his house. Wego was generally believed to be Chiang's blood son, rather than the adopted child that he was, and his mother Chiang's former mistress. Worse, the Three People's Principles Youth Corps, which Ching-kuo took over at his father's behest to build up his power base, published a book about Chiang entitled *Long Live the Director-General,* in which Ching-kuo's mother was mentioned but Madame Chiang was not. The book was handed out to all Youth Corps members before being pulled, presumably at Mayling's insistence.

But most devastating to Mayling's emotional state was a widening breach in her marriage, and a subsequent frenzy of gossip. Protest could not be articulated openly, so discontent with the Kuomintang regime and with life after seven years of war found expression in the form of rumors that quickly gained wide currency, growing more outlandish with each retelling. There was no more satisfying target than the proud and puritanical Mayling, who had no shortage of enemies. In 1944 most non-Communist Chinese still had faith in Chiang Kai-shek, but his prestige had declined markedly. Criticism of his leadership was mounting at home as well as abroad. There was tremendous resentment of the Kuomintang and its military leaders, who had, it was felt, enriched themselves at the expense of the Chinese people. Great personal fortunes had been amassed by leaders who had previously been poor struggling revolutionaries. Many felt that Chiang and the Soong clan acted as though China were their "private preserve." Among intellectuals there was little respect for Madame Chiang, who was seen as a "vain woman without any real influence on the Generalissimo." Madame Kung was widely criticized for her financial dealings. T. V. Soong was seen as a good administrator but an autocrat. Madame Sun Yat-sen alone was universally respected by Chinese liberals.

Mayling went almost annually to Hong Kong for medical treatment, and each time she departed rumors that there was a marital rift in the Chiang household arose. These were invariably dismissed as "smear stories" fed to "leftist intelligentsia" by the Communists. But now, there appeared to be some truth to the gossip. The Generalissimo was said to be displeased that Madame Chiang had failed in her mission to America and had stayed away so long, against his wishes.

In April 1944 the U.S. ambassador to China, Clarence E. Gauss, wrote the secretary of state that Mayling had lately been entrusted with delivery of an important message from Roosevelt to Chiang and had not only delayed delivery but had tried to have the message "toned down." Reports of "domestic intranquility" in the presidential household were mounting. For several months Chiang had been in an "irascible" mood and Mayling was urging her American doctor to tell her husband she should go abroad for a rest. Gauss advised the War Department to cease using her as a conduit for messages.

By May, Chungking was "literally seething" with tales of the Chiangs' domestic troubles. John S. Service reported to Washington that if Madame openly broke with her husband, the family dynasty would be split and the effects in China and abroad would be serious, resulting in a "great loss of prestige" to both the Generalissimo and the Madame. "The prevalence and belief of these stories, and the humorous elaborations which are passed around, are at least indications of the unpopularity of the Madame (it is generally regarded by Chinese as a joke at her expense) and the decline in respect for both her and the Generalissimo," Service wrote. Mayling's strong Christian views on marital infidelity were well known; several government officials had suddenly lost their jobs because their wives had brought their husband's peccadilloes to her attention. Chiang's critics viewed the controversy as proof of the hypocrisy of his Christian and New Life moralizing, showing he was little more than an old-fashioned warlord after all.

Some reports held that Chiang had resumed relations with his third wife, Jennie Chen, while Mayling was away in the U.S.; others said that he was involved with a younger woman, variously said to be living in Chiang's house or in seclusion elsewhere as she was about to bear his child. Madame Chiang, it was said, now referred to Chiang as "that man," and complained that he put his teeth in only when he was going to see "that woman." She allegedly went in her husband's bedroom, found a pair of pumps under the bed, and threw them out the window, hitting a guard on the head. Chiang supposedly did not receive any visitors for four days because he had a bruise on his head from a flower vase, incurred in an altercation with his wife.

True or otherwise, there were verifiable indications that all was not well in the Chiang household. Since returning to China the previous summer Mayling had stayed mostly at Madame Kung's house. She avoided social and public appearances; on the rare occasions she was seen with the Generalissimo they appeared cool toward each other. Her skin complaint, which doctors attributed to nervous strain, returned with a vengeance and she seemed irritable. But it was thought that the stakes were so high that she would simply swallow her pride and put up with the situation.

Concerned, Roosevelt dispatched Vice President Wallace to China in June 1944. Before Wallace's departure, Roosevelt spoke of China's inflation problem, the strained relationship between China and Russia, and the "lack of domestic felicity" between China's first couple. He told Wallace it was up to him to play "Cupid" to bring Chiang and Madame together again. On tensions between the Nationalists and the Communists, Roosevelt said: "Let me get them all in the same room, with good chairs to sit on, where they can put their feet on the table, where they can have cold beer to drink and good cigars to smoke. Then I will knock their heads together and we will settle everything."

Wallace traveled to China via Russia with John Carter Vincent, a China expert in the State Department, and Owen Lattimore, Chiang's former adviser. Both regarded the Kuomintang government with a jaundiced eye. Mayling told Lattimore she wished to go abroad for medical treatment and asked Wallace to mention her health to Chiang, which suggested she was having difficulty persuading him to let her leave. She even pulled down her stockings to show Lattimore her skin troubles.

Wallace and Vincent also visited Madame Sun Yat-sen in Chungking. She complained of undemocratic conditions in China, which she felt accounted for the lack of popular support for the government. "Madame Sun's depth and sincerity of feeling is more impressive than her political acumen but she is significant as an inspiration to Chinese liberals," Wallace reported to Roosevelt.

Wallace got an earful in China. He heard a story about an "amusement" house in Kunming named Megwa, or "American Joy Club," run by Chinese businessmen for the entertainment of American servicemen. When leaks concerning troop movements were traced to girls working in the club, Stilwell ordered the place shut down; besides, American boys were contracting diseases from the girls. From the Burma front Stilwell received orders to report to Chungking. When he arrived he was confronted by

Madame Chiang and Chennault. She objected to his closing the club, which was for the "amusement of American boys who are doing so much for us," and ordered it reopened. Wallace also heard that when Mayling returned from America in 1943 her plane was loaded with luxury items. The coolies could hardly be restrained from looting the cargo, most of which allegedly was sold on the black market for exorbitant prices.

Roosevelt pressed Wallace for a U.S. military mission to Yenan, the Communist stronghold, which Chiang naturally opposed, knowing it would be tantamount to American recognition of the Communist regime. Chiang insisted to Wallace that although the Comintern had been dissolved in 1943, the Chinese Communists were still under the orders of Russia. He said the Chinese Communists were "not men of good faith." Under duress, he eventually agreed to the Yenan mission. Wallace returned to the U.S., concluding China was near collapse and Chiang "at best a short term investment."

Soon afterward an American group headed for Yenan on what was dubbed the "Dixie Mission." The Americans were "dazzled" by what they found there. "Chungking was simply waiting for the end of the war. . . . Up in Yenan—they had nothing . . . [yet] the whole atmosphere was just full of confidence and enthusiasm," Service recounted later. "They were absolutely sure that they were winning." The mood was congenial and informal. Mao Zedong might drop by for a chat in the evening, and visitors could see him and his colleagues on short notice. The Americans were impressed that in contrast to wartime Chungking, things got done promptly and efficiently in Yenan, and people were outgoing and cooperative. Everyone grew their own vegetables, even Mao. Service had been in gloomy Chungking a long time, "maybe too long," he said, later conceding, "Maybe I'd lost my perspective a little bit." Even Stalin regarded the Chinese Communists as "Oleomargarine" Communists. But while Americans swooned at the blandishments of the gentle and earthy "agrarian reformers" in Yenan, the Japanese were under no illusions. An intercepted Japanese diplomatic telegram called the Chinese Communists "even more radical than Moscow" and "practically a mob of anarchist[s]."

By July Mayling was seriously ill with "nervous exhaustion" and insomnia. Comdr. Frank Harrington, assistant U.S. naval attaché and her physician, warned H. H. Kung he "could not promise she would retain her sanity" if she did not leave China soon. Dr. Harrington believed her persistent rash resulted from nervous strain over relations with her husband. It was decided she would seek medical treatment abroad.

On the eve of her departure, Chiang and Mayling held a tea party for about sixty senior government officials, diplomats, missionaries, foreign correspondents, and a group of women from Madame Chiang's advisory council at the Generalissimo's summer residence in the hills outside Chungking. Chiang, clad in an unadorned khaki gabardine suit, stood and addressed the gathering with force and emotion. Everyone stopped eating and listened in rapt attention. He felt the time had come to speak frankly on a certain matter in order to "uphold the revolution." Malicious rumors about his personal life had been circulating widely for some time, he said, and had become a matter not only of social gossip but of sarcastic comment, even among his comrades. Apart from his wife, only one true friend had come forward to tell him of the rumors—among them that he had a mistress and that she had borne a child by him. He categorically denied there was the remotest truth to any of it. He and Madame Chiang had started the New Life Movement in 1934 to raise the moral standard of the nation. His destiny was linked with that of the nation and any stain upon him as a leader was a stain upon China. If his moral standards were lax, how could he face the people and lead the government? He felt ashamed of himself because his character was not great enough to imbue the people with absolute faith in him. An attack on his integrity was an attack on China. He became extremely agitated during his forty-five-minute speech, and his voice frequently rose to a high pitch. He finished to great applause.

Mayling then rose. She spoke quietly and slowly in Chinese, but when she restated her remarks in English she did so with passion. She wore a plain blue and white flowered dress with green earrings, white gloves, and white shoes. She said she had received many letters concerning the rumors. "I felt it my duty, not as a wife, but as a true patriot, to acquaint the Generalissimo with these rumors," she told listeners. "Never for a moment did I stoop or demean myself by believing them nor did I ask him if they were true. If I had doubted the Generalissimo, I should have insulted him. I believe perfectly in his integrity, in his honor, in his personality, in his leadership. I have been married to him for seventeen years. I have been with him through all his trials and I know every facet in his integrity. I hope no one has given credence to these malicious slanders." She was heartily applauded. The event was declared "off the record," but Madame told reporters they could tell their friends if they wished.

The tea party naturally became the subject of lively comment in China. Some Chinese felt the denial of extramarital peccadilloes was contrary to Chinese tradition, and only served to confirm the stories in their minds and to lower Chiang's prestige. Others held that another period of separation, and Madame Chiang's temporary removal from the Chinese scene, would allow him to strengthen his position at home.

Looking pale and listless, Mayling departed on July 9 in secrecy to avoid Japanese bombers. Her party included her sister Eling, niece Jeanette and nephew Louis, two maids, a cook, two servants, and a secretary. She arrived in Rio de Janeiro on July 13, 1944, where she stayed at a villa on Broccio Island in Guanhari Bay. Neither the U.S. ambassador to Brazil nor Brazil's foreign minister "knew what the real motive was for her coming here (which is hardly a suitable place for treating skin trouble) and were somewhat bewildered." British sources suggested the trip was to inspect her "substantial investments" there.

The next day the rumors surfaced in Drew Pearson's syndicated column. U.S. relations with China were "bad," palace politics were "intense," newsmen were "virtual prisoners" under Chinese censorship. The warlords didn't like Madame Chiang and didn't want to fight the Japanese. "Madame Chiang has hard sledding," Pearson wrote. "She is childless, sentiment is with the General when he goes to another wife. . . . Madame Chiang is his third. . . . Now there is talk of a girl, sixteen, in the palace, the niece of a warlord who wants to get Chiang away from American ideas."

By this time it was clear that there was an "extremely serious rift" between the first couple, the U.S. ambassador in Chungking reported to Washington. Madame Chiang had been heard to make bitter reference to "all the trouble she has had with him." Madame Kung had discussed the matter with foreigners and it "weighed heavily upon her mind" as well as those of other family members. Chiang's remarks at the "fantastic" tea party, identifying himself with the Chinese nation, closely resembled the Nazi pronouncement that "Hitler is Germany and Germany is Hitler."

The "explanation" for the rumors, given out in an international semi-official countercampaign by friends and supporters of the Chiangs, was that

Ching-kuo had had an extramarital affair that had produced twin boys—which was true—and that the Generalissimo could not help but be pleased that he now had grandchildren of pure Chinese blood. It was explained that he had given orders for a house in Chungking to be made ready for the new mother and children, with funds for her care and police protection. Misunderstanding had arisen because it was widely assumed that the lady in question was his own mistress—or so it was explained.

Under normal circumstances such rumors would not have caused much concern in China, as concubinage, although declared illegal in 1936, was still widely accepted. Among those men whose wives were childless, it was expected, such were the societal pressures to produce offspring. But given Chiang's ardent protestations of his Christian faith the matter was closely scrutinized, and coming in tandem with his deteriorating military position it gave his enemies new ammunition. An intercepted letter quoted Mayling's former private secretary as saying that the by now famous "tea party" was held chiefly "to hoodwink foreigners." But Mayling left China not only because of husband troubles, but also because "she saw all of her hopes and plans relating to the country as a whole going to pieces before her eyes."

Meanwhile, tensions in the China theatre of war were mounting, with Stilwell at the apex once again. Soon after Cairo, Stilwell launched his cherished Burma offensive, and by the spring of 1944 Chennault's supplies were reduced to a trickle. Japanese troops launched an offensive that threatened large chunks of what little territory remained under Nationalist control, as well as many of Chennault's airbases. On April 16 three Japanese divisions crossed the Yellow River and streamed across the flat wheat fields of Henan province. The ill-supplied Chinese army was forced into retreat. Chennault had only ninety functioning planes with which to harass the enemy and disrupt supply lines. The Japanese then advanced into the rice fields of Hunan province, destroying some of China's best agricultural lands and precipitating further famine.

Despite the danger, Stilwell withheld ammunition from Chinese forces, resulting in the loss of the key city of Hengyang after a lengthy siege. The Hengyang debacle was interpreted by Stilwell's supporters as demonstrating the weakness of Chennault's air strategy. When Chennault proposed to Stilwell that some of the Hump tonnage be diverted to China's land forces to enable them to retake the city, Stilwell refused, writing his wife: "If this crisis were just sufficient to get rid of the Peanut without entirely wrecking the ship, it would be worth it." The Communists, he argued, were China's "only visible hope." Chiang tried to get control of Lend-Lease supplies, but Stilwell would not budge. "If the G-mo gets distribution [of Lend-Lease] I am sunk," he wrote in his diary. "The Reds will get nothing."

During his mission to China in the summer of 1944, Wallace had consulted with all parties and recommended to Roosevelt that Stilwell be replaced by a senior officer who could win the trust and confidence of Chiang. But when Chiang asked for troops to be withdrawn from Burma to protect Kunming, Stilwell accused Chiang of conserving his military resources to fight the Communists once the U.S. had won the war against Japan for him. Roosevelt responded by promoting Stilwell to four-star general and transferring him from Burma to China to command all Chinese forces—including the Communists—and reporting directly to Chiang.

The move was a dramatic shift in Roosevelt's position on China in the less than eight months since the two leaders had met in Cairo, where Roosevelt insisted that Chiang be treated as the leader of a great power. During that brief period, the prestige of the Nationalist Chinese government had plummeted precipitously as the Communist star had risen. The Communists' supporters asserted, improbably, that the Communists alone were fighting the Japanese while the Nationalists were doing little more than containing the Communists. But Stilwell's promotion put him in an untenable position, a fact that canny Roosevelt surely would have foreseen. Although officially Stilwell was subordinate to Chiang, in practice he looked to Washington for marching orders. He could not serve two masters.

Before the bombshell about Stilwell was dropped, Chiang asked Roosevelt to send a personal representative to China. Roosevelt shared Chiang's distrust of the State Department and dispatched Maj. Gen. Patrick J. Hurley, former secretary of war under the Hoover administration. The colorful self-made millionaire from Oklahoma was named ambassador soon after arriving in China in August 1943. He was utterly committed to supporting Chiang Kai-shek, and in this he clashed with foreign service officers in China, most of whom thought that Communist as well as Nationalist forces should be used to fight the Japanese. Hurley soon became famous for demonstrating a high, piercing Choctaw battle cry at Chinese banquets.

On September 19, Chiang was in a meeting with Hurley, T. V. Soong, minister of war He Yingqin, and others when Stilwell appeared bearing a letter from Roosevelt outlining Stilwell's new position and Chiang's evident demotion. Chiang invited him to join the discussion. Stilwell demurred, instead asking Hurley to step outside the room. When Hurley read the letter, he tried to persuade Stilwell not to deliver it because as drafted it would clearly be unacceptable to any head of state. But Stilwell said he had been directed to deliver it in person, and he insisted on doing so. When Chiang read the translation, all he said was "I understand." But once the Americans left, Chiang broke down in tears. He could not let such an insult pass unanswered. Stilwell would have to go. Soong warned Chiang of the possible repercussions of Stilwell's recall, but Chiang was "adamant" that retaining Stilwell would make him a "prisoner in his own house." Chiang called the episode the "greatest humiliation" of his life. Stilwell, not one to pass up an opportunity for schadenfreude, celebrated what he regarded as his triumph over "Peanut" by indulging his penchant for biting doggerel in an exultant letter to his wife. A few days later, Chiang asked Roosevelt for Stilwell to be replaced. Roosevelt finally ordered Stilwell's recall in mid-October 1944. Regarding the Stilwell imbroglio, Chiang wrote in his diary: "The pain that it has given me was almost beyond belief. . . . Fortunately Sino-American relations have not been wrecked by it." Gen. Albert C. Wedemeyer was appointed chief of staff of the China theatre of war in Stilwell's place. British officials were gleeful at the "wholesale debunking" of China under way in America.

Stilwell departed, but not before giving his side of the story in interviews with Brooks Atkinson of the *New York Times* and Theodore White of *Time*. The *Times* devoted four pages to the story in an article that sparked a torrent of attacks in the American press against Chiang Kai-shek and the Nationalist Chinese government. Feigning unconcern, Chiang wrote in his diary: "My conscience is clear and I don't care what they say about me."

In early September 1944 Mayling left Brazil for New York, where she was admitted to Columbia-Presbyterian Hospital on September 11. The nature of her illness was not disclosed. After she'd had a brief secret stay at Johns Hopkins Hospital in Baltimore, her physicians, Dr. Loeb and Dr. Dana Atchley, issued a statement on October 8, saying that Madame Chiang continued to suffer from the "physical incapacitation" that had brought her to the U.S. Her slow progress was due to a "severe state of exhaustion" caused by the "unremitting pursuit of her important work despite prolonged illness with all its attendant physical distress." An eventual complete recovery was assured, but continued treatment and a "long, rigidly-restricted and uninterrupted convalescence" were essential. She would be under treatment for much of the next year, alternating periods at home with hospital stays.

Although her doctors had strictly forbidden any visitors, British diplomat Berkeley Gage and his family were secretly permitted to see Mayling on October 14, 1944, at River Oaks, her "modest" seventeen-room Tudor residence in Riverdale, overlooking the Hudson. She told him it cost only $350 a month to rent, including $150 for the gardener, probably to counter news reports that she had rented an expensive mansion. Her only companions were her nephew David and niece Jeanette. Gage was "deeply shocked" by her tired appearance. She seemed "listless and despondent" about her health. She still had a rash and was unable to sleep properly due to the irritation. She also kept moving her fingers, "as if suffering from some muscular or nervous pain." Her doctors had told her she must remain quietly in the U.S. for at least six months if she wished to recover, but her uncomprehending husband "kept asking her to come back." She was "frankly gloomy" about the military situation in China. "I was filled with compassion for Madame, who, used to being in the center of things, now finds herself faced with the choice of either isolating herself in the U.S. and risking her position in China, or disobeying the doctors by returning to China and risking a nervous breakdown," Gage wrote. The only outdoor recreation she was allowed was to rake leaves for a few minutes a day.

Apocryphal or no, the rumors of a marital split took on a life of their own in Chinese circles. Even devoted friends of the first couple who initially dismissed the story came to believe it was substantially true, and were "bitterly disappointed." Some blamed the Generalissimo for his "selfishness in forgetting the country to satisfy his own whims." Although her friends knew Mayling was "too much of a Christian" to countenance the domiciling of another woman in her home, some felt she should have allowed the "good of the country" to prevail over personal resentment. They blamed her absence from Chungking for the acrimonious split between Chiang and Stilwell, and the subsequent barrage of attacks on China in the

American press. Many friends attested to her immense influence over her husband; others said her influence was overestimated. Most believed her health troubles would be cured by marital reconciliation and freedom from worry.

Churchill viewed the notion of China as one of the world's great powers an "absolute farce." He was vindicated when in early February 1945, Roosevelt met Churchill and Stalin in the Soviet city of Yalta on the Black Sea, where the pledges made at Teheran were formalized in a secret accord. The USSR would join the war against Japan on condition that former tsarist rights in Manchuria were restored. Roosevelt raised with Stalin the difficulty of talking to the Chinese, since whatever was said to them became general knowledge within a day, the president said. Stalin replied that there was no immediate necessity to speak to the Chinese. He assured Roosevelt that the Chinese Communists were merely "radish" Communists—red outside but white inside. Meanwhile, Chiang fretted that Churchill and Stalin might band together, to China's detriment. "Will Britain and Russia try to sacrifice China as I have feared?" he wrote in his diary. But he never suspected that his hero, Roosevelt, was double-dealing. The president ceded to Moscow a naval base at Port Arthur, joint control of key railways and access to the port of Dalien, and protection of Soviet interests in Manchuria, in an accord that partially contradicted the Cairo Declaration.

No announcement was made of the Yalta pact. Chiang never heard a word from Roosevelt. But rumors circulated, and he learned the details from China's ambassador to the U.S. in mid-March. "Has China really been sold out at Yalta?" he wrote in anguish. If true, "All the ideals and purposes for which we have been fighting in this war will become illusory." For the Nationalists, the very word "Yalta" became synonymous with betrayal— one they came to believe paved the way for the Communist takeover of China.

In early April 1945 Roosevelt dispatched General Hurley to London and Moscow to seek support for America's continued policy of backing the Nationalist Chinese government. Branding America's China policy the "great American illusion," Churchill agreed but demanded a quid pro quo: American men and aid to help reconquer Britain's Far East colonies. Hurley countered that America should use her resources to defeat Japan rather than "dissipate them in the reconquest of colonial territory." Churchill vehemently disagreed and told Hurley: "Hong Kong will be eliminated from the British Empire only over my dead body." He asserted Britain "would ask for nothing and would give up nothing." Hurley retorted that President Roosevelt had given him the British Empire, which was lost up until the time America entered the war.

American missionary Frank Price, one of Chiang's advisers, arrived in New York from China in April 1945 bearing a letter to Mayling from Chiang, who had asked him to deliver it in person. He called several times and finally spoke with Madame Kung, who told him Madame's doctors had ordered her not to see visitors. Price wrote Mayling that the Generalissimo was in good health. "He speaks of you often in our conversations and always with gentleness and affection," Price wrote. "He is a lonely man today in many ways; he wants and needs you. But he also knows how important is your physical recovery and the restoration of your mental and spiritual vigor if you are to take up again your great service for China." There was no reply. Still under treatment, Mayling was "extremely shocked" to hear of the death of President Roosevelt on April 12. His sudden passing was a heavy psychological blow to her and Chiang, who had looked to the president with great admiration and faith, and her recovery was set back by the news.

She was finally released from the hospital in May 1945, but remained under outpatient care, and doctors advised her to remain in the U.S. until at least October. She was still highly nervous and had problems eating and sleeping. When sleep would not come she read or wrote into the night, or took a drive up the Henry Hudson Parkway with David Kung. She began studying the American social security system and working on a plan to bring it to Chinese workers. In June 1945 she went on a rare outing to visit Westfield State Farm, a women's state penitentiary in Bedford Hills, New York. Accompanied by two Secret Service men, she inspected cottages, workshops, classrooms, and the nursery. She chatted earnestly with matrons and inmates to gather information for the reform of China's prison system.

Mayling's former aide, William Donald, had been interned by the Japanese in the Philippines from 1941 to 1945, his fellow internees carefully concealing his true identity from the Japanese. By the time he emerged from captivity he was ill with lung cancer. Now, in the early summer of 1945, he visited the U.S. and saw Mayling in New York. She asked him to work for China again, but he declined, citing poor health. Donald told others he felt the success of the Communist movement was due to popular dissatisfaction with growing corruption in Chiang's regime. He was convinced that it would be impossible for Chiang to unify China without a thorough housecleaning of his own government.

Donald's influence on Mayling had been enormous, but her influence on him was perhaps at least as great. A friend with whom Donald stayed in the U.S. noted that he showed much "confusion" about China. Sometimes he defended Chiang's government as doing the best it could under difficult conditions; sometimes he severely criticized it. But not once did he criticize Madame Chiang. "He always went out of his way to remove any possible impression that he considered her to blame for any of the things that had gone wrong." Donald told this friend that he might write his memoirs after all, but following his visit with Mayling he abandoned the idea "because he could not write unless he could tell the truth and he couldn't tell the truth without offending people in China to whom he had been very close." He turned down a large advance from a British publishing firm.

On July 28, Radio Tokyo announced that the Japanese government would continue to fight. The U.S. dropped the first atomic bomb, on Hiroshima, on August 5, 7:15 P.M. Washington time. On August 9 the second atomic bomb was dropped, on Nagasaki. The next day Radio Tokyo announced that the government was prepared to surrender. Stalin finally did declare war on Japan, but only on August 8—three days after the Hiroshima bombing. Japan formally and unconditionally surrendered on August 14, 1945. Stalin demanded that the Soviet Union and the U.S. jointly command the occupation of Japan. President Harry Truman, who as vice president had succeeded Roosevelt, ignored the demand.

On the day of the Japanese surrender, Mayling thanked Americans in a radio address for their "sympathetic and unwavering understanding" of China during eight years of war. She spoke of the "sobering task of formulating a truly Christian peace" and warned that the secret of the atomic bomb would find its way into the hands of a "greedy and unprincipled enemy" and "may yet cause the destruction of the greater part of humanity." Man's scientific ingenuity was "far ahead of his spiritual maturity" and unless addressed, the bloodshed and sacrifice of the war would be in vain.

Her health recovered, Mayling traveled to Washington, where on the morning of August 29 she met President Truman in the White House. She questioned him on the future of Korea and Indochina. He said Korea would be placed under trusteeship by the U.S., China, the Soviet Union, and Britain. Mayling said she did not recall Britain having been included as a trustee. She asked about Vietnam, of which she recalled Roosevelt having spoken of trusteeship as well. Truman replied that in his recent discussions with Gen. Charles de Gaulle of France it had been agreed that immediate steps would be taken toward giving Vietnam its independence. Mayling asked about the future of India, observing that Churchill "saw red" whenever the subject arose. Truman laughed and replied that Churchill was still "seeing red" over India but he hoped that Britain's new Labour government would be less rigid. She raised the problem of China's postwar reconstruction and asked whether Truman was familiar with Roosevelt's intentions. Truman replied that he and Roosevelt had discussed the matter many times. Mayling said the essence of the difficulty in China was to "improve the masses on a consumer level" while simultaneously building the country's production capacity. Truman said he hoped that he and Chiang could meet and sit down to talk over these problems. Mayling said that was precisely the message Chiang had asked her to deliver to Truman. She left for China that same afternoon.

A week later, after a fourteen-month separation, Chiang met Mayling at the airport in Chungking wearing a long Chinese gown and a sun helmet. Upon landing in a U.S. Army transport, she appeared well and smiled and waved to those who had come to greet her, including Madame Sun Yat-sen and H. H. Kung. She found the Generalissimo in good health but "somewhat thin," she wrote Eleanor Roosevelt.

For China, fourteen years of Japanese invasion was officially over. "Fifty years of national humiliation, as well as the indignities and insults that I have endured, are being washed away," Chiang wrote in his diary. "But while old wrongs have now passed into history, we are in danger of being engulfed by new ones." In eight years of war, 1.32 million Chinese soldiers died in combat, 1.76 million were wounded, and 130,000 were missing, according to official figures. Among the civilian population the number of dead and wounded, due to war, malnutrition, and illness, was far greater. On September 9 Chiang wrote: "The crisis with which our nation is faced today is more serious than at any other time since the Japanese invasion of Mukden on September 18, 1931. If we are not careful . . . [Stalin] and Mao Tse-tung will exploit the situation and plunge China into chaos and anarchy."

Chapter Sixteen
The Storm Center

The storm center of the world has gradually shifted to China. Whoever understands that mighty empire—socially, politically, economically and religiously—has a key to politics for the next 500 years.
—Secretary of State John Hay, 1899

C hiang Kai-shek was universally vilified, with some justification, for having run an ineffectual campaign against the Japanese in the Second World War. Yet he successfully executed his "magnetic strategy" of tying down millions of Japanese troops in China so that they and their weapons could not be utilized elsewhere, while refusing to surrender, a feat appreciated by Roosevelt, if not by Churchill. Where Chiang failed disastrously was not in waging the war but in winning the peace. General Wedemeyer foreshadowed this in a letter to General Marshall written just days before the Japanese surrender. "At times his trust and dependence are almost childlike," General Wedemeyer wrote of the Nationalist leader, who often asked him for advice. "He has many intricate problems and frankly I have determined that he is not equipped either mentally or in training or experience to cope with most of them." As true as this was in war, it was to prove much more so in peace.

After Japan's defeat, the mood in China was jubilant. But the logistical challenges ahead were staggering, and postwar planning nil. Japan had well over 2 million armed troops in China and Manchuria and 1.75 million civilians. Despite enormous losses, the Nationalists still had 2.7 million troops and the Communists had nearly 1 million. U.S. forces had to transport the Japanese troops and civilians back to Japan, a massive undertaking. Enemy-occupied territory had to be surrendered. Thousands of internees from Japanese prison camps—businessmen, professors, missionaries—needed to be repatriated. But more serious even than the challenges of recovering former enemy territory and repatriating millions of Japanese troops and civilians was the looming crisis between the Nationalists and the Communists. The long-simmering conflict had been kept under wraps by the exigencies of the war of resistance against Japan, but now, despite Ambassador Hurley's mediation efforts, it threatened to burst into flame.

Hurley wasted no time in bringing the two sides together. He personally escorted Mao Zedong from Yenan to Chungking, arriving on August 28, 1945, for six weeks of talks. The endeavor began inauspiciously when Chiang Kai-shek sent a deputy to meet Mao at the airport in a deliberate show of superiority. The Communist leader, clad in a conspicuously new suit and hat, looked like a "country bumpkin" as he stepped down from the plane. Dinners with the two leaders were awkward affairs, because Mao was fond of drinking and became expansive and humorous, but Chiang was a teetotaler and inept at small talk. Many banquets were held in Mao's honor during his six-week visit, including one hosted by Madame Sun Yat-sen. During one dinner, Mao raised his glass in a toast to his rival: "Long Live Chairman Chiang!" Minutes later Mao learned that a Communist official had been killed en route to the dinner—while riding in the car that Mao usually used.

Press baron Henry Luce visited Chungking in October 1945, having been prevented by the State Department from going to China since before Pearl Harbor. He attended a dinner in Mao's honor during which the Communist leader said in a speech that China must find unity under Chiang Kai-shek. Mao was surprised to see Luce and gazed at him with "intense but not unfriendly curiosity." Luce tried to strike up conversation with Mao, who had a "peasant-like" face and wore a "sloppy" uniform, but Mao confined his remarks to "polite grunts," Luce recounted. After dinner together one evening Mayling stressed to Luce the "terrible responsibility" the government had, now that the war was over, not to "disappoint the hopes of the people." Luce made an extended tour of north China and wrote her a lengthy letter outlining his impressions and suggestions on the recovery of Japanese-occupied lands, the Communist problem, the restoration of business activity, the attitude of the American military, and freedom of the Chinese press.

While the rival Chinese leaders "negotiated" in Chungking, their respective forces in the field scrimmaged for territory and spoils. The Soviet Union, having swiftly taken control of Manchuria following the Japanese surrender, turned over enormous stockpiles of Japanese arms and ammunition to the Communists. Communist forces marched into Manchuria to claim it before Chiang could dispatch enough of his own troops there to secure the region. Elsewhere, the rival forces jostled for control as Mao and Chiang agreed in principle to establish a political democracy, as envisioned by Sun Yat-sen, under which freedom of speech and press, as well as rule of law, would be guaranteed; to unify China's armed forces under Chiang Kai-shek; to convene a national people's congress; and to hold local elections. Mao left Chungking on October 11, 1945.

In America, there was in the autumn of 1945 tremendous pressure from the public for the demobilization of American armed forces in China, and this was Truman's chief concern. He had no intention of becoming embroiled in fratricidal warfare in China. His instructions were that "Americans must not participate in clashes between Chinese Forces; and that Americans must not be employed to facilitate central government operations against dissident groups within China," Wedemeyer wrote Chiang. The stick backing up U.S. policy in China was aid: "The extent to which political stability is being achieved in China under a unified, fully representative government is regarded by the U.S. as a basic consideration which will at all times govern the furnishing of economic, military or other assistance to China."

The U.S. demanded that China reduce its existing large military forces to fifty divisions. No Chinese occupational forces were to be sent to Korea and Japan, as all available troops were needed to secure China, Formosa, and Manchuria, Wedemeyer informed Chiang. This came as a heavy blow to Chiang's vision of China as a global power, and Wedemeyer's suggestion that perhaps China could send token forces to Korea and Japan later was little consolation. Chiang's hopes for playing a dominant role in Asia in the postwar era were further dashed by the dictum that North French Indochina was to be occupied by French and not Chinese forces, as he had wished.

Meanwhile, within their own territories, the Nationalists were doing little to further their cause. After the Japanese surrender, all people in occupied areas were treated as collaborators. The Nationalists confiscated private enterprises, jailed people, and commandeered private property. Some people were collaborators, but mostly because they had no choice, and when it served Nationalist purposes, some who had willingly collaborated were put into positions of power. These tactics earned the Nationalist government a tremendous amount of ill will. Corruption accompanied the Nationalists' return to power in Manchuria and elsewhere. O. Edmund Clubb, a foreign service officer, witnessed "carpet-bagging, looting, taking over of desirable residences." Manchuria—dubbed the "tinder box of Asia"—was a great prize, coveted equally by the Nationalists, Communist Chinese, and Soviets, whose tsarist-era claims at Yalta the Nationalists were reluctantly compelled to accept. The region had not only strategic importance but great reserves of natural resources—coal, iron, and other minerals—and industry and agriculture that the Japanese had developed substantially since 1931. There were large smelters at Mukden and Anshan, and coal at Fushun. The Chinese eventually recovered most of the Japanese-built industrial plants in Manchuria, but only after the Soviets had already spirited away most of the equipment, down to the light switches. Heavy industry was left nearly at a standstill.

But the Nationalists' undoing stemmed in the end from the fact that they could not stabilize the economy. The government's policies of inflationary finance—i.e., its overreliance on the printing press—had carried it through the Second World War, but came home to roost after 1945 when the long-simmering civil war began in earnest. The surge in popular feeling after the defeat of the Japanese was swiftly followed by great disappointment in the areas over which the Nationalists regained control, due both to shabby treatment of the populace and, even more so, to worsening economic conditions. This was compounded by widespread rumors of corruption among the men Chiang Kai-shek sent to administer recovered territories.

In November 1945, Hurley returned to Washington, where he resigned abruptly and angrily. His resignation letter bitterly charged the career foreign service officers in the American embassy in Chungking and in the State Department with disloyalty and sabotage of his efforts. He publicly charged that America's China policy was being molded by people with Communist leanings, and suggested a Communist conspiracy had infected the State Department. The seeds of McCarthyism had been planted. Hurley was subsequently replaced as ambassador by John Leighton Stuart, a missionary educator who had spent much of his life in China.

On learning of Hurley's resignation, Truman immediately telephoned General Marshall at his country estate in Leesburg, Virginia. "General, I want you to go to China for me," the president said. Marshall replied, "Why yes, Mr. President, of course," and quickly hung up the phone. Truman was tremendously impressed by Marshall's strong sense of duty to his commander in chief, but the real reason Marshall answered as he did was more prosaic. His wife, Katherine, was within earshot and he did not want her to know how brief his much-deserved retirement as army chief of staff would be. He hoped to break the news gently to her, but when she turned on the radio a few minutes later, his appointment was announced on the news. Katherine had been looking forward to spending time with her husband after the hectic war years, and she was terribly upset by what she called Truman's "bitter blow." Marshall later told Truman, "There was the devil to pay."

The president wanted to send Marshall to China as a special envoy to negotiate a peace between the Nationalists and the Communists. With his enormous worldwide prestige, Marshall was unquestionably the best man for the job. He was one of the most effective and lauded military commanders of his era, a man used to succeeding in every endeavor he tackled. But the notion that the warring Chinese forces could be harmoniously brought together into one government was ill-conceived from the start.

Marshall had long shown a keen interest in the Far East. As a lieutenant colonel, he had requested assignment to the Army's Fifteenth Regiment, stationed in Tientsin, China. Arriving there in 1924, Marshall learned enough Chinese to be conversant and cemented a friendship with Maj. Joseph Stilwell. He left China in early 1927, shortly before Chiang Kai-shek established the Nanking government. Marshall was suspicious of Chiang's "radicalism"—a notion shared by most Westerners in China at the time. Some of Marshall's views on China then seem startlingly prophetic in view of the tempests that were to come. Riots in Shanghai, he predicted in late 1926, were a harbinger of demands for abolishing the unequal treaties between China and the West. "How the Powers should deal with China," he wrote Gen. John Pershing, under whom he had served as aide-de-camp, "is a question almost impossible to answer. There has been so much wrong-doing on both sides. . . . There is so much of bitter hatred in the hearts of these people and so much of important business interests involved, that a normal solution can never be found." He hoped that "sufficient tact and wisdom will be displayed by foreigners to avoid violent phases during the trying time that is approaching." He could have been writing about the mission he was given in 1945.

The revered general was nearing sixty-five when he headed for China in December 1945, his face grown haggard but his blue eyes as piercing as ever. On his arrival in Chungking on December 22, Mayling told the press, "I wish him every success. He is an able and forthright man." Though her words lacked the ring of optimism, she ventured the belief that although China faced many difficulties, people were inspired by the fact that "for the first time in eight years they are breathing air."

Since her return to China in September, Mayling had been keeping a low profile while quietly resuming her previous activities. She was deeply stung when in early December Eleanor Roosevelt said publicly of her that "she can talk beautifully about democracy, but she does not know how to live democracy." With Marshall's arrival Mayling resumed a more public role. In addition to interpreting during meetings between the American envoy and her husband, she often met privately with Marshall and reported back to Chiang. But Edwin Locke, Truman's personal representative to China at the time, brought his own interpreter to meetings with Chiang because Mayling "had a way of taking over the negotiation" and would summarize five minutes of remarks by saying, "He's just talking a lot of nonsense about so-and-so." However, Marshall soon found that she was the only interpreter who was not afraid to tell Chiang the truth.

Marshall moved quickly, and succeeded in bringing about the signing of a Nationalist-Communist truce on January 10, 1946. January 25, 1946, was proclaimed as the first day in eighteen years on which there was no fighting in China, but all the while skirmishes continued between the two sides in many parts of the country.

In late January 1946, when the Russians were threatening not to withdraw from Manchuria, Chiang dispatched Mayling to Changchun as her husband's "special messenger of friendship." Bearing thirty thousand boxes of Chinese candy to sweeten Sino-Soviet relations and a sackful of medals with which to decorate Soviet army officers, she arrived in deep snow and subzero temperatures bundled in a fur hat, beaver coat, and padded silk gown. She was to hand-deliver a message from Chiang to Marshal Rodion Malinovsky, thanking him for restoring Manchuria to Chinese sovereignty. The Russian commander was ostensibly not in town—possibly a deliberate snub—but Mayling inspected an orphanage and visited wounded soldiers. Chiang Ching-kuo, who accompanied her, interpreted at a banquet, where Manchurian brandy instead of vodka was served to make many toasts to Stalin and Chiang. Mayling hailed Stalin's "military genius and wise, foresighted statesmanship." In a concession to her femininity, her hosts provided her port wine, a glass of which she raised to propose a toast to the speedy reunion of the Russian forces so long in Manchuria with their families at home. The hint was not lost on her unamused hosts. The tires on her plane were slashed and she was advised to leave quickly.

London-born journalist Freda Utley, who had first met Mayling in Hankow in 1938, visited her again during the last days of the Chungking capital, in early 1946. "Miss Utley," Mayling exclaimed in her candid manner, "I did not recognize you for a moment, you have grown so much fatter!" In China, this was a compliment, but not coming from Mayling. Utley found her "less hard and sure of herself. . . . She showed the keen discernment of old concerning both the international situation and Chinese politics, but she spoke of the death and suffering she had seen with feeling and in terms of humanity, not national pride." Although she had fully recovered from her illness, she was not the same "confident, ebullient First Lady of China I had known in 1938," Utley observed.

The conversation turned to the peace talks under way between the Nationalists and the Communists. "People should believe in one another until insincerity is proved," Mayling argued. "I have seen too much war and death not to want to try everything possible to avoid more bloodshed and suffering." Now, it seemed, she was in favor of reaching a settlement, whereas in 1938 she had been more hostile and distrustful of the Communists than even her husband. Chiang had changed too, Utley noted. He had aged much faster than his wife, and now looked elderly beside her. He seemed tired, weary of the tasks history had assigned to him. Gone was his serene confidence. His manner was more relaxed; no longer did one feel the urge to stand at attention in his presence. He seemed both "more human and more melancholy."

When Chiang and Madame first visited Shanghai in early 1946, such was his prestige that millions of people poured into the streets to welcome him. But the takeover was not well planned and the city underwent a "wild scrimmage for spoils," in the words of K. C. Wu, who became mayor of Shanghai in May 1946. The way various government agencies went about taking over so-called enemy property was "simply abominable. . . . They behaved like conquerors to their own people." Their sense of humor grim but undulled, Shanghai sophisticates dubbed the arrivals from the central government "Chungking man"—an allusion to the "Peking man" of pale-ontology. The "Chunking man," it was said, was interested only in the "five zi"—*tiaozi* (gold bars), *fangzi* (houses), *nuzi* (girls), *chezi* (cars), and *guanzi* (restaurants). But people dared not openly protest at the "carpet-baggers" lest they be branded collaborators and suffer reprisals. The take-over of Japanese-occupied areas across China was managed terribly, and corruption reached "truly unprecedented proportions" as civilian and military officials scrambled to appropriate formerly Japanese-owned prop-erty. The government was so preoccupied by the negotiations with the Communists that it was not fully aware of the situation in the recovered territories for some time. Not until the spring of 1946 was a centralized bu-reau established with the aim of managing recovered enemy factories and property.

In early spring Marshall traveled to Washington to argue for further financial aid for China, and in April he returned to Chungking with his reluctant wife. "I have one desire—To have the entire administration & *their wives* sent out here to stay and let me bid them a farewell of 'How nice you are going to China with your husband,'" Katherine Marshall wrote a friend upon arrival. They soon moved to Nanking, which she found more agreeable. She saw her husband only at meals due to a steady stream of callers, including the Mesdames Chiang, Sun, and Zhou Enlai's wife Deng Yingchao. The Marshalls often dined with the Chiangs, who "simply cant [sic] do enough for us & she is now fix-ing us a home in the mountains for the hot weather."

The Marshalls soon got a taste of China's notorious "bamboo wireless." Katherine made a weekend trip with Mayling to Shanghai, and out of that uneventful visit the Chinese press cooked up a marital spat between the American envoy and his wife, who had supposedly left Nanking in a huff. Marshall wrote of the incident to his protégé Gen. Dwight D. Eisenhower, wryly calling it a "commentary on the virulence of the present propaganda warfare" between the Nationalists and the Communists. Mayling showered Katherine with gifts, including dresses made by her own tailor and jade earrings and other jewelry. "She does so much I feel embarrised [sic]," Katherine wrote. "Every day she sends me something."

The Nationalist government officially decamped from the wartime capital, Chungking, and returned to Nanking on May 1, 1946. Chiang and Mayling moved back into their two-story redbrick house in the compound of what was formerly the Central Military Academy in Nanking, located near the airport and in the shadow of Purple Mountain. They preferred this modest building to what Chiang's aides saw as the obvious choice: a rambling white-plaster palace built for Wang Jingwei, the puppet president under the Japanese, and subsequently sold to the U.S. to house its embassy.

In the brief time that Marshall had been away, the January cease-fire, which meant little without his physical presence, had fallen apart. In his absence both sides violated the accord, scrambling for control in Manchuria, and skirmishes persisted even after his return. His prestige and negotiating abilities, formidable as they were, could not cut through the byzantine thicket of mutual mistrust that was Chinese politics. To his dismay, he found his motives called into question. Even the Chiangs were less than receptive, behind the welcoming front. "She told me that Marshall's attitude was impatient and rude and he was very insulting to our party and its military cadres," Chiang recorded in his diary on June 29, 1946, referring to Mayling's version of a conversation she had had with the American envoy. "Marshall was arrogant and proud of the fact that the U.S. Congress passed a bill to grant military aid to China and regarded that as his 'personal accomplishment.'" Marshall warned Truman that peace talks were at an impasse.

In addition to the Nationalists and the Communists, there was by this time what was loosely termed the "third force"—a term used to describe several small political groups comprised of non-Communist intellectuals and liberals who wanted to prevent civil war, and who felt that all Chinese should work together. The "third force" was purely political, with no military arm. Marshall hoped it could help bring about a resolution to the conflict, but by the end of June 1946, the truce was acknowledged to have broken down. At Chiang's urging, Marshall stayed on; however, fighting was spreading and the chances of mediating a lasting political settlement were growing dimmer. At the same time anti-American sentiment was rising among the Chinese, fanned by strong anti-American statements by Mao and the Communist party.

As Marshall shuttled between the Communists and the Nationalists, vainly trying to negotiate a peace, the Communist party secretly prepared an elaborate blueprint for turning Chinese and international public opinion against the U.S. and the Nationalist government. "The American Imperialists have taken away their false mask and begun to levy war upon the people of China directly," asserted a party document dated July 7, 1946. The U.S. was "attempting to strangle China to death. . . . The crisis of the Chinese Race has seriously started!" America's true ambition was to take over the world, the paper claimed, and to do so secretly planned to establish a Manchurian base from which to attack the Soviet Union. The Americans wished to foment civil war in China as a pretext for invasion. "Cunning" Marshall's mediation efforts were "empty talk." The Communist party called for a propaganda campaign in schools and organizations across China to change the public image of America as a "friend" to that of a nation of "evil will." The paper called on party workers in China and overseas to mobilize to break the ties between the Nationalists and the American people, to isolate the Nationalists, and even to confuse and incite conflict among the American people themselves. Whether by design or happenstance, events were to unfold in ways that bore an astonishing resemblance to the aims of the propaganda campaign as outlined in the document.

In July 1946 Katherine Marshall was taken to the summer retreat at Kuling, high above the Yangtze River, up six miles of stone steps. Founded in the nineteenth century by the British, the resort was "beautiful beyond description," she wrote, with scenery "that makes Switzerland look mild."

She memorably described the trip by sedan chair, borne by six coolies, in a letter to her husband, who remained in the Nanking "inferno" below:

> With the Whole Yanksee valley below the views were magnificent but I could not enjoy them for the panting & condition of the coolies. They were soaking wet & would change position on the chairs with out stopping. Only three times on that 4500 foot climb they stopped to rest. . . . Half way up the cool air struck us—and what a relief. As we came in sight of Cooling [Kuling] village we saw a long procession coming down. It was Madame & all her retainers coming to meet us—She had her chair carried beside mine where it was wide enough so we could talk. She looked very cute & smart in a blue woolen slack suit & was all smiles. When we got to the town of Cooling there was quite an ovation. Two little girls presented flowers to Madame & me. . . . [There] was a long banner across the street—"Welcome General Marshall—The Angle [sic] of Peace." A huge poster of the Generallissimo on one side and one of you [Marshall] on the other. The street on either side was packed with people all smiling & waving. It was very touching such a welcome—even if it was ment [sic] for you.

Mayling had prepared a cottage for the Marshalls next to her own, and the two ladies lunched together daily. Mayling was known to occasionally produce Coca-Cola from a cool grotto where she had several cases stashed away, thanks to coolies who carried the quintessentially American elixir up the mountain.

Despite Madame Chiang's exertions, by then even Katherine sensed that the general's task was beyond hope, though she did write a friend, "He never says die and maby he will wear the Chineese down instead of their doing him in." Marshall sympathized with Mayling and liked her. He was not entirely insensitive to her physical charms. He felt that she was in an impossible situation. "The Chinese don't trust her because she's too Westernized; the Westerners don't trust her because she's too much Chinese," he told an aide. But he thought she had a salutary influence on her husband. "She does . . . exercise a certain amount of restraint on Chiang," Marshall said privately. "She keeps him from making more of a fool of himself than [he otherwise] by inclination would."

Truman's patience was wearing thin. He did not think much of the Chiangs or the Nationalist government. He told Vice President Wallace he had never met the Generalissimo "but he had met Madame Chiang and he did not like her." The Kuomintang was "just like any other dictatorship [and] you couldn't trust it as far as human rights were concerned." By August Truman was ready to call off Marshall's mission. "It is with deep regret that I am forced to the conclusion that [Marshall's] efforts have apparently proved unavailing," he wrote Chiang. "Unless convincing proof is shortly forthcoming that genuine progress is being made toward a peaceful settlement of China's internal problems, it must be expected that American opinion will not continue in its generous attitude towards your nation. It will, therefore, be necessary for me to redefine and explain the position of the United States to the American people."

American opinion was already shifting, and *Thunder Out of China* gave it a push. Penned by Theodore H. White and Annalee Jacoby, former *Time* correspondents in China, the 1946 best-seller was a vivid and compelling indictment of Chiang Kai-shek and the Kuomintang for corruption, repression, and ineptitude. Although not Communists themselves, the authors admired the Chinese Communists, and argued that the best course of action for the U.S. would be to drop its unqualified support for the Nationalist government and adopt a neutral stance in China's civil war so as to be positioned to foster democracy in the future. Continued American backing of the autocratic Chiang Kai-shek was misguided and not in America's interest. The book was "honeycombed with factual errors and distortions of the truth," missionary Frank Price, longtime adviser to the Chiangs, reported to Mayling. "The facts are one-third wrong and conclusions two-thirds wrong." Regardless, the book's essential truths made it tremendously influential.

Marshall, too, grew disenchanted with the behavior of his hosts. One incident in particular raised doubts in his mind as to the Chiangs' motives. A delegation of ordinary people had come to see Chiang Kai-shek. As they waited they were attacked by a "mob," Marshall later recounted, during which an old woman and others were severely beaten.

I went to the Madame (the generalissimo was there, too) and said, this is a most terrible thing. The generalissimo said he would have to check. I said, you have your army headquarters here and many of your troops, and yet this thing [i.e., the attack] went on from seven to twelve [midnight]. I asked Madame to go to the hospital. She didn't want to go, but she went. I said to the generalissimo, what you are saying is, your army is completely impotent and I can't swallow that at all. His foot just went a wiggling, as it did when he was angry or upset.

As Marshall strove valiantly, if quixotically, to bring peace to China, William H. Donald, Mayling's loyal propagandist, lay ill. He was taken to Honolulu for treatment and told his right lung had collapsed. He wanted to die in his adopted homeland, so in early 1946 Mayling and Chiang sent Hollington Tong to Hawaii to bring him back to China. She set him up at the Country Hospital in Shanghai with an air-conditioned room—a rare luxury—and decorated it with bright curtains, wall hangings, a rug, a big easy chair, and orchids from Formosa. Her staff consulted daily with the head nurse to see if there was anything he needed. "They are very kind to me. They allow me to buy nothing, and anticipate all of my wants, even to the point of embarrassment," Donald wrote. Mayling visited often, as did many other friends, but Donald was distressed by China's worsening circumstances. "Hell is let loose all over the place, and the end is not yet. I want to weep," he wrote a friend. He had seen China throw off the Manchus, and struggle to unify and rid itself of the Japanese. Now China was on the verge of being overtaken by communism, to his mind far worse than the Japanese.

As Donald lay dying, he called for Mayling. Her plane was delayed and he anxiously listened for her footsteps in the hallway. Upon arriving she said, "Gran, here's your boss." She read him the Twenty-third Psalm and then the Ninety-first. Before she left, he kissed her hand and said: "Take care of yourself." "China's Best Friend" died on November 9, 1946, and was buried in International Cemetery near Mayling's mother.

* * *

As autumn turned to winter, conflict between the Nationalists and the Communists continued to escalate in a thinly veiled resumption of civil war, and the economic situation deteriorated. "My battle out here is never ending, with both ends playing against the middle—which is me," Marshall had written Eisenhower in September. By November 1946, Marshall's mediation efforts were effectively over. The great general had from the start been faced with tremendous problems, Mayling wrote Wedemeyer, but "his patience, persistence and desire to be of help to China have won the admiration of all our people except that of those who, for selfish reasons, berate him for what he is not and for what he did not do."

On December 1, 1946, Marshall met with Chiang for three hours. Mayling interpreted. The time for diplomatic niceties—not Marshall's strong suit in any case—was long past. He said to Madame Chiang, "I will tell you something, but it is so strong, you may not want to translate it. Don't translate if it goes too far." He then addressed Chiang: "You have broken agreements, you have gone counter to plans. People have said you were a modern George Washington, but after these things they will never say it again." Mayling nodded and said, "I want him to hear it." As she translated Marshall's remarks, Chiang sat expressionless, but his feelings were betrayed by a bobbing foot.

Marshall continued. Military expenditures were running at four times income and gobbling up as much as 90 percent of the government budget, fueling inflation as the government resorted to the printing press to finance the war. The situation made fertile soil for the Communists, who were poised to take advantage of the escalating problems. Marshall predicted that a financial crisis would precede military victory. He refrained from mentioning the growing public disapproval of Kuomintang leadership, or the government's potential collapse. But his point was clear. "His old foot went round and round and almost hit the ceiling," Marshall said of Chiang later.

After Madame Chiang had translated, Chiang unleashed an hour-long rebuttal. His false teeth clicking as he spoke, he told Marshall he was convinced that the Communists had never held the remotest intention of cooperating. The Communist party was controlled by Moscow, and the only way to counter Soviet machinations in China was to defeat the Communists. The Soviets understood nothing but force. The Nationalists, he claimed, could bring down the Communist armies in eight to ten months, long before any economic collapse. The U.S. should revise its China policy in favor of the Nationalists, he said. Nonetheless, he remained open to peace talks with the Communists.

Marshall was unimpressed by Chiang's arguments. After nearly a year in China, he wanted to go home. In response to Marshall's report of the meeting, Truman gave him permission to end the mission. Marshall declined Chiang's offer to stay on as an adviser.

In early January 1947 Truman ordered his China envoy to report to Washington for consultation. Marshall knew that meant the president wanted to appoint him secretary of state. He replied via Dean Acheson: "My answer is in the affirmative if that continues to be his desire. My personal reaction is something else."

Mayling and her husband met with Marshall on January 7. Their final conversation was one of dramatic intensity. Chiang repeated his invitation to Marshall to continue his valuable service to China as his adviser, pleading with great earnestness and offering Marshall all his powers and pledging to cooperate fully. Marshall replied merely that he appreciated the honor. He was leaving China a tired and frustrated man.

Frank Rounds, *World Report* correspondent, was one of the few among Nanking's foreign press corps who got up early to see Marshall leave. At five o'clock in the morning on January 8, 1947, he went to Marshall's residence and watched him pack. "Members of his staff were running up and down stairs with suitcases and swords and mementos of many kinds," Rounds recalled. "Some were still being crated and rushed into cars to go out to the airfield." A thin blanket of snow covered the cabbage fields on the way to the airfield. Finally Marshall's staff got everything into his private plane.

The "Tiger of Peace," as the Chinese called Marshall, stood on the tarmac on that cold, clear morning before a C-54 with five stars emblazoned on its tail, waiting to carry him home. A sad little group stood by, waiting for the final breach. Mayling and her husband drove up in their new bulletproof Cadillac as the aircraft's engines started. She wore a handsome heavy beaver coat. Chiang, Ambassador John Leighton Stuart, and T. V. Soong, now finance minister, were there too. Marshall said his goodbyes to Stuart and the Chinese officials who had risen early to see him off.

He greeted Mayling somberly. "Come back soon," she insisted. The first couple boarded for a few minutes to say good-bye. After they emerged, the plane took off, sweeping over Purple Mountain and Sun Yat-sen's tomb. China's "Most Fairly Friend" was gone. Mayling turned to her brother T. V. and said, "Shall we have a cup of coffee?"

As arranged, the State Department released Marshall's final report—labeled a "personal statement"—an hour after his departure. In it he described the Chinese situation as "intricate and confused." The greatest obstacle to peace, he said, was the "complete, almost overwhelming suspicion" between the Nationalists and the Communists. Each side "sought only to take counsel of their own fears . . . and were susceptible to every evil suggestion or possibility." He wrote of patrol clashes that were "deliberately magnified into large offensive actions. The distortion of the facts was utilized by both sides to heap condemnation on the other." He spoke of his "struggling against almost insurmountable and maddening obstacles to bring some measure of peace to China." He blamed the breakdown in negotiations on a "dominant group of reactionaries" in the Nationalist government "who have been opposed, in my opinion, to almost every effort I have made to influence the formation of a genuine coalition government."

On the Communist side, although there were liberals, the "dyed-in-the-wool Communists do not hesitate at the most drastic measures to gain their end . . . without any regard to the immediate suffering of the people involved." He condemned the "very harmful and immensely provocative" Communist propaganda. "I wish to state to the American people that in the deliberate misrepresentation and abuse of the action, policies and purposes of our Government this propaganda has been without regard for the truth . . . and has given plain evidence of a determined purpose of mislead[ing] the Chinese people and the world and to arouse a bitter hatred of Americans. It has been difficult to remain silent in the midst of such public abuse and wholesale disregard of the facts, but a denial would merely lead to the necessity of daily denials." The Nationalists had also made misrepresentations, but not of the "vicious" nature of the Communist propaganda.

Marshall decried some in the Kuomintang who were "interested in the preservation of their own feudal control of China" and had sabotaged the first truce reached in early 1946. Although a soldier himself he deplored the "dominating influence" of the military, which "accentuates the weakness of civil government in China." His efforts to forge a settlement had been frustrated time and again by extremists on both sides. The only "salvation" of the situation as he saw it would be the assumption of leadership by the liberals in the government and in the minority parties, a "splendid group of men" who at the moment lacked political power. Among these were "young men who have turned to the Communists in disgust at the corruption evident in the local governments—men who would put the interest of the Chinese people above the ruthless measures to establish a Communist ideology in the immediate future."

In the U.S., Marshall's candid statement was interpreted as wishing the Chinese a "blistering plague on both your houses," as the *Los Angeles Times* put it. Chiang, in a feeble attempt to make the best of a catastrophe, called the statement "friendly and constructive." Mao's second-in-command, Zhou Enlai, agreed with Marshall's description of the Kuomintang reactionaries, but regretted Marshall "did not point out that Chiang Kai-shek himself is the leader of this reactionary group."

Just hours after the release of his statement, while his army transport flew east over the Pacific, Marshall's appointment was leaked to White House reporters. Three weeks later he was sworn in as the fiftieth secretary of state, the first career military man to hold the post. The professional soldier who had fought in two world wars came to the post with one overarching conviction: that the only way to be sure of winning a third world war was to prevent it.

In retrospect, it is evident that neither side was negotiating in good faith. The Communists, despite what was said publicly, never had any intention of submitting themselves to the role of opposition party under Kuomintang leadership of a democratic state, or even of forging a coalition government; they wanted nothing less than absolute power. It is equally clear that the Nationalists were similarly unwilling to genuinely cooperate with the Communists. Given America's long-standing aid to and friendship for the Nationalist government, Chiang felt fully justified in assuming Washington would back him should peace with the Communists prove unattainable. Among the Nationalists, there was also an expectation that before long there would be war between the U.S. and the Soviet Union and that "China would profit from that war"; therefore there was no real need to compromise with the Communists. Quite understandably, the Communists saw no point in making concessions either because they too expected the U.S. to back the Chiangs. It was Marshall's lack of credibility as a truly impartial mediator in the eyes of both sides that was at the heart of his mission's failure. Mao Zedong later derided the mission as a "crude farce."

The end of the Marshall Mission was a turning point. It was the failure of a sincere if misguided effort to bring peace and reconciliation to China, and a fateful day in history. Some said the mission was doomed from the start. Most of all, perhaps, Marshall blamed himself for his failure. "I tried to please everyone," he later observed. "The result was that by the time I left, nobody trusted me." After Marshall's departure the Communists became "blatantly bumptious," in the words of Ambassador Stuart.

In practice China's problems after the war were so enormous as to be virtually insoluble for Chiang. There was the lack of adequate plans for postwar reconstruction and revitalization of the shattered economy; widespread destruction of infrastructure; and galloping inflation. The mood of the people after eight years of war and millions of lives lost was one of frustration and desperation, but Chiang regarded economic, social, political, and agricultural reforms as secondary to unifying the country and building a strong central government.

Lenin once said that the best way to destroy the capitalist system was to debase the currency. By 1945 it was, arguably, already too late to save China from communism because of the impact of inflation, which Chiang continued to underestimate. He was convinced that as China's economy was largely agrarian, it was less susceptible to economic and financial turmoil. The economic problems were compounded by the fact that Nationalists did not have an effective political organization, especially at the grass roots. They had no compelling political doctrine and were unable to offer a credible alternative to the Communists.

For her part, Mayling held greater appeal for foreigners than for many of her own countrymen. This was illustrated in a telling vignette that took place not long after Marshall's departure in early 1947. Two young American military officers went to a Chinese opera performance at the Majestic Theatre in Shanghai, held for American servicemen in the port city. Madame Chiang and Madame Sun Yat-sen were there, with the Generalissimo beside his wife. Mei Lan-fang, the great Chinese female impersonator, was singing in falsetto. The two Americans were utterly dazzled by the beautiful sisters, whom they had never seen in person. One of the officers, who hailed from Montana, could not resist ogling Madame Chiang with unabashed rapture during the performance. Suddenly Mayling turned and caught his admiring gaze, with its childlike frankness, held it steadily, and slowly broke into a warm, brilliant smile that lit up her face. He grinned back at her. Her diamond earrings flashed. Then she did something the two young officers would never forget: she gave the American boy far from home a slow, knowing wink before turning back to Mei Lan-fang.

On leaving China in the summer of 1947, Frank Rounds met Mayling for a farewell interview at her Nanking home. Rounds had asked to learn some "intimate details" about the Chiangs' family life, so Mayling showed him a little shrine where she said the Generalissimo prayed every day. Then they had tea in front of a fireplace, while military aides stood at attention. Madame Chiang looked "extraordinarily beautiful" that day, Rounds recalled. As the interview drew to a close he said he felt she had an opportunity to be a modern-day Joan of Arc. "But you've got to take off those rubies and those emeralds, and you've got to get out into the fields," he told her. "You've got to take off that silk and put on padded clothes. That's the only way you're going to save China." Mayling got up and walked the length of the room to the door. Then she turned to him and said, "Mr. Rounds, will you have another piece of cake?"

Chapter Seventeen
Taiwan's Sorrow

There are tremendous difficulties in the way of regarding Chinese officialdom with anything like feelings of confidence and respect. . . . This countless host, from the viceroy down to the lowest yamen member [bureaucrat], goes on the fundamentally pernicious principle that the country was made for the mandarins, and not the mandarins for the country.

—Reverend William Campbell, Presbyterian
missionary on Formosa, circa 1896

The Taiwanese historian Lien Heng wrote in 1920 that Taiwan's sorrow was that it had no history. That was not precisely true, of course; it had been inhabited by tribesmen for millennia. China's emperors, however, paid scant attention to the island, daunted by its treacherous waters, precipitous coastline, untamed malarial jungles, and fierce head-hunting warriors.

If Lien meant that Taiwan had no voice in its own history, it was true that a succession of foreign rulers had dominated the island since its "discovery" by the West in 1490. Portuguese mariners struck by its soaring mountains and verdant jungles called it *Ilha Formosa*—"Beautiful Isle." Long known to the West as Formosa, the island's Chinese name—Taiwan, or "Terraced Bay"—did not come into use until the late twentieth century. In 1624 the Dutch East India Company established a trading post in the south, later ousting Spanish traders from the north to take control of the island. The Dutch built forts, evangelized, and traded until 1661, when they were themselves driven out by the pirate-warrior Koxinga, a half-Japanese, half-Chinese pirate-adventurer. From his base on Taiwan, Koxinga—known to the Chinese as Zheng Chenggong—embarked on a quixotic quest to restore China's

Ming dynasty, but was defeated by Qing forces in 1683. Under Qing rule the Formosans were notoriously rebellious. "Every three years a disorder, and every five years a rebellion," it was said. In 1887 the Qing government made Taiwan a Chinese province, only to cede the island to Japan in 1895 under the terms of the treaty of Shimonoseki.

At the end of the Second World War, Chiang Kai-shek sent troops to take over Taiwan after the Japanese surrender, as had been provided in the Cairo Declaration. The island of six million had two hundred thousand aboriginal tribesmen; the rest were immigrants from the coastal Chinese provinces of Fukien and Guangdong, and included many Hakka. Over three centuries, these independent-minded pioneers mixed with the Dutch, aboriginals, and later Japanese. They began to see themselves as "native" Taiwanese, forging an ethnic identity distinct from mainland Chinese. Still, during the Japanese occupation many Taiwanese felt a sentimental yearning to return to the motherland. In 1945, they greeted the arriving Chinese with enormous enthusiasm, far more than people in formerly Japanese-occupied areas on the mainland. For their part, Chinese viewed the island as a wild and barbarous frontier.

Japan had developed Taiwan's industry and infrastructure as a launch pad for its imperialist march into Southeast Asia, with the island's farmland serving as granary for the home islands. During the long occupation the Japanese improved education, health standards, and public services. Train and road networks were developed and even rural villages were electrified. Literacy became widespread. The Japanese trained thirty thousand Taiwanese doctors, more physicians than existed in the whole of mainland China. In Asia, the Taiwanese standard of living was second only to Japan. As well, Taiwanese enjoyed a strict but clean legal system under Japanese rule. During the war the colonial rulers promoted assimilation, restricting Chinese publications and compelling Taiwanese to worship at Shinto shrines and adopt Japanese names. In 1945 most Taiwanese looked forward to life under a Chinese government, because they revered the Generalissimo, believed in Sun Yat-sen's Three People's Principles, and looked forward to participating in public life in a way that had been impossible under Japanese rule.

However, disillusionment quickly set in as mainlanders, inevitably seen as carpetbaggers, arrived. They felt racially superior to the Taiwanese, whom

they viewed as culturally polluted by the Japanese. The new administration returned the initial enthusiastic welcome by visiting upon the Taiwanese "oppression, economic extortion, political tyranny, inefficiency,
corruption, and [bestowing upon the Taiwanese] the status of a conquered
people," a U.S. diplomat wrote Washington. "The island was administered
solely for the benefit of a plague of mainland officials who swarmed in to
loot the local economy for personal gain." One Nationalist official later said
the men sent to the island "just treated the Formosans like dirt."

Feelings of superiority ran both ways. Happy to be rid of the Japanese, the
islanders soon found they liked their new masters less. "We think of the
Japanese as dogs and the Chinese as pigs," one islander told *Time* magazine.
"A dog eats, but he protects. A pig just eats." Taiwanese derided Chinese
conscripts who gaped at elevators because they had never seen them before, or who stole bicycles but had to carry them off on their backs because
they did not know how to ride them. Taiwanese called mainlanders *Ah-shan*
(mountain people) and themselves *Ah-hai* (sea people). Islanders who cooperated with Chinese were disparaged as *Ban-shan* (half-mountains).

On October 21, 1946, Chiang and Mayling visited Taiwan. After a three-
hour flight from Nanking, they smiled and waved as they stepped on Taiwanese soil for the first time. Taiwan provincial governor Chen Yi's
Packard, previously used by Gen. Ando Rikichi, the last Japanese governor
of the island, whisked them up to the Japanese royal family's former retreat
on Grass Mountain. Some suggested—prophetically—that with its cool
breezes, hot sulfur springs, and magnificent scenery, Grass Mountain could
become another presidential resort. As news of their arrival spread, many
people traveled to the capital and waited for days in the hope of catching
a glimpse of the Generalissimo and his famous wife. People thronged the
streets and teahouses buzzed with talk of the first couple; newspaper sales
soared. At a rally Chiang called on the Taiwanese to rebuild the island as
a model province of China, and promised islanders equal treatment with
mainland compatriots. The Chiangs departed for China on October 27.

But behind the carefully staged welcome, Chiang's "model province"
was simmering with tensions as mainland officials extorted businessmen
and confiscated property on charges of collaboration. Officials appropriated
former Japanese property that Taiwanese considered rightfully theirs, and
forcibly conscripted Taiwanese men. Taiwanese were barred from many

administrative posts. The economy deteriorated as prices soared and un-employment rose. Scattered rice riots broke out. Language differences between Taiwanese and mainlanders led to misunderstandings that turned violent, and that were emblematic of a misunderstanding far more pro-found. Taiwanese fury and hatred of the new arrivals bewildered main-landers, who sincerely believed they were liberating the islanders from fifty years of slavery and could not comprehend why the Taiwanese had such re-gard for the Japanese, who had killed millions of mainland compatriots. For their part, the Taiwanese deeply resented being treated as a conquered people by those with whom they shared the same ancestors.

All that was missing was the spark. One night in late February 1947, agents of the government's Monopoly Bureau—which controlled the manu-facture and sale of cigarettes, alcohol, camphor, matches, and opium—pistol-whipped (and killed, by some accounts) an elderly widow selling contraband cigarettes. An angry crowd attacked the agents, who shot at random and killed a man. The next day a large crowd of Taiwanese marched on the Monopoly Bureau, demanding a hearing, and were fired on without warning by machine guns. The incident quickly escalated into an island-wide rebellion. Angry mobs shouting "Taiwanese want revenge now!" "Kill the pigs!" and "Let Taiwan rule itself!" sprang up. A thousand mainlanders were killed.

Shortly after midnight on March 9, reinforcements dispatched from Nanking landed. There began an island-wide bloodbath, with widespread and indiscriminate killing and looting by Chinese troops. Up to thirty thou-sand Formosans died in a "reign of terror" lasting three weeks. Thousands more were arrested. When word of the rebellion and its aftermath reached Chiang, he blamed the Communists. He replaced the governor and some reforms were made.

The tragic episode, known as the 2-28 Incident for the date on which it erupted, was a tremendous blow to the Nationalist government's prestige—and, more critically, to its hopes for American aid. Nanking's failure to curb the rapacity of the Taiwan administration was bad enough, but the brutally inept handling of the uprising aroused horror. The event weakened the legitimacy of the Nationalist government's already tenuous claim over the island in the eyes of Taiwanese and foreigners alike. Taiwanese lead-ers wanted the island to become an independent state and brought their case to Nanking, but were sent away without a hearing. Some American diplomats supported Taiwanese aspirations for self-rule. "If—and only if— enlightened political and economic administration is set up in Taiwan, would American involvement or even government aid be justified," warned a U.S. consular report. The nascent Taiwanese independence movement had been decimated by the 2-28 Incident, yet even as the movement went underground, it was galvanized by the event, which became its defining moment.

Truman subsequently declared that the U.S. would aid countries threatened by communism—*European* countries—and in a June 1947 commencement speech at Harvard, Marshall launched a multibillion-dollar European recovery scheme. While Europe would get the Marshall Plan and billions of dollars in aid, China would get little more than sympathy. Alarmed by China's slide into chaos, in the summer of 1947 Truman dispatched General Wedemeyer to China to survey the situation and propose a fresh China policy. The Nebraska native and staunch supporter of the Nationalist government submitted his report to Truman following his return to the U.S. in the late summer. In the controversial report, Wedemeyer argued that the U.S. should intervene in China, under certain conditions. First, China should ask to place Manchuria under UN trusteeship; second, China had to reform its finances, government, and army and accept American military and economic advisers. Marshall immediately ordered the report classified and took no action. On the one hand it recommended supporting the Nationalists financially and militarily, which he and Truman had no intention of doing, and on the other hand it was extremely candid as to the Nationalists' shortcomings, and would have angered their supporters in the U.S. Although not published, the report's essential conclusions— intended to "jolt" the Nationalist government into action, as Wedemeyer put it—became known.

Wedemeyer's departure marked a turning point. Mayling became increasingly despondent over the Nationalist regime's predicament, and concurred with the American general's assessment that the Nationalists' fundamental problem was "spiritual bankruptcy." Her mood could not have been helped by the fact that her sister Eling and brother-in-law H. H. Kung packed their bags and "retired" to New York soon after Wedemeyer left, no doubt having seen the writing on the wall.

In early 1948 Marshall again wrote Mayling, pressing her to "drop everything" and visit his wife and him. She declined, pleading duties. "I wish that the world we had all so hopefully fought for during those trying war years were now a reality, for if possible we all are, I think, even a little more tired and worn than during those years," she replied in a despairing tone on March 16. "Certainly we had brighter hopes then. But now as then, the fight is still on. . . . I suppose we must struggle on." In the April issue of the Wellesley alumni magazine she complained of "deliberate distortion and misrepresentation" of China's problems. "Doubtless the situation in this country is bad, but the reasons underlying the misery are certainly not those usually cited by those who have tried to make a good case for the Chinese Communists."

By the spring of 1948 anti-Chiang pressures were intensifying, which may have explained Mayling's reluctance to leave China at that moment to visit the Marshalls. Dissident Kuomintang groups were becoming quite active, especially the Hong Kong–based KMT Revolutionary Committee, comprised mostly of former Nationalist officials and small-party members, which formed the nucleus of the "Third Force" that the U.S. later helped finance. T. V. Soong and Li Zongren, a former warlord from Guangxi province and a Chiang rival, were both in contact with this group, as was Madame Sun Yat-sen. That spring the new Kuomintang-controlled National Assembly, established under the 1946 constitution, elected Chiang president of the Nationalist government, making him the official head of state for the first time in his two decades as China's strongman. Chiang backed Sun Yat-sen's son Sun Fo as his vice president, but the disgruntled assembly, in a rare display of defiance, elected Li Zongren instead in a secret ballot. As one of the "liberals" Marshall gave favorable mention to in his parting statement, Li was widely seen as an alternative to Chiang's leadership. Having secured the presidency, Chiang soon afterward declared martial law and suspended the constitution, turning the presidency into an all-powerful post.

By August 1948 the government was in dire financial straits, as hyperinflation outpaced the printing press. A major contributing factor to postwar inflation under Nationalist rule was the policy adopted concerning the "puppet currency" issued by the Wang Jingwei regime that had been installed in Japanese-controlled territory. The puppet currency had been far more stable than the scrip issued by Chungking, but as a matter of pride, at the end of the Second World War Chiang's government elected to fix an exchange rate for the puppet currency that was far lower than its actual value, rendering it nearly worthless. The consequence of this catastrophic decision was in effect to spread the spiraling inflation in Nationalist-controlled China to the rest of the country.

Past experience notwithstanding, Chiang Kai-shek clung to the delusion that the inexorable laws of economics could be defeated by force. Draconian currency reforms were introduced, with the ostensible aim of halting inflation. Under penalty of death, citizens were ordered to surrender all gold, silver, and foreign exchange to back a new currency called the Gold Yuan. Prices were frozen at mid-August levels. The reforms were intended to be nationwide but in execution were largely limited to Shanghai, to which Chiang dispatched his elder son to oversee enforcement.

Chiang Ching-kuo's grasp of economics was no stronger than his father's, but he had a reputation for ruthlessness. "Chiang the Blue Heaven," as he styled himself after a famously incorruptible and beloved official of a long-ago dynasty, zealously targeted Shanghai's affluent, whom he regarded as the source of the country's evils, in enforcing the reforms. "Their wealth and foreign-style homes are built on the skeletons of the people," he wrote in his diary, in a tone oddly redolent of Communist rhetoric. He boasted he would not only swat flies, but go after tigers too, contrary to the old proverb.

Predictably, there was a mad scramble to buy goods and shops were emptied. Producers took their wares elsewhere, as prices were still rising in other cities. Shanghai was soon short of food and medical supplies. Ching-kuo's agents arrested people for failing to surrender bullion and foreign exchange, for engaging in speculation, or for hoarding, and sent them to a special court. Half a dozen were promptly shot as examples. Then, in late August, the press reported that David Kung, armed with advance knowledge of the currency reforms, had profited mightily through speculation. Ching-kuo, no friend of the Kung-Soong clans, was itching to arrest him, but Mayling flew to Shanghai to protect her favorite nephew and threatened to leave the country if he was arrested. "You are brothers," she told Ching-kuo, although in fact they were stepcousins. "You have no reason to fight each other." The firm through which Kung made the transactions in question was linked to Du Yuesheng, Shanghai's most powerful underworld leader and a major benefactor of the Kuomintang. On September 2 Ching-kuo arrested Du's eldest son, Du Weiping, on charges of illegal stock trading to take the rap for Kung.

Du Yuesheng, infuriated by the arrest of his son, who was to receive capital punishment, tipped off Ching-kuo to violations by Kung's Yangtze Development Corporation. A search revealed the firm had stockpiled two thousand bales of cotton yarn, a hundred cars, five hundred cases of woolen goods, and two hundred cases of medicine. David Kung was accused of illegal hoarding. Charges were dropped, but only after, as newspapers reported, Aunt Mayling made a second trip to Shanghai by special plane from Nanking on October 1 to intercede once again on her nephew's behalf. Kung paid a substantial settlement, estimated at $6 million, to the government in return for safe passage to New York. After his son's release Du Yuesheng closed up shop and moved to Hong Kong. Other leading Shanghai merchants followed suit.

The Gold Yuan collapsed soon after as the notes became virtual wastepaper. The debacle amounted to calculated confiscation of private assets, and drove many embittered Chinese into the arms of the Communists. The episode illustrated why many Chinese did not love the Communists more, but merely disliked them less, than the Nationalists, whose remaining popular support, sapped by eleven years of war, had been shattered.

That China's "royal family," as the Chiang-Kung-Soong clan was dubbed, had large sums of money was undisputed; how much and how it was made remains the subject of vigorous debate. A close associate of the Kung and Soong clan estimated that on the mainland, Madame and H. H. Kung had amassed a fortune of $30 million, and that altogether their children had made a similar amount. T. V. Soong, according to this source, made $20 million. It was widely reported elsewhere that the clan's fortune ran into the billions, dispersed among accounts and investments on four continents. The truth, perhaps, lay somewhere in between. In any case, the family's wealth was stupendous by any measure, and particularly in the context of the appalling poverty of China.

The extended family made money through both official and unofficial channels. K. C. Wu, who for many years held senior government posts under

Chiang Kai-shek and later became one of Chiang's fiercest critics, charitably asserted that in a technical sense the clan could probably claim to have made every cent legally. But even allowing for China's weak legal system, it is virtually certain that much if not most of the money was made through means not merely ethically dubious but illegal—inside information, connections, influence, and kickbacks. The clan "empire" included privately owned businesses, such as the Yangtze Development Corporation. T. V. Soong controlled the China Development Company, officially a government concern. The empire also included government agencies or concerns over which the clan exercised control, such as the Central Trust of China, a subsidiary of the Central Bank, which David Kung controlled, although it was nominally headed by a government official. The Central Trust was responsible for government procurement, affording Kung ample opportunity to pocket kickbacks or commissions on government purchases of commodities and matériel. It was extremely difficult to get foreign exchange at the time, but Kung's associates ran the foreign exchange bureau of the finance ministry, so he could. For most importers red tape was prohibitive, but Kung could get priority to import commodities scarce in China, making huge profits.

While it was evident that Eling's children carried out their nefarious activities at least in part under Mayling's protection, it is unclear to what extent she was aware of those activities. K. C. Wu argued that she had been "much more sinned against" than she was a sinner, her two chief weaknesses being vanity and pliancy. "When she keeps good company she can be good, but when she keeps bad company she can be very bad," Wu said. "Her greatest misfortune is that she has had bad company most of her life." The most evil influence on her was her eldest sister, who could twist her around her little finger, he believed. Wu called Madame Kung the "shrewdest, most capable and absolutely unscrupulous character" he had ever known. However, Wu's characterization of Mayling as, at worst, ignorant and malleable appears naive in retrospect.

Chiang Kai-shek led a relatively spartan lifestyle, and even his opponents insisted he was not personally corrupt. This may, perhaps, have been true in the limited sense that he apparently did not take bribes or use his position for personal enrichment as such. But he was certainly corrupt in the larger sense that he saw no distinction between the assets of the state and his own. If he wanted funds for whatever purpose, he simply ordered the Central Bank to put them at his disposal. The many corrupt men around him were forced to be more creative. Some of Chiang's generals, for instance, pocketed the salaries of their troops to speculate in stocks or hoard goods to sell later for profit, paying their soldiers late, when the value of the salary had been dissipated by inflation. They padded their ranks with "paper soldiers" and monks dragged from monasteries to get more provisions and salaries. But Chiang valued loyalty over ability, so he turned a blind eye.

As time passed Chiang became increasingly unwilling to listen to adverse facts, much less adverse views. None of those around him dared to express an opinion; instead they guessed what Chiang most wanted to hear and advised him accordingly. If things went wrong, he blamed subordinates. By November 1948 things were going very wrong. At the end of the war the Nationalist forces held superiority by a factor of four to one in combat troops and light arms, held a virtual monopoly on heavy equipment, and controlled the air force. Three years later the Nationalists had lost the upper hand in both men and weapons, and the Communists were marching from victory to victory. The catastrophic loss of the vast, rich territory of Manchuria in October 1948, along with four hundred thousand troops, including the Nationalists' finest division, and their weapons and equipment, left the Communists poised to pounce on North China. Gen. David Barr, head of the U.S. military adviser group in Nanking, attributed China's military debacles to "the world's worst leadership" and deplorable morale. "No battle has been lost since my arrival due to lack of ammunition or equipment," he wrote Washington.

In response to his impending defeat, Chiang intensified his Cassandra-like warnings of a looming third world war in a desperate bid to get American support. He told the *New York Herald Tribune* that when Japan invaded Manchuria in 1931, he had warned that a second world war had begun. Now he warned the world that with the Communist conquest of Manchuria, a third world war had commenced.

Inflation was galloping. Mobs roamed the streets looting and students held antiwar protests. Typically, Chiang attributed the rising chaos to Communist propaganda: "The leftist intellectuals, college professors, and editorial writers have accused the government of all sorts of alleged crimes and misdeeds," he wrote. "This is a Communist-staged campaign to discredit [me]. It is amazing that even our military and party personnel have been affected. . . . This is more deadly . . . than the most powerful military weapons." Whatever the cause, Chiang's mandate from heaven had clearly run out. "He couldn't be elected dog-catcher even in his native village," wrote Randall Gould, editor of the *Shanghai Evening Post & Mercury.* Gould blamed Henry Luce for fostering "a Chinese governing-class psychology of childish grab together with childish pouting for more."

Popular disillusionment with Kuomintang rule, however, was only part of the reason why so many Chinese, especially intellectuals and students, but also merchants and industrialists, civil servants and hundreds of thousands of soldiers, were siding with the Communists. The Communists had built a reputation for effectiveness, honesty, and credibility, and from their rural base had shown themselves to be China's most dynamic political force. They had become known for keeping their word, carrying out their policies, and correcting their mistakes. The exemplary behavior of Communist military and civilian personnel in areas they occupied contrasted sharply with the often abominable behavior of the Nationalists.

Although the Communists said that their ultimate goal was to communize China, they insisted that aim would take many years, and during the interim they would build a "democratic" society with room for all, be they intellectual, peasant, worker, landlord, or bourgeois capitalist. Due to the Communists' high credibility, many Chinese cast aside whatever misgivings they may have had and believed them.

The Communists strived to apply their revolutionary principles to solving China's practical realities, while Chiang Kai-shek attempted to mold China and its people to fit his lofty theories of what he thought China should be— as in, for example, the failed New Life Movement. Mao insisted that the Communist party should become close to the people, and thus earned their trust, while Chiang tried to distance himself from the ordinary people, thus alienating himself from them. This was the fundamental reason why the Communists were able to appeal so effectively to the hearts and minds of the Chinese people in the 1940s, and Chiang was not.

Mayling and Chiang pinned their hopes for an American rescue on a win by New York's Republican governor Thomas Dewey in the 1948 presidential elections. The Nationalist government was believed to have contributed $2 million to the Dewey campaign through H. H. Kung's Universal Trading Company. As returns came in, Mayling followed anxiously. As predicted, Dewey jumped to an early lead and was seemingly well on his way to victory, but Truman went on to pull off an incredible upset.

It was clear that without fresh aid the Nationalist armies faced certain defeat. The Communists controlled much of the north and west and were sweeping south toward the capital. On November 9, while Truman relaxed in Key West, Chiang sent him an urgent appeal. "If we fail to stem the tide, China may be lost to democracy," he wrote. "As a co-defender of democracy . . . I appeal to you for speedy and increased military assistance and for a firm statement of American policy in support of the cause for which my Government is fighting." Truman merely acknowledged the message, and nixed a proposal to invite Chiang to America to explain his case in person.

Mayling telephoned Marshall, and then announced plans to go to the U.S. herself to appeal for help. A decade earlier, the fiery Madame Chiang vowed she would not go to America on a begging mission. Now, pride cast to the wind, she was going uninvited.

As the Nationalists' position deteriorated, Capt. Walther Stennes continued to give Mayling his advice, however unpalatable, until she finally begged him, "Please don't tell me of any more things that are going wrong; I just don't want to know." Now, as she prepared to leave, he told her morale was so low her departure might have a devastating effect. "Madame, at this moment it is impossible for you to go to America," the Prussian said. "If you leave us, people will not know what to think. Things are very bad and there is little time left. All you can do is stay and fight it out in China, and, if necessary, we must die in China."

"Captain Stennes," she replied with a sad smile, "you have never been afraid to say unpleasant things. I think that, if no one else were left, you would still be at my side telling me the awkward truth. I must go to America, because without their help we cannot go on fighting. But you need not worry; I shall only be away three weeks, so I shall be back in China in time to die." Chiang was dubious about the value of the trip, but did not stop her from going. Despite the circumstances, he displayed a baffling serenity, "almost an exaltation of spirit," Ambassador John Leighton Stuart reported to Marshall.

Publisher Roy Howard worried about the "hazards" of her mission. "All the Communistic and anti-Chinese influences in the country will seek to discredit the Madame and her objectives," he warned a Nationalist diplomat. He hoped her trip would not be entrusted to the "young gentleman who balled things up so badly for her in 1943"—i.e., David Kung. "Sometimes this job of attempting to help the Chinese, even to the extent of helping them to help themselves, becomes a bit discouraging," he lamented.

Before her departure from China in late November 1948, Mayling broadcast a desperate appeal to Americans: "If Communism prevails in China, you, my friends, will ultimately also be suffering," she warned, offering an early incarnation of the famously controversial domino theory to bolster her case for American aid. "If China falls, all of Asia goes. And certainly Asia's importance to peace is not one whit less than Europe's." She would never set foot on her native soil again.

A Navy DC-4 plane provided by Truman carried Mayling and her party to the U.S. The day she landed in San Francisco, American embassy staff began to leave Nanking, as Communist forces pushed inexorably nearer the Nationalist capital. Her visit, Mayling said, was made "in a private capacity for the purpose of informing her friends in the United States regarding the real facts of the situation in China." Marshall sent his personal plane, the *Sacred Cow*, to bring her to Washington. He could not greet her, as he was in Walter Reed Hospital having a right kidney removed for a nonmalignant cyst, so he sent Katherine. He knew Mayling was waiting for an invitation to see the president—an invitation that might not materialize.

Mayling looked tired as she disembarked from the *Sacred Cow* on December 1, and avoided newsreel cameras. She was ushered past a legion of reporters into a State Department Cadillac. They followed her to Dodona Manor, the Marshalls' country estate in Leesburg, Virginia, where she recovered her spirits and obligingly sat for photographs and bantered with reporters. When asked what kind of fur her coat was made from, she spelled out: "N-u-t-r-i-a." Glancing at Mrs. Marshall's mink, she added, "It's an old fur coat, and it's out of style, but it's warm." Her sense of humor was intact. When the two ladies posed together, Mayling asked, "Are we supposed to look at each other lovingly?" When she mentioned it was her wedding anniversary, Mrs. Marshall said they must celebrate. "Just being here is celebration enough!" Mayling replied.

Madame Chiang was met with cool courtesy but no enthusiasm in Washington, even in Foggy Bottom, where her friend Marshall reigned over the State Department. Her presence made people in the halls of power uncomfortable. Officially, U.S. policy toward China had not changed, but support had been dropped in all but name as the Nationalists' plight grew more desperate by the day. Since the end of World War Two America had given nearly $2.5 billion in aid to the Nationalist Chinese government, but it was obvious to all but the most credulous observers that the Nationalists had given up the fight.

Privately, the Chiangs blamed the U.S. for the Communist victories, both because of Roosevelt's concessions at Yalta and because Marshall had cut aid in order to try to force Chiang to bring Communists into his government. These accusations were not given credence in the administration, but nonetheless there was in Washington a sense of guilt underlying the smug satisfaction that came from blaming the Nationalists for their ostensibly self-inflicted woes. The White House made no official comment, but the president of the Export-Import Bank, William McChesney Martin, declared the Nationalist government of China "a poor business risk." Texas senator Tom Connally, who had lavished praise on Mayling in 1943, said bluntly: "Chiang is a generalissimo—except that he never goes out in the field and generalissimos."

Publisher Henry Luce did his utmost to help the Nationalist cause, putting Chiang on the cover of the December 6, 1948, issue of *Time*—the eighth time the nationalist leader had graced the magazine's cover. *Time* warned that the Communists were "overrunning China like lava" and that the prestige of the Generalissimo had "sunk lower than the Yangtze." The Communists might "turn the world against us," one article warned. "Our objective in China is not that of aiding our friends. It is to roll back Communism in order to save our own—and Chinese—necks."

Truman agreed to see Madame Chiang, but made clear that there was nothing she could possibly say that would make him change his position. No date for the meeting was immediately set. Mayling visited Marshall briefly at the hospital on the evening of December 2, and then again for a longer meeting the next day. Beforehand Marshall had asked for a last-minute briefing from adviser George F. Kennan, the State Department's director of policy planning and renowned author of the "containment" theory, the basis for America's cold-war policies toward communism. Kennan had advised him to express concern and sympathy for China's predicament, but to tactfully make clear that "the whole idea of the National Government of China being saved at this time by things this country could do is a great misunderstanding." The Nationalists' military reverses were not due to a lack of arms or economic assistance, nor even to the lack of a "momentary fillip" to Chinese morale the appointment of an American commander in chief might bring, but rather to the absence of a "vital 'something,'" Kennan wrote.

In a meeting with Marshall at the hospital lasting nearly four hours, Mayling made several urgent requests on her husband's behalf. She asked that the White House make a statement supporting the Nationalist government and opposing communism in Asia; that the U.S. send an outstanding American military man to China to be the "spark plug" behind the Nationalist government's military effort, along with American officers to see to it that incompetent Chinese staff officers followed through on orders; and that a capable economic adviser be sent to reform the Nationalist government's finances, accompanied by massive economic aid to the tune of $3 billion over three years. All aid, both military and financial, would be administered by the Americans. According to Mayling, Chiang had even offered to step down if it was in the national interest. It is unclear how sincere Chiang was in his intentions, but in essence he was making the astonishing offer of virtually turning over his government and armies to the U.S. in return for aid.

Mayling stressed to Marshall the gravity of the situation, but refuted reports that thirty-three Nationalist divisions had surrendered to the Communists, asserting it was only twelve. Most of her husband's military commanders and political associates were ineffective, she told Marshall, insisting he would shed those who were incompetent. She said the government planned to abandon Nanking and make a stand in southeast China. The Generalissimo would support whomever the U.S. government sent.

Marshall gave her no encouragement. He had discussed the matter with Truman and ruled out any public statement of support, as it would have to be so watered down as to do more harm than good. He told her it was "highly inadvisable" for the U.S. to place a man in China under the present circumstances and that in any event he could not succeed without virtually taking over the government. As for aid, Marshall pointed out, the Republican-controlled Congress had cut the $463 million aid bill signed by Truman in April 1948 down to $400 million, despite the fact that the Republicans were arguing in favor of more aid to China. It was evident that Mayling's intended knight in shining armor had simply refused to get on his white horse.

Although Mayling returned to Leesburg empty-handed, she optimistically reported back to Chiang that she had clarified with Marshall a number of major "misunderstandings," and that in any case the matter of the request for U.S. aid was not one that could be resolved in a few days. Chiang, however, perceived that her efforts were proving of no use and in a telegram dated December 7 told her not to press the matter further, and urged her to hurry back to China after seeing Truman. She replied that she could not immediately return because she was hopeful of a positive outcome in further talks with Marshall, who she claimed seemed to be coming around, and added in a conspiratorial tone that she was undertaking "extremely complex" work that she could not write about in a telegram. She told Chiang to disregard the many "speculative" news reports concerning her visit to Washington. She also insisted he strictly forbid the foreign ministry and embassy officials in Washington from making public comments—a reflection of her rivalry with the foreign ministry, which had no option but to submit to her de facto control of foreign policy.

Marshall, meanwhile, underwent surgery, and to cheer him up Mayling wrote him a tongue-in-cheek battle report from the Dodona Manor "front." Often conscripted into duty by his wife, Marshall doubtless appreciated the letter, which began:

Top Secret
For Your Eyes Only
Report for General Flicker

While you are lolling in "silken" sheets, all is not quiet on the Home Front.

1. On the morning of December Seventh, 130 giant caliber daffodils of the Holland type were planted by first raking detonating leaves off flower-bed borders, digging fox-holes strategically placed in

trenches, camouflaging positions through putting soil firmly down, and finally re-raking leaves to keep off enemy frost.

2. After three hours of courageous and hard labour of outstanding bravery and endurance (this deserves at least a *bleeding heart* decoration) aggravated by combat nerves in waiting for field report from the hospital, whole company including unskilled labour did fatigue duty by imbibing Coca-Cola. . . .

Two "harrowing" hours on kitchen duty followed, for which Mayling submitted a "bill" of $6.50. "Deputy Commander" Katherine promised that if Mayling refrained from mutiny, a strawberry ice cream soda would be forthcoming, and argued that "since billeting in present bivouac, undersigned [Mayling] has rounder cheeks, better colour, and a noticeable increase in girth," and that therefore any financial claim was "invalid." Mayling countered that the assertion was "undemocratic, unfair, and discriminatory," adding:

Is there no justice? Hence this SOS to the Commanding General to get out of *them* silken sheets.
Home, sweet home was never like this!
Undersigned calls upon high heavens to witness this un-China treatment. . . .
Awaiting prompt and immediate Congressional attention, à la [Senator Tom] Connally, as due one who is on the soil of the Pilgrim Mothers—Down with slave labour!
Respectfully Submitted,
Una—Ex—Pluribus.
P.S. What is minus a kidney? Am I not . . . minus spleen?

The letter jokingly alluded to the tremendous controversy generated by her silk bed linens during her 1943 White House visit, and poked fun at her government's authoritarian tendencies and at the notoriously lavish entertainment designed to woo guests to the Nationalist cause. Mayling was clearly basking in her holiday from China. Even her old enemy insomnia vanished, perhaps due to Katherine's forced exertions.

On December 10 Mayling saw Truman, his wife Bess, and daughter Margaret for a five o'clock tea at Blair House—the Trumans had lately moved into the presidential guesthouse while the White House underwent renovations—along with Mrs. Marshall. Afterward Mayling met with the president privately and told him of the troubles faced by her husband and his government. When she emerged, reporters asked, "Madame Chiang, were you successful?" She replied: "I am sorry—no comment." The White House said merely that she had stated her case to the president and he had listened "sympathetically." She cabled her husband to be patient.

Wellington Koo, the Nationalist Chinese ambassador in Washington, subsequently complained to American officials that Mayling had come to the U.S. on a "girlish whim." He then said he had been "authorized" to offer the officials a "solution" to the problem of aid to China. At this "eleventh hour and fifty-ninth minute," China's ruling clan was willing to use its private fortunes to underwrite a loan of a billion dollars. The origin of the funds would be kept secret from the Chinese and American public. China could not withdraw funds from the World Bank because China was a member "on paper only," Koo said. The country's share in the bank was paid for by the U.S. government, a fact of which neither the American nor Chinese public was aware. The administration did not pursue the outlandish offer, which was probably a desperate bluff.

While Mayling lobbied Washington, General David Barr, commander of the U.S. Military Advisory Group in Nanking, warned that the Nationalists were doomed. In a December 18 report, he argued that further aid would have little impact, but cautioned that aid currently being given "should not be withdrawn abruptly . . . as such action would be widely condemned and would place the United States in an unfavorable light in the eyes of the world." The only reason for the U.S. to support the Nationalist government if it were forced to retreat to Taiwan would be to provide a base for future operations against the Communists should the Chinese people revolt, and to "curb Chinese subjugation and exploitation of the Taiwanese."

Mayling spent Christmas with Katherine Marshall, whose husband was still confined to the hospital. On Christmas Day the Chinese Communists broadcast a list of forty-three "war criminals." Chiang topped the roster; Mayling had the dubious honor of being the only woman on the list, which included T. V. Soong, H. H. Kung, and other top Nationalist officials, warlords, and diplomats, some living abroad. She continued to press Marshall for a change in U.S. policy to back her husband's government, even enlisting his wife to relay messages on her behalf. In an apparent effort to buoy Chiang's spirits, she wrote him in a December 28 telegram that Truman might announce a change in China policy within the week.

Chiang did not buy this and repeatedly pleaded with her to return to China. She replied, perhaps disingenuously, that American public opinion was changing in favor of the Nationalists and, besides, she could not leave now as there was much more work to be done. In recent days, she wrote on New Year's Day, she had been quietly meeting with leading congressional Republicans to lobby for aid. Her husband's armies, meanwhile, were fast disintegrating. In the two-month battle of Hsuchow ending on January 11, the Nationalists suffered at least three hundred thousand casualties. The Communists lost even more through the use of "human wave" tactics, but they now controlled the area north of the Yangtze River. The two armies massed on opposite banks of the mighty river. On January 14, Mao countered Chiang's peace proposal with what amounted to a demand for unconditional surrender. It was purely for show. The Communists could have crossed the Yangtze and taken Nanking at will.

Chapter Eighteen
Madame General

It is either in your hearts to love us or your hearts have been turned from us.

—Madame Chiang Kai-shek

In early January 1949 Mayling retreated into virtual seclusion at the Kung family residence in Riverdale, New York, declining a multitude of requests to make speeches and appearances. Behind the scenes she tried to rally support among Republican party, military, and church leaders. She asked the major Protestant denominations to publicly back her husband, but they refused. She wasted no time licking her wounds, however, quickly regrouping to plot a new strategy of attack. As her husband lost ground at home, she opened a second front in America, taking the battle from the Great Wall to Capitol Hill. From her base in the Bronx mansion above the Hudson, she took charge of Nationalist lobbying forces in the U.S., marshaling the formidable powers of command for which she had years ago earned the epithet "Madamissimo." On the advice of her husband's supporters in Congress, she plunged into spearheading a revamped lobbying campaign to secure aid for Chiang's government.

Nationalist lobbying in the U.S. was nothing new. Agents both overt and covert, mercenary and volunteer, had plied Washington at least since T. V. Soong lobbied for aid during the early years of the Second World War. In April 1948 the Nationalists had hired a professional lobbyist, William J. Goodwin, who promoted the Nationalist cause on Capitol Hill and arranged for the release of favorable publicity. Nationalist lobbying and publicity efforts had been mostly standard fare—putting a positive spin on events, advancing legitimate albeit exaggerated arguments, entertaining. But following Madame Chiang's appearance on the American scene

Madame Chiang Kai-shek with Eleanor Roosevelt on the White House lawn, 1943. *(Courtesy of Kuomintang Archives)*

Franklin D. Roosevelt meeting Madame Chiang at Washington's Union Station on her arrival in the capital in February 1943. *(Imperial War Museum, London, NYP 19607)*

Madame Chiang Kai-shek addressing the U.S. Congress on February 19, 1943, at the start of her sensational American tour, during which she called for American backing of Nationalist China in the war against Japan. *(CSU Archives/Everett Collection)*

Wellesley's most celebrated alumna created a fashion furor when she took a much-publicized stroll across the college's snow-covered campus wearing slacks during her 1943 American tour. She appears here with Wellesley president Mildred McAfee, who is wearing a Navy WAVES uniform. *(Imperial War Museum, London, NYP 6841)*

Madame Chiang with nephews Louis (far left) and David (far right) Kung, and niece Jeanette Kung (second from left) during her 1943 American tour. *(Imperial War Museum, London, NYP 6752)*

New York's Chinatown welcomes Madame Chiang Kai-shek during her 1943 American tour. *(Courtesy of Kuomintang Archives)*

A candid moment at the Cairo Conference in late 1943. Official photographs depict Madame Chiang seated alongside her husband, Roosevelt, and Churchill, although she was not a head of state. *(Imperial War Museum, London, E 26546)*

The Chiangs with General Joseph Stilwell, commander of American forces in China, who clashed with Chiang and was recalled by President Roosevelt in 1944. *(The George C. Marshall Research Library, Lexington, VA, SC 134625)*

"I'd Like To Get You On A Slow Boat To China"

This cartoon, which depicts Madame Chiang vamping Uncle Sam, was published following her arrival in Washington to seek massive American aid to rescue her husband's government and prevent China from falling into the hands of the communists. *(A 1948 Herblock Cartoon, copyright by the Herb Block Foundation)*

The legendary American general Douglas MacArthur kissing Madame Chiang's hand on departing from embattled Formosa (Taiwan) on August 3, 1950, not long after the outbreak of the Korean War. The famous kiss aroused controversy in the United States. *(© Bettmann/CORBIS)*

Vice-president Richard Nixon and his wife, Patricia, with the
Chiangs during a 1953 visit to Taipei. A strident anti-Communist,
Nixon was long one of Nationalist China's staunchest supporters.
(Courtesy of Kuomintang Archives)

Roy Howard, publisher of Scripps-Howard newspapers, visiting the Chiangs
in Taipei in 1955. Howard served as Eisenhower's unofficial envoy to the
Nationalist Chinese leaders. *(Courtesy of Kuomintang Archives)*

Chiang Kai-shek and Madame Chiang with his son from his first marriage, Chiang Ching-kuo (right), circa 1955 on Taiwan. Although stepmother and stepson appeared to get along in public, in private they were sometimes at odds. *(Hulton Archive/Getty Images)*

Mayling painting with Chiang looking on. She took up the brush in 1951 and before long became an accomplished amateur painter in the Chinese style. *(Courtesy of Kuomintang Archives)*

Madame Chiang at Chiang Kai-shek's funeral in 1975, flanked by her stepsons Chiang Ching-kuo (left) and Wego Chiang (right). *(Courtesy of Kuomintang Archives)*

Madame Chiang, accompanied by her grandson Chiang Hsiao-yung (second from left), as she returned to Taiwan in September 1994 to visit her beloved niece, Jeanette Kung, who was dying of cancer. Taiwanese president Lee Teng-hui (rear) and his wife, Tseng Wen-hui, greeted Madame Chiang on her arrival at the airport. *(United Daily News)*

in December 1948, the loose-knit organization that came to be known as the China Lobby changed tack, adopting as its preferred methods financial inducements and even direct intervention in American politics, accompanied by—still more ominously—slander, intimidation, and demagoguery. A key tenet of the reinvigorated campaign would be to convince Congress and the American public that the United States government and in particular certain individuals within it were responsible for the crisis the Nationalists now faced.

Madame Chiang was not only aware of these new, more aggressive tactics, but actively involved in their implementation. So deep was her cynicism—and so great her desperation—that she showed not the slightest qualm or hesitation in turning from persuasion to bribery of elected American representatives, although she did take great pains to prevent herself from being directly linked to lobbying activities. On January 8, 1949, she cabled Chiang for at least $200,000 to hire American publicity consultants to carry out lobbying efforts. The funds would be used to "encourage," as she phrased it, members of Congress as well as the American public to back the Nationalist government. She would direct the initiative, she wrote Chiang, but hastened to reassure him that no funds would pass through her hands. For the task of paymaster, she recruited nephew Louis Kung, who was nicknamed "the Major" or "the little fellow." Chiang replied that this matter could not be answered by telegram, since if it leaked there would be consequences, and again begged her to return.

Mayling, however, had no intention of leaving her new self-appointed command. On January 12 she invited Roy Howard and his wife, Margaret, to dinner at the Kungs' Riverdale home as part of her efforts to influence opinion leaders. She was in "excellent health," reported Howard, "beautiful as always," and appeared entirely relaxed. She had spoken with her husband several times of late, and discussed her unsuccessful visit to Washington "without the slightest evidence of hurt or rancor." She expressed great friendship for the Marshalls, and if she was disappointed that she was unable to change the secretary of state's thinking on China, Howard saw no sign of it. She insisted Truman had treated her with "great courtesy and kindness." Truman, she felt, took his cue on China policy from Marshall, who had long since ruled out any possibility of giving China sufficient aid to save the country from communism. She was convinced Americans would one day realize the terrible consequences of this error. She admitted she had "no doubt that there had been graft, dishonesty and misuse of funds" in China, though perhaps no more so than elsewhere. She appeared to be sustained, Howard thought, by a combination of "Christian fortitude and Oriental fatalism."

Fatalism, Oriental or otherwise, simply was not Mayling's métier, but it was true that she had become more religious over the years. She believed that she received "spiritual guidance" from God, who, she claimed, spoke to her both when she was awake and in her dreams. During the tumultuous days of early 1949, one morning she heard what she believed to be a divine message, in the form of an inner voice that said in Chinese, "You will have sixteen days of spinach soup." Puzzled, she consulted her sister Eling, who pointed out that if the Chinese word for spinach soup—*botang*—was pronounced with different tones, it meant waves and upheavals. Sure enough, for sixteen days uncertainty emanated from China. On the sixteenth day, Mayling received word from Chiang that he would "retire" from the presidency.

After Chiang stepped down on January 21, Vice President Li Zongren became acting president and Chiang retreated to his ancestral village. However, he remained head of the Kuomintang, as well as commander in chief of the armed forces, and therefore in practice still held the reins of political, military, and, not least, financial power. During this period, he made certain that funds would not fall into Communist hands, in part by depositing untold millions of dollars of government funds into overseas private bank accounts held in the names of loyal associates or into numbered accounts. Chiang had always sought his beloved hills of Xikou in times of turmoil, but it is doubtful they gave him much solace now—especially as he knew he might never see them again. On the very day Chiang left office, Dean Acheson became U.S. secretary of state, Marshall having resigned due to health reasons. Marshall had been friendly if unhelpful, but Acheson viewed the Nationalists with thinly disguised disdain. At the same time, the Communists took Beijing, and Nanking sank into chaos as the government fled to Canton.

T. V. Soong, serving as governor of Guangdong province, took Chiang's resignation as his cue to decamp. While millions of Chinese families were being torn asunder by civil war, or finding themselves trapped in China by circumstance amid the chaotic exodus, T. V. and his family left for an extended sojourn in Europe, arriving in the U.S. in June. Soong was by no means alone; during the turmoil and uncertainty of the late 1940s a host of Nationalist party and government leaders left for Hong Kong or exile in the West. They included Chiang's longtime lieutenant Chen Lifu, leader of the powerful C. C. Clique and one of the "reactionaries" Marshall had condemned at the conclusion of his mission. Chen settled in New Jersey and set himself up as a chicken farmer.

On January 27, 1949, Mayling cabled Chiang to press him again for cash urgently needed to fund her lobbying initiative on Capitol Hill, as well as among Protestant groups and in high-level military circles. The Catholic archbishop of Nanking, Paul Yu Pin, a close associate of the Chiangs who had lately taken refuge in the U.S., also needed funds for his lobbying efforts in Catholic circles. Yu was nicknamed the "political monk." She asked Chiang whether, of the $2 million of government funds held in the account of Gen. P. T. Mow, he would permit up to $200,000 to be withdrawn for lobbying purposes. Mow, a nephew of Chiang's first wife, headed the Nationalist Chinese air force procurement office in the U.S. He was a favorite of Mayling's, and his implication in the Chinese air force corruption scandal of the late 1930s had not hampered his career.

Although Chiang's response is not known, it was apparently in the affirmative, for Mayling's lobbying efforts in Congress soon began bearing fruit. On February 7, fifty-one Republican representatives presented Truman with an urgent inquiry regarding plans for the support of Nationalist China. Not long after, Sen. Pat McCarran, a Nevada Democrat, introduced a bill to provide the Nationalists a $1.5 billion loan, which was subsequently turned down by Congress.

As the Nationalists' military predicament worsened, Mayling intensified her lobbying efforts, gathering the faithful about her at the Kung residence in Riverdale for regular strategy talks. "I am now holding meetings each Tuesday with [General] P. T. Mow, [Nationalist UN delegate] Li Weiguo and others to give them orders on everything" concerning the lobby effort, she wrote Chiang, referring to a clutch of trusted operatives in the U.S. Besides her relatives—H. H. Kung, T. V. Soong, and Louis Kung—these included Yu Guohua, delegate to the World Bank; Gen. Peter T. K. Pee, military attaché at the embassy in Washington; UN representative

Tsiang T'ing-fu; Chen Lifu; and Chen Chih-mai, counselor at the embassy. In 1938 General Mow had been implicated in the air force corruption scandal that Mayling had investigated during her tenure as head of China's aviation ministry, but curiously was now closer than ever to the Chiangs. These men all wielded power well beyond their rank, and often reported directly to Chiang. In addition to official funds to carry out their regular work, they were given separate accounts from various branches of government for use at Chiang's discretion.

Her frequent protestations of lofty democratic principles notwithstanding, Mayling urged Chiang to sabotage acting president Li Zongren, suggesting several schemes to this end, and to maneuver himself back to the presidency as quickly as possible. Chiang replied on February 1 to say that his "retirement" served a number of useful purposes and told her to halt all her propaganda efforts and requests for aid from the U.S., and quickly return to China. In any case, Chiang added loftily, for the next two decades he would be critical to peace not only in China but in the world, so there was no urgent need to beg for aid at this time. He ordered her to give $10,000 to Bishop Yu for lobbying expenses, for which he would reimburse her shortly, and asked whether she had received a transfer for an unspecified sum that he had recently sent.

Chiang needed no encouragement from his wife when it came to preventing Li Zongren from exercising any real power. His success in this goal is illustrated by the fact that although after becoming acting president Li ordered the release of Zhang Xueliang and Yang Hucheng, Chiang's kidnappers in Xi'an, the secret police refused to carry out Li's order because they were still controlled by Chiang. Instead, Chiang ordered the execution of not only Yang but his entire family. Only one son survived, because he had joined the Communists. Zhang had already been secretly transferred to Taiwan in late 1946, where he remained in detention.

In early March Chiang sent Mayling three cables pleading with her to return, but she declined, insisting she must stay in the U.S. to direct her behind-the-scenes lobbying efforts. She instead dispatched nephew Louis Kung to China to meet with Chiang at his native village in the mountains. The purpose of Louis's mission was not revealed in telegrams, but it was probably to courier cash or bullion as well as to discuss U.S. lobbying efforts.

After becoming acting president, Li Zongren had immediately begun peace negotiations with the Communists in the vain hope of keeping them north of the Yangtze. But in an indication of the abysmal state of morale on the Nationalist side, a Kuomintang peace delegation dispatched to Beijing for peace talks defected en masse to the Communists after negotiations broke down. On April 20 the People's Liberation Army crossed the Yangtze. Nanking was captured with hardly a shot. Chiang, still in Xikou, paid a final visit to the graves of his ancestors and after a few days in Shanghai traveled briefly to Taiwan, where he would henceforth be based. There agriculture minister Tso Chun-sheng visited him in May. Wearing a blue scholar's gown, the "retired" Nationalist leader looked healthy and optimistic, betraying no sign of sadness or panic. The first thing he said was "Now Mao Tse-tung can't hit me!" which struck Tso as an "infantile" remark. Chiang was courteous, and even escorted Tso to his car as he left. "What a difference from the Mr. Chiang of Nanking days!" Tso marveled. "He reminded me of an old monk in a dilapidated temple—what a sorry sight."

Mayling wrote Chiang on May 6 that she had learned Britain was urging the U.S. government to recognize the Communists as China's governing authority. She proposed a nationwide propaganda campaign in the U.S. to forestall this possibility and to generate sympathy among the American public—and ultimately to secure more American aid. Chiang promptly agreed, complaining that Britain was "selling out" its wartime ally.

Under Madame Chiang's direction, the shadowy group that came to be known as the China Lobby was galvanized from a loose-knit, unfocused political movement within the Republican party into a powerful and effective political operation. On the American side, it was peopled by a constellation of isolationists, members of the Republican old guard, religious groups, and others who for diverse motives, ideological as well as commercial, shared a passion for Nationalist China, and spearheaded by paid American publicity agents.

For the Republicans, who had been shut out of the White House since 1932, the alliance with Chinese interests was a serendipitous marriage of convenience. Although they had taken control of Congress in 1946, they were bitter about having lost the 1948 presidential election. The China debacle made a handy stick with which to bludgeon the Democrats, whom lobbyists accused of having sold out the Nationalists. The State Department, they charged, was "soft" on communism and to blame for the "loss" of China. Mayling was looked to as the spiritual leader of the movement, whose luminaries included her friends Henry Luce, Republican congressman Walter H. Judd, New Hampshire senator Styles Bridges, Gen. Albert Wedemeyer, and a young congressman from California named Richard Nixon. Many others linked to the Lobby were her close friends, family, and protégés.

Among the most potent forces behind the China Lobby was a businessman named Alfred Kohlberg, who since 1916 had been importing embroidered linens from China and selling them under the prosaic name "Kohlkerchiefs." Mayling was on cordial terms with Kohlberg, whom she had first met in 1946 in Nanking. After her return to the U.S. in late 1948 Kohlberg began working closely with her and other Lobby operatives, particularly Counselor Chen Chih-mai. He attended at least one of the strategy meetings presided over by Madame Chiang in Riverdale, in early 1949. In person Kohlberg was disarming and affable, but underneath the smooth exterior lurked an ideological crusader of fanatical zeal. He was convinced that the international Communist movement, under the aegis of Moscow, had a secret blueprint for world conquest. Anyone who disagreed with him was a Communist, a pinko, or, at best, a "pro-Communist."

Kohlberg ran his own homegrown news service, dispatching with the aid of assistants a constant flow of pro-Nationalist China information to some two thousand newspapers and publications. He financed and ran the anti-Communist American China Policy Association and the magazine *Plain Talk* (later renamed *Freeman*). He had long held that there was a Communist "conspiracy" in the State Department, and in the Nationalist Chinese he found a willing audience for his theories.

Kohlberg was a master at planting innuendo and casting doubt on the loyalties of his targets. A typical example of his modus operandi was a letter to a *Los Angeles Daily News* columnist, commenting on a speech by Eleanor Roosevelt: "I think I may know more about Asia than Mrs. Roosevelt, and possibly, although I don't feel at all sure about it, more about Communism." He claimed to finance his anti-Communist campaign from the profits of his successful business, an assertion that appeared to be borne out when the Bureau of Internal Revenue, after extensive investigation, found only that he was due a slight tax refund from 1946 and 1947. Kohlberg took delight in taunting the Treasury Department, which in a letter to the secretary of the treasury following the failed investigation he called a "cat's-paw" of the Communists. It is nonetheless possible that he received cash payments from the China Lobby.

On May 19 Mayling telegraphed Chiang twice to press for more funds, so that her lobbying organization could "use cash to counter" what she called anti-Chiang propaganda that Communists were spreading in America. "At my request Senator Pat McCarran today attacked Secretary of State Acheson during a Senate Appropriations Committee hearing . . . accusing Acheson of conspiring with the Soviet Union to abandon the Far East and recognize the Communist Chinese government," she proudly reported, adding that Acheson was forced to deny the charge and compelled to promise an "investigation" of the State Department's Far Eastern Affairs Division's policy toward China. In closing she wrote: "In order to prevent my recent close relations with Congress from leaking out, please immediately destroy this secret code book 1421." Chiang replied to warn her not to mention the lobbying campaign or congressmen's names in telegrams, as they might be intercepted.

As the Communists marched on Shanghai, Mayling urged Chiang to prevent weapons, factories, and other key assets in the city from falling into Communist hands. Shanghai fell on May 27. Hundreds of thousands of refugees fled to Taiwan, and many thousands more were stranded. Families were torn apart in the rush to leave, in many cases permanently. Days later Mayling complained to her husband that following the Communist takeover of Shanghai the U.S. government had received telephone calls reporting that the situation in the city was fine. "I had asked you to destroy communication links between Shanghai and the outside world but it was not done," she wrote. "This increases the possibility that the US will recognize the Communist government." She peppered Chiang with suggestions to thwart the Communists, including bombing Chinese airports, flooding Communist-occupied areas with fake currency to disrupt the economy, and sending secret agents into Communist territory to prevent foreign and overseas Chinese industrialists from returning and reestablishing their business operations.

On taking office in January 1949 Secretary of State Acheson had ordered a review of Sino-American ties. In late June 1949 Mayling learned that the State Department had completed a document that blamed Chiang Kai-shek entirely for the "loss" of China, and was preparing to publish it. Alarmed, she warned Chiang and lobbied vigorously to prevent its release, or at least to have its conclusions modified. The China White Paper, as the report was called, was a 1,054-page tome of government documents, cables, and reports, including the suppressed Wedemeyer Report, amounting to a postmortem conducted while the body still breathed. Chiang Kai-shek was written off entirely, and it was assumed Taiwan would soon be overrun by Communists. The U.S. was preoccupied with rebuilding Europe and molding Japan in its own image. The report mounted a robust defense of U.S. policy, and placed blame for the China debacle squarely on the Nationalists' own corruption and incompetence, Chiang's obstinacy, and poor leadership. "We picked a bad horse," Truman said privately. In essence, the White Paper was a unilateral announcement that China was lost to communism and that the U.S. had washed its hands of the matter.

Acheson wanted to publish the incendiary document, arguing it would silence the "primitives." Chiang objected on the grounds that it would give "moral support" to the Communists, but Congressman Judd urged him not to oppose publication because the American public would see that as a "confession of guilt." A debate within the administration over whether to publish the White Paper ensued.

As if on cue, on June 30, 1949, Mao Zedong launched an anti-American salvo, saying China was "united in a common struggle" with the international anti-imperialist front headed by the Soviet Union. "You have to choose between the alternative of either killing the tiger or being eaten by it," Mao proclaimed. He credited Moscow and the "masses" in America with helping to cause the Nationalist downfall. He promised to create a "people's democratic dictatorship" in China in which "the people" would have the right to voice their opinions and "lackeys of imperialism"—landlords, bureaucratic capitalists, and Kuomintang members—would not.

In America, meanwhile, accusations that the Soongs, Kungs, and other wealthy and well-connected Chinese were hiding ill-gotten gains in the U.S. grew louder. There was talk of freezing Nationalist Chinese financial interests in the U.S. In May 1949 Truman ordered the FBI to launch a secret inquiry. John Edgar Hoover, FBI director, instructed field offices to give the investigation "preferred and expeditious attention." Despite exhaustive investigation, the FBI was apparently unable to fully substantiate the claims. Banks were reluctant to supply information on privacy grounds and the FBI was either unable or unwilling to force them to do so.

In late July Mayling reported to Chiang that a measure to furnish aid to Nationalist China had failed to pass a congressional appropriations committee (she did not specify House or Senate). She would continue to try to "use"—as she put it—some members of the committee to propose at least $100 million in U.S. military aid to the Nationalists at its next meeting. "The exact amount is still under negotiation, but in order to persuade a certain number of members we must first promise to contribute to their next re-election campaigns," she wrote, asking Chiang to remit funds. She closed by saying that this telegram was "extremely confidential" and ordered him to discard the codebook used to decipher the telegram's code.

At that moment Chiang was busily attempting to forge an anti-Communist alliance in the Pacific. To this end he visited South Korean president Syngman Rhee and Elpidio Quirino, president of the Philippines. En route back to Taiwan, he learned of the August 5 release of the White Paper. Chiang was infuriated by the document's conclusion that he was solely responsible for losing China, but remained silent. Instead, he sent $800,000 to Mayling's associates in the U.S., part of which was used to retain an American public relations firm named Allied Syndicates. Officially hired by the Bank of China, the firm's task was to prevent both U.S. recognition of the Communist Chinese and confiscation of Nationalist Chinese assets in the U.S. to hand them over to the Communists.

In America, the effect of the White Paper was electric. The growls of Acheson's "primitives" were not silenced; instead they rose to a full-throated roar. As Acheson ruefully observed, the paper's conclusions were "unpalatable to believers in American omnipotence, to whom every goal unattained is explicable only by incompetence or treason." Marshall was attacked by congressmen on both sides of the aisle, but his virtually unassailable reputation saved him from serious harm. He removed himself from the storm, taking his wife and Mayling on vacation to Raquette Lake in the Adirondacks, at the former estate of financier J. P. Morgan. Once the dust had settled, Mayling spent a weekend in September with the Marshalls in

Virginia. Soon afterward she invited them for "chicken-tails" and dinner in New York, promising to fix the general "a real stinker" and prepare his favorite Chinese dish, longevity noodles. Then they went to see the Broadway hit *South Pacific.*

At the time the White Paper was released, a debate raged in the State Department and in the U.S. government over the essential nature of the Chinese Communists and their relationship with Russian communism, which was by then being regarded as a threat. An underlying premise of the White Paper was that the Chinese Communists were not true Communists, but merely social and agrarian reformers, and that they were not directed by Moscow. This misconception was nurtured by the Chinese Communists and accepted by Western sympathizers—dubbed "parlor pinks" by detractors—many of whom were idealistic and well-intentioned intellectuals for whom communism was appealing as the antithesis of the fascism that had so recently threatened to engulf the world.

Whether this conventional wisdom was the result of a calculated vilification campaign orchestrated by the Communists, as supporters of the Nationalists contended, or an organic shift fueled by influential books such as *Thunder Out of China* remains the subject of debate. Only later was it recognized that there was no fundamental distinction between communism as a political force in Asia and in Russia. The movement in China emphasized agriculture over Marx's original focus on industry, but Moscow was nonetheless the Jerusalem of the Chinese communist movement, even though Beijing and Moscow were sometimes at odds.

Adding sting to the debate was the enormous disillusionment across America with the Nationalist government, even among its most devoted supporters, the American Protestant churches. There was widespread dismay that the massive military and economic aid that the U.S. had given China had apparently been squandered. Churchgoing Americans could not comprehend how Chiang Kai-shek, the man they had supported for so long with pennies and prayers, was now on the brink of losing half a billion souls to "godless" communism. They felt duped, even betrayed, by the Christian Generalissimo and his glamorous wife.

Yet another current in the maelstrom of 1949 was the debate over the military value of Taiwan to the Nationalists and to the U.S. Views diverged sharply in the high echelons of Washington. The State Department wished to write off China and Taiwan entirely, while the Joint Chiefs of Staff saw Taiwan as a crucial link in the strategic defense perimeter of the western Pacific.

As recriminations flew fast and furiously in Washington during the spring and summer of 1949, Chiang Kai-shek quietly sent to Taiwan troops, large quantities of munitions, and China's entire foreign exchange and gold and silver bullion reserves of some $400 million. He also transferred to Taiwan an enormous collection of priceless artworks from the Imperial Palace in Beijing. Once this was learned in America, Chiang was severely criticized. Mayling wrote him on September 13 to urge him to resume control of the government as soon as possible, as she and their American friends were finding it difficult to defend his actions, given that he had no nominal authority to have taken them. When one senator argued in a meeting with Acheson that Chiang "took the only feasible course," the secretary of state heatedly replied that Chiang's action was "absolutely wrong and that no fair view of the situation could permit of any other judgment."

It was also in September 1949 that Chiang hatched the ill-conceived scheme of secretly offering Wedemeyer, through an intermediary, $5 million to give up his military career in the U.S. to go to China to help Chiang fight the Communists. Wedemeyer politely declined the offer, saying that if Chiang's government had such a large sum of funds, public or private, it should be used instead for the welfare of the Chinese people and to repel the Communists.

Taiwan was soon loaded with the best units of the Nationalist army and ample matériel. The Nationalists' morale was surprisingly good—at least they had put a ninety-mile moat between them and the Communists. But among Taiwanese, bitterness lingered over the 2-28 Incident, and it was exacerbated by the waves of mainland refugees, rich and poor, who were flooding in. Many came in fishing junks, landing on beaches. Shanghai industrialists dismantled factories wholesale and shipped them across the Taiwan Strait. By July 1949 over a million Chinese had come, swelling the population to 7.2 million. Chiang's secret police cast a security net over the island, arresting suspected Communists as well as Taiwanese advocating independence or foreign intervention.

Washington, meanwhile, wrestled with the question of what to do about Taiwan. State Department China expert John Paton Davies argued that giving more aid to Chiang would be "throwing good money after bad," and added that "efficiency, leadership and morale are not export products which can be shipped to him on an assistance program." The National Security Council recommended that the U.S. should make abundantly clear to Chiang that "the lessons to be drawn from developments on the mainland and from previous Formosan reactions to Chinese rule will not be overlooked," while secretly forging ties with leaders of the Taiwanese independence movement.

The State Department and the military intelligence concurred with the CIA's prediction that "failing U.S. military occupation and control, a non-Communist regime on Taiwan probably will succumb to the Chinese Communists by the end of 1950." The British Foreign Office agreed, and argued that the question of diplomatic recognition of the Communist regime "should be considered on a basis of practical convenience rather than of sentiment." But the State Department had a ticklish problem—that of washing its hands of the China debacle without appearing to be ignobly and unceremoniously dumping its wartime ally. American prestige, it was felt, was riding on America's self-image as an altruistic, fair, and honest "friend" of China—an image not widely shared among the Chinese themselves.

One school of thought in Washington held that the best way to get rid of the Taiwan "problem" was to let the Communists take over, but the Pentagon wanted to keep the "unsinkable aircraft carrier," as Taiwan was dubbed. The U.S. government, however, was sensitive to Communist propaganda concerning American motives in Asia and took pains not to be accused of imperialistic designs on Taiwan. In early 1949, the State Department had produced a secret memorandum discussing the island's ambiguous legal status. One interpretation was that China had "full title" to the island by virtue of the Cairo Declaration, the other that China did not possess title to the island at all. The detailed report considered how Taiwan might be administered under a UN trusteeship, later either to become independent or to form an association with China.

Some in the State Department favored Taiwanese independence. A top-secret draft statement prepared for the secretary of state stated that the U.S. "no longer regards the Declaration of Cairo applicable in so far as Formosa is concerned," and was prepared to consider with the UN "measures whereby the Formosans may be protected against mis-rule and afforded an opportunity freely to express their wishes with respect to the future status of Formosa." But the statement was not made public.

When Mao Zedong proclaimed the founding of the People's Republic of China with Beijing as its capital on October 1, 1949, Mayling's sister Ching Ling was among those standing with him on the balcony overlooking Tiananmen Square at that historic moment. She had remained in Shanghai after the city fell to the Communists in May 1949. She was determined to remain in China to help from within rather than, in her biting words, "leave my country and retreat to a small white Connecticut farmhouse and prepare my memoir for a tall, thin American publisher." Although she had not joined the Communist party, she was named to the largely honorary post of deputy chairman of the Communist government. The Soviet Union recognized the new government the following day.

The Communists took Canton in October. Chiang moved the Nationalist capital back to Chungking, but snowballing defections by local warlords shattered his hopes of making a last stand there. As Communist General Deng Xiaoping's forces neared Chengdu in early December, Chiang left Chinese soil for the last time, arriving on Taiwan by December 11. Lively debate ensued in the U.S., with many arguing that it was in the American interest to forge a working relationship with the new regime. The State Department notified diplomats that the loss of Taiwan was expected soon, and instructed them to take the position that the island was of no strategic importance and that the Chinese alone were responsible for its fate.

Mayling, meanwhile, fretted over the fate of a large quantity of Chinese tungsten ore stored in Hong Kong. On January 1, 1950, she telegraphed Chiang to urge him to transfer ownership of the ore into the name of an unspecified American company (one controlled by the Kungs, perhaps), as she feared that when Britain recognized the Communist government, the valuable commodity would wind up in Communist hands. She offered to sell it on the U.S. market, where it could fetch higher prices. "It would be a pity to suffer such a financial loss," she wrote. Chiang ordered that she drop the matter to avoid giving enemies an excuse to "slander" them.

On January 5, 1950, Truman announced that the U.S. had "no predatory designs" on Taiwan, did not wish to establish military bases on the island "at this time," and had no intention of becoming involved, militarily or otherwise, in China's civil conflict. Then he delivered the coup de grâce: "The United States Government will not provide military aid or advice to Chinese forces on Formosa. In the view of the United States Government, the resources on Formosa are adequate to enable them to obtain the items which they might consider necessary for the defense of the Island." As if on cue, the next day London recognized the Communist government in Beijing. The Communists had in effect been bestowed an engraved invitation to seize Taiwan.

Feeling angry, betrayed, humiliated, and defeated, Mayling was faced with the choice of taking permanent refuge in America, as her entire family and many friends had done, or rejoining her husband to make a symbolic last stand. From halfway around the globe she had watched in despair as city after city, province after province, fell and once-loyal army officers defected en masse to the Communists. By day she plotted and lobbied; by night she was racked by insomnia and stricken by a "vast bleakness," as she described the renewed bout of depression. When her husband finally withdrew to Taiwan, smaller than the smallest of mainland provinces, "The world wrote off our China and some of our erstwhile friends and allies recognized the Communist regime," she wrote bitterly. "I then determined that no matter what the future held, since I could do no more for my country in America, I would return to share the fate of my husband and my people on Formosa."

Friends and relatives tried to dissuade her, fearing that she was headed to certain death, and pointed out that her "sacrifice" would be in vain as it was only a matter of weeks, perhaps days, before Taiwan fell too. "I shall feel very anxious about you and frankly I would be happier if your husband were to join you here," Eleanor Roosevelt wrote her in a concerned, motherly tone. "The people of China seem to have made their decision and I doubt if Formosa can stand out against it. I understand your feelings and they are courageous but sometimes the things that courage can lead one into . . . serve no real good and certainly there is very little that you can do now in Formosa." Mayling did not reply.

But Mayling had made up her mind. "I felt . . . that life was meaningless if I survived while China perished," she wrote. "How could I let my husband face the greatest setback of his life without me at his side?" One day at dawn an "ethereal Voice" told her: "All is right." She went to her sister Eling, who asked, "What has happened? Your face looks radiant." Mayling replied that God had spoken to her and she was going "home" by the first available plane. Without another word of protest, Eling—who had been trying to persuade Mayling to stay in America—helped her pack. Mayling wondered to what sort of "home" she was headed. Not to China, but to Taiwan—a mere "dot on the map." There she would join people who were not "duped," as she phrased it, by the Communists, who had chosen freedom and left possessions and even family behind. And—of course—she would be joining her husband as well. At last, after receiving divine reassurance, she later wrote, she knew that that was what she should do.

But it was not Mayling's style to slink away with her tail between her legs. She could not leave America without responding to what she perceived as grievous insults to the dignity of her country, her husband, and herself. It was time to emerge from seclusion for a dramatic reappearance on the American stage. As she pondered her final riposte, she arranged for a fund of more than a million dollars to be placed at the disposal of Counselor Chen Chih-mai, Alfred Kohlberg's close associate, for lobbying purposes.

On Sunday, January 8, 1950, she gave a defiant and emotional farewell speech over NBC's national television and radio network. Staged for maximum impact, her parting statement was a carefully scripted virtuoso performance worthy of Scarlett O'Hara in Selznick's cinematic epic *Gone With the Wind*. Wearing a simple black silk Chinese dress with an austere high collar, she sat before a microphone at her sister's house in Riverdale and spoke in a soft but firm voice. Though she may have looked delicate and tiny, her words and tone oozed righteously aggrieved martyrdom.

She was sad to leave America, where, she said, she had received "much of the inspiration for whatever I have been able to do for my people." She was returning to Chinese soil. "I shall return to my people on the island of Formosa, the fortress of our hopes, the citadel of our battle," she said. "With or without help we shall fight," she told her nationwide audience. "We are not defeated." The world was now divided in a "gigantic conflict" between good and evil, between liberty and communism. China, "abandoned and alone, now shoulders the only rifle in the defense of liberty."

Her husband, she said, was first among the world's statesmen to see through the "lie" of communism. He was the first to fight the Communists, and had been doing so for more than twenty years. "A few years ago he was exalted for [his] courage and tenacity. . . . Now he is pilloried. Times have changed, but the man has not changed." She went on, her voice charged with emotion:

"Already the moral weaklings are deserting us. It is with heavy heart that I note that a former ally, Britain, which sacrificed millions of lives on the altar of freedom, has now been taken by its leaders into the wilderness of intrigue. Britain has bartered the soul of a nation for a few pieces of silver. I say, 'For shame,' to Britain. One day these pieces of silver will bear interest in British blood, sweat and tears on the battleground of freedom. That which is morally wrong can never be politically right."

To Americans, she spoke of the "long friendship" between China and the U.S. "Your name among us will always be treasured for its friendship and kindliness. . . . I can ask the American people for nothing more. When a nation, like a man, does an act of justice it must be of his conscience, and not by request or demand. . . . Perhaps you will think me proud. My friends, my country is humbled. Our government is on an island in the ocean.

"At such a time, no pleading can be with dignity. It is either in your hearts to love us or your hearts have been turned from us. It is either in your mind and your will to aid China in her struggle for liberty, or you have abandoned liberty. . . . We stand with empty but willing hands. We stand humble, tired, crying for peace and rest . . . but we shall not give up the fight for liberty. . . . History records with devastating truth that right will prevail."

As she boarded a Trans World Airlines jet, she thanked China's friends. "I wish you all the luck in the world," she said. "God bless you. Goodbye."

PART IV

Chapter Nineteen
The Resurrection

We have just been through the valley of death. We have touched the rock bottom of desolation, darkness and despair. But if the night is at its darkest, the dawn is at hand . . .

—Madame Chiang Kai-shek

Crowds of supporters turned out to greet Mayling at stopovers in San Francisco, Honolulu, and Manila as she made the journey to Taiwan. She was mid-flight when on January 12, 1950, Secretary of State Dean Acheson told Washington's National Press Club that Taiwan and Korea lay outside the U.S. defense perimeter, a pivotal remark that drew little attention at the time.

During the long trip, she thought of her husband and their many tumultuous years together. She recalled the public pledge they made on their wedding day to work for the unity and uplifting of China, and felt "sick at heart" at the character assassinations against him, and others, so cleverly foisted—as she saw it—on the world by Communist propagandists. "When the water recedes, the stones will appear," she claimed to have told herself, citing a Chinese proverb. "Nothing remains hidden. Time and God will vindicate them." But her mind was filled with questions and doubts. Why had the Communists won? Why had she failed to secure American aid? Could she have done more? And finally, "What could I do now?" The answer, she realized suddenly, was more spiritual than material; all along she had been "using God" instead of "letting God use me." She thought of starting a prayer group, but "quailed" self-consciously, fearing her friends would think her, as she had once regarded her mother, self-righteous and "over-pious."

She arrived on Taiwan on January 13, having not seen her husband in over a year. Looking forward to a quiet reunion, she was dismayed to see throngs of well-wishers rush to greet her as she disembarked, crowding out Chiang. When he managed to reach her, they only shook hands stiffly and smiled, as Chinese mores made a public embrace unthinkable. Before departing the airfield, they paused together and silently gazed westward, as if trying to see the mainland beyond the horizon. "On this island we would pick up the pieces and rebuild," she thought.

Rebuilding was one matter; forgiving was another. The Chiangs felt abandoned and betrayed by the West. Britain was an especial target of venom. Mayling spoke with the bitterest contempt of London's recognition of Beijing, likening it to British prime minister Neville Chamberlain's appeasement of Hitler at Munich in 1938. Her husband, in contrast, was convinced that Britain's China policy was motivated by a desire to strengthen the Communists so that the ultimate battle against communism would take place in Asia rather than in Europe. Mayling was careful to mute her anger at the U.S., as she still hoped for an eventual rescue by Washington.

Beijing blustered its intention to "liberate" Taiwan, heightening fears of an imminent invasion. In January Beijing tried to unseat Taipei from the UN Security Council and complained at the "unjustified" delay when the organization did not immediately move to oust the Nationalist Chinese. The State Department found itself in an awkward predicament: senior officials did not wish to lift a finger on behalf of the Nationalists but were extremely anxious to avoid giving the impression that the U.S. had ingloriously delivered the final blow to the Nationalist resistance on Taiwan when the anticipated Communist takeover occurred.

For Americans, the early days of 1950 were a time of national soul-searching and painful realization of the limits of American omnipotence. Still reeling from the "loss" of China, Americans were rattled by a barrage of blows that fueled the mass hysteria rising against communism. On the eve of Mayling's arrival on Taiwan, Joseph Alsop, syndicated columnist and wartime aide to General Chennault, authored a scathing riposte to the China White Paper in the influential *Saturday Evening Post*. Alsop challenged the White Paper's essential conclusion that Chiang was the author of his own doom: "If you have kicked a drowning friend briskly in the face as he sank for the second and third times, you cannot later explain that he was doomed anyway because he was such a bad swimmer."

The China experts in the foreign service had served China to the Communists, he charged in the incendiary article, "like a trussed bird on a platter."

Then, on January 21, Alger Hiss, suspected spy and a former senior State Department official who accompanied Roosevelt to Yalta, was convicted of perjury before a federal grand jury for denying that he had passed documents to the Soviet Union. His friend Dean Acheson famously told the press, "I do not intend to turn my back on Alger Hiss." Hiss's conviction was a great victory for the House Committee on Un-American Activities, a congressional Communist-hunting panel. On February 3, Klaus Fuchs, a German-born physicist who had helped develop the atomic bomb, confessed he had passed critical information to the Soviets. With Fuchs's help the Soviets succeeded in detonating their first atomic bomb in the summer of 1949, dismaying Americans over the end of their nuclear monopoly.

Alarm turned to hysteria when on February 9, a scant month after Mayling's departure, the junior Republican senator from Wisconsin publicly charged the State Department with harboring 205 Communist party members in its ranks. He claimed to have a list and said their presence was known to the secretary of state, in effect accusing Acheson of treason. Sen. Joseph McCarthy's charges became a national sensation, unleashing a vicious witch hunt that ravaged the lives of countless individuals, some guilty, some naive, many innocent. The notorious McCarthy era, one of the darkest hours in American history, had begun.

McCarthyism could not have wielded the power it did were it not for the China Lobby, which helped to lay the groundwork for the senator's charges. Alfred Kohlberg met with McCarthy and quickly harnessed him to the China Lobby agenda. It was a perfect match: a demagogue in search of a cause and a cause in search of an unscrupulous firebrand.

Fueled by fear and loathing of communism, the China Lobby quickly gained broad support across America. Its central tenet—that if only the U.S. government would give Chiang Kai-shek the necessary backing he could fight his way back to the mainland and turn the tide against the spread of communism in Asia—became accepted wisdom in many quarters. A staunch Chiang supporter, California Republican Sen. William Knowland—dubbed "the Senator from Formosa"—expressed the fears of many in arguing that if Taiwan and South Korea fell to communism, Japan and the

Philippines would be next in line, and the U.S. defensive perimeter might be pulled back to the California coast. The motives of many Lobby followers were sincere, if misguided, but the ugly truth was that they too had blood on their hands, for operatives such as Kohlberg and Chen Chih-mai worked hand-in-glove with McCarthy and his cohorts, feeding the infamous senator rumors, half-truths, hearsay, and distortions, which he used unverified to denounce and destroy. Kohlberg relished his role as "agitator, prophet and Cassandra," wrote an interviewer in the *New York Post*. "Not only does he enjoy it but he . . . plays [it] with a deadly skill." The same might have been said of Mayling.

Such was the power of the China Lobby in American politics that anyone remotely critical of the Nationalist government was quickly labeled a Communist, or a sympathizer. The Lobby's tactics were intimidation, innuendo, and character assassination. Lauchlin Currie, Harry Dexter White, and Alger Hiss, all formerly well-placed officials in the Roosevelt administration, had already been charged with espionage during the House Committee on Un-American Activities hearings in 1948, and Chiang Kai-shek's partisans seized on their cases to accuse them of sabotaging the Nationalist government. These men were shown to have been Soviet agents. But beginning in March 1950 with Owen Lattimore, the respected Asia scholar who had been Roosevelt's representative to Chiang Kai-shek in the early 1940s, a generation of respected China experts, many of them in the U.S. foreign service, were groundlessly and unfairly denounced as Communists. Many were men whom Mayling knew personally, some well; in addition to Lattimore, these included John S. Service, John Carter Vincent, and John Paton Davies, who came under scrutiny in 1951.

Numerous figures in the entertainment industry were also targeted. During the McCarthy era, many promising careers were torpedoed, and many innocent victims were driven into exile or even to suicide. For nearly two decades the China Lobby would wield enormous influence over America's China policy, curtailing academic freedom and stifling dissenting voices by forcing potential critics into "psychic preventative detention." Criticism of Chiang Kai-shek on the part of Americans became tantamount to disloyalty, even treason. Apart from the notorious senator, Kohlberg perhaps bears greater responsibility for the McCarthy era than any other individual. Mayling, too, is far from blameless.

* * *

Cut loose but undaunted, Chiang resumed the presidency on March 1, 1950, prompting former acting president Li Zongren, who had fled to New York for "medical treatment" in December 1949, to denounce Chiang as a dictator. Chiang defiantly vowed to lead his loyal followers, a bedraggled band of two million refugees, to recover their homeland. Here on his island redoubt, the embattled Generalissimo pledged to forge a model Chinese province and a beacon of prosperity and freedom for Chinese compatriots on the mainland. These were brave dreams. The notion of a "return to the mainland" by military force was recognized as pure fantasy by the Americans, but diplomats were careful not to speak of this to the Chiangs. Unrealistic as the idea was, it served the crucial purpose of buoying morale among Chiang's followers.

In fact, Chiang Kai-shek, Mayling, and their followers were fervently praying they could hold Taiwan until the advent of a third world war, an American rescue, or a sheer miracle. Taiwan was just 1/260th of the mainland's size and less than 2 percent of its population. The Taiwan Strait, the Chiangs believed, was all that stood between them and annihilation. They expected a mass invasion in early summer, before the typhoon season. Ching-kuo made arrangements for his father to take asylum in the Philippines if needed.

Chiang appointed K. C. Wu, a former Shanghai mayor as popular among Americans as Chinese, governor of Taiwan. For the island's top military post, Chiang appointed Gen. Sun Li-jen, a graduate of Virginia Military Institute who had been close to Stilwell and T. V. Soong. He named George Yeh, a graduate of Amherst College and Oxford, foreign minister. Mayling strongly backed these members of the "American faction," whose appointments were designed to please Washington.

In April 1950 Mayling established the Chinese Women's Anti-Communist Aggression League to help destitute refugee soldiers and their families, who were squatting in temples and schools. She appealed to the business community to help build housing for the soldiers, enlisting wives of the island's business leaders. The Women's League, as her group came to be known, built numerous "military villages" with basic housing for tens of thousands of soldiers and their dependents. Many soldiers posted on the frontline islands in the Taiwan Strait had families on Taiwan with no means of support, so Mayling spearheaded efforts to train the women to do household and handicraft work. She dispatched groups of women to visit troops and bring them presents and food. She initiated many other projects, including teaching Mandarin Chinese to Taiwanese women, providing first aid courses, and visiting the sick and wounded in hospitals.

Emma Mills, Mayling's friend from Wellesley, visited Taiwan in the spring of 1950. She was struck by what she saw as evidence of Mayling's "Wellesley training" in her friend's businesslike response to the situation on beleaguered Taiwan. Mills toured the Women's League headquarters, where Mayling "had all the women busy" in a volunteer "sewing factory" making a million sets of underwear for soldiers from bolts of unbleached muslin. They raised money to buy material for uniforms through drives, theatricals, auctions, and dances. Mills found the wives of senior government officials and military officers bent over twenty-eight old Japanese sewing machines. There were not enough machines to go around so they took turns. Mayling sewed a T-shirt.

The two college friends relaxed in the sulfur hot spring baths at a Japanese villa in the mountains. Mayling griped about her husband's subordinates, complaining that General Sun Li-jen was "getting out of hand—too much inflated by publicity." Mayling was likely aware that senior Washington officials were drawing up plans to oust Chiang and replace him with either Sun or the respected scholar-diplomat Hu Shih, and then make Taiwan a UN trusteeship. But she may never have learned that in early June, Sun sent a secret letter to Assistant Secretary of State Dean Rusk proposing to lead a coup against Chiang and requesting U.S. backing. As for K. C. Wu and his wife, Edith, "Mayling is jealous of both these people, thinks he is a great publicity seeker," Mills recorded in her diary.

Back in the U.S., Mills hit the lecture circuit, advocating American support for the Nationalist government, now effectively in exile, in Taipei. Prospects appeared dim. A State Department memorandum flatly stated, "The US does not recognize the present regime on Formosa as the ultimate solution." By May the situation was precarious. There was bad blood between mainlanders and Taiwanese; there were food and housing shortages. American intelligence reported that large numbers of troops, fighters, and junks were massing along the southeast China coast in preparation for an assault. The State Department warned Americans to leave, assuming Taiwan would topple in a matter of months. American aid had been cut off, and the upkeep of the troops was a huge financial burden. "We were at our wits' end," Wu said.

At that critical juncture, an American syndicated columnist, Constantine Brown, claimed H. H. Kung and T. V. Soong had a billion dollars deposited in the U.S., and asked why these "high-minded and patriotic Chinese citizens" did not lend $300 million to the cash-strapped Nationalist government. This would "not exactly impoverish them" and would impress Congress and Americans as an example of "unselfish patriotism." It could hardly have been a more inopportune moment to begin wooing the U.S. again, but the Chiangs were desperate. They dispatched trusted aide Hollington Tong to sound out John Foster Dulles, consultant to Secretary of State Acheson.

Dulles bluntly told Tong that there was no possibility of any "bargaining." There had been in America a "complete loss of confidence in the will of the Nationalist forces to fight," Dulles said, adding they had ample resources to defend Taiwan themselves if they so wished. He cited rumors circulating that many Nationalist leaders, including Chiang, were planning to leave the island for safer shores. He pointedly reminded Tong that in 1943 Madame Chiang told Roosevelt, "God helps those who help themselves." Dulles declared that now was an excellent time for the Nationalists to "take that to heart." It is doubtful Tong relayed this last barb to Mayling.

Privately, however, Dulles favored preventing a Communist takeover of Taiwan. He urged in a May 18 memorandum that the U.S., to shore up American prestige in the Far East, "take a dramatic and strong stand that shows our confidence and resolution." Taiwan had strategic advantages, and the U.S. had a "moral responsibility" toward its native inhabitants. "If we do not act," he warned, "it will be everywhere interpreted that we are making another retreat because we do not dare risk war." Dulles added prophetically that such an interpretation would invite adventurism elsewhere.

Mayling then wrote Secretary of Defense Louis Johnson, asking him to visit Taiwan. Acheson dismissed the idea as "most undesirable." All else having failed, Mayling turned once again to her old friend "General Flicker," as she called George Marshall, after his boyhood nickname. Marshall was retired now and running the American Red Cross, but he still had influence. Swallowing her pride, she wrote him a long, heartfelt letter pleading for military aid to match the Russian-backed military buildup in China and to counter the looming Communist assault. "Undoubtedly we will experience devastating air raids in the very near future," she wrote, in her most persuasive style. "But here on this beautiful Island . . . we will carry on the task of fighting for the freedom of our people. . . . No effort will be too great, no sacrifice will be spared. This Island . . . will serve to harass and drain the Russians just as the British Isles drained Hitler." She took pains to promise that any aid would be controlled by U.S. personnel.

It was a last-ditch, long-shot plea. Marshall did not even bother to reply, perhaps because he had just sent her a breezy letter detailing his and Katherine's travels. On June 23 Secretary Acheson publicly reiterated that American policy remained unchanged—the U.S. would not intervene in Taiwan. Truman rejected not only a call by the Far Eastern commander, Gen. Douglas MacArthur, for military aid to Chiang, but also General Sun's coup proposal and the plans of Rusk and other policy makers to unseat Chiang and make Taiwan a UN protectorate.

Just two days later, at dawn on June 25, 1950, Communist North Korean troops crossed the 38th parallel into South Korea. The U.S. was caught entirely off guard, unaware that Kim Il-sung had been planning the assault for months and had secured the permission of both Stalin and Mao. For Taipei, this was the awaited godsend—not quite the hoped-for third world war, but sufficient to catapult the Nationalist government from almost certain doom into a strategically crucial position. U.S. support was now ensured. Unknown to either the Americans or Taipei, Mao had already postponed the invasion of Taiwan until the summer of 1951, perhaps due to advance knowledge of Kim's plans.

Washington immediately concluded that the North Korean invasion was not merely an internal incident but part of a wider Communist offensive in Asia. Truman dispatched naval, air, and ground forces to aid South Korea. He ordered the Seventh Fleet to "neutralize" the Taiwan Strait and enforce a cease-fire between the two Chinas. The Seventh Fleet had the navy's biggest carriers and bristled with the most advanced weaponry of the day—atomic weapons, guided missiles, planes that could destroy the Communist Chinese air force. The occupation of Taiwan by Communist forces, Truman declared, would be a "direct threat" to the Pacific area and to U.S. forces in the region.

Chiang, Mayling, and Ching-kuo quickly huddled with other senior officials. Chiang promptly offered to send thirty-three thousand Nationalist troops to join UN forces in Korea, but MacArthur declined on grounds they were of unknown quality, would require extensive support, and "would be an albatross around our neck for months." Moreover, their diversion to Korea would invite attack on Taiwan.

The Joint Chiefs of Staff asked MacArthur to visit Taiwan to survey military requirements if capture of the island was to be prevented. He proceeded to Taiwan in late July 1950, over the disapproval of the State Department. The brilliant and famously egotistical general admired the Chiangs, and the feeling was mutual. He shared not only Mayling's political views but also her penchant for drama. Quite unexpectedly, and in front of news photographers, he seized her hand and planted on it a theatrical kiss—decidedly not a Chinese custom—that took her by surprise and made headlines across America. In the photographs she looked both shocked and delighted. MacArthur later claimed astonishment that his visit created a "furor" in the American press. On August 1, Mayling sent Marshall a detailed eight-page report of MacArthur's visit, typed by herself with two fingers, as she had yet to find an English-language secretary. She neglected to mention the by now famous hand-kissing incident.

MacArthur, she informed Marshall, arrived with a party of forty-eight instead of the twelve expected, precipitating a scramble to find enough accommodations. After a three-hour briefing in the map room, during the height of the tropical summer, with no air-conditioning and under bright, hot lights, MacArthur met with Chiang and Mayling alone. He appreciated the Generalissimo's "generous" offer to send Nationalist troops to Korea but said that would endanger Taiwan's defense. On the question of defending the offshore islands, MacArthur's advice was "not to give up an inch of land."

At the end of the conference, the three took a drive before the Chiangs saw MacArthur off. Chiang told the commander that there had been requests from various quarters, including the guerrillas, that Mayling be appointed head of the Nationalist-led guerrilla movement on the mainland. He asked the American general what he thought. MacArthur appeared to take the question quite seriously, and replied that he thought it would be fine as far as the effectiveness of the work was concerned, and that certainly she would be the last person the enemy would suspect—a vital consideration in guerrilla operations. But he warned that whoever headed the movement would be in tremendous danger and would be subjected to tortures worse than death if caught. "I would not like to see you in such danger," he told Mayling before departing. "I have long left personal considerations behind," she claimed to have replied. "My only objective is to serve my country in the best way possible." She had already picked a group of people who were willing to conduct sabotage and demolition work behind enemy lines on the mainland, and whether she headed the operations or not, she hoped to get some experts to train them. MacArthur promised to wire Washington on the matter.

It is unclear how seriously Chiang Kai-shek considered installing his wife as clandestine operations chief. Perhaps he wanted to sound out the American commander to see if Americans would back the proposition; or maybe he secretly wanted MacArthur to respond negatively in order to dissuade his wife.

Belying her brave tone, Mayling confided to Marshall that she had been exhausted and ill with the summer heat and humidity and could get a good night's sleep only after moving the household to higher elevation on Grass Mountain. It was evident she yearned to be free from the unremitting pressure of being Madame Chiang Kai-shek, helpmeet to the dethroned Generalissimo of China. "I think of you and Mrs. Marshall often and of the lovely leisurely life at Raquette Lake, the soft lapping waves on the side of the row-boat, and oh, so nostalgically of the cool evenings in front of the roaring fires in the lounge, and best of all, the absence of 'Musts,'" she wrote, recalling their trip to the Adirondacks a year earlier. "No must to see people, no must to make speeches, no must to smile when my facial muscles ache, no must to race against time."

But more than nostalgia haunted her on that remote outpost along the eastern frontier of the Iron Curtain. She was lonely. "I know you are ever so busy, but when I get your letters you and Mrs. Marshall do not seem so far away," she wrote in a rare plaintive tone. "This island feels very isolated sometimes, and of all my friends in America, you two are among the very few who have any idea of what my life in China is like, and you seem very close when I hear from you."

Marshall replied with unconcealed dismay at the notion of Mayling heading up the guerrilla movement on the mainland. "I think this would be a terrible responsibility for you to take not only from the viewpoint of danger but also considering your uncertain state of health as you would be bound to suffer heavily from the hard living during such an enterprise," he warned. And indeed, her health was suffering. By late summer she had a persistent "humidity rash," she wrote Emma Mills, and had to take daily thyroid supplements, as well as injections of calcium and penicillin.

Chiang ultimately appointed his son, Ching-kuo, head of guerrilla operations, but Mayling was by no means sidelined. Not only did she retain her position as her husband's chief adviser on political and diplomatic relations with the U.S., but her unofficial portfolio was expanded to include a senior liaison role between U.S. intelligence services and her husband on intelligence and paramilitary operations; after all, her loyalty was beyond question. Soon the CIA was supporting several units of Nationalist special forces totaling some nineteen thousand men on Taiwan, under Ching-kuo's command, trained to carry out covert action. Sometimes Mayling clashed with Ching-kuo over differences in policy concerning intelligence and clandestine operations. But they kept their conflicts well hidden and met separately with the Gimo, as Chiang was called, on contentious matters.

Even after the Korean War broke out, the legal status of Taiwan continued to be the subject of vigorous debate. The State Department's position remained that the Nationalists were holding Taiwan "in trust," and that a Communist takeover by force would mean that Beijing merely assumed the same "uncleared title." Taipei's position resembled a government in exile, weakening the rationale for not recognizing Beijing. Policy questions abounded. Having declared that the Seventh Fleet would "prevent any attack on Formosa," what were the limits of U.S. responsibility? Did that mean the U.S. would defend Taiwan until the Chinese Communist regime ceased to be a threat? Should the offshore islands be defended too? What attitude should the U.S. take toward internal affairs, especially the Taiwan independence movement and repression under Chiang? What if the UN tried to establish a trusteeship? Should a military aid program to Taiwan simply be a "sterilizing operation without a blood transfusion," or something more?

Some quarters in the State Department were deeply chagrined that Chiang Kai-shek had been rehabilitated by circumstances. "The inspiration of anything connected with CKS is the Gimo's desire that everything be molded to serve his personal ends, which can be summed up in one word, 'power,'" one memorandum, dated August 10, 1950, noted caustically, if accurately. "If he was perhaps somewhat subdued before, the introduction of the Seventh Fleet into the picture, combined with the visit to Formosa of General MacArthur, has patently . . . [served] to restore in him his congenital belief in his own infallibility—assuming that that belief had ever flagged in his autocratic breast it is reasonably certain that CKS [now] believes that he has a fresh opportunity to ride back to the mainland on the coat-tails of Uncle Sugar—if only the US can be caused to fight, at most, the Soviet Union, or at least, Communist China."

Truman, too, harbored a "violent animosity" toward Chiang, in MacArthur's words. On August 25, he wrote to Trygve Lie, head of the UN, stressing that any U.S. action in Taiwan was "without prejudice to the future political settlement of the status of the island." The U.S., he added, would welcome UN consideration of Taiwan's case. The Pentagon, however, had no intention of allowing Truman to hand Taiwan over to the UN, a move tantamount to serving up the island on a platter to the Communists. The strategic consequences, the Joint Chiefs of Staff warned, would be "so seriously detrimental" to U.S. security that Taiwan's fate could not be left to the UN. It was wartime, and brass hats prevailed.

By late summer, victory seemed ensured in the Korean conflict. MacArthur masterminded a brilliant but highly risky amphibious landing at Inchon on September 15 that was the pinnacle of his illustrious military career. The overextended North Korean army collapsed. At Thanksgiving MacArthur said American troops would be home for Christmas. Just three days later the U.S. was confronted with a terrible shock: three hundred thousand Chinese "volunteers" crossed the Yalu River, which served as the border with North Korea, and attacked American forces. China had entered the war. Truman's order to neutralize the Taiwan Strait freed up Communist armies to move north to Manchuria, and the Americans were quickly driven into a pell-mell retreat.

MacArthur, backed by irate China Lobbyists, demanded a showdown with "Red China"—World War III, in other words. He requested the fresh Nationalist troops that he had earlier spurned, and was disgruntled when the Joint Chiefs balked. Truman was adamantly opposed to an all-out war, and from the original goal of uniting the Korean peninsula he reduced U.S.

war aims to maintaining the status quo antebellum. As Truman's chief of staff, Gen. Omar Bradley, said, "It would be the wrong war in the wrong place at the wrong time against the wrong enemy."

The escalation of the Korean conflict cemented Chiang's position as a valued American protégé. Any lingering notions in Washington of removing him, handing Taiwan over to the UN, or forging a rapprochement with Beijing were obliterated overnight. Chiang was a living symbol of resistance to communism in a region in which such staunch anti-Communist allies were in short supply.

The "unsinkable aircraft carrier" quickly became an "unsinkable station" for the CIA. In the two decades that began with the Korean War, Taiwan was the principal base for gathering intelligence and waging clandestine war against Communist China. The CIA provided the Nationalist government with a "cornucopia" of funds, weapons, supplies, and training for guerrilla operations. The agency's station in Taipei soon mushroomed to six hundred staff, plus thousands of Chinese and Americans engaged in intelligence-gathering activities.

The airline that Chennault had founded in 1946, Civil Air Transport, was the only Chinese airline that did not defect to the Communists. In 1950 the CIA had secretly bought C.A.T. for use in clandestine missions. Intriguingly, the "privately owned" C.A.T. doubled as Taipei's flag carrier for many years. For public consumption Chennault remained an owner of the airline while it ran routine passenger and cargo flights and provided air support in the Korean and Indochinese conflicts. It also carried out covert operations and surveillance of enemy territory and supported the 1.6 million guerrillas Chiang claimed were active on the mainland. The airline subsequently became legendary during the Vietnam War as Air America.

As a Christmas gift, in 1950 T. V. Soong sent his sister a dehumidifier to combat the Taiwanese damp that continued to retrouble her skin. "I wish you were here," Mayling wrote to thank him. She added in a chastising tone, "I think it was a great mistake that you did not come back when I repeatedly asked you to come. When another opportunity comes for you to return you ought to do so for, after all, China is our country and we must see to it that it is free from the iron curtain." She was apparently oblivious to the fact that her brother was not welcome on Taiwan, but he knew better. It is not clear exactly why he had not returned when summoned by his sister, but evidently there had been something of an acrimonious break, for in early June 1950 Taipei had announced Soong's "resignation" from the Kuomintang following his refusal to return to Taiwan. In reporting the news, the *New York Times* called him "one of the wealthiest men in the world."

Mayling's apparent refusal to recognize the rift between her brother and the Nationalist regime was an example of what an American official who visited the Chiangs in early 1951 termed "blank spots in their mental processes." He was surprised to hear Mayling state matter-of-factly that the Nationalist government would be back on the mainland "next year." Still more perplexing was her revelation that she and her husband were trying to persuade H. H. Kung to come to Taiwan as finance minister. She spoke in "glowing terms" of his "great genius" in running China's finances during the war against Japan, and appeared to have no grasp whatsoever of the disastrous impression that would be created in America and Taiwan were Kung to rejoin the Nationalist government.

In a 1951 New Year speech, Chiang called the Communist takeover of the mainland "my personal humiliation and the deep regret of my life." His wife, however, had recovered her old bravado. Even as UN forces in Korea suffered huge losses, Mayling did not attempt to disguise her satisfaction at the turn of events in Asia. "Evidently the American public is getting educated, and from recent signs I would say that the State Department, too, is learning its lesson," she wrote Emma Mills in a smug tone. "It is just too bad that my predictions became realities in so short a time." When American friends tried to console her after she failed to persuade the U.S. to aid the Nationalist government in 1948–49, she replied she had come "to tell your people . . . that what China was suffering then would eventually be the fate that America would have to face," she wrote Mills. "Having acted according to the dictates of my own conscience, instead of feeling sorry for China or for myself, I only felt sorry for America and the American friends that they paid so little heed to what I pointed out." But all that was past and now it was time to "buckle down and . . . pull ourselves out of this mess and mire by our bootstraps."

At the start of the Korean War, Congress passed a $40 million aid bill for Taiwan. When aid finally began to trickle in, it was in the form of commodities. As the new U.S. ambassador to Taipei, Karl Rankin, with whom the Chiangs had become very friendly, prepared to return to Washington for consultation in early 1951, he met with the Chiangs. When Chiang stressed his urgent need for fighter planes and military equipment, Mayling interjected, "He expects you to bring home the bacon." Rankin replied that even General MacArthur had been unable to deliver what Chiang was asking for. In a rare attempt at humor, Chiang countered that MacArthur had not left his wife behind as a hostage. In light of events that followed, the joke was more sinister than amusing.

Mayling, meanwhile, was becoming openly evangelistic as her religious feelings intensified. Shifting from the earlier approach of soft-pedaling their beliefs, by 1951 the Chiangs were publicly extolling the virtues of Christian life. Their religious activities and remarks were given wide play in the state-controlled press, although just a fraction of Taiwan residents were Christian. Mayling invited American missionaries to "bring the Gospel" to her sewing ladies during the ten-minute daily break from making clothes for soldiers. The missionaries felt resistance, but hoped they were "planting the seed."

On Good Friday 1951, Chiang and Mayling led worship services broadcast across the island. They each gave sermons on Christ's crucifixion, his in Chinese and hers in English, beginning an annual tradition. She wrote her own and edited his. "On the eve of the crucifixion what a cataclysmic struggle raged in our Lord's breast as He accepted God's will," she wrote, with a fervor suggesting that it was her husband and the loss of the mainland she had in mind more than the biblical episode. "I venture to think that His spiritual agony on that occasion transcended even the pain of the actual crucifixion. . . . He came to the world to save the world. . . . Is it any wonder then that He felt that His mission was not complete? Give Him more time, a little more time, He pleaded. Yet when God made known his bidding, our Lord bowed to it in sublime submission." The strained parallels between Jesus and Chiang were evidence that she and Chiang were endeavoring to create a Christ-like cult around the Nationalist leader.

Chiang was not the only military leader in the Far East nurturing a God complex. General MacArthur was still calling for all-out war against China. He wanted to drop atomic bombs on the mainland; he called for a naval blockade. He demanded massive troop reinforcements. Truman and Marshall, who had been called back from retirement to be secretary of defense, were resolutely opposed to broadening the conflict. Truman called the proposed assault on China a "gigantic booby trap" set by the Russians. On April 11, 1951, Truman's patience finally reached its limit, and he relieved MacArthur of his command. His firing became a great cause célèbre and left the China Lobby rabid.

The China Lobby had long been a thorn in Truman's side. Now that its patron saint had been ousted, the president ordered a multiagency investigation into its dealings. The FBI trailed suspected operatives while the Bureau of Internal Revenue audited them. Large sums of American aid money given to the Nationalist government, it was alleged, had been transferred back to the U.S. and were being used for bribery, propaganda work, and political campaign contributions, with the goal of influencing American policy. Investigators were told that a large sum was withdrawn from the Bank of China and turned over to Madame Chiang for these purposes during her 1949 visit to America. "This suggests to some a closed circuit of American dollars flowing from Congress to the Nationalists and back again in the form of lobbying activities for still more money for Chiang," Sen. Wayne Morse declared in June 1951.

There were persistent reports that Taipei had since 1949 been giving cash contributions to members of the U.S. Congress from both parties in return for support of Taiwan. The payments were said to be taken from government coffers and delivered by couriers, some of whom were relatives of Madame Chiang. Columnist Drew Pearson told President Eisenhower that former Defense Secretary Louis Johnson once offered him $10,000 if he would make a favorable mention of H. H. Kung in his column. This was said to be typical of how the China Lobby worked.

An extensive investigation produced "very little in connection with the search for a China Lobby as such," but Treasury reports illuminated corruption and graft in the Nationalist government during and after the war. There were "indications but no clear proof" of "direct financial transactions" between Nationalist Chinese sympathizers and American political figures. Neither were investigators able to prove that funds derived from corruption and profiteering with U.S. aid money were recycled back to the U.S. in the form of cash payments, propaganda, and political influence. A report concluded that a congressional investigation of the "China Lobby as such involves a grave risking of failure," but suggested that Kung family wealth, which according to the Treasury was derived in part from wartime profiteering, was partly behind the China Lobby. Mayling's nephew Louis Kung served as an intermediary for his father in political circles and was said to be "one of the key people who handles cash transactions in Washington."

In April 1952 the Washington *Reporter* published a lengthy exposé on the China Lobby entitled "Washington's Darkest Mystery." A dragon menaced from the cover. The magazine called the Lobby a partnership of "fear, ambition, and greed . . . a nondescript tentacular affair that manages to use the craft of professional operators and the good will of well-intentioned amateurs." It preyed on the bewilderment of the American people over the "loss" of China and exerted "relentless" pressure on American policy. The magazine detailed connections, payoffs, and corruption, naming few sources.

As in years past, Mayling's nephews, Louis and David Kung, were at the center of controversy. As scrutiny of the China Lobby mounted in 1951, she pulled strings to get Louis appointed a counselor of the Nationalist Chinese embassy in Washington, just as she had seen that he was promoted from major to colonel in the Nationalist army, though he had done no soldiering since the war. The diplomatic post gave him virtual immunity from China Lobby investigators. David Kung was implicated in a scandal written up in Drew Pearson's influential "Washington Merry-Go-Round" column. He had allegedly sold 123 tons of tin illegally to Communist China. Pearson also charged that Mayling's brother T. L. Soong cornered the soybean market "at the expense of the American public" by buying up huge quantities of soybeans just before China invaded North Korea. Prices subsequently soared and Soong allegedly sold at a profit of $30 million.

Mayling, however, sailed through the storm unscathed. She was occasionally mentioned in investigation reports—one stated that while she was in the U.S. in 1943, she withdrew some $600,000 in cash from bank accounts—but nothing of substance could be pinned to her. Congressman Walter Judd later denied that she "ran" the China Lobby as charged. "No one was more involved in the effort to keep China out of Communist hands than I, and if she was operating it, I wish I could have seen more evidence of that, and especially some financial support of our efforts," Judd wrote, a remark that in retrospect appears disingenuous.

In September 1951 Marshall resigned as secretary of defense. He refused to write his memoirs, despite an offer of a million dollars. He later lent his prestigious name to the Committee of One Million, a front organization for the China Lobby founded in 1953 with an impressive lineup of supporters whose purpose was to keep Communist China out of the UN. Mayling thanked her old friend by giving him a number of paintings she herself had done, which he hung at Dodona Manor.

Mayling did not play quite the same high-profile role in Taiwan as she had on the mainland, and she was less active in the political realm, at least publicly. She had previously been renowned for behaving as though she were royalty and keeping people waiting, or showing off, especially in front of foreigners, not realizing the negative impression she was creating. But after the Nationalist government was forced to take refuge on Taiwan, she became more subdued, rarely attempting to upstage her husband. Her influence over him had diminished, but she still wielded substantial power, although it was not always decisive. He naturally had his own strongly held views, and sometimes they clashed. She remained particularly influential in the realm of foreign affairs, especially in personnel appointments in the foreign ministry and the diplomatic corps. She also kept a hand in senior military appointments, and nurtured the careers of favorites. Often she eased military protégés into diplomatic careers.

Chiang cultivated an air of sagelike serenity in public but in private had a "terrible" temper, which he vented on his aides when he was unable to get what he wanted in meetings with high-level American visitors. His subordinates universally regarded *laoxiansheng*—"The Old Man"—with respect and fear. When Chiang was in an angry mood, important decisions were delayed due to his refusal to consider matters before him. Senior government and party officials would rely on Madame Chiang to take him for a walk in the garden to calm him down and put him in an amenable mood.

Mayling remained invaluable to Chiang, particularly in entertaining the many foreign friends and dignitaries deemed susceptible to and worthy of "the charm treatment." Military maneuvers held for junketing officers were so frequent that it became a joke that more ammunition was expended putting on displays than would have been needed to repel a Communist attack. "The China treatment," as the red-carpet reception given to visitors was known, was adroitly varied to suit the guest, and an audience with Madame Chiang was usually a key component.

Perhaps to demonstrate her retreat—if not removal—from politics, in the spring of 1951 Mayling took up painting, then much in vogue. Churchill, Eisenhower, and Clare Boothe Luce had all picked up the paintbrush in midlife. She hired two master painters, Zheng Manqing, who specialized in flowers, and Huang Chunbi, renowned for landscape painting, and took lessons three afternoons a week from two to six P.M. Chiang was skeptical. "If you had any talent in painting, you would have discovered it before," he told her. "You'll never be any good at it at your age." But Mayling was a quick study. Soon guests had difficulty believing that the paintings were hers, and it was rumored that her teachers had painted them. To dispel doubts, her teachers suggested hosting a dinner with twenty renowned painters at her residence. After the meal, she and one of her teachers together painted a large painting. She painted first—a tall pine tree. The guests were surprised and impressed, but Chiang insisted that they admired the painting only because she had painted it. "I do not think you are that good," he said.

Evidently his was the only note of skepticism in a chorus of praise. After just five months of lessons, Mayling ingenuously wrote Emma Mills, artists and connoisseurs of Chinese painting were telling her she had the "possibilities of a great artist . . . perhaps the greatest living artist." This she found "astounding" but "wonderful." She sent photographs of her paintings to her sister Eling to seek the opinion of experts at the Metropolitan Museum of Art. "It seems that my brush work is extraordinary," she wrote Mills, and she had a natural sense of rhythm, proportion, and perspective. "As you know I dabble a little bit in writing and music, but I thought that painting was what I could never do. Now it seems that it is just the thing I can best do." She acknowledged it sounded conceited to say that, but she believed the Chinese experts because, oddly, it was "no effort" at all for her to paint. "Painting is the most absorbing occupation I have known in my life," she wrote. "When I am at work, I forget everything in the world, and I wish that I could spend all my time in doing nothing but painting and painting."

By the late summer of 1951 Mayling was giving indications she might abandon her other activities to concentrate on painting. She found solace in painting, especially at night when she had trouble sleeping. When a visiting American official asked if she had read Churchill's well-known book *Painting as a Pastime,* she replied she had not and added tartly that for her, painting was not a "pastime." After seeing her at work, the official was convinced that she had a "rather big talent" and suggested to Henry Luce that a spread on her paintings would make a "timely, highly photogenic, and generally fascinating *Life* feature." Luce agreed and showcased a number of her paintings in the October 13, 1952, issue of the magazine. "Like most Chinese artists, she paints pines so well you can almost hear wind wailing through the boughs," gushed the description of one painting. Mayling ordered five hundred reprints, which she gave as gifts to friends and acquaintances.

Despite blandishments to the contrary, Madame Chiang was not destined to enter the pantheon of great Chinese artists. She did, however, become a highly accomplished amateur, and brought her own style to her work. "Most Chinese paintings don't tell you anything," she once said. She used her paintings to express an idea, a Western concept.

Whatever their earlier marital differences may have been, by the early 1950s Mayling and Chiang appeared to have patched matters up, at least for public consumption. They called each other "Dar"—short for "Darling"—and lived in the same room with a screen separating their beds. They strolled together almost daily in the gardens of their residence, surrounded by bodyguards, who were alerted by a system of bells—one ding for Chiang, two dings for Madame, and three for both. They frequently vacationed together at a dozen presidential residences scattered around the island.

Still, Mayling and her husband led very different lives. She liked Western cuisine; he preferred Chinese. She liked air-conditioning; he used a fan. He neither smoked nor drank, but she smoked menthol cigarettes. He rose at six in the morning and retired early. She rose with him for morning devotions but afterward returned to bed until midday, because she liked to stay up late into the night watching movies, reading, writing, or painting. After she went back to sleep, Chiang would stroll onto the second-floor balcony, reading aloud from his dog-eared Bible, and turn to the east and bow. Then he would read from a Chinese translation of *Streams in the Desert*, a book of religious devotions, underlining passages he liked and writing comments in the margins.

Soon after arriving on Taiwan, Mayling had gathered a handful of her closest friends "to pray together for the fate of China and for the world according to His will." Both her mother and sister Eling had led prayer groups, which were common in America but unknown in Taiwan. Citing the axiom "The family that prays together, stays together," Mayling asked: "Would it not also be true that a nation that prays together, stays together?" The Wednesday afternoon ladies' prayer group, which met at the presidential residence in Shihlin, became a tradition that lasted decades. It was a nondenominational group consisting mostly of the wives of high-ranking military and government officials, nearly all mainland refugees.

Many members were doubtless genuine in their religious sentiments, but some joined because they wanted to be close to Madame Chiang, or because they hoped to advance their husbands' careers. An invitation to join the Chiangs' inner circle was a coveted honor few would refuse, but the wife of a three-star army general did. Mayling invited her to the Wednesday prayer group and tea and cake after. When the general's wife replied that she was diabetic and could not eat sweets, Mayling commented, "My dog has diabetes." The general's wife was deeply offended and declined.

The Chiangs built a small chapel on the grounds of their residence and named it *Kaige Tang*—Victory Song Chapel. The church became very exclusive and many people worshipped there because the Chiangs did. Occasionally ambassadors and other foreign guests attended too; President Eisenhower once came to Sunday service.

There were two divergent currents to Mayling's faith—an intellectual, analytical faith that stemmed from her Wellesley education, and her mother's zealous, almost charismatic, faith. After arriving on Taiwan Mayling's proselytizing streak grew increasingly pronounced. On Christmas Eve, she timed dinner so that it would be finished just before the evening church service, so she could say to all the guests, "Let's go to church!" One of her most prized—and unlikely—converts was the famous Young Marshal. In late 1946 Zhang Xueliang was brought over to Taiwan, where, still in captivity, he passed the time studying Ming dynasty history and cultivating orchids. His mistress, Edith Zhao, was allowed to come to Taiwan with him. Initially he was kept under house arrest in the countryside near Hsinchu; later he was transferred to the Taipei suburb of Peitou, in the foothills of Yangmingshan. Evidently he was depressed, because in May 1950 Mayling told Emma Mills she was visiting him to "cheer him up." Occasionally his boyhood friend and financial adviser James C. Elder, now residing in the U.S., was permitted to visit him.

The Young Marshal once said that his relationship with Chiang Kai-shek was politically inimical but emotionally like father and son. If that was so, Madame Chiang was like a mother. She could not give him his freedom, and it is not clear that she would have done so, although she did once raise the matter with General Marshall, who knew Zhang well. Marshall did not reply. "This fellow had taken [Chiang] prisoner and I didn't think I ought to stick my finger in that pot at all," he later said.

Madame Chiang took Zhang under her wing. When at one point he told her that he was studying Buddhism, she sighed and fell silent. "You're off on the wrong track again," she said finally. She gave him a copy of *Streams in the Desert,* Chiang's favorite book, and sent Hollington Tong to tutor him in Christianity. Zhang polished his English by translating into Chinese one of the books on Christianity that she gave him. She often took him to the Victory Song Chapel with her, even though he was supposed to be under house arrest. By dint of her efforts, he eventually became a devout Christian. With Madame Chiang's encouragement and assistance, in July 1964 her captive convert and Edith Zhao, who also became a Christian, were married after thirty years together. This notwithstanding, it was rumored that Chiang Ching-kuo sometimes took the Young Marshal out for a late-night soiree, complete with drinking and ladies.

Even as she wooed converts, Madame Chiang was "tormented" by "startling" spiritual questions, wrote her friend Grace Oursler, widow of *Liberty* magazine editor Fulton Oursler. When would civilization find a "new answer" to war? When should a "good Christian" fight? How far should appeasement be taken? How would Christ fight communism? Is war ever justifiable? Can one condone wrong in others and wrong done to others and still be a good Christian? Mayling told Oursler of a controversy in Taiwan in which she demanded the removal of a government official on grounds that he should not be allowed to apply one set of rules in public affairs and another—"shoddy and evil"—in his private life. Wasn't prayer needed "as ammunition" and "spiritual discipline" as urgently as military training in this time of world crisis? Not content with merely posing questions, during a subsequent visit to the U.S. she summoned to her apartment a group of religious leaders to consult with them. "I felt these were part of a truly religious soul's personal struggle and did not realize she intended seeking as authoritative an answer as possible," wrote Oursler.

Even after starting the prayer group, Mayling wrote, God to her was still an "impersonal" power, and she "flinched" from anything mystical. But one day she underwent what she termed an "old-fashioned conversion." While reading the biblical story of the crucifixion, which she had pondered many times before, she claimed to have suddenly realized for the first time that Christ's suffering was for her. "I cried and cried, overcome with my own unworthiness," she wrote. "It was a peculiar sensation, at once great grief and great release. I can count the times I have wept since I have grown up . . . for as children we were taught not to show emotion, and to abhor sentimentality." From then on she claimed to be "not only intellectually convinced but personally attached" to God. Infused with new religious fervor, she found solace in viewing her personal trials as well as those of the Nationalist Chinese government in biblical terms: "In these days of national tribulation," she told Nationalist followers in her 1952 Easter broadcast, "we do not need to be reminded of the relevance of Resurrection to each . . . of us or to nations."

Chapter Twenty
Cold War, White Terror

A ruler must of necessity do some evil things, but when he does them he should let someone else bear the full responsibility.

—from the Chinese classic on statecraft
Book of the Warring States

The outward calm of sleepy Taipei, with its unpaved streets and lone traffic light, belied a climate of fear and paranoia, for 1950s Taiwan was in the grip of the Cold War and the "White Terror."

After resuming the presidency in March 1950 Chiang Kai-shek appointed a group of loyal followers to a powerful Central Reform Committee, from which Mayling was tellingly excluded. Thus began an intense period of collective soul-searching. Chiang and the committee quietly held a series of sober meetings to examine what had gone wrong on the mainland and what lessons could be drawn from the humiliating experience. This proved to be one instance where some of the lessons of history were actually learned. The committee recommended sweeping reforms in the Kuomintang and a purge of corrupt and incompetent members, as well as those who had defected to the Communists. With a firm nudge from Washington, Taipei's leadership committed to extensive land reforms promised but never carried out on the mainland. The corruption, profiteering, and nepotism rife under Nationalist rule on the mainland would (in theory) not be tolerated—at any rate, not to the same degree. Private enterprise would be encouraged rather than stifled. Over the decades, these early decisions would prove critical.

From the start it was clear that Mayling's relatives were not welcome on Taiwan. The Soong and Kung families were by this time not only thoroughly discredited but nearly universally reviled. Mayling was heavily criticized for interfering in matters of state, and became acutely sensitive to such accusations. In a shift from the highly public governing partnership she had enjoyed with her husband on the mainland, she was compelled to revert to a more traditional wifely role, at least for public consumption. But there was another reason behind this change. While Mayling was in America from late 1948 to early 1950, Chiang Ching-kuo replaced her as Chiang's constant companion. Slowly, he had managed to win his father's complete confidence, and now rivaled his stepmother as the person with the most influence over Chiang Kai-shek.

On the surface they appeared to get along, but in fact Mayling and her stepson were like "fire and water." Underlying their mutual antagonism was not, as might be supposed, a clash in political convictions, but a struggle over who would be closest to the aging Generalissimo. As Ching-kuo's influence grew, Mayling's waned in proportion. Mayling never fully regained her perch, but the struggle persisted for decades. As late as the mid-1960s Ching-kuo complained to an acquaintance that his efforts over the years had been hampered by "the opposition of Madame Chiang, who had been trying to turn the President against him" ever since he returned from Russia in the late 1930s.

Ching-kuo's thinking was shaped by life experiences vastly different from those of Mayling. All they had in common was Chiang and an extended sojourn abroad during formative years of their youth. But Mayling's life of privilege in America was a far cry from Ching-kuo's stay in Russia. Cut off from family and effectively a hostage, after April 1927 he worked variously in a mine, a factory, and a labor camp. When Stalin's great purges stalked Russia in the mid-1930s, with every footstep outside the door Ching-kuo feared he would be arrested. One day he was, and he thought it meant the end. But instead of prison he was sent to Moscow, where he was brought before Stalin and told he would be sent home. Ching-kuo left with great admiration for certain facets of Russian life. He was especially impressed by the way he was able to advance himself through hard work and education. In Russia Ching-kuo had labored with his hands, working shoulder-to-shoulder with ordinary people. The experience gave him something utterly lacking in his father and stepmother and the elite coterie surrounding them—empathy for and the ability to connect with the common man. It also gave him an egalitarian streak, and a distaste for pomp and circumstance.

Ching-kuo was a very different personality from his reserved and austere father. He was much more outgoing and informal. Around the Generalissimo was an atmosphere of hushed reverence entirely absent with Ching-kuo. In the early years on Taiwan, when his face was not well known, he often traveled around the island alone. Once, driving his jeep on the east coast, he picked up a couple of military officers hitching a ride to Taipei. Not recognizing him, they gave him twenty Taiwan dollars for the lift—which he kept because "it would have embarrassed them to realize who I was."

Before he rose to high positions he liked parties and enjoyed a drink. He was a formidable player of a popular Chinese drinking game in which the loser must down a drink. Ching-kuo was so good that sometimes he let himself lose just to give the other person "face." After being diagnosed with diabetes he was advised not to drink and had aides do the drinking for him. On social occasions his affability and down-to-earth manner were extremely disarming to critics. "On a one-to-one basis he could be very charming," recalled a former American intelligence officer.

But for all his sociability, Ching-kuo was a "lone wolf." His position was ensured, and so, unlike his father, he had no need to be buttressed by henchmen. Like his father, in choosing subordinates he valued loyalty and obedience over education and expertise, but as he was not reliant on them to keep himself in power he felt no compunction about firing or transferring them. He was a very "Stalinistic" character; if someone got in his way he soon regretted it. He was also a very dutiful son who did everything his father said. After the 2-28 Incident, Chiang realized he had to secure his control over Taiwan. The government had already occupied the island militarily, but it saw itself threatened by communism and the Taiwanese independence movement. This was where Ching-kuo's experience was useful, so Chiang put him in charge of military intelligence. His actual power far exceeded his official position—lieutenant general and chief of the defense ministry's political warfare department—because he controlled most of the numerous security, secret, and regular police and intelligence organizations. Ching-kuo sized up the important people on the island—who they were, what they did, and how they could be manipulated. In this respect he was "more of a Communist than the Communists."

From 1949, when he took charge of the island's security forces, Ching-kuo embarked on what amounted to a reign of terror. Tens of thousands of people were imprisoned, killed, or mysteriously disappeared over the next few decades on Formosa. Initially the focus of repression was the Communists, but once the Korean War was under way attention shifted to Taiwan independence supporters and even foreigners. David Osborn, who worked for the U.S. Information Service in Taiwan, discovered that his house servants were submitting reports on him to the Kuomintang and even to Alfred Kohlberg of the China Lobby. Many of Osborn's Taiwanese friends were arrested and accused of being independence activists.

Ching-kuo's techniques were redolent of Soviet Russia—house-to-house searches, arrest without warrant, detention without trial, checks and counterchecks on the loyalty of officials and others, constant watch on the daily movements of each member of even the remotest communities, brainwashing, midnight knocks on the door. His hundred-thousand-member Chinese Anticommunist National Salvation Youth Corps—the Taiwanese incarnation of the Three People's Principles Youth Corps on the mainland—was rigidly disciplined and highly indoctrinated, and influenced if not controlled most high school and university students on the island. The organization was used to spy for seditious activity and to recruit young talent for the Kuomintang and the government. At rallies, Ching-kuo could turn the Hitleresque group into a "horde of screaming worshippers." Still, while the police on Formosa were "ubiquitous and sometimes harsh," British diplomats reported a surprising amount of criticism of the government both in the press and in private conversation.

Of alleged Communists and other political detainees, about 15 percent were executed. For the rest Ching-kuo established a high-security political prison camp on Green Island off southeastern Taiwan. At the euphemistically named New Life Institute, the "students" had no fixed terms but were released according to progress in reforming their thinking, reforms that were often encouraged by torture. Ching-kuo took great pride in the "institute" and once boasted to American visitors he was showing around Green Island that 95 percent of the "students" were sent back to Taiwan after reeducation in the Three People's Principles. The guests politely inquired what happened to the other 5 percent. "Oh, we don't hurt them," Ching-kuo replied cheerfully. "We give them a boat, food supplies and a radio, and send them back to the Chinese mainland. After three or four days, we start sending radio messages to them asking: 'When are you going to report?' And the Communists take care of them."

In 1950 Ching-kuo established and headed a political affairs department in the defense ministry to introduce political and psychological training into the armed forces. "Political officers" were installed in the ranks of the military alongside regular officers to ensure the loyalty of troops. Ching-kuo was also the force behind state-sponsored prostitution in the military. Perhaps in a bid to offset the demoralizing effect of the new political commissar system, his political affairs department set up and ran thirty-seven "tea houses" for the troops, with nearly a thousand "hostesses." The "hostess" recruits were dispatched to the frontline islands in the Taiwan Strait for six-month engagements. If Mayling was aware of the practice she did not publicly complain.

In contrast to her strained ties with Ching-kuo, Mayling was very close to Wego, her husband's adopted younger son. Maj. Gen. Wego Chiang was cosmopolitan and Western in outlook, unlike his brother, and although a military man by training, he had a rather emotional character. He joined groups such as Taipei's English-speaking Rotary Club. Ching-kuo spoke Russian but his English was limited. Wego spoke good English and from his years in Nazi Germany his colloquial German was excellent. He even spoke a little of the Taiwanese dialect. He was less ambitious than Ching-kuo and untainted by links with the notorious security forces. Perhaps at Mayling's urging, Chiang kept the Armored Force—the tank division—under the separate command of Wego Chiang, as a check on the power of Gen. Sun Li-jen, army commander in chief.

In much the same way that he used Ching-kuo, Chiang also used his wife to carry out unpleasant missions. At his behest she often served as message-bearer or moderator between Chiang and his subordinates, directly or through their wives. She allowed herself to be used in this peculiar role in the power struggle that unfolded between her stepson and Taiwan Governor K. C. Wu.

Soon after the Nationalist government fled to Taiwan, Chiang grew jealous of Wu and began to mistrust him. When Mayling returned from the U.S. in January 1950, she arranged for a large group of American press to visit, the first such delegation since the loss of the mainland. Chiang and other officials held press conferences, but reporters focused on the charismatic and articulate governor. This was not appreciated. Wu further annoyed Chiang by pushing for democratic reforms. Reluctantly, Chiang permitted free local elections. Wu privately urged Chiang to allow opposition parties, and argued that the Kuomintang should be supported not by the government treasury, but by member contributions. Chiang said he would consider the suggestions. Matters were not helped when *Time* put Wu on the cover of its August 7, 1950, issue and carried an article singing his praises.

Meanwhile, Wu and his wife, Edith, became so close to the first couple that they dined with them several times a week. But by the autumn of 1950, Wu had already clashed with Chiang's powerful son. Many arrests were being made despite Wu's efforts to stop unlawful detentions. He later learned that Ching-kuo secretly controlled all the various police forces, both open and secret, and that certain branches of the secret police were ordered to make regular reports on Chiang's subordinates. After Wu discovered that his own staff were reporting on him, he tried to resign in early 1952. "If Your Excellency loves Ching-kuo your son, you must not let him head the secret police," Wu told Chiang. "For . . . relying on your backing . . . he will become a target of hatred among the people." Chiang replied that he had a headache and wished to hear no more. Shortly afterward the Generalissimo and Madame Chiang unexpectedly appeared at the door of Wu's house on Chinese New Year's Day, saying they wished to pay their respects to his parents. This was a rare honor. After the formalities, Chiang casually told Wu that his proposed reforms to the military courts—namely that no arrests of civilians should be made without a warrant from the provincial police department, over which Wu had direct control—would be approved. Wu's resignation was returned the next day.

In the summer of 1952 the Wus' eldest daughter was to be married in the U.S. When Mayling heard of this, she strongly urged Edith Wu to attend the wedding and to bring their two sons along and place them in American schools, but the Wus were worried about the expense. The next day Mayling visited Mrs. Wu and told her that Chiang would like to give the Wus a gift of $10,000. K. C. Wu said they must decline the "kind offer," as it would be from the public treasury, and if discovered would cause criticism. Mrs. Wu relayed this to Mayling, who insisted that the money was from their own personal funds, but did not press the matter. Wu decided to send his elder son to the U.S. with his wife, but to keep the younger son on Taiwan to finish high school. After the wedding, Edith Wu received a visit at her New York hotel from Yu Kuo-hua, Chiang's former private secretary and a protégé of Madame Chiang. Yu tried to hand Mrs. Wu $10,000. She refused to accept, but Yu simply left without taking the cash.

Since arriving on Taiwan Mayling had been troubled intermittently by her neurodermatitis, as her skin condition was called, but in late 1951 it took a turn for the worse. Her doctor prescribed what was then a new "miracle" drug, ACTH (adrenocorticotropic hormone). Her skin cleared up in two days, but she could not sleep more than two or three hours a night. A week later the rash reappeared and she had to take another dose. "With the strenuous life I lead here with its resultant tensions and anxieties, my system cannot cope with it without the extra lift from the medicine," she wrote her friend Emma Mills.

It is possible that her anxiety resulted at least in part from an inner struggle to reconcile her professed democratic and Christian values with the reality of the repressive regime she was complicit in perpetuating, first on the mainland and now on Taiwan. Although she wrote and spoke often and self-righteously of democratic principles, in practice her loyalties lay first and foremost not with lofty ideals but with her husband, and so his principles became hers. She seemed unable to face up to this inconsistency between her professed values and the unbecoming role she played, but it took a psychic toll. The unremitting stress of keeping up the façade may have contributed to her skin problems, nervous breakdowns, chronic insomnia, and, ultimately, as she intimated to Mills, dependency on medication.

Her nerves were not helped by a famous and personally embarrassing case. In August 1951, Chiang ordered Gen. P. T. Mow, Mayling's protégé, who was deputy chief of staff of the Chinese Air Force liaison office in Washington, back to Taipei after he charged the Taiwan government with corruption in purchases. He refused to return, and subsequently absconded to Mexico with $7 million in Nationalist funds. The case was extremely embarrassing to Taipei, not least because Gen. Mow knew all of the unsavory details of China Lobby activities.

Mayling continued to take ACTH over the next year despite the fact that it made her look "awfully swollen and puffy." The effects were disastrous. By June 1952 her condition was so severe that she tried to persuade her doctor to fly to Taipei from New York to treat her. In August she was forced to seek treatment in the U.S. She wanted to charter a plane, but Wu cautioned that at a time when Taiwan needed so much American aid, it would not be wise. He suggested instead that she take a commercial flight on Pan-American Airlines, which she did. Requesting that no pictures be taken, Mayling left on August 9 for Honolulu. She hoped she could be successfully treated there and return home, but she was forced to continue to San Francisco, where she entered Franklin Hospital on August 17. At the height of the attack her face and body swelled and her skin darkened. Doctors ordered a strict diet—eggs, dairy products, and certain other foods were prohibited. She was also ordered to avoid direct sunlight.

U.S. ambassador to Taipei Karl Rankin and his wife, Pauline, visited her in the hospital a month later. They found her feeling somewhat better and impatient to get back to Taiwan, but still very "nervous" and seeing almost no visitors. She was continuing to take ACTH, and her doctors had told her an extended stay in the U.S. was needed for recovery. In mid-October, after two months in Franklin Hospital, she flew to New York, where she stayed with her sister Eling, who had lately purchased an estate called Hillcrest in Lattington, Long Island. She began X-ray therapy at the dermatologist, as well as dental work.

The illness forced Mayling to miss the sixth congress of the Kuomintang, held in Taipei in October 1952. Her absence was seen as bad news for the "enlightened" Western-educated officials in the government—K. C. Wu, George Yeh, Sun Li-jen—in their struggle against the "authoritarians," namely Chiang Ching-kuo. In a sign of her diminished political stature, Mayling was ousted from the party's central committee in party elections. Ching-kuo, who had no political presence during the last congress in 1945, won the second-highest number of votes, a reflection of his vastly increased power. K. C. Wu leaped from forty-ninth to seventh place.

The Republican candidate, Dwight D. Eisenhower, defeated Democrat Adlai Stevenson in the 1952 U.S. presidential election. "As you may well imagine, we are indeed delighted," Mayling wrote to congratulate the much-decorated Second World War general. Aware that the president-elect planned a trip to Korea, she sounded him out on a side trip to Taiwan. "Our facilities are meager and life there is rather austere, but we shall do everything to make your visit pleasurable," she ventured. "If such an invitation would not embarrass you, we shall send it immediately." Eisenhower politely declined. She wanted to go home, but shortly before Christmas suffered another skin outbreak.

The new president was much more favorably inclined toward the Nationalist Chinese government than Truman had been. In February 1953, soon after taking office, Eisenhower "unleashed" Chiang Kai-shek by lifting Truman's order preventing Nationalist military action against the mainland. Then he sent a handwritten note to Mayling inviting her to "drop in" for tea at the White House in early March. "While I know of no subject of common and pressing intent that could not be handled through normal channels, Mrs. Eisenhower and I would be delighted" to see you, he wrote. John Foster Dulles, who had replaced Acheson as secretary of state, and his wife were out of town so Undersecretary of State Walter B. Smith and his wife joined the gathering, along with the Chinese ambassador, Wellington Koo, and his wife. Mayling also met with Marshall, who told her he was meeting with every Chinese who asked to see him in the hope that one of them could offer a practical plan to help "Free China," as Taiwan was often referred to.

On Taiwan, civil liberties continued to decline and there were wholesale arrests by Ching-kuo's security apparatus. Wu was dismayed to find that the provincial police department was issuing blank arrest warrants. He himself was still being spied on by the secret police; his household servants were reporting on him and his phones were tapped. In early 1953 Wu tried to resign again, but Chiang rejected his resignation. Wu then went with his wife to Sun-Moon Lake on "sick leave," vowing he would neither return nor receive visitors until his resignation was accepted.

While Wu was sequestered at Sun-Moon Lake in March 1953, Mayling visited Wellesley with classmates. There she made her only public appearance of the seven-month trip to the U.S., giving a speech on Taiwan's economic development. She told a group of American students to enjoy themselves at college, but admonished a Japanese student sponsored by a scholarship in Mayling's name to "study hard, because we Oriental women have a harder time ahead." Immediately afterward she suddenly left for

Taiwan, against the advice of her doctors. She did not even tell her friend Emma Mills why she had to leave so unexpectedly. At the airport she told reporters she "had to get home" because "I have a lot of work to do."

Wu knew why Mayling had rushed back to Taiwan. If he succeeded in resigning, Ching-kuo's hand would be strengthened and her position weakened. Wu was in a quandary. If he came down from the mountains to greet her, as courtesy demanded, he would appear irresolute; if he did not, according to Chinese etiquette, it would be rude. So he did the only thing he could in the circumstances—he sent his wife.

Edith Wu took the five-hour drive from Sun-Moon Lake to the airport. After Mayling stepped down from the plane and greeted Chiang, she took Mrs. Wu's hand. "I came back because of K. C.," she whispered. "Will you please ask K. C. to come down from Sun-Moon Lake right away." She added, "I am quite surprised that he did not come to see me here." Mrs. Wu told her he would not come down. Mayling replied that she would go back to Sun-Moon Lake with Mrs. Wu the next day. Knowing the phone was tapped and her conversation would be immediately reported back to Chiang younger and senior, Mrs. Wu called her husband from their home in Taipei and told him what Mayling had said. Wu said if Madame Chiang wished to come see him that was fine, but he would not come down.

The next day Mayling asked Mrs. Wu to visit her. "You must tell K. C. to come down and take up the governorship right away," she told Mrs. Wu during the visit. "I originally intended to go up to Sun-Moon Lake with you to see K. C., but now the Generalissimo is absolutely angry at K. C. and forbids me to go. So you better tell him to come down here." Mrs. Wu said her husband was a very stubborn man but she would telephone him again. Wu's answer was that he wished to resign and if Chiang was angry he could go ahead and accept his resignation, but he would not come down. Mrs. Wu reported the conversation to Mayling.

A few hours later, Mayling sent her private secretary, Bill Sun, to Mrs. Wu's house. He said that the Generalissimo was now furious and would not allow Mayling to speak to Mrs. Wu again unless K. C. came down from the mountains and returned to his office immediately. Mrs. Wu replied that she and Madame Chiang had been personal friends for a long time, but if the Madame did not wish to see her again, she had no desire to see her either. Sun rushed back to report to Mayling. Soon afterward he called Mrs. Wu and said Mayling wanted to see her in her office at the Women's League headquarters, instead of at her residence. When they met, Mayling said, "If K. C. doesn't want to come down and go back to his office, can he come down to see me personally without letting the public know?" Wu finally relented out of courtesy.

Wu was acutely aware he had to be extremely careful. He knew Mayling sensed the trouble was over Chiang Ching-kuo, but he could not say so directly. He had learned she could not be relied upon to be discreet; moreover, she had no real power to make decisions, and might even make tensions worse. He recalled the time an executive from a government-owned monopoly, the Taiwan Match Company, had been arrested and falsely charged with being a Communist. The Chiangs and the Wus had met for lunch shortly afterward. Before Chiang arrived, Mayling casually asked Wu if he had had any disagreements with Ching-kuo's secret police. Wu mentioned the case of the match executive. Her temper flared. The instant her husband stepped into the room, she stood and demanded impulsively, "Do you know what your son has been doing?" which of course he did. Chiang's habitual forced smile vanished. The Wus were deeply embarrassed. In an effort to dispel the awkward mood, Wu suggested they begin eating. But Mayling instead grabbed Wu by one hand and his wife by the other and with the words "Let's go," marched out, leaving the "old man" by himself. From then on, Wu had stopped confiding in her.

Wu came down from Sun-Moon Lake and met Mayling at the presidential residence while Chiang was out. She took his hand and led him to the far corner of the verandah to talk, saying that there were hidden microphones installed everywhere else. When she asked why he wanted to resign, Wu spoke vaguely of "difficulties" and claimed he was "tired." She replied she had heard he was tired of Chiang's leadership. Wu denied this; to the contrary, he was willing to become Chiang's secretary if the Generalissimo so wished, but he would not resume the governorship.

Then Mayling again sent Bill Sun to see Wu's wife. If the trouble was Chiang Ching-kuo, Sun asked, why didn't Wu cooperate with Madame Chiang and Premier Chen Cheng to get Ching-kuo fired? Wu knew that all the power lay in the hands of father and son. He also felt Mayling's offer might be a trap, so in reply he quoted a proverb: "It is not for those who are not close enough to try to stand between those who are so close together."

The Wus headed back to the mountain resort on Easter Sunday 1953. En route, the driver checked the car because it had been handling oddly and found that the steering mechanism had been deliberately tampered with, in such a way that the car could have easily gone out of control, causing the passengers to plunge to their deaths on the treacherous mountain roads. Wu was deeply alarmed.

Undeterred, Mayling sent Wu's brother-in-law to Sun-Moon Lake to press Wu to return to Taipei. But Wu wanted to find out if Chiang knew about what he felt certain was an attempt on his life. He wrote a letter to Chiang alluding to a story from the Chinese classics. Quoting a famous loyal official about to be executed by his king on a false charge, Wu wrote, "My crime is worthy of death, but my sovereign is always wise." He ended the letter with a request to see Chiang, knowing that if Chiang knew about the ostensible murder attempt, he would refuse to see him. There was no reply.

Convinced his life was in peril, Wu pondered for days before coming up with a strategy. He called Arthur Goul, an Associated Press reporter who was returning to the United States. Since the phones were tapped, he knew Ching-kuo would find out. He visited Goul's house in Taipei and made the reporter swear on a Bible to obey his instructions. "Governor, why are you being so melodramatic?" Goul asked. Wu told him the story about the car and gave him letters of introduction to a number of his prominent American friends, including Gen. Albert Wedemeyer, publisher Roy Howard, and Col. Robert McCormick of the *Chicago Tribune*. If anything untoward happened to Wu, Goul was to tell them the full story.

The next day Goul was unexpectedly summoned to see Madame Chiang, which he found odd, as he did not know her personally. She offered him a job as her secretary for six months, for which she would pay him $10,000. Suspecting her intent was to keep him in Taiwan, he politely declined.

Wu applied for passports for himself, his wife, and his son. He got no response even after writing directly to Chiang Kai-shek, and Foreign Minister George Yeh could not help. So Wu wrote a personal plea to Madame Chiang asking her to intercede on his behalf. He had received several invitations to attend conferences in the U.S., he informed her, and if the passports were not issued, he would be forced to write his American friends to say the passports had been denied. Mayling took action, and before long she informed George Yeh that the Generalissimo had agreed to issue passports for Wu and his wife, but not for their son. Wu insisted he must have a passport for the boy, but Yeh told him that Chiang had specifically ruled it out. Soon after the passports were issued Mayling visited Mrs. Wu. She asked how long they planned to stay in the U.S. Mrs. Wu replied, "Indefinitely." Mayling evidently pretended she did not believe it, for she said, "Tso-chun, you don't know how hard living in America is. I bet you and K. C. will return in three months."

Wu requested a meeting with Chiang to bid him farewell before their departure on May 24, but received no reply. So Edith Wu wrote to Madame Chiang to say that if she had time, they would like to call on her before leaving. They heard nothing for several days. On the eve of their departure, Madame Chiang called Wu by military telephone to say they were on holiday in the mountains and could not personally see them off, but she would send Bill Sun on her behalf, and Chiang would send Ching-kuo on his behalf. She paused to speak with her husband. Then she said into the phone, "The Gimo wants me to give you a message. He wants you to take along the [complete] works of Dr. Sun Yat-sen to read them over on your trip to America." Wu was furious, but evenly asked Madame to thank her husband for the suggestion. "Please tell him I have read Dr. Sun's works very thoroughly," he said, "and please ask him to do the same."

By mid-1953 the disappearance of K. C. Wu from public view, combined with mounting reports of Chiang Ching-kuo's nefarious activities, was causing alarm among Taipei's American "friends." In a letter to "My dear Mayling," Roy Howard voiced concern that "Free China" was no longer getting the sort of favorable publicity it had when K. C. Wu was governor. The "ever-active American enemies" of Nationalist China, Howard warned, "exploited to the maximum" reports of Ching-kuo's activities. Mayling carefully avoided addressing Howard's concerns in her reply, but undoubtedly relayed the message to her husband.

To remove him from the scene temporarily, in September 1953 Ching-kuo was sent to the U.S. for three months as an official guest of the Defense Department. It was his first trip to a foreign country apart from the Soviet Union, and it was hoped in both the Departments of Defense and State that it would broaden his "intellectual horizon" and give him a salutary taste of American democracy. He toured military posts and installations.

He met with Eisenhower, CIA chief Allen Dulles, and his brother Secretary of State John Foster Dulles, who scolded Ching-kuo for being "rough" in handling security matters. Ching-kuo only murmured inaudibly in reply.

Mayling was quick to take advantage of Ching-kuo's absence. She used her influence to have a ban on Christian evangelism in the armed services and military hospitals rescinded shortly after his departure, as the ban, imposed by Ching-kuo, interfered with "God's work." She and her prayer meeting sponsored twenty five chaplains to minister in military hospitals, military prisons, and the army.

While Ching-kuo was touring America, one of Taipei's staunchest American friends made his first visit to Taiwan. In the summer of 1953, Eisenhower had dispatched Vice President Richard Nixon on a goodwill tour of Asia, in the days when such whirlwind extravaganzas were taken seriously. His grueling nineteen-country itinerary reached Taiwan in early November. The China Lobby stalwart, who as senator from California had spearheaded the investigation of Alger Hiss and attacked Acheson as responsible for the "loss" of China, conferred with Chiang for eight hours, with Madame Chiang and interpreters the only others present. Chiang waxed eloquent on his hopes of reconquering the mainland and reuniting the country under his leadership, but Nixon delivered a firm message from Eisenhower that Chiang could expect no military support for any invasion he might contemplate launching.

Nixon soon found that Mayling was much more than her husband's translator. "I believe Madame Chiang's intelligence, persuasiveness, and moral force could have made her an important leader in her own right," he later wrote. She and the vice president shared a passion for secrecy, as evidenced by the fact that a memorandum of the conversations at the meetings—which bore Mayling's editorial touch—was shown to Ambassador Rankin, but he was not permitted to keep a copy. Intriguingly, it was on this tour that Nixon showed the first hint of his flexibility on China; he told a British official in Singapore that—despite the virulent hostility to communism expressed in his 1950 and 1952 campaign speeches—he was open to the idea of bringing Beijing into the UN, if it became more "reasonable."

In December 1953, Ching-kuo returned to Taiwan deeply impressed, he claimed, with the "inner strength" of the American people. Social order in Russia was accomplished through terror, he noted, while in the U.S. the people were "automatically order-conscious." He also observed that although there were many rich people in America, it was impossible to tell the wealthy from those who were not. The trip evidently boosted Ching-kuo's standing at home, because he took over Mayling's position as senior liaison with the CIA and U.S. military intelligence. CIA station chiefs were told to place high priority on building close ties with Chiang's son.

From their self-imposed exile in a modest hotel in Evanston, Illinois, the Wus anxiously watched and waited. During the six months since leaving Taiwan they had written to Madame Chiang three times asking her to help secure a passport for their fourteen-year-old son, Hsiu-huang, so he could join them in America. Madame replied twice to say that she could not do anything. So when they received a telephone call one day in late November from Madame's nephew Louis Kung, they hoped that at long last she had succeeded in getting the passport. But Louis then hand-delivered a letter from Madame Chiang, which said only that her husband wanted Wu to return to Taiwan to serve as secretary-general of the presidential office. Wu consulted Wedemeyer, who recommended he write her back stressing the urgency of adopting democratic reforms.

As 1953 drew to a close, the Wus grew increasingly desperate to get their younger son out of Taiwan. Since his arrival in the U.S. in May 1953, Wu had kept his silence on his troubles with Chiang's regime, privately telling the full story only to Roy Howard and Gardner Cowles, now publisher of *Look* magazine. It was obvious that Chiang was holding the son as a hostage to keep Wu quiet.

In early 1954 Wu finally went public. In an open letter dated February 27 to the National Assembly in Taipei, he charged the Chiang government and the Kuomintang with running an undemocratic police state modeled on that of the Communists and "entirely devoted to the purpose of perpetuating its power." He attacked the Soviet-style political commissar system Ching-kuo had set up in the armed forces, saying it had devastated troop morale. "If we want to employ these troops just for the purpose of giving reviews and parades, it may be feasible," he wrote. "If we want to use them to fight for the recovery of the mainland, I cannot help shuddering at the thought!" Wu charged that the secret police were "so rampant

[that] Formosa has become virtually a police state." Countless innocent people had been illegally arrested and detained, tortured, or blackmailed. "Every time . . . I think of this, I cannot but feel an ache in my heart," he wrote. He criticized the Youth Corps as being modeled after the Hitler Youth and Communist youth organizations. He attacked press restrictions and arrests of reporters.

Chiang's government responded with "foaming indignation," in the words of *Time* magazine. It suppressed Wu's letter and unleashed a barrage of official propaganda accusing Wu of dereliction of duty, corruption, and treason. It labeled his charges "malicious" and accused him of giving "aid and comfort" to the Communists. He was expelled from the Kuomintang. Wu published his letter in the U.S. and penned a series of frank letters to Chiang. "The trouble with Your Excellency is your own selfishness. . . . Your love of power is greater than your love of the country," Wu wrote in a particularly biting missive dated April 3, 1954. Chiang Ching-kuo, Wu charged, had "no understanding whatever" of democracy and was a "great obstacle" to political progress. He urged Chiang to send Ching-kuo away from Taiwan until after the recovery of the mainland. "Your Excellency may [then] become cleared of any charge . . . that you entertain any ulterior motive of setting up a dynasty," Wu wrote.

Alfred Kohlberg of the China Lobby branded Wu's charge that Chiang had designs on his life a "delusion," but Wu's criticisms made headlines across America and compromised what little prestige Chiang's government had left. In the wake of the furor, Wu's son was finally granted a passport and allowed to join his family. Washington was keenly aware that democratic reforms were needed on Taiwan to attract popular American support for the Nationalist regime, but did little to push for change.

Distressed and embarrassed as she was by the acrimonious public break between her husband and her longtime protégé, Mayling's skin troubles flared up again. Her condition quickly became so serious that yet again she found it impossible to sleep without drugs. She needed to go back to America for treatment but dreaded the trip in her condition, fearing she might be swamped by reporters and Chinese-Americans, and that she might offend people by ignoring them. Chiang asked Pauline Rankin, the American ambassador's wife, to visit Mayling before she left. Mrs. Rankin found her "evidently very depressed and implied K. C. Wu's recent activities were [an] important contributing cause of her present illness." Mayling hurried back to the U.S. on a Nationalist Air Force plane, arriving in San Francisco on April 29, 1954. She checked into Franklin Hospital immediately.

A month later she was resting in the California countryside. "Progress is somewhat slow but I think the balmy California weather and the medical care will eventually affect [sic] a cure," she wrote Wellington Koo. Her doctors suspected her skin problems were caused by some sort of allergy and said that when her skin healed sufficiently they would carry out allergy tests. She proceeded for further treatment to New York, where an American friend, Dorothy Thomas, visited her in the hospital. Still quite ill, Mayling could not have anything touching her skin. A bamboo cage had been constructed for her and the bedcovers were put over it.

In the summer of 1954 a crisis erupted over the offshore islands of Quemoy and Matsu, small heavily fortified islands near the China coast that remained in Nationalist Chinese hands. Nationalist and Communist forces exchanged heavy artillery barrages, sparking fears of another war in the Far East just one year after the Korean armistice. By late August Mayling was sufficiently recovered to become the first woman in the history of the American Legion to deliver the main address at its annual banquet. Other speakers included President Eisenhower; Adm. Arthur W. Radford, chairman of the Joint Chiefs of Staff; and New York's influential Cardinal Francis Joseph Spellman. As long as the Taiwan "footstool" remained free from Communist control, she told listeners, the Chinese people had a sanctuary of freedom. "We Chinese will not be slaves long. This I promise you."

She returned to Franklin Hospital in San Francisco for a checkup before heading back to Taiwan, expecting to stay just a few days, but on arriving had another flare-up of hives. It was eventually traced to a new vitamin B pill the doctors had prescribed. "We found that it had not only liver, but fish liver as well, and as I am allergic to both fish and liver, you can well imagine what were the effects," she wrote a friend. She finally returned to Taipei in late October 1954.

With skirmishes over the offshore islands continuing as the U.S. deliberated on a response, *Life* magazine's Asia correspondent John Osborne had what he called a "fascinating" experience during an afternoon tea with the Chiangs in early January 1955. "I was treated to a knockdown argument between her and the Gimo, he holding that the US was to be trusted in the long term and she that it should not be trusted for a moment," Osborne wrote to Luce's deputy, C. D. Jackson. "Both called on me to support their views, the Madame throwing the Democratic record at me and the Gimo testing my confidence (as I then asserted it) in the long term good sense and good faith of the US. Boy, did I sweat!" Osborne left convinced that all he had heard about Madame Chiang in the last year was true—that she now harbored an "ingrained distrust and dislike of all things American."

Even as her faith in America plunged, Taipei's American champions were fighting an uphill battle to improve Taiwan's tarnished international image. Britain charged the U.S. with denying the existence of the Communist regime on the mainland. Dulles countered that the U.S. knew well that the Beijing regime existed and tartly declared: "It is, however, one thing to recognize evil as a fact; it is another thing to take evil to one's breast and call it good." Henry Luce was annoyed when Churchill approached him with the old idea of making Taiwan a UN trusteeship, a plan still backed by some U.S. congressmen. "US opinion is overwhelmingly for keeping 'the Reds' out of the UN but it is by no means equally strong for Formosa," Luce wrote ruefully to John Osborne. "Even those who are for Formosa (more or less) are rather apologetically for it. People are even more apologetically for Chiang—if they are for him at all." Churchill conceded the U.S. had a "duty of honor" to prevent Taiwan from being overrun by the Communists and to protect its inhabitants from meeting a fate similar to that of the alleged two million Chinese on the mainland who had been liquidated in Communist purges, but he was concerned as to whether the Americans viewed Chiang as tenant or owner of Taiwan.

Taiwan's ambiguous legal status notwithstanding, by this time the U.S. was developing the island as a showcase for American aid. Along with Japan, Taiwan became an essential part of the new American vision of a "free" Asia, economically at least. The U.S. was eager to see "Free China," as Taiwan was called, prosper as a model for "democracy" in its competition with the Soviet Union, and the Republic of China was held up as a counterpoint to the People's Republic of China. Using economic aid as both carrot and stick, Washington steered Taiwan in the direction of becoming an industrialized and modern country. Ultimately the U.S. aimed to make Taiwan self-sufficient from U.S. aid to serve as an example for other American aid recipients.

Meanwhile, pressure from the China Lobby as well as continuing conflict over the disputed coastal islands helped push Washington into forging a Sino-American Mutual Defense Treaty with Taipei, signed on December 2, 1954. For Taipei, which had long lobbied for the treaty, the pact gave while it took away: It made clear U.S. determination to defend Taiwan and Penghu from Communist attack, but it also put a leash on Chiang once again by restraining him from launching any attack against the mainland. It also mollified the China Lobby by formalizing Taiwan's position as a fortified link in the "island chain" in the Western Pacific, and as an integral part of the U.S. "containment" strategy against Communist aggression. Taiwan's position was further secured, and the U.S. was further invested in Taiwan.

Secretary of State Dulles visited Taipei in early March 1955 to formally put the treaty into effect. Just weeks before the P.R.C. had forced the Nationalists to withdraw from the Dachen Islands, but did not take Quemoy and Matsu despite heavy bombardment. The U.S. Navy's Seventh Fleet helped evacuate 18,000 civilians and 15,000 troops and the Communists took the islands days later. The incident had rattled Taipei's leadership, and Dulles was sympathetic to Chiang's argument that a formal cease-fire between the Nationalists and the Communists over Quemoy and Matsu would lead to an inevitable collapse of morale on Taiwan. As she invariably did when high-level foreign visitors were present, Mayling joined the meetings, but she said little.

After Dulles's return to Washington, Eisenhower dispatched Roy Howard to Taipei in late March to sound out Chiang on the contentious issue of the offshore islands. Eisenhower hoped to persuade Chiang to abandon Quemoy and Matsu, but for Chiang the islands' symbolic significance far outweighed any practical considerations involved in keeping them. As they were officially territory of Fujian province, the tiny outposts furnished the only thread of legitimacy, however tenuous, to his claim to rule all China. Howard saw the president at the White House before departing. "He approved of my ideas and added a few of his own, which he said he would like to have me put over, not as his ideas but as my reporter's point of view," Howard wrote in his diary.

Howard and his wife Margaret met the Chiangs at Sun-Moon Lake. Mayling interpreted during many hours of talks, punctuated by a boat ride on the lake accompanied by several boatloads of security guards. "I became convinced that Chiang intends to defend Quemoy and Matsu if he has to do it alone," Howard wrote. "His reason is that if he does not do so he is sunk anyway." Chiang's rationale was that he could afford defeat but not retreat because that would result in the "complete collapse" of his army. Eisenhower later told Howard that he had a "great deal of admiration" for the Chiangs, but thought they were "unnecessarily complicating the situation" as the military significance of the islands to either the "Reds" or the Nationalists was small.

Mayling took the opportunity of Howard's visit to brief him on a fashion show she had recently organized, at which Ching-kuo's henchmen—probably his Youth Corps—had staged a violent "demonstration." Publicly denouncing the event as frivolous, given that it was wartime, they disrupted the show, to which the diplomatic corps had been invited, even overturning diplomats' cars. Alarmed by Ching-kuo's growing power, Howard feared for Mayling's personal safety should Chiang die suddenly, and made detailed plans to get her out of Taiwan immediately in the event that occurred. Howard advised Chiang to send Ching-kuo to the U.S. for a year or two of study, both to remove him from the scene before he could do more harm and to try to instill in him democratic values. Howard left Taiwan convinced that young Chiang was "insidious" and "bears watching."

If Mayling's political clout was waning, her financial clout was on the rise. In 1955, during this time of straitened circumstances, Chiang Kai-shek— presumably at the urging of his wife—ordered the finance ministry to impose a special duty on importers. This new duty, euphemistically billed as a "military welfare donation," was in fact a tax on all imported goods. All proceeds went not to defense, but to the Women's League, and thus importers became involuntary contributors to the organization's coffers. A similar "donation," again destined for the Women's League, was exacted from every movie theatre ticket sold. In this way Madame Chiang controlled a stream of funds that was initially modest but grew substantially in later years as Taiwan's economy strengthened. As the accounts of the Women's League were not subject to scrutiny, even by members, Madame was free to dispose of the funds as she wished, accountable to no one.

* * *

Against the backdrop of the continuing Quemoy-Matsu crisis in 1955, one of the most infamous—and perplexing—incidents of Chiang rule on Taiwan unfolded. Gen. Maxwell D. Taylor, who had been commander of the U.S. Far East Command in Tokyo, visited Taiwan in May 1955 en route to Washington to take up the post of army chief of staff. Along with the Chiangs and other members of the military and diplomatic corps, he viewed military exercises in Pingtung, a base in the south of Taiwan. All seemed to go impressively well. Afterward the Chiangs invited Ambassador Rankin and his wife to fly back to Taipei with them on their personal plane. The Rankins chatted with Mayling while Chiang rested and read from a book of Chinese classics. Nothing seemed amiss.

Later, however, it "emerged" that a group of officers in the Chinese army had supposedly seized the occasion of Taylor's visit to present certain demands and other matters to Chiang during the military display. Gen. Sun Li-jen, who had been removed as army commander in 1954 and was now Chiang's chief of staff, was held responsible, and his military career was brought to an abrupt end due to what was labeled a Communist-inspired "coup plot." Some three hundred people were implicated and over a hundred officers were arrested and charged in the alleged conspiracy against the Generalissimo. Some were sent to the notorious Green Island and others were executed as Communists.

The affair caused a great stir. General Sun was a favorite of American military leaders. The Chinese called him the "Ever Victorious General" for his successful military record. Concern over the case reached the highest levels in Washington. Senior military officials were appalled. Admiral Radford declared that "something must be quite bad" in the Chinese army for so many officers from so many different units to join the alleged mutiny. It was true that tensions were high due to Ching-kuo's political commissar system. Louis Kung told Howard that Sun's ousting was the "handiwork" of Chiang Ching-kuo. The exact details remain unclear to the present day, but it is now generally accepted that Ching-kuo fabricated the entire incident to frame Sun and remove him as a rival, while taking advantage of the opportunity to purge the army.

On August 20, 1955, it was publicly announced that Sun had "resigned" as an admission of negligence in connection with the alleged coup plot and Communist spy ring in the army. Howard sent Mayling a stern letter, dated August 22, objecting to Sun's ousting, terming it "a stupid move." He strongly advised the Nationalist government to give Sun "a clean bill of health for the benefit of the Free China [cause] with the present administration"—clearly implying that Eisenhower, too, was displeased. Mayling did not reply to Howard's admonitions. Sun was charged with failure to properly supervise subordinates and placed under house arrest. Ambassador Rankin visited Sun later at his home in central Taiwan and found him "comfortably installed" with his family and "enjoying his rose garden."

Mention of Sun's name was henceforth taboo under Chiang rule. The government embarked on a campaign to destroy his legacy, banning books on his military exploits, airbrushing his image from photographs, and removing his name from monuments.

With Wu and Sun out of the way, Ching-kuo's rivals for power in the *meiguo pai*—the so-called American faction in the Nationalist government, of which Mayling was the spiritual leader—had been almost entirely purged. They had in any case outlived their usefulness, now that American support was ensured due to the Korean War and the 1954 mutual defense pact. Mayling was regarded as "too Americanized," and the Li-jen Sun episode threw into stark relief the erosion in her standing since its peak during the Sino-Japanese war. Ching-kuo was by now running the country on a day-to-day basis, while his father, at sixty-eight, had embraced his preferred role of elder statesman. Isolated in an ivory tower, the aging Generalissimo pored over Confucian texts, the Bible, and *Streams in the Desert*, making major decisions while leaving the dirty work to his son. Ching-kuo's only remaining rival was Vice President Chen Cheng, with whom he struggled for power until Chen's death a decade later.

In late 1955 Mayling went to the U.S. once again, apparently to lobby the Eisenhower administration to carry out defense commitments to Taiwan. A year later, December 1, 1956, she and Chiang celebrated their thirtieth wedding anniversary, regretting that the "National Revolution" to which they'd dedicated themselves when they were married remained unachieved. "My wife and I share an acute consciousness of failure in not living up to the lofty ideals instilled in us by our mothers," Chiang wrote piously. "It was their constant and cherished expectation that we return thanks to the State by delivering our people from evil and suffering." They pledged to rededicate themselves to the "supreme task to which we are called."

* * *

Taiwan residents were ambivalent about the American role on the island. The U.S. military was in Taiwan officially in an advisory capacity, not as an occupying force, as charged by Beijing. Nevertheless the highly visible American presence—large billboards proclaimed a U.S. military area in Taipei as "Freedom Village," for instance—at times affronted nationalistic sensibilities, resulting in friction. Taiwan's ties with its great patron were severely tested when on May 24, 1957, rioters sacked the American embassy in Taipei. The incident erupted when the widow of a man who had been shot by an American sergeant staged a tearful one-woman protest in front of the embassy with her little daughter in her lap. She objected to the American court-martial verdict acquitting the sergeant, who claimed the man had peeped in the window of his quarters as his wife was dressing. Embassy officials tried to mollify the widow's demands for financial compensation with vague promises to look into the matter, but soon a crowd began to gather. A handful of curious onlookers soon swelled into an angry mob of ten thousand. The mob destroyed embassy buildings and injured several staff. Looters scattered files and furniture in the street and smashed embassy cars. Rioters pulled down the American flag and hoisted the Nationalist flag. When police were belatedly called in, they stood by and did little to stop the rioting, which went on for most of the afternoon.

American eyewitnesses reported seeing large groups of Youth Corps members in the melee, but Ching-kuo afterward disingenuously claimed they "just happened to be there." Army troops were not called to the scene to quell the riot, ostensibly because they were participating in air raid exercises. Ching-kuo was harshly criticized by U.S. officials for not putting a stop to the violence, but the administration was so deeply invested in its relationship with Taipei that Eisenhower, disgruntled though he was, chose to confine his reaction to mild protestations and hand-wringing.

The murky episode, which some suspected may have been deliberately staged to obtain U.S. documents held in embassy files, or simply to teach the U.S. a lesson, did nothing to improve the younger Chiang's already unsavory reputation in Washington, where he was still mistrusted in some quarters as a sinister character who might one day deliver Taiwan to the Communists. When the Veterans Administration not long after invited Ching-kuo to inspect veterans' facilities in the U.S., several ranking

Republican senators, some staunch supporters of Chiang, strongly protested and the invitation was rescinded. By this time Ching-kuo was privately tiring of his role as his father's "lackey," as foreign minister George Yeh put it to the new American ambassador, Everett Drumwright. Obliged as he was to carry out and shoulder blame for many "unpleasant tasks" at his father's bidding, Ching-kuo had begun to chafe under Chiang's "iron control" and wished to give up his military posts in favor of positions in the economic arena.

Taiwan's economic prospects did appear decidedly grim. The island was beset with despair, shame, and uncertainty. The government's answer to all problems seemed to be to hide in unreality while awaiting the cherished "return to the mainland." Ubiquitous slogans on the evils of the Red Chinese regime and the coming "counterattack" were plastered on walls, proclaimed over the airwaves, and even printed on matchbooks. The island had the flavor of an armed camp, with soldiers much in evidence, constant reminders of the threat of Communist spies, and frequent air raid drills. Austerity was a dominant theme and the lion's share of the government budget—much of it supplied by the U.S.—went to military expenses. Taiwan had an estimated six hundred thousand men under arms in the 1950s and 1960s—or 5 pecent of the population, proportionally higher than any other nation.

The Philippines was rated by economists as having far greater prospects for prosperity. Taiwan's population was surging by 4 percent a year and the island was forced to import food in order to feed the population. People were poorly dressed, most wearing wooden shoes, if any. The sight of young mothers waddling along with protruding bellies, an infant strapped on their back and a toddler on each hand, was common. Shacks housing mainland refugees abounded in the major cities. The capital's mostly human-powered traffic—bicycles, pedicabs, and pull-carts—was regulated by a solitary traffic light; the tallest buildings soared to all of four stories. Unemployment was high, jobs were scarce, and inflation cut into salaries. Agriculture aside, economic activity was largely confined to petty retail trade. The chief economic improvement the government could point to was land reform, which Chiang had refused to carry out on the mainland for fear of alienating his power base, but which was easily executed on Taiwan because the landlords were the politically powerless Taiwanese.

The political climate discouraged investment and Taiwan seemed guaranteed to remain a declining agrarian economy. The mainland was widely depicted as being on the march, while Taiwan was seen as indulging in daydreaming and posturing.

Chiang's followers wrestled constantly with the conflict between their absolute faith that they would soon go back "home" and the painful reality that the likelihood this dream would be realized was extremely remote. Even a simple matter such as putting in a vegetable garden became a difficult decision. "Is it worth planting these tomatoes?" asked one refugee. "Am I not surrendering to despair if I put in trees—am I not admitting to myself that I may be here forever?"

In their homeland, meanwhile, the political and economic situation went from bad to worse. Early purges and famines were followed by the ill-fated "Hundred Flowers" campaign to encourage political dissent. Then, in 1957, Mao abruptly chopped off flowers' heads in the antirightist campaign, sending some three hundred thousand intellectuals to labor camps or to their deaths. Most catastrophic of all was the "Great Leap Forward" that began in 1958, when Chairman Mao launched an astonishingly ill-conceived modernization policy intended to catapult China virtually overnight to the level of the industrialized West, both technologically and economically. Among other measures, the rural public was compelled to turn over every scrap of iron to feed thousands of small smelting furnaces across the country in order to produce steel. In the mad frenzy, farmers melted down plows while harvests rotted in the fields, precipitating widespread famine.

Divided by ideology and geography, Mayling and her sister Ching Ling had been out of contact since the late 1940s. Publicly, Ching Ling followed the party line, attacking the West and extolling the virtues of life under communism. She frequently attacked the U.S., both during the Korean War and after. "Children should know that Chairman Mao and the Communist Party are the Saviors of the People and that U.S. imperialism and the reactionaries are big scoundrels" was a typical sample of her published writings. In 1951 she was awarded the Stalin Peace Prize. She lent her name to international Communist organizations, and was sent to "friendly" countries as an ambassadress for the Beijing regime. The Nationalists regarded her as politically naive at best and at worst a traitor for allowing herself to be used by the Communists.

But private reports emerged suggesting all was not well in Madame Sun's lacquered cage. In the spring of 1952 Nehru's sister and Mayling's onetime friend, Nan Pandit, visited China. She met twice with Ching Ling in Shanghai but was surprised to find her confined to virtual seclusion and extraordinarily uncommunicative, appearing "bitter" at the world and unwilling to converse in English. Madame Sun was surrounded at all times by several Chinese, and her activities and contacts were evidently monitored. An unrelenting "hate campaign" against the U.S. was in full swing. Pandit carried a letter from Eleanor Roosevelt to Madame Sun, appealing to her to use her influence to help foreign nationals in detention or under house arrest in China. But under the circumstances Pandit thought it inadvisable to deliver the letter. She concluded, as she told an American diplomat, that Madame Sun was "living retired life and has had halo of saint cast about her by Commies but is removed from reality of Chi[nese] politics."

In a December 1955 visit to India as Nehru's guest, Ching Ling publicly attacked the U.S. for its "occupation" of Taiwan and "interference" in the "liberation" of the disputed offshore islands. But at a state banquet in her honor, a guest reported that she seemed "ill at ease" and, surrounded by Chinese associates, barely spoke. When asked if she was a Communist, she replied in the negative. When asked if she approved of Chiang Kai-shek's regime on Taiwan, she said she did not as there were many differences between her late husband's revolutionary ideals and those of Chiang. But when asked if she was still a Christian, like her sister, she said that she was. The guest received the unmistakable impression Ching Ling did not approve of the Communist regime.

Chapter Twenty-one

Return to the Mainland

Faith is the substance of things hoped for, the evidence of things not seen.
—The Bible, Hebrews 11:1

In the mid-1950s, Chiang and Mayling turned their minds to producing his-and-her books in an apparent attempt to salvage their damaged images—and egos—in the eyes of the American public. Mayling's book had much to do with her growing religious faith. Her friend Grace Oursler, a fellow Christian, visited Taipei in early 1955 and for eighteen days and nights she and Mayling worked together on *The Sure Victory*, a venture aided by their common affliction, insomnia. The book was a "labor of love"—Mayling's defense of herself and her husband, and their role in China's civil war, disguised as a spiritual manifesto.

The two women were close, and Mayling confided in Oursler. Back in the U.S., Oursler pleaded with Mayling to let her write an article to counter what she termed the "miasma of ill feeling" toward Mayling and her husband that had been created by their "enemies." Since her return from Taiwan, Oursler lamented, she had been asked no fewer than four times whether she had slept on silk sheets. "I only wish with all my heart, especially in the light of the new book by Emily Hahn, who continually stresses that you and the Generalissimo have no family, that I could mention miscarriages under the hardships that you have endured," Oursler wrote Mayling in a letter dated April 1955, referring to a recent unauthorized biography of Chiang Kai-shek. "In other words, dear friend, it seems a shame that a person who loves you cannot say for you the things you very naturally would not say for yourself." Oursler enclosed a draft article entitled "What She Is Like" for Mayling's reaction.

Mayling was horrified. First, she abhorred "personal publicity," she replied in a stinging rebuke to Oursler. Second, the article was "peppered" with inaccuracies. And third, her husband insisted that "the public should not invade our home." For that reason she had never allowed herself to be portrayed on stage, film, or television. Mayling bridled at Oursler's assertion in the article that she was accustomed to great wealth. "I have been used to comforts and have never known poverty, it is true, but I have not been used to great wealth," she countered, rather naively. "I appreciate more than I can tell you your great affection for me and your desire to write something which would counteract malicious propaganda. I have been in political life long enough to realize, however, that inevitably in politics there is mudslinging and when there is nothing for the enemy to attack he usually fabricates. I have also learned that one can never catch up with a written lie and the more one persists, the greater aid and comfort one gives to the enemy; therefore the best thing is to rise above it and not let it get under one's skin. In time, truth will out." She claimed to concur with George Bernard Shaw, who had carved on his mantelpiece the words: "They say, what do they say?—let them say."

Harper & Brothers, meanwhile, rejected *The Sure Victory*. An editor commented that the draft was "moving" but suffered from "leaks of egoism, little traces of spiritual pride and 'Christian' tribalism." Especially problematic was the line: "Wherein have I failed that even the mainland has been lost?" The editor noted acidly, "The unconscious majesty here is pretty hard to take. The lady is taking a great deal upon herself. . . . The 'I am China' touch, which, even if it were valid, has no place in this piece." Thanks to Oursler's careful shepherding, *Reader's Digest* ran a condensed version in its August 1955 issue, and the publishing house Fleming Revell subsequently published the book.

In 1956 Chiang produced a manuscript, penned largely by associates. It was the story of his titanic struggle against communism—part history, part apologia, part defense, part confession. Henry Luce had been pushing the "extremely important" work for several years, and promised to run installments in *Life*. "When this project will have run its publishing course, your thoughts will have been conveyed to a tremendous section of the American people," the publisher wrote Chiang.

During her 1955–56 visit to the U.S., Mayling was introduced to Roger Straus, publisher at Farrar, Straus, Cudahy. Straus was captivated. "She was a good-looking woman even as a mature woman—she was then of a certain age—and obviously smart as hell," he said later. "She was brilliant . . . well-dressed and well jeweled, and had a great presence. She was very cool, very aloof, but I found her a most intriguing character."

Chiang's book was "atypical" of Farrar's list, and Straus "brooded" over whether to publish it. He thought it would sell only modestly but felt it was a historical document that should be published. The real reason he decided to publish the book, however, was because Madame Chiang had told him she was writing her autobiography, "and that I wanted very badly, because I had always [thought] . . . she was a far more interesting person than her husband from the point of view of a book publisher." Mayling had led Straus to believe that she had many notes and journals she was using to write her memoir, and he was convinced it would be a "fascinating" book. She had given him the impression that the reason she was not rushing to publish was because she and Chiang were not getting along and would not have agreed on much of what she was writing. This seemed plausible, since at that point she had been in the U.S. for some time and there were stories circulating that she was estranged from her husband. Straus subsequently made a "substantial and attractive" offer for Chiang's book. "This was my ploy, really, to get her book," he said.

Madame Chiang closely supervised and edited the English translation of her husband's book, the Chinese edition of which had appeared in Taiwan in 1956 and quickly became required reading for Nationalist party members, government officials, and students. At her insistence the more violently antiforeign language was edited out of the English version. She demanded that galley proofs of the book be sent to her for review before publication, and was livid when they were not. To the publisher's chagrin, Chiang refused to hold a press conference or even do interviews to publicize the book, which appeared in 1957 as *Soviet Russia in China*. The book was nonetheless an unexpected success and was soon reprinted.

Mayling insisted on holding up the third printing in order to make changes, and again demanded to see the galleys. The costs of printing a revised edition were "enormously" high, Straus wrote, and such an undertaking, "under ordinary circumstances, would not warrant further consideration." But what Madame Chiang wanted, Madame Chiang got—textual revisions plus a new cover design, a new book jacket, and the addition of a map. By December 1957, 17,500 copies had been sold in the U.S. In mid-1958 it went into a fourth printing. Straus later discovered that the CIA was distributing the book widely, which helped to explain the robust sales.

Mindful of her coquettish half-promise, Straus later tried to entice Mayling to write a book "that has been very close to our hearts for several years past." There would, he argued, be "enormous interest . . . to hear from you directly of all the trials and tribulations as well as the victories and achievements . . . during these last confused years. . . . You have, we are sure, a great deal to say and we are confident that [it] is not only of paramount importance at this time to the English-speaking world but also . . . for the historical record." Mayling replied coolly that "at the present time" she was not contemplating publication of her memoirs. It is doubtful she ever had the remotest intention of doing so.

The "evil" of communism had divided the world and created a new "dark age," Chiang Kai-shek declared in his 1958 Good Friday sermon. In hers, Madame Chiang pointed to anti-Communist uprisings in Eastern Europe and China, and lauded those who chose death over "compromise with the Anti-Christ." She ended with a biblical quote: "Faith is the substance of things hoped for, the evidence of things not seen."

The thing hoped for, of course, was a return to the mainland. But faith alone, it seemed, would not be enough. American help was needed. And faith in American help sprang eternal, despite all evidence to the contrary. Earlier failures notwithstanding, Mayling plotted a triumphal return to the American spotlight. "While there is deep antagonism among the [American] people for Red China, Formosa is almost forgotten," her old friend George Sokolsky, by this time a right-wing syndicated columnist, warned her on the eve of her trip. In a diplomatic attempt to persuade her to tone down her notoriously florid and opaque oratorical style while in America, he enclosed a copy of the Gettysburg Address as a reminder that "the genius of Lincoln was that he understood that English is a terse language, rich in its simplicity and only true when readily understood."

Mayling arrived in New York in late May 1958 and met with Roy Howard, who strongly advised her to concentrate on one major speech on Taiwan's value to the democratic world and to "cut out the talk of a return to the mainland." But she ignored him and instead took the advice of Secretary of State John Foster Dulles, who told her she should take every opportunity to speak on "the evils of Communism." She plunged once again into her role as the most visible and colorful publicist for the Nationalist cause, making several speeches in quick succession, overnight becoming one of the nation's most sought-after speakers. Although controversy and shifting public sentiment had dimmed her appeal, *Newsweek* observed dryly, "The years have served only to cast her exotic beauty into a mature mold, and have taken none of her personal charm, keenness of intellect, or oratorical ardor."

World communism was "on the offensive," Mayling declared in an interview, vowing that the Nationalists would recover the mainland—alone, if necessary. "We are going to do our own fighting. . . . In fact, we don't want you to fight for us. If you did, the Communists would make capital of it, and say, 'see, they have to have a foreign power to help them.'" She insisted she was not on an official mission, but allowed: "I am my husband's wife." Unofficially or not, she was in rare form. Sokolsky's pointed references to the virtues of the Gettysburg Address were cast to the wind. As she collected an honorary degree from the University of Michigan in early July, she attacked "intellectuals" who argued for disarmament on grounds that Communist domination was preferable to nuclear destruction, saying they were victims of "self-hypnosis" and "sequacious reasoning" who had "confused the need for peace with survival at any cost."

In mid-July, Mayling lunched at the White House with President and Mrs. Eisenhower. The gathering resembled a war council of her closest American allies, and included government, military, and religious leaders. The gold table service was used for only the second time during the Eisenhower administration. On July 17 she gave a speech to Washington's National Press Club, having sent Sokolsky a draft beforehand. He advised she tone down her "bull's-eye attacks" on U.S. policy, cautioning that she would be criticized for trying to "stir up a war mood." She instead attacked those who supported recognition of Communist China. She was only the fourth woman to address the prestigious organization in its fifty years of existence. When she spoke before the club it was still men-only; women could not attend the banquet and were sequestered in the balcony instead.

As Madame Chiang lobbied America, her old friend Claire Lee Chennault lay dying of lung cancer. She was godmother to his two daughters with Anna Chan, a young Chinese news reporter he had married after divorcing his first wife, with whom he had eight children, in 1946. During his illness Mayling visited him several times in Washington and in New Orleans, where he was being treated by Dr. Alton Ochsner, among the first physicians to speak out on the evils of smoking. Ironically, the World War II hero—and inveterate smoker—had recently appeared in a cigarette advertisement. Mayling praised the old Flying Tiger for his "wonderful fighting spirit" and his devotion to China's cause during her darkest hour. He died on July 27, 1958, and was buried in Arlington National Cemetery.

The message of Madame Chiang's tour took on new urgency when on August 23, 1958, the Communist Chinese launched a fresh artillery barrage on the island of Quemoy. The goal was apparently more psychological than military—the Communists wanted to deprive the island of supplies, and perhaps oust the Nationalists from the islands, but mostly they hoped to wear down morale. The U.S. decided again not to take military action, reflecting the long-held feeling that the remote flyspeck islands were not worth the life of a single American boy. But to Chiang Kai-shek, the frontline islands remained of critical importance, as they represented the last toeholds for the Nationalist government on the mainland.

Days after the 1958 Taiwan Straits crisis erupted, Madame spoke at the eighty-first annual dinner of the American Bar Association, the first woman ever to deliver the keynote address. She criticized Washington for refusing to act in the Quemoy crisis: "We call ourselves civilized and we advocate the use of moral force to condemn international wrong," she said. "Yet at the first sign of . . . violence we forgo our principles as well as our moral right to excoriate the evil and the evildoer. Can this . . . bring world peace?" She cited Munich, Yalta, and Korea as examples of political folly. Addressing the American Legion Auxiliary, she condemned what she called the attitude of "accommodating at all costs" the "wily" Communists. She denounced those who had "fallen for the fallacies of appeasement"— coexistence, trade and cultural exchange with "Red" China, and the "two-China myth." Quoting from the play *Lysistrata,* she called for a "Chorus of Women" working to make the world free.

Her inflammatory speeches were arousing concerns in Washington that she was "rocking the diplomatic boat," wrote *Newsweek.* "Biting the hand that feeds" might have been a more apt analogy. On *Meet the Press,* she told a nationwide television audience that people on the mainland were asking why Taiwan did not use nuclear weapons against the Communist regime. She asserted that a Nationalist counterattack against the mainland was growing nearer every day "because we are responding to the cries of suffering of the tortured, oppressed people" there. Not everyone agreed with her "fiery" arguments, but most Americans, even her critics, "couldn't help liking the way the tiny, courageous woman threw her punches straight from the shoulder," *Newsweek* observed.

Six weeks after the onslaught on Quemoy began, Beijing suspended bombardment—and subsequently announced that it would shell on odd-numbered days only. Dulles dismissed this odd declaration as "fantastic." In his view, the Chinese Communists wanted to keep Quemoy "as a sort of 'whipping boy' to be lashed whenever there are 'intrusions' by the United States or acts by the Chinese Nationalists which indicate lack of 'repentance.'" This he denounced as "mere sadistic terrorism."

The Communists were displeased when Dulles visited Taiwan in October 1958, and shelled Quemoy with the secretary of state en route. In Taiwan he tried to promote what he called a "new concept" of the Nationalist mission. He urged Chiang to renounce the use of force as a means to reconquer the mainland, thereby strengthening the Nationalists' moral position by putting Taiwan in the same position as West Germany, South Korea, and South Vietnam. Chiang refused but finally agreed that his government's principal means of achieving its mission of recovering the motherland would be by keeping Sun Yat-sen's principles alive in the minds and hearts of the Chinese people, and not by the use of force. But Dulles failed to impress upon Chiang the "unwisdom of attaching and identifying his cause with two pieces of real estate which perhaps, in this uncertain world, could not always be defended under all conceivable circumstances." Immediately on his return Dulles and his wife telephoned Madame Chiang in New York and gave her a report on the visit and on her husband. "We do not accept the present Communist regime in China as permanent," Dulles wrote John Cabot Lodge after his visit. "How quickly it will change, I do not know. But that it will change, I do not doubt."

As Madame Chiang traveled about the U.S., enjoying her return to the limelight, Chiang Kai-shek's banished former wife, Jennie Chen, was secretly preparing a memoir of her relationship with the Nationalist Chinese leader. Since leaving China in August 1927 she was said to have studied at university for several years before returning to Hong Kong at the age of twenty-five. She later moved back to China and lived there quietly, remaining even after the Communist takeover, managing to escape to Hong Kong only in the late 1950s. Chiang Ching-kuo had quietly sent Jennie funds for many years, perhaps partly out of sympathy for her plight, but mainly to keep her quiet. However, after her daughter fell ill and medical expenses mounted, Chen's limited means compelled her to seek other options. Her efforts to produce a memoir did not escape the notice of Ching-kuo's spy network. Chen Li-fu, Chiang's erstwhile henchman, who had been living in "retirement" in the U.S. since the late 1940s, was enlisted to dissuade her. Jennie knew Chen Li-fu from the days of the Canton government in the 1920s. "I believe that if you depend on selling your memoirs to get money for medical expenses, that is . . . destroying one person to save the other," he wrote Jennie in a letter as cruel as it was menacing. "Your adopted daughter's sickness cannot be cured. This you may regard as superstition but the matter has cause and effect involved although you may not wish it so."

Chen wrote Jennie again in April 1959: "I hear that you are again listening to people's urgings and intend to publish some kind of book. For your own sake and for your own good, I, Li-fu think it most unwise," Chiang's old enforcer warned. "There will be one hundred injuries and not even one single benefit. . . . It is my hope that you will, once again, maintain your own great magnanimous personality as always, emphasize on friendship (for Chiang Kai-shek) and look lightly on material profit. Don't allow evil people to use you." Jennie apparently put the memoir aside. It is doubtful that Madame Chiang was ever informed of the matter.

Mayling returned to Taiwan in the early summer of 1959, shortly after attending John Foster Dulles's funeral, at which she sat in the front pew. Her visit had made headlines but not much of an impression. In June 1960 Eisenhower visited Taipei with his son John and daughter-in-law. On the eve of his arrival the Chinese Communists resumed bombardment of Quemoy, which he decried as an "outrageous act of aggression." Eisenhower's visit was hoped to encourage Taiwan, that "staunch but frustrated ally," and offset "sensitivities" over the large American presence there. It was meant to "reaffirm that we consider our Asian friends neither as mendicants nor as anti-Communist pawns," but as valued allies in the struggle against communism. Mayling sat in on the meetings and said little, but Eisenhower's briefing materials spoke volumes. Her biography was longer than her husband's, and the American president was warned: "While charming and gracious in public, she is a high-strung woman whose private life reportedly is marked by occasional outbursts of temper."

Chiang told Eisenhower that his visit had brought "cheer and courage." The president expressed surprise at how healthy, happy, and well dressed the people on the streets looked, and it was true that the economy was picking up slightly. He was especially impressed, he said, with the "sweet and lovely looks" of the Chinese girls. Chiang claimed with pride that there were no beggars in Taiwan. The Generalissimo then dismissed talk of a split between Moscow and Beijing. The Communists were at the bottom of nearly all the troubles in Asia and the key to stability in the region, he said, was to bring about the downfall of the Chinese Communist regime, not militarily but by fomenting uprisings. Eisenhower agreed but cautioned that care must be taken not to cause the kind of "debacle" that had occurred in Hungary. Chiang pleaded for U.S. backing for "Pegasus," a plan intended to "subvert" the Beijing regime through guerrilla operations that would spark revolt across the mainland. He insisted that the U.S. need only provide airplanes and telecommunications equipment. Eisenhower merely promised to study the plan.

The American president joined the Chiangs at Sunday church service at the Victory Song Chapel. "I cannot tell you how impressed I am with the evidence of the thriving democracy that you have established in a relatively short time here," he wrote Chiang on departing. He later sent Mayling one of his landscape paintings, and she sent Eisenhower's son John one of her bamboo paintings.

During the hard-fought 1960 U.S. presidential campaign, Sen. John F. Kennedy argued in a crucial televised debate with Nixon on October 13 that the Nationalist-held offshore islands of Quemoy and Matsu were "indefensible" and "not worth the bones of a single American soldier." Taipei was reported to be bitterly disappointed when Nixon lost the November election. Despite his campaign rhetoric, once elected Kennedy made no move to compel Taipei to abandon the islands. Soon after taking office he sent Vice President Lyndon Johnson on a round-the-world trip. The Johnsons initially received a frosty reception in Taipei. Madame Chiang was supposed to show Lady Bird around while Chiang hosted Johnson. "She was very cold and curt to Lady Bird," recalled Sarah McClendon, a reporter accompanying Johnson. "She came and spoke to us, said, 'Hello. Here's the school. Do you want to see the children? I've got business back at the government,' and promptly left her." Chiang gave Johnson the cold shoulder and refused to hold a joint press conference, apparently because he believed Johnson had been sent to lecture him.

McClendon was annoyed because she and fellow reporters were obviously not going to get a scrap of news, so she told the Nationalist press handlers that when she returned to Washington she would tell the Chiangs' friend Sen. Styles Bridges, a New Hampshire Republican, that Chiang would not meet Johnson or give out any information. The press office called within the hour to invite Johnson to a press conference in the garden with Madame and the Generalissimo. Johnson was never the wiser. He assured the Chiangs on Kennedy's behalf that the U.S. stood by them "today, tomorrow and every day to come."

In spite of this assurance, Taipei faced increasing diplomatic isolation. The mood in America had changed. There was no longer an immediate fear that a third world war might break out. Interest had shifted from Asia to other trouble spots. Roy Howard warned Mayling of rising apathy in the U.S. toward "Red" China's entry into the UN. The argument long held by the British, that one could not ignore the existence of six hundred million people indefinitely, was becoming widely accepted.

A firestorm arose when in 1961 Mongolia applied to join the UN. Chiang had signed the 1945 Yalta treaty providing for Mongolian independence but later repudiated the accord. Taipei claimed sovereignty over what it called "Outer Mongolia," and Chiang insisted he would veto its entry to the UN. But Mongolia's candidacy was packaged with a group of African countries supportive of the Kuomintang, and to veto Mongolia would alienate them. U.S. diplomats tried to persuade Chiang that this would not be a wise move. Chang Chun, one of Chiang's top aides, responded defiantly: "The UN is not that important," he told a U.S. diplomat. "If we get kicked out, we'll get back in when we recover the mainland. If we don't recover the mainland, we're finished anyway."

Roy Howard pressed Mayling to support Mongolia's entry in the ultimate interest of keeping Communist China out. "As I am sure you realize, the loss of this fight in the UN would not only be a staggering blow to Free China, but it would also be a body blow to American prestige in the UN and the world," he wrote on September 9. He pleaded with her to persuade the Generalissimo to abstain from the Mongolia vote, rather than veto it, an action that could easily spark a backlash that would see the unseating of Taipei from the UN Security Council and its replacement with Beijing. In the end Chiang reluctantly abstained, and Mongolia became a member.

By this time Chiang Kai-shek was an impatient and desperate man. The passing years had brought him no closer to his cherished dream of a return to the mainland. It was tempting to compare the aging Gimo to the seventeenth-century pirate-warrior Koxinga, who with his followers hunkered down on Taiwan, never to return to China, and whose hated enemies, the Qing dynasty, ultimately annexed the island. Now seventy-four, Chiang saw his health deteriorating, and he was afraid he would not live to get back to the mainland. He told associates that he absolutely refused to be buried on Taiwan. He was forced to stand by and watch helplessly as the Great Leap Forward took its disastrous course, eventually killing some thirty million Chinese in possibly the greatest famine in history. He worried about his prestige among not only his followers on Taiwan but also the people on the mainland, whom he saw as looking to him for deliverance. Chiang saw it as not only his responsibility but his destiny to liberate his shackled people and restore his reputation before he died.

Year after year, Chiang appealed to his mainland compatriots to rise up against their Communist masters. Year after year, he pledged to personally lead his forces into battle to liberate them. But as time went by it grew harder to perpetuate the unfulfilled myth except by cranking up the volume. By March of 1962 propaganda about the "return to the mainland" reached a fever pitch and certain quarters were abuzz over the anticipated "counterattack," which Chiang called a "sacred mission." This time, however, there was substance behind the noise. Chiang believed that the turbulence in China in the wake of a series of vicious political campaigns and the catastrophic Great Leap Forward had left the people on the mainland deeply disaffected and that now conditions were ripe for revolt. He secretly began serious preparations for an attack. The Communists got wind of the preparations and moved additional air units to the area across the strait from Taiwan. Chiang did not inform the U.S. of his plans, but they were inevitably discovered.

Alarmed, President Kennedy dispatched the assistant secretary of state for Far Eastern affairs, Averell Harriman, to Taipei. Harriman had first met the Chiangs in Cairo, and Mayling, he claimed, had occupied "a warm spot in his heart" ever since. Chiang said he needed planes from the U.S. to drop personnel into mainland China, with the aim of organizing an uprising. He was confident that the Chinese Communist regime was on the verge of collapse. The people would overwhelmingly support an uprising against the "hated regime," he told the envoy, insisting the "opportunity now present is not of man's creation, but is God's gift." In restoring freedom to the mainland he would be "carrying out God's will and God would be on our side." He hoped President Kennedy would become a "second Lincoln" and free the enslaved Chinese people on the mainland. Neither the passion nor the logic of Chiang's arguments impressed Harriman, who was convinced that Chiang was trying to entice the U.S. into war with China by drawing it into larger air drops and intelligence-gathering schemes on the mainland. The envoy told the Chiangs there should be full consultation and agreement on any proposed action. Kennedy was intrigued by the idea of clandestine operations, but Harriman advised the president to resist.

Undeterred, just weeks after Harriman's visit Chiang issued a fiery Youth Day Statement comparing China's present mood to that before the 1911 revolution. He proclaimed that the "anti-communist revolution" would erupt at any moment and he would lead a "Holy Expedition" from Taiwan. He exhorted young men in the armed forces to "dedicate themselves to the revolutionary Holy War." After several more months of intense rhetoric emanating from Taipei, Kennedy finally made a strong public statement in June 1962 in which he reinforced the long-standing U.S. position that it would not back a Taiwanese military adventure on the mainland.

Chiang's fervor subsequently receded for a time, though perhaps more due to the fact that he was suffering from a recurrence of prostate trouble than in response to Kennedy's words. In July 1962 Mayling appealed to T. V. Soong, now in New York, to help secure an eminent American physician for her husband. The problem, she wrote her brother, was that against her advice an earlier operation had been done by an army physician. She had argued with Chiang that except during wartime, no top-flight doctor would work in the armed forces. She blamed herself for not having "acted according to my own judgment regardless of all opposition," as she would have when she was "much younger and more impulsive." The result was that her husband needed another operation on the tumor. "I dread the ordeal, as last time I accompanied the patient to the hospital, I developed an acute dermatitis, and I am just getting over it after two months of intense itching," she wrote. She urged T. V. to telephone their eldest sister Eling to wish her a happy birthday, "for the older I grow, the more convinced am I of the wisdom of the saying 'Blood is thicker than water.'"

Soong engaged an American specialist to treat Chiang on short notice. He evidently patched up ties with Eling, because he later visited her in Los Angeles. "We were very much cheered by the confrontation Kennedy put up to Khrushchev," he wrote Mayling, referring to the Cuban missile crisis of October 1962. He added optimistically, and incomprehensibly, "This is the beginning of a new chapter in history, and affords renewed hope of returning to our homeland."

In August, C. D. Jackson of *Time* and *Life* visited Taiwan. Mayling personally intervened to get him a coveted tour of Quemoy. She gave him the presidential plane and assigned an admiral to escort him in the hope that he could counteract the "nonsense" spread by those who derided the island as a "worthless piece of real estate." Jackson succumbed to the charm treatment. He was deeply impressed by what he saw on Quemoy, and even more impressed by Madame Chiang. He interviewed the Chiangs in their summer residence high up in Yangmingshan—an honor reserved for most favored guests. Madame looked "very, very beautiful and many years younger than her reported early sixties," he reported. He admired the paintings on the wall and was surprised to learn they were her work. She planned to auction them off to raise funds for her pet charities.

Chiang, recovering from prostate surgery, looked pale and thin. But when the conversation turned to recent riots in mainland China, he said to Jackson with great intensity: "Tell your people to look for extraordinary developments next winter and spring. Something big is going to happen." Jackson asked Chiang whether, if there were upheavals on the mainland and people there appealed for military aid, he would help them without American approval. Before he could reply, Mayling interjected, "Well, under these circumstances do you think President Kennedy would sit and do nothing?"

Chiang answered vaguely that he would feel it his duty as a Chinese to do what he could, despite potential "escalation." Mayling again pressed Jackson: "But how do you think the American people would feel?" Jackson replied that if a revolt met with initial success then everybody would want to "get on the bandwagon." He pointed out that when the East Germans put up the Berlin Wall, the U.S. responded only after seventy-two hours of consultations, but this did not mean that the president was "doing nothing." Chiang replied, "Well, Quemoy is our Berlin." Jackson left utterly convinced that Quemoy was among the "most important outer bastions of the Free World."

An American vice admiral who visited soon after found Chiang fuming in suspicious fury over the Warsaw talks, a fitful series of parleys between Washington and Beijing that had begun in 1955, and represented the only direct contacts between the two in the absence of diplomatic relations. Instead of charm, the guest was treated to a blistering tirade from the Generalissimo, with Mayling looking on. Chiang condemned America's "shaking hands" with the Communists and said bitterly that the U.S. government seemed "unable to recognize friend from foe."

Nothing, it seemed, could cool Chiang's ardor. In early 1963 he promised to personally lead the counterattack, but said he would launch it only after an uprising on the mainland. "We cannot stay on this island forever," he said. He did not ask for U.S. troop support but still hoped for logistical, spiritual, and moral support from America. Mayling, too, seemed oblivious to reality. She sent Soong copies of her collected speeches, and particularly stressed one in which she argued that conventional weapons, not nuclear, "will ultimately decide the fate of the third world war." Her tone suggested she assumed that such a war was inevitable. Soong replied that American military leaders believed Chiang realized that without American backing his planned attack on the mainland could not be carried out, and felt that he was "talking a blue streak" on invasion to keep up civilian and military morale.

Soong also warned Mayling to consider carefully a formal invitation that her nephew David Kung had learned the Kennedy administration planned to extend her to visit the U.S. The American policy of noninvolvement remained unchanged, he said, as confirmed by several of "our friends," including Luce, Howard, and Douglas MacArthur, who had pointed out to Soong that given that Kennedy had refused to back the Bay of Pigs invasion ninety miles from U.S. shores, it was unreasonable to expect he would back an expeditionary force from Taiwan. "This should serve as a warning to personages in Taiwan, who may be carried away by . . . portents of closer relationships with the U.S., and thus dream of U.S. support for an invasion," Soong wrote. "If you were requested to accept the invitation in the hope that you could obtain US support of an invasion now, you will be greatly disappointed. Your visit is our last card; it must not be used lightly. . . . Remember if you come you cannot afford to fail." No invitation materialized.

Chiang continued to push the idea of guerrilla action on the mainland. In September 1963 he dispatched Ching-kuo to Washington to seek backing for guerrilla operations. The American response was essentially "dropping a few crumbs and showing we were sympathetic but not much else," said a former diplomat.

In late 1963 Jennie Chen's memoir resurfaced. She was working with the Australian-Chinese Lee brothers, James and William, who were trying to find an American publisher. By this time Chen was sixty years old and still living in Hong Kong. An American editor, Lawrence Hill, shopped the politically explosive book around and was told Doubleday wanted it. Contacted by Hill, Chiang's longtime lieutenant, Chen Li-fu, said that when he was Chiang's secretary in the 1920s, Jennie Chen lived with Chiang as his "hostess." He denied having written her threatening letters.

Taiwan representatives subsequently offered Jennie $100,000 not to publish the book, whose contents would have proven extremely embarrassing for Chiang and Madame Chiang, as well as for the U.S. government. Hill's office was ransacked; he was harassed with threatening phone calls; he was investigated by the FBI. One night he was attacked by unknown assailants and beaten unconscious. Doubleday withdrew its offer; no other publisher would touch it. Hill later heard that Jennie Chen had taken the hush money from Taiwan and in return had handed over the manuscript.

Preoccupied with nursing her ailing husband, in November 1962 Mayling persuaded her favorite niece, Jeanette Kung, to come to Taiwan from the U.S. to oversee her many charitable and other activities. Brusque, mannish, domineering, and utterly devoted to Madame, Jeanette was intelligent and capable but often offended people. She was universally disliked, it seemed, and her temper was notorious. But Mayling came to rely heavily on her niece, who wielded great influence over her.

When Madame Chiang was young, she had worn her brother T. V.'s handed-down clothes. So when Jeanette was a little girl, Mayling once suggested that she wear long-sleeved boys' clothes to help clear up a persistent skin ailment, which flared up on exposure to sunlight. But her headstrong niece liked boyish attire so much that from then on she refused to wear dresses, and her parents indulged her. As an adult Jeanette wore the floor-length dark gown traditionally worn by Chinese men or a Western man's suit and tie, and kept her hair cropped short in a masculine cut. She was said to carry a gun—illegal in Taiwan. She never married and was whispered to have a female lover. All of this was cause for raised eyebrows in conservative Chinese society. Mayling was wracked with guilt, because she blamed herself for ruining her niece's chances for marriage. She once even introduced Jeanette to a promising candidate, a military man, but the match was not meant to be—a fact evident to all, apparently, but the well-meaning aunt.

Chiang Kai-shek and Ching-kuo tolerated Jeanette only because Mayling adored her—so much so that rumors persisted that Jeanette was in fact Mayling's own daughter. Improbable as this was, the intense relationship between the two was an enigma even to those close to the family.

Mayling put Jeanette in charge of the Grand Hotel, the Huahsin schools, the Cheng Hsin Hospital, and even the Women's League. Thereafter Jeanette was called *zong jingli*—general manager—by all, even Chiang

Kai-shek. As on the mainland, Mayling sponsored an orphanage that doubled as a school, supported by a fund comprised of private donations from Taiwan and abroad as well as government contributions. In the late 1950s an Australian Chinese had left a substantial bequest to the orphanage in the name of "Madame Chiang of Chungking." Beijing tried to claim the funds and the battle went to court, which ruled in Taipei's favor.

Mayling visited the Huahsin schools, of which there were several for boys and girls of different ages, at least several times a week, and often brought foreign guests. She looked into every detail. "She checked the children's clothes to see if they were warm enough; she tested the food to see if it was good enough," said Lin Chien-yeh, a former principal of one school. She was especially concerned with table manners and hygiene, and taught the children how to hold their chopsticks properly and to eat soup without slurping. She lectured the children on how to behave and encouraged them to be diligent in their work and in their studies. Students were required to take a Bible study class once a week, to pray before meals, and to attend Sunday service, but they did not have to convert. The students called her "Mama." For many, she was the only mother they had ever known, and they continued to regard her with unalloyed adoration long after graduation.

At holidays many of the children either had no family to go home to or could not afford to make the trip, so Mayling invited them to her residence for a holiday meal. She would seat the smallest children by her side and cut their food for them. She took a particular interest in some students, including an aboriginal boy named Kuo Yuan-chih, a member of Taiwan's celebrated Little League team that in 1969 won the first of the island's seventeen Little League world championships (albeit amid accusations of cheating). When at one stage the team was to be disbanded, she had the school take charge of it. After Kuo had attended a single semester he went home to his village and was unable to return because his family could not afford to buy a train ticket. Mayling arranged payment of not only the train fare but later Kuo's tuition at Fu Jen Catholic University. He became one of Taiwan's best professional baseball players, and was recruited to play in Japan.

In the early 1960s Mayling built a center for children with polio. The Cheng Hsin Rehabilitation Center had space for four hundred patients and a waiting list of twice that number. She also supervised the construction of the immense Grand Hotel, built in an imposing and elaborate traditional Chinese architectural style, on a rise overlooking the capital. Taipei then lacked five-star hotels, and visiting foreign dignitaries needed a suitable place to stay. The Chiangs inspected construction several times a week. Mayling chose everything from décor to management to menu. For decades the Grand Hotel boasted the only swimming pool in the capital.

Mayling's brother T. A.'s boys had come to stay with her nearly every summer since the late 1950s. She had recruited a handful of sons of senior government officials and military officers as playmates for her nephews. One was Johnny Ni, whose father was navy commander in chief. She treated them all like grandkids, letting them watch her as she painted and showing movies after dinner. When her nephews had returned to the U.S. for school, Mayling insisted Johnny and the other boys have lunch with her each Sunday after church. She made them take Bible study classes, and in 1963 she asked them to come to church services late Christmas Eve to be baptized, but they said they could not because they had school the next day. Distressed, Mayling asked the education minister to declare Christmas Day a school holiday, but he declined on grounds that then Buddha's birthday would have to be made a holiday too. She was not to be deterred. At her urging, in 1963 Chiang's cabinet passed a law declaring December 25 a national holiday, Constitution Day, in honor of the date in 1946 on which the legislature passed the first constitution. Johnny Ni and five other boys were baptized that Christmas Eve.

Mayling's skin condition had improved, but in the summer of 1963 she began to suffer from recurring painful attacks of gallstones. Finally, in late January 1964, she underwent surgery in Taipei with a team of two American and three Chinese doctors. While she was under the knife, France announced the establishment of diplomatic relations with Beijing. Fearing other governments might follow suit, Chiang called the move a "matter of life and death." While recovering, Mayling denounced the move as "opportunistic and unprincipled." It was part of a pattern of "defiance impregnated by an emotionalism of a special Gaullist brand of French grandeur bidding for hemispheric leadership," she fumed in a letter to Clare Boothe Luce. Taipei unilaterally severed diplomatic ties with Paris.

On October 16, 1964, shortly before the American presidential election, China detonated its first nuclear bomb. An emotional Chiang told a visiting

State Department official that American assurances about the defense of Taiwan were insufficient to allay fears. If the U.S. were a real friend it would do more, he said. As it was, the people of Taiwan felt their American friends were in effect "asking that they wait for death."

In May 1965, China test-dropped its first nuclear weapon from an aircraft, thereby proving it had weapons capability. Madame Chiang prepared for another trip to America. Although about sixty-seven years of age and a great-grandmother by marriage, she looked like a woman in her early forties and her figure was "exquisite," gushed an article. She shared with widowed Jacqueline Kennedy a place on the annual Gallup list of the ten "most admired women" in the world. In late August 1965, she flew to the U.S. after an absence of over five years for what would be her final public speaking tour. On arrival in San Francisco she held a news conference in which she declared that seating "Red China" in the UN would be a violation of principle. There could not be two Chinas, she insisted. Arriving in New York soon after, on stepping down from the plane she made an impassioned plea for the U.S. to immediately attack and destroy atomic installations in mainland China. "We should try to cut out the cancer before it permeates any further," she said, her silver air force wings pinned to her left shoulder. Beijing's possession of atomic weapons put the world in jeopardy, she insisted.

A Taiwanese independence advocate, writing in the September 7 edition of the *New York Times*, accused her of "warmongering" to satisfy the ambitions of a small band of Nationalist leaders. Recovery of the Chinese mainland was a "lost cause," he argued. Most of the island's residents— and the Taiwanese who accounted for 70 percent of the Nationalist armed forces—did not share the aspiration to "return to a land where they have never lived." Taiwan's future lay in its conversion into an independent country where its ten million Taiwanese and two million Chinese could live together amicably, he argued. Mayling responded publicly by calling the letter "strange and wayward" and saying she hoped the writer would "mend his ways." She added, "Formosa is a province of China. Formosans are Chinese just as we are all Chinese."

She immediately proceeded to Washington, where she was met at Union Station by Mrs. Dean Rusk, the wife of the secretary of state, and hundreds of well-wishers. When a reporter asked her why she'd made the trip, she responded by asking him if he ever read the papers. "It has been printed day after day," she said tartly. "I have been invited here by many friends. They want to see me and I want to see them." No meeting had been set up with President Johnson, but he was expected to drop in at a tea with Mrs. Johnson scheduled for September 14.

The tone of news reports on Madame Chiang was generally "un-friendly," Henry Luce noted in a memo. "While 'they' can't quite equate her with Madame Nhu, they come as close to it as they can," he wrote, referring to the former First Lady of Vietnam, dubbed the "Dragon Lady" in the West. In Luce's view, Mayling was an "outstandingly charming, in-telligent and gracious person. She does indeed hold very strong convictions which, it seems to me, she has expressed with moderation." She clearly outshone her stepson, Ching-kuo, now defense minister, who visited Wash-ington on his father's behalf at the same time. He dutifully called on her daily in her presidential suite at the Shoreham Hotel.

The purpose of Ching-kuo's visit was to promote a plan to seize five southwestern Chinese provinces, which he laid before Secretary of De-fense Robert McNamara. Chiang Kai-shek, who had dispatched Ching-kuo to Washington on the mission, insisted there could be no solution to the problem in Vietnam until the problem of Communist China was settled. This plan, Chiang argued, would cut off Communist Chinese support to trouble spots in Southeast Asia. "In dealing with Asian problems your country should listen more than it now does to the advice of Asians," he told American embassy officials. Ching-kuo paid unstinting lip service to his father's return-to-the-mainland ethos, but privately he told an ac-quaintance that the only way it could come about was through an anti-Communist revolution on the mainland, which he viewed as unlikely.

Madame Chiang brushed off questions about whether Nationalist China might quit the UN if Beijing were admitted. She said she could no more en-vision the Chinese Communists in the world body than she could envision herself "flying in the air without an airplane." It was comebacks such as this that led one writer to call her the nearest a woman has ever come to being another Winston Churchill. "She has that bulldog strength that inspires strength in others. She has a great gift of words and a blinding belief in her cause." She also had "a little of Billy Graham" in her, the reporter added. As she talked, her eyes "often fixed on the ceiling, like an evangelist."

Mayling was treated politely by the administration, but it was evident her views were not given much credence. During her tea date at the White House, she and Lady Bird Johnson met in the Yellow Oval Room with Mrs. Dean Rusk, the widowed Mrs. John Foster Dulles, and one of Madame Chiang's nephews. Lady Bird reminisced about a memorable pedicab ride she and her husband took during their twenty-two-hour visit to Taiwan, during which they caught a glimpse into the frog leg industry, learning that the irrigation canals in the rice paddies they saw doubled as frog-raising ponds. Then the president arrived and gave Madame Chiang a personal tour of the historic rooms of the White House.

Secretary of State Rusk held a dinner in her honor. Defense Secretary McNamara attended, as well as the Chinese ambassador and two senators. A spirited discussion ensued. Mayling expressed concern over the recent explosion of a nuclear device by the Chinese Communists. She argued that the "ChiComs" were not rational men; they were "insane with power" and would resort to any means to obtain their objectives. She insisted that the only sensible course of action for the U.S. was to take out Chinese nuclear installations with conventional weapons, destroying their capability before it reached dangerous proportions. Secretary McNamara countered that the Chinese Communists' response to such action would be "violent" and that given their enormous manpower, the U.S. might be forced to resort to nuclear weapons and face world condemnation. Mayling disagreed, saying nuclear weapons would not have to be used, but McNamara countered that it would be impossible for the U.S. to use manpower in Asia against such numeric odds. Mayling replied that she hoped it was thoroughly understood that the Republic of China did not propose the use of any American troops.

In October 1965 a U.S. Air Force plane carried her on a sentimental journey to Wesleyan College in Macon, Georgia, her first visit since 1943. A deluge of dignitaries, alumnae, and trustees descended on Macon for the event. She had requested that sirens sound for her motorcade, and rolled down her windows to listen. To the thousands of students and guests she said she was delighted to be home again, and tears sprang to her eyes when the school's alma mater was played. After exhorting her audience that "ladies should be ladylike," she advised students: "Work . . . work harder, and despair never." Unable to resist touching on politics, she decried "soft thinking" as "lethal" to a nation. Many listeners were moved to tears.

Mayling certainly was not lacking detractors, but her popularity among a wide swath of Americans was hardly dented by them, judging by the huge number of requests she received from across the country to make speeches and television appearances. But she seemed out of step with the times. Her appearance and style were strongly reminiscent of her wartime visit more than two decades earlier. She seemed "very much the same unruffled, stunningly attired, defeat-defying figure of decades ago," noted *Newsweek*. "The world had changed, but not the Missimo." She lost her composure only momentarily, when asked to reconcile conflicting reports of her age. "What does it matter whether I am sixty-four or sixty-seven or something else?" she asked. "You can tell the age of a person not by the calendar but by his or her character and willingness to be of service to the world."

Returning to New York in September, she tried to rally faltering support for her husband's government in Chinatown, where, waving a white lace handkerchief to cheering crowds, she rode in a bubble-top limousine up Mott Street behind a Chinese school marching band playing "Sidewalks of New York" and "When the Saints Go Marching In." Plainclothes policemen hustled her into the Chinese Community Center at 62 Mott Street, where she spoke in Mandarin to about five hundred Chinese Americans. Her remarks had to be translated into Cantonese.

She often labored over her speeches for a month or two. She once asked her press secretary, Loh I-Chung, a graduate of the Columbia School of Journalism, to help draft them, but he declined, as he did not approve of her writing style or her use of what he termed "those $64,000 words." In early December she visited Wellesley, met with old school friends, and spoke to an overflow crowd of more than sixteen hundred students, faculty, and alumnae. After delivering a strident attack on "ambivalent thinking," which she said helped the cause of Communist imperialism, she received a standing ovation.

In March 1966 Mayling visited New York's International Flower Show, where she admired the calla lilies. When she said she had not had much luck growing them in her garden in Taipei after importing them from America, she was told American experts got theirs from Belgium. During this period, her godson, Ulick Gage, visited her in New York. Gage was surprised to find her reading *The Thoughts of Chairman Mao* and asked why. She countered, "Why should I not be reading it? I like to be well-informed."

That month she again addressed the National Press Club in Washington. The speech was largely ignored by newspapers, but the *New Yorker* magazine poked fun at her incomprehensible language. A grand ballroom full of "dropped jaws and popped eyes" greeted her talk, as listeners struggled to decipher what she meant by such sentences as: "*Das Kapital*, by appropriating only the 'Hegelian Triad'—thesis, antithesis, and synthesis—which is part and parcel of the necessary progression of Hegelian schematic thought and applying it to the theme of social evils and injustices, whilst discarding the Hegelian schema of harmonizing Greek ontology with Kantian psychology and the concept of the 'true Being,' has built within Marxism the endemic limitations which cannot permit its synthesis to continue sound and healthy ad infinitum." Stooping to conquer had never been her métier, and she was not about to start now.

By April 1966 her "unofficial" visit, during which she had delivered seven speeches, held two press conferences, and made one television appearance, had stretched into seven months, and its continued purpose was the subject of press speculation. Her speeches and doings were now relegated to the society and gossip pages of the newspapers rather than the news sections. Critics suggested she was trying to persuade the administration to back landings of Nationalist troops on the Chinese mainland as part of the escalating Vietnam conflict. Meanwhile, she had become one of New York's most elusive and exclusive celebrities. She exchanged her Central Park view for one of the East River, moving from the Fifth Avenue apartment of T. V. Soong into a luxury cooperative apartment near Gracie Mansion bought by David Kung.

By this time Taipei's hold on its UN seat was precarious. Through a series of unintended reprieves, from the Korean War to the Quemoy crisis to the Vietnam War, the Nationalist government had managed to cling to its illusory perch as the sole government of China. At the height of the Cold War, during the 1950s and early 1960s, there had been enormous hostility toward Communist China. Some fifty-four thousand Americans had been killed in Korea. There were Beijing-backed Communist movements across Indochina and Southeast Asia. Anti-Communist alarm had been magnified when in 1956 Soviet leader Nikita Khrushchev had famously beat his shoe against his desk in the UN before shouting to U.S. representatives, "We will

bury you!" Americans had been convinced Beijing was on a drive to take over
Asia, and that Beijing was a proxy for Moscow in its bid to take over the
world. The few lone voices who argued the U.S. should change its policy on
China, or that recognition of Taipei was a fiction, were severely criticized.

But by 1966, that hostility had begun to ease. The admission of "Red"
China to the UN was being widely debated. The U.S. was struggling to
muster enough votes to keep its protégé Taipei on the Security Council.
There was a key Senate hearing on China policy in 1966, at which renowned China scholars John Fairbank and A. Doak Barnett testified.
Barnett coined the phrase "containment without isolation," which became
the basis for a subtle policy shift. American officials tried to prepare the
Chiangs for whatever might come, and attempted to persuade them to
accept a seat in the General Assembly, if worse came to worse, with Beijing
occupying the Security Council seat. But the Chiangs adamantly refused
to countenance recognition of "two Chinas."

The cost to the U.S. of maintaining diplomatic ties with Taipei at the
expense of ties with Beijing was becoming untenable. Pressures for change
mounted from all sides. "We make a pretense of believing that the twelve
million people on Taiwan, and not the seven hundred million in continental China, represent the great historical political entity known as China and
that the Chinese Communist regime is not here to stay, but may be swept
away almost any time by the [Nationalists] on Taiwan," wrote the American
ambassador to Tokyo, Edwin O. Reischauer, in an August 11, 1966, dispatch
to Secretary of State Rusk. "I feel that it is highly damaging to ourselves and
to our policies that we make the pretense of doing so. It is confusing to the
American people, it distresses almost all of our major allies, including the
Japanese, and it angers many of the less-developed nations, who sometimes
interpret our seeming scorn for Peking as a broader scorn for all less developed nations." Working toward "peaceful coexistence" with Communist
China was the "one and only realistic objective," he argued, and the only way
to find an international approach to containing Communist China's expan-
sionism. "We lose face by letting our basic policies seem to be determined
by the peculiar sensitivities of a small country like Taiwan."

Reischauer's views were by now widely held, but Mayling remained militant. In August 1966 she reiterated the long-standing claim that her government would "liberate our people" on the mainland, telling American media,

"There is no possibility of coexistence." It would not be liberation by force, she asserted, adding in contradictory fashion, "We're going back for what is rightfully ours, although we'll have to use force." When pressed as to when the "liberation" might take place, she indicated it would be "in our lifetime." She insisted, "There can be no two Chinas. There is only one China, and I cannot conceive of the Red regime on the mainland being admitted" to the UN.

But by mid-1966, China's Great Proletarian Cultural Revolution was under way. Reports of atrocities and persecution committed by hordes of Red Guards run amok were seeping out of the country as a decade of chaos began. Meanwhile, Washington and Beijing remained at odds. A senior Beijing official branded the U.S. a "completely barbaric country." Secretary of State Rusk, who viewed Beijing as irrational and intransigent, dismissed both Mao and Chiang as "old men in a hurry." The political turmoil in China, combined with the escalating undeclared war in Vietnam against Ho Chi Minh and the Communist north, ostensibly backed by Beijing, ensured that better ties with Red China were out of the question for the foreseeable future. Thanks to yet another serendipitous reprieve, Taipei was once again granted a stay of execution.

Madame Chiang continued to make speeches in the summer and autumn of 1966 as the Cultural Revolution swept China, gathering fury as it went and leaving chaos in its wake. Red Guards dug up and ransacked the Soong family tomb in Shanghai, earning a rebuke from Zhou Enlai after Soong Ching Ling wrote him to complain. Mayling derided the movement as a pogrom divested of the "frou-frou of Maoism" designed to perpetuate the Communist regime. By this time morale in Taiwan concerning American policy was "tragically low," reported U.S. diplomats. Chiang Kai-shek and his son were "dispirited and discouraged." Because of her long stay away, there was gossip in Taiwan that Madame and Chiang were estranged. The State Department judged that her efforts to rouse American audiences had had "minimal impact" and discouraged any further propaganda campaigns.

But by October 1966 she had yet to return home, even missing the annual "Double Ten" festivities marking the anniversary of the 1911 revolution. Patience was wearing thin. Senator J. W. Fulbright, chairman of the Senate Foreign Relations Committee, complained she was making speeches calling on the U.S. to "use its power to overthrow Red China." There was inordinate speculation and gossip concerning her prolonged stay in the U.S. A foreign ministry protégé insisted her only reason for staying so long was that she liked America and greatly needed a change of scenery. After fifteen months in America, she finally returned to Taiwan in late 1966. At La Guardia Airport, her plane taxied out to the runway and was about to take off when it unexpectedly stopped and came back to the gate. She had forgotten to thank the Secret Service men who had looked after her during her visit. Some of them were moved to tears.

According to one account, shortly after her return Mayling went to inspect a new residence Chiang was building for them on Yangmingshan, an elaborate structure with classic Chinese architectural elements, at a cost of $2 million. She instructed the builders to change the position of the bathroom window. They complied. A few days later Chiang visited the site and asked them to change it back again, which they did. When Madame Chiang returned and saw the window, she threatened her husband that if he did not change it back to the way she wanted it she would never stay in the house.

Back in Taiwan, Mayling continued to campaign for U.S. help in toppling the Beijing regime, seemingly oblivious to the implausibility of the notion. In March 1967, during a visit by Sen. Harry F. Byrd Jr., Mayling launched into a heartrending and apparently entirely sincere plea for U.S. backing for her government's return to the mainland. All that was needed, she claimed, was logistical support; no American lives would be lost. Byrd firmly told her that the American people were in no way prepared for the risks of such a venture, especially given that the military commitment in Vietnam was proving larger than anticipated.

This message was underscored by former vice president Nixon, who visited Taiwan in April. He met with Mayling and Chiang in one of their villas by the Shihmen Reservoir near Taipei. They tried to persuade him that given the chaos of the Cultural Revolution, the time was ripe for the "counterattack." Nixon expressed sympathy but told them it was "unthinkable" that the U.S. could underwrite a Nationalist attack on the mainland. Logistical support might not be enough and the U.S. might find itself embroiled in a long and inconclusive war, a venture the American people would not support.

Henry Luce, the press baron who helped shape America's relations with China, died in early 1967. It was the end of an era. "We have indeed lost a true friend who had loyally stood by us whenever our country had to steer through a stormy course," Mayling wrote to his widow. "Moreover, he also served as the voice of human conscience with unerring judgement and dauntless courage in every moral issue of our day." In August, H. H. Kung died suddenly at the age of eighty-six. Mayling rushed back to attend the memorial service at New York City's Marble Collegiate Church. Mourners included Richard Nixon and Cardinal Spellman. Kung's remains were taken to the family mausoleum at Ferncliff Cemetery in Westchester County, New York, for temporary entombment pending permanent burial in China following the anticipated reconquest.

Taiwan, meanwhile, was rapidly transforming from an underdeveloped backwater into a self-sufficient economic force. The land-to-the-tiller program was an enormous success, underpinning the island's middle class and setting the stage for industrialization. The U.S. pumped over $1.4 billion into Taiwan between 1951 and 1965, the year American aid was halted. By then 85 percent of the island's farmland was tilled by farmers who owned it, leading to large increases in agricultural production. The economy was still farm-based—Taiwan was the world's leading exporter of bananas in 1965, and the second-biggest sugar exporter. But as war against the mainland, or a Communist invasion of Taiwan, seemed increasingly unlikely, foreign investment was trickling in. Manufacturing and trade took off. Western electronics firms built factories and Taiwanese manufacturers gained strength, laying the foundation for Taiwan's future vibrant—and unheralded—prosperity.

Chiang never relinquished his dream of recovering the mainland, but he finally abandoned plans for a counterattack. Thwarted in the pursuit of his cherished dream, his interest in a goal that was once but a distant second—building a prosperous Taiwan—seemed to grow. During a convivial dinner with Congressman Walter Judd and other American visitors in late September 1967, the Generalissimo's mood turned philosophical. It was probably "providential," he said, that the mainland had been lost when it had. Twenty years on Taiwan, undisturbed by conflict and turmoil, had given him a chance to show the world what he could do, he claimed, adding that the great progress on Taiwan could never have been achieved on the mainland, where he was faced with the constant pressures of the Communist threat. Many of the programs so successful on Taiwan, he said, had failed in China because of subversion and the government's inability to devote sufficient attention to them due to civil war. He gave a toast, vowing to spend his ninetieth birthday on the mainland. Mao Zedong, Chiang said, was unwittingly doing all that could be hoped for to speed the Nationalist government's return; the best strategy was to sit and wait. He then recited four proverbs:

> The bees steal from one flower only to pollinate another;
> Whom the gods would destroy they first make mad;
> The mills of fate grind exceedingly slow but exceedingly fine;
> It is always darkest before the stars come out.

Chiang could not have known that the night was about to get darker. As he spoke, his old friend Richard Nixon was poised to publish a pivotal article in the October 1967 issue of the influential journal *Foreign Affairs*. The arch anti-Communist, who had spent two decades attacking "Red" China, now argued that the U.S. could no longer afford to ignore the world's most populous country, which contained a quarter of the world's population. "Any American policy towards Asia must come urgently to grips with the reality of China," Nixon wrote. "This does not mean rushing to grant recognition to Peking. . . . But we simply cannot afford to have China forever outside the family of nations, there to nurture its fantasies, cherish its hates, and threaten its neighbors."

Chapter Twenty-two
Death of a
Failed Messiah

If when I die I am still a dictator, I will certainly go down into the oblivion of all dictators. If, on the other hand, I succeed in establishing a truly stable foundation for a democratic government, I will live forever in every home in China.

—Chiang Kai-shek

As the 1960s drew to a close, Madame Chiang seemed to become increasingly consumed by the desire to cling to the status quo. But when in an unprecedented political comeback Americans elected Richard Nixon president in November 1968, the wind began to shift. U.S. diplomats tried to psychologically prepare Taipei for détente between Washington and Beijing. Although they did not know what was coming or when, they knew the current situation could not last forever. But the Chiangs and many of their followers remained bitterly and unalterably opposed to any recognition of geopolitical realities.

In the years since his first visit to Taipei in November 1953, Nixon had remained in contact with the Chiangs, visiting frequently and forming "a personal friendship that I valued greatly," as he later wrote. Indeed, during his visits he stayed at the Chiangs' guesthouse, and the Chiangs' staff observed that Nixon was so close to them that they treated him as though he were their son. After losing the California gubernatorial election in 1962, Nixon joined the New York law firm Mudge, Rose. He had found the Generalissimo gracious during his years in the political wilderness and commercially accommodating when he once sought to negotiate a lucrative franchise on behalf of a client, Pepsi-Cola. Nixon's home was decorated with gifts of Oriental rugs from Madame Chiang, a candelabra from Syngman Rhee, and a Persian rug from the Shah of Iran. And according to the Chiangs' staff, a large, heavy leather suitcase had appeared at the Chiang residence one day in the autumn of 1968. They learned that the mysterious suitcase was stuffed with U.S. banknotes Chiang had ordered from the Central Bank, and was destined for the coffers of the Republican party ahead of the November 1968 elections.

Soon after taking up residence in the White House in early 1969, Nixon sought to establish diplomatic ties with Mongolia. On hearing this Chiang was shocked and dismayed that his friend Nixon, of all people, would suggest such a move. "If the U.S. can recognize Mongolia 'today,' there is no reason why U.S. recognition of Peking could not follow 'tomorrow,' and abandonment of Taiwan 'day after tomorrow,'" Chiang told Walter McConaughy, the American ambassador to Taipei. On learning of Chiang's violent reaction, Nixon asked the State Department to shelve recognition plans. "He feels the move is not worth taking over Chiang Kai-shek's objections," wrote the national security adviser, Henry Kissinger.

In late February 1969 Mayling's youngest brother, T. A. Soong, died of a heart attack on a business trip to Hong Kong. Mayling's old friends the Wedemeyers were visiting Taipei when she heard the news; she later apologized for being "poor company" during their visit. She flew from Taipei to the West Coast under heavy security to attend a memorial service in San Francisco, where T. A. had lived. The trip was supposed to be entirely secret, but word leaked out after the aircraft made an unexpected landing at Wake Island and was reported missing. Through tears, Mayling would say to reporters only that it was a personal trip. All the siblings but Madame Sun were there, and "although it was a sad reunion we were fortified by our family closeness," she wrote Wedemeyer.

After the funeral T. V. wrote to her, taking issue with a suggestion she had made that their nephew Louis Kung was "not very stable." He wrote with feeling:

> We have just lost a brother. I felt that God will punish me if
> I do not voice my opinion of Louis. Like every human being
> Louis has his faults, but he has the capacity of dreaming.
> When Nixon was defeated in the 1960 presidential election, &
> soundly routed in the governorship of California, he himself

thought his political life was over and said so. Louis was one of the very few who believed that Nixon's qualities would some day raise him to the presidency, and supported and encouraged Nixon not to despair. The part he played in the 1968 election you must have known already. The close ties between him and Nixon <u>is our most precious asset</u>. It should not be wasted. . . . Autumn will come soon when China's seat in the UN will be hotly contested. The sands are running out fast.

If Mayling was blind to the fact that Taipei's days as the "capital of China" were numbered, T. V. was not. "The pro-Communist left, the intellectuals and most public men are all in favor of Communist China, with not a single dissenting voice raised," he added in the letter, suggesting that Mayling ask Chiang to bring Louis onboard to campaign for Taipei in the U.S., and citing Louis's "effective" role in the "so-called 'China Lobby.'" Nothing came of it.

The presidential staff had long held that the Yangmingshan residence had bad feng shui, or spiritual harmony. Mayling supposedly did not believe in feng shui, but in any case did not like staying there. On September 16, 1969, as she and Chiang headed up the winding mountain road to Yangmingshan in their limousine, a military jeep on its way down rounded a corner at high speed, forcing the lead car in the presidential motorcade to stop suddenly. The Chiangs' limousine forcefully rear-ended it, and the thick bulletproof glass barrier between the driver and the rear passenger seat shattered and fell onto their laps. Chiang had his dentures knocked out and was lightly injured, but Mayling had severe whiplash and seriously injured her arms and legs. They were taken to the hospital.

The accident was kept tightly under wraps. When President Nixon learned of it in mid-November, he expressed concern and offered to send a noted New York osteopathic physician to Taiwan to treat them. They declined. By then Mayling had regained some use of her arms but was still unable to walk. Her recovery was slow, and four months after the accident she was still unable to use her right hand well enough to sign letters. Several months after that she began receiving visitors again, although she had not appeared in public since the accident. "Every day . . . [when] I go into my study and look with longing at my latest unfinished painting [I wish] that I could pick up a brush and put on the finishing touches," she wrote the Wedemeyers.

As a new decade approached, Taipei's leadership was on the defensive. Because the government nominally supported Sun Yat-sen's political philosophy, which called for democracy following a period of political tutelage, they were forced to admit that the ultimate goal was democracy—unlike Beijing, which had no such goal. So in a peculiar sense the political opposition to Chiang's regime—mainly Taiwanese independence supporters and disaffected mainlanders—was in a strong position.

The Legislative Yuan—or parliament—and the National Assembly were rubber-stamp institutions comprised almost entirely of mainlanders, whose positions were sinecures as Chiang had suspended elections until the recovery of the mainland. For decades the government had used the tired excuse that as the nation was in a state of war it could not introduce full democracy, although Chiang did permit elections for local assemblies and mayors on Taiwan. Candidates were forbidden to criticize Chiang's leadership or raise sensitive issues such as the counterattack. In essence democracy, such as it was, was little more than a contest for spoils and a façade for foreign consumption, intended to show the island was not ruled entirely by mainlanders. Even though opposition candidates were allowed to run as independents, it was a one-party state. Henry Kao, a native Taiwanese, ran as an independent and was twice elected Taipei mayor in the 1950s. This so embarrassed the Kuomintang that Chiang decided the mayoral post should be an appointed position. Then he cleverly appointed Kao, who served in the post for several more terms.

Although the opposition had a presence in political life, Taiwan remained a highly repressive police state. There was military training in schools; informants were ubiquitous; the media were tightly restricted. There was a climate of intellectual and artistic stagnation. Native Taiwanese were not alone in being dissatisfied with the political situation; many mainlanders, too, were unhappy, not only with the political repression and lack of democratic progress, but also with the corruption and inefficiency in the government. There was increasingly the widespread feeling that the leadership was out of step with the times.

For two decades U.S. efforts to promote democracy on Taiwan had been feeble if not nil, but this was beginning to change. Washington had remained silent amid a storm of international protest when Lei Zhen, a former Nationalist official whose *Free China* magazine had become a symbol of liberal criticism of the regime, was imprisoned in September 1960 on sedition charges after attempting to form an opposition party with native Taiwanese politicians. Lei had committed the "double heresy" of doubting the myth of the return to the mainland and calling for self-government on Taiwan.

Officially, American policy in the 1950s and 1960s was to take positions only in the economic realm, and not to impose American political ideals on the Nationalist government. In practice, however, Washington was effectively complicit in Chiang's politically repressive police state simply by virtue of the fact that the U.S. was until 1965 keeping the regime militarily and financially afloat. Perhaps the best illustration of how the Nationalists used American aid to repress political opposition and bolster Chiang's regime—and Nationalist rule was far more repressive on the island than it had been on the mainland—was the 1949–53 land reform program.

Devised and carried out by the Joint Commission on Rural Reconstruction, a bilateral organization financed by the U.S. and staffed by American and Chinese experts, the reforms were in part an effort to make amends for having failed to carry out agrarian reforms on the mainland, where they would have alienated the Chinese gentry, the Nationalists' support base. They greatly increased agricultural production and, not incidentally, wiped out the economic base of the landlord class, the only group capable of viable political opposition to the Nationalists, while somewhat mollifying Taiwanese discontented over the 2-28 Incident, political oppression, and military conscription. Ultimately the land reforms fundamentally transformed the structure of Taiwanese society in ways similar to the postwar land reforms undertaken in Japan, creating a nation of small landholders and in effect redistributing wealth more equally.

In one infamous episode, Washington overtly stepped beyond its putative hands-off policy into collaboration with the Nationalist regime—on American soil, no less. When Asia scholar Ross Y. Koen tried to publish a book entitled *The China Lobby in American Politics* in 1960, under pressure from Taipei and the China Lobby the U.S. government banned the book.

The publisher was forced to destroy four thousand copies that had been printed, and many of the eight hundred that had already circulated were either stolen from library shelves by Nationalist or China Lobby agents and replaced with *The Red China Lobby*, or placed under lock and key by university libraries across the U.S. America's cherished press freedoms, it seems, took a back seat to preserving the image of Washington's Far Eastern ally.

But there were glimmers of change in the American position, although Washington would not begin to pressure Taipei for political reform until the 1970s. In May 1964, the State Department's legal adviser Leonard C. Meeker drafted a secret position paper arguing that the U.S. had a "strong interest" in preserving Taiwan's self-determination, through fostering the idea of a Taiwan separate from China—either independent or autonomous. The best way to "preclude a Nationalist accommodation" with Beijing after Chiang Kai-shek passed from the scene was to promote economic development and a political evolution that would bring native Taiwanese to the fore.

When Peng Ming-min, chairman of the political science department at National Taiwan University and a leader of the underground independence movement, was arrested and court-martialed in 1964 for issuing a "Manifesto to Save Taiwan," there was an international outcry and protests from such figures as Henry Kissinger, Peng's former professor, and Harvard China scholar John K. Fairbank. Peng spent fourteen months in military prison before Chiang bowed to pressure and commuted his eight-year sentence to lifetime house arrest. After Peng managed to escape detention in January 1970, Chiang accused the CIA of aiding his flight into exile, where Peng was granted asylum in Sweden and two years later settled in the U.S.

In another famous case of persecution under "White Terror," the renowned writer and poet Bo Yang translated into Chinese a Popeye cartoon in which Popeye was depicted in a boat holding Swee'Pea, pointing toward a distant island, and saying, "I will be king of that island and you will be my darling prince." Chiang Kai-shek was infuriated by the implication that he was grooming Ching-kuo as his heir apparent—its evident truth notwithstanding—and in 1968 had Bo Yang imprisoned on Green Island without trial. The writer narrowly escaped death and was finally released in 1977 under pressure from the U.S. and international human rights groups.

Having been promoted to vice premier in 1969, in late April 1970 Ching-kuo visited Washington, where on April 24 two Taiwanese independence activists attempted to assassinate him at his hotel. A shot was fired before the men were arrested. Unharmed, Ching-kuo brushed off the incident and coolly continued with his schedule, meeting Nixon before dinner that same day. In conversation afterward with Secretary of State William P. Rogers, Ching-kuo dismissed the independence movement, long a taboo subject in Taiwan, as having no roots on the island. It was cultivated abroad, he claimed, by a "handful of people who are dissatisfied or have inordinate ambitions."

The *Time* magazine issue covering the attempt on Ching-kuo's life was banned in Taiwan—not because of the incident, but because the article stated that resentment of Chiang family rule was rising in Taiwan and that the people feared Ching-kuo might one day deliver the island to the Communists. Chiang Kai-shek subsequently broke decades of official silence on the subject to denounce the independence movement as, implausibly, a "Communist plot."

The Nationalist regime, and Mayling personally, suffered a series of shocks in 1971. She was recovering from surgery in March on her right leg, still troubling her a year and a half after the car accident, when news broke of Beijing's surprise invitation to the U.S. table tennis team to visit China. From April 11 to 17, Americans followed delightedly as the team, along with five American journalists, toured the Great Wall, chatted with ordinary Chinese, and were told by Zhou Enlai that they had opened a "new page" in Sino-U.S. relations. Famously dubbed "Ping-Pong diplomacy," it was the first time Americans, apart from Edgar Snow and a few other sympathizers, had been allowed in China since 1949. Soon after, Nixon met with Anna Chennault, widow of the World War II hero and now a well-heeled Washington hostess and Republican party fund-raiser, who over the years had been close to the China Lobby. In her newest guise as unofficial emissary between Taipei, Washington, and Beijing, she told Nixon of Chiang's concern over the visit of the U.S. team to the mainland. Nixon replied cryptically that relations between Washington and Taipei were "entering a new stage requiring greater consultation and understanding between the two nations" and reiterated America's friendship and commitment to the Republic of China on Taiwan.

This hardly reassuring message was soon followed by news of T. V. Soong's sudden death at seventy-seven in San Francisco. Mayling planned to go to the U.S. for the funeral, but ideology trumped family sentiment, and she canceled at the last minute after news reports said her long-estranged sister Ching Ling might attend too. Mayling was already airborne when she abruptly had the plane turn around and head back to Taiwan for fear of a "United Front trap" set by Beijing. The government, Ching-kuo told Ambassador McConaughy, could not risk the "embarrassment" of having Madame Chiang attend if there was a chance that Madame Sun might show up. In fact, Ching Ling did not attend.

Mayling's reversal underscored Chiang's rejection of U.S. pressure for direct negotiations between Beijing and Taipei over the future status of Taiwan. All appeals to Taipei for a more flexible policy vis-à-vis the mainland were bitterly spurned. So strong were Chiang's objections to increased contacts that Taipei's consular agencies overseas were instructed to revoke Taiwan visas if the passport-holder had visited the mainland.

In his will, filed in New York City, T. V. Soong's assets at the time of his death were listed at an improbably low $10.5 million. After taxes, fees, and payments to creditors, the residual estate was said to be worth only some $2.7 million. If Soong had once ranked among the richest men in the world, his billions had long since been salted away elsewhere. It is virtually certain that he had kept substantial assets offshore, where they would be impossible to trace, or had them transferred under the names of his children or other family members, who likewise may have kept the funds in overseas accounts.

Writing her widowed sister-in-law Laura Soong, in thanks for sending her a volume of Chinese paintings that had belonged to T. V., Mayling complained that the summer of 1971 had been "difficult and hot." Her maid, who had been with her since her wedding, had died, and both she and Chiang had caught the Asian flu. But Mayling did not allude to the most difficult event of that summer.

After months of secret contacts, in early July Nixon had dispatched Kissinger to Beijing on a super-secret mission: to pave the way for America's establishing relations with the People's Republic of China. In discussions before the trip, Kissinger vowed to Nixon that Beijing "cannot trick us out of Taiwan." In meetings between July 9 and 11, Zhou and Kissinger discussed a future trip by Nixon to China, but Zhou stressed that first an understanding must be reached that Taiwan—which he called the most "crucial issue" in relations between China and the U.S.—belonged to China. "That place is no great use for you, but a great wound for us," Zhou said. Kissinger reassured his counterpart that the U.S. did not propose "two Chinas" or "one China, one Taiwan," and that neither would it encourage the Taiwan independence movement. But he evaded Zhou's repeated demands that Washington agree that Taiwan belonged to China by saying the question would ultimately "take care of itself."

Just as the secret diplomatic venture was about to become public, Nixon—perhaps seized by a sudden pang of guilt—dispatched his old friend Don Kendall, chairman of Pepsi-Cola, to Taiwan. He instructed Kendall to personally deliver a verbal message to the unsuspecting Generalissimo: "Whatever the future may hold, I'll never forget my old friend." Kendall had no idea what the words meant. Upon being given the message, Chiang nodded gravely and said nothing.

When Nixon went on television on July 15 to announce the rapprochement with China and his plans to visit Beijing, the Taipei leadership was "thunderstruck," U.S. Ambassador McConaughy wrote the secretary of state. The initial reaction of the Kuomintang regime was one of shock, anger, and anti-American bitterness. But it was soon recognized that an emotional response would only give satisfaction to Taipei's enemies, and the government put up a front of calm and self-confidence. The Taiwanese people were rather more ambivalent. There was anger at the U.S., mingled with fear that it might abandon Taiwan and dread of a takeover of the island by Communist China. But there was also a certain glee at the discomfiture of Chiang's government, and hope that the day when the island would be governed by Taiwanese, not mainlanders, was now closer. There was also an acute awareness among the Taiwanese that they had a vested interest in the island's continued stability and prosperity.

Nixon greatly valued his friendship with Chiang, he later wrote, claiming that he found the rapprochement with Beijing "a profoundly wrenching personal experience." His consternation was plain in a draft telegram explaining his action to Chiang. "I deeply regret that I was not able to inform you at an earlier date of the substance of my announcement of July 15," he wrote. "The steps which I have recommended were taken because I believe it has become imperative in this age to break down barriers of hostility and suspicion that have grown over the years and could threaten the peace of the world. The people of free Asian nations should be the first to benefit from efforts to lower tensions in relations between the United States and the People's Republic of China." In an earlier draft he had added, "I am sorry that our actions have been so disturbing to the Republic of China." But the apology was subsequently crossed out and changed to "I recognize that these actions are disturbing to the Republic of China." Nixon went on to assure Chiang that Americans would continue to "cherish their friendship" with his country and that defense commitments would be honored. He closed by asserting that he was "proud" of his long personal association with Chiang.

Nixon's letter did nothing to mollify the Chiangs and their inner circle, who behind a frosty façade of stoicism privately vented their anger, furiously branding the American president "ungrateful" and worse. The earthshaking revelation of Kissinger's trip to Beijing was followed in early August by Washington's announcement that the administration would support Beijing's entry into, but not Taipei's exclusion from, the UN. The news plunged Taipei's rattled ruling elite into a frenzy of debate, and Madame Chiang was at the center of the discussions. She continued to play an influential role in foreign affairs, particularly where important matters were concerned, so much so that some called her the government's de facto foreign minister. Ching-kuo was firmly entrenched in many areas of government, but the foreign ministry remained her undisputed fiefdom, and she handpicked senior officials and ambassadors.

Madame Chiang's nephew David Kung, termed Taipei's "underground ambassador" to the U.S. due to his intimate ties with his aunt and his role in carrying out sensitive political missions for her, flew in from New York. He affected the title of "Dr.," despite not having received a doctorate from Harvard, although in 1954 he did complete a dissertation entitled "Some Illustrations of the Development of the Theory of Tyrannicide in the West." Never married, David kept a low profile, occupying himself by handling the Kung family investments while carrying out China Lobby activities at his aunt's behest. At Madame Chiang's insistence, and over

Ching-kuo's opposition, Chiang had appointed him a national policy adviser. On this occasion David tried to persuade Chiang Kai-shek to adopt a more flexible diplomatic policy, arguing that in order to preserve its basic interests, Taipei should try to maintain representation in the UN, even if Beijing took over the Security Council seat, adopting the model of East and West Germany for the time being and leaving the question of territorial claims for later. To withdraw would be to dig one's own grave and would threaten the Republic of China's very survival. But Chiang and Ching-kuo both remained violently opposed to compromise, insisting that "the Chinese race would not be betrayed twice." If Beijing entered the UN, then Taipei would withdraw. Any other response was tantamount to appeasement—attempting to "make the tiger give up its pelt."

Soon the presidential residence—dubbed the "Palace"—was divided into two factions, one led by David and Jeanette Kung and favoring a pragmatic approach, the other led by Chiang and Ching-kuo and adamantly rejecting coexistence with the Communist "bandits." Madame Chiang found herself caught in the middle of the acrimonious split, not knowing which side to take. The controversy so upset Chiang that in August, his heart illness flared up. David Kung returned to New York, but the debate continued.

Nixon dispatched Ronald Reagan, then governor of California, to Taipei for the Double Ten celebration, this year marking the sixtieth anniversary of the 1911 revolution. The festivities were dampened by the imminent threat to Taipei's continued recognition as the "rightful" government of China, and even to its seat at the UN. At a 250,000-strong rally, Chiang and Mayling made their customary five-minute appearance on the balcony of the presidential palace. The crowd had just finished singing "Our Great Leader." Dressed in a military uniform, the eighty-four-year-old president, in a high, quavering voice, led the crowd in chanting "Long Live the Revolution of 1911" and "Long Live the Republic of China." The crowd responded by chanting "Long Live the President." Students had practiced for a month to deliver that one line.

The real purpose of Reagan's visit, of course, was to explain the greatest reversal in American foreign policy in more than two decades to Chiang Kai-shek, who regarded it as yet another in a litany of betrayals. Although Reagan privately disapproved of Nixon's moves toward normalizing relations with

Beijing, he publicly defended it. On this visit, he also broke the news to Chiang of Nixon's plans to visit Beijing the following February. Chiang countered that he feared Nixon would be "embarrassed" by Communist "treachery" and insisted Taipei would never concede to any claim over the island by the Beijing regime.

Foreign Minister S. K. Chow and the delegation to the UN conferred with Chiang before leaving for New York for the UN session in the autumn of 1971. Madame Chiang was also present. The U.S. had made it clear that it would support two resolutions in the UN that session: the IQV, or important question variation, namely to admit Beijing to the UN, and the DRC, or dual representation complex, which would offer both regimes simultaneous membership. Together the resolutions were designed to open the door to Beijing while safeguarding the Republic of China, which had been a founding member of the world organization. It was a given that once votes were tallied Taipei's Security Council seat would be handed to Beijing, but Washington hoped to salvage a seat for Taipei in the General Assembly. This scenario would place Beijing and Taipei on a similar footing as other divided nations, namely Korea and Germany, whose rival governments were both represented in the UN. Most of Taipei's diplomatic allies had advised the ROC government to support the two resolutions.

At the meeting with Chiang, Chow and Huang Shao-gu, secretary-general of the National Security Council, argued in favor of publicly supporting the two resolutions proposed by Washington. No one seemed opposed; Chiang too appeared resigned to accepting that course of action and moved to conclude the meeting. As he began to make a few closing remarks, Madame Chiang, who had been silent, suddenly asked to take the floor. "*Ren you renge, guo you guoge,*" she declared. "Just as a person must have integrity, so must a nation." Her words galvanized Chiang and swayed the mood of the group. A decision was then made that there could be no public support of the resolutions.

As it happened, Henry Kissinger was again visiting Beijing when the pivotal UN votes took place in New York, serving only to weaken Taipei's position. On the brink of expulsion, Taipei withdrew from the organization on October 25, 1971. Even if the ROC delegation had supported the two resolutions, it was uncertain that Taipei could have mustered enough votes to receive a General Assembly seat; in any case, that seat might have been

snatched away in a few years once Beijing consolidated its position sufficiently to obtain the necessary two-thirds majority needed to expel a UN
member. Madame Chiang had advocated defiance over potentially futile
compromise, in the face of certain humiliation.

The strain of the UN imbroglio affected the eighty-four-year-old
Chiang's health, not only causing his heart condition to worsen, but giving
him severe constipation. A few weeks after the UN withdrawal, because his
doctor was not available, Chiang ordered one of his aides to give him anal
suppositories to relieve the pain. The inexpert aide inadvertently perfo-
rated Chiang's anus in the process, causing him to bleed profusely. When
doctors determined what had happened, Chiang was incensed and ordered
the aide imprisoned. Ching-kuo was about to have him court-martialed when
another aide suggested that the man instead be temporarily placed in a detention room in the presidential residence, so word of the incident would
not leak out. Chiang did not recover for over a month. Madame Chiang
was subsequently often heard to harshly curse the aide, blaming him for
her husband's worsening health. She was so angry that only five years
later did she allow the aide to be released from detention, after others
pleaded on his behalf.

Taipei's effective banishment from the UN precipitated breaks with
many countries and a wave of emigration from the island. Among the politically aware, Taiwanese or mainlander, there was recognition that the
successive shocks, especially the UN rejection of Taipei's claim to represent China, had severely undermined the Nationalist government's
very rationale for existence. At the same time, among residents who stayed
the shocks heightened awareness of a sense of shared fate, regardless of
ethnic background.

At the presidential residence, reality was slow to sink in. In his New
Year's message of 1972, Chiang called recent events a "temporary setback"
on the way to "eventual victory" in recovery of the mainland and exhorted
his followers to remain resolute and self-reliant in the face of "slander and
insult." He declared, "We shall never coexist with traitorous Maoists" and
quashed rumors of secret contacts with Beijing, asserting the only contacts
were those of "blood and steel." Mayling wrote Mrs. Wedemeyer on January 7 that the mood of "our people" was captured in the words of Saint
Paul: "We are troubled on every side yet not distressed; we are perplexed

yet not in despair; persecuted but not forsaken; cast down but not destroyed." She hoped, improbably, that there would be "an awakening to the true situation" soon.

Her hopes were not fulfilled. Nixon proceeded as planned to Beijing in February 1972. On landing he shook hands with Premier Zhou Enlai, the gesture that John Foster Dulles had refused so many years before. The American president was struck by the contrast between Mao and Chiang. The "robust, earthy" Mao exhibited an "animal magnetism" despite slouching in his chair like a "sack of potatoes"; the thin, ascetic Chiang sat up "ramrod-straight as if his backbone were made of steel." Mao displayed a "relaxed, uninhibited" sense of humor, but Nixon had never known Chiang to attempt humor of any kind. Chiang was orderly; Mao was unkempt and sloppy.

Mao mentioned that in a recent speech Chiang had called the Beijing leadership "bandits." Nixon asked what *he* called the Nationalist leaders. Mao laughed. Zhou Enlai said that they called them "Chiang Kai-shek's clique" and sometimes called Chiang "a bandit. . . . Anyway, we abuse each other." Nixon was surprised to learn that the Communist leaders were strangely ambivalent in their attitude toward their vanquished erstwhile rival. "As Communists, they hated him; as Chinese, they respected and even admired him. In all my discussions with Chiang he never expressed any reciprocal respect." Mao said to Nixon, "Our common old friend Generalissimo Chiang Kai-shek doesn't approve of this," meaning their meeting, and added, "The history of our friendship with him is much longer than the history of your friendship with him."

As for Mao's wife, Jiang Qing, Nixon wrote, "I have never met a more cold, graceless person." The contrast between her and Madame Chiang was far more striking than that between their husbands. "Madame Chiang was civilized, beautifully groomed, very feminine, yet very strong," Nixon wrote. "Jiang Qing was tough, humorless, totally unfeminine, the ideal prototype of the sexless, fanatical Communist woman." Although she hosted the American president at a performance of a well-known play, *The Red Detachment of Women,* she did not approve of Nixon's visit and demanded sharply, "Why did you not come to China before now?"

The linchpin of Nixon's negotiation sessions in Beijing was the understanding reached on Taiwan. In a virtuoso display of diplomacy-speak, the key clause of the February 28 Shanghai communique, the joint statement issued at the conclusion of the talks, read: "The United States acknowledges that all Chinese on either side of the Taiwan Strait maintain there is but one China, and that Taiwan is a part of China. The United States Government does not challenge that position. It reaffirms its interest in a peaceful settlement of the Taiwan question by the Chinese themselves." With this deceptively simple yet carefully crafted formula the U.S. was able to preserve the letter if not the spirit of its relationship with the Nationalist government while satisfying Beijing. By "acknowledging" the position of "all Chinese," without in fact agreeing with it, Washington cleverly avoided taking any position on the intractable issue. Glaringly absent, of course, was any mention of Taiwanese aspirations.

It was Nixon's most glorious moment. As the architect of the historic rapprochement between the world's most populous country and its most powerful, he toasted his hosts before departing, "This was the week that changed the world."

For the Nationalists, it was the beginning of the end. During the twilight period of Washington's formal diplomatic relations with Taipei, there was, in the words of one U.S. diplomat, a "hand-holding operation" to gradually ease the leadership on Taiwan into accepting the inevitable. It was evident that there would be a switch in U.S. diplomatic relations to Beijing from Taipei, but no one knew when. There was still considerable opposition to the move in Congress and in U.S. political circles, and strong support for Chiang Kai-shek. There was also recognition that the mainland was in a sorry state with the political upheavals of the Cultural Revolution. While Taiwan was no paradigm of democratic virtue, anyone who still took the earlier line that Communist China was a model democracy was being laughed at. But even though there was no hurry to switch recognition, it was only a matter of time before it happened.

In the wake of Nixon's visit to Beijing, Chiang Kai-shek became increasingly isolated, and his health deteriorated. His natural inclination to brood in solitude before making important decisions rather than seeking a variety of views from his advisers became more pronounced. About the only person who saw him alone was his wife, who took charge of his medical care, and her exclusive access to him allowed her to exert inordinate—and to some minds unconstructive—influence over him. One senior government

official complained to American diplomats that her influence was ultracon-
servative and geared toward "selfish" preservation of her own preeminent
position at all costs, without regard to the urgent need to adapt to the current critical situation. In any case, there was no one else, not even Ching-
kuo, who dared to voice any opinion counter to Chiang's views. The only
person who was not afraid to do so was his wife, but her views were if anything more uncompromising and inflexible than his own.

In the face of Taipei's deepening diplomatic isolation, Mayling was by
turns defiant and philosophical. In April 1972 she told a Women's League
tea that the willingness of world leaders to appease the Chinese Communists had created a "shameful and deplorable atmosphere in the world
today." But in early June she wrote Emma Mills, "What is of import is not
what happens, but how we react to it. Life would indeed be monotonous
if every day the sun shines and there is no mist or rain. The beauty of a
Chinese painting depends as much on the empty spaces as on the drawn
lines."

Madame Chiang did not appear to heed her own philosophical musings
when it came to her husband's health, which declined rapidly after Nixon's
visit to Beijing. Over the next few years she became obsessed by the desire to keep him alive, as though he were immortal, and spared no effort or
expense. Already suffering from heart disease, in the early summer of 1972
Chiang Kai-shek caught pneumonia. From then on he was president in
name only. He was mostly confined to bed and while still mentally alert,
he was physically quite weak. His last public appearance was on July 18,
1972. The American embassy reported to Washington that a number of
prominent foreign guests who would ordinarily have merited an audience
with him were being received by Madame Chiang alone. Diplomats were
led to believe that her husband was growing less intelligible, so she had become his "spokesman." It was noted that neither husband nor wife made
their customary appearance on the balcony of the presidential palace during the annual mass rally on Double Ten.

The truth was that Chiang was not merely ailing, but had in fact fallen
into a coma, on July 22. His sudden collapse precipitated chaos among his
rattled staff, but Madame Chiang immediately rose to the occasion, taking
charge like a battlefield commander, as she barked orders while receiving
reports of her husband's condition from medical staff. In her mind secrecy

was paramount, and she issued strict orders that the entire secretarial and medical staff of the presidential residence were not to take any days off, including weekends, until further notice, nor contact their families. If family members telephoned to inquire, they were to be told that their loved ones had been sent to the south of Taiwan on urgent official business for an indefinite time period. She stoically prepared for the worst and began planning funeral arrangements.

Anxious hours turned into days and days into weeks, but Chiang showed no sign of returning to consciousness. His body bristled with tubes and he had to be put in fresh clothes, turned, and massaged almost constantly as doctors struggled to keep him alive. With the help of Jeanette Kung, Madame Chiang closely followed all aspects of his treatment, often coming into conflict with his large medical staff.

The running of the country was now in the hands of Ching-kuo, who had been promoted to premier in May 1972. He turned his attention from the military sphere to economic development and initiated ten major infrastructure projects. Coming at the time of the global oil crisis, the government's investment boosted the economy and helped Taiwan ride out the crisis. As ever, political opposition was equated with treason, perhaps even more so since the attempt on Ching-kuo's life in the U.S.

Despite his heavy responsibilities, Ching-kuo remained an enigmatic figure. He adopted the image of civilian statesman, favoring shirtsleeves and windbreakers over military attire, but remained suspicious of American-style democracy. He did not appear to be an ideologue of any sort, and his style was an unlikely mix of Puritanism, Leninism, and Confucianism, with a vaguely populist flavor. "I must do something for the people," he had been heard to say privately. Ching-kuo chafed against the Kuomintang's old guard, who blocked his attempts to modernize the government and to appoint more Taiwanese and young people. After being promoted to premier, Ching-kuo quickly moved to undermine and curb the powers of these conservative comrades of his father, who included elements of the military, the National Assembly, and the legislature. He launched a stringent ten-point code dubbed the "Ten Commandments," cracking down on the corruption that his father had long tolerated among loyal associates. Under the austerity campaign officials were served notice that they were not to hold expensive gala banquets or ribbon-cuttings, or to frequent nightclubs and girlie bars, in order to reduce opportunities for corruption. He banned the playing of mah-jongg in government buildings.

Ching-kuo also moved to recruit Taiwanese and technocrats, plucking from obscurity a political neophyte named Lee Teng-hui and bringing him into the government as minister without portfolio. A modest, scholarly man and a devout Christian, the Taiwanese native held a PhD in agricultural economics from Cornell University. Because he lacked political experience or a power base, he was not on the radar screen as one of a group of elite Taiwanese thought to have a political future.

As the summer of 1972 gave way to autumn, there was no change in Chiang's condition. He had been moved to the Veterans' Hospital, where his wife and Jeanette Kung each stayed in nearby rooms and Ching-kuo slept in a small room attached to his father's. Although Madame Chiang had gone to inordinate lengths to keep the truth of Chiang's condition from the public, rumors inevitably circulated. It was evident to the public that he was severely ill, or possibly even dead, but no explanation was offered for his disappearance from public view. Mayling paused from caring for her husband only long enough to break her silence on Taipei's humiliating diplomatic reversals, publishing a vitriolic tract in which she condemned the many governments that had chosen to recognize the People's Republic of China over the past year. "By giving the stamp of approbation to the proverbial Cain they have deigned to dignify the enslavement of the Chinese people on the mainland as if conferring a blessing," she railed bitterly. "And this they call friendship for the seven hundred million Chinese people!"

In January 1973, after half a year in a coma, Chiang regained consciousness, amid much rejoicing on the part of his wife, family, and staff. His seemingly miraculous return from the brink served as testimony to his extraordinary catlike resilience, personal as much as political; and it doubtless buttressed his image as China's messiah, at least in the eyes of those in his inner circle who were inclined to view his recovery as a Christ-like "resurrection." Physically he was extremely weak, but mentally he was surprisingly alert, and his memory did not appear to have been affected. However, his inability to move about left him frustrated and irascible toward his exhausted staff, who worked in shifts, never leaving the hospital. In hot weather he insisted that they fan him by hand day and night, as he disliked both air-conditioning and electric fans.

For many months after regaining consciousness, Chiang was still not well enough to reappear in public. In April 1973 Mayling wrote Wedemeyer, who was about to depart for Taiwan, to say that her husband was convalescing from a severe bout of "pneumonia" and would not be able to see him during his visit. "Let come what will come, God's will is well come," she added, with respect to Taipei's shifting diplomatic circumstances, and stoutly claimed: "The President and I have the same faith today that we had in the darkest days of World War II." It is uncertain whether Chiang was well enough to be concerned with geopolitics, but by mid-1973 he had recovered sufficiently that he could be propped up in a chair. Madame Chiang seized the opportunity to dispel rumors swirling as to his condition. To "prove" that he was not only alive and well but running the government, she arranged to have a photograph of him with his grandson, Chiang Hsiao-yung, taken at the latter's wedding and released to the press.

At the end of September 1973 Madame Chiang hurriedly left for New York, where Eling Kung was hospitalized with an unknown illness. For the second year in a row, Chiang did not make his customary appearance at the Double Ten rally. While in the U.S. Mayling was diagnosed with breast cancer, but opted to return to Taiwan after just two weeks; Eling died four days after she left. Back in Taipei, Mayling elected to have radiation treatment rather than surgery. Her condition was kept a closely guarded secret, even from her ailing husband. While she was having a mastectomy the following year, he asked why she did not come to visit him twice a day as usual. He was told she had gone on a brief trip to America.

In early 1974, Ambassador McConaughy was about to retire from the diplomatic service and return to the U.S. Madame Chiang fretted for a long time over whether Chiang should see the envoy before his departure. She feared that if he did not, it would be perceived as bad manners and could negatively affect Taipei's fragile relations with Washington. She decided that on March 25, 1974, she and Chiang, by this time eighty-seven, would host a farewell dinner for the ambassador. It would be the first time Chiang had received foreign guests since July 1972.

But Chiang's doctors were extremely concerned, and insisted that he could not be taken off his heart monitor for more than a few minutes, let alone through an entire dinner. After all, his heart had stopped beating and his staff had revived him a number of times before, and the intervals between such incidents were growing shorter. If one occurred during the meal, they might not be able to resuscitate him. Madame Chiang resolutely insisted upon going ahead, arguing that for the future of the nation, they must take the risk.

Every detail of the dinner had to be elaborately choreographed. At the appointed hour, Chiang was propped up in his chair to await the ambassador's arrival. Medical staff were hidden close by the dining room, with oxygen and emergency equipment at the ready. Aides hovered anxiously nearby. During the dinner Chiang's facial expression seemed unnatural and he slurred his words, gasping for air when he spoke. Madame Chiang expertly covered for him by "explaining" to McConaughy what her husband was trying to say, but there was no disguising that the president's condition was extremely serious.

Within months of Nixon's triumphal visit to Beijing, the pinnacle of his political career, the American president became embroiled in what became known as the Watergate scandal. Watergate nipped at his presidency until early August 1974, when a transcript of a secret tape made in the Oval Office was released, directly linking Nixon to a cover-up of the infamous burglary of Democratic party offices. With impeachment looming, he resigned. "We have unlocked the doors that for a quarter of a century stood between the United States and the People's Republic of China," he said in his resignation speech. "We must now ensure that the one quarter of the world's people who live in the People's Republic of China will be and remain not our enemies but our friends."

Madame Chiang immediately took him to task—not for his misdeeds in office, but for his assertion regarding China. "The unlocking of the doors of the mainland would indeed be a very good thing were it true," she declared in a statement. "Unlocking the doors means free egress and ingress. The pity of it all is that no compatriots of ours are permitted to leave the country and their enforced serfdom."

After the death of influential newsman Drew Pearson in 1969, his stepson had edited his diaries into a book and a bidding war broke out among the big publishing houses. Pearson had been political gossip columnist extraordinaire for decades. His nationally syndicated column and radio program had been hard-hitting enough, but the truly outrageous tales he had saved for his diary. Holt, Rinehart and Winston published the book in 1974. It claimed Madame Chiang had had an extramarital affair with Wendell Willkie in the early 1940s; it also alleged that the daughters of senior Chinese generals had slept with American military officers during the war in order to obtain military secrets. Madame Chiang was furious and instructed Taipei's Information Office, the de facto consulate in New York, to sue the publisher for several million dollars. Two years later, the case was settled, with an apology extracted from Holt along with a promise to remove the offending material from future printings.

In early 1975 Chiang's health took a turn for the worse. This time, though, there would be no reprieve. As the Generalissimo lay on his deathbed, Mayling released an odd, rambling, and bitter thirty-two-page rant replete with archaic and obscure words attacking the U.S., which she claimed was plagued by "malaise" and declining international prestige. She began by excoriating the U.S.'s policy of détente with Beijing, but inexplicably went on to inveigh against everything from the use of marijuana and other illicit drugs by America's younger generation to the fashion of long hair among its young men, racial tensions in Boston, and welfare fraud. "What has become of the Great American Dream, refined through time, encompassing decency, fortitude, resourcefulness, generosity of spirit, and propriety—which were attributes highly regarded when I was a child in the United States?" she railed. "What has happened to the America of 1942 and 1943 [with its] strength, patriotism and infectious enthusiasm?" It was as though she blamed the U.S. for not helping her husband fulfill his dream of apotheosis as China's messiah before his demise.

As death approached, Chiang was said to have called his wife and his elder son to his bedside, asked them to put their hands together, and made them promise him that they would get along well and treat each other like mother and son. Chiang died of a heart attack just before midnight on April 5, 1975, at the age of eighty-eight. Ironically, it was Tomb-Sweeping Day, a traditional holiday for commemorating the dead.

The news hit the island like a "mighty emotional earthquake," one mourner in Taipei told Reverend Billy Graham. U.S. embassy staff in Taipei toyed with the idea of drafting a two-word telegram for the ambassador to sign reporting the grave news back to Washington: "Peanut planted." But they decided that Ambassador Leonard Unger would not appreciate this, even in jest.

Chiang had written in his last testament that he considered himself a disciple of Jesus Christ and a follower of Sun Yat-sen, in that order. His lifelong goals, he wrote, had been to realize the Three People's Principles, recover the mainland, rejuvenate China's national culture, and remain in the democratic camp. Mayling's confident calligraphic signature topped the list of witnesses; Ching-kuo's came only third.

Nixon lauded his "friend" Chiang Kai-shek as a "man of keen intellect, of great gallantry and of unwavering dedication to those principles in which he so fervently believed" and called him one of the "giants" of modern history. Mayling received hundreds of messages of condolence, including ones from Henry Ford II, chairman of the Ford Motor Company; Ronald Reagan; Reverend Billy Graham; and Hiram Fong, the first U.S. senator of Chinese descent.

A few days after Chiang died, the Shihlin residence's head gardener, Fang Yun-ho, received an urgent telephone call at six in the morning. Madame Chiang was looking for him. During Chiang's prolonged illness, the president's staff had ordered Fang to replace all the white flowers in the gardens of the Shihlin residence with red ones, owing to a Chinese superstition that white was associated with death and red was an auspicious color. Madame Chiang told the gardener that a Protestant funeral service would be held in a few days and that all the flowers had to be changed to white in time for the service, because foreigners were coming and it would be embarrassing. "She was very upset," recalled Fang. "She held my hand and said, 'I know this is very difficult for you, but *wei le guojia de mianzi*—to preserve our nation's face—we must change the flowers.'" So at great effort Fang dug up all the red flowers and replaced them with white ones in time for the service.

Over a period of five days, more than two and a half million people filed past Chiang's glass-topped coffin to pay their last respects by bowing three times. Among them was Young Marshal Zhang Xueliang, whom, still under house arrest, Madame Chiang brought for a final glimpse of his captor.

Vice President Nelson A. Rockefeller flew to Taipei to represent the American government at Chiang's funeral; the U.S. was the only major power to send an official representative, although two former Japanese prime ministers were on hand—much to Beijing's fury. The UN sent no one. The U.S. administration had originally planned to send a relatively low-level official, the secretary of agriculture, but Rockefeller was named at the last moment after the intervention of Anna Chennault. Madame Chiang knew nothing about this.

The state funeral was held in Taipei's Sun Yat-sen Memorial Hall on April 16. The entire diplomatic corps had been drilled in how to go up in groups of three to the podium and bow three times from the hips to Chiang's portrait in a gesture of respect. Chiang's favorite books were placed inside his coffin—the Bible, Sun Yat-sen's *Three Principles of the People,* a book of Tang dynasty poetry, and *Streams in the Desert.* With Ching-kuo and Wego at her side, Madame Chiang fought back tears as the glass-topped coffin bearing her husband's body was closed. She wore dark glasses and appeared ashen and tired as she bowed three times. Ching-kuo broke down and wept. The coffin was surrounded by calla lilies and a white cross of chrysanthemums stood at its foot. Chow Lien-hwa, the Chiangs' minister, read the Twenty-third Psalm and a children's choir sang "Nearer My God to Thee."

Covered with yellow and white chrysanthemums, the hearse made its way to the Generalissimo's summer retreat, Tzu Hu—Lake of Mercy. A minute's silence was observed across the country. As the forty-mile funeral cortege set off on that warm and humid spring day, the crowds keened and bands played dirges interspersed with renditions of "Auld Lang Syne." Roadside tables were stacked with offerings of burning incense, fruit, flowers, and candles, in accordance with Chinese tradition. Millions of people lined the route, in some places ten deep. "Even in my benumbed state of shock and grief I became aware of a receding surge of humanity as hundreds knelt or prostrated themselves to pay their last respects on the hot asphalt roads," Madame Chiang later wrote the Wedemeyers of the trip to Tzu Hu. "Many of them were so overcome, so broken in their sorrow that my heart went out to them. Somehow my own sorrow became of little importance subsumed in their grief. It has been my resolve to serve them in their dedication to continue the President's call for freedom from fear, freedom from want, and freedom from slavery." While Madame Chiang labored under the delusion that the prostrate millions were grieving for their beloved leader, in reality the mass outpouring of emotion was not so much grief for the dictator, who was feared but not loved, but anguish over the shattering of their long-cherished dream of returning to the mainland.

Chiang's remains were taken to a square redbrick villa with a central courtyard nestled in the side of a wooded mountain. He had chosen the locale because it reminded him of his ancestral home. There he would lie in temporary entombment above ground pending the recovery of the mainland, when he would be transported for final burial in his ancestral village.

A memorial service for Chiang Kai-shek held in Washington's National Cathedral was filled to capacity with sixteen hundred mourners. Reverend Billy Graham praised Chiang as a man of "unashamed" faith, adding that Taiwan stood as a "living memorial" to him. Graham concluded by quoting St. Paul, imprisoned in Rome and near death: "I have fought the good fight, I have finished the race, I have kept the faith." Gen. Albert C. Wedemeyer told listeners that Chiang once wrote, "If when I die I am still a dictator, I will certainly go down into the oblivion of all dictators. If, on the other hand, I succeed in establishing a truly stable foundation for a democratic government, I will live forever in every home in China." Wedemeyer said that although Chiang was unable to do so on the Chinese mainland, on Taiwan he had laid "a cornerstone of freedom," a foundation on which future generations could build with confidence.

In the months that followed, Mayling found her husband's death difficult to accept. It felt as though he were off on a trip, she wrote Emma Mills, and she was still marveling at the outpouring of national grief. She began planning for a huge memorial park to be built for the late president in downtown Taipei; it would be the crowning touch in the cult of Chiang. Once the park was completed, in its center would stand a five-story concrete complex encased in over a thousand tons of white Vermont marble, with Chinese flourishes and a two-story statue of Chiang, seated in the manner of Lincoln at the latter's memorial in Washington. The resemblance in pose to that of the Great Emancipator could not have been accidental.

On September 17, 1975, Mayling left Taiwan for the U.S. for "urgent medical treatment," as it was officially explained. She was seen off at Sungshan Military Airport by Ching-kuo and a hundred other friends, family, and officials, including Ambassador Unger. Before departing on the presidential plane with seventeen attendants and a large stack of baggage, she released a rambling emotional statement that sounded more like a farewell speech than that of someone going away on a short visit. During her husband's long illness and the period of "great sorrow" she felt after his death, her own health had deteriorated, she stated. She did not disclose the nature of her illness, but it was reported abroad that she had recently had two operations for breast cancer.

She urged her husband's followers to keep the faith. "Without frost and snow people won't realize the toughness of the pine and the cypress tree," she said, citing a Chinese proverb. "For . . . forty-eight springs and autumns I lived together with the President and we exhorted each other," she said. "Now I am [alone] facing a portrait of President Chiang Kai-shek with [his] gentle smile. But I feel as if he were still alive and still standing by me . . . when I close my eyes in prayer."

Mayling's departure was not entirely for health reasons. She and Ching-kuo had dutifully kept their promise to Chiang to be good to each other, but they were both extremely opinionated and had very different ideas on many subjects, particularly concerning relations with the U.S. After Chiang died, it was said, she tried to throw her weight around. In response, Ching-kuo coolly played the role of devoted son—which was ironic, because everyone knew how much he and Mayling disliked each other. Her Kung relatives pushed her to make a bid for Kuomintang leadership, but Ching-kuo was elected chairman with no opposition two weeks after Chiang's funeral. Finally she said, "Better to leave you alone—you can do what you want. I'm going to the US."

While she was being treated in New York for pains in her neck and left leg caused by the auto accident six years earlier, she came down with a severe case of shingles. Disregarding the advice of her doctors, she insisted on returning to Taiwan in April 1976 for the first anniversary of Chiang Kai-shek's death. In Taipei she slipped and fell in the bath, hitting her head. For many months she was unable to use her left hand and walked with a cane. In August 1976 Mayling flew back to the U.S. to resume medical treatment. She checked into Baltimore's Johns Hopkins Hospital for ten days under an assumed name. She proceeded to New York in mid-September to recuperate at the Kung estate on Long Island, where for the duration of her stay in the U.S. she was cared for by her nephew and niece, David and Rosamond Kung, the elder of Eling Kung's two daughters, along with a secretary and nursing staff. Mayling informed an associate in Taipei that once her health improved, "I shall return home to work for the big plan of recovering mainland China" from the Communists.

Chiang the vanquished had met his demise deeply bitter toward his nemesis, but Mao Zedong, who could afford to be magnanimous in victory, had taken to calling Chiang his "old friend." About the only thing they had agreed upon was that Taiwan should be brought back into the bosom of the motherland, but neither of them lived to see that dream come true.

Mao did not have long to exult over his government's dramatic elevation in international status, or the humiliation and demise of his erstwhile rival—1976 was a cursed year in the People's Republic of China. First Premier Zhou Enlai died, then Gen. Zhu De, Mao's comrade-in-arms. A massive earthquake struck Tangshan, in Hebei province, killing 240,000 people. Finally, on September 9, 1976, on the anniversary of the Autumn Harvest Uprising, which he claimed marked the start of his revolutionary career, Mao died. As he lay dying, he quoted the Chinese proverb that final judgment can be made only once a person lay in his coffin. "In retrospect, I have done two major things during my whole life," he mused. "One is the years-long struggle with Chiang Kai-shek, which resulted in Chiang's running to Taiwan. . . . The other one is the Cultural Revolution." As for recovering Taiwan, he said, that would require time and the efforts of the next generation.

Still in the U.S., Mayling had been virtually bedridden for nine months with shingles and her injuries, and was now having to learn how to walk again. "With continuous physiotherapy and exercise I am making much progress," she wrote Wedemeyer in January 1977. Mentally, at least, she was back in form. After thanking him for a book he had sent her, she moved on to a favorite theme, arguing that the world emerged from the Second World War "worse off" than before. "In the Free World's naivete, it has brought on more cruelty, more misery, more shackles and more perdition for the human beings it vaunts to save," she argued. "I know some will immediately dispute what I am saying here but I think history will bear out my thinking and those who think as I do and have the gumption to say so will be proven right."

By early 1977 Mayling felt well enough to make an extended visit to her nephew Louis Kung, who had moved to Houston and in 1961 founded Westland Oil Development Corporation. Nixon's former campaign operative was by now an eccentric oil tycoon and married to Hollywood actress Debra Paget. While Madame Chiang and her husband had once merely hoped for a third world war, "Major" Kung was actually preparing for one. He had purchased a fifteen-hundred-acre tract of land in Montgomery, Texas, where he was building an office building with an elaborate security system and bulletproof windows that doubled as his residence. But an entrance between fortified twin pagodas led to the pièce de résistance: a vast, nuclear-proof underground bunker bigger and more elaborate than Hitler's. The forty-thousand-square-foot compound, seventy feet below ground, had its own power generation capability and was designed to accommodate up to fifteen hundred people for ninety days in the event of a Communist nuclear attack. As well as living space, a factory, and offices for Kung's employees, the compound included fitness facilities, saunas, detention cells, a hospital, and a morgue, complete with body bags. The office building and bunker complex had been built at a cost of $24 million.

After a time in Texas, Madame Chiang returned to stay at the Kungs' Long Island estate, where she remained in virtual seclusion. She did not mingle with the local populace while staying at Hillcrest, where she had her own suite, but took long walks on the heavily wooded grounds. She failed to return to Taiwan for Ching-kuo's presidential inauguration in the spring of 1978. Nassau County police provided extra protection at the Lattingtown estate, and when she went into New York City to see her doctors she was guarded by Secret Service men. When she ventured out to the hairdresser, it was arranged in advance that she would be the only patron in the salon while she was being coiffed. In the late 1970s, Madame Chiang moved into a duplex cooperative apartment purchased for her by David Kung on Manhattan's Upper East Side. It was in an exclusive building on Eighty-fourth Street off Gracie Square Park, a stone's throw from the East River. The opulent prewar apartment at 10 Gracie

Square had eighteen rooms, including seven bedrooms and eight baths, a private elevator, servants' quarters, several fireplaces, and East River views. There she would be closer to doctors and friends.

On December 15, 1978, without warning, President Jimmy Carter made a televised address announcing that Washington would establish full diplomatic relations with Beijing and sever ties with Taipei. Though long expected, the break was a traumatic surprise and Taipei's leadership did not take it well. Warren Christopher, deputy secretary of state, led a State Department delegation to Taiwan to work out a blueprint for future U.S. relations with Taipei. Upon their arrival a surreal scenario transpired, one strangely reminiscent of the 1957 American embassy riot.

There was a massive demonstration at the Sungshan airport as Christopher and his delegation landed. When they tried to leave the airport, their limousine was caught in a frenzied sea of angry protesters. The departing U.S. ambassador, Leonard Unger, wanted to take a back road to his residence to get away from the demonstrations, but the driver refused; he was evidently under instructions to drive the car and its hapless occupants directly into a "real mob scene," as Unger later described it. Surrounded by parked trucks with government-controlled network television cameras on their roofs filming the entire proceedings, their motorcade was stuck in the mob, which chanted anti-American slogans and poked sticks through the windows of their cars, cutting the Americans on their faces till they bled profusely of superficial wounds. It was never made clear who engineered the protest, but given that the island was still under martial law, the authorities could have easily prevented or at least curbed it had they desired to do so. The incident was evidently staged to humiliate the Americans, though they were only messengers, rather than architects, of the policy.

On December 31, 1978, the U.S. officially broke off diplomatic ties with Taipei, and a day later recognized Beijing. In late January, Deng Xiaoping, China's new premier, visited the U.S. A few months later the U.S. Congress, where feelings that we were abandoning a friend ran high, passed the Taiwan Relations Act, which guaranteed continued unofficial but substantive ties with Taipei through a private, nonprofit entity that mimicked the functions of an embassy.

Soon afterward, Madame Chiang broke years of public silence. In the late 1970s a wave of "boat people" fled Vietnam, as the Communist government expelled ethnic Chinese. Outraged, Madame Chiang took out a half-page advertisement in the *New York Times* on July 20, 1979, condemning the Vietnamese authorities. In English and Chinese she called the mass expulsion "genocide" and a "diabolical policy" devised to extort property from the victims. She appealed to large countries to absorb the flood of refugees, and called on the public to condemn such "wanton acts of inhumanity, lest such tragedies be repeated elsewhere on earth." Similar notices appeared in the *Washington Post* and the *Los Angeles Times*. Each showed a photograph of Madame Chiang from her younger days. The Chinese version of the ad appeared to have been written in her own calligraphy.

Chapter Twenty-three

Resurgam

The biggest lie perpetrated on the whole world in the history of mankind has at last been called to task.

—Madame Chiang Kai-shek

I n early 1981 Madame Sun Yat-sen fell critically ill with leukemia and heart disease. Two years after Deng Xiaoping had ascended to power, China was just beginning to heal the wounds of the Mao era and recover from the devastation of the Cultural Revolution. Economic and agricultural reforms engineered by the pragmatic Deng—who famously said that it did not matter whether a cat was white or black as long as it caught mice— were starting to reshape the country.

As she lay dying, Ching Ling requested to see her younger sister. China's official media mounted a campaign to persuade Madame Chiang to return to her native soil from the U.S. and visit her long-estranged sister before she died, or, failing that, to attend her funeral. Madame Chiang made no response. The invitation was vetoed by Taipei on grounds that her presence in China would be used by Beijing to imply a reconciliation of sorts between the two governments. Taipei still resolutely maintained its long-standing "three nos" policy toward the People's Republic—no contacts, no negotiations, no compromise.

In her final days, Ching Ling, regarded as a national saint, was anointed honorary president of the People's Republic of China. She was also made a member of the Communist party she had steadfastly refused to join for more than half a century—arousing speculation that the move was taken without her knowledge or permission. Ching Ling died in Beijing on May 29, 1981, at the age of ninety. "Comrade Soong Chingling's death is a great loss to our country," an official announcement ran. She was a "great patriotic, democratic, internationalist and Communist fighter and out-standing state leader of China." On the day of her death more than fifty party and state leaders, relatives from overseas, and friends filed past her bedside to pay their last respects. A period of national mourning was de-clared, during which her body lay in state for three days in the Great Hall of the People near Tiananmen Square. She was given a full state funeral and buried in Shanghai near her parents and her beloved maid.

Madame Chiang had always been a prolific correspondent; as she aged she became prolix, and her opinions did not mellow with the years. She often penned lengthy diatribes to like-minded friends, many about past history, some concerned with current events, which she saw through her own unique lens. In a letter to Wedemeyer dated July 26, 1980, she called American gratitude a "fragile flower" and bitterly wrote that the U.S. had "manipulated and used" China during her hour of need. In Decem-ber, Mrs. Douglas MacArthur escaped lightly with birthday congratulations and jasmine tea from Taiwan. Wedemeyer must have been somewhat baffled by a New Year's greeting that read: "May 1981 see an amelioration of pernicious Communism in the decline both morally and substantively, be it from the Russian Bear or the Chinese Serpent."

Walter Judd was treated to a seven-page missive dated March 6, 1982, that began by lauding his recent appearance denouncing communism on the television program *Firing Line* and that then segued into a vigorous defense of her husband and herself. "What really has the US benefited from the fall of China into Communist hands?" she asked. "We were not given the time to prove that we were sincere in our intentions and that we knew how to ac-complish our goal for our people," she complained bitterly. After seventy years in practice, communism was obviously morally and intellectually bank-rupt, and an economic failure, she argued, asking how it could still "mesmer-ize" people. "There is a sucker born every minute," she wrote.

In May 1982 she wrote a rambling five-page letter to President Ronald Reagan praising him for alerting the American public to the "perils" of Soviet Russia. He never saw her letter, but signed a polite reply drafted by aides. Reagan had a sympathetic, even protective attitude toward Taiwan, and during the Reagan years the U.S. was more solicitous of Taiwan's in-terests than it had been under the Carter administration. There was a strong feeling in the administration and in Congress that the U.S. had an obligation to see that Taiwan was not left defenseless. After the formal break in diplomatic relations in 1979, the ground rules stressed that there was to be no "official contact" between the two governments. In practice this meant that U.S. officials could not meet with Taiwanese officials in their offices, and vice versa. So they met in restaurants, hotels, or at home. Other countries followed suit.

Reagan visited China—which he still quaintly called "Red China"—in April 1984. It was his first visit to a Communist country. Deng told Reagan that Taiwan was "the knot in our relationship." More than a decade after Kissinger had assured Mao and Zhou that the problem of Taiwan would "take care of itself," that prediction had yet to materialize. Reagan stuck to the State Department script and said the U.S. would honor existing accords. As to Taiwan's future, he gave the formulaic response that it was a matter for China and Taiwan to work out peacefully between themselves.

Zhou Enlai's widow, Deng Yingchao, a respected Communist revolutionary in her own right, wrote Mayling a letter, which she showed to Ching-kuo. The letter was not released, but in February 1984 Mayling published a letter in reply in which she lectured pedantically on the checkered history of Kuomintang-Communist cooperation. She lamented that the Communist party was now putting Deng Yingchao in an awkward position by using her to make a "peace overture." Mayling recalled meeting the widow in Chungking during the war. "Since then, I have often wondered why you should be obsessed by Marxism authored by an anti-god German Jew," Mayling wrote. She closed by asserting that "the real China is now in Taiwan."

In April 1984 Mayling sent Wedemeyer a copy of *Conversations With Mikhail Borodin*, a book she had written in the late 1970s from notes dating back to early 1927, when she met with the Russian revolutionary. It was "wrong and unnecessary," she wrote Wedemeyer, to use the atomic bomb at the end of World War II. Truman's "impulsiveness" would long haunt America. "I feel sorry for the U.S.—so well intentioned and yet so naive!" she mused, adding the far-fetched claim, "Many problems troubling us today would have been nonexistent but for the fall of China." In the early 1980s, she visited the Wedemeyers at least once at Friends Advice, their estate in Boyds, Maryland. But in 1985 she took a "rain check" on grounds of old age.

Though Madame Chiang's legs were still troubling her, she would not use crutches. When visitors come to her Gracie Square duplex, she insisted on walking down the stairs herself to greet them. She was invariably immaculately dressed, alert, and extremely well informed on relations between Washington and Taipei. Her staff were amazed by the effort she put into her physical recovery. She never revealed to visitors how much painful and difficult physical therapy she was required to do. She displayed tremendous perseverance, doing even more exercises than doctors ordered.

Whatever their past disagreements may have been, Madame Chiang and her stepson were in close contact during the 1980s. Ching-kuo instructed Fredrick Chien, Taipei's de facto ambassador in Washington, to report to her on what he was doing—whom he met, what was said—even on matters Chien did not think he ought to be telling her. While she was in New York, there was almost daily cable and fax traffic between her and Ching-kuo, who wrote letters longhand in ink brush and faxed them across. He seemed to value her views.

But while Madame Chiang's health was gradually improving, old age—and diabetes—was taking a toll on Ching-kuo. When he was first diagnosed with the disorder in the early 1950s, Mayling had urged him to give up drinking, which he did for a time. But while the elder Chiang had followed doctors' orders to the letter, Ching-kuo was a "disobedient patient." Though he insisted on keeping his medical condition a secret from the public, reports appeared in Chinese media overseas. In the 1980s the press began to speculate on "dynastic succession," but there was no sign that he was grooming his sons to succeed him. In 1984 he had chosen Lee Teng-hui as his vice president, a largely ceremonial post. Lee, an unassuming agriculture expert, was the first Taiwan-born official in the position. By then Ching-kuo was nearly blind and running the country from a wheelchair.

The Nationalist government, meanwhile, was coming under increasing pressure, from both the U.S. government and the Taiwanese people, to dismantle Taiwan's police state and introduce democratic reforms. Since Mayling had left Taiwan in 1976, there had been growing agitation for political freedom, to which the government had responded with an odd combination of sophistication and brutality. In the "Formosa Incident" of 1979, the government had arrested and jailed many leaders of Taiwan's underground opposition movement after a demonstration calling for democracy and Taiwanese independence. They were defended by Chen Shui-bian, a young maritime attorney who subsequently entered opposition politics.

The case galvanized the opposition movement and ultimately made it more difficult for the government to resist popular demands for political reform. But as Taipei's remaining political allies quickly shifted recognition to Beijing, the country slipped into diplomatic limbo. The island's uncertain political future sparked a wave of emigration as many Taiwan residents lost confidence and decided to start afresh elsewhere. Discontent with the Chiang family regime grew.

In the early 1980s, a university professor and government critic died in Taiwan after mysteriously "falling" from the roof of a building. The mother and twin daughters of an opposition politician were murdered. Neither crime was ever solved. The long arm of the police state was not confined to Taiwan. Taiwanese students and professors in the U.S. were watched by Taiwan security agents and interrogated on returning to the island. In 1984, Henry Liu, a Taiwanese journalist who wrote a biography critical of Chiang Ching-kuo, was assassinated in California by Taiwanese agents. The U.S. Department of Justice subsequently sent an investigation team to Taiwan and gave lie-detector tests to several senior officials. It emerged that Taipei's military intelligence chief had asked the Bamboo Union Gang, an organized crime syndicate comprised of mainlanders on Taiwan, to "teach him a lesson." One of Ching-kuo's sons, Chiang Hsiao-wu, was implicated, and whatever hopes he may have entertained of following in his father's footsteps ended with the Liu murder case. He had been president of the state-owned Broadcasting Corporation of China and later moved into foreign affairs, serving as Taipei's de facto ambassador to Singapore and then Tokyo.

The same year a book entitled *The Soong Dynasty*, a compelling indictment of the Soongs and Chiang Kai-shek's rule in China, was published in the U.S. and became a best seller. In response the Nationalist government not only banned the book in Taiwan, but also mounted a campaign in America to discredit the book and its author, Sterling Seagrave. Madame Chiang was said to have been instrumental in the effort, in which American friends and academics were enlisted to refute the book's charges of corruption, incompetence, and ruthlessness.

During local elections in November 1985, opposition politicians openly criticized the Chiang family and the Nationalist party. After failing to be elected as county chief, Chen Shui-bian and his wife, Wu Shu-chen, walked through the streets thanking voters. Suddenly a truck veered off the road at high speed, hitting Wu and paralyzing her from the waist down. The truck's driver said the brakes malfunctioned, but they were later found to be in normal working order. Despite these and other incidents, Ching-kuo—dubbed the "Teflon Buddha"—enjoyed considerable popularity and was rarely blamed for the actions of subordinates.

Ironically, management of the economy—one of the chief causes of the Nationalist regime's collapse on the Chinese mainland—had by the mid-1980s proven to be the most spectacularly successful aspect of Nationalist rule on Taiwan. The economy and the stock and property markets were booming, lifting Taiwan's large middle class, which had effectively been created by the land-to-the-tiller reforms undertaken due to American pressure in the 1950s, to sudden prosperity. This newfound affluence in turn intensified popular demand for political freedom. Opposition politicians dared to call openly for Taiwanese independence. These government opponents, who had no party affiliation as Taiwan was still a one-party state, were winning a greater share of contested seats in local polls.

As Chiang Ching-kuo's health deteriorated, his thoughts turned to his legacy. He calculated that he would be regarded more favorably by history if he ushered in democracy. South Korea's democratic growing pains had not gone unnoticed, and Marcos's humiliating exit as Philippine president in February 1986 heightened the urgency for reform. Ching-kuo recognized that Taiwan's security and international stature would be enhanced if Taiwan moved toward democracy. In any case it was by now clear that he could no longer resist popular demands for liberalization, and controlled reforms would be a way of preempting the independence movement. Defying the long-standing ban on opposition parties, in September 1986 government opponents established the Democratic Progressive Party (DPP), whose chief tenet was Taiwanese independence. Ironically, they chose as the venue for the launch the Grand Hotel, Madame Chiang's pet project and a monument to imperial Chinese splendor.

*   *   *

During her long stay in America, Madame Chiang's thoughts often turned to the nearly half century of life spent with her late husband. Memories of "periods of great tension, days of deep anxieties, of reverses suffered and overcome flashed in kaleidoscopic sequences through my mind," she wrote in a 1986 essay. Through it all, "our constant concern was for the success of our national cause. How we hoped, prayed, and worked that the destiny of our country would be commensurate to our efforts so that she will truly be an ineluctible stabilizing force for world peace."

After more than ten years in the U.S., she returned to Taiwan in October 1986 to observe the anniversary of Chiang's hundredth birthday. She arrived on a China Airlines flight chartered for herself and her entourage, planning to return to New York after a brief stay. The visit stretched into five years.

Madame Chiang's unexpected resurfacing on Taiwan came at a politically sensitive moment and breathed new life into the fading hopes of the old guard, the Kuomintang's *yuanlao pai*, which felt threatened by the resurgent Taiwanese independence movement. She still held two Nationalist party positions: chairman of the party's central advisory committee—an exalted albeit largely honorific post—and head of the party women's group. Her arrival ignited intense speculation that she had returned to interfere in the succession to her ailing stepson, Ching-kuo, who had begun to call for an end to martial law and the repeal of a ban on the formation of new political parties. His push for political liberalization was welcomed by the opposition and his supporters, but the older Kuomintang conservatives— among whom Madame Chiang remained influential—were rabid.

At a memorial rally for Chiang Kai-shek Mayling told fifty thousand listeners that she hoped the principles for which the Nationalist party stood would shine over the mainland again. Her voice was so soft that the microphones had to be turned up so the crowd could hear her, but her face appeared animated and little changed from decades earlier. She stood unaided to deliver her speech, though she sat in a wheelchair for the remainder of the rally. The famous speech was entitled "*Resurgam,*" Latin for "I shall rise again"—the same title she had given a series of controversial articles she wrote in the late 1930s. "Although living abroad during recent years, I have closely followed the domestic scene with joy and concern as if I were always on home soil," she said. She came back to "be with my countrymen and family members and to witness the progress and prosperity of Taiwan, which is our base for national renaissance." Newspapers published her speech in full.

The capital was soon buzzing with theories as to her intentions. Some believed she had come back to Taiwan simply because she wanted to spend her final days on Chinese soil. But the *Resurgam* message was taken literally by many, who suspected she wanted to make a grab for power in her old age and assume the presidency after the demise of her stepson. It was widely believed that at the very least she wanted to install the younger generation of the Chiang family in power in order to perpetuate the family dynasty.

After eleven years out of the political limelight, Madame Chiang began holding meetings and tea parties with a select group of family, friends, officials, and military figures at her residence in Shihlin. She gave no hint of her intentions, but dissidents feared she might try to derail her stepson's plans for political reform. When two dissident magazines suggested that she was trying to marshal opposition to the reforms, the magazines were promptly seized by the Garrison Command, Taiwan's chief security agency. Undaunted, publishers reprinted the confiscated editions. Newsstands hid the offending journals under the counter and sold them on request.

Although nearing the tenth decade of her life, Madame Chiang still cast a long and mystifying shadow over Taiwan politics. While her supporters said she backed political reform—and she had always proclaimed herself to be democratic—her public utterances seemed calculated to inspire quite the opposite interpretation. In a lengthy essay published in the Taiwanese papers in early December 1986, she criticized recent local elections as marked by "clodhopping boorishness and uncivilized geste of discourteous unseemliness." Democracy, she argued, "should not be imported lock, stock and barrel from abroad. For us democracy should be built on the Three People's Principles." She added: "There is instant coffee and instant tea but only charlatanry could provide instant democracy." She closed by saying a nation's deadliest enemies lived within—an apparent reference to independence activists. In a speech to the American Chamber of Commerce, she attacked the news media and warned that if democratic societies sank into chaos, communism could triumph.

Listeners took her remarks to mean that Taiwan should move slowly toward democracy—if at all.

In a gesture of respect, Chiang Ching-kuo visited Mayling almost daily, sometimes for breakfast, sometimes just to say hello. At one public function, in an effort to dispel long-standing rumors that they did not get along, the government told newspapers to stress that Madame Chiang and her stepson were "intimately holding hands." Ching-kuo was said to have consulted her on the question of his successor. She expressed her approval of Vice President Lee Teng-hui, who shared her religious beliefs. "This man is a Christian, so he cannot be a bad person!" she told her stepson.

From his wheelchair, Ching-kuo battled hard-line opposition and hurriedly carried out political and economic reforms. He knew he was racing against time, for diabetes was ravaging his body. On July 15, 1987, he rescinded martial law and the ban on forming political parties. He allowed Taiwanese residents to visit relatives on the mainland for the first time. He pushed through economic reforms. He gave more political power to islanders, famously declaring that he, too, was a Taiwanese. Finally, from his deathbed, on January 8, 1988, he lifted all restrictions on the press— the pièce de résistance of his drive for political reform. He died on January 13 at the age of seventy-seven. The six-decade political dynasty of the Chiang family had ended.

Vice President Lee Teng-hui was sworn in as president hours later. In an apparent effort to mollify the old guard, he appeared on television and made a rhetorical appeal to unite the country and fulfill the great mission of recovering the mainland that Chiang Ching-kuo had been unable to finish. This meant he would not abandon the cardinal tenet of Kuomintang rule on Taiwan—the dream of eventual reunification with China. Decoded, it meant he would not make any moves toward independence. Some native-born Taiwanese called for a declaration of Taiwanese independence, but the majority of people on the island wanted self-determination and democratic reform under the status quo, rather than formal independence.

In stark contrast to the death of his father, there was no national outpouring of emotion at Ching-kuo's death, and apart from a modest funeral life was business as usual—in part testimony to Ching-kuo's refusal to encourage the creation of a personal cult. Madame Chiang was not seen at his funeral, but was later spotted in a black limousine near his mausoleum.

At the time of his succession to the presidency, Lee Teng-hui was re-garded as a mild scholar with neither a political base nor a flair for cutthroat politics. The bureaucracy, the party, and the military were in the hands of powerful mainlanders. It was widely assumed that the devout Christian, who had often said he would like to become a missionary when he retired, would merely be a transitional figure who would head the government in name only. The man could hardly have been more underestimated.

Not long after Lee ascended to the presidency, it was said, he secretly met with leaders of the opposition Democratic Progressive Party, who asked him to lead Taiwan to formal independence. "Just give me time" was his legendary reply. Although perhaps apocryphal, the story gained wide currency in Taiwanese political circles, and as the years unfolded Lee's actions lent credence to the tale.

In the days following Ching-kuo's death, Madame Chiang wrote a let-ter to the Kuomintang leadership, arguing that the party should not rush to appoint an acting chairman; instead, the post should be filled by mem-bers of the party's senior decision-making body on a rotating basis. But party leaders had already committed to deciding the matter immediately, to avoid leaving the party rudderless and prolonging uncertainty surround-ing the succession. There was consensus that the new president should be named Kuomintang chairman, a position at least as powerful as the presi-dency. Making Lee chairman as well as head of state—like both Chiangs before him—was seen as critical to ensuring Taiwan's continued political stability. This view was reinforced by a verbal message from President Ronald Reagan to Lee expressing American support for the constitutional process that had carried Lee to the presidency.

Undaunted, Madame Chiang continued to pressure party leadership to follow her wishes. At a key meeting during which the chairmanship was to be voted on, Premier Yu Guohua, her longtime protégé, presided. He stalled for two hours, having even removed the matter from the agenda. Finally, James Soong, a young moderate mainlander party member, abruptly stood up and spoke in support of making Lee Teng-hui chairman and pro-posed to put the question to an immediate vote. Although Soong had spo-ken out of turn, Yu could delay no longer, and the resulting vote was nearly unanimous. Madame Chiang responded by writing to say to party leaders that she had only suggested that the matter should be handled according to party rules. There was no ulterior motive, she asserted; she was "loyal to the party and a patriot" first and foremost. Trying to dispel negative interpretations of her motives, she said, "I supported [Lee] at the beginning, and I'm not going to go against him today."

Although her real power was negligible, Madame Chiang's words still carried weight and she was still paid ritual obeisance. Both President Lee and James Soong called on her to pay their respects after the nomination, though perhaps more to prevent her from losing "face" than out of a genuine respect for her views. Whatever its true purpose may have been, her letter was widely interpreted as the Kung-Soong clan's rising from the ashes to interfere in Taiwan's political process in an unwarranted and unwanted manner. The depth of suspicion among much of the public, combined with the lack of transparency in her backstage intriguing, generated enormous resentment and left her thoroughly discredited among a large section of the population. Press reports questioned whether she had acted according to her own will or whether she may have been unduly influenced by her family members. Another suggestion was that she had been encouraged to write the controversial letter by "Royalists," or members of the "palace faction," who wanted the party chairmanship for themselves or at least hoped to undercut the authority of the new Taiwan-born president. At ninety-one years of age, the newly unshackled press asked, could Madame Chiang be fully cognizant of the current political mood? The incident also shone an unpleasant spotlight on the waning influence of the conservative old guard of the party—influence that would never again be resurrected.

Two weeks after Chiang Ching-kuo's death the cabinet announced that Young Marshal Zhang Xueliang, now hardly "young" at ninety, had been freed after more than half a century in captivity. Gen. Sun Li-jen was also released, after thirty-three years under house arrest, and died two years later.

In June 1988, Madame Chiang made her first public appearance since the previous December, at a Women's League tea. She addressed the audience, attacking those who criticized her, the Chiang family, and her late husband's record as a leader. It was unfair to use modern standards to judge the past because conditions were different, she said. Though constructive criticism was good, a person's name could be destroyed overnight by slander. The older generation in Taiwan had survived Japanese occupation, but "I hope those who have never experienced those hardships can be cautious enough not to be confused by those infiltrating Taiwan or attempting to affect social peace, our national image and various accomplishments by the armed forces and the people here," she warned, obliquely referring to Taiwanese independence activists who were returning to the island from years spent in exile. "We must not forget that if there are rights, there are obligations too. Democracy and freedom have their limits. Democracy must be ruled by law, while freedom means not violating others' freedom."

In July the Kuomintang held its thirteenth party congress, the first in seven years. Madame Chiang emerged from seclusion to laud the Kuomintang's "glorious" history in her role as chairwoman of the Party's Central Advisory Committee. The twelve hundred delegates gave her a standing ovation as she haltingly walked across the stage with the aid of a cane in the Chungshan Building high up on Yangmingshan, wearing a white printed *qipao*—the long Chinese dress with high collar and slit sides—with black piping and a black vest, her still jet-black hair pulled back in a bun.

As the widow of Chiang Kai-shek, and the only senior living member of the clan that had dominated Chinese politics and history for over half a century, she remained a potent symbol of the party's past and the patron saint of its old guard. Behind her hung a huge portrait of Sun Yat-sen in a gold frame; she faced another of her late husband. A painting of her stepson hung to her right. She did not directly endorse the choice of Lee Teng-hui as chairman, but her presence was an unmistakable nod of tacit approval.

In a weak but firm voice she greeted the congress, saying, "How are you, comrades?" drawing applause and a response of "fine" from listeners. Her throat bothered her, so she asked Li Huan, the party's secretary-general, to read her fifteen-minute speech, rumored to have been penned by David Kung. In it, she noted that the historic Marco Polo Bridge Incident that had touched off the Sino-Japanese war had taken place fifty-one years earlier. She recounted her memories of the first national party congress, held in Canton in 1924. "At that time all our participant comrades displayed by word and action their vigor and loyalty to the Party and the country," she said. "I was present myself. I heard in person our Tsungli [Sun Yat-sen] elucidate us on the need for organizing a strong political party which could restructure our country." She reminded the audience that her father was one of Sun's close associates, and that he had given protection to comrades, raised funds for the revolutionary cause, and hosted secret meetings at their family home. As a result her father was at one time wanted by the Manchu government, which had offered a reward for his arrest, forcing the family to seek refuge in Japan.

"We are facing a critical moment as our senior members are retiring and are succeeded by new blood," she told delegates. "Among the old Kuomintang members with gray hair and who now walk in faltering paces are warriors who fought battle after battle or outstanding leaders who made important contributions to our country in the years long past," she said. The old guard's contribution to the party and the nation should never be ignored. "We should create a new era without forgetting the past," she said, adding that the party was like a tree, with an "old trunk and new branches."

She went on to warn the party to beware "publicity-seekers" and "trendy and outré ideas," alluding to the notion of Taiwanese independence or the concept of "one China, one Taiwan." She scolded the media, saying that they must confine opinions and criticisms to the editorial column. She asserted that the nation's founder, Dr. Sun Yat-sen, had founded the party in order to create a harmonious state comprised of China's five different ethnic groups. "It is self-evident that there should be no 'independence,' for we all belong to the Han race." She noted that the Americans fought a bloody civil war to preserve their union. She called on party members to unite under the leadership of the chairman and to uphold democracy, improve the economy, and honor the party's "glorious" history. The applause was deafening as President Lee shook her hand. Waving a white handkerchief, she left to another standing ovation.

At the conference, Lee was confirmed as Kuomintang chairman. His assumption of the party post was widely seen as reinforcing democratic change, since Lee was a Taiwanese native and much of the party power remained in the hands of mainlanders. Had he not been made chairman, many argued, he might have been a weak and ineffective president, since for so long "party" had been synonymous with "state." But later some observers felt Madame Chiang might have been right after all—separating the presidency from the chairmanship of the dominant political party might have done more to promote democracy, by decoupling party and state. Only two members of the Chiang family were nominated to key party posts: John Chang, one of Ching-kuo's illegitimate twin sons who had risen through the ranks to deputy foreign minister; and Chiang Hsiao-yung, Ching-kuo's (legitimate) third son, who ran a number of party-owned business enterprises.

In November 1988, Madame Chiang announced that she would return to America in early 1989, and her niece and nephew David and Rosamond Kung arrived in Taiwan to help their sister Jeanette prepare for Madame's departure. But the discovery of an ovarian tumor derailed Madame's plans. Her personal physician was flown in from America to treat her and her right ovary was removed in early 1989.

Jeanette Kung insisted on complete secrecy about the illness, which naturally led to inaccurate speculation in the press as to its exact nature. When Madame Chiang had suffered breast cancer in the 1970s, Jeanette was infuriated after reports of her illness leaked out. Some outstanding physicians at the Veterans' General Hospital were forced to resign. "Why do Madame Chiang's relatives surround her medical condition with such an air of mystery?" mused *The Journalist,* a leading Taiwanese newsweekly, in February 1989. Her residence was run like a "feudal kingdom," the magazine commented. Her handlers claimed to be acting according to her wishes, but they were creating a distorted image of the former First Lady. She had virtually no contact with or understanding of the world outside her family and staff, and the Taiwanese people had still less understanding of her. She was so isolated, *The Journalist* observed, that she had become a foreigner in her own land.

When newspapers reported in April 1989 that Madame Chiang planned to return to America, fifty veterans rallied outside the Chiang Kai-shek Memorial Hall appealing to her not to abandon them. They begged her to help them cash in property deeds issued by the Nationalist government as compensation after the retreat to Taiwan in 1949. The deeds promised holders title to land on the mainland, to be occupied once the mainland was recovered from the Communists. Her surviving stepson, Wego Chiang, explained to them that she was recovering from surgery and still loved Taiwan and did not plan to go abroad.

In November 1989, President Lee called on Madame Chiang at her Shihlin residence. They met for two hours one afternoon and discussed an upcoming military reshuffle, among other matters. Gen. Hau Pei-tsun, a protégé of Madame's and for the last eight years chief of the general staff, was expected to become defense minister. He had served as chief aide to Chiang Kai-shek from 1965 to 1970 on Madame Chiang's recommendation, and she'd promoted his career thereafter.

Madame Chiang apparently had planned to live out her days on the island. But the political situation was changing rapidly. She was upset with changes in the Kuomintang and the administration of President Lee, especially his "Taiwanization" policies, which entailed giving more key posts to native Taiwanese. Jeanette Kung was determined that she stay on the island, and Madame Chiang was reluctant to leave her favorite niece, and so she once again delayed her departure. But she resented persistent reports that she was trying to interfere in senior personnel changes and in the running of government. Her pride was deeply wounded, and she believed the rumors were intended to hurt her and even drive her away. This in part stemmed from the difficulty she had in adjusting to the newly unfettered and rambunctious press, now openly critical of her and her family. "This is my country; I have a right to live on my own soil," she was heard to say.

In the spring of 1989, Madame Chiang watched as protesters marched across China calling for democracy. When tanks rolled into Tiananmen Square, killing untold numbers of democracy demonstrators on June 4, 1989, she swiftly condemned the leadership in Beijing. In a statement to the media, she wrote of her "indescribable horror" at news that armed troops were used to "wantonly slaughter" peaceful students and workers. "I pray that the regime run amok will cease butchering en masse the innocents. . . . All the students wanted initially was dialogue with this inhuman, diabolic regime for freedom of person and expression. And for this natural yearning, they were murdered in cold blood." She instructed the Women's League to donate $5 million Taiwan to help mainland compatriots affected by the massacre.

A week after the massacre, Madame Chiang was awarded an honorary doctorate of law by Boston University on the institution's 150th anniversary. President George H. W. Bush, François Mitterrand, and King Hussein of Jordan also received the degree, but hers was the only one conferred off-campus. The university's president, John Silber, who traveled to Taiwan for the ceremony, lauded Madame Chiang as a woman of "indomitable spirit and personal courage" who remained America's "true and honest friend." Standing with the aid of a cane, she began by saying she was recovering from a severe allergic reaction to an antibiotic that had necessitated several months in the hospital, and that her medications made her "woozy," for which she asked listeners' patience. She then bitterly condemned the "satanic carnage" at Tiananmen Square carried out by the "dastardly Communist poltroons." Widespread demonstrations and "spontaneous general uprisings" on the mainland showed that the Chinese people were saying, "We can't take it any more! . . . You are nothing but demoniac butchers!" she declared. "The biggest lie perpetrated on the whole world in the history of mankind has at last been called to task," she concluded triumphantly. "After some seventy-five years, Communism is bankrupt."

Chapter Twenty-four
Diva at Dusk

How could we forget?

—Bob Dole

As the decade of the 1990s began, Madame Chiang remained on Tai-wan, still apparently undecided about whether to return to New York. As she entered her twilight years—she was now about ninety-three—her famed imperious manner had softened, and she was not as intimidating as she used to be. She had become more introspective and, like her mother, more devout, and spent hours reading religious books. She liked to play down her role in history, telling friends she was "just a simple Christian." Her health was reasonably good, but her short-term memory was fading. Still, she was alert, and her mind was clear. Her thoughts often returned to the past, recalling in great detail events of decades earlier—what she said to her husband, where they went, how they faced a particular problem. She remained particular about her appearance, still had her hair done and wore makeup, jewelry, and elegant silk dresses. The only thing that had diminished with age was the height of her heels.

Age did not, however, prevent Madame Chiang from remaining in control of the National Women's League, as it was now called. In 1990 she appointed Cecilia Koo, wife of Koo Chen-fu, a prominent Taiwanese industrialist and senior Kuomintang member, to replace her as secretary-general of the organization, which boasted two hundred thousand members, while she retained the title of chairman. As Taiwan's economy entered its "miracle" phase in the 1970s and 1980s, the funds collected by the Women's League via the "military welfare donation" tax exacted on imports had grown exponentially. The "donation" had finally been scrapped in 1989, after industry associations complained, but Madame Chiang still controlled the organization's assets. Since the League's accounts remained a closely guarded secret and were not subject to the scrutiny of any government agency or even by its membership, only a handful of key people knew the extent of its holdings, which were thought to be substantial. In the late 1990s there was talk of a government probe into the League's finances, but nothing came of it.

Madame Chiang kept in touch with old friends, including the Young Marshal, whom she occasionally took out to lunch at the Grand Hotel. Since the death of Chiang Ching-kuo the government had repeatedly denied that Zhang Xueliang was still under house arrest, but he was not seen in public until June 1990—for the first time since 1936—when he celebrated his ninetieth birthday. During the event he referred to himself as the "sinner of sinners." Madame Chiang often told friends, "*Women duibuqi Hanqing!*" She meant that "we"—presumably herself, her husband, and her stepson—had deeply wronged Zhang, whom she always called by his personal name, Hanqing. It was an interesting statement, considering that although she failed on the promise she made in Xi'an to ensure that Zhang would go free, it was she, he believed, who prevented her husband from executing the "young fellow."

Madame Chiang continued to appear in public occasionally, and her often controversial utterances still commanded attention. In an April 1991 speech to the Women's League, Madame denounced the "mindless" violence in Taiwan's now rambunctious legislature and what she called a trend toward evil and decadence. It was true that passions ran high during legislative debates and sometimes erupted into vigorous melees among lawmakers. People's lives had become materially richer, bringing "greed and reckless acts," she lectured, calling it "shameful" that the nation's parliament was ridiculed abroad as a "circus."

In July, Madame Chiang addressed an art conference hosted by the National Palace Museum, which held the vast trove of Chinese antiquities taken from the Imperial Palace in Beijing that the Nationalists had transferred to Taiwan in the late 1940s. She had been instrumental in the establishment of the Palace Museum in 1965, and formerly chaired its advisory board. It was widely rumored that she had long firmly controlled the museum through its director, Qin Xiaoyi, and often borrowed pieces from its collections for private viewing at her homes in Taipei and New York.

At the conference, she called on Western countries and Japan to return Chinese antiquities looted during the late Qing dynasty and the Sino-Japanese war. European paintings stolen during the Second World War, she argued, were being returned to their original owners. Her appeal sparked wide discussion and caused consternation at the foreign ministry. Officials warned that the matter of negotiating for the return of artifacts to their rightful owners was extremely complex to begin with and further complicated by Taiwan's peculiar diplomatic status. Given that the countries in question recognized the PRC as the only legal government of China, it was unlikely that the objects would be turned over to Taiwan.

Madame Chiang had hoped, it seemed, to spend her final years on Taiwan, but the political environment was changing rapidly, and she grew uncomfortable. As a potent symbol of the ancien régime, she became a target of protest, and anti-Kuomintang activists demonstrated outside the gates of her Shihlin residence. The opposition Democratic Progressive Party was gaining power. Politicians freely criticized the Chiang era, verbally attacked family members, and called for Taiwanese independence, a notion she found anathema.

In September 1991, word emerged that Madame Chiang would soon return to the U.S., symbolically marking the end of the Chiang family's influence on the island. A China Airlines plane was chartered for her, her luggage, and a huge entourage, which included a personal medical staff. The country's flagship carrier chose its best and most experienced pilots and flight attendants, and the first-class cabin was converted into a sleeping compartment for her. On September 21 she was seen off at the airport by President Lee Teng-hui and other senior officials and family members in a "private" farewell from which the news media were banned. She took up residence in her Manhattan apartment once again.

A few weeks after she left, five Taipei city councillors from the opposition Democratic Progressive Party went to her Shihlin residence and tried to enter in order to "measure" the property, claiming that the land belonged to the Taipei municipal government and that the thirty hectares of land should be transferred from military to city control and opened to the public. They were stopped at the gates by police.

Then in 1992, the long-suppressed memoir penned by Chiang's former wife Jennie Chen, which had been discovered in an archive, was published in Taiwan. Wego Chiang, retired and still living in Taiwan, denounced it as an attempt to smear his father's reputation and an "insult" to his father and Jennie alike. "Jennie was a nice lady. She never would have written anything like that," Chiang's adopted son said. He recalled meeting Chen for the first time when he was six years old. "I had just returned from a tour of Whampoa Island with my father when I found a young lady at our residence in Canton," he said. "Because my father was busy with his revolutionary work, I gradually developed an intimate friendship with Jennie. . . . She was a tender, elegant woman." He never saw her again after she was sent to the U.S., in August 1927, but said his brother Ching-kuo had later arranged for her financial support. The book appeared in English in America two years later, but protected as she was by her family and aides, it is unlikely Madame ever knew of its publication.

In 1993, Zhang Xueliang and his wife were permitted to leave Taiwan for Hawaii, where he applied to immigrate to America and was subsequently issued a green card. There, in the Golden Dragon luxury apartment complex, one of the most colorful and beloved characters in modern Chinese history lived out his twilight years, spending time with relatives, going to church, and taking an occasional wheelchair ride by the sea. He received repeated entreaties from official quarters in the PRC, including one from the mayor of Shenyang (previously called Mukden), Zhang's former Manchurian stronghold, that he return to live in China.

The 1990s in Taiwan witnessed the complete dismantling of the Chiang legacy, as nearly all vestiges of the family's four-decade dictatorship were erased. It was a period of tremendous transition, from the early tentative euphoria at the end of military rule and the one-party state to vigorous opposition-led democracy. Thousands of political prisoners were freed; hundreds of new publications were launched; thousands of grassroots associations, foundations, and citizens' groups of every stripe—forbidden under martial law— were formed; lively political call-in shows flourished on pirate radio stations; wires carrying still illegal cable television programs festooned the alleys of Taipei, supplying more interesting fare than the three networks then controlled by the Kuomintang. The last blacklisted dissident returned from exile in 1993, was arrested briefly on arrival, and was then released.

It is ironic that while Madame Chiang and her family were tumbling from grace in Taiwan, a wave of revisionism began in the People's Republic of

China regarding the Chiang dynasty's role in China's modern history. Even as Beijing heaped abuse on Lee Teng-hui, calling him a "splittist" determined to seek Taiwanese independence, the former Nationalist leaders were unofficially rehabilitated—not least because they shared with PRC leaders a passionate belief that Taiwan was an irrevocable part of China. A more balanced view of the Chiangs' strengths and shortcomings as leaders, as well as a recognition of their contributions to China, was slowly emerging. Doubtless their celebrity status and commercial cachet aided their rehabilitation, as cash-strapped local governments sought to attract tourists. In Nanking, the Chiang residence was restored to its former glory. The church where they had worshipped was renamed "Mayling's Temple." Chiang's ancestral home at Fenghua was preserved and became a popular destination for Chinese tourists. Chiang family graves desecrated by Red Guards during the Cultural Revolution were repaired. Even the Soong family's humble ancestral home on Hainan Island was preserved as a historic site.

In September 1994 Madame Chiang returned to Taiwan to see her beloved niece Jeanette Kung, who was dying of colon cancer. She had always treated Jeanette like a daughter and had been heavily reliant on her during her own illnesses. Due to time considerations she did not charter a plane, but booked the entire first-class cabin on a China Airlines commercial flight instead. Under fire for giving her special treatment when she left in 1991, the foreign ministry forced her to use a diplomatic passport for the first time instead of the special *laissez-passer* she had used for years. Normally only diplomats and spouses could obtain diplomatic passports, but the foreign ministry could issue them at its discretion, with cabinet approval. The new passport was rushed through in time for her trip. She brought with her two doctors from the U.S.

Back on Taiwan soil for what would be the last time, Madame Chiang, now ninety-seven, briefly entered the spotlight once again. Despite the long flight, she emerged from the plane impeccably dressed, and smiled brightly for the cameras. She walked with the support of aides, accompanied by her favorite stepgrandson, Chiang Hsiao-yung. President Lee Teng-hui was among the many officials, associates, and friends waiting to greet her. Avoiding politics, they spoke of religious matters only.

She arrived to a lively spectacle typical of Taiwan in the mid-1990s, but was whisked out of the airport in order to avoid the two hundred protesting taxi drivers waiting to "welcome" her. Hundreds of riot police were on hand to prevent violence. She visited her husband's mausoleum before seeing her niece. She returned to America a week later, and Jeanette died on November 8 at the age of seventy-five.

Madame's relationship with her favorite niece remained a mystery. The old rumors that Jeanette was in fact her daughter persisted. Improbable as that was, their connection was so powerful, a friend observed, that whenever Madame looked at Jeanette it was as though she "loses her own soul." Whatever Jeanette said, Madame Chiang did without question. After her death, Jeanette's remains were sent to the U.S. and placed in the family crypt at Ferncliff Cemetery in Hartsdale, New York. Madame Chiang asked to be left alone in the tomb, and stayed by her niece's coffin for half an hour.

On February 28, 1995, during a ceremony establishing a memorial to honor the event's victims, President Lee Teng-hui made a public apology on behalf of the government for the 2-28 Incident. But while this first step toward healing nearly half a century of bitterness was being taken, efforts to dismantle the legacy of the Chiang cult were gathering steam as opposition-controlled local governments across Taiwan began removing hundreds of statues of Chiang Kai-shek. Stella Chen, a legislator from the Democratic Progressive Party, made a deliberate show of defacing the statues, she said at the time, in order to encourage people to stop blindly worshipping political idols. By now, few people displayed a portrait of Chiang Kai-shek in their homes, as had been de rigueur in the past. The newly elected opposition mayor of Taipei, Chen Shui-bian, announced that portraits of both Chiangs, father and son, would be removed from municipal offices and schools, and that only portraits of Sun Yat-sen and President Lee Teng-hui would remain.

In June 1995 the administration of U.S. president Bill Clinton finally gave in to unremitting congressional pressure and permitted President Lee to make a controversial trip to visit his alma mater, Cornell University. It was the first trip to the U.S. by a sitting leader of Taiwan. Although billed as a private visit, it received much media attention, and its political significance was not lost on Beijing. The irate PRC government tried to block the trip. In a deluge of vitriolic attacks, official Chinese media accused Lee of using "political hallucinogenic drugs" to mask his moves toward Taiwanese independence. He was labeled a dictator who used tricks to stay in power. But Lee remained defiant. He and his wife sent Madame Chiang two dozen roses during their trip.

The following month, the U.S. Congress hosted a reception in Madame Chiang's honor, to mark the fiftieth anniversary of the end of World War II. Even at ninety-eight, she was a lightning rod for controversy. The July 1995 event came at an especially tense moment in Sino-U.S. relations, amid squabbling over China's alleged human rights abuses, President Lee Teng-hui's controversial June visit to America, and Beijing's furious reaction. House Speaker Newt Gingrich had lately called for diplomatic recognition of Taipei, but quickly backpedaled after being reminded of U.S. treaty obligations to Beijing. On the eve of the reception on Capitol Hill, Beijing test-fired two missiles in the sea near Taiwan to drive home its ire. Ironically, there was no formal complaint from Beijing over the congressional reception, but Taiwan's Democratic Progressive Party objected to the event, saying that Madame Chiang was "one has-been despot better left ignored." Independence advocates called her invitation to Capitol Hill a "slap in the face" to countless Taiwanese who had died in the 2-28 Incident and at the hands of Chiang Kai-shek's secret police.

Illinois Democrat Paul Simon and Bob Dole, a Kansas Republican who was Senate majority leader and his party's presidential candidate, sponsored the reception. Simon pushed for a Senate resolution backing Taipei's bid for UN membership. None of the three former presidents invited to the event attended. Clinton administration officials were also invited, but stayed away for fear of offending Beijing. Some of Beijing's fiercest critics in the Senate attended, including Jesse Helms, a North Carolina Republican and chairman of the Senate Foreign Relations Committee; Strom Thurmond, a South Carolina Republican who chaired the Senate Armed Services Committee; and the Wyoming Republican Alan Simpson. Simon, the son of Lutheran missionaries in Shanghai, downplayed politics in favor of the event's historical significance. Noting that Madame Chiang was the only major figure still living from the World War II era, he termed the event a "gesture of friendship" to the Chinese people. "I thought she was dead," said a former Flying Tiger who attended, calling her a "great lady."

Madame Chiang's last public appearance in Washington had been her address to the National Press Club in 1966. Taiwan's television networks broadcast the event live—at 4:30 A.M., Taiwan time—and aired special programs about her life. Congressmen lined up to shake the hand of the tiny ninety-eight-year-old woman with jet-black hair and jade earrings. She was elegantly attired in a Chinese gown and appeared animated, alert, and in good health. Seated in a chair in the marbled Senate Caucus Room in the Russell Senate Office Building, with stepgrandson Chiang Hsiao-yung at her side, she read her remarks in a steady, firm voice in her characteristically elegant English.

"I'm happy that you remember an old friend from China who was a wartime ally," she said to the more than three hundred guests. She added she believed that "the combined effort of our two countries laid the foundation for the final victory of World War Two." Echoing the remarks she had made before Congress in 1943, she said, "I will always look on America as my second home, and it is good to be back home today."

Never one to shy away from sensitive subjects, she added that in retrospect it was clear that the Three People's Principles of Dr. Sun Yat-sen had triumphed over communism. "When the Chinese people are considering the future of their country, they should know what to choose—democracy, not authoritarianism," she declared, blithely oblivious to the fact that the Chiang regime, first on the mainland and then on Taiwan, had been anything but democratic. Looking back on the Second World War, she said, "I cannot help but reflect upon the tragedy of that war and those years of blood and tears, neither can I forget the moral courage evinced by both the peoples of the United States and China fighting shoulder to shoulder. Today I would also like to take this opportunity to express my heartfelt gratitude to the people of the United States for their moral and material support extended to my country, the Republic of China." She closed by saying, "God bless you all!"

She chatted and laughed with Senator Thurmond, the oldest member of Congress and five years her junior. Tricia Nixon Cox, the late President Nixon's daughter, was also there. Large black-and-white photographs of Madame Chiang with her husband, the Roosevelts, Churchill, Chennault, Eisenhower, Marshall, and other wartime figures hung on the walls. "My grandmother was very happy, and I have not seen her enjoying herself so much for a long time," Chiang Hsiao-yung said. He added that she was extremely moved to see that American congressmen as well as overseas

Chinese still remembered and admired her. "It was an honor for my grandmother and an honor for the Chinese people," he said.

In March 1996 she previewed an exhibition of Chinese art and treasures from the National Palace Museum in Taiwan at the Metropolitan Museum of Art. She smiled and shook hands with well-wishers, including ninety-four-year-old philanthropist Brooke Astor. She toured the show of 450 vases, paintings, carvings, and other pieces from the Palace Museum's 600,000-piece collection, mainly by wheelchair, though she walked through two galleries. When photographers urged her to pose before a tenth-century portrait of Sun T'ai-Tsu, the first Sung dynasty emperor, she joked, "I'll break the cameras!" Some of those present thought she was being self-deprecating about her looks, but the *New York Times* sinisterly interpreted the remark as threatening physical damage to photographic equipment if photographers had the temerity to take her picture. The Metropolitan Museum's director, Philippe de Montebello, personally escorted her. "She is clearly a grande dame and a calm and serene presence," he said.

Madame Chiang kept herself informed of current events but declined to comment on tensions across the Taiwan Strait, which were then on high boil. Taiwan's first democratic presidential elections were just days away. Incumbent Lee Teng-hui was pitted against former political prisoner Peng Ming-min, lately returned from exile and regarded as the "godfather" of the Taiwanese independence movement, running as the Democratic Progressive Party's candidate on a platform of Taiwanese independence. Kuomintang politicians discontented with Lee Teng-hui had broken with the party to field two independent candidates, both calling for eventual unification with China.

In an apparent effort to influence the outcome of the controversial polls, Beijing issued threatening statements and conducted missile tests in waters near the island. In response, Washington dispatched the aircraft carrier USS *Independence* to provide a stabilizing presence; the unsubtle symbolism was lost on no one. Madame Chiang did allude obliquely to the tensions. "She spoke with majesty of the enduring and unifying quality of art in times of political turmoil," noted de Montebello. Much to the chagrin of Beijing, the despised Lee Teng-hui handily won the historic March 23, 1996, election, with Peng coming in second.

Dismayed at the poll result, Wego Chiang asked the Kuomintang to explore the possibility of burying his father and brother on the mainland, as he feared their remains might be desecrated by political activists opposed to the Chiang family. His request was in part spurred by recent moves engineered by opposition government officials to remove statues and images of Chiang Kai-shek from Taiwan. Wego wanted the elder Chiang to be buried in Nanking, with Sun Yat-sen, and his father to be put to earth in his ancestral village in Zhejiang province.

Wego's appeal prompted more than ten thousand people to flock to see the mausoleums of the two leaders. The issue was effectively quashed when a senior Beijing official handling Taiwan affairs under the PRC's State Council—or cabinet—said that the time was not right to rebury the two leaders on the mainland. The Kuomintang decided that reburial would not take place until Taiwan had peacefully unified with China. In response, Chiang Hsiao-yung lambasted the ruling party for dragging its feet. When asked if reburial in China meant surrendering the late leaders' bodies to the enemy, he declared bitterly he would rather let the remains of the two Chiangs be "whipped" by the enemy than by "our own people."

A few months after the 1996 presidential election, the extensive gardens of Madame Chiang's Shihlin residence were opened as a public park, but the residence itself remained closed and under military security. Visitors strolled the ten acres of gardens, wooded paths, and tea pavilions, lounged on the grass beneath palm trees, admired Madame Chiang's rose garden, and toured the guesthouse where Eisenhower, Nixon, and a host of other foreign dignitaries had stayed. They peered into the tiny chapel where the first couple had worshipped with the social elite of Taipei, and toured the greenhouse that still housed her extensive collection of orchids.

To celebrate Madame Chiang's hundredth birthday, March 20, 1997, a delegation from Taiwan, including Madame Cecilia Koo, former premier Hau Pei-tsun, Wego Chiang, and a group of Madame's orphans traveled to New York for the occasion. Days later, a Hong Kong law firm, Tsang, Chan & Woo, presented a surprise anonymous gift of $6 million in the names of the three Soong sisters to Wesleyan College in Georgia. Wesleyan's president, Bob Ackerman, at first thought the fax—dated March 27, 1997—might be an April Fools' prank. He soon discovered that this "joke" was the largest bequest the college had ever received. He was informed that the money had to be removed from Hong Kong before the British colony was to be handed over to China on July 1, 1997. Ohio's Oberlin College received a bequest in the same amount in the name of H. H. Kung.

Madame Chiang and Wego had remained very close, and he visited her frequently during her years in New York. They regarded each other as mother and son. In October 1997, her favorite stepson died. Soon after, a Taiwan scholar announced that as a child Chiang Kai-shek had been bitten on the genitals by a dog and left infertile. Refusing to reveal his sources, the scholar claimed that, like Wego, Ching-kuo was not Chiang's blood son. Although the veracity of this rather far-fetched claim was dubious, the story made banner headlines in Taiwanese and Hong Kong newspapers and sparked wide comment. Madame Chiang's niece Rosamond Kung emerged to bitterly condemn the assertions as hurtful "nonsense." In an effort to counter the claim she offered a doubtful story of her own: that Madame Chiang was pregnant with Chiang's child in the autumn of 1937 when she had a car accident and had miscarried as a result. This was the last time her aunt was pregnant, Kung claimed, adding that Madame Chiang adored children and had hoped for a child since her marriage, and that after the accident her spirits were extremely low.

In December 1997, on the sixtieth anniversary of the Rape of Nanking, Madame Chiang sharply criticized "historical revisionists" in Japan who refused to accept responsibility for war crimes and even denied they had taken place. Scenes of battle, destruction, and misery from that painful period of Chinese history remained fresh in her mind. Chinese culture was a "force for peace," she wrote, that would ultimately dispatch communism to the scrap heap of history.

In 1998, Madame Chiang's spirits were good and she had the health of an eighty-year-old, her niece told a news reporter. By the mid-1990s, the urticaria that had long plagued her appeared to have completely cleared up, and her food allergies had subsided. But she was quite hard of hearing and visitors had to speak slowly and loudly or to write messages on a board kept nearby for that purpose. She had given up smoking Salem menthol cigarettes only a few years earlier. She was still quite alert, but used a wheelchair most of the time; still, even in the late 1990s she walked up and down the stairs in her apartment for exercise, with the help of her staff. She painted and practiced Chinese calligraphy with brush and ink, at least until 1997. She devoted much time to reading the Bible and the *New York Times,* and to prayer. After a severe earthquake jolted central Taiwan in September 1999, she directed the Women's League to donate $3 million to relief efforts, and instructed Huahsin, one of her schools, to take in children orphaned by the deadly quake.

As the years went by, Madame Chiang became increasingly isolated from the world, cloistered and surrounded by a large entourage. After David Kung died in August 1992, his sister Rosamond took over as Madame's primary companion and gatekeeper. Dozens of security, nursing, and household staff—many of them sent out from Taiwan on one- or two-year engagements—worked in three eight-hour shifts. Once or twice a week Madame would be taken, complete with entourage, to do a little "window shopping" at Saks Fifth Avenue from her wheelchair, to eat in a restaurant, or to take a spin around town. She liked to visit Grant's Tomb and see the Christmas show at Radio City Music Hall.

Far from tempering with time, the family predilection for secrecy and paranoia became if anything more pronounced. When Madame Chiang went to New York Presbyterian Hospital for medical checkups, hospital staff were ordered to clear the floor while she was whisked in through a back entrance by her security staff. She kept three small dogs, two Bijons and a Yorkshire terrier, which posed no problems, but at one stage some of her well-heeled neighbors complained about an infestation of cockroaches. After repeated complaints, exterminators were finally permitted into her apartment. Inspectors dispatched afterward to ensure that the offending pests had been removed claimed, improbably, to have discovered a closetful of gold bars.

Each year on her birthday family and faithful made an annual pilgrimage to pay their respects. Subordinates and protégés from Taiwan would fly to New York, and family came from far and near to see her. Always impeccably dressed and made up, looking at least twenty years younger than she was, Madame would rise to the occasion. Even into her twilight years she still wore her beloved air force wings pin. Only an honored few from the inner circle were invited to attend the annual birthday festivities. She looked forward to visits by old friends, so much so that for several days before and after a visit, her old complaint, insomnia, would return. Much as she enjoyed the visits, they left her exhausted for a week, to the dismay of nurses and aides. She liked to play games and joke with guests, whose visits lifted her spirits and left her full of memories of the past.

Occasionally she would become impatient with her attendants, who carefully protected and cared for her like a national treasure. One year a group of former students from her orphanage schools came to pay their respects on her birthday. Carrying a store-bought cake with them as they entered the apartment, they greeted her as "Chiang Mama" and wished her happy birthday. Her nurse had warned the staff not to let her eat any oily cake. Her security staff told the visitors that Madame Chiang could not eat any foods that had not undergone a security inspection. But in a rare display of defiance, Madame cut herself a piece of cake and took a bite before the security staff had a chance to stop her. "Is there a problem?" she asked.

The secret to her long life was her "resolute faith," said Cecilia Koo. "She has no fears, no worries." Once when Koo visited her, Madame Chiang had a cold and was coughing. Koo patted her on the back. Madame said, "Don't worry, God is with me." But at times her longevity must have seemed more a burden than a blessing, as she outlived one after another of her family members. In 1998 she was heard to ask, "Why does God want me to live so long?"

After Louis Kung died in November 1996 of cancer, the only one of the Kung children left was Rosamond. Ching-kuo's eldest son, Hsiao-wen, had died of diabetes-related complications in April 1989 at the age of fifty-three, and his second son, Hsiao-wu, died in July 1991 from the same condition, at forty-six. In February 1993, Ching-kuo's fifty-one-year-old out-of-wedlock son Winston Chang, then president of Soochow University, was struck by a cerebral hemorrhage while on a trip to China and died after returning to Taiwan. Then Ching-kuo's third son, Hsiao-yung, died from esophageal cancer in December 1996 at the age of forty-eight, leaving Winston's brother John Chang, who had by then risen to become Taipei's foreign minister and Kuomintang secretary-general, the last of Ching-kuo's five sons still living.

The deaths led to talk of a "curse" on the third generation of the Chiang family, supposedly due to the fact that the two elder Chiangs had not been properly put to earth, as Chinese tradition dictates. John Chang had asked to be formally recognized as a member of the Chiang family as early as 1991, but was ignored for fear of offending Ching-kuo's widow, Faina, by this time in her eighties and in poor health. In January 1998, Chang asked to pay a courtesy visit on Madame Chiang during a trip to New York, but was refused.

In 1998 the National Women's League, of which Madame Chiang was still titular head, gave $1.75 million to Wellesley to establish an endowed chair in Chinese culture. Madame dispatched Cecilia Koo to the International Cemetery in Shanghai to place flowers on her parents' grave, her views of the Chinese government seemingly having softened slightly by this time. She told acquaintances that there had been progress on the mainland and that the Beijing leadership had taken some positive steps.

In the summer of 1998, the remaining Kung family members sold the Hillcrest mansion, built in 1913 and purchased by the Kungs in 1949, to New York developer Irwin Stillman for an estimated $2.8 million. On December 10, 1998, a small advertisement ran in the Locust Valley, Long Island, *Leader*, announcing that on December 12, Madame Chiang's Long Island estate would be opened for a preview of its contents, subsequently to be auctioned. Proving the efficiency of the bamboo grapevine, an astonishing torrent of more than ten thousand people, mostly Chinese Americans, poured into the village of Lattingtown to see where Chinese royalty lived. They snarled Long Island traffic for miles in all directions for hours, creating an unexpected headache for local police, who set up roadblocks and turned away the overwhelming majority of would-be tourists.

The house had been inaccurately billed—presumably for marketing purposes—as "Madame Chiang's" home and the items as "hers," but few if any of the paintings, furniture, housewares, and bric-a-brac on display actually belonged to her. A family member later grumbled that many of "Madame's" belongings were brought in from outside for the occasion. None of this, however, deterred the huge crowds of tourists that materialized from up and down the East Coast to catch a glimpse—and maybe buy a piece—of Chinese history on the block. The majority of visitors who succeeded in getting to the mansion were less interested in buying than in taking pictures of themselves in front of the house or in the various rooms. "We totally underestimated the importance of Madame Chiang Kai-shek," admitted Gary Braswell, the Norwalk, Connecticut, gallery owner who handled the auction.

Some Chinese visitors felt it was a pity that "Madame's" house and belongings were being sold to foreigners. Others were surprised to learn that the household objects of China's royal family were, after all, rather ordinary—most of the things on display were such as would be found in the average grandmother's attic. The most valuable items were an automated cathedral clock that sold for $64,000 and a pair of French chandeliers that went for $62,500. A bed, purported to be Madame Chiang's, sold for $8,000. Stillman subsequently resold the property for nearly double what he had paid for it.

Toward the end of her life, Madame Chiang devoted a great deal of thought to the controversial issue of her final resting place. She told relatives and friends that she wanted to be buried back on the mainland with her husband at the Sun Yat-sen Mausoleum in Nanking. If Chiang could not be buried beside Sun Yat-sen for political reasons, she would like to be buried with her husband in his native village in Zhejiang province. She recognized, however, that for political reasons it was unlikely that she and Chiang could be buried together, in which case she wished to be buried in Shanghai with her parents and her sister Ching Ling in the family plot.

When her ruminations became public, they sparked wide discussion. The Kuomintang leadership in Taiwan reiterated that the remains of Chiang father and son could not be moved to the mainland until the democratization of China had taken place. Madame Chiang agreed, but suggested that in the interim the two late presidents' remains could be formally buried at Wuzhishan, a military cemetery set high in the mountains outside Taipei and featuring panoramic views. There, it was agreed, the feng shui was better (although Madame Chiang did not believe in feng shui, everyone else did). Besides, Chinese tradition dictates that a body must be buried in the earth, so the state of temporary entombment in which the bodies of Chiang father and son had rested since their deaths was inauspicious. Madame knew her remains would probably have to lie in temporary estate above ground with her family tomb in the U.S. to await eventual return to China. There was never any suggestion that she might be buried in Taiwan, from either her or her family members, lending credence to the charges of Taiwan independence advocates that she cared nothing for the island. Tellingly, Ching-kuo had made clear that he wished one day to be buried beside his mother in his native village.

In January 2000 an exhibition of Madame Chiang's paintings and calligraphy in New York City, held at the Brooklyn headquarters of the Chinese-language newspaper *World Journal*, attracted more than thirteen thousand visitors. She attended the opening, touring the galleries in a wheelchair. Held as Taiwan's second democratic presidential elections approached, and as tensions—both with China and on Taiwan itself—were seething, the exhibit took on the air of a celebration of a bygone era. The highlight of the show was a spare ink brush painting of a lotus among water lilies. Entitled *Lotus: A Gentleman Among Flowers,* the painting itself was unremarkable, but the inscription was priceless. Chiang Kai-shek had written in calligraphy and stamped with a red seal the following words: "In a pure wind, I smell fragrance from afar. Sitting across from my wife, I forget the heat of the summer." To traditional Chinese, the public expression of such intimate thoughts was shocking. So popular was the show, which included works by other Chinese artists as well, that it was subsequently taken to San Francisco's Asian Art Museum, followed by a stint in a Los Angeles museum.

At the age of 102, more or less, Madame Chiang remained an honorary member of the Kuomintang's central advisory committee. She had not intervened in Taiwanese politics since her disastrous foray following Chiang Ching-kuo's death. But as the March 2000 presidential elections drew near, it appeared that the Kuomintang's five-decade grip on power would be snatched away by the opposition Democratic Progressive Party. In a controversial letter purportedly dictated and signed by her, Madame Chiang publicly endorsed the Kuomintang candidate, Lien Chan. It appeared to be a bid to rally support among her small but fiercely loyal band of followers, many of whom had turned away from the party to back James Soong, the popular Kuomintang maverick. Soong was running as an independent, threatening to split Kuomintang voters and hand victory to the Democratic Progressive Party.

Taiwan faced a "painful choice" in this critical election, Madame Chiang wrote. "Once we stumble, it will lead our country and people into a disaster from which there is no return," the letter warned, arguing that Lien would usher in a new era in relations with China and lead the country toward democracy. Lien thanked her for her backing and promised stability and prosperity, but Soong derided his opponent, saying "Who's he trying to fool with Madame Chiang's letter?" Even her protégé, former premier Hau Pei-tsun, questioned the authenticity of the letter, noting that the signature was penned in the firm hand of decades past, not the spidery hand that he had witnessed in recent years. Even if the letter was authentic, it was extremely unlikely that Madame Chiang was fully aware of the true political situation in Taiwan.

The candidate of the Democratic Progressive Party, Chen Shui-bian, won the historic election, toppling the Kuomintang. James Soong came in second, and Lien Chan suffered a humiliating defeat, getting just 23 percent of the vote. Immediately after voting in the historic March 18 poll, a delegation of friends from Taiwan flew to New York to celebrate Madame Chiang's birthday, but no one told her the outcome of the election for fear of upsetting her. A few months later, with her permission, the new government announced Madame Chiang's Shihlin residence would be converted into a research center for studies of the Chiang-Soong family and modern Chinese history. The new government also moved to right some of the wrongs committed under Kuomintang rule. February 28 was declared a national holiday, and in January 2001 the Control Yuan, a government watchdog agency, posthumously exonerated the late General Sun Li-jen of all charges of wrongdoing, declaring there was "no evidence" that Sun had been involved in the alleged 1955 coup attempt against Chiang Kai-shek.

Lee Teng-hui had not led Taiwan to a formal declaration of independence during twelve years in office, as he had once allegedly promised he would, but he had brought it immeasurably closer to that day, despite vociferous protests from Beijing. His successor played down his party's central tenet of independence, arguing that determination of Taiwan's status must await a future plebiscite. On her 104th birthday, on March 6, 2001, Madame Chiang received emissaries from the new president, Chen Shui-bian, for the first time since the change in government. On retirement Lee Teng-hui began to openly advocate Taiwanese independence and to criticize Beijing, confirming the worst suspicions of his detractors.

In October 2001, Madame Chiang's old friend and most famous Christian convert, the Young Marshal, died at age 100. China's president, Jiang Zemin, hailed the world's longest-serving political prisoner as a great Chinese patriot. It is not known whether Madame was told of his death.

On her 105th birthday in 2002, Madame Chiang appeared wearing a deep purple brocaded *qipao* and jade necklace, bracelet, and rings to greet fifty family members and well-wishers. She was healthy and in good spirits, quite alert, and smiling and waving at guests. She seemed delighted when students from her school, Huahsin, came from Taiwan to perform a traditional Chinese dance for her. After the performance, she even joked with guests, asking them, "Why aren't you clapping?" But she appeared bored when a Kuomintang official gave her a report on party business. She did not eat lunch with the group as she usually did, returning upstairs to rest after greeting guests.

In March 2003, Taiwan officials and friends gathered at her Manhattan residence for the annual birthday celebration, but for the first time the guest of honor was absent. She had just checked out of the hospital, where she stayed for two weeks to be treated for a cold and a cough. At a separate birthday event held in Flushing, Queens, home to a large Chinese-American community, some two hundred elderly veterans honored the lady whose life spanned three centuries. One veteran of China's civil war spoke with emotion of his memories of coming to Taiwan from China: how they hoped to fight their way back to the mainland; how hard life had been in the 1950s, when they ate little more than rice and pickled vegetables and lived in soldiers' housing made of sheet metal. But worse than the physical deprivation, he said, was living with the feeling of incalculable sorrow that permeated their lives, and hearing people secretly crying at night through the thin walls of the military village.

After catching a cold and showing signs of pneumonia, Madame Chiang died peacefully at home at 11:17 p.m. on October 23, 2003, taking a century of secrets with her. Several close family members were with her when she died. New York's three Chinese dailies tore apart their front pages to inform their readers of her passing by morning, a day ahead of other newspapers.

The next morning, as her body was taken from the apartment into a waiting hearse, photographers tussled with New York City police called in by relatives to prevent them from taking pictures of the dead woman. Taiwan's President Chen announced that mourning and funeral arrangements for the former First Lady would be treated as a state event, and ordered flags to be flown at half-mast. A shrine was set up in Taipei's Chiang Kai-shek Memorial Hall. Some of the mourners who visited sobbed uncontrollably and had to be assisted from the site.

President George W. Bush called Madame Chiang a "close friend" of the U.S., especially during the "defining struggles" of the last century, and expressed condolences to her family. "Generations of Americans will always remember and respect her intelligence and strength of character," he said. Bells tolled at Wesleyan College in Macon, Georgia, in her memory, and a moment of silence was observed.

The public reaction in Taiwan was polarized and passionate. Plutarch's adage "Of the dead say nothing but good" was ignored. Some deified her to the status of sainthood; others reviled her as a corrupt, scheming, and ruthless modern-day Empress Dowager—the power behind the throne.

Two hundred thousand Taiwanese took to the streets in the south to appeal for formal independence from mainland China. In the capital, several thousand protesters marched in a counterdemonstration to oppose Taiwanese independence. Vice President Annette Lu told marchers that the death of Madame Chiang marked the end of Chiang dynasty influence and the beginning of a new era. Surprisingly, given her vehement opposition to the Madame's political views, the onetime anti-Chiang firebrand and former political prisoner under Chiang family rule called her a "human treasure" who represented "kindness, beauty and wisdom. . . . She is a great woman whose life bridged three centuries." Lu added, "The love-hate tensions between the Chiang dynasty and China and the tension and confrontation between the two sides of the Taiwan Strait must now end."

Not everyone was so charitable. The *Taipei Times* voiced the feelings of many in calling her the twentieth century's "most evil woman." An editorial, entitled "So long and good riddance," concluded: "[Madame Chiang] valued only money and power, tried to secure Taiwan as a fiefdom for her awful family and left in a huff when she failed. The only good thing she ever did for Taiwan was to leave it. Now this evil and corrupt woman is where she belongs—in Hell."

Just two days after her death, former president Lee Teng-hui publicly asserted that Madame Chiang's popularity and success in America was due not to diplomatic skill and charm but to bribery. He claimed that she had offered President Roosevelt "Chinese cuisine," by which he meant "old, dirty customs characteristic of the Chinese." The Roosevelt clan had business interests in China and she gave them special favors, he alleged, without providing any sources for his charges.

In the PRC, ironically, she was showered with unwonted praise. In contrast to the colorful invective Beijing habitually hurled at opponents, in death Madame Chiang was treated like a long-lost prodigal princess instead of the top war criminal the Communist party branded her as in the late 1940s. Chinese leaders called her "a noted and influential person in the modern era of Chinese history," praising her for fighting the Japanese, opposing separatism, and hoping for peaceful reunification of Taiwan with the motherland and national prosperity. The government expressed "deep condolences" to her family. Beijing even offered to send its ambassador in Washington to the funeral, creating some consternation. Internet chat rooms in China were filled with messages from people declaring their respect and admiration for Madame Chiang, one calling her "the pride of the Chinese nation." Mass-circulation newspapers carried favorable reports about her long career, particularly her role as a diplomat on her husband's behalf.

Controversial as she had been in life, it was hardly surprising that her funeral arrangements were vexed by politics. By coincidence, President Chen had been scheduled to be in New York during the time of the funeral to accept a human-rights award. Surviving members of the Chiang, Kung, and Soong families debated whether the funeral should be held during Chen's visit so he could drape the Republic of China flag over Madame Chiang's coffin. But some relatives opposed the idea because of her implacable ideological differences with Chen. "She devoted her entire life to defending the Republic of China," even cutting ties with her sister Ching Ling, said Fang Chih-yi, Chiang Hsiao-yung's widow. "I believe that she would not allow a president who does not recognize the Republic of China to drape the flag." There were concerns about whether Chen's unfurling of the national flag at a public event might unnecessarily inflame tensions with Beijing and annoy American officials. In the end it was decided that Chen would simply present the flag to Madame Chiang's relatives in a private visit, and the memorial service would be delayed until after his departure.

On arrival in New York, President Chen immediately went to pay his respects to the former First Lady. At her ninth-floor apartment at 10 Gracie Square, he bowed before a memorial and handed a Republic of China flag to Wego Chiang's son, Chiang Hsiao-kang. Noting her contributions to the nation, Chen gave her a posthumous commendation on behalf of his government, despite opposition from members of his administration. He shook hands with family members. It was an extraordinary and deeply ironic spectacle—the longtime campaigner for Taiwanese independence and defender of political dissidents persecuted under Chiang rule paying homage to the leading spokesman of a government that many Taiwanese regarded as a repressive, autocratic, and corrupt colonial regime; and the once-powerful family who had openly campaigned against him in the presidential election three years earlier receiving the politician who opposed nearly everything Madame Chiang stood for.

The funeral was held at St. Bartholomew's Church on the corner of Park Avenue and Fiftieth Street in midtown Manhattan on November 5, 2003. The church was completely full, with about fifteen hundred mourners. Curiously, given Madame Chiang's intense desire for security and privacy while alive, there appeared to be no security at the church. Many Chinese reporters and television crews waited outside on the front steps on that gray and misty morning. The mourners were mostly middle-aged and older people, virtually all Chinese, some of them "warphans" who had been rescued by the orphanages she founded in China and on Taiwan. Two rows of flower bouquets lined the center aisle—champagne roses, purple orchids, and white rhododendrons. She had a twofold prayer, mourners were told: that China would be free, and that China might become a Christian country. The Chinese version of "Amazing Grace," one of her favorite hymns, was sung a capella.

Fredrick Chien, former aide to Chiang Kai-shek and former foreign minister, called her Chiang Kai-shek's *liangban*—better half. "We all thought she was an outstanding foreign relations expert," he told listeners. Former vice president Lien Chan called her a symbol of Chinese-American friendship. Sen. Bob Dole said her name was synonymous with the tortured history of modern China and called her one of the most influential women of the twentieth century. "To meet her once is to remember her always," he said, describing how he had met her at the 1995 congressional reception, when she had appeared physically delicate but her spirit was still indomitable. Recalling that on that occasion she had said she was glad Americans remembered an old friend, Dole asked, "How could we forget?" Sen. Paul Simon recounted how when he had introduced his son Mark to her at the reception, she had asked, "Are you a good son?" and he'd blushed and stammered. "She was still sharp."

Her longtime pastor, Reverend Chow Lien-hwa, said she combined the best of East and West. During the Sino-Japanese war, she'd mobilized women to care for the wounded, bereaved families, and orphans—a Western concept that had to be applied using Chinese methods. She could also be unusually thoughtful and generous, he said. Once when the wife of a political opponent of her husband was in the hospital, Madame Chiang sent someone to the hospital to take her measurements and make padded cotton outfits for her, sent flowers, and paid the medical bills. The woman was not even the man's legal wife. "We are all God's creatures, but she is God's masterpiece," Reverend Chow said, adding she would forever remain "the First Lady of First Ladies."

Even more politically sensitive than the funeral was the issue of where she was to be buried. After days of discussion, the family decided to place her coffin "temporarily" in the family mausoleum at Ferncliff Cemetery in Hartsdale, New York, pending the long-awaited unification with China. Ferncliff Cemetery is the final resting place of such varied luminaries as actress Judy Garland and political activist Malcolm X.

After more than a decade of debate, a tomb was finally built for Chiang Kai-shek and Chiang Ching-kuo at the military cemetery in Wuzhishan, high in the mountains of Taipei county. By mid-2006 the two Chiangs' remains were at long last set to be properly buried there. Ching-kuo's wife, Faina, who had died in December 2004 at the age of eighty-eight, was also set to be buried in the new tomb, beside her husband. But tellingly, Madame Chiang's remains still rested in New York.

Madame Chiang's old adversary Winston Churchill once declared, "History will be kind to me for I intend to write it." He is also alleged to have said that old age had one benefit—one could have the last word on one's enemies. Churchill lived to be ninety-one and wrote an abundance of books. Madame Chiang outlived all her contemporaries, but steadfastly refused to write her own story. It is partly as a consequence of this, perhaps, that history has not always been kind.

Epilogue

"My name is Ozymandias, king of kings:
Look on my works, ye mighty, and despair!"

—Percy Bysshe Shelley

Shelley's mythical monarch left behind only ruins in the desert sand. Madame Chiang Kai-shek bequeathed a legacy far more complex. It may be too early to pass definitive judgment on China's "Madame Majestic," not least because her reputation in the eyes of Chinese people the world over remains polarized and in flux. But this extraordinary woman has assumed such mythic proportions in the turbulent history of modern China's relationship with the West—especially the United States—as well as in the popular imagination of her compatriots and Americans alike, that it behooves us to search for patterns of meaning in the intricate and multihued tapestry of her life.

The allegories seen, of course, depend on the eye of the beholder.

A corps of devoted followers on Taiwan call her "China's Eternal First Lady," a reverential epithet that suggests a legacy not merely lasting but immortal—even divine. Indeed, it is not difficult to imagine that one day soon the faithful will beatify her into the pantheon of Chinese deities and heroes, alongside the Boddhisattva Guanyin, goddess of mercy, and the warrior princess Mulan.

Madame Chiang held many titles in her long lifetime, but ultimately it was from her position as the wife of Chiang Kai-shek that she derived her power and prestige. Ironically, the claim to First Ladyship of China is technically tenuous. For two decades after their marriage, Chiang Kai-shek was not head of state but a military dictator. Madame Chiang officially became First Lady in the spring of 1948, when the National

Assembly elected Chiang president of the Nationalist Chinese government, which by no means controlled all of the country. Less than a year
later, in January 1949, he resigned. After fleeing to Taiwan, he resumed
the presidency of "China" on March 1, 1950, but despite protestations to
the contrary, his government's rule was confined to the island—as was
his First Lady's domain.

The nuances behind Madame Chiang's position are emblematic of the
tensions between reality and myth in the most important role of her life,
that of being the public face of China to the West. How was it that this
daughter of the Chinese Christian enclave of nineteenth-century colonial
Shanghai, a tiny hybrid society perched on the margins of East and West,
could ever claim to represent China? Madame Chiang's rise to international prominence was as improbable as it was meteoric, and her subsequent fall from grace as spectacular as it was predictable.

As a young woman Mayling Soong embarked on a quest not so much
for a husband as for a cause to which to fasten herself, and this she found
in Chiang Kai-shek. In this endeavor she followed in the footsteps of her
older sister Ching Ling, who had married Sun Yat-sen for much the same
reasons. Inspired perhaps as much by sibling rivalry as her own need to
be "the best" at whatever she did, Madame Chiang set out to match her
sister and then to outshine her. In marrying Chiang, she took on many of
his values, beliefs, and attitudes as her own, to such an extent that it became difficult to know where he ended and she began. The role of wife
and helpmeet to the self-anointed Christ of China was the role in which
Mayling came to see herself, and it might be said that she succeeded brilliantly in this, the calling to which she had been born and bred. For although Chiang Kai-shek was not a minister like her father, she came to
see her warrior husband as the divinely ordained savior of the Chinese
people, just as he did. It was a self-serving belief and one that justified
any end.

A question that continues to fascinate Chinese observers in particular
is whether the Chiangs' union was a "political marriage." The question
is usually posed as though in marriage, ambition and love are mutually exclusive, but in this instance, at least, they were not. Theirs was first and
foremost a grand political partnership, the like of which has rarely been
seen, in which each used the other to further his and her own towering

ambitions. That notwithstanding, love was by no means absent; it was simply secondary.

It was, however, a partnership founded upon a delusion—that Chiang was the messiah of China. Certainly he loved her in his own way; her love for him, at least initially, was melded with hero worship, and appears to have waxed and waned over the decades. Nonetheless, however low her affections for him as a husband may have ebbed, she remained steadfastly loyal to him as a leader, although perhaps as much to preserve her own image as out of love for him. For all her inveighing against the Chinese obsession with notions of "face," she was supremely concerned with the preservation of her own, and appeared unaware of any contradiction. In private she sometimes clashed with her husband, but in public she went to enormous lengths to keep up the façade of a devoted marriage. It would have been shameful and a great loss of face to do otherwise, according to traditional Chinese thinking, which held that the "husband sings and wife follows." On the occasions that her views varied from his, it was generally over matters of style or personality rather than principle.

During the 1930s and early 1940s, Madame Chiang Kai-shek became to the West a compelling figure on many levels. There she was seen as the ideal of a "Westernized" Asian woman, and as a positive image of a China that was on the march to modernity. In the United States she was embraced as the living embodiment of America's cultural good intentions in the world, as a shining example of well-educated modern womanhood, and as ambassadress from China to the U.S. and vice versa. She was looked up to as a woman accepted as an equal (or nearly so) in a world dominated by men, at a time when most women, even in the ostensibly advanced Western countries, were seen as members of a lesser class. These were images that she actively encouraged, and many—although not all—Westerners accepted such depictions at face value.

In contrast, Madame Chiang was admired by her countrymen as a Chinese celebrated by the predominantly Caucasian West at a time when Chinese were discriminated against, legally and socially, not only abroad, but in their own country. She is revered by some of her compatriots as a valiant fighter for the rights and status of the Chinese race. Konshin Shah, former translator and pilot for Chiang Kai-shek, a diplomat in his government, and a protégé of Madame Chiang, is representative of Chinese who remain fiercely loyal to the memory of the Chiangs, for reasons of national pride. "For me, Generalissimo and Madame Chiang rescued us from being a downtrodden country," he argues with great vehemence and emotion. In prewar Shanghai, "sailors from any country could kick me for no reason, and they would not be punished." Foreign seamen often got roaring drunk, then smashed shops and attacked Chinese with impunity, because they had virtual immunity under colonial extraterritoriality laws. "My generation regards the Chiangs as a godsent couple for uplifting our country to an equal status in the world. Even today the Communists are benefiting from all they did for China," Shah maintains, with bitterness in his voice.

It is true that under Chiang rule on the mainland, the Nationalist Chinese government succeeded in nominally unifying a country fractured by warlordism. It mounted a war of resistance against the invading Japanese. It finagled a seat at the international table as one of the "Big Four" Allied powers during the Second World War, albeit in practice as junior partner. Together the Chiangs made China a force to be reckoned with and treated with far greater respect by the Western powers than China ever had been before. Extraterritoriality laws were repealed; the Republic of China became a founding member of the United Nations and secured a seat on the UN Security Council; and overt colonialism in China ended (with the exception of Hong Kong and Macao, which remained colonies of Britain and Portugal until 1997 and 1999, respectively). Indeed, it would appear that the Communists ultimately reaped the rewards of these achievements, to which Madame Chiang contributed not inconsiderably, especially after Beijing was admitted to the UN as a member of the Security Council.

But for all the positive aspects of Madame Chiang's political legacy on the Chinese mainland, that legacy was unfortunately undercut by another encapsulated by the old refrain "power corrupts." This was corruption not only in the narrow sense of graft, but in a far broader and more insidious form—a corruption of the personality or spirit that reverberated through China's ruling clan and the Nationalist government.

America fell in love with a fantasy of China embodied by Madame Chiang Kai-shek. Pearl S. Buck wrote in the May 10, 1943, issue of *Life* magazine that Americans saw in Madame Chiang "someone whom they were able to understand—not a remote and esoteric creature who might have stepped from a Chinese fan, but a modern woman, a woman who is at home in any country; and through her China has for millions of Americans suddenly become a modern nation."

She appealed to American men and women in different ways. Predictably, men were intrigued by her slim figure, slinky dresses, and exotic looks. But more important she appealed to their sense of chivalry and machismo, and moreover to their sense of the American national mission of rescuing the fair damsel in distress—in this instance China, as personified by Madame Chiang Kai-shek. To American women, her attraction was more complex. By 1943 large numbers of American women had joined the labor force for the first time, many in traditionally "male" occupations—as workers in munitions factories, as farm laborers, in the armed forces, and as nurses in combat zones. Madame Chiang tapped into the unexpressed and unfulfilled aspirations of American women, whose worth had historically rested upon their roles as wives and mothers, but who were discovering that the war was giving them opportunities in the realm of men—opportunities for changing their status and self-image as women.

Enter Madame Chiang, feminine, photogenic, and a devoted wife, and, although she had no children of her own, a surrogate mother to tens of thousands of China's "warphans." Yet she was fiercely intelligent and outspoken, an influential figure not only in the Nationalist Chinese government, but an international stateswoman, sparring with the most formidable men on the world stage. Loved or hated, she was a woman to be reckoned with, not only by dint of her position but by force of personality. Unlike most political wives, she was not content to stay in the shadow of her husband, or to confine herself to domestic and social issues as did Eleanor Roosevelt, the historical figure to whom she perhaps most closely compares. She fearlessly tackled the biggest and prickliest issues of the day— Allied war strategy, colonialism, racism, and postwar geopolitics.

Yet the more successful she was at dazzling the West, the more she alienated her fellow countrymen. It cannot be emphasized strongly enough that although it may not have appeared so to most Americans in the 1930s, '40s, and '50s, let alone today, Madame Chiang and her family lived a lifestyle that was shockingly luxurious and extravagant, even decadent, in the eyes of ordinary Chinese. The irony, of course, is that without her veneer of cosmopolitan sophistication and glamour she could not have attracted so much

American attention, admiration, and sympathy for China. To achieve this goal she felt she had to not merely follow American standards, but outdo them, even competing with American First Ladies. However, it is perfectly true that the image of an educated, Westernized, and glamorous Chinese First Lady did much to torpedo the prevailing American stereotypes of a backward and ignorant China, not to mention the laundryman stereotype of Chinese in America.

To many Chinese, on the other hand, her popularity in America was disturbing, even disgusting, as though she were pandering to Americans, figuratively prostituting herself—and by extension China—to obtain aid for a feminized, emasculated China. This injured sense of national pride, consciously or unconsciously felt, helps to explain the vehemence with which she is despised by some Chinese. Her deliberate strategy of "showing off" soon backfired in America too. Many Americans, once the initial flush of infatuation faded, began to see Mayling's charms as an act, and acidly noted the glaring disparity between what they viewed as her ostentation and prima donna behavior and the abject poverty in which the overwhelming majority of Chinese people lived. This growing perception set in motion a backlash in the form of a compulsion to demonize.

Madame Chiang, in contrast, never seemed to be conscious of the vast gulf, both psychological and material, that existed between her and most of her 450 million compatriots. If she was at all aware of the gap, that awareness only served to reinforce her deeply ingrained sense of entitlement, rather than to awaken her to the true needs, feelings, and aspirations of the Chinese people. Ultimately, that insensitivity—attitudes shared by her family, apart from her sister Ching Ling, and social class—was as much a contributing factor in the downfall of the Chiangs on the mainland as corruption, oppression, or any of the other ills of the Nationalist regime.

We have a tendency to view people, and especially public figures, as being static, their personalities, motivations, and attitudes fixed in stone. While some people mellow with age, Madame Chiang did the reverse, perhaps as a result of her increasing isolation from reality as the years went by, combined with the intensification of some personality flaws, which flourished unchecked. Her early hopes and dreams for China's advancement, buoyed by an earnest if naive idealism, appear to have been genuine, although for her— as was true for many of her contemporaries—democracy finished a distinct if not distant second behind nationalism. In other words, she was convinced that making China strong, independent, and prosperous took precedence over making China democratic, and that Western-style democracy was probably unworkable for China anyway.

But at some point she seemed to undergo a shift from idealistic and relatively well intentioned to brittle, rigid, self-righteous, and dogmatic. It is difficult to say when the change took place. It may have been during her 1943 trip to the United States, or perhaps during the post-1945 period of civil war between the Communists and the Nationalists. Certainly by the time she left for America in 1948 to seek aid she had turned profoundly cynical.

The Nationalist defeat at the hands of the Communists was a traumatic personal experience from which she never fully recovered. Her deep sense of personal failure may have been compounded by old rivalries with her sister Ching Ling, who had sided with the victorious Communists. Following her return to Taiwan, after a brief period of soul-searching, she appeared to become consumed by bitterness and injured pride. She became increasingly rigid in her thinking and views, and the flashing wit and sparkling humor of her younger years evaporated, to be replaced by bombast and Christian piety. As the years went by, her capacity for self-reflection seemed to diminish to the vanishing point. In her public persona, she became a one-dimensional battle-ax, an iconic caricature of herself.

When Madame Chiang and China failed to deliver on America's fairy-tale expectations and "lost" China to communism, the natural response was to wreak vengeance upon her, deserved or otherwise. Where once she had been built up to superhuman proportions, she was torn down. She was always an icon to be revered or an idol to be smashed, never a mere mortal. But in a manifestation of Madame Chiang's staying power among Americans, despite her slide from grace Americans voted her to the Gallup Organization's poll of the world's ten most admired women no fewer than seventeen times after 1948, when the poll began.

Why does the name of Madame Chiang Kai-shek continue to arouse such emotion, even in death? Inevitably, women who step out of the narrow confines of their prescribed roles are seen as threatening and even dangerous, in China as elsewhere. Politically active and opinionated wives of leaders typically serve as lightning rods for their husbands, but unlike their husbands, they tend to be variously attacked or adored not so much for what they have done, but for what they symbolize. So it is with Madame Chiang. As with such figures as Eleanor Roosevelt, Evita Perón, and Hillary Clinton, those who hated the husband hated his wife far more.

For the Chinese, she provokes emotion because she is a symbol of China's tortured history over the last century, a history that polarized the Chinese people and left wounds that have yet to heal. In the drama, Madame Chiang is invariably—and usually unfavorably—contrasted with her saintly sister Ching Ling. For nearly half a century the two sisters trumpeted their political beliefs from the ramparts on either side of the great ideological divide of the twentieth century. For some Americans, she is a symbol of the spirit of the Allies as they battled fascist aggression during World War II, and a symbol of the Cold War "democratic" front against the spreading menace of communism. For others, Madame Chiang will always be seen as vividly emblematic of the ills of her husband's Kuomintang regime and the corruption of her family.

She was beautiful, vain, witty, spirited, capricious, scheming, selfish, and driven. She was brilliant, yet as naive as a small child, and for her the ends justified any means. She was immensely melodramatic and grandiose, and possessed an enormous sense of entitlement. She had not the slightest compunction about using her arsenal of wile, guile, and ruse to get what she wanted. She masqueraded as virtuous and loyal wife, matron of charitable causes, devout Christian, and font of democratic values. Along with all her triumphs she had many secret sorrows.

One can come to no other conclusion but that she was a fascinating woman of great political and personal weakness, who regarded herself not as simply leading or representing China but as (along with her husband) *being* China. Whatever they did, they were convinced, was for the benefit of China. Hence her frequent references to "my people" and "our people," which speak to her sense of ownership—the role of lord rather than servant, parent rather than equal.

She grandly claimed to be working for China, but in fact she was working to preserve her husband's dictatorship and her own position. Despite her frequent and lofty rhetoric about democratic principles and ideals, and her failed attempts at reforming the Chinese by castigating and shaming them, as evidenced by the New Life Movement and her *Resurgam* articles in the 1930s, she did nothing to change the nature of her husband's rule in China or on Taiwan—party dictatorship in name, one-man dictatorship in practice. Instead she worked tirelessly to reinforce his position, both at home and abroad. She was his most loyal confidant and his regime's most visible and outspoken propagandist to the outside world.

Madame Chiang never saw the repressive nature of Kuomintang rule as problematic, and so was apparently incapable of comprehending why the Chinese people had chosen communism over her husband. For all her education and experiences in America, she seemed unable or unwilling to fully appreciate the spirit of the democratic political system. It is difficult to know to what degree her exposure to hypocrisy, corruption, and injustice in America's much-vaunted democracy allowed her to justify her own—and to justify repression as a necessity of political life. It is easy to forget, for instance, that when Madame Chiang made her celebrated 1943 American tour, as one of the "colored" races she could have been barred from restaurants, hotels, and other public venues in large parts of the country. This was, however, a fact of which she was undoubtedly acutely aware. Then as now the American version of democracy had glaring flaws, which would have made her cynical, but that does not explain why she so deliberately and profoundly distorted the meaning of democracy to apply it to her husband's government.

Neither does it explain why she felt it necessary to try to bribe elected U.S. representatives not only to give aid to her husband's government, but to denounce as Communists loyal Americans who for legitimate reasons opposed supporting the Nationalist regime. It is as yet unclear to what degree she was complicit in one of the most shameful periods in recent American history, but there is no doubt that she helped lay the groundwork for the McCarthy witch hunts that began a scant month after her departure from the U.S.

It has been argued that during the Second World War and during the Cold War era that followed, when the world was polarized into two camps, if a government was allied with the industrialized West and opposed to communism then it was, ipso facto, democratic. This may well have been the defense Madame Chiang would have used herself, had she been challenged. While perhaps tolerable under wartime exigencies, the use of this rationale by the Chiangs to justify—and by the U.S. to back—a regime that was far from democratic was otherwise dubious.

Ironically, although the Chinese are generally convinced that Madame Chiang was totally "Westernized," and often criticize or dismiss her for that reason, in the most crucial sense her mentality and behavior were utterly "Chinese." In fact her "Western" traits—such as her outspokenness and concern for sanitation—were largely superficial while her allegiance to her Chinese cultural heritage ran far deeper, serving as the wellspring of her values, motivations, and behavior.

The most significant of her "Chinese" values was her unquestioning and absolute loyalty to clan and personality over principle. In the traditional Chinese worldview, any commitment to abstract principles, to an ideology, or to a cause was relegated to a distant second behind personal loyalties. Concern for *renqing*, or human feelings, was the most cherished value in Chinese culture. The practical manifestation of this ethical belief was that each individual Chinese was inextricably enmeshed in a web of relationships bound together by interlocking reciprocal favors, in which to refuse to perform a requested favor, however unethical or undesirable it might be, for a member of one's clan or social group was a virtual crime that could carry considerable repercussions. This belief system served a critical function in a society in which political turmoil, oppression, war, natural disaster, famine, and the absence of a reliable legal system were the norm for millennia; survival depended on personal ties.

In the modern society that the Chiangs were ostensibly trying to create on the Chinese mainland during the 1930s, however, placing *renqing* above law and principle was a maladaptive coping mechanism that deformed and stunted the growth of the institutions on which modern nations are founded. Sadly, Madame Chiang not only played out this tradition that pervaded Chinese society, but seemed oblivious to the ethical dubiousness of her actions, let alone the consequences. When there was a conflict between principle and clan, she invariably sided with family, and in so doing not only inflicted unimaginable damage to her own image and that of her husband in the eyes of the public, but undermined the very foundations of the Nationalist Chinese government. While most people were obviously not in a position to "buck" traditional Chinese ethical and behavioral norms, she surely was, and that she did not do so was not merely a personal failing but, more critically, an enormous liability for her husband's government and ultimately for her beleaguered country.

Although on the surface Madame Chiang appeared to be a strong and independent woman, this could hardly have been further from the truth. Not only was she reliant upon the services of a substantial entourage of servants, secretaries, and other minions from the moment she returned to China in her late teens, but for all her apparent outspokenness she was also very much dependent upon, and even submissive to, the authority of both her family and her husband. Within a few years after returning to China from the U.S., she had relinquished her American identity and re-assimilated into China's highly status-conscious and hierarchical society, as manifested in her social class. Lacking self-reliance or firm values of her own, she was instead molded by those on whom she depended for her position and livelihood. She lacked the strength, vision, courage, or willingness to independently arrive at, or mount a sustained defense of, her own set of values in the face of familial and social pressures, let alone to defy them entirely.

Inevitably one must confront the apparent contradiction between Madame Chiang's professed Christianity and her complicity in her husband's oppressive regime. Scholars have tended to ignore or dismiss the religious beliefs of Madame Chiang and her husband as a subject not meriting serious inquiry. Clearly, however, religious beliefs have animated the political beliefs of leaders past and present, tyrant and democrat alike, and have been used to buttress leaders' actions in crucial ways. Madame Chiang was sometimes heard to say that if everyone were a Christian, the world would be a better place. The statement strains credulity—especially if she meant to suggest if everyone were a Christian in the manner of her and her family.

However genuine Madame Chiang's beliefs appear to have been, there is no doubt that they served practical ends beyond the obvious spiritual aims. They imbued her and her husband with the notion that they had been divinely chosen to rule China—in other words, the ancient mandate of heaven. They reinforced the Chiangs' sense of entitlement and their belief that they were superior to and set apart from ordinary Chinese. The Chiangs' religious beliefs also helped to beguile Westerners, especially Americans, into believing that the Chiangs shared their cultural and moral values and that with them at the helm, China was on the road to Western-style democracy. The Chiangs' Christian faith also served to differentiate them from the "godless" Communists, thereby making it more difficult for overwhelmingly Christian America to abandon the Nationalist government.

Ironically, both Marxism and fascism are similar to Christianity, in that they are all messianic belief systems that promise a transcendent new world to followers. Marxism is, in a sense, religion stripped of the supernatural, while fascist regimes have often attempted to co-opt religion to serve their own ends. In both instances the language of religion is infused into political ideologies to induce followers to worship a mortal rather than a divine being. "God gave the Savior to the German people," in the words of Hitler's deputy Hermann Göring. "We have faith, deep and unshakeable faith, that he [Hitler] was sent to us by God to save Germany." Chiang tried, with less success, to infuse his countrymen with essentially the same notion. He and his wife used Christianity to inspire, justify, and perpetuate his messiah complex. He variously attempted to fashion himself as a great sage in the Chinese tradition and as a great spiritual leader like Jesus Christ or Gandhi. He did not, however, attempt to adopt Christianity as the state religion of China, as the fourth-century emperor Constantine did for the Roman Empire; neither did he actively proselytize as his wife did. Chiang did succeed in creating a personal cult, with Madame Chiang as chief acolyte and a minor deity in her own right.

Ultimately we cannot know the authenticity of Madame Chiang's religious beliefs or those of her husband. It is safe to say that many of their actions ran diametrically counter to the tenets of Christianity. It is difficult to see how corruption, police-state repression, and "reeducation" camps combined with wholesale arrests, disappearances, torture, and execution of political dissidents in the name of defending the nation against communism can be consistent with the teachings of the figure to whom Chiang ostensibly looked as his greatest inspiration in life.

Madame Chiang's intensifying religiosity may have been an attempt to mask, deflect, or compensate for deeper psychic ills. The more passionately and often she expressed her Christian beliefs, the more one is tempted to wonder whether "the lady doth protest too much." It is not entirely clear whether her constellation of recurring and mysterious health problems may have been a result of her personality conflicts or if the health problems may have helped shape her personality. She was clearly preoccupied with her health to an inordinate degree, and over the course of her long life suffered from a dizzying array of illnesses, conditions, and symptoms, for which she consulted innumerable doctors and tried countless treatments and medications. Hypochondria is a tempting diagnosis, but probably inaccurate. Her health problems appear to have been quite real; whether they also had a psychosomatic component is open to question.

It is evident that Madame Chiang had a textbook case of narcissism, with many of the classic traits, including haughtiness; grandiosity; a need for admiration and adulation; a sense of entitlement; unreasonable expectations of favored treatment; an insistence on unquestioning compliance with demands; and extreme sensitivity to even the slightest criticism, combined with a tendency to lash out in defiant counterattack. Like Madame Chiang, narcissists are often highly seductive and manipulative, tend to be charismatic and charming, and are often high achievers.

She appeared to have been chastened, at least temporarily, by the demise of her husband's regime on the Chinese mainland, but her grandiosity and sense of entitlement grew unabated. This was clearly manifested in her belief that she was a great painter. Taking up the palette at midlife, by dint of application she became an accomplished amateur painter, for which she was duly lauded. It is unlikely, though, that other amateur Taiwanese painters, however talented, could have had their works minted into postage stamps, as were Madame Chiang's.

What is not clear is whether Madame Chiang's narcissism occurred in association with, or even as a result of, other conditions. Narcissism is often linked to such psychological disorders as manic depression (bipolar disorder)—of which she showed symptoms—and can be brought on by chronic substance abuse. Many of her symptoms were consistent with drug addiction. Indeed, on several occasions, Madame Chiang confided to friends that she was unable to sleep without sleeping medications, and it is true that one of her chronic complaints over the decades was insomnia—which itself is often the result of a high tolerance built up by an overuse of sleeping medications. While she was undergoing medical treatment in New York from December 1942 to May 1943, one of the drugs she was prescribed to take several times daily was the sleeping medication chloral hydrate, best known today as the "date rape" drug. This drug, itself highly habit-forming, was also sometimes administered to ease withdrawal from heroin and other addictive drugs. Even at normal doses, however, it causes gastrointestinal distress—another of Madame Chiang's chronic complaints. In the 1800s there were many chloral hydrate addicts, including the English poet and painter Dante Gabriel Rossetti and the German philosopher Friedrich Nietzsche.

It appears likely that Madame Chiang was at least an episodic if not a chronic substance abuser, which would help to explain the need for a series of mysterious—and mysteriously lengthy—inpatient hospital stays and periods of seclusion under medical treatment that she underwent from the 1930s into the 1950s. Another hint may be found in decrypted U.S.-based Soviet spy communications, in which Madame Chiang is alleged to be a "narcotics addict" in a July 19, 1943, report to Moscow. Given her history of depressive spells interspersed with periods of intense activity dating back to her late teens, it may be that Madame Chiang's medication use began as an attempt to self-medicate her psychological issues—probably bipolar disorder—only for the "cure" to become a problem in itself.

As for Madame Chiang's persistent recurring skin rashes, diagnosed variously as chronic or acute urticaria (hives), they were indeed very real and debilitating. Urticaria is one of the most excruciating dermatological conditions, and may have been a contributing factor in the bouts of depression and anxiety that she was prone to. In turn, it is thought that stress and other psychological factors can play a role in bringing on hives. Urticaria can be caused by many things, including infections, autoimmune disorders, antibiotics, and shellfish, and the cause is not always identifiable; it can be a reaction to use or abuse of certain medications, especially in people prone to allergies. One article in a medical journal argues that in the case of acute urticaria, "medication use is often the culprit." The article further states that opiates "have been shown to induce or exacerbate urticaria."

Madame Chiang was also repeatedly diagnosed with and treated for what was variously described as "nervous fatigue," "nervous breakdown," "nervous collapse," or neurasthenia, a fashionable late-nineteenth-century diagnosis that was still in use into the mid-twentieth century. An important pre-Freudian psychological concept once known as a "disease of the affluent," neurasthenia was based on the now discredited premise that every human being had a fixed amount of nervous energy that was thought to drive the electrically powered nervous system. A breakdown in the system was characterized by tiredness, weakness, lethargy, and dyspepsia, and was difficult to treat. The modern-day equivalent of neurasthenia is the condition known as chronic fatigue syndrome, which is sometimes regarded as a psychological disorder and is often associated with depression, bipolar disorder, or chronic infection.

In the absence of her medical records, it is difficult to know the exact nature of Madame Chiang's health problems. It is possible that even if those records were accessible, her problems might still be unclear, as even the many eminent doctors whom she consulted were unable to fully resolve her manifold health issues. Understanding and diagnosis of mental illness and addiction were in their infancy in the 1930s through the 1960s. Treatments were largely experimental, and often made problems worse. At the very least, this exploration shows that Madame Chiang, however unlikely it may seem in view of her longevity and formidable persona, was a physically, psychologically, and emotionally fragile woman. Despite her struggles with debilitating illnesses, both physical and psychological, her achievements and contributions were tremendous. In this respect she can be seen as a sympathetic and human figure, and even admired for her tenacity and perseverance. She may serve as inspiration for those who suffer from psychological disorders, particularly in Chinese culture, where there is little awareness or understanding of mental illness and addiction, and the stigma and shame attached to these conditions remain enormous.

Today, a generation of Chinese *liuxuesheng*, or students studying abroad, are sojourning in America, just as privileged Chinese students did a century ago. What of their American experience will these future leaders of government, business, and society carry back to China, and how will they use that experience? In the late nineteenth and early twentieth centuries, returned Chinese students, despite their minuscule numbers relative to the Chinese population, wrought immense changes in their homeland. What values, beliefs, and ideals—or even animosities—will the generation of Chinese studying in America today infuse into the China of tomorrow?

Will this generation of returning students have the idealism and hope for the future of China that many of their intellectual antecedents from all points on the political spectrum had—those who helped foment revolution and tried to free China from foreign oppression, bring their homeland into the modern age, and help the voiceless legions of poor? These were the reformers of the May Fourth movement, the idealists among Sun Yat-sen's followers, and the romantics of the Chinese Communist party in its earlier days.

Or will the *liuxuesheng* of today follow the path of other returned students in the decades after the 1911 revolution? Will they become classist, clan-oriented, corrupt, and cynical, besotted with getting rich in the new capitalist-with-Chinese-characteristics China, seeking only to secure their own position and that of their clan? Will they speak beautifully of democracy in Harvard-accented English, but practice a one-party capitalist dictatorship disconcertingly reminiscent of Kuomintang rule? Will they, as Madame Chiang evidently did, adopt the attitude (to paraphrase the literary prophet George Orwell) "We are all Chinese, but some of us are more Chinese than others"?

Madame Chiang's life serves as an object lesson for Americans as much as for Chinese. Americans, then as now, tend to be easily enraptured by personality and readily beguiled by the illusion of American-style "friendliness" and superficial familiarity with the American argot and the lexicon of "American values." Americans love to manufacture heroes, and are invariably terribly disappointed when they turn out to be human beings. This was certainly true in the case of Madame Chiang Kai-shek.

A key component of Madame Chiang's historical legacy is surely the fact that she used her understanding of the American mind to help keep Taiwan positioned as the "knot" in the Sino-U.S. relationship. But she may never have fully appreciated the ambiguity of the American role on Taiwan in the second half of the twentieth century. While the U.S. government was very much complicit in Chiang Kai-shek's repressive regime, particularly in its early decades on the island, Washington quietly promoted political reform on Taiwan and is in some measure responsible for its peaceful transition to genuine democracy. Since 1950 Taiwan has evolved from a showcase for American aid into a showcase for American nation-building prowess into, finally, a showcase for American-inspired democracy. In the ties between the world's only superpower and its leading potential challenger, Taiwan of course remains the "knot."

For women, Madame Chiang's legacy is ambiguous, with attributes both admirable and troubling. She called herself a feminist long before the notion became fashionable. With her husband she was chosen "Man and Wife of the Year" by *Time* magazine in 1937. She is one of only four women—the others being Wallis Simpson, Queen Elizabeth II, and Corazon Aquino—to be so recognized since 1927, when the annual anointment began as "Man of the Year." She was only the second woman in history to address the United States Congress, and the first woman of color.

Whatever her shortcomings, personal or political, women will inevitably look to Madame Chiang Kai-shek as a role model—albeit not without reservations—simply by virtue of the fact that there have been so few female world leaders. Any women in history who overcame obstacles to achieve international prominence will serve as trailblazers—as well as object lessons in what not to do. Nearly all members of this tiny club achieved their positions through birth or marriage and Madame Chiang was no exception. But unlike the others, she tried to take on a mantle that transcended national boundaries. It is perhaps easy to underestimate the depth of ambition, vision, and audacity required to attempt the task of imagining herself as a world figure, and to conclude that what China needed was a female ambassador to the West. In this respect her achievement was unprecedented.

There is no doubt that Madame Chiang was a deeply flawed heroine. Yet even as she is remembered with ambivalence, she is admired for her courage, indomitable spirit, passion for life—and utter imperviousness to change. She was that rare creature who stuck resolutely to her beliefs, however misguided some of them may have been, through the decades and the trials. And she was ultimately vindicated in at least one respect. After having spent more than half a century bitterly condemning communism, she lived to see the fall of the Berlin Wall, followed by the collapse of the Soviet Union. She witnessed China's abandonment of socialism in all but name, and the decisive repudiation of communism as the bankrupt ideology she had long insisted it was.

The story of Madame Chiang Kai-shek is in the end a tragic one—not because she was humiliatingly tossed from her exalted pedestal as First Lady of China; not because much of her public persona was a masquerade; but because she failed in the rare opportunity that she was given to transform her country. She began by being part of the solution to China's ills but, sadly, ended up being part of the problem.

When Americans saw her, they saw neither the real China nor the real Madame Chiang Kai-shek, so inevitably their perceptions were riddled with false beliefs. Thus is her life ultimately a metaphor for the great century-long misunderstanding between the United States and China, and the uneasy ambivalence that persists in the relationship today.

Notes

NOTES FOR CHAPTER ONE

5   *What is natural to woman:* Wilson, 4. *Mayling Soong was born:* The year of Mayling Soong's birth is in dispute. It is agreed that her birth date was the twelfth day of the second month of the Chinese lunar calendar, which corresponds to sometime in February or March, depending on the year, according to the Gregorian calendar used in the West. In the absence of documentary evidence, it is unclear if she was born in 1897, 1898, or 1899, as has variously been claimed. There is evidence to support and contradict each claim. *Sink of iniquity:* quoted in Couling, 517.

6   *Higher and a better civilization:* Wilson, 2–3. *Playful Soong children:* Hahn, *The Soong Sisters,* 27–28. *Soong's American eccentricities:* Ibid., 28–29.

7   *You upstart, you!:* quoted in Burke, 32–33.

8   *I must ask God:* MCKS, "I Confess My Faith." Methodist Church pamphlet, mid-1930s. Wesleyan. *Excessively pious:* MCKS, "The Power of Prayer," *Reader's Digest,* Aug 1955. *Conveniently thirsty:* MCKS, "I Confess My Faith." Wesleyan. *First girls' primary schools established in 1907:* Bays, 215.

9   *Women's education critical to spreading gospel:* Ibid., 228. *Degrading systems:* quoted in Bays, 211. *Missionaries subversive:* Fairbank, *Missionary Enterprise,* 2. *Girls' schools challenged Confucianism:* Bays, 228–30. *Missionaries contributed to China's great revolution:* Fairbank, *Missionary Enterprise,* 2–3. *Mother Soong's studies:* MCKS, "Message on the Mayling Soong Foundation," ca. 1942. President's Office, Chiang, Mayling Soong. WCA.

10   *Gospel of gentility:* quoted in Bays, 211–12. *Idealized vision:* Ibid., 228–29. *Mayling at McTyeire:* Hahn, *Soong Sisters,* 44–46. *Little Lantern:* Ibid., 41.

NOTES FOR CHAPTER TWO

11   *They have borne the light:* *Go Forward,* February 1909, 17. Tuan Fang made the remarks in New York on 2 February 1906.

12   *Soong's parents:* Lin Shiluan, 1116. His mother died in 1917. *Soong's adoption:* Ibid.

13   *Penguins:* Epstein, *Woman in World History,* 14. *China cannot borrow:* *New York Times,* 23 Jul 1881.

14   *B. C. Wan and S. C. New:* Box 1, Chinese Educational Mission Papers; Thesis: Chris Robyn, "Building the Bridge: The Chinese Educational Mission to the United States: A Sino-American Historico-Cultural Synthesis, 1872–1881," 1996, Appendix 0, 156. CHS. *Soong on the* **Gallatin***:* Ensign Arthur Tourtellot, "C. J. Soong and the US Coast Guard," U.S. Naval Institute Proceedings, Feb 1949, 201–3. 28b: Charlie Soong.

Webb Papers. UNC. *"My little friend Harrie":* unidentified newspaper article, 28b: Charlie Soong. Webb Papers. UNC. *Coast Guard records:* US Coast Guard to George Sokolsky, 6 Jun 1933. 267/3, Sokolsky Papers. Hoover. *Revival meeting:* Letter to the editor, *North Carolina Christian Advocate,* 19 Dec 1995, 3.

15   *Honorable discharge:* D. Osborn Bettencourt, "The Gallatin." *Dukes County Intelligencer,* Nov 1970. *Send him up:* Powell, 330–31. *Description of Carr:* Webb, 104; Powell, 330–31. *Listen, brethren:* Julian S. Carr, sermon, 1889, #141, Folder 33, Carr Papers. UNC. *He came to my house:* quoted in "General Carr and the Education of Charlie Soong," Costen J. Harrell, *General Julian S. Carr: Greathearted Citizen.* Durham, North Carolina, Seeman Printery Inc., 1946.

16   *Great hurry:* quoted in Burke, 8–9. *China was the lodestar:* quoted in Fairbank, *Missionary Enterprise,* 356. *Missionary statesmen:* Fairbank, *Missionary Enterprise,* 63. *Manifest Destiny:* Ibid., 356. *How can we better:* quoted in Fairbank, *Missionary Enterprise,* 347.

17   *Especially commissioned:* Fairbank, *Missionary Enterprise,* 353–54. *Big business:* Ibid., 8, 61–62. *Moral and cultural superiority:* Ibid., 7. *Leave them alone:* Mark Twain, "The United States of Lyncherdom," 1901. http://etext.lib.virginia.edu/railton/enam482e/lyncherdom.html.

18   *Cherokee Indians at Trinity:* Webb, 125. *Was doing very well . . . idols of heathenism:* Durham District Conference Minutes, 1885–1895, North Carolina Conference, Methodist Episcopal Church, South. Charles Soong Collection. Duke (Archives).

19   *We thought better:* McTyeire to Allen, 8 Jul 1885. Allen Papers, Box 15/5. Emory. *Brightest . . . Chinaman:* R. A. Young to Allen, 18 Aug 1885. Box 15/5, Allen Papers. Emory. *Denationalized Chinaman:* quoted in Burke, 34. "Located" meant assigned to a fixed parish, as opposed to preaching from town to town as a "circuit rider."

20   *I felt more homelike in America:* Soong to Annie Southgate, 14 Jun 1886. Charles Soong Papers. Duke. *Intellectual approach:* Fairbank, *Missionary Enterprise,* 165. Burke, 34–35. *Description of Allen:* Burke, 34–35; Emory University press release, "Jin Professorship Honors Emory/China Connection," 24 Mar 2000; "A Missionary Memorialized," *Oxford Outlook,* Spring 1998, Oxford College, Emory. www.geocities.com/heartland/plains/8692/youngj.html. *He hated very much:* Allen to R. A. Young, 25 Jan 1886. Box 15/5, Allen Papers. Emory.

21   *A great work is before you:* Allen to Soong, 20 Jan 1886. Box 15/5, Allen Papers. Emory. *Ignores my privileges:* Soong to Annie Southgate, 14 Jun 1886. Charles Soong Papers. Duke. *Sent to Kunshan:* Burke, 36; Soong to James Southgate, 4 Feb 1887. Charles Soong Papers. Duke. *Her parents' favorite:* *Who's Who in China 1931;* Hahn, 22–23. *Soong's wedding:* Lin Bowen, 27.

22   *Asked to be located:* Clark, 30. *Soong's business ventures:* Hahn, *Soong Sisters,* 24; Couling, 124.

23   *Sun sought to enlist Triads in revolution:* Schiffrin, 357.

24   *Worked day and night:* Hahn, *Soong Sisters,* 22–23.

NOTES FOR CHAPTER THREE

25   *Now is the time:* quoted in Fairbank, *Missionary Enterprise,* 357.

27   *Roosevelt apologized:* Hahn, *Soong Sisters,* 49. *Immoral, degraded and worthless race:* quoted in McClellan, 70. *Then I don't want to be a doctor:* quoted in Hahn, *Soong Sisters,* 50. *Mayling in sailor suit:* photo from *Summit Herald,* 21 May 1942. *Mayling's*

Summit playmate: "Fell Flat on Face Dancing, Wrote Mme. Chang [sic] to Chum," *Brooklyn Eagle,* 9 Mar 1942.

28   *Blindman's buff:* Articles, Mygatt. *Reading habits of Mayling and Ching Ling: Summit Herald,* 21 May 1942. *Yesterday I nearly drowned:* Mayling Soong to Emmie Donner, 8 Jul 1908. Reproduced in Articles, Mygatt. *Friend Francis Moulton:* Articles, Mygatt. *Not admitted to public schools: Christian Science Monitor,* 10 Apr 1943. *Mrs. Burks:* Articles, Thomson.

29   *Pardon me, I am a southerner:* quoted in Articles, Thomson. *China-painted:* Ibid. *She will never learn:* "Amazing Life of Madame Chiang," *Macon Telegraph,* 26 Jun 1943. *Silk dresses:* "Chapel Hill Man Knew China's Famous First Lady in School," Durham, N.C., *Herald-Sun,* 13 Dec 1942.

30   *Mayling's studies at Piedmont:* Mary C. Lane, Piedmont College Archivist, to author, 29 Oct 2001. *The cultured hostess:* Piedmont College Catalogue, 1909–1910, p. 36. *Always smiling:* "Atlantan Recalls Madame Chiang as Girl," unidentified newspaper, ca. Jun 1943. Piedmont. *All these people:* MCKS to George C. Bellingrath, 30 Jun 1938. *The Piedmont Announcements,* Sep 1938. Piedmont. *The beauty of forgiveness:* Articles, Ainsworth.

31   *Prayed to the Lord to let her pass:* Ibid. *I do not wish to play:* "Before Meeting Mme. Chiang Kai-shek," *Worcester Sunday Telegram,* 7 Mar 1943. *The big girls had secrets:* Hahn, *The Soong Sisters,* 52. *Romantic little souls:* Articles, Ainsworth. *The Tri-Puellates:* Ibid.

32   *A campus newsletter:* Hahn, *The Soong Sisters,* 54. *Full of pep:* "Social Sidelights," *Macon Telegraph,* 25 Jun 1943. *Not embarrassed:* Articles, Ainsworth. *Sergeant-at-arms:* Ibid. *The Billy Crows:* Clark, 52. *Proud of her intellectual abilities:* Hahn, *The Soong Sisters,* 55. *Mayling's taste for big words:* Ibid., 52. *Good bye, Macon:* "Amazing Life of Madame Chiang," *Macon Telegraph,* 26 Jun 1943.

NOTES FOR CHAPTER FOUR

34   *The Higher Education of Women:* "Notes of Mr. Durant's Sermon on 'The Spirit of the College,'" Boston, Frank Wood, Printer, 1890. *I am Southern:* Articles, Reinhardt. *Hot confederate:* Mayling Soong to EDM, 18 Aug 1919. Mills Papers. WCA. *Well, I reckon:* Articles, Harrington.

35   *Heroines of their own lives:* Nora Ephron, Wellesley Commencement Address, 1996. www. Wellesley.edu/publicaffairs/commencement/1996/speechesnephron.html. *Senior Prom:* Hackett, 192–93.

36   *Pacifist movement:* Ibid., 191. *Relief funds:* Ibid., 197. *She kept up an awful thinking:* Articles, Tuell. *Perhaps I:* MCKS, *The Sure Victory,* MCKS, 11–12. *Quiet amusement:* Mary O'Leary, "Recall College Career of Mme. Chiang Kai-shek." Worcester *Evening Gazette,* 17 Aug 1937.

37   *Tuell's observations of Mayling's character:* Articles, Tuell. *She would work good and hard:* "Mayling Soong Chiang" manuscript, 10. Box 7: MCKS. Hull Papers. Columbia. *Cross as a bear:* Mayling Soong to EDM, 10 Aug 1921. Mills Papers. WCA. *Mayling joins Tizzie:* Article 1, Section 2 of the TZE Constitution. Courtesy Tau Zeta Epsilon Society. Wellesley. *But you don't know how to ride a bicycle:* Unidentified Los Angeles newspaper, ca. 1 Apr 1943 (n.d.). Class of 1917, Alumnae: Mayling Soong and her Classmates. WCA. *Expected by her people:* Articles, Reinhardt.

38   *Zealous desire:* Ibid. *China's contributions to civilization:* Hahn, *The Soong Sisters,* 94. *Fur coat:* Reminiscences of Tso Shun-sheng, 114. COHC. Columbia. *I can help China:*

quoted in Epstein, *Woman in World History*, 35. ***Diagnosed with Bright's disease:*** C. J. Soong to T. V. Soong, 3 May 1915, 6 Aug 1915. Folder 1, Soong Collection. Duke (Archives). ***Mayling supported Ching Ling:*** Epstein, *Woman in World History*, 209.

39   *I was never so hurt:* quoted in Burke, 265. ***Brief engagement:*** Articles, Harrington; Seagrave, 140. ***Nice Chinese boy:*** Hahn, *The Soong Sisters*, 94.

40   *The only thing oriental about me is my face:* Ibid., 95. ***Golden fleece:*** Class of 1917 yearbook, *Legenda* 1917. ***Marched forth:*** 1917 graduation materials, Class of 1917, Box 1: General (of Students): 1915–1917. WCA.

NOTES FOR CHAPTER FIVE

41   *The profession of marriage:* Mayling Soong to EDM, 25 May 1919. Mills Papers. WCA. *If ever I have any influence:* Mayling Soong to EDM, 4 Jul 1917. Mills Papers.

42   *If God lets Shanghai endure:* quoted in Dong, 1.

43   *Head servant of servants:* Dong, 35. ***Foreigner's fart:*** Fenby, 134. ***Shanghai house:*** Mayling Soong to EDM, 7 Aug 1917. ***Shared floor with T. V.:*** Mayling Soong to EDM, 12 Nov 1917. *I have complete control:* Mayling Soong to EDM, 7 Aug 1917. ***Called her sir:*** Mayling to EDM, 28 Sep 1917. ***We have five maids:*** Mayling Soong to EDM, 7 Aug 1917.

44   *Terribly strict:* Mayling Soong to EDM, 21 Mar 1920. ***Too embarrassing:*** Mayling Soong to EDM, 10 Aug 1921. ***It seems very queer:*** Mayling Soong to EDM, 7 Aug 1917. ***Foreign devils:*** Mayling Soong to EDM, 15 Dec 1917. ***Things Oriental:*** Ibid. *The Oriental mind:* Mayling Soong to EDM, 28 Dec 1917.

45   *These servants simply don't know how to clean:* Hahn, *The Soong Sisters*, 106–7. ***Years in democratic America:*** Mayling Soong to EDM, 28 Sep 1917. ***We actually bought:*** Mayling Soong to EDM, 11 Oct 1917. ***Gone native:*** Dong, 34. ***Talk of the town:*** Articles, Sokolsky.

46   *Nora an inspiration:* Dong, 147. *I like them:* Mayling Soong to EDM, 7 Aug 1917.

47   *The way the family scorns him:* Mayling Soong to EDM, 16 Aug 1917. ***Met my fate:*** Ibid. *Strictly chaperoned:* Mayling Soong to EDM, 15 Sep 1917. ***Semi-intellectual confabs:*** Mayling Soong to EDM, 13 Jan 1918. *I just feel my mental powers:* Mayling Soong to EDM, 15 Sep 1917. ***Eagerly awaited:*** Mayling Soong to EDM, 16 Aug 1917. ***Respectable jobs for women virtually nonexistent:*** Dong, 146–47. *The life I am leading:* Mayling Soong to EDM, 26 Oct 1917.

48   *As a human being:* Mayling Soong to EDM, 13 Feb 1918. ***He is very clever:*** Mayling Soong to EDM, 12 Nov 1917. ***Too much mushy love-making:*** Mayling Soong to EDM, 7 Dec 1917. ***Would you like to be found:*** Mayling Soong to EDM, 8 Feb 1918. ***Scared to death:*** Mayling Soong to EDM, 7 Dec 1917.

49   *Hypodermic treatment:* Mayling Soong to EDM, 26 Oct 1917. ***Cried out of pure nervousness:*** Mayling Soong to EDM, 4 Nov 1917. ***Much bepowdered:*** Mayling Soong to EDM, 12 Nov 1917. *I am seized with:* Mayling Soong to EDM, 7 Dec 1917. ***Dada, I don't know:*** Mayling Soong to EDM, 13 Jan 1918. *I shall never marry without money:* Mayling Soong to EDM, 31 Jan 1918.

50   *Reading aloud:* Sophie C. Hart, "Wellesley Women in China," *Wellesley Quarterly*, Jan 1919. *I have such a hot temper:* Mayling Soong to EDM, 19 Mar 1918. ***Sending her off:*** Mayling Soong to EDM, 11 Apr 1918. *I lie awake nights:* Mayling Soong to EDM, n.d. *Awful row:* Mayling Soong to EDM, 19 Mar 1918. ***As I am anxious:*** Mayling Soong to EDM, 13 Feb 1918. ***Sweated:*** Mayling Soong to EDM, received 28 May 1918. *I believe in prayer:* Mayling Soong to EDM, 29 Apr 1918.

51   *I am going almost crazy:* Mayling Soong to EDM, received 28 May 1918. *Prayer room:* "Today's Talk," George Matthew Adams, *Houston Chronicle,* 16 Apr 1943. *You know how my family feels:* Mayling Soong to EDM, n.d. *He understands:* Mayling Soong to EDM, 29 Jun 1918.

52   *I rather like the work:* Mayling Soong to EDM, 6 Mar 1918. *Shanghai's evils:* Mayling Soong to EDM, 15 Aug 1918. *So much misery everywhere:* Mayling Soong to EDM, 7 Dec 1917. *I do hate:* Mayling Soong to EDM, 24 Aug 1918. *Mental exercise:* Mayling Soong to EDM, 21 Sept 1918.

53   *Paint poison:* Mayling Soong to EDM, 20 Sep 1918. *Buick hit a child:* Mayling Soong to EDM, 19 Oct 1918. *Visited Tianjin:* Mayling Soong to EDM, 14 Nov 1918. *I go to the managers:* Mayling Soong to EDM, postmarked 7 Dec 1918.

54   *Rottenest sermons:* Mayling Soong to EDM, 7 Jan 1919. *Chinese politics is impossible:* Mayling Soong to EDM, 7 Dec 1917.

55   *What our government:* Mayling Soong to EDM, 6 Mar 1919. *Might is Right:* Mayling Soong to EDM, 6 Mar 1919. *Intellectual revolution:* Chow, 359.

56   *I feel that this boycott:* Mayling Soong to EDM, 5 Jun 1919. *Even I:* Mayling Soong to EDM, 15 Jun 1919. *Hysterical letter:* Mayling Soong to EDM, 9 Apr 1919.

57   *The profession of marriage:* Mayling Soong to EDM, 25 May 1919. *The question of sex:* Mayling Soong to EDM, 9 Jul 1919. *I am dreadfully bored:* Mayling Soong to EDM, 24 Jul 1919. *Jeanette born:* Mayling Soong to EDM, 9 Sep 1919.

58   *My circle of friends:* Mayling Soong to EDM, 18 Nov 1919. *The Celestials:* Mayling Soong to EDM, 24 Jul 1919. *Tommyrot:* Mayling Soong to EDM, 9 Sep 1919. *I think I am:* Mayling Soong to EDM, 5 Sep 1920.

59   *Friends are very nice:* Mayling Soong to EDM, 11 Oct 1920. *Climbing rocky hill paths:* Mayling Soong to EDM, 28 Feb 1921.

60   *If I really had something:* Mayling Soong to EDM, 28 Apr 1921. *Vibrant joy:* Ibid. *I cannot seem to get away:* Mayling Soong to EDM, 28 Apr 1921. *Frantic telegrams:* Mayling Soong to EDM, 21 Apr 1921, 25 May 1921. *We had a beautiful time:* Mayling Soong to EDM, 25 May 1921. *I am too darned independent:* Mayling Soong to EDM, 6 Jul 1921.

61   *Silk factories:* Rose Hum Lee, "Madame Chiang's Children," *Survey Graphic,* Apr 1943. *Reflected glory:* Mayling Soong to ?, 11 Jun 1922. Mills Papers. WCA. *Liu appeared embarrassed:* Thomas Lu Keng, interview with author, 27 Jan 1998. See also Wang Fong, *Soong Meiling,* 194–99.

NOTES FOR CHAPTER SIX

63   *Here was my opportunity:* Articles, Chiang. *Wild and ungovernable:* Loh, 32. Loh's book is a psychological study of Chiang as a young man.

64   *Chiang's psychosomatic dysfunction:* Loh, 32. *Abandoned himself:* Loh, 24. *Madame Yao:* Lin Bowen, 83–84. *Brains of Sun's movement:* George Sokolsky, 29–30, OHRO. Columbia.

65   *You have a fiery temper:* quoted in Loh, 35. *Unsuitable for society:* quoted in Loh, 44. *I am given to lust:* quoted in Loh, 32. *Taken advantage:* Loh, 38. *Few social acquaintances:* Loh, 44–45. *Whenever you are despondent:* quoted in Loh, 39. *My nature will be purified:* quoted in Loh, 62. *A glorious stature:* quoted in Loh, 62. *Attempted seduction:* Chen, 15–16. This detail of Chen's account is impossible to verify. Although the book contains errors in dates and historical events, her account is regarded as essentially

true. *Undying love:* Chen, 33. *Date of Chiang's marriage to Jennie Chen:* Chen, 38. *Zhang served as master of ceremonies at Chiang's wedding:* Chen, 38.

66   *Sapling caught in a typhoon:* Chen, 59. *Jennie left infertile:* Chen, 83–85. *Past transgressions:* quoted in Loh, 64. *Kaleidoscopic patchwork:* Jordan, x. *Sun opposed Communism:* Jacobs, 112. *When a man is drowning:* Asie/Chine/538, 129. Archives Diplomatiques. *National bourgeois revolution:* Jordan, 45–46; Jacobs, 147. *Sun finds a Lafayette:* Jacobs, 126.

67   *Borodin on human nature:* "Personal Observations of Chiang Kai-shek: 1926–1945." Box 87, Folder: "United Forces China Theater: China —Politics and Government, General." Wedemeyer Papers. Hoover. *Borodin's mission:* Ibid. *Genius:* Jacobs, 145.

68   *You have shown us the path:* Jacobs, 132. *Jennie became Chiang's secretary:* Chen, 168–69. *Chiang a moody, tempestuous soul:* Gannett, 28–31. *Chiang humiliated soldiers:* Chen, 155. *A series of tantrums and shoutings:* Chen, 167. *Carcass of a horse:* W. H. Donald to Harold K. Hochschild, 21 Nov 1924. Hochschild Papers. Columbia. *Chiang proposed to Ching Ling:* Snow, 85.

69   *Jennie adopted a baby girl:* Chen, xxiii. *Ching-kuo to Moscow:* Taylor, 25–33. *Catalytic charisma:* Jordan, 6. *Ningpo Napoleon:* Chiang was not in fact from Ningpo, a region near Shanghai.

70   *Red General:* Jordan, 33. *Soviet report on Chiang's character:* WO 208/182, May 1926. TNA. *First meeting:* Lin, 83.

71   *Chiang made the revolution stick:* Articles, Sokolsky. *Strutted like a peacock:* Chen, 186. *You must be sensible:* quoted in Chen, 186–87. *Only a middle-class housewife:* Ibid., 190. *But a bad temper:* Ibid., 191.

72   *David Kung accompanied Chiang:* Hahn, *The Soong Sisters,* 129. *Mayling strikes up correspondence with Chiang:* Chen, 209. *Dear Big Brother:* quoted in Chen, 216. *Sun insisted:* Jacobs, 112. *Mayling Darling:* quoted in Hahn, *Chiang Kai-shek,* 87.

73   *Borodin description:* MCKS, *Conversations with Mikhail Borodin,* 6–9. *Borodin's sermonizing:* Ibid.

74   *Très intrigante:* 12 Fév 1927, 128. Serie: Asie 1918–1940. Sous-serie: Chine, Vol. 193. Archives Diplomatiques. *Eling's bargain:* Chen, 236–38. *Political marriage:* Ibid., 237–42. *Look at you constantly:* quoted in Chen, 41–42. *Longing for Little Sister May:* Articles, Chen, *Aiji,* 4.

75   *Squeezed lemon:* quoted in Jordan, 123. *Party purification:* Jordan, 123. *Betrayal:* Ibid., 123–24. *Down with the traitor:* *Time,* Apr 1927, 25. *I do not know you:* quoted in Taylor, 42. *Chiang's reaction:* Taylor, 44. *Armed takeover:* Jordan, 136.

76   *Ching Ling denounced Chiang; Mayling dispatched to Hankow:* Epstein, *Woman in World History,* 172–73. *The only man:* quoted in Jacobs, 280. *Wet nurse to the revolution:* San Francisco News, 2. *Borodin ill:* Jacobs, 259. *KMT a toilet:* quoted in Jacobs, 200. After fleeing to Russia, Borodin edited the *Moscow Daily News,* but ultimately fell victim to Stalin's caprice and perished in the Siberian gulag in 1951. He was posthumously rehabilitated under Khrushchev. *Neither traitor nor fence-sitter:* quoted in Epstein, *Woman in World History,* 197. *Cancerous force:* Epstein, *Woman in World History,* 198. [Soong Ching Ling, *Struggle for New China,* Beijing, Foreign Languages Press, 1952, 8–11.]

77   *Revolution is inevitable:* "Madame Sun's withdrawal," *Nation,* 21 Sep 1927. *Enhance his greatness:* *NYT,* 16 Aug 1927. *May the Great Buddha smite me:* Chen, 251–53. *Madame Chiang Speaks:* San Francisco Chronicle, 9 Sep 1927.

78   *Chiang denies having wife:* Washington Star, 20 Sep 1927. *Mayling confirms engagement:* San Francisco Chronicle, 22 Sep 1927; AP, Shanghai, 21 Sep 1927. *I am very excited:*

quoted in Articles, Chen, *Aiji*, 4. **Liu Jiwen:** Liu's previous interest in Mayling apparently did not earn him Chiang Kai-shek's enmity. He embarked on a distinguished political career. In 1927 Chiang appointed Liu mayor of Nanking, a plum post in the new national capital. In 1929 he was elected to the Central Executive Committee, the Kuomintang's highest governing body. In 1930 he began a stint as superintendent of customs in Shanghai. In 1932 he was appointed mayor of Canton, where he served for four years, subsequently becoming a vice minister in the Ministry of Audit. He went to Taiwan in the late 1940s with the Kuomintang. In 1956 he flew to the United States to seek treatment for cancer, and died there the following year. **Mother Soong refused to see Chiang:** Hahn, *The Soong Sisters*, 138. **Outstanding warrants:** C. E. Gauss to J. V. A. MacMurray, 29 Nov 1926, "Criminal Record of Chiang Kai-shek." RG 59, CDF (1910–29), M-329, Roll #56, Frames 495–96. NARA.

79   **Chiang declares he divorced first wife in 1921:** *Shen Bao*, 2 Oct 1927, A14. Oddly, the original printing of the letter in *Shen Bao* could not be located. At that time in China, a man could divorce his wife simply by publishing an announcement to that effect. A woman, however, had to prove abandonment, cruelty, or the like, and the father invariably received custody of children regardless of the circumstances. Ironically, Mayling later helped to pass laws affording married women greater legal protection. **Chiang obtains permission:** Hahn, *The Soong Sisters*, 138–39; *Shen Bao*, 6 Oct 1927, A5. **Chemistry:** George Sokolsky, 21–22, OHRO. Columbia. Articles, Sokolsky. **Rather dead than wed:** quoted in Epstein, *Woman in World History*, 209. **Marriage of opportunism:** quoted in Snow, *Journey*, 85. **Joan of Arc:** Snow, *Journey*, 91. **Could it not be:** Snow, *Journey*, 85–86.

80   **No marriage after divorce:** Burke, 343. **Fifteen hundred invitations:** *Shen Bao*, 30 Nov 1927, A14. **Chiang's wedding statement:** *Shen Bao*, 1 Dec 1927.

81   **Bitter ridicule:** Reverend Timothy Tingfang Lew, *North Carolina Christian Advocate*, 6 May 1943, 7. **Chiang appeared uncomfortable:** Smith, Whitey, 51–52. **Description of wedding:** *North-China Daily News, Shanghai Times, China Press, North-China Herald, South China Morning Post*, 2 Dec 1927; also Smith, Whitey, 51–52.

82   **Wedding movie in theatres:** *Shen Bao*, 2 Dec 1927, A1; 4 Dec 1927, A3. **Pagan idols:** Oursler, 351–52. **Chiang a heroic figure:** Articles, Sokolsky. **Here was my opportunity:** Articles, MCKS.

NOTES FOR CHAPTER SEVEN

85   **I have the greatest blessings:** Mayling Soong Chiang to Sophie Chantal Hart, 17 Jan 1934, Class of 1917: MCKS Correspondence (n.d.) 1916–80. WCA. **Honeymoon cut short:** Hahn, *The Soong Sisters*, 143. **Tea party:** Jeffrey Stuart Abrams. "James Marshall McHugh: An American Encounter With Chiang Kai-shek, 1937–1942," 4. McHugh Papers, Cornell.

86   **Chiang in love:** James McHugh, unpublished CKS memoir, Chapter 1, page 3. McHugh Papers, Cornell. **Claimed to represent China:** Eastman, *Abortive Revolution*, 271–72. **Bled the Kuomintang:** Eastman, 7–8. **Nanking's ancient, crumbling glory:** Hahn, *The Soong Sisters*, 143. **Nanking a village:** W. H. Donald to Emily Hahn, n.d. Hahn Mss, Box 6: 1939–1953: Soong Sisters Correspondence, Hahn Papers. Indiana University. **Strolling site:** Hahn, *Chiang Kai-shek*, 137.

87   **First Couple's love cottage:** "Former Residence of Chiang Kai-shek," *Shanghai Star*, 3 Jul 2002. The Chiangs' former love nest is now part of the Shanghai Conservatory of

Music on Dongping Road. They later acquired other residences. One, at Guling (Kuling, at Lushan)—a summer retreat high above the Yangtze settled by the English in the nineteenth century—was called *Mei Lu;* another, in Hangzhou, was named the *Cheng Lu.* **The only woman:** W. H. Donald to Emily Hahn, n.d. Box 6: 1939–1953: Soong Sisters Correspondence. Hahn Papers. Indiana. **Aunk, aunk:** George Sokolsky, 70, OHRO. Columbia. **Painful silence:** Conversation with Hu Shih and V. K. Ting, 3 Jul 1934. Johnson Papers, Box 54, 135. LOC. **Mayling retired from public eye:** George E. Sokolsky, "The First Family of China: The Soongs," *New York Times Magazine,* 15 Nov 1931. **Led hospital campaign:** *Washington Star,* 27 Apr 1928. **Officers' Moral Endeavor Association:** W. H. Donald to Emily Hahn, n.d. Box 6: 1939–1953: Soong Sisters Correspondence. Hahn Papers. Indiana. **New and creative spirit:** Nelson T. Johnson to Stanley K. Hornbeck, 25 Jun 1934. Box 23, Johnson Papers. LOC. **Huang and the OMEA:** Hahn, *The Soong Sisters,* 146–47. **Revolutionary blood:** W. H. Donald to Emily Hahn, n.d. Box 6: 1939–1953: Soong Sisters Correspondence. Hahn Papers. Indiana.

88   **Dark, dirty, pestiferous holes:** "China's First Lady Big Helpmate," *Newport News,* 15 Apr 1937. **Description of schools:** Sues, 116. **Students revere Mayling:** unidentified newspaper clipping, 31 Oct 1933. Class of 1917: MCKS, Articles about MCKS (1927–37). WCA.

89   **Mayling served as legislator: China Handbook:** *1937–43,* Chinese Ministry of Information, 1943, Macmillan. **Knowledge of things:** "Undifferentiated Optimism," speech before the American Bar Association, 28 Aug 1958. *Madame Chiang Kai-shek: Selected Speeches 1958–1959,* 46. **New family law:** *North-China Daily News,* 13 June 1931. **Kiss me, Lampson:** quoted in Hahn, *Chiang Kai-shek,* 138.

90   **Madame's favorite magazines:** Gunther, 207. **My place is at the front:** "Chinese General's Wife Is Only Woman Aide-de-Camp," *Worcester Sunday Telegram,* 3 Feb 1935. **Purely Chinese:** W. H. Donald to Emily Hahn, n.d. Box 6: 1939–1953: Soong Sisters Correspondence. Hahn Papers. Indiana. **At the front:** Mayling Soong Chiang to Sophie Chantal Hart, 17 Jan 1934. Class of 1917: MCKS Correspondence (n.d.) 1916–80. WCA; Hahn, 148. **In the dead of night:** Mayling Soong Chiang to Sophie Chantal Hart, 17 Jan 1934. Class of 1917: MCKS Correspondence (n.d.) 1916–80. WCA.

91   **I think from this:** Mayling Soong Chiang to Sophie Chantal Hart, 17 Jan 1934. Class of 1917: MCKS Correspondence (n.d.) 1916–80. WCA. **Miscarriage:** Articles, Chen, *Aiji,* 10–11.

92   **KMT killed Mao's first wife:** Spence, 405. **Powderkeg:** Eastman, *Abortive Revolution,* 275. **Considerable progress:** Eastman, *Abortive Revolution,* 271–72.

93   **We would indeed feel hopeless:** unidentified newspaper clipping, 31 Oct 1933. Class of 1917: MCKS, Articles about MCKS (1927–37). WCA. **Nanking government "Eurasian":** Samuel G. Blythe, "Complicated China," *Saturday Evening Post,* 14 Feb 1931. **Reign of terror:** Spence, 413. **Our Christian Generalissimo:** quoted in Chang, 75.

94   **Young Marshal ill with "typhoid":** Abend, 150–51.

95   **Not international policemen:** "To my Alma Mater: to America," 13 Jun 1942 speech. Mayling Soong Chiang, *We Chinese Women,* 41. **Cloak of patriotism:** MCKS, "The Crossroad: Survival or Destruction," speech delivered April 20, 1957, to Rotary Club in Taipei. **Mayling gains tremendous influence:** Clarence E. Gauss to Nelson T. Johnson, 23 Sep 1934. Box 23, Johnson Papers. LOC. **Wellesley stride:** "Wellesley in the World," Elizabeth Anne Bradstreet, n.d. Class of 1917: MCKS, Articles about MCKS (1927–37). WCA.

96   *Chiang's baptism:* "Together They Lead China," pamphlet, Hollington Tong, 1958, Public Affairs Press, Washington, D.C. Located in Wedemeyer Papers, Box 108, File: China: 1957–73. Hoover. Also "Chiang Kai-shek: Why He Became a Christian," by a "Shanghai Correspondent," 2 Dec 1930. WO 208/182. TNA.

96   *I feel the need:* "The Debt of the President of China to America," *North Carolina Christian Advocate,* 29 Jan 1931. *Methodism in his madness:* Burke, 347. *Rice Christian: New York Herald Tribune,* 26 Oct 1930. *Compared to Constantine:* "Personal Observations of Chiang Kai-shek," Box 87, Folder "United Forces China Theater: China—Politics and Government, General." Wedemeyer Papers. Hoover. *Number of Chinese Christians (in 1928):* "A Chinese Youth Looks at China," Philip Meng, *World Call,* May 1941.

97   *If he is a Christian:* Epstein, *Woman in World History,* 209. *I shall be responsible:* CKS, "Some Reflections on My Fiftieth Birthday," *Hsiung,* 373–78. *Mother would pray me through:* Articles, Chiang. *Mother, you are so powerful:* Mayling Soong Chiang, *The Sure Victory,* 10; Articles, Chiang. *Assassination attempt foiled by Mayling's dreams:* Oursler, 349–52. An attempt was made on Chiang's life on or about August 28, 1929, at the Chiangs' house at No. 9 Route Francois Garnier. It is unclear whether Mayling's dream occurred then or on another occasion. See Edwin S. Cunningham to secretary of state, 8 Nov 1929. ICP, RG 59, CDF 1910–29, M-329, Roll #86, Frames 415–21. NARA.

98   *Mother-in-law of the country:* North-China Daily News, 25 Jul 1931. *Ching Ling attended funeral:* Macon Telegraph, 18 Aug 1931. *Dark despair:* Articles, Chiang.

NOTES FOR CHAPTER EIGHT

99   *Outward beauty:* MCKS, "New Life in China," *Forum,* Jun 1935. *Down with the Soong dynasty: North-China Daily News,* 24 Jul 1931.

100 *Tzu Hsi's pearls:* Seagrave, *Dragon Lady,* 461–62. *Mayling at bottom of Yangtze:* Abend, 117. *That woman:* quoted in Hahn, *Chiang Kai-shek,* 190. *China for the Soongs:* Epstein, *Woman in World History,* 235–36; Articles, Sokolsky.

101 *It is now undeniable:* "MCKS Brings American Way to China," *Virginian-Pilot,* 21 Feb 1943. *The Chinese revolution has failed:* Eastman, *Abortive Revolution,* 1. *Inappropriate methods:* Franklin L. Ho, 291, COHP. Columbia. *Corruption flourished:* Eastman, *Abortive Revolution,* 16–20. *Integrating force:* James C. Thomson, Jr., 165. *Christian spirit of service:* Ibid., 154. *Moral regeneration:* Articles, Dirlik, 945–46.

102 *Revival of the spirit:* MCKS, "New Life in China," *Forum,* Jun 1935. *New Life derived in part from Samurai Bushido:* James C. Thomson, Jr., 153. *Both revolutionary and conservative:* Articles, Dirlik, 947. Dirlik argues the New Life Movement was intended to lay the groundwork for a KMT version of the Communists' Cultural Revolution, to which it bears some similarity. (945–46, 976.) *Knowledge and morality:* Articles, Dirlik, 954. *Foreign signs banned:* China Intel. Sum. No. 58, Mar 1934. WO 208/182. TNA. *We are giving the people what the Communists promised:* quoted in Auden, 57.

103 *Reverend Shepherd advised Chiangs: Marlboro Enterprise,* 29 Feb 1940. *What would Borodin do:* quoted in James C. Thomson, Jr., 176–78. *World's Greatest Evangelistic Opportunity:* James C. Thomson, Jr., 231. *Mayling translated Oxford Group literature:* "Personal Observations of Chiang Kai-shek," Box 87, "United Forces China Theater: China—Politics and Government, General." Wedemeyer Papers, Hoover.

104 *Christian revolutionary:* Auden, 41–42. *Spiritual guidance:* L. H. Roots, Lecture, Royal Central Asian Society, 1 Dec 1938. WO 208/182. TNA. *Quiet time:* Ibid. *Bishop Roots*

met Chiangs: Johnson to Stanley Hornbeck, 26 Jun 1934. Box 23, Johnson Papers. LOC. *Four virtues:* James C. Thomson, Jr., 156–57. New Life's "four virtues" are reminiscent of the Oxford Group's "four absolutes"—honesty, purity, unselfishness, and love. *Oxford Group targeted society leaders:* Edwin C. Hill, "The Oxford Movement," *Boston American,* 2 Sep 1937; *Example and exhortation:* Utley, 198. *The virtue of the gentleman is like wind:* Confucius, Book XII, Verse 19, 115–16; Articles, Dirlik, 970.

105   *Mayling controlled the New Life Movement:* F. Tillman Durdin, "Worth Twenty Divisions," *NYT Magazine,* 4 Sep 1941. *I sometimes despair:* New Life Movement materials, undated. Class of 1917: MCKS, Articles about MCKS (1938). WCA. *The regeneration of China:* MCKS, "You Must Change Man's Character," unidentified periodical, 12 Dec 1935. Class of 1917: MCKS, Articles by Gen. & MCKS (1930–37). WCA. *Salvation from within: Macon Telegraph,* 22 Feb 1937. *As water is craved by the famishing:* Message from MCKS to Australian Women's Conference, 5 Apr 1938. Class of 1917: MCKS Correspondence (n.d. 1916–80). WCA. *Like wildfire:* MCKS, "New Life in China," *Forum,* Jun 1935. *Cross in the background:* James C. Thomson, Jr., 187.

106   *Boy Scouts:* The Chinese Scout movement began soon after the 1911 revolution. *New Life dictums:* Jim Marshall, "China's Girl Boss," *Collier's,* 10 Apr 1937; Lin Yutang, "Chiang's Virtues," *Literary Digest,* 27 Feb 1937; "The New Life Movement and its Significance," Box 54, 148, Johnson Papers. LOC. *Housewives' leagues:* Alice Tisdale Hobart, "China's Great Lady," *American Girl,* Feb 1943. *Stupid, overzealous, dizzy:* quoted in Auden, 58.

107   *New Deal:* Lin Yutang, "Chiang's Virtues," *Literary Digest,* 27 Feb 1937. *Gigantic task:* CKS (translated by MCKS), "Outline of the New Life Movement" (pamphlet). Box 108, 1935 Foreign File—China. Howard Papers. LOC. *Bore rather than inspire:* Articles, Dirlik, 953. *Burst of laughter:* Lin Yutang, "Chiang's Virtues," *Literary Digest,* 27 Feb 1937. *Chiang took realistic view of opium trade:* Nelson T. Johnson to Stanley K. Hornbeck, 31 May 1934. Box 23, Johnson Papers. LOC. *Confucian cobwebs:* Soong Ching Ling, 97; *comments on New Life:* Soong Ching Ling, 92–104. *The aim of revolution:* Utley, 14–15. *Shallow:* Sir Anthony Jenkinson, "She Is the World's First Lady," *Daily Sketch,* 1 Jun 1938.

108   *Mayling counters criticism:* MCKS, "New Life in China," *Forum,* Jun 1935. *Grow men:* "China's First Lady Big Helpmate," *Newport News,* 15 Apr 1937. *Biggest thing the Kuomintang has done:* Gunther, 208. *Greatest nation in the world:* Fulton Oursler, "China's Strong Woman Talks," *Liberty,* 7 Aug 1937. Oursler and his wife, Grace Perkins Oursler, were Oxford Group members and close friends of Madame Chiang. *New Life's inherent contradictions:* Articles, Dirlik, 975–76. *Anguished patriots:* James C. Thomson, Jr., 224.

109   *Sufficiently pure:* "The New Life Movement and its Significance," Box 54, 148. Johnson Papers. LOC. In 1935 Johnson's post was upgraded to ambassador when the American legation became an embassy.

110   *Very quick mind:* Arthur N. Young, oral history interview, 22–23. www.trumanlibrary .org/oralhist/young. Young was an American economist who advised the Chinese government from 1929 to 1946. *Soong's American ways:* George E. Sokolsky, "The First Family of China: The Soongs," *New York Times Magazine,* 15 Nov 1931.

111   *Forty-five percent of budget going to national defense:* James C. Thomson, Jr., 15. *T. V. supported Zhang Xueliang:* Conversation with V. K. Ting and Hu Shih, 19 Mar 1933. Johnson Papers, Box 53, 320. LOC. *Washington's $50 million loan:* James C. Thomson, Jr., 23. *T. V.'s sarcasm:* Box 53, p. 324, 4 Nov 1933, Johnson Papers.

LOC; George Sokolsky, OHRO, Columbia; Articles, Sokolsky. *Mayling had failed:* Diaries of Sir Alexander Frederick Whyte, Vol. 8, 36–54, MSS EUR D761. OIO, British Library.

112 *Soong's ambitions:* Ibid. *Impertinent snort:* Ibid., Vol. 8, 44. *Feather-pillow head:* Diaries of Sir Alexander Frederick Whyte, Vol. 8, 39, MSS EUR D761. OIO, British Library. *Mayling's astounding statement:* Johnson to Stanley K. Hornbeck, 31 May 1934. Box 23, Johnson Papers. LOC. *Rake-off:* Johnson to Stanley K. Hornbeck, 31 May 1934. Box 23. Johnson Papers. LOC.

NOTES FOR CHAPTER NINE

114 *How do you know him:* Documentaries, *Zhang Xueliang*. *Anger:* Documentaries, *Zhang Xueliang*.

115 *Zhang ambitionless:* Memorandum of conversation, 9 Apr 1931. Box 51, Johnson Papers. LOC. *We are making progress:* quoted in Chapter 24: Outreach. www.llu.edu/info/legacy. *Zhang's secretary:* At some point Zhao became Zhang's mistress. They married decades later. *Great vitality:* MCKS, *China at the Crossroads*, 123.

116 *Soong's plot:* Hong Kong to War Office, Telegram 3269, Desp. 18 Dec 1936. WO 208/182. TNA. *Insufferably stupid:* quoted in Selle, 290. *China should be ashamed:* Ibid. *You were wonderful:* Ibid., 290–91. *Gran:* Apparently short for Grandpa.

117 *Shoot a lot of people:* Selle, 295. *Jumble and a miserable business:* quoted in Selle, 301. *Too much for me:* Ibid., 302. *Gissimo and Missimo:* Selle, 306. *Roughage and refuge:* Archibald Clark Kerr to Foreign Office, 13 May 1940. FO 371/24702. TNA. *Patriot's Soliloquy:* quoted in Selle, 314–15.

118 *I am sorry:* Thomas W. Lamont to Johnson, 19 May 1936. Box 29, Johnson Papers. LOC.

119 *Mayling agreed with Donald:* W. H. Donald interview, 26 Jan 1937. WO 208/182. TNA. *High spirits:* Statement by H. H. Kung, Jun 1937. Wheeler Papers. Cornell. *Why do you Chinese fight us:* H. B. Elliston, "China's No. 1 White Boy," *Saturday Evening Post*, 19 Mar 1938.

120 *Inhuman is he:* Han, 148. *Scolding:* Franklin Ho, 168–69, COHP. Columbia. *Nervous breakdown:* Johnson to Stanley K. Hornbeck, 19 Oct 1936. Box 29, Johnson Papers. LOC. *Breaks out in a rash:* Johnson to Stanley K. Hornbeck, 19 Oct 1936. Box 29, Johnson Papers. LOC. An early attack of Mayling's recurring urticaria, or hives. *Kung's premonition:* H. H. Kung, COHP. Columbia.

121 *Blue Shirts:* Articles, Youwei and Billingsley. *Stimulate his awakening:* "Mme. Chiang's Own Story of the Sian Rebellion Crisis," *NYT*, 16 Apr 1937.

122 *Kill me:* NYT, 21 Apr 1937. Chiang's account of the kidnapping. *Let me do the work:* NYT, 21 Apr 1937. *Unreasonable woman:* NYT, 16 Apr 1937. *Mayling took command:* W. H. Donald interview, 26 Jan 1937. WO 208/182. TNA.

123 *If he is killed:* Lattimore, 140–41. *Unhealthy obsession:* NYT, 16 Apr 1937. *Woman pleading:* NYT, 16 Apr 1937. *Chiang cried:* "Notes on the Sian Incident," 1936 (Copy 1), 117. Box 17: Sian Incident. Nym Wales Collection. Hoover. *Live ass:* W. H. Donald interview, 26 Jan 1937. WO 208/182. TNA.

124 *I would have done the same:* quoted in Snow, *Journey*, 94. *Mayling telephoned Ching Ling:* Epstein, 318–19. *Stab in the back:* Telegram No. 244, 17 Dec 1936. WO 208/182. TNA. *Zhang's statement:* Hallet Abend to *NYT*, n.d. Box 28, Johnson Papers. LOC.

125 *Zhou Enlai:* Articles, Youwei and Billingsley.

126   *MCKS upset:* Sebie Biggs Smith, 47. OHRO. Columbia. *Mayling ordered end to bomb-ing:* W. H. Donald interview, 26 Jan 1937. WO 208/182. TNA. *Deadly cargo:* Hallet Abend to *NYT*, n.d. Box 28, Johnson Papers. LOC. *Man to man:* Chiang, *China at the Crossroads,* 114. *Things messed up:* Chiang, *China at the Crossroads,* 114–15. *Tiger's lair:* Chiang, *China at the Crossroads,* 116. *Wanted to cry: NYT*, 24 Apr 1937.

127   *Scolds those of whom he has high hopes:* Chiang, *China at the Crossroads,* 120–21. *Spiritual guidance:* Chiang, *China at the Crossroads,* 123. *Chiang eventually persuaded:* Sir Hughe Knatchbull-Hugessen to Foreign Office, Telegram No. 946, 30 Dec 1936. WO 208/182. TNA. *Hand of God:* Hallet Abend to *NYT*, n.d. Box 28, Johnson Papers. LOC. *Settlement terms:* W. H. Donald interview, 26 Jan 1937. WO 208/182. TNA.

128   *Chiang promised nothing:* Zhou Enlai, interview with Nym Wales (Helen Snow), 22 Jun 1937. "Notes on the Sian Incident, 1936" (Copy 1), 189. Box 17: Sian Incident. Nym Wales Collection. Hoover. *By nature:* Johnson to secretary of state, 12 Jan 1937. Box 32, Johnson Papers. LOC. *Chiang resigns:* Johnson to secretary of state, 12 Jan 1937. Box 32, Johnson Papers. LOC. *Mayling urged Chiang:* Documentaries, *Zhang Xueliang. Lenient punishment:* Johnson to secretary of state, 12 Jan 1937. Box 32, Johnson Papers. LOC.

129   *The only man:* William H. Donald to Roy W. Howard, 2 May 1938. Box 146: 1938—Foreign File—China. Howard Papers. LOC. *Special pardon:* Johnson to secretary of state, 12 Jan 1937. Box 32, Johnson Papers. LOC. *Converting Zhang:* R. G. Howe to Sir Hughe Knatchbull-Hugessen, 28 Dec 1936. WO 208/182. TNA. *The only reason:* Documentaries, *Zhang Xueliang. Phantasmagoria:* W. H. Donald interview, 26 Jan 1937. WO 208/182. TNA. *Chiang changed tune:* Johnson to Stanley K. Hornbeck, 6 Feb 1937. Box 32, Johnson Papers. LOC.

130   *Mayling threatened Chiang:* W. H. Donald interview, 26 Jan 1937. WO 208/182. TNA. *Donald attacked:* W. H. Donald interview, 26 Jan 1937. WO 208/182. TNA. *Picturesque:* "The Chiang Kai-shek Saga," *NYT*, 16 Apr 1937. *She cannot take all the credit:* Chen Li-fu, Office Files, Box 48: Sian Incident, COHP. Columbia.

131   *Penetrating intelligence: NYT*, 18 Apr 1937. *Dictates to the dictator: Boston Post*, 9 May 1937.

NOTES FOR CHAPTER TEN

132   *Heel-clicking German officer:* Sues, 148. *That man Stennes:* quoted in Drage, 104.

133   *Casual, unaffected friendliness:* Drage, 107. *Greater than Hitler:* quoted in Drage, 110. *Missing interpreter:* Drage, 119–20. *Behead American missionaries:* Robert E. van Patten, "Before Flying Tigers," *Air Force,* Jun 1999.

134   *Airsickness:* Hahn, *Chiang Kai-shek,* 183. *Russians threatened to stop sending planes:* Utley, 8. *Nervous breakdown:* Knatchbull Huggessen to Foreign Office, 26 Apr 1937. WO 208/182/61783. TNA. *Madame Kung's corruption:* Memorandum of conversation, 24 May 1937, J. Hall Paxton; Willys R. Peck to Johnson, 7 Jun 1937. Box 32, Johnson Papers. LOC.

135   *General Zhou:* referred to as "General Tzau," also known as Chow Chih-jo. *Sisterly struggle:* Willys R. Peck to Johnson, 7 Jun 1937. Box 32, Johnson Papers. LOC. *Gamecock of the wilderness:* Alsop, 165.

136   *Major not impressive rank:* Sebie Biggs Smith, 52, OHRO, Columbia. *Princess:* quoted in Tuchman, 217. *Illegal anti-Japanese actions:* Spence, 445. *Unpardonable crime:* quoted in Spence, 445. *Through the roof: NYT*, 6 Mar 1938.

137 *Planes reduced to nineteen: NYT,* 6 Mar 1938. *That doesn't matter:* quoted in Leonard, 132. *Long Bar patrons:* Drage, 127. *Damned fools:* quoted in Leonard, 142.

138 *China is not afraid: NYT,* 29 Aug 1937. *Hill of ants: Time,* 3 Jan 1938. *Appeal to Chinese women: NYT,* 1 Aug 1937. *Mayling's office: NYT,* 2 Sep 1937. *Swivel chair on a tiger rug: Literary Digest,* 29 Aug 1936.

139 *Pusillanimity:* MCKS, "China and Japan—What Is Going to Happen?" *Liberty,* 4 Sep 1937. *Fair chance:* MCKS, "China and Japan—What Is Going to Happen?" *Liberty,* 4 Sep 1937. *Accessory to this mass murder: NYT,* 12 Sep 1937. *You may blame:* Sues, 158–62. *Propaganda and retreat:* Sues, 158–62.

140 *Fighting heart of a lioness:* Sues, 167. *Nervous breakdown:* Sues, 158–62. *Mayling visits gas victims: Evening Star,* 14 Oct 1937.

141 *Mayling decries American embargo: Forum,* Dec 1937. *Joan of Arc: Evening Star,* 16 Oct 1937. *We are left alone: Asia,* Jul 1938. *Flies through the air:* Selle, 340. *Out of a gutter:* Selle, 340. *It hurts me to breathe: Time,* 1 Mar 1937.

142 *John Rabe:* Rabe was later dubbed "China's Oskar Schindler." He was persecuted by the Nazis on his return to Germany. Mayling sent him money for food and necessities. *Rape of Nanking:* Chang, Iris, 4. The incident is treated lightly in Japanese school textbooks, and despite overwhelming evidence, a small but influential segment of Japanese society continues to deny that atrocities occurred. *Chiang lifted ban: NYT,* 7 Apr 1938.

143 *History, grown weary:* Auden, 40. *Do poets like cake:* quoted in Auden, 55–60. *Was this the face:* quoted in Gunther, *Inside Asia,* 205–8. *My visit:* London *Times,* 14 Jan 1938; also 15 Jan 1938. *In the dog house:* James M. McHugh to "Skipper," 20 Mar 1938. McHugh Papers. Cornell.

144 *Damned business:* quoted in Selle, 318. *Cog in China's defense: Atlanta Constitution,* 30 Mar 1933. *Strain on the Generalissimo: Atlanta Constitution,* 30 Mar 1933. *Strain of war activities: Boston Globe,* 2 Mar 1938. *Zhou demoted:* Memorandum for the ambassador, 28 Feb 1938. Box 2, McHugh Papers. Cornell. *Views unprintable: NYT,* 12 Jun 1938. *What have the democracies done for us: NYT,* 12 Jun 1938. *When this war:* MCKS to Mrs. Theodore Roosevelt Jr., 22 Apr 1938. Box 27, Special Correspondence 1938–40, MCKS. Theodore Roosevelt Jr. Papers. LOC.

145 *Begging expedition: NYT,* 10 July 1938. *Generalissimo does not want me to go: Sunday Star,* 24 Apr 1938. *Bombed into Godmaternity:* Gage, 76; Articles, Gage. *How are your children:* quoted in Auden, 59–60; Boorman, 331. *If Japanese planes: Sunday Star,* 9 Jan 1937.

146 *Welter of blood and ruin:* MCKS, "An Open Letter to My Alma Mater," 20 Mar 1938; *Wellesley Magazine,* Jun 1938. *Chiang used public purse:* Franklin Ho, 156, COHP. Columbia. *The Generalissimo wants money:* Ibid. *They danced and played:* Carlson, 282. *Last drop of coolie blood:* quoted in Carlson, 284.

147 *Son gone away:* quoted in Taylor, 63. *Generalissimo wished Ching-kuo would return:* Taylor, 70; Tsiang T'ing-fu, COHP. Columbia. *Letter of apology:* Taylor, 79. *That is not my mother: Time,* 3 Jan 1938. *Mayling slipped Ching-kuo cash:* Taylor, 80.

148 *Wego took part in Anschluss:* Taylor, 101. *Mayling met Wego in 1940:* Taylor, 101–2. *Big bourgeoisie:* quoted in Taylor, 87–88. *Ching-kuo called his father "The Old Man":* Taylor, 97. *Unsatisfactory:* James C. Elder to Roy W. Howard, 12 Apr 1938. Box 146: 1938—Foreign File—China. Howard Papers. LOC. *Great deal of mystery:* Roy W. Howard to W. H. Donald, 18 Apr 1938. Box 146: 1938—Foreign File—China. Howard Papers. LOC. *A lot of blather:* Roy W. Howard to Clarence Kuangson Young, 18 Apr 1938. Box 146: 1938—Foreign File—China. Howard Papers. LOC. *Wait for*

a chance: W. H. Donald to Roy W. Howard, 2 May 1938. Box 146: 1938—Foreign File—China. Howard Papers. LOC.

149   *The people must be prevented from fooling themselves:* W. H. Donald to Roy W. Howard, 2 May 1938. Box 146: 1938—Foreign File—China. Howard Papers. LOC. *Not easy to be both a good German and an honorable man:* Drage, 117. *A spoon may be licked: NYT,* 18 Sep 1938. *Rain of explosives:* William H. Donald to Roy W. Howard, 21 Jan 1939. Box 157: 1939—Foreign File—China. Howard Papers. LOC. *Magnetic strategy:* Mayling Soong Chiang, *We Chinese Women,* 37. *Trying to fight a jelly:* William H. Donald to Roy W. Howard, 21 Jan 1939. Box 157: 1939—Foreign File—China. Howard Papers. LOC. *Iron nerves:* Drage, 111.

NOTES FOR CHAPTER ELEVEN

152   *Lines of coffins:* Mayling Soong Chiang to Emma DeLong Mills, 10 May 1939. Class of 1917, Alumnae: Mayling Soong and her classmates. WCA. *Handouts are demoralizing: NYT,* 29 Jan 1939. *Tiny living statue in the midst of carnage:* Selle, 348.

153   *The shades of night: NYT,* 29 Nov 1940. *Bowl of Rice:* Theodore Roosevelt Jr. to MCKS, 6 Mar 1940. Box 27, Special Correspondence 1938–40: MCKS, Theodore Roosevelt Jr. Papers. LOC. *Sentimental feeling about China: NYT,* 12 Jun 1941. *Stopped cold in its tracks: NYT,* 12 Jun 1941. *As much joy:* Newspaper clipping, 3 Nov 1941. Class of 1917: MCKS, Articles about MCKS (9/1941–8/1942). WCA. *Worth twenty divisions: NYT Magazine,* 14 Sep 1941.

154   *Reprehensible bunch:* Paul Frillmann, 120–21, OHRO. Columbia. *Flying Tigers:* Soong to Claire Chennault, 14 Mar 1949. Soong Papers, 61.4. Hoover. *My boys:* Speech to AVG, 17 Apr 1942. Reel 1, Chennault Papers. LOC. *She treats us like we were nitwits:* quoted in Sues, 166. *Leading lady:* Gage, 104. *Chennault's base:* Merry, 132.

155   *Driven most men:* Report No. 1–39, 10 Apr 1938. Box 2, McHugh Papers. Cornell. *Opposed and obstructed:* Report No. 1–39, 10 Apr 1938. Box 2, McHugh Papers. Cornell. *If I say the wrong thing:* Col. John M. Williams, 62, OHRO. Columbia. *Overpaid:* Chennault to MCKS, 12 Feb 1942. Reel 1, Chennault Papers. LOC. *Without you:* Chennault to MCKS, 27 Nov 1941. Reel 1, Claire Lee Chennault Papers. LOC.

156   *Laughing and chattering like schoolgirls:* Chang Jung, 79. *My Red sister:* Fr. Thaddeus Yang, "The Chinese Adventure of an Indonesian Monk," 7 Jan 1971. http://www.valyermo.com/mnk-yng2.html. *Childlike figure:* Chang Jung, 54. *There is a great woman:* [Frances Gunther] to Jawaharlal Nehru, 14 Apr 1938. Volume 29, 153–57, Nehru Papers. NML. *I didn't fall in love:* quoted in Snow, *Journey,* 88. *Bitter laughter:* Rand, 241. *Would never have remarried:* Snow, *Journey,* 91. *Fuzzy and criss-crossed:* Rand, 241. *Flip-flops:* quoted in Rand, 241. *Capable of anything:* quoted in Chang Jung, 82. *Generalissimo:* quoted in Rand, 240. *Betrayal:* quoted in Snow, *Journey,* 85. *Much worse:* Ibid., 91. *Less than the others:* Ibid., 95.

157   *The Sage:* quoted in Chang Jung, 80. *She's very clever:* quoted in Snow, *Journey,* 90. *See what I have brought back:* quoted in Endicott, 145.

158   *Sea of troubles: Asia,* Jul 1939. *That's because: Asia,* Jul 1939. *Blind to shortcomings: Asia,* Jul 1939. *Had their knives out:* James M. McHugh to "Garnet," 25 May 1940. Box 1, McHugh Papers. Cornell. *Grandfather:* Box 5, Folder 222, 59–68, Frances Gunther Papers. Harvard.

159   *Debunk Sun Yat-sen:* W. H. Donald to Theodore Roosevelt Jr., 20 Mar 1941. Box 27, Special Correspondence, W. H. Donald. Theodore Roosevelt Jr. Papers. LOC. *Im-*

practical visionary: James McHugh, CKS memoir, manuscript, chapter 1, p. 15. McHugh Papers. Cornell. *Tell to their faces:* Asia Trip Notes, Box 5, Folder 222. 59–68. Frances Gunther Papers. Harvard. *Malodorous bone:* Hahn, *Chiang Kai-shek,* 234. *Some persons even you cannot criticize:* quoted in Selle, 349. *Sheean's article; Lin Yutang's reply: New York Herald Tribune,* ? Nov 1941 and 7 Dec 1941.

160 *Inimical totalitarians . . . traitor:* Clark Kerr to Foreign Office, 13 May 1940. FO 371/24702. TNA. *I hope it is genuine:* Clark Kerr to Foreign Office, 13 May 1940. FO 371/24702. TNA. *I am not at war with Germany:* quoted in Selle, 349. *Genuinely upset:* James M. McHugh to "Garnet," 25 May 1940. Box 1, McHugh Papers. Cornell. *Stennes a Soviet agent:* http://archives.his.com/intelforum/2000-May/msg000 72.html; http://english.pravda.ru/society/2003/02/11/43255.html. *Messenger boy:* Memo to the ambassador, 6 Jun 1940. Box 3, McHugh Papers. Cornell.

161 *Slackness a strangling national habit:* MCKS, *China Shall Rise Again,* 19. *Inspire all delinquents:* Ibid., 55. *National spiritual mobilization:* Ibid., 56. *Stinging disgrace:* Ibid., 30. *Creeping paralysis:* Ibid., 33. *Self-seeking and stupidity:* Ibid., 34. *If we are worthy:* Ibid., 35. *Cankerous growths:* Ibid., 55.

162 *Refuge for incompetents:* Ibid., 43–44. *Grand Army:* Ibid., 45. *Exposure of national weaknesses:* Ibid., ix. *We have been virtually abandoned: Liberty,* 21 Dec 1940. *Cutting off heads:* Franklin L. Ho, 251, COHP. Columbia.

163 *Some 2.6 million Chinese soldiers dead:* Spence, 460. *Whispering campaign:* Johnson to secretary of state, 18 Oct 1940. PSF, Box 174. China—Diplomatic Aspects (Folder 1). Truman. *Currie fell hard:* Vincent to?, "Wednesday, the 9th" [1941]. Box 1, McHugh Papers. Cornell. *Opportune:* Memorandum of conversation, 13 Apr 1941. Box 1, McHugh Papers. Cornell. *Disillusionment:* Memorandum of conversation, 13 Apr 1941. Box 1, McHugh Papers. Cornell. *Grown in dignity: Sunday Star,* 24 Apr 1938.

164 *Madame Chiang fairly radiated charm:* Carlson, 130. *Greatest woman:* Hedin, 66. *Hard, shallow and selfish:* Vincent to?, "Wednesday, the 9th" [1941]. Box 1, McHugh Papers. Cornell. *Olympian self-possession, brilliant black eyes:* Carlson, 130. *Endicott protested:* Hahn, *China to Me,* 127. Also Endicott, 148–49. *So many Communists:* quoted in Endicott, 150–51.

165 *Cholera germ:* Endicott, 151. *We are not trying:* quoted in Gellhorn, 57–58. *I guess that'll teach you:* Ibid., 57–58. *Malaria and dengue fever:* MCKS to Clare Boothe Luce, 15 Aug 1941. 101/5, Clare Boothe Luce Papers. LOC.

166 *Spiritual desolation:* MCKS, *The Sure Victory,* 18. *I was like a top:* Ibid., 15–16. *Spiritual blindness:* Ibid., 18–19. *Hate the evil:* Ibid., 19. *Her nature:* Memorandum, 23 Aug 1941. Box 1, McHugh Papers. Cornell. *We feel we have earned: Foreign Relations,* 1941, Volume IV, 552–53. *Psychological results: Foreign Relations,* 1941, Volume IV, 552–53.

NOTES FOR CHAPTER TWELVE

168 *India is like a beautiful woman:* Victor Sassoon to "Mickey" Hahn, 18 Mar 1945. Box 2, Hahn Papers. Indiana. *Well-meaning but incurably meddlesome:* Mansergh, Vol. 3, 253. *Deeply-rooted suspicion:* Mansergh, Vol. 3, 256.

169 *Invade the Western world:* Henry Wallace Diary, Vol. 18, 3199, OHRO. Columbia. *Chiang demanded participation:* Conversation with CKS, 31 Jul 1941. 49/9, Lattimore Papers. LOC. *Chiang's rancorous tirade:* Lattimore, 164.

170   *To attempt to manage Chiang:* Mansergh, Vol. 1, 102. *Pan-Asiatic malaise:* Mansergh, Vol. 1, 114.

171   *Very grave mistake:* Mansergh, Vol. 1, 120–21. *Niggling impractical creatures:* Mansergh, Vol. 1, 108. *Beyond doubt:* Wilson Papers, 1.5 (Diaries), 10 Feb 1942. Georgetown. *Dramatic and spectacular:* Wilson Papers, 1.5 (Diaries), 10 Feb 1942. Georgetown. *India's heart . . . kindred spirit . . . spiritual bonds . . . one look:* Hindustan Times, 10 Feb 1942, 11 Feb 1942. *Amusing study:* Mansergh, Vol. 1, 136–37.

172   *Mark the hours:* MCKS to Nehru, n.d., Vol. 13, 207–9. Nehru Papers. NML. *I am India:* Hindustan Times, 11 Feb 1942. *Star of hope:* Hindustan Times, 12 Feb 1942. *The old world:* Ibid. *We must have liberty to fight:* Hindustan Times, 13 Feb 1942. *I pray:* Hindustan Times, 16 Feb 1942.

173   *Devotion of an emperor:* Ibid. *Nehru turned somersaults:* Tong, 179–80. *If things do go wrong in Burma:* Eden to prime minister, 12 Feb 1942. PREM 4/45/3. TNA. *Great mistake:* Churchill to Eden, 13 Feb 1942, PREM 4/45/3. TNA.

174   *They do not even admit your country:* Foreign Relations, China series 42, 33–34. *Hoped for better luck with Gandhi:* Mansergh, Vol. 1, 213. *Not changed an atom:* Ibid., 236. *Most critical moment:* Hindustan Times, 22 Feb 1942. *Applauded Chiang's courage:* Hindustan Times, 24 Feb 1942. *Meddlesome Marshal:* The Dawn, 1 Mar 1942. *It is unfortunate:* Ibid. *Quite failed to understand:* Mansergh, Vol. 1, 185. *Madame is a very clever and competent little lady:* Ibid.

175   *Not averse to a flirtation:* Wilson Papers, 1.5 (Diaries), 18 Feb 1942. Georgetown. *We shall leave nothing undone:* MCKS to Nehru, 22 Feb 1942. Vol. 13, 85–89, Nehru Papers. NML. *Deep impression:* Nehru, 28 Feb 1942, Vol. 19, 227–31, Nehru Papers. NML. *Noble wife:* "Cable to Chairman," 24 Jun 1942, Soong Papers, 62.1. Hoover. *You may count on us:* MCKS to Nehru, 2 May 1942. Vol. 13, 197–99, Nehru Papers. NML. *Backward boy:* Foreign Office to Washington, Telegram No. 1450, 5 Mar 1942. L/P&S/12/2315 (Coll 11/25(S)). OIO. British Library. *Neither racial affinity nor common destiny:* Mansergh, Vol. 1, 448.

176   *Break with Gandhi:* Ibid., 837. *Practically universal:* Seymour to FO, No. 371, 26 Mar 1942. FO 371/31626. TNA. *Feeling of superiority:* Ibid. *Chinese intolerant:* Anglo-Chinese Relations, minutes, 28 Mar 1942. PRO FO 371/31626. TNA. *Situation there unspeakably dangerous:* To Currie, 12 Apr 1942. Vol. 13, 165, Nehru Papers. NML. *The imp in me:* MCKS to Nehru, 22 Apr 1942. Vol. 13, Nehru Papers, NML.

177   *Utterly disheartened:* Ibid. *Woman's touch:* Ibid. *I felt headachy:* Ibid. *Madame, if I die:* Tong, 184. "First Lady Hopes US Will Continue Firm Vietnam Stand," Chinese News Service, 19 Mar 1965. Box 175: "CKS and MCKS, General, 1960–1972." Judd Papers. Hoover.

178   *If China is really an ally:* MCKS to Currie, 18 May 1942. Currie Papers, Box 1. Hoover. *Forlorn client:* Memorandum to the president, n.d. Soong Papers, 37.14. Hoover. *Double-crossing:* CKS to Soong, 1 Jan 1942; 2 Jan 1942. Soong Papers, 59.6. Hoover. *Pawn in the game:* CKS to Soong, 19 Apr [1942?]. Soong Papers, 36.5. Hoover. *Critical carping:* John de La Vallette to Ashley Clarke, 26 Apr 1942. FO 371/31626. TNA. *Where I suppose we fail:* Anglo-Chinese Relations, minutes, 16 Jun 1942. FO 371/31626. TNA.

179   *Mischievous and ignorant:* Mansergh, Vol. 2, 674. *Disastrous effect:* Chiang to Roosevelt (via "Chairman," i.e., Soong), 11 Aug 1942. Soong Papers, 62.1. Hoover. *Thirteen colonies:* Roosevelt to CKS, No. 516, 13 Aug 1942. Soong Papers, 62.1. Hoover. *Cherchez la Femme:* Kimball, 563. *I think the best rule:* Mansergh, Vol. 2, 832. *Chinese Raj:* Ashley Clarke to Sir David Monteath, 20 Jan 1943. L/P&S/12/2315 (Coll 11/25

(S)); D. T. Monteath to Ashley Clarke, 25 Jan 1943. L/P&S/12/2315, OIO. British Library; also Mansergh, Vol. 3, 314–15. *What is it:* Mansergh, Vol. 5, 647–8. *With such dynamite:* MCKS to Nehru, 22 Apr 1942. Vol. 13, 180 (approx.), Nehru Papers. NML.

180 *Arrogant belief: NYT Magazine,* 19 Apr 1942. *Ruthless and shameless: Atlantic Monthly,* May 1942. *The time has past:* MCKS broadcast, 13 Jun 1942, Class of 1917: MCKS, Speeches by MCKS (n.d., 1938–45). WCA. *Indiscreet and unfriendly woman:* Anglo-Chinese Relations, 26 Jun 1942. FO 371/31626. TNA. *What right has she:* Ibid. *China's claim pathetic:* Sino-British Relations, 7 Jul 1942. FO 371/31626. TNA. *At Washington:* Churchill, Vol. 4, 133.

181 *Such being the case:* quoted in Tuchman, 311-13. *Mad as hell:* Ibid. *Chiang's demands bluff:* Gauss to secretary of state, No. 514, 14 Jul 1942. PSF, Box 174, File: China—Diplomatic Aspects, Pt. II. *Chinese have been built up:* Ibid. *Greatest living woman . . . tragic figure: Atlanta Constitution,* 26 Jul 1942.

182 *You are bound:* CBL to MCKS, 25 Aug 1942. 110/4, Clare Boothe Luce Papers. LOC. *Free spirit:* quoted in *Current Biography,* 1940. *Overwhelming magnetism:* Cowles, 65. *Another Lincoln: Current Biography,* 1943. *Roosevelt's puppy (named Fala):* Henry Wallace Diary, Vol. 13, 2366. Columbia. *Willkie rambunctious:* Ibid., 2365.

183 *Well insulated from pollution:* quoted in Tuchman, 332. *Fallen so much in love:* quoted in Neal, 254. *Most charming woman: Life,* 26 Apr 1943. *One of her easiest conquests:* Davies, 255. *Smelled like raw beef:* quoted in Tuchman, 335. *Chiang strangely quiet:* Willkie, 168–70. *Agrarian awakening:* Ibid., 176. *Howl and howl: NYT,* 5 Oct 1942. *Very disturbing personality:* quoted in Davies, 256; *NYT,* 5 Oct 1942.

184 *Killed by kindness:* quoted in Neal, 253–54. *Silver platter:* Sues, 166. *Colonial days are past:* Willkie, 251. *Liquidation of the British Empire: NYT,* 11 Nov 1942. *I want you to meet my other sister:* quoted in Willkie, 178.

185–86 *Mayling's affair with Willkie:* Cowles, 88–90. The veracity of Cowles's account of the alleged affair cannot be verified, but there is no apparent motive for him to have invented the episode, about which he told columnist Drew Pearson in the 1940s and later recounted in a privately published memoir.

186 *Educate us:* Willkie, 178–79. *He is all you led us to expect:* MCKS to CBL, 6 Oct 1942. 110/4, Clare Boothe Luce Papers, LOC. *Soul kiss:* Abell, 388. *Ultimate test of charm: Look,* Dec 1942. *Willkie drinking:* Wallace Diary, 29 Oct 1942, Vol. 10, 1927. Columbia. *Ballerina . . . girls of Bagdad:* Wallace Diary, Vol. 10, 1927. Columbia.

187 *Pepper was required:* quoted in Tuchman, 336–40. *Kicking an old lady:* Ibid., 305.

188 *Certain influences:* Ibid., 306–8. *Resentful of American influence:* Chennault to MCKS, 27 Nov 1941. Chennault Papers. Hoover. *Nippon planes:* MCKS to Chennault, 13 May 1942. AVG. Chennault Papers. Hoover. *The hell they are:* quoted in Tuchman, 311.

189 *Chiang's only true friend:* Ibid., 317–18.

NOTES FOR CHAPTER THIRTEEN

193 *Discourteous:* Viceroy to secretary of state (for India), 27 Nov 1942. FO 371/31710, TNA. *Worrying about insult:* 30 Nov 1942. FO 371/31710. TNA.

194 *You'd better watch your step:* quoted in Tully, 330–31. *This state:* Loeb and Atchley to CKS, 2 May 1943. Soong Papers, 63.16. Hoover. *Infeasible:* quoted in Sherwood, 660–61. *Madame Lin:* Frances Gunther to "Madame Lin," 11 Feb 1945. Box 5, Folder 219, File 76. Gunther Papers. Harvard. *Your wife:* FDR to CKS, 3 Dec 1942. Soong Papers, 62.2. Hoover.

195 *Subject to her command:* Willkie to "Miss D'un," 11 Dec 1947. MCKS file, Willkie Papers. Indiana. *Because the Generalissimo:* St. Louis *Star-Times,* 12 Dec 1942. *Furious at leak:* 7 May 1943. RG 226, Entry 210, Box 401, File 11. NARA. *Aftermath of horror . . . hypodermics:* Box 5, Folder 219, File 76, Gunther Papers, Harvard. *Poor Nehru:* Ibid. *Bitter and unhappy:* Douglas Auchincloss to Henry Luce, 28 Jan 1943. *Time-Life* Archives. *Still in a nervous state:* Washington to Foreign Office, 30 Jan 1943. FO 371/ 35775. TNA.

196 *Adulation:* Tong, 188. *Takes your breath away: Seattle Post-Intelligencer,* 19 Feb 1943. *Most Americans:* quoted in Stowe, 47. *Recklessly romantic:* Stowe, 37. *Dreamy unreality:* Steele, 23.

197 *Armchair Marco Polo:* Caniff, 16. *Confucius say: South China Morning Post,* 1 Apr 1940. *Washee-washee agents: Boston Herald,* 17 Feb 1943. *After all she is only a Chinese:* quoted in Lattimore, 141. *Vast amount:* Helen Hull, unidentified magazine, n.d. [ca. April 1943]. Wesleyan.

198 *Strict regimen:* Robert Loeb to T. V. Soong, 25 Feb 1943. 63.16, Soong Papers. Hoover. "Chloral" is chloral hydrate, a hypnotic or sleeping medication. It is a controlled narcotic, popularly known as the "date rape" drug, or "Mickey Finn," as it has a knockout effect when mixed with alcohol. When taken alone, dependency soon results. Despite its addictive qualities, her doctors may have used it to wean her off another narcotic considered more harmful. Or they may have used it simply to treat her "exhaustion," on the premise that inevitable dependency on chloral hydrate was the lesser of two evils. We cannot know for certain, in the absence of her medical records. Miller, 79–81. *Do my best:* Soong to Loeb, 26 Feb 1943. Soong Papers, 63.16. Hoover. *Beautifully serene:* Mayling Soong Chiang to Eleanor Roosevelt, 14 Feb 1943. Series 100, Box 1675, 1943, Special Folder—Mme Chiang. Eleanor Roosevelt Papers. FDR Library. *I think a girl:* Reminiscences of H. H. Kung, 141–42. COHP. Columbia. *Confusion:* Parks, 74. *My boy:* quoted in Roosevelt, 282–84.

199 *Tying down:* MCKS to Wedemeyer, 26 Jul 1980. Box 31: Correspondence: CKS & MCKS 1971–1988. Wedemeyer Papers. Hoover. *The President only smiled:* Joseph Chiang, "Currie," 27 Feb 1943. Soong Papers, 63.16. Hoover.

200 *Electric with anticipation:* McNaughton to McConaughy, 18 Feb 1943. *Time-Life* Archives. *Beautifully flashing legs:* Frank McNaughton to James McConaughy, 18 Feb 1943, *Time-Life* Archives.

201 *Mayling's congressional speeches: New York Herald Tribune, NYT, Washington Post,* and other newspapers, 19 Feb 1943. *Excessive if applied to the Madonna:* to Ashley Clarke, 2 Mar 1943. FO 371/35775, TNA. *Georgia softness:* unidentified newspaper, 19 Feb 1943. *China's lissome Joan of Arc: Los Angeles Examiner,* 19 Feb 1943.

202 *Spiritual ally:* Articles, Shih, "Eros."

204 *Emerald phrases:* Frank McNaughton to James McConaughy, 18 Feb 1943. *Time-Life* Archives. *Soul of China:* unidentified newspaper, 19 Feb 1943. *Too, too Wellesley:* Manfred Gottfried to T. S. Matthews, n.d., Chiang Kai-shek (Mme). *Time-Life* Archives. *Pixillated:* 26 Feb 1943. FO 371/35775. TNA. *Churchill was but a memory:* Watkins to David Hurlburd, 19 Feb 1943. *Time-Life* Archives.

205 *Women correspondents:* Eleanor Roosevelt to Madame Chiang, 11 Feb 1943. Series 100, Box 1675, 1943, Special Folder—Mme Chiang. Anna Eleanor Roosevelt Papers. FDR. *Too bad:* Watkins to David Hurlburd, 19 Feb 1943. *Time-Life* Archives. *Tiny:* Ibid. *Madame's press conference with Roosevelt: Complete Presidential Press Conferences of Franklin D. Roosevelt,* Vol. 21, 157–67. Da Capo Press, New York, 1972.

207 *Chinese can get away:* to Ashley Clarke, 2 Mar 1943. FO 371/35775. TNA. *Madame's silk sheets:* Parks, 96–97. *Profoundly disturbed:* Robert Loeb to Soong, 25 Feb 1943. Soong Papers, 63.16. Hoover. *Thought all Chinese:* Roosevelt, 282–84.

208 *Calling the coolies:* quoted in Tully, 331. *As hard as steel:* Roosevelt, 282–84. *Gentle and sweet character:* quoted in Roosevelt, 282–84. *Nonplussed:* Marion Dickerman, 162, OHRO. Columbia.

209 *We do not want promises:* quoted in Sherwood, 706–7. *Roosevelt scared stiff:* to Ashley Clarke, 2 Mar 1943. FO 371/35775. TNA. *Fingers crossed:* Wallace Diary, Vol. 15, 2687. Columbia. *Feminine mind:* Ibid., Vol. 18, 3200. *Press conference: Complete Presidential Press Conferences of Franklin D. Roosevelt*, Vol. 21, 157–67. Da Capo Press, New York, 1972.

210 *Transparent honesty of a friend:* Neal, 257. *Mayling's tête-à-tête with Cowles:* Cowles, 88–90. *Mayling nervous:* "Mayling Soong Chiang" manuscript, 1. Box 7: MCKS. Hull Papers. Columbia.

211 *Avenging angel:* unidentified news article. *Next month's* Vogue: *Time*, 15 Mar 1943. *Madison Square Garden speech:* WO 208/270A. TNA. *She is a marvel:* Carl Sandburg newspaper column, n.d. Mar 1943. *Radically and consistently:* Robert Loeb to L. K. Kung, 4 Mar 1943. Soong Papers, 63.16. Hoover. *Admonished her audience: Christian Science Monitor*, 10 Apr 1943.

212 *Butterfly:* Class of 1917: Alumnae: Mayling Soong and her classmates. WCA. *Mayling's Wellesley visit: The (Wellesley) Townsman*, 11 Mar 1943. *I was fat then: Christian Science Monitor*, 10 Apr 1943.

213 *Will I corrupt their morals: Wellesley College News*, 11 Mar 1943. *Strong emotions: Wellesley College News*, 11 Mar 1943. *Indehiscence and mawkish:* A cenote is an underground reservoir; indehiscence is a state afflicting certain maturing plants that are unable to open and discharge their seeds.

214 *Her slacks have ruined: Boston Traveler*, 8 Mar 1943. *Wellesley rules the WAVEs: Wellesley College News*, 11 Mar 1943. *It is safe to say: Boston Post*, 9 Mar 1943. *If Madame is a product: Boston Daily Globe*, 8 Mar 1943. *Foreign Office minutes concerning Madame Chiang visit:* 7 Dec 1942. FO 371/31710. TNA.

215 *Americans pathological:* Eden to Hardinge, 12 Dec 1942. FO 371/31710. TNA. *Coals of fire:* Proposed visit to England of Madame C.K.S., Mar 1943. FO 371/35775. TNA.

NOTES FOR CHAPTER FOURTEEN

216 *Rightful position:* Vincent to secretary of state, 19 Mar 1943. PSF, Box 174, China—Diplomatic Aspects, Part III. Truman. *Man across the street:* John S. and Caroline Service, Vol. I, 180–82. FAOHP. Georgetown.

217 *Build a backfire:* Ibid. *Hell of a good newspaperman:* Ibid. *Currie tracked Madame's finances:* Currie Papers, Box 3. Hoover. *Soong family most influential in China:* Memorandum, John Edgar Hoover to Lawrence M. C. Smith, chief, Special War Policies Unit, 15 Jan 1943. Materials furnished to the author by the Department of Justice in response to a Freedom of Information Act inquiry.

218 *Could be expected:* Memorandum re: Soong Family, L. B. Nichols to Mr. Tolson, 8 Feb 1943. Materials furnished to the author by the Department of Justice in response to a Freedom of Information Act inquiry. *For their own personal use:* H. H. Kung, Registration Act, China Lobby, 18 Dec 1951. Materials furnished to the author by the Department of Justice in response to a Freedom of Information Act inquiry. *Slander campaign:* B. A. Garside, n.d. Box 5. ABMAC Collection. Columbia.

219   *The reason I did not like to use other people's sheets:* MCKS to Grace Perkins Oursler, 2 May 1955. Series I, Box 1, Folder 17, Oursler Papers. Georgetown. *Dogs eating human bodies: Time,* 22 Mar 1943. *Mayling confronted Luce:* White, *In Search of History,* 161. *Impossible to exaggerate her loveliness: Fortune,* Sep 1941.

220   *Beautiful, tart and brittle:* White, *In Search of History,* 143. *Extravagant:* 14 Jun 1943. RG 226, Entry 210, Box 401, File 11. NARA. *Doesn't care a darn:* 6 Oct 1943. RG 226, Entry 210, Box 401, File 11. NARA. *Why don't you:* 24 Jun 1943. RG 226, Entry 210, Box 401, File 11. NARA.

221   *Stupidity:* 23 Jun 1943. RG 226, Entry 210, Box 401, File 11. NARA. *Second fiddle:* 14 Apr 1943. RG 226, Entry 210, Box 401, File 11. NARA. *High, wide and handsome: Chicago Sun,* 21 Mar 1943. *Message to the Negro press: Christian Science Monitor, Chicago Sun,* 23 Mar 1943.

222   *Fairy tales: Christian Century,* 31 Mar 1943. *Children want their dollies: Chicago Sun,* 23 Mar 1943; 20 Mar 1943, WO 208/270A, TNA. *Though our two countries: Chicago Sun,* 23 Mar 1943.

223   *There she is:* quoted in Tong, 190–91. *Hell of a fight:* 19 Apr 1943. RG 226, Entry 210, Box 401, File 11. NARA.

224   *Hollywood Bowl speech: New York Herald Tribune,* 5 Apr 1943. *Selznick's Hollywood pageant:* David Thomson, 386–90. *Ghastly memories: New York Herald Tribune,* 5 Apr 1943.

225   *I gotta get my laundry:* www.grimsociety.com/wayback/janwb.html. *Mayling mystified:* Roosevelt, 286–87.

225–26   *His-and-her books: New York Times Book Review,* 18 Apr 1943.

226   *Comprador-feudalist fascism:* Neils, 98. *China's Destiny:* Chiang's book was eventually published in the U.S. in 1947, in watered-down form.

227   *Angels don't throw cards:* Wendell Willkie to MCKS, 19 Apr 1943. MCKS Folder, Wilkie Papers. Indiana. *The Gospel According to Hoyle* is a book of card tricks with Christian messages, designed for evangelistic purposes. *Perpetual adolescent:* Wallace Diary, Vol. 14, 2467. Columbia. *Newfoundland dog:* Ibid. *World vision:* Halifax to Foreign Office, 20 Apr 1943. WO 208/270A. TNA. *Mischievous statements:* Mansergh, Vol. 3, 928.

228   *Indian response:* Soong to MCKS, 20 Apr 1943. Soong Papers, 63.16. Hoover. *Madame is a devoted friend:* Soong to Consul General Pao, 26 Apr 1943. Soong Papers, 63.16. Hoover. *Befuddle a credulous world:* quoted in Furuya, 753. *Stilwell:* "Why We Lost China, I," *Saturday Evening Post,* 7 Jan 1950. *Vacillating tricky undependable old scoundrel:* quoted in Tuchman, 371.

229   *I have won for China:* quoted in Alsop, 216–20.

230   *Soong's discussion with Churchill:* Soong Papers, 61.6. Hoover. *Really was provocative:* Soong Papers, 61.6. Hoover.

231   *China consciousness:* "Address to Ladies of Congressional Members," 20 May 1966. Judd papers, Box 175: CKS & MCKS, General, 1960–1972. Hoover. *Luce's soul-searching memo:* "Private Memorandum on Pearl Buck's article on China," March 1943. Time-Life Archives. *Buck's article: Life,* 10 May 1943.

232   *To the President:* Moran, 131. *Little yellow men:* quoted in Moran, 599. *My dear Sister:* Soong to MCKS, 18 May 1943. Soong Papers, 63.12. Hoover. *Floor at the Ritz:* Prime minister to foreign secretary, 21 May 1943. PREM 4/28/7. TNA.

233   *Would not kow-tow:* Box 5, Folder 219, File 76, Gunther Papers. Harvard. Churchill is identified as "X" in Gunther's notes. *Anglo-Saxons superior:* Wallace Diary, Vol. 14, 2476–7. Columbia.

234   *Let's hope:* 11 Jun 1943. FO 371/35776. TNA. *These irritations:* Schedule A, Box 30, Soong
       Papers. Hoover. *Ochlocracy an inchoate rococo of mob rule:* FO 371/35776. TNA. *I feel
       as if:* unidentified newspaper clipping, n.d. Wesleyan. *Living symbol: NYT,* 27 Jun 1943.

235   *No, you can't clean this dress:* Ann Maria Domingos, interview with author, 29 Jun
       1998. *I hate his guts:* 25 Jun 1943, 12 Aug 1943, 6 Oct 1943. RG 226, Entry 210, Box
       401, File 11. NARA. *Meeting with Roosevelt:* Wallace Diary, Vol. 14, 2538. Columbia.

236   *The weather:* Drew Pearson, "Washington Merry-Go-Round," 6 Sep 1943, unidenti-
       fied newspaper. *Nearly left us guests:* 10 Jul 1943, unidentified newspaper clippings.
       Where the hell: 25 Apr 1944. RG 226, Entry 210, Box 401, File 11. NARA.

237   *Generalissimo was livid:* Arthur N. Young, oral history interview, 158–63. Truman.
       Arrival reenacted: 25 Apr 1944. RG 226, Entry 210, Box 401, File 11. NARA. *Spiri-
       tual lift: NYT,* 11 Jul 1943.

NOTES FOR CHAPTER FIFTEEN

238   *American public disillusionment: Foreign Relations,* 1943, China, 80–81. *Hanson Baldwin
       article: NYT,* 20 Jul 1943.

239   *Subservience:* MCKS to Soong, 18 Jul 1943. Soong Papers, 62.1. Hoover. *I shall never
       forget:* Willkie to "My dear May," 14 Aug 1943. Mme. Chiang folder. Willkie Papers.
       Indiana University. *I did not know Mr. Willkie:* MCKS to Harry Barnard, 28 Aug 1973.
       US History mss. Indiana. *Made up her mind:* Mountbatten to Cripps, 30 Oct 1943.
       Mountbatten Papers, MB1/C59/6. Southampton.

240   *I've prayed with him:* Belden, 435. *Two intelligent dames:* Stilwell, 224. *Snow White:*
       quoted in Belden, 434–35. *This was all balderdash:* Stilwell, 232–33.

241   *Row between CKS and Soong:* Articles, Alsop, "Why We Lost China," Part I. *If elder
       sister had been a man:* quoted in Alsop, 223–27. *Carton de Wiart: Current Biography,*
       1940. *Stilwell is most friendly:* Carton de Wiart to Mountbatten, 20 Dec 1943. MB1/
       C42/4 (1–4). Mountbatten Papers. Southampton. *Surface:* Carton de Wiart to "Pug"
       Ismay, 26 Feb 1944. CAB 127/27. TNA.

242   *Peacemaker:* quoted in Tully, 270.

243   *Now let me get this straight:* Stilwell, 225. *Ghastly waste of time:* quoted in Tuchman,
       404. *Medieval machinery:* J.C.S. 127th Meeting, Sextant Conference, 22 Nov 1943.
       RG 165, Entry 421, File 337, Box 257. NARA. *Stop your outrageous talking:* Marshall,
       605. *Feminine Super All-Highest:* Mansergh, Vol. 4, 501–3. *If you allow me: NYT,* 6 Sep
       1965. *Little Lady at Big Conference: New York Mirror,* 9 Jan 1944. *Terrible old man:*
       "First Lady Hopes US Will Continue Firm Vietnam Stand," Chinese News Service,
       19 Mar 1965. Box 175: CKS & MCKS, General, 1960–1972. Judd Papers. Hoover.

244   *Remarkable and charming:* Churchill, Vol 5, 328–29. *China an even older country:* "Con-
       fidential," n.d. MB1/C42/26 (1–3), Mountbatten Papers. Southampton. *Eye trouble:*
       MCKS to Mrs. Helen Reid, 2 Dec 1943. Reid Family Papers, Box D59. LOC. *Noth-
       ing:* Moran, 130–31. *The talks:* Churchill, Vol. 5, 328. *Flat promise:* Memorandum for
       the president, 3 Sep 1945. PSF. Truman.

245   *Considerable impatience . . . from the very top:* Frank Dorn to Wendell J. Coates, 7 May
       1969. Dorn Papers, 6.4. Hoover. *Worked out an arrangement:* Wallace Diary, 23 Jul
       1946. Vol. 27, 4854. Columbia. *Anxiety and apprehension:* quoted in Furuya, 785–86.

246   *Stalin spoke disparagingly:* Churchill, Vol. 5, 318. *Nervous breakdown:* MCKS to Mrs.
       Helen Reid, 2 Dec 1943. Reid Family Papers, Box D59. LOC. *Electric: Foreign Rela-*

tions, 1943, China, 179. *Chiang threatened: Foreign Relations*, 1943, China, 482–83. Also Gauss to secretary of state, 16 Jan 1944. President's secretary's file, Box 175, File: US-China Supply. Truman Library. *Tell them to go jump:* quoted in Jean Edward Smith, 175.

247   *Relieve me of the torture:* MCKS to Eleanor Roosevelt, 29 Feb 1944. Eleanor Roosevelt's White House Papers, Special Folder, Series 100, Personal Letters, Box 1715. FDR. *They are trying:* MCKS to Eleanor Roosevelt, 19 Apr 1944. Eleanor Roosevelt's White House Papers, Special Folder, Series 100, Personal Letters, Box 1715. FDR. *Bad blood:* "Confidential," n.d. MB1/C42/26 (1–3). Mountbatten Papers, Southampton. *Sparkling political cocktail: Current Biography*, 1944. *First Lady of China Too Chic: Boston Post*, 20 Feb 1944.

248   *What exactly is wrong: Foreign Relations*, 1944, China, 38. *Soong countered: Foreign Relations*, 1944, China, 51–52. *Adler lampooned Chiang's book:* No. 2700, 17 Jun 1944. RG 59, CDF 1940–44, Box 5849. NARA. *Ching-kuo given lavish budget:* C. E. Gauss to secretary of state, 21 Apr 1944 and 5 Apr 1944. RG 59, LM 65, Reel 11. NARA. *Ching-kuo's advancement:* C. E. Gauss to secretary of state, 21 Apr 1944 and 5 Apr 1944. RG 59, LM 65, Reel 11. NARA.

249   *Private preserve:* General Chiang Kai-shek, Consul-General Kunming to Washington, 1 Aug 1944. RG 59, CDF 1940–44, Box 5844. NARA. *Smear stories:* Tong, 198–99. *Generalissimo displeased:* Chinese Political Situation, 27 Feb 1945. RG 226–OSS, Entry 210, Box 160, Folder 1. NARA.

250   *Domestic intranquility:* Gauss to secretary of state, 24 Apr 1944. RG 59, CDF 1940–44, Box 5849. NARA. *Literally seething:* "Domestic Troubles in the Chiang Household," 10 May 1944. McHugh Papers, Box 3. Cornell. *The prevalence and belief:* "Domestic Troubles in the Chiang Household," 10 May 1944. McHugh Papers, Box 3. Cornell. *That man:* "Domestic Troubles in the Chiang Household," 10 May 1944. McHugh Papers, Box 3. Cornell. *indications:* "Domestic Troubles in the Chiang Household," 10 May 1944. McHugh Papers, Box 3. Cornell.

251   *Cupid:* Wallace Diary, 8 May 1944. Vol. 19, 3319. Columbia. *Let me get them all in the same room:* Ibid., 3346. *Mayling pulled down her stockings:* Lattimore, 186. *Madame Sun's depth: Foreign Relations*, 1944, China, 240–44. *Amusement:* Abell, 60. Wallace Diary, Vol. 22, 4024–45. Columbia.

252   *Not men of good faith:* "American Attitude Toward Kuomintang-Communist Relations During the Hurley Mission," RG 59, Entry 399A, Box 13, File: TS 1948—Chicom-Kuomintang Relations. NARA. *Chiang is at best:* Furuya, 815. *Americans dazzled by Yenan:* John S. and Caroline Service, Oral History Project, Vol. II, 218–22. Georgetown. *Oleomargarine communists:* K. C. Wu to Soong, 27 Apr 1945. Soong Papers, 36.41. Hoover. *Even more radical than Moscow:* 7 Dec 1944. RG 457, Entry 9032, Box 519, File Decrypted Diplomatic Traffic. NARA. *Could not promise:* Hahn to Mrs. Lewis, 1 Aug 1945. Box 2. Hahn Papers. Indiana.

253   *Chiang and Mayling deny rumors at tea party:* Chungking to secretary of state, 9 Jul 1944; 11 July 1944. RG 59, CDF 1940–44, Box 5849. NARA.

254   *Departed for Brazil:* 10 Jul 1944. Soong Papers, 62.2. Hoover. *Bewildered:* Rio de Janeiro to Foreign Office, 11 Jul 1944. FO 371/41590. TNA. *Investments:* 26 Jul 1944. RG 226, Entry 210, Box 401, File 11. NARA. *Drew Pearson's column: New York Mirror*, 10 Jul 1944. *Extremely serious rift:* No. 2761, Chungking to secretary of state, 11 Jul 1944. RG 59, Entry CDF 1940–44, Box 5849. NARA.

255   *Hoodwink:* Extract from letter dated 30 Dec 1944. WO 208/270A. TNA. *If this crisis:* Stilwell, 307.

256   *Only visible hope:* Stilwell, 317. *If the G-mo:* Stilwell, 331.

257   *I understand:* quoted in Alsop, 241. *Prisoner in his own house:* Soong to T. A. Soong, 30 Sep 1944. Soong Papers, 36.18. Hoover. *Greatest humiliation:* quoted in Furuya, 808–9. *Stilwell celebrated:* Stilwell, 333. *The pain:* quoted in Furuya, 814. *Wholesale debunking:* Mansergh, Vol. 5, 191. *My conscience:* quoted in Furuya, 815. Stilwell died on October 12, 1946, of stomach cancer. *Patient at Johns Hopkins: Boston Post,* 29 Sep 1944. *Physical incapacitation: NYT,* 8 Oct 1944.

258   *Gage visit to Mayling:* Berkeley Gage to "Benito," 30 Oct 1944. FO 371/41590. TNA. *Disappointed:* 21 Nov 1944. RG 226, Entry 210, Box 401, File 11. NARA.

259   *Absolute farce:* Churchill, Vol. 6, 701. *Talking to the Chinese:* "US Wartime Commitments and Negotiations Affecting China . . . ," n.d. RG 59, 399A, Box 14, Files. TS-Taiwan 1948. NARA. *Radish communists:* quoted in Taylor, 122. *Will Britain and Russia:* quoted in Furuya, 821. *Has China really:* Ibid., 822. *American illusion:* Hurley to secretary of state, 14 Apr 1945. Box 306: Yalta. Harriman Papers. LOC.

260   *Hong Kong will be eliminated:* Ibid. *He speaks of you often:* Frank Price to MCKS, 21 Apr 1945. Price Papers, 2.12. Marshall. *Extremely shocked: NYT,* 14 Apr 1945; *Washington Times,* 19 Jul 1945.

261   *He always went:* Harold K. Hochschild to Earle Albert Selle, 3 Feb 1947; 31 Jan 1947. W. H. Donald Letters, Hochschild Papers. Columbia. *Sympathetic and unwavering understanding: Contemporary China,* 20 Aug 1945. Box 175. Judd Papers. Hoover.

262   *Saw red: Foreign Relations,* 1945, Vol. 7, 540–42. *Improve the masses: Foreign Relations,* 1945, Vol. 7, 540–42. *Somewhat thin:* MCKS to Eleanor Roosevelt, 18 Sep 1945. Anna Eleanor Roosevelt Correspondence, 1945–52, Box 3269: MCKS. FDR. *Fifty years of national humiliation:* quoted in Furuya, 831.

263   *The crisis with which our nation is faced today:* Ibid., 832.

NOTES FOR CHAPTER SIXTEEN

264   *Storm center: Life,* 13 Dec 1948, Letters to the Editor. *At times his trust:* Wedemeyer to Marshall, 1 Aug 1945. Marshall Papers, Box 90. Marshall.

265   *Long Live Chairman Chiang:* Reminiscences of Tso Shun-sheng, 220–22. COHP. Columbia. *Polite grunts:* Luce's Chungking diary, October 1945. *Time-Life* Archives. *Terrible responsibility:* Luce's Chungking diary, October 1945. *Time-Life* Archives. Owing to her duties in Washington, Clare, who in 1942 had been elected a Republican senator from Connecticut, did not join Luce on the trip. *Luce wrote Mayling:* Luce to MCKS, 28 Oct 1945. *Time-Life* Archives.

266   *Americans must not participate:* Wedemeyer to the Generalissimo, 10 Nov 1945. Box 303: China-General, Harriman Papers. LOC. *No Chinese forces in Korea:* Wedemeyer to the Generalissimo, 10 Nov 1945. Box 303: China-General, Harriman Papers. LOC.

267   *Carpetbagging:* O. Edmund Clubb, 39. Truman. *Inflationary finance:* Pepper, 424.

268   *Seeds of McCarthyism:* O. Edmund Clubb, 34. Truman. *General, I want:* Edwin A. Locke, oral history interview, 79–80. Truman. *Bitter blow:* quoted in Pogue, 29–30. *Devil to pay: NYT,* 25 Jan 1956. *Radicalism:* quoted in Stoler, 53. *How the Powers should deal with China:* Ibid. *I wish him every success: New York Herald Tribune,* 1 Jan 1946.

269   *She can talk beautifully:* Associated Press, 4 Dec 1945. *A lot of nonsense:* Edwin A. Locke, oral history interview, 61. Truman. *Special messenger: London Times,* 26 Jan 1946.

270   *Stalin's military genius: NYT,* 24 Jan 1946. *Tires on plane slashed: NYT,* 27 Jan 1946. *Miss Utley:* quoted in Utley, *Last Chance,* 131–33. *People should believe:* Ibid.

271 *Simply abominable . . . Chungking man:* Dr. Wu Kuo-Cheng, COHP. Columbia. *Truly unprecedented proportions:* Pepper, 424. *I have one desire:* Bland, 574. *Simply can't do enough:* Bland, 575.

272 *Commentary on the virulence:* Bland, 575. *She does so much:* Bland, 578. *She told me that Marshall's attitude:* Bland, 160.

273 *Communist anti-American campaign:* "Directions of Anti-America Propaganda," 7 Jul 1946. Soong Papers, 61.11. Hoover.

274 *Katherine Marshall's trip to Kuling:* Bland, 579–80. *Mayling produced Coca-Cola:* Frank Rounds, Vol. 1, 55–56. Columbia. *He never says die:* Bland, 580. *The Chinese don't trust her:* John F. Melby, oral history interview, www.trumanlibrary.org /oralhist/melby2.htm.

275 *He had met:* Wallace Diary, 23 Jul 1946. Vol. 27, 4854. Columbia. *It is with deep regret:* Wellington Koo to T. V. Soong, 14 Aug 1946. Soong Papers, 37.14. Hoover. *Honeycombed:* Frank Price to MCKS, 21 Jan 1947. Price Papers, 2.12. Marshall.

276 *I went to the Madame:* Marshall, 575. *Kind:* Donald to Hochschild, 15 Apr 1946. Hochschild Papers, Columbia. *Boss:* Ida du Mars to K. C. Li, 12 Nov 1946. Hochschild Papers, Columbia.

277 *My battle:* Marshall to Eisenhower, 17 Sep 1946. Marshall Papers, 122/42. Marshall. *Desire to be of help:* MCKS to Wedemeyer, 14 Nov 1946. Wedemeyer Papers, Box 92. Hoover. *I will tell you something:* Marshall, 571. *His old foot:* quoted in Beal, 313.

278 *My answer:* quoted in Acheson, *Present,* 210. *Their final conversation:* U.S. News & World Report, 1 Oct 1954. *Members of his staff:* Frank Rounds, Vol. 1, 81-82. Columbia.

279 *Come back soon: Time,* 20 Jan 1947. *Coffee:* Frank Rounds, Vol. 1, 81–82. Columbia. *Marshall's personal statement:* "General Marshall Leaves China," 8 Jan 1947. Box 2, China file: General, 1948. Melby Papers. Truman Library. *Dyed-in-the-wool Communists:* Ibid. *Interested in the preservation:* Ibid.

280 *Blistering plague: Los Angeles Times,* 8 Jan 1947. *Friendly and constructive: NYT,* 13 Jan 1947. *Did not point out: NYT,* 15 Jan 1947. *China would profit:* O. Edmund Clubb. Truman.

281 *Crude farce: Selected Works of Mao Zedong,* Beijing, Foreign Languages Press, 1969. Vol. IV, 434. http://ptb.sunhost.be/marx2mao/mao/FLS49.html. *I tried to please everyone:* quoted in Bidault, 144. *Blatantly bumptious: Foreign Relations,* 1947, Vol. 7, 51. *Credible alternative:* William Wells, interview with author, 29 Jun 1998.

282 *The wink: The New Yorker,* 12 Apr 1947. *Piece of cake:* Frank Rounds, Vol. 1, 58–59. Columbia.

NOTES FOR CHAPTER SEVENTEEN

283 *Made for the mandarins:* Pickering, 97. *Taiwan's sorrow: General History of Taiwan,* Lien Heng, 1920, cited on Wikipedia.org, under Lien Chan.

284 *Every three years:* quoted in Mancall, 148.

285 *Plague of mainland officials:* 2 Sep 1947. No. 971, Box 2: China-General, 1947. Melby Papers, Truman. *Dirt:* Dr. Wu Kuo-Cheng, 8, COHP. Columbia. *A dog eats: Time,* 4 Jul 1949. *Chinese conscripts gaped at elevators:* Allan Shackelton. *Formosa Calling: An Eyewitness Account of Conditions in Taiwan During the February 28th, 1947 Incident.* Chevy Chase: Taiwan Publishing Company and Taiwan Communiqué, 1998.

286 *Taiwanese want revenge now:* quoted in Lai, et al., 105–7.

287 *If—and only if:* Memorandum on Taiwan, Nanking to secretary of state, 21 Apr 1947; "Taiwan" report, 9 Aug 1947. RG 59, Entry 1108, Box 2: Formosa. NARA.

Jolt the government: Wedemeyer to "Leighton" [Stuart], 3 Sep 1947. Melby Papers, Box 2. Truman. *Spiritual bankruptcy:* Rev. David E. Morken, "A Recounting," 1998, www.morken.com/lifestories/dmorken/index7.html; *Foreign Relations,* 1948, Vol. 7, 226.

288 *Nothing would delight my soul:* MCKS to Marshall, 16 Mar 1948. 60/45, Marshall Papers. Marshall. *Doubtless the situation: Wellesley Magazine,* Apr 1948.

289 *Source of the country's evils:* 28 Oct 1948, No. 446. Lewis Clark to secretary of state. Box 3: China-General, 1948. Melby Papers, Truman. *Their wealth and foreign-style homes:* quoted in Spence, 503. *You are brothers:* quoted in Taylor, 160.

290 *David King's activities:* Shanghai to secretary of state, 2 Sep 1948, 3 Sep 1948. RG 59, CDF 1945–49, LM 184, Roll 58, Frames 495–97. NARA. *Tu Yueh-sheng tipped off Chiang Ching-kuo:* Shanghai to secretary of state, 6 Oct 1948. RG 59, CDF 1945–49, LM-184, Roll 50 Frames 628–29. NARA. *David Kung paid a settlement:* Taylor, 160–61. *Gold Yuan collapsed:* Li Han-hun, Dr. Wu Kuo-Cheng, 76–78. COHP. Columbia. *China's "royal family" fortune:* Dr. Wu Kuo-cheng, 322–23. Columbia.

291 *Much more sinned against:* Dr. Wu Kuo-cheng, 325. Columbia. *When she keeps good company:* Dr. Wu Kuo-cheng, 346–47. Columbia.

292 *World's worst leadership:* "Quotations from Telegrams . . . ," n.d. RG 59, Entry 399A, Box 13: TS-China Aid Program 1948. NARA. *Third world war:* Memorandum to secretary of state, No. 458, 5 Nov 1948. Box 3: China-General, 1948. Melby Papers, Truman. *Communist-staged campaign:* quoted in Furuya, 901.

293 *Chiang couldn't be elected dog-catcher:* Randall Gould to Roy Howard, 25 Nov 1948. Box 235: 1948—Foreign File—China, Howard Papers. LOC. *Communists a credible and dynamic force:* Pepper, 427–35. *Communists close to the people:* Ibid., 435. *Nationalists contributed to Dewey's campaign:* Memorandum: "Evidence of Corruption in the Chinese Government," 22 Jul 1949. RG 59, Entry 399A, Box 16: TS-White Paper. NARA.

294 *If we fail to stem the tide:* 9 Nov 1948. RG 59, Entry 399A, Box 13: TS—Chiang—1948. NARA. *Don't tell me any more:* quoted in Drage, 176. *Chiang's exaltation of spirit: Foreign Relations,* 1948, Vol. 7, 626. *Hazards of her mission:* Roy Howard to N.C. Nyi, 29 Nov 1948. Box 235: 1948—Foreign File—China. Howard Papers, LOC.

295 *If Communism prevails: Newsweek,* 6 Dec 1948. The term "domino theory" was coined in 1954. *The real facts of the situation:* Memorandum of conversation, 26 Nov 1948. RG 59, Central Decimal Files 1945–49, LM-184, Roll 26, Frame 239. NARA. *I'm so dizzy: Newsweek,* 13 Dec 1948. *Mayling bantered with reporters: Time,* 13 Dec 1948; *Newsweek,* 13 Dec 1948.

296 *Poor business risk . . . Chiang is a generalissimo: Newsweek,* 13 Dec 1948. *Overrunning China like lava: Time,* 6 Dec 1948.

297 *Great misunderstanding:* Suggested statement to Madame Chiang, George F. Kennan, 2 Dec 1948. RG 59, Entry 399A, Box 13: TS—Chiang—1948. NARA. *Spark plug:* Memorandum of conversation with Madame Chiang, 3 Dec 1948. PSF. Truman. CKS to MCKS, 1 Dec 1948, Jiashu. AH. *Highly inadvisable:* Memorandum of conversation with Madame Chiang, 3 Dec 1948. PSF. Truman.

298 *Misunderstandings:* MCKS to CKS, 5 Dec 1948, 9 Dec 1948. Jiang Zhongzheng Dangan, Tejiao Wendian, Lingxiushigongzhibu—Duimeiwaijiao, Diwuceshangce. CKS to MCKS, 7 Dec 1948, Jiashu. AH. *Top Secret Report for General Flicker:* MCKS to Marshall, n.d. [Dec 1948]. Marshall Papers, 60.46. Marshall.

300 *Were you successful: Time,* 20 Dec 1948. *Patient:* MCKS to CKS, 12 Dec 1948, 13 Dec 1948, 15 Dec 1948. CKS Files, Tejiaowendian, Lingxiushigongzhibu—Duimeiwaijiao, Diwuceshangce. AH. *Girlish whim:* Memorandum: MCKS, 15 Dec 1948. Truman

Papers, PSF. Truman. *Should not be withdrawn:* Barr to Maddocks, 18 Dec 1948. RG 59, Entry 399A, Box 13: Ts-Internal Situation 1948. NARA.

301   *Truman might announce change:* MCKS to CKS, 28 Dec 1947. CKS Files, Tejiaowendian, Lingxiushigongzhibu—Duimeiwaijiao, Diwuceshangce. AH. *Chiang pleaded:* CKS to MCKS, 28 Dec 1948. CKS Files, Jiashu. AH. *Meeting with congressional leaders:* MCKS to CKS, 1 Jan 1948. CKS Files, Tejiaowendian, Lingxiushigongzhibu—Duimeiwaijiao, Diwuceshangce. AH.

NOTES FOR CHAPTER EIGHTEEN

302   *Madame General: The Reporter,* 29 Apr 1952. *In your hearts:* MCKS's Farewell Address, 8 Jan 1950. Reid Family Papers, Box D94. LOC.

303   *China Lobby changed tack: The Reporter,* 15 Apr 1952. *The U.S. responsible for Nationalist predicament:* Koen, 95. *Mayling requests $200,000:* MCKS to CKS, 8 Jan 1948. CKS Files, Tejiaowendian, Lingxiushigongzhibu—Duimeiwaijiao, Diwuceshangce. AH. *The Major . . . the little fellow: The Reporter,* 15 Apr 1952, 20. *If the matter leaked:* CKS to MCKS, 14 Jan 1948. Jiashu. AH. *Howard's observations:* Roy Howard, "Strictly Confidential Memorandum," 14 Jan 1949. Courtesy Pamela Howard. *Great courtesy:* Ibid.

304   *Christian fortitude:* Ibid. *Sixteen days of spinach soup:* quoted in Oursler, 349. *Nationalist funds transferred into private accounts: The Reporter,* 29 Apr 1952, 8.

305   *Mayling repeats demand for funds:* MCKS to CKS, 27 Jan 1949. CKS Files, Tejiaowendian, Lingxiushigongzhibu—Duimeiwaijiao, Diwuceshangce. AH. *Mayling's efforts bore fruit:* Koen, 95. *Holding meetings each Tuesday:* MCKS to CKS, n.d. (A596), CKS Files, Tejiaowendian, Diwucexiace, Lingxiushigongzhibu, Lingdaogemingwaijiao—Duimeiguanxi. AH.

306   *Chiang's men in U.S. had access to multiple accounts: The Reporter,* 29 Apr 1952. *Mayling urged Chiang to sabotage:* MCKS to CKS, 27 Jan 1949. CKS Files, Tejiaowendian, Lingxiushigongzhibu—Duimeiwaijiao, Diwuceshangce. AH. *Chiang asked if Mayling had received funds:* CKS to MCKS, 1 Feb 1949. CKS Files, Jiashu. AH.

307   *Now Mao Tse-tung can't hit me:* Tso Chun-sheng, 273–75, COHP. Columbia. *Selling out:* MCKS to CKS, 6 May 1949. CKS Files, Tejiao Wendian, Lingxiushigongzhibu—Duimeiwaijiao, Diwuceshangce. CKS to MCKS, 6 May 1949. Jiashu. AH.

308   *Kohlberg participated in strategy meeting: The Reporter,* 29 Apr 1952. *I think I may know:* Kohlberg to Leslie E. Claypool, 8 Apr 1952. Box 30: China Lobby. Kohlberg Papers. Hoover.

309   *Cat's-paw:* Kohlberg to secretary of the treasury, 20 Sep 1950. Box 30: China Lobby, Kohlberg Papers. Hoover. *Use cash to counter:* MCKS to CKS, 19 May 1949, A256 and A262. CKS Files, Tejiaowendian, Lingxiushigongzhibu—Duimeiwaijiao, Diwuceshangce. AH. *At my request . . . destroy code book:* Ibid. *Chiang warned not to mention names:* CKS to MCKS, 21 May 1949. CKS Files, Jiashu. AH. *Mayling urged Chiang:* MCKS to CKS, 8 May 1949. CKS Files, Tejiaowendian, Lingxiushigongzhibu—Duimeiwaijiao, Diwuceshangce. AH. *I had asked you:* MCKS to CKS, 2 Jun 1949. CKS Files, Tejiaowendian, Lingxiushigongzhibu—Duimeiwaijiao, Diwuceshangce. AH. *Bombing airports:* MCKS to CKS, n.d. (A596), CKS Files, Tejiaowendian, Diwucexiace, Lingxiushigongzhibu, Lingdaogemingwaijiao—Duimeiguanxi. AH.

310   *Mayling lobbied against White Paper:* MCKS to CKS, 16 Jul 1949. CKS Files, Tejiaowendian, Diwucexiace, Lingxiushigongzhibu, Lingdaogemingwaijiao—

Duimeiguanxi. AH. *We picked a bad horse:* quoted in McCullough, 744. *Silence the primitives:* quoted in Cray, 675. *Moral support: NYT,* 24 Jul 1949. *Confession of guilt:* Judd to CKS, 30 Jul 1949. Box 163: CKS & MCKS 1940–82. Judd Papers. Hoover. *Mao's speech: NYT,* 1 Jul 1949.

311   *Preferred and expeditious:* Hoover to SACs, n.d.; Hoover to FBI San Francisco, 13 May 1949. Materials furnished to the author by the Department of Justice in response to a Freedom of Information Act inquiry. *FBI investigation:* Director and SAC New York from Phila, n.d. Materials furnished to the author by the Department of Justice in response to a Freedom of Information Act inquiry. *The exact amount:* MCKS to CKS, 23 Jul 1949. CKS Files, Tejiaowendian, Diwucexiace, Lingxiushigongzhibu, Lingdaogemingwaijiao—Duimeiguanxi. AH. *Chiang furious:* Dr. Wu Kuo-Cheng, 110. Columbia. *Unpalatable to believers:* quoted in Cray, 675.

312   *Chicken-tails:* MCKS to Marshall, 26 Sep 1949. Marshall Papers, 60.46. Marshall.

313   *Mayling urged Chiang to resume control:* MCKS to CKS, 13 Sep 1949. CKS Files, Tejiaowendian, Diwucexiace, Lingxiushigongzhibu, Lingdaogemingwaijiao—Duimeiguanxi. AH. *Only feasible course:* Memorandum of conversation, 30 Nov 1949. Acheson Records, Box 74. Truman. *Chiang offered Wedemeyer $5 million: The Reporter,* 29 Apr 1952. Also mentioned in MCKS to CKS, 13 Sep 1949. CKS Files, Tejiaowendian, Diwucexiace, Lingxiushigongzhibu, Lingdaogemingwaijiao—Duimeiguanxi. AH.

314   *Throwing good money:* "Comments on September 20th Draft of Formosa Paper," 21 Sep 1949. RG 59, Entry 399A, Box 16: File TS-Taiwan 1949. NARA. *Lessons:* "Summary of NSC Policy Decisions Regarding China," n.d. RG 59, Entry 399A, Box 16: TS-US Policy Toward Nationalist China 1949. NARA. *Failing military occupation:* "Problem: US Policy toward Formosa," n.d. RG 59, Entry 399A, Box 14: TS-American Policy Toward Formosa, 1949. NARA. *Should be considered:* RG 59, Entry 3990, Box 15: TS-Resistance. NARA. *Full title:* "Questions Relating to a Possible Trusteeship for Formosa," 7 Jan 1949. RG 84, Entry 3259A: TS Eyes Only, Box 1. NARA. *No longer regards:* "Proposed Statement to Be Issued by the Secretary of State," 15 Apr 1949. RG 59, Entry 399A, 16: TS-Taiwan-1949. NARA.

315   *Leave my country:* Frank E. Taylor to Madame Sun, 12 Aug 1969. Box 1: 1969. Taylor Papers. Indiana. *It would be a pity:* MCKS to CKS, 1 Jan 1950. Jiashu. AH. *Slander:* CKS to MCKS, 2 Jan 1950. Jiashu. AH. *No predatory designs:* Statement by the president, 5 Jan 1950. RG 59, Entry 399A, Box 17: TS-NSC Papers. NARA.

316   *The world wrote off our China:* MCKS, *The Sure Victory,* 21–22. *I shall feel:* Eleanor Roosevelt to MCKS, 9 Jan 1949 [should be 1950]. Anna Eleanor Roosevelt Correspondence, 1945–52, Box 3269: MCKS. FDR. *Life was meaningless:* MCKS, *The Sure Victory,* 22–23.

317   *Ethereal Voice:* Ibid., 23–24. *Dot on the map:* Ibid., 24. *A million dollars at Chen Chihmai's disposal: The Reporter,* 29 Apr 1952, 7.

317–8   *Mayling's farewell speech:* MCKS's Farewell Address, 8 Jan 1950. Reid Family Papers, Box D94. LOC.

318   *I wish you all the luck:* Associated Press, 10 Jan 1950.

NOTES FOR CHAPTER NINETEEN

321   *We have just been through:* "Easter Broadcast," MCKS, 11 Apr 1952. Selected speeches on religion by president and MCKS. Box 175: CKS & MCKS, General, 1930–1959.

Judd Papers. Hoover. *When the water recedes:* MCKS, *The Sure Victory,* 24–27. *Overpious:* Ibid., 27–28. *On this island:* Ibid., 29.

322   *Recognition of Beijing like Munich: Foreign Relations,* 1950, Vol. 6, 280–83. *Unjustified delay: NYT,* 4 Feb 1950. *Alsop's "Why We Lost China" article:* Articles, Alsop.

323   *I do not intend to turn my back:* Truman, 759. *Kohlberg briefed McCarthy: The Reporter,* 29 Apr 1952.

324   *He enjoys his present role: New York Post,* 15 Jul 1951. *Currie, White, and Hiss:* See Haynes & Klehr, *Venona. Psychic preventative detention:* Koen, xii. *Criticism of Chiang tantamount to treason:* Koen, 49.

325   *Asylum arrangements:* Taylor, 196.

326   *Wellesley training:* EDM to MCKS, 21 Aug 1975. Mills Papers. WCA. *Sun getting out of hand:* Diary of Mills's trip to Taiwan, Apr–May 1950, 34. Mills Papers. WCA. *Washington officials plotting coup to replace Chiang with Sun:* Taylor, 197–98. *Sun proposes coup:* Taylor, 198. *Mayling jealous of Wu:* Diary of Mills's trip to Taiwan, Apr–May 1950. Mills Papers. WCA. *The US does not recognize:* "Memorandum," n.d. [circa Mar 1950]. RG 59, Entry 399A, Box 16: TS-Taiwan, 1949. NARA.

327   *We were at our wits' end:* Dr. Wu Kuo-cheng, 170. Columbia. *High-minded:* H. H. Kung to Constantine Brown, 13 Jul 1950. Sokolsky Papers, 108.10. Hoover. *Complete loss: Foreign Relations,* 1950, Vol. 6, 343. *Take a dramatic and strong stand:* "The United States faces a new and critical period," 18 May 1950. RG 59, Entry 399A, Box 17: TS-US Policy Toward China, 1950. NARA. *Most undesirable:* Acheson to Johnson, 8 Jun 1950. RG 59, Entry 599A, Box 17: TS-US Policy Toward China, 1950. NARA.

328   *Undoubtedly we will experience:* MCKS to Marshall, 23 May 1950. Marshall Papers, 60.47. Marshall. *Breezy, chatty letter:* Marshall to MCKS, 29 May 1950. Marshall Papers, 60.47. Marshall.

329   *An albatross:* "Chinese Nationalists," 30 June 1950. PSF. Truman. *Astonishment at furor:* MacArthur, 340. *Not to give up an inch:* MCKS to Marshall, 1 Aug 1950. Marshall Papers, 60.47. Marshall.

330   *I would not like to see you in such danger:* MCKS to Marshall, 1 Aug 1950. Marshall Papers, 60.47. Marshall. *Grass Mountain:* Chiang soon after changed the name of Grass Mountain to "Yangmingshan" (Yangming Mountain) after Wang Yangming, a Ming philosopher he admired. *I think of you:* MCKS to Marshall, 1 Aug 1950. Marshall Papers, 60.47. Marshall. *I know you are ever so busy:* MCKS to Marshall, 1 Aug 1950. Marshall Papers, 60.47. Marshall.

331   *I think this would be:* Marshall to MCKS, 5 Sep 1950. Marshall Papers, 60.47. Marshall. *Humidity rash:* MCKS to EDM, 26 Sep 1950. Mills Papers. WCA. *Mayling became senior intelligence liaison:* Taylor, 207. *CIA-supported covert action forces:* Taylor, 207. *Conflicts between Mayling and Ching-kuo:* Taylor, 208. *In trust . . . uncleared title:* Cavendish W. Cannon to Mr. Jessup, 28 Aug 1950. RG 59, Entry 599A, Box 17: TS-US Policy Toward China, 1950. NARA. The legal term "uncleared title" applies to property whose legal ownership cannot be determined or is in dispute. *A sterilizing operation:* "Check List on China and Formosa," n.d. RG 59, Entry 399A, Box 17: TS-NSC Papers, 1950. NARA.

332   *The inspiration of anything:* 10 Aug 1950. RG 59, Entry 399a, Box 17: TS-Resistance. NARA.

333   *Violent animosity:* MacArthur, 341. *Without prejudice to the future:* quoted in MacArthur, 342. *Seriously detrimental:* quoted in MacArthur, 343.

334   *The wrong war:* quoted in Ambrose, 241. *Unsinkable station . . . cornucopia:* Taylor, 206–7. *I wish:* MCKS to Soong, 14 Feb 1951. Soong Papers, 63.13. Hoover.

334   *One of the wealthiest men:* NYT, 10 Jun 1950. ***Blank spots in their mental processes:*** *Foreign Relations,* 1951, Vol. 7, 1824. ***My personal:*** RG 59, Entry CDF 1950–54, Box 4218. NARA. ***Evidently:*** MCKS to EDM, 26 Jan 1951. Mills Papers. WCA.

335   *He expects you to bring home the bacon:* Rankin, 91. ***Bring the gospel:*** E. H. Hamilton to "Dear Friends All," 14 Nov 1959, Box 175: CKS and MCKS, Correspondence relating to, 1943-82. Judd Papers. Hoover. ***On the eve:*** "An Easter Message," MCKS, 23 Mar 1951. Selected speeches on religion by president and MCKS, Box 175: CKS & MCKS, General, 1930–1959. Judd Papers. Hoover.

336   *Gigantic booby trap:* quoted in McCullough, 817. ***Funds given to Madame Chiang:*** "China Lobby," n.d. PSF, Box 161: China Lobby, State Department. Truman. ***This suggests to some:*** Congressional Record, 11 Jun 1951, A3456. ***Pearson told Eisenhower:*** Abell, 212. ***Very little:*** Memorandum, Jim Lanigan to Ted Tannenwald, 10 Sep 1951. PSF, Box 161, China Lobby, State Department. Truman. ***Indications but no clear proof:*** Memorandum, James S. Lanigan to Theodore Tannenwald, Jr., 9 Oct 1951. PSF, Box 161, China Lobby, US Chamber of Commerce. Truman.

337   *Washington's Darkest Mystery:* The Reporter, 15 Apr 1952. ***Louis Kung made counselor:*** Rankin to Department of State, Aug 1953. RG 59, CDF 1950–54, LM-152, Roll #10, Frames 149–50. NARA. ***Drew Pearson's accusations:*** Washington Post, 2 Jul 1951, 16 Jul 1951. ***No one was more involved:*** Walter H. Judd to Robert C. Armstrong, 10 Mar 1982. Box 175: CKS & MCKS, Correspondence relating to, 1943–1982, Judd Papers. Hoover.

338   *Chiang's terrible temper:* USIS Taipei to USIA, 12 Jul 1955. RG 84, Entry 3258—Taiwan Consulate, Confidential File, Box 18, File 361.1-CKS. NARA.

339   *If you had any talent:* Emily Hahn, "The Old Boys," The New Yorker, 7 Nov 1953. ***I do not think:*** Hsiung Wan, interview with author, 28 Feb 1998. ***Great artist:*** MCKS to EDM, 21 Oct 1951. Mills Papers. WCA.

340   *Painting not a pastime:* Robert W. Barnett to Henry R. Luce, 7 Jan 1952. RG 59, CDF 1950–54, Box 4218. NARA. ***Most Chinese paintings:*** Chow Lien-hwa, speaking at memorial service for MCKS, 5 Nov 2003. ***Call each other Dar:*** Hsiung Wan, interview with author, 28 Feb 1998. ***Painted at night:*** "First Lady Hopes US Will Continue Firm Vietnam Stand," Chinese News Service, 19 Mar 1965. Box 175: CKS & MCKS, General, 1960–1972. Judd Papers. Hoover.

341   *Chiang's dog-eared Bible:* Congressional Record—Senate, 21 Apr 1975, S6339. ***Pray together:*** MCKS, The Sure Victory; Reader's Digest, Aug 1955. ***My dog has diabetes:*** Ren Nienzhen, grandmother of author's husband, as told to author. ***Two currents:*** Chow Lien-hwa, interview with author, 26 May 1998. ***Let's go to church:*** Ibid.

342   *To cheer him up:* diary of Mills's trip to Taiwan, Apr–May 1950, 35. Mills Papers. WCA. ***This fellow:*** Marshall, 367. ***You're off on the wrong track:*** Documentaries, Zhang Xueliang, Part 4. ***Tormented:*** GPO, "How This Came to Be Written," GPO to Kenneth Payne, 29 Sep 1954. Series I, Box 1, Folder 17, Oursler Papers. Georgetown.

343   *Flinched:* MCKS, The Sure Victory, 33. ***Conversion:*** Ibid., 34–35; Reader's Digest, Aug 1955. ***In these days:*** "Easter Broadcast," MCKS, 11 Apr 1952. Selected speeches on religion by president and MCKS, Box 175: CKS & MCKS, General, 1930–1959. Judd Papers. Hoover.

NOTES FOR CHAPTER TWENTY

344   *Soul-searching:* Rubinstein, 321–22; Arthur Hummel, FAOHP. Georgetown. ***Fire and water:*** Reminiscences of Dr. Wu Kuo-cheng, 319–21. Columbia. ***Opposition:***

AmEmbassy Taipei to Department of State, 10 Jun 1966. RG 59, SNF (1964–66), Files Pol-15-1, Box 2034. NARA. *Ching-kuo admired aspects of Russian life:* Rankin to Department of State, 31 Mar 1953. RG 59, CDF 1950–54, LM-152, Roll #24, Frames 640–41. NARA.

346   *It would have embarrassed them:* American consulate general, Hong Kong, to Department of State, 10 Nov 1955. RG 59, CDF 1955–59, Box 3937. NARA. *Enjoyed a drink:* Oscar Armstrong, FAOHP, 36. Georgetown. *Very charming:* William Wells, interview with author, 29 Jun 1998. *Lone wolf:* Rankin to Department of State, 15 Mar 1954. RG 59, CDF 1950–54, Box 4218. NARA. *If someone got in his way:* William Wells, interview with author, 29 Jun 1998. *More of a Communist:* Ibid.

347   *Friends arrested:* David L. Osborn, FAOHP. Georgetown. *Horde of screaming worshippers:* American consulate general, Hong Kong, to Department of State, 10 Nov 1955. RG 59, CDF 1955–59, Box 3937. NARA. See also Rubinstein, 323. *Surprising amount:* E. H. Jacobs-Larkom to J. S. H. Shattock, 26 May 1953. FO 371/105213. TNA. *Students:* Taylor, 192. *We don't hurt them:* Walter E. Jenkins, 16. FAOHP. Georgetown.

348   *Political officers:* Rubinstein, 323. *Teahouses and hostesses:* Taylor, 214.

349   *Wu urged Chiang:* Kerr, "Dr. K. C. Wu's Views on the Police State and General Chiang Ching-kuo," *Formosa Betrayed,* Appendix II. www.romanization.com/books/formosabetrayed/appendix2.html. *If Your Excellency loves Ching-kuo:* Ibid. *Kind offer:* Wu Kuo-cheng, 213–14. Columbia.

350   *Yu Kuo-ha's visit:* Ibid., 214–15. *The strenuous life:* MCKS to EDM, 5 Dec 1951. Mills Papers. WCA. *Mao Bangchu case: The Reporter,* 15 Apr. 1952.

351   *Awfully swollen:* MCKS to EDM, 10 Jun 1952. Mills Papers. WCA. *At the height of the attack:* Emily Hahn, "The Old Boys." *The New Yorker,* 7 Nov 1953. *Rankin found her nervous:* Rankin, 146. *X-ray therapy:* MCKS to ER, 24 Oct 1952. Anna Eleanor Roosevelt Correspondence, 1945–52, Box 3269: MCKS. FDR. *Enlightened officials:* FC1019/75, FO 371/99241. TNA. *As you may well:* MCKS to Eisenhower, 7 Nov 1952. Eisenhower to MCKS, 14 Nov 1952. Eisenhower Papers (Ann Whitman File), International Series, Box 10: Formosa (China) 1952–57 (7). Eisenhower.

352   *Another outbreak:* MCKS to Wedemeyer, 18 Dec 1952. Box 31, Correspondence: CKS & MCKS 1951–1970. Wedemeyer Papers. Hoover. *While I know:* Eisenhower to MCKS, 26 Feb 1953. White House Social Office, Records 1952–61, Box 2. Eisenhower. *Study hard:* unidentified magazine clipping, n.d. WCA.

353   *I have a lot of work to do: NYT,* 23 Mar 1953. *I came back because of K. C.:* Dr. Wu Kuo-cheng, 248–50. Columbia.

354   *If K. C. doesn't want:* Ibid. *Do you know:* Ibid., 250–52; 320–21. *It is not for those:* Ibid., 250–53.

355   *My crime is worthy of death:* Ibid., 265. *Governor, why:* Ibid., 268–70. *Madame offered Goul job:* Ibid., 270–71.

356   *You don't know:* Ibid., 270–71. *The Gimo:* Ibid., 276–77. *My Dear:* Roy Howard to MCKS, 31 Aug 1953. Howard Archive. Indiana. *Intellectual horizon:* quoted in Taylor, 219.

357   *Rough: Foreign Relations,* 1952–54, Vol. 14, 251–53. *God's work:* Rankin to Department of State, 12 Oct 1953. RG 59, CDF 1950–54, LM 152, Roll #10, Frames 487–88. NARA. *I believe:* Nixon, *Leaders,* 242–43. *Reasonable:* Quoted in Aitken, 227. *Inner strength of the American people:* Karl Rankin to Department of State, 10 Nov 1953. RG 59, Entry CDF 1950–54, File 033–9311, Box 182. NARA.

358   *Ching-kuo took over Mayling's position:* Taylor, 221. *Wu wrote Madame:* Dr. Wu Kuo-cheng, 290–91. Columbia. *Wu's letter to the National Assembly:* Kerr, "Dr. K. C. Wu's

Views on the Police State and General Chiang Ching-kuo," *Formosa Betrayed*, Appendix II. www.romanization.com/books/formosabetrayed/appendix2.html.

359   *Foaming indignation: Time*, 29 Mar 1954. *Malicious . . . aid and comfort: Time*, 22 Mar 1954. *No understanding:* Kerr, "Dr. K. C. Wu's Views on the Police State and General Chiang Ching-kuo," *Formosa Betrayed*, Appendix II. www.romanization.com/books/formosabetrayed/appendix2.html. *Delusion:* Alfred Kohlberg to Robert R. McCormick, 5 Apr 1954. Box 28: Chicago Newspaper Clippings and Correspondence. Kohlberg Papers. Hoover. *Evidently very depressed:* Ambassador Rankin to secretary of state, 21 Apr 1954. RG 59, CDF 1950–54, Box 4218. NARA.

360   *Progress:* MCKS to Wellington Koo, 28 May 1954. Koo Papers. Columbia. *Bamboo cage:* Dorothy R. Thomas, OHRO. Columbia. *We Chinese will not be slaves: NYT,* 31 Aug 1954. *It had not only liver:* MCKS to GPO, 8 Nov 1954. Series I, Box 1, Folder 17, Oursler Papers. Georgetown. *I was treated to a knockdown argument:* John Osborne to C. D. Jackson, 19 Jan 1955. Jackson Papers, Box 40: CKS & MCKS (2). Eisenhower. *Take evil to one's breast:* quoted in C. D. Jackson to John K. Jessup, 24 Mar 1955. Jackson Papers, Box 40: CKS & MCKS (2). Eisenhower.

361   *US opinion:* Henry Luce to John Osborne, 27 Aug 1954. *Time-Life* Archives. *Duty:* W. S. C. to foreign secretary, 10 Oct 1954. FO 371/110234. TNA. *Showcase for American aid:* Mancall, 60–61, 110; Rubinstein, 330–31, 336.

362   *Containment strategy:* Mancall, 107. *Put a leash on Chiang:* Rubinstein, 326. *Mayling said little:* 6 Mar 1955. Eisenhower Papers (Ann Whitman File), International Series, Box 10: Formosa (China) 1952–57 (4). Eisenhower. *He approved:* Roy Howard Diaries, 24 Feb 1955. Courtesy Pamela Howard.

363   *Sunk anyway:* Ibid., 20 Mar 1955. *Collapse:* Ibid., 22 Mar 1955. *Great deal of admiration:* Howard's Eisenhower memorandum, 3 Aug 1955. Courtesy Pamela Howard. *Howard advised Chiang to send Ching-kuo to U.S.:* Roy Howard Diaries, 22 Mar 1955. Courtesy Pamela Howard. *Howard found Chiang insidious:* Top-secret memorandum, 25 Mar 1955. RG 84, Entry 3259B, File 2, Box 1. NARA. *Women's League financed by import taxes: Ziyou Shibao,* 9 Apr 1995; *Minzhong Daily News,* 8 Aug 1997.

364   *Something must be quite bad:* quoted in Taylor, 232. *Handiwork:* Roy Howard Diaries, 18 Aug 1955. Courtesy Pamela Howard. *Exact details unclear: Taipei Times,* 10 Jan 2001. *Admission of negligence:* Boorman, Vol. 3, 167.

365   *Stupid move:* Roy Howard Diaries, 22 Aug 1955, 16 Sep 1955. Courtesy Pamela Howard. *Sun enjoying his rose garden:* Rankin, 272–73. *Americanized:* Conversation with Mrs. Lina Tai, 23 Oct 1956. RG 59, CDF 1955–59, Box 3937. NARA. *My wife:* Hollington K. Tong, *Together They Lead China,* 10. Public Affairs Press, Washington, 1958. Box 108: China 1957–1973. Wedemeyer Papers. Hoover.

366   *Just happened to be there:* Dulles to AmEmbassy Taipei, 22 Mar 1958. RG 59, CDF 1955–59, Box 3937. NARA.

366   *Ching-kuo his father's lackey:* Taipei to secretary of state, 23 Mar 1958. RG 59, CDF 1955–59, Box 3937. NARA. *Six hundred thousand men under arms:* Mancall, 91.

368   *Is it worth:* Emily Hahn, "It's Not Home," *The New Yorker,* 24 Oct 1953. *Children should know: NYT,* 30 May 1981.

369   *Halo of saint: Foreign Relations,* 1952–1954, Vol. 14, 63–65, 73–75. *Ching Ling attacked U.S. for "occupation" of Taiwan:* Cooper to secretary of state, 21 Dec 1955. RG 59, CDF 1955–59, File 033-9391, Box 70. NARA. *Ching Ling ill at ease, uncommunicative:* Henry C. Ramsey to Department of State, 11 Jan 1955. RG 59, CDF 1955–59, File 033-9391, Box 70. NARA. *Ching Ling still a Christian:* Ibid.

370   *Oursler visited Taipei:* GPO, "How This Came to Be Written," Oursler Papers, Series I, 1/17. Georgetown. *Labor of love:* MCKS to GPO, 27 Sep 1955; Fleming H. Revell, Office Memo, 14 Sep 1955. Oursler Papers, Series I, 1/17. Georgetown. *Miasma:* GPO to George Sokolsky, 9 Aug 1955. Oursler Papers, Series I, 1/17. Georgetown. *I only wish with all my heart:* GPO to MCKS, 21 Apr 1955. Oursler Papers, Series I, 1/17. Georgetown.

371   *I have been used to comforts:* MCKS to GPO, 2 May 1955. Oursler Series I, 1/17. Georgetown. *I appreciate:* MCKS to GPO, 2 May 1955. Oursler Papers, Series I, 1/17. Georgetown. *Leaks of egoism:* John B. Chambers, Harper & Brothers, n.d. Oursler Papers, Series I, 1/17. Georgetown. *When this project:* Luce to CKS, 21 May 1957. Jackson Papers, Box 40: CKS & MCKS (1). Eisenhower.

372   *Good-looking:* Roger W. Straus, 620, OHRO. Columbia. *Atypical:* Reminiscences of Roger W. Straus, OHRO. Columbia. *Very badly:* Roger W. Straus, 618, OHRO. Columbia. *Substantial and attractive:* Jackson to MCKS, 11 Mar 1957. Jackson Papers, Box 40: CKS & MCKS (1). Eisenhower. *Ploy:* Roger W. Straus, 619, OHRO. Columbia. *Proofs not sent:* Col. Harold Riegelman to Hollington K. Tong, 25 Jun 1957. Jackson Papers, Box 40: CKS & MCKS (1). Eisenhower.

373   *Under ordinary circumstances:* Roger Straus to Riegelman, 18 Dec 1957. Box 60, FSG Papers. NYPL. *Very close to our hearts:* Roger Straus to MCKS, 23 Aug 1960. Box 60, FSG Papers. NYPL. *At the present time:* MCKS to Roger Straus, 17 Nov 1960. Box 60, FSG Papers. NYPL. *New dark age:* Chinese News Service, 11 Apr 1958. Kohlberg Papers, Box 32: Chinese News Service 1958–59. Hoover. *Compromise with the Anti-Christ:* Chinese News Service, 11 Apr 1958. Kohlberg Papers, Box 32: Chinese News Service 1958–59. Hoover. *Faith is the substance:* The Bible, Hebrews, chapter 11, verse 1. *While there is deep antagonism:* Sokolsky to MCKS, 12 May 1958. Sokolsky Papers, 35/16. Hoover.

374   *Cut out the talk:* Roy Howard Diaries, 6 Jul 1958. Courtesy Pamela Howard. *Evils:* CKS & MCKS, oral history interview, 38–39. Princeton. *The years have served only:* *Newsweek*, 6 Oct 1958. *We are going to do our own fighting:* *NYT*, 28 Jun 1958. *Self-hypnosis:* MCKS, "Existence on Sufferance," 10 Jul 1958. *Bull's-eye:* Sokolsky to MCKS, 5 Jul 1958. Sokolsky Papers, 35/16. Hoover.

375   *Wonderful fighting spirit: Time,* 21 Jul 1958; unidentified clipping. *We call ourselves civilized:* MCKS, *Selected Speeches 1943–82,* 114. *Accommodating:* Chinese News Service, 28 Aug 1958, 4 Sep 1958. Kohlberg Papers, Box 28: CKS & MCKS. Hoover.

376   *Because we are responding: Newsweek,* 6 Oct 1958. *Quemoy as whipping boy:* Dulles to Selwyn Lloyd, 24 Oct 1958. Dulles Papers, 1951–59. JFD Chronological Series, Box 16: Oct 1958 (2). Eisenhower. *Mere sadistic terrorism:* Dulles to John Cabot Lodge, 29 Oct 1958. Dulles Papers, 1951–59. JFD Chronological Series, Box 16: Oct 1958 (1). Eisenhower. *New concept of their mission:* Dulles to Sidney E. Smith, 27 Oct 1958. Dulles Papers, 1951–59. JFD Chronological Series, Box 16: Oct 1958 (1). Eisenhower. *Unwisdom of attaching:* NSC Memorandum, 31 Oct 1958. Eisenhower Papers, Ann Whitman File, NSC Series, Box 10: 384th Meeting of the NSC. Eisenhower. *Dulles reported to Madame Chiang:* Dulles to CKS, 29 Oct 1958. Dulles Papers, 1951–59. JFD Chronological Series, Box 16: Oct 1958 (1). Eisenhower. *We do not accept:* Dulles to John Cabot Lodge, 29 Oct 1958. Dulles Papers, 1951–59. JFD Chronological Series, Box 16: Oct 1958 (1). Eisenhower.

377   *I believe that if you depend:* Chen Li-fu to "Miss Che-ju," 20 Mar ?. Connor Papers, "Secret Years of Chiang Kai-shek." Columbia. *I hear that you are again:* Chen Li-fu to "Miss Che Ju," 4 Apr 1959. Connor Papers, "Secret Years of Chiang Kai-shek." Columbia.

378   *Outrageous act:* Eisenhower to CKS, 19 Jun 1960. Eisenhower Papers, Ann Whitman File, International Series, Box 12: Formosa (China) (Far East Trip), 6/12–26/60 (14). Eisenhower. *Staunch:* President's Far Eastern Trip, 8 Jun 1960. Eisenhower Papers, White House Central Files, 1953–61, Confidential File, 1953–61, Subject Series, Box 57: President's Trip to Russia, Japan and Far East—1960. Eisenhower. *While charming:* Ibid., 3 Jun 1960. *Cheer and courage . . . sweet and lovely looks:* White House Office, Staff Secretary: Records of Carroll, Goodpaster, Minnich, and Russell, 1952–61. International Trips and Meetings, Box 12: Far East Trip, June 1960. Eisenhower.

379   *Indefensible:* Third Kennedy-Nixon Debate, transcript, 13 Oct 1960. Commission on Presidential Debates, www.debates.org. *Show Lady Bird:* Sarah McClendon, 92–3. OHRO. Columbia. *Today, tomorrow and every day to come: Evening Star,* 15 Sep 1965.

380   *The UN is not that important:* Ralph Clough, interview with author, 6 Jul 1998. *As I am sure you realise:* Roy Howard to MCKS, 9 Sep 1961. Howard Archive, Indiana. *Abstain:* Roy Howard to MCKS, 16 Sep 1961. Howard Archive, Indiana. *Refused to be buried:* AmEmbassy Taipei to Dept. of State, 17 Nov 1965. RG 59, SNF (1964–66), Pol 15–1 Chinat, Box 2034. NARA. *Sacred mission:* Mancall, 12.

381   *Taiwan preparing for attack on mainland:* AmEmbassy to SecState, 20 Mar 1962. RG 59, CDF (1960–63), Box 2149. NARA. *Warm spot:* Soong to MCKS, 1 Sep 1963. Soong Papers, 63.12. Hoover. *Opportunity now present is not of man's creation:* Memorandum of Conversation, 14 Mar 1962. RG 59, CDF 1960–63), Box 2149. NARA. *Holy Expedition:* Ralph Clough to secretary of state, 29 Mar 1962. RG 59, CDF (1960–63), Box 2149. NARA.

382   *My own judgment:* MCKS to "My Dear Brother," 2 Jul 1962. Soong Papers, 63.13. Hoover. *Cheered:* Soong to MCKS, 31 Oct 1962. Soong Papers, 63.12. Hoover. *Nonsense:* MCKS to C. D. Jackson, 5 Oct 1962. Jackson Papers, Box 40: CKS & MCKS (1). Eisenhower. *Very, very beautiful:* "Overseas Report (Confidential) #6 from C. D. Jackson," 21 Aug 1962. Jackson Papers, 1931–67, Box 113: World Trip, Reports Mailed, 1962 (3). Eisenhower.

383   *Tell your people:* Ibid. *But how do you think the American people would feel? . . . Quemoy is our Berlin:* Ibid. *outer bastions:* C. D. Jackson to MCKS, 13 Sep 1962. Jackson Papers, Box 40: CKS & MCKS (1). Eisenhower. *Friend from foe:* Taipei to secretary of state, 27 Aug 1962. RG 59 CDF (1960–63), Box 2152. NARA. *We cannot stay on this island forever:* AmEmbassy to Department of State, 18 Feb 1963. RG 59, SNF (1963) Chinat-Pol-15, Box 3868. NARA. *Third world war:* MCKS to Soong, 28 Mar 1963. Soong Papers, 63.13. Hoover.

384   *Blue streak:* Soong to MCKS, 27 Apr 1963. Soong Papers, 63.12. Hoover. *Dropping a few crumbs:* Ralph Clough, interview with author, 6 Jul 1998. *Jennie Chen's memoir:* "Chiang's Other Wife," North America News Alliance, 11–12 Apr 1964. "Secret Years of Chiang Kai-shek," Connor Papers. Columbia. Lawrence Hill later founded Hill & Wang, the publisher, with Arthur Wang.

385   *Hush money:* "Chiang's Other Wife," North American News Alliance, 11–12 Apr 1964. "Secret Years of Chiang Kai-shek," Connor Papers. Columbia. *Jeanette in Taiwan:* Wang Fong, *Wo zai Jiang Jieshi fuzi shenbian,* 145–46. *Wracked with guilt:* Hsiung Wan, interview with author, 28 Feb 1998.

386 *Checked clothes:* Lin Chien-yeh, interview with author, 12 Nov 2001. *Polio rehabilitation center:* London Times, 8 Oct 1971.

387 *Christmas declared Constitution Day:* Johnny Ni, interview with author, 6 Feb 1998; www.gio.gov.tw/info/festival_c/law_e/law.htm. Constitution Day remained a national holiday until 1997, when it was declared a working holiday as part of measures cutting the workweek from six days to five. *Matter of life and death:* AmEmbassy Taipei to SecState, 26 Jan 1964. RG 59, SNF (1964–66), Pol Affairs & Rels. Chinat-US, Box 2040. NARA. *Opportunistic and unprincipled:* MCKS to Clare Boothe Luce, 31 Jan 1964. Clare Boothe Luce Papers, 220.3. LOC.

388 *Wait for death:* Foreign Relations, 1964–1968, Vol. XXX, 115–16. *Exquisite figure:* Evening Star, 29 Aug 1965. *Cut out the cancer:* NYT, 30 Aug 1965. *Warmongering:* NYT, 7 Sep 1965. *Formosa is a province of China:* NYT, 8 Sep 1965.

389 *No meeting had been set up with President Johnson:* Evening Star, 8 Sep 1965. *Unfriendly:* Henry R. Luce to Mr. Donovan, 9 Sep 1965. *Time-Life* Archives. *In dealing with Asian problems:* AmEmbassy Taipei to SecState, 31 Dec 1965. RG 59, SNF (1964–66), Pol. Affairs & Rels. Chinat-US, Box 2040. NARA. *Ching-kuo gave lip service:* AmEmbassy Taipei to Department of State, 10 Jun 1966. RG 59, SNF (1964–66), Pol-15-1, Box 2034. NARA. *Flying in the air without an airplane:* NYT, 8 Sep 1965. *MCKS another Winston Churchill:* Evening Star, 19 Sep 1965. *President gave Madame Chiang a personal tour:* Evening Star, 15 Sep 1965.

390 *ChiComs insane with power:* Foreign Relations, 1964–1968, Vol. XXX, 207–9. *Ladies should be ladylike:* Macon Telegraph, Atlanta Constitution, Atlanta Journal, 21 Oct 1965. *Atlanta Journal and Constitution Magazine,* 28 Nov 1965. *Bulletin of Wesleyan College,* Jan 1966. Wesleyan.

391 *Unruffled:* Newsweek, 6 Sept. 1965. *What does it matter:* NYT, 6 Sep 1965. *Chinatown speech:* Newsweek, 6 Sep 1965; NYT, 6 Sep 1965. *Did not approve:* I-Chung Loh, interview with author, 12 Jan 1998. *Ambivalent thinking:* NYT, 8 Dec 1965.

392 *I like to be well-informed:* Articles, Gage. *Grand ballroom full of dropped jaws:* The New Yorker, n.d. [circa March 1966]. *Elusive and exclusive:* NYT, 17 Apr 1966. *We will bury you:* http://news.bbc.co.uk/1/hi/uk_politics/2368397.stm.

393 *We make a pretense:* AmEmbassy Tokyo to SecState, 11 Aug 1966. Harriman Papers, Box 443: China-Taiwan. LOC. *Liberate our people:* unidentified newspaper clipping, 8 Aug 1966.

394 *Completely barbaric country:* AmEmbassy Tokyo to SecState, 16 Sep 1966. Box 443: China-Taiwan. Harriman Papers. LOC. *Old men in a hurry:* Memorandum of conversation, 22 Sep 1966. Box 443: China-Taiwan. Harriman Papers. LOC. *Frou-frou:* MCKS, "The Divine Right of Maoist Myth," 30 Aug 1966. Box 31: Correspondence: CKS & MCKS 1971–1988. Wedemeyer Papers. Hoover. *Morale tragically low; gossip that MCKS estranged from husband:* Foreign Relations, 1964–1968, Vol. XXX, 286–88. *Minimal impact:* Foreign Relations, 1964–1968, Vol. XXX, 296. *Use its power:* Evening Star, 4 Oct 1966.

395 *Needed a change of scenery:* AmEmbassy Taipei to Department of State, 14 Jun 1967. RG 59, SNF (1967–69), Pol 15-1 Chinat, Box 1984. NARA. *Moved to tears:* I-Chung Loh, interview with author, 12 Jan 1998. *Threatened Chiang:* Hsiung Wan, interview with author, 28 Feb 1998. *Plea for U.S. backing:* AmEmbassy Taipei to Department of State, 5 Apr 1967. RG 59, SNF (1967–69), Pol-15-1 Chinat, Box 1984. NARA. *Unthinkable:* AmEmbassy Taipei to Department of State, 28 Apr 1967. Box 443: China-Taiwan, Harriman Papers. LOC. *We have indeed lost a true friend:* "To Time for Luce Obit from Andrews," rec'd 3/2/67. *Time-Life* Archives.

396 **H. H. Kung's death:** *NYT,* 16 Aug 1967. **Self-sufficient:** "Free China Today," *American Legion Magazine,* May 1966. **Providential:** AmEmbassy Taipei to Department of State, 30 Sep 1967. RG 59, SNF (1967–69), Pol 15-1 Chinat, Box 1984. NARA.

397 *American policy toward Asia:* Richard Nixon, "Asia After Vietnam," *Foreign Affairs,* Oct 1967.

NOTES FOR CHAPTER TWENTY-TWO

398 *If when I die:* Congressional Record—Senate, 21 Apr 1975, S6340; *NYT,* 16 Apr 1975, 17 Apr 1975; *London Times,* 17 Apr 1975. **Personal friendship:** Nixon, *Leaders,* 242–43. **Their own son:** Wang Fong, *Soong Meiling,* 342.

399 *Mysterious leather suitcase:* Wang Fong, *Soong Meiling,* 339–45. *If the US can recognize:* May 1969, RG 59, SNF (1967–69): Political Affairs & Relations Chinat-US, Box 1613. NARA. *He feels:* Kissinger to acting secretary of state, 15 May 1969. RG 59, Entry SNF (1967–69): Political Affairs & Relations Chinat-US, Box 1613. NARA. *Sad reunion:* MCKS to Wedemeyer, 24 April 1969. Box 31, Correspondence: CKS & MCKS, 1950–70. Wedemeyer Papers. Hoover. *Louis not very stable:* T. V. Soong to "Dear Sister," 22 Mar 1969. Soong Papers, 63.12. Hoover.

400 *Car accident:* Wang Fong, *Wo zai Jiang Jieshi fuzi shenbian,* 182–86. *Nixon offered assistance:* Ambassador McConaughy to Armstrong, 21 Nov 1969. RG 59, SNF (1967–69), Files Pol 15-1 Chinat, Box 1984. NARA. *Every day:* MCKS to General & Mrs. Wedemeyer, 4 Apr 1970. Box 31, Correspondence: CKS & MCKS 1951–1970. Wedemeyer Papers. Hoover.

401 *Taipei on the defensive:* Ralph Clough, interview with author, 6 Jul 1998. *Democracy a façade:* Mancall, 60.

402 *Double heresy:* Mancall, 62–64, 126. *Land reforms:* Mancall, 5, 59, 75. *China Lobby book banned:* Koen, ix.

403 *Strong interest:* L. C. Meeker, "China," draft, 14 May 1964. RG 59, SNF (1964–66), Poll Chinat-US, Box 2040. NARA. *Kissinger protested Peng's arrest:* ttp://students .washington.cdu/taiwanuw/peng/dr_mingmin_peng.htm. *Popeye cartoon:* http://en .wikipedia.org/wiki/Bo_Yang.

404 *Handful of people who are dissatisfied:* Memorandum, 6 May 1970. RG 59, SNF (1970–73), Pol 7 Chinat, Box 2202. NARA. **Time issue banned:** AmEmbassy Taipei to Department of State, 20 May 1970. RG 59, SNF (1970–73), Pol 15-1 Chinat, Box 2203. NARA. *Independence movement a Communist plot:* AmEmbassy Taipei to Department of State, 5 Jun 1970. RG 59, SNF (1970–73), Pol 15-1 Chinat, Box 2203. NARA. *New page:* Ray Cline to Acting Secretary Irwin, Intelligence Brief, "Communist-China/US: Peking's People's Diplomacy: A 'New Page' in Sino-American Relations," 14 Apr 1971. http://www.gwu.edu/~nsarchiv/NSAEBB/NSAEBB66/ch-13.pdf. *Entering a new stage:* AmEmbassy Taipei to SecState, 15 Apr 1971. RG 59, SNF (1970–73), Pol 18—Chinat, Box 2204. NARA.

405 *Fear of United Front trap:* AmEmbassy Taipei to SecState, 30 Apr 1971. RG 59, SNF (1970–73), Pol 7—Chinat, Box 2202. NARA. *T. V. Soong's estate:* Soong's will can be found in probate records held at the New York County Surrogate's Court, 31 Chambers Street, New York City. There is a copy in the Soong Papers at Hoover. See also William S. Youngman to Sterling Seagrave, 18 Mar 1985. Soong Papers, 64.2. Hoover. *Summer of 1971 difficult:* MCKS to Mrs. T. V. Soong, 1 Sep. 1971. Soong Papers, 63.13. Hoover.

406   *Cannot trick us:* Record of Nixon-Kissinger telephone conversation discussing Zhou's message and possible envoys to China, 27 Apr 1971, 3. http://www.gwu.edu/~nsarchiv/NSAEBB/NSAEBB66/ch-18.pdf. *Great wound:* Memcon, Kissinger and Zhou, 11 Jul 1971, 11. www.gwu.edu/~nsarchiv/NSAEBB/NSAEBB66/ch-38.pdf. *Take care of itself:* Memcon, Kissinger, and Zhou, 10 July 1971, Afternoon (12:10 p.m.-6:00 p.m.), with cover memo by Lord, 6 Aug 1971, 16. www.gwu.edu/~nsarchiv/NSAEBB/NSAEBB66/ch-35.pdf. *Whatever the future may hold:* quoted in Aitken, 428. *Thunderstruck:* AmEmbassy Taipei to SecState, 23 Jul 1971. RG 59, SNF (1970–73), Pol 15-2 Chinat, Box 2203. NARA. *Taiwanese reaction ambivalent:* Intelligence Note, 15 Feb 1972. RG 59, SNF (1970–73), Pol 1—Chinat, Box 2202. NARA. *Nixon later wrote of Chiang:* Nixon, *Leaders*, 242. *I deeply regret:* Department of State to Ambassador McConaughy, 17 Jul 1971. RG 59, SNF (1970–73), Pol 15-1 Chinat, Box 2203. NARA.

407   *Nixon ungrateful:* quoted in Wang Fong, *Soong Meiling*, 98. *Kung's tyrannicide thesis:* Kung's dissertation is held at Boston Public Library, Miami University (Ohio), and Tamkang University on Taiwan.

408   *The Chinese race would not be betrayed twice:* Wang Fong, *Song Meiling*, 97–98; *Zhongguo Shibao*, 17 Mar 1997. *Long Live the President:* *NYT*, 11 Oct 1971.

409   *Chiang feared Nixon would be embarrassed:* AmEmbassy Taipei to SecState, 15 Oct 1971. RG 59, SNF (1971–72), DEF-1 Chinat-US, Box 1698. NARA. *Guo you guoge:* Fredrick Chien, interview with author, 5 Feb 1998.

410   *The anus incident:* Wang Fong, *Wo zai Jiang Jieshi fuzi shenbian*, 187–90. *Sense of shared fate:* Intelligence Note, 15 Feb 1972. RG 59, SNF (1970–73), Pol 1—Chinat, Box 2202. NARA. *Temporary setback:* AmEmbassy Taipei to SecState, 3 Jan 1972. RG 59, SNF (1970–73), Pol 15-1 Chinat, Box 2203. NARA. *We are troubled:* MCKS to Mrs. Wedemeyer, 7 Jan 1972. Box 31, Correspondence: CKS & MCKS 1971–1988, Wedemeyer Papers. Hoover.

411   *Mao robust:* Nixon, *Leaders*, 238, 241. *Chiang never expressed reciprocal respect:* *Leaders*, 241–42. *The history of our friendship with him:* Nixon, *Leaders*, 241. *Madame Chiang was civilized:* Nixon, *Leaders*, 242–43. *Why did you not come:* Nixon, *Leaders*, 2430.

412   *Shanghai Communiqué:* www.taiwandocuments.org/communique01 *This was the week that changed the world:* Aitken, 432. *Hand-holding operation:* Frank Burnet, FAOHP. Georgetown.

413   *Selfish preservation:* AmEmbassy Taipei to Department of State, 24 Mar 1972. RG 59, SNF (1970–73), Pol Chinat, Box 2202. NARA. *Shameful and deplorable:* *NYT*, 20 Apr 1972. *What is of import:* MCKS to EDM, 8 Jun 1972. Mills Papers. WCA. *Chiang fell into coma:* Wang Fong, *Wo zai Jiang Jiesh fuzi shenbian*, 208–10.

414   *I must do something:* AmEmbassy Taipei to Department of State, 10 Apr 1970. RG 59, SNF (1970–73), Pol 15-1 Chinat, Box 2203. NARA. *Ten Commandments:* AmEmbassy Taipei to Department of State, 13 Sep 1972. RG 59, SNF (1970–73), Pol 15-1 Chinat, Box 2203. NARA.

415   *Stamps:* MCKS, "Anti-Practiced Moral Cowardice and Anti-Marginal Thinking," 17 Nov 1972. Class of 1917: MCKS—Speeches by MCKS (1950–72.) WCA.

416   *Let come what will come:* MCKS to Wedemeyer, 16 Apr 1973. Box 31: Correspondence: CKS & MCKS 1971–1988. Wedemeyer Papers. Hoover. *Prove:* Wang Fong, *Wo zai Jiang Jieshi fuzi shenbian*, 233. *Mastectomy:* *Far Eastern Economic Review*, 10 Oct 1975. *Fretted:* Wang Fong, *Wo zai Jiang Jieshi fuzi shenbian*, 235–36.

417   *Unlocking the doors:* *Los Angeles Times*, 11 Aug 1974. *Pearson diaries:* I-Chung Loh, interview with author, 12 Jan 1998.

418   *What has become:* MCKS, "We Do Beschrei It," 6 Mar 1975. Class of 1917: MCKS, Articles by Generalissimo & MCKS (1950–88). WCA. *Emotional earthquake:* Congressional Record—Senate, 21 Apr 1975, S6336. *Peanut planted:* Frank Burnet, FAOHP. Georgetown.

419   *Our nation's face:* Fang Yun-ho, interview with author, 30 Mar 1998. *Final glimpse:* Documentaries, *Zhang Xueliang,* Part 4.

420   *Intervention:* Anna Chennault, interview with author, 1 Jul 1998. *Benumbed state:* MCKS to Mrs. Wedemeyer, 3 May 1975. Wedemeyer Papers, Box 31. Hoover.

421   *Billy Graham, Wedemeyer laud Chiang:* Congressional Record—Senate, 21 Apr 1975, S6340; *NYT,* 16 Apr 1975, 17 Apr 1975; *London Times,* 17 Apr 1975. *Off on a trip:* MCKS to EDM, 13 May 1975. Mills Papers. WCA. *Memorial Park: Burlington Free Press,* 8 Jun 1980. *Madame Chiang's departure: Far Eastern Economic Review,* 10 Oct 1975; *London Times,* 17 Sep 1975; *NYT,* 18 Sep 1975; "News from China," 17 Sep 1975. Box 175, Judd Papers. Hoover.

422   *Better to leave:* Hsiung Wan, interview with author, 28 Feb 1998. *Slipped and fell:* MCKS to EDM, 15 Jun 1976. Mills Papers, WCA. *Medical treatment:* MCKS to Mrs. Wilber M. Brucker, 23 Sep 1976. Box 1: Correspondence 1956–76, MCKS. Brucker Papers, Michigan.

423   *I shall return home: NYT,* 4 Nov 1976. *In retrospect:* "Rediscovering Lost History: Reunification Endeavors in 1975" (translated from Guangming Ribao, 11 Oct 2002). www.china.org.cn/english/2002/oct/45515.htm. MCKS to Wedemeyer, 26 Jan 1977. Box 31, Wedemeyer Papers. Hoover.

424   *Kung moved to Houston: Houston Chronicle,* 13 May 1997. *Louis Kung's bunker: Houston Business Journal,* 15 Dec 2003; *Montgomery County News,* 29 Sep 2004, 6 Oct 2004. *Madame in seclusion: NYT,* 19 May 1978. *Madame Chiang's apartment:* After Madame Chiang's death the duplex at 10 Gracie Square was sold to William S. Taubman, a shopping center developer, for an estimated $12.5 million. (www.nytimes.com, 20 Jun 2004.)

425   *Christopher's trip to Taipei:* Leonard Unger, 81–83, FAOHP. Georgetown.

426   *Genocide: NYT,* 20 Jul 1979.

NOTES FOR CHAPTER TWENTY-THREE

427   *Ching Ling wished to see Mayling:* "Rediscovering Lost History: Reunification Endeavors in 1975" (from *Guangming Ribao*), www.china.org.cn. *Comrade Soong Ching Ling's death: NYT,* 30 May 1981.

428   *Manipulated and used:* MCKS to Albert Wedemeyer, 26 Jul 1980. Box 31: Correspondence: CKS & MCKS 1971–88, Wedemeyer Papers. Hoover. *Birthday congratulations:* MCKS to Mrs. Douglas MacArthur, 20 Dec 1980. Box 31, Wedemeyer Papers. Hoover. *Amelioration:* MCKS to General & Mrs. Albert C. Wedemeyer, 10 Jan 1981. Box 31, Wedemeyer Papers. Hoover. *What really has the US benefited:* MCKS to Dr. Walter Judd, 6 Mar 1982. Judd Papers. Hoover. *Letter to Reagan:* MCKS to "Mr. President," 10 May 1982; Ronald Reagan to MCKS, 13 Aug 1982. WHORM casefile ND016:087862. Reagan Library.

429   *Knot in our relationship:* Cannon, 481. *Mayling's reply to Deng Yingchao's letter: Asian Outlook,* Apr 1984. *Wrong and unnecessary:* MCKS to General A. C. Wedemeyer, 9 Apr 1984. Box 31, Wedemeyer Papers. Hoover.

430   *Disobedient patient: China Times,* 25 Nov 2002. *Ching-kuo consulted Madame:* Fredrick Chien, interview with author, 5 Feb 1998.

431 *Teach him a lesson:* David Dean, interview with author, 2 Jul 1998.

432 *Teflon Buddha: Washington Post,* 12 Dec 1985. *Management of the economy:* Rubinstein, 324.

433 *Periods of great tension:* MCKS, "*Sursum Corda,*" *China Post,* 6 Dec 1986. *Chiang's hundredth birthday:* His official birthday was October 31, 1887, but in accordance with Chinese custom the centennial was celebrated a year early. *Although living abroad: Los Angeles Times,* 1 Nov 1986.

434 *Clodhopping boorishness:* MCKS, "*Sursum Corda.*" *China Post,* 6 Dec 1986. *Attacked media:* MCKS, "And Shall It Be See Ye To It?" *China Post,* 9 Dec 1986.

435 *Intimately holding hands: Wall Street Journal,* 3 Feb 1988. *This man is a Christian: Ziyou Shibao,* 22 Sep 1991.

437 *Loyal to the party and a patriot: Taipei Times,* 16 May 2004. *I supported him at the beginning: Ziyou Shibao,* 22 Sep 1991. *Was she fully cognizant: Ziyou Shibao,* 30 Jan 1988.

438 *I hope: China Post,* 10 June 1988. *Kuomintang's glorious history: NYT,* 9 Jul 1988. *Madame's party congress speech: China Post,* 9 Jul 1988; "Madame Chiang Kai-shek's Address," courtesy *China Post;* Taiwanese newspapers.

440 *Foreigner in her own land: The Journalist Weekly,* 6–19 Feb 1989.

441 *This is my country: Ziyou Shibao,* 29 Aug 1990; *Zili Zaobao,* 29 May 1989. *I pray that the regime run amok: China Post,* 6 Jun 1989.

442 *Satanic carnage: China Post,* 13 Jun 1989; partial copy of speech, courtesy *China Post.*

NOTES FOR CHAPTER TWENTY-FOUR

443 *Women's League:* Cecilia Koo, interview with author, 2 Mar 1998. *Women's League financed by import taxes: Ziyou Shibao,* 9 Apr 1995; *Minzhong Ribao,* 8 Aug 1997.

444 *Sinner of sinners:* unidentified newspaper clipping. 11 Dec 1990. *Women duibuqi Hanqing: United Daily News,* 6 Mar 1999. *Zhang believed Madame Chiang saved his life: United Daily News,* 6 Mar 1999. *Madame Chiang denounced violence: China Post,* 18 Apr 1991. *MCKS calls for return of Chinese antiquities:* unidentified newspaper article, circa July 1991.

445 *Jennie was a nice lady: China Post,* n.d.

446 *Shenyang mayor invited Young Marshal to visit: Central Daily News,* 5 Sep 1997.

448 *Loses her own soul:* Lu Keng, interview with author, 26 January, 1998. *Political hallucinogenic drugs:* 25 July 1995, Reuter.

449 *Slap in the face:* Taiwan Communique No. 66, June 1995. www.taiwandc.org. *I thought she was dead: NYT,* 24 Jul 1995.

450 *I'm happy that you remember an old friend: Los Angeles Times,* 27 Jul 1995. *When the Chinese people are considering: China News,* 28 Jul 1995. *My grandmother was very happy: China News,* 29 Jul 1995.

451 *I'll break the cameras:* Associated Press, 12 Mar 1996; *NYT,* 12 Mar 1996. *She spoke with majesty:* Associated Press, 12 Mar 1996; *Time,* 25 Mar 1996.

452 *Whipped by the enemy: China News,* 24 Aug 1996. *Anonymous donation to Wesleyan: Wesleyan College News,* Summer 1997.

453 *Chiang's alleged infertility hurtful nonsense: China Times,* 5 Oct 1997. Rosamond Kung's assertion that Mayling miscarried during the October 1937 car accident is perplexing. It seems unlikely that after one or more miscarriages, Mayling would have been crossing a war zone. It is more likely that she would have headed to the relative safety of Hong Kong for the duration of her pregnancy—if indeed she was pregnant. *His-*

torical revisionists: United Daily News, 14 Dec 1997. *Madame's urticaria:* Hsiung Wan, interview with author, 28 Feb 1998. *Instructed Women's League to donate $3 million: United Daily News,* 24 Sep 1999.

454 *Cockroach infestation:* David Patrick Columbia's Social Diary, 27 Oct 2003. www.newyorksocialdiary.com/socialdiary/2003/socialdiary10_27_03.php.

455 *Is there a problem: China Times,* 28 Mar 1999. *God is with me:* Cecilia Koo, interview with author, 2 Mar 1998. *Why does God: Zhongguo Shibao,* 3 Mar 1998. *Louis Kung's death:* Kung lost his bunker and office complex in 1987 after his company went bankrupt. His brother David, who controlled the Kung family assets, refused to bail him out. The complex was later purchased by real estate investors, and in the late 1990s, a group of Republic of Texas separatists considered buying it to serve as their new capital. As of 2005, the complex was being used as a data storage facility. *Houston Business Journal,* 15 Dec 2003; *Montgomery County News,* 29 Sep 2004, 6 Oct 2004. *Madame refused to see John Chang: United Daily News,* 27 Jan 1998, 9 Feb 1998. In the summer of 2000, John Chang returned to the mainland in search of his Chiang family roots. He was welcomed by the extended clan in the ancestral village of Xikou, in Fenghua county, Zhejiang province. But he remained persona non grata with the Chiang family. In March 2005, not long after the death of Faina Chiang in December 2004, John Chang announced that he had officially changed his name to Chiang, and his children would follow suit.

456 *Hillcrest sold:* (Long Island) *Newsday,* 17 Aug 1998. *Underestimated:* Reuters, 30 Jan 1999; Artnet.com, 8 Feb 1999; (Locust Valley) *Leader,* 17 Dec 1998.

458 *In a pure wind: Asiaweek,* Mar 2000. *Madame Chiang's letter: United Daily News,* 15 Mar 2000; *Taipei Times,* 15 Mar 2000; Associated Press, 14 Mar 2000. *Authenticity of letter:* Hau Pei-tsun, interview with author, 5 Jul 2000.

459 *Madame Chiang not told of election result:* Ibid. *Sun Li-jen exonerated: Taipei Times,* 10 Jan 2001. *Why aren't you clapping: China Times,* 27 Mar 2002.

460 *Close friend:* www.whitehouse.gov, 24 Oct 2003.

461 *Human treasure: Taipei Times,* 25 Oct 2003, 26 Oct 2003; *Taiwan News* 26 Oct 2003. *Twentieth century's most evil woman: Taipei Times,* 27 Oct 2003. *Chinese cuisine: China Times,* 26 Oct 2003; *Taiwan News,* 26 Oct 2003. Lee, it should be noted, was not averse to favors himself. While president, he accepted from a Taiwanese businessman a gift of an expensive luxury house on an elite golf course and, when criticized, insisted there was nothing wrong with his action. He also steered Taiwan on a course of "pragmatic diplomacy," a cornerstone of which amounted to buying diplomatic recognition from mostly small poor countries with dictatorial regimes. He once publicly offered the United Nations $2 billion in return for granting Taiwan membership. *Noted and influential person:* Associated Press, 25 Oct 2003.

462 *Pride of the Chinese nation: Taipei Times,* 26 Oct 2003. *She devoted her entire life: Taipei Times,* 28 Oct 2003.

464 *History will be kind:* www .quotationspage.com/quotes/Sir_Winston_ Churchill/.

NOTES FOR EPILOGUE

465 *My name:* From the 1817 sonnet "Ozymandias of Egypt."

467 *For me:* Konshin Shah, interview with author, 3 Mar 1998.

469 *Alienated her fellow countrymen:* For many of the ideas in this and the next several paragraphs I am indebted to Wang Ke-wen.

474   *Human feelings:* Eastman, 295.

476   *God gave the Savior:* quoted in *Hitler's Elite: Shocking Profiles of the Reich's Most Notorious Henchmen,* Berkeley Books, 1990. Cited on www.nobeliefs.com/henchmen.htm. *Protest:* from *Hamlet,* Act III, Scene ii, line 239.

477   *Narcissistic traits: Diagnostic and Statistical Manual of Mental Disorders, Fourth Edition (DSM-IV).* American Psychiatric Association, Washington, DC, 1994. Reproduced at http://behavenet.com/capsules/disorders/narcissisticpd.htm. *Chloral hydrate used to ease withdrawal:* Miller, 79–81.

478   *Narcotics addict:* quoted in Haynes and Klehr, 214. *Medication use is often the culprit:* Supriya Varadarajulu, "Urticaria and Angiodema." *Postgraduate Medicine,* May 2005, Vol. 117, Issue 5, 25-31. *Chronic fatigue syndrome once called neurasthenia:* B. Evengard et al. "Chronic Fatigue Syndrome: New Insights and Old Ignorance," *Journal of Internal Medicine,* Nov 1999, Vol. 246, Issue 5, 455–69.

479   *Madame Chiang's health problems:* For insights on this subject I am indebted to Mavis Humes Baird, a psychotherapist living in New York City.

480   *Feminist:* Chinese News Service, 28 Aug 1958. Box 28: CKS & MCKS. Kohlberg Papers. Hoover.

Bibliography

Manuscripts

AH   Academia Historica, Taipei
                       Chiang Kai-shek Papers (Jiang Zhongzheng Zongtong Dang'an)
                              Jiashu
                              Tejiaowenjian

Archives Diplomatiques, Ministère des Affaires Étrangères, Paris

British Library   Oriental & India Office (OIO)
                       Diaries of Sir Alexander Frederick Whyte

Columbia   Butler Library, Columbia University
                       Oral History Research Office (OHRO)
                              Reminiscences of Marion Dickerman, Paul Frillmann, Frank Rounds, Sebie Biggs Smith, Roger W. Straus, Dorothy R. Thomas, Col. John M. Williams
                       Rare Book and Manuscript Library (RBML)
                              ABMAC Collection
                              Peter & Edith Chang Papers
                              Chinese Oral History Project (COHP)
                                     Reminiscences of H. H. Kung, Li Han-hun, Franklin L. Ho, Tsiang T'ing-fu, Tso Shun-sheng, K. C. Wu
                              Ginny Connor Papers
                              Harold K. Hochschild Papers
                              VK Wellington Koo Papers
                              Henry A. Wallace Diary

CHS   Connecticut Historical Society
                       Chinese Educational Mission Papers

Cornell   Rare & Manuscript Collections, Carl A. Kroch Library, Cornell University
                       James Marshall McHugh Papers
                       William Reginald Wheeler Papers

Duke	Rare Book, Manuscript, and Special Collections Library, Duke University
	Charles Jones Soong Papers
	Duke University Archives
	Charles Jones Soong Collection
Eisenhower	Dwight D. Eisenhower Library
	DDE: Papers as President of the U.S., 1953–1961 (Eisenhower Papers)
	White House Social Office, Records 1952–61
	John Foster Dulles Papers
	C. D. Jackson Papers
Emory	Special Collections, Robert W. Woodruff Library, Emory University
	Young John Allen Papers
	William B. Burke Papers
FDR	Franklin D. Roosevelt Memorial Library
	Anna Eleanor Roosevelt Papers
	Lauchlin Currie Papers
Georgetown	Lauinger Library, Georgetown University
	Fulton Oursler Papers
	Grace Perkins Oursler (GPO) Papers
	Thomas Murray Wilson Papers
	Foreign Affairs Oral History Project (FAOHP): Oscar Armstrong, Arthur Hummel, Walter E. Jenkins, David L. Osborn
Harvard	Schlesinger Library, Radcliffe Institute, Harvard University
	Frances Fineman Gunther Papers
	Theodore H. White Papers
HKPRO	Hong Kong Public Records Office
Hoover	Hoover Institution Archives, Stanford University
	Claire L. Chennault Papers
	Lauchlin Currie Papers
	Walter H. Judd Papers
	Alfred Kohlberg Papers
	George E. Sokolsky Papers
	T. V. Soong Papers
	Nym Wales Papers
	Albert C. Wedemeyer Papers
Indiana	Manuscripts Department, Lilly Library, Indiana University
	Emily Hahn Papers
	Frank E. Taylor Papers
	Wendell Willkie Papers

Weil Journalism Library, Indiana University
   Roy W. Howard Archive

KMT   Kuomintang (Nationalist Party) Archives, Taipei, Taiwan
   Madame Chiang Kai-shek's 1943 Trip to the United States (a collection of newspaper clippings)
   Photograph collections

LOC   Manuscript Division, Library of Congress
   W. Averell Harriman Papers
   Roy W. Howard Papers
   Nelson T. Johnson Papers
   Owen Lattimore Papers
   Clare Boothe Luce Papers
   Henry Luce Papers
   NAACP Records

Marshall   George C. Marshall Foundation
   George C. Marshall Papers
   Frank Price Papers

Michigan   Bentley Historical Library, University of Michigan
   Clara Brucker Papers

NARA   National Archives and Records Administration

Nixon   Richard Nixon Library and Birthplace, Yorba Linda, California

NML   Nehru Memorial Library, New Delhi
   Jawaharlal Nehru Papers

NYPL   New York Public Library
   Farrar, Straus & Giroux (FSG) Papers

Piedmont   Piedmont College Archives

Princeton   Rare Books and Special Collections, Seeley G. Mudd Manuscript Library, Princeton University
   Karl L. Rankin Papers

Reagan   Ronald Reagan Presidential Library, Simi Valley, California

SOAS   School of African & Oriental Studies, University of London

Southampton   Special Collections, Hartley Library, University of Southampton
   Papers of Louis, Earl Mountbatten of Burma

TNA   Public Record Office, The National Archives of the United Kingdom
   Cabinet Office Files (CAB)
   Foreign Office Files (FO)
   Prime Minister's Office Files (PREM)
   War Office Files (WO)

Truman   Truman Library
                       President's Secretary's Files (PSF)
                       Truman Papers
                       John F. Melby Papers
                       Oral History Interviews: O. Edmund Clubb,
                       Edwin A. Locke, John F. Melby
UNC   University of North Carolina at Chapel Hill
                       Southern Historical Collection
                       Julian S. Carr Papers
                       Mena F. Webb Papers
WCA   Wellesley College Archives, Wellesley College
                       Emma DeLong Mills [EDM] Papers
                       Hetty Shepard Papers
                       Class of 1917 Papers
Wesleyan   Wesleyan College Archives
                       Soong Collection

Interviews

Anna Chennault, Fredrick Chien, Chang Chun-ting, Chin Hsiao-yi, Chow
    Lien-hwa, Ralph Clough, David Dean, Ann Maria Domingos, Fang Yun-
    ho, Hau Pei-tsun, Hsiung Wan, Arthur Hummel, I Fu-en, Cecilia Koo,
    Lin Chien-yeh, I-Cheng Loh, Lu Keng, Margaret Pei, Robert L. Scott,
    Konshin Shah, William Wells.

Documentaries

Zhang Xueliang, 1901–2001: A Century of Memories of the Young Marshal.
    Documentary. Interviews by Guo Guanying, Zhou Yukou. Produced by
    Dahao Broadcasting Company. Released by Himalaya Foundation.
    Copyright © Himalaya Foundation, 2001.
Madame Chiang Kai-shek: A Legend Across Three Centuries (Shiji Soong Meiling).
    Produced and released by (Taiwan) Public Television Cultural
    Foundation, [ca. 2003].

Articles

Ainsworth, Mrs. W. N. "Mayling Soong as a Schoolgirl." Soong Collection,
    Wesleyan.
Alsop, Joseph. "Why We Lost China," Parts 1–3. *The Saturday Evening Post,* 7,
    14, and 21 Jan 1950.
Chen Jinjin. "Cong Aiji kan Jiang, Soong qingai," *Jindai Zhonggou Funu Yanjiu,*
    Vol. 11 (Dec 2003). Institute of Modern History, Academia Sinica.
Chiang, Soong Mayling. "What Religion Means to Me." *Forum,* Mar 1934.

Dirlik, Arif. "The Ideological Foundations of the New Life Movement: A Study in Counterrevolution." *Journal of Asian Studies*, Aug 1975.

Harrington, Jean. "Madame Chiang Kai-shek (Mei-ling Soong), '17." *The Wellesley Magazine*, Feb 1938.

Mygatt, Emmie [Donner]. "Fellow Student Recalls Early Days of Mei-ling Soong, Now Mme. Chiang Kai-shek." *Washington Post*, 6 Sept 1942.

Reinhardt, Grace K. "Knew Dictator's Wellesley Wife." *New York Sun*, 2 Jan 1937.

Shih, Chih-yu. "The Eros of International Politics: Madame Chiang Kai-shek and the Question of the State in China." Courtesy Shih Chih-yu.

Sokolsky, George E., "The Soongs of China." *Atlantic Monthly*, Feb 1937, 185–88.

Thomson, Eunice. "Wesleyan and the Soong Sisters." *Chattanooga Sunday Times*, 13 Mar 1938.

Tuell, Annie K. "Recollections by Miss Tuell, Miss Mills," n.d. Class of 1917: MCKS, General: Biographical Information. WCA.

Xu Youwei, and Billingsley, Philip. "Behind the Scenes of the Xi'an Incident: The Case of the Lixingshe." *China Quarterly*, Jun 1998.

Other Sources

Congressional Record, U.S. Government Printing Office

Foreign Relations of the United States, Department of State, Washington, D.C. *(Foreign Relations)*

New York Times (NYT)

Books

Abell, Tyler. *Drew Pearson Diaries 1949–59*. New York: Holt, Rinehart & Winston, 1974.

Abend, Hallett. *My Life in China: 1926–41*. New York: Harcourt Brace, 1943.

Acheson, Dean. *Sketches from Life of Men I Have Known*. New York: Harper, 1961.

———. *Present at the Creation: My Years in the State Department*. New York: Norton, 1969.

Aitken, Jonathan. *Nixon: A Life*. Washington, D.C.: Regnery Publishing, 1993.

Alsop, Joseph W. *I've Seen the Best of It: Memoirs*. New York: Norton, 1992.

Ambrose, Stephen E. *Nixon*. New York: Simon & Schuster, 1987.

Auden, W. H., and Isherwood, Christopher. *Journey to a War*. London: Faber & Faber, 1973.

Ball, Terrence, and Dagger, Richard. *Political Ideologies and the Democratic Ideal*. New York: Longman, 1998.

Bays, Daniel H., ed. *Christianity in China: From the Eighteenth Century to the Present*. Palo Alto, Calif.: Stanford University Press, 1996.

Beal, John Robinson. *Marshall in China*. Garden City, N.Y.: Doubleday, 1970.

Belden, Jack. *China Shakes the World*. London: Victor Gollanz, 1951.

Bergère, Marie-Claire. *The Golden Age of the Chinese Bourgeoisie, 1911–1937*. Translated by Janet Lloyd. New York: Cambridge University Press, 1989.

———. *Sun Yat-sen*. [Paris], Fayard, 1994,

Berkov, Robert. *Strong Man of China: The Story of Chiang Kai-shek*. New York: Books for Libraries Press, 1970.

Bidault, Georges. *Resistance: The Political Antobiography of Georges Bidault* (translated from the French by Marianne Sinclair). New York: F. A. Praeger, 1967.

Bland, Larry I., ed. *George C. Marshall's Mediation Mission to China*. Lexington, Va.: George C. Marshall Foundation, 1998.

Booker, Edna Lee. *Flight From China*. New York: Macmillan, 1945.

———. *News Is My Job: A Correspondent in War-Torn China*. New York: Macmillan, 1940.

Bright, J. *Madame Chiang Kai-shek*. Lahore, India: Hero Publications, 1943.

Buck, Pearl S. *China As I See It*. New York: John Day, 1970.

Burke, James. *My Father in China*. New York: Farrar & Rinehart, 1942.

Caniff, Milton. *Terry and the Pirates: China Journey*, New York: Nostalgia Press, 1977.

Cannon, Lou. *President Reagan: The Role of a Lifetime*. New York: Simon & Schuster, 1991.

Carlson, Evans F. *Twin Stars of China*. New York: Dodd, Mead & Company, 1940.

Chang, Iris. *Rape of Nanking*. New York: Basic Books, 1997.

Chang, Jung. *Mme Sun Yat-sen (Soong Ching-ling)*. London: Penguin, 1986.

Ch'en, Chieh-ju. *Chiang Kai-shek's Secret Past: The Memoir of His Second Wife, Chen Chieh-ju*. Lloyd E. Eastman, ed. Boulder, Colo.: Westview Press, 1993.

Chiang, Kai-shek. *All We Are and All We Have: Speeches and Messages Since Pearl Harbor. December 9, 1941–November 17, 1942*. New York: Chinese News Service, 1948.

Chiang, Kai-shek, and Chiang Kai-shek, Madame. *China at the Crossroads*. New York: Doubleday, Doran, 1937.

———. *China in Peace and War*. London: Hurst & Blackett, 1940.

———. *China Shall Rise Again*. London: Hurst & Blackett, 1941.

———. *Conversations with Mikhail Borodin*. [Taipei]: World Anti-communist League, 1977.

———. *Leaves from a Book of Travels*. n.d.

———. *Madame Chiang Kai-shek: Selected Speeches 1943–1982*. No publisher listed.

———. *Madame Chiang Kai-shek: Selected Speeches 1958–1959*. No publisher listed.

———. *Selected Speeches*. Taipei: Government Information Office, 1957.

———. *The Sure Victory*. Westwood, N.J.: Fleming H. Revell, 1955.

————. *This Is Our China.* New York and London: Harper & Brothers, 1940.

————. *War Messages and Other Selections.* Hankow: The China Information Committee, 1938.

————. *We Chinese Women: Speeches and Writings During the First United Nations Year (February 12, 1942–November 16, 1942).* New York: Chinese News Service, n.d.

Chin, Hsiao-yi, ed. *Zhongguo Xiandaishi Cidian.* Taipei: Jindai Zhongguo Chubanshe, 1985.

Chow, Tse-tsung. *The May Fourth Movement: Intellectual Revolution in Modern China.* Cambridge, Mass.: Harvard University Press, 1960.

Churchill, Winston S. *The Second World War.* Boston: Houghton Mifflin, 1950.

Clark, Elmer T. *The Chiangs of China.* New York: Abingdon-Cokesbury Press, ca. 1943.

Coble, Parks, Jr. *The Shanghai Capitalists and the Nationalist Government, 1927–1937.* Cambridge, Mass.: Harvard University Press, 1980.

Confucius. *The Analects.* Translated by D. C. Lau. London: Penguin Books, 1979.

Converse, Florence. *The Story of Wellesley.* Boston: Little, Brown, 1915.

Couling, Samuel. *Encyclopaedia Sinica.* Hong Kong: Oxford University Press, 1983.

Cowles, Fleur. *She Made Friends and Kept Them: An Anecdotal Memoir.* New York: HarperCollins, 1996.

Cowles, Gardner. *Mike Looks Back: The Memoirs of Gardner Cowles, Founder of Look Magazine.* New York: G. Cowles, 1985.

Cray, Ed. *General of the Army.* New York: Norton, 1990.

Crozier, Brian. *The Man Who Lost China: The First Full Biography of Chiang Kai-shek.* New York: Charles Scribner's Sons, 1976.

Curtis, Richard. *Chiang Kai-shek.* New York: Hawthorn Books, 1969.

Davies, John Paton. *Dragon by the Tail.* New York: Norton, 1972.

Davis, Benjamin O., Jr. *Benjamin O. Davis Jr., American: An Autobiography.* Washington, D.C.: Smithsonian Institution Press, 1991.

Dong, Stella. *Shanghai: The Rise and Fall of a Decadent City.* New York: William Morrow, 2000.

Dowd, Jerome. *The Life of Braxton Craven.* Durham, N.C.: Duke University Press, 1939.

Dumas, Freda Payne. *A Guerry Genealogy: Ancestors and Some Descendants of William Barnett Guerry.* Ozark, Mo.: Dogwood Printing, 1994.

Eastman, Lloyd E. *The Abortive Revolution: China Under Nationalist Rule, 1927–1937.* Cambridge, Mass.: Harvard University Press, 1990.

Eden, Anthony. *The Reckoning.* Boston: Houghton Mifflin, 1965.

Eisenhower, Dwight D. *Mandate for Change: 1953–56.* New York: Doubleday, 1963.

Epstein, Israel. *The Unfinished Revolution in China.* Boston: Little, Brown, 1947.

————. *Woman in World History: Life and Times of Soong Ching Ling (Mme. Sun Yat-sen)*. Beijing: New World Press, 1995.

Esherick, Joseph W., ed. *Lost Chance in China: The World War II Despatches of John S. Service*. New York: Random House, 1974.

Fairbank, John King. *China: A New History*. Cambridge, Mass.: Harvard University Press, 1992.

————. *The Missionary Enterprise in China and America*. Cambridge, Mass.: Harvard University Press, 1974.

Fenby, Jonathon. *Chiang Kai-shek: China's Generalissimo and the Nation He Lost*. New York: Carroll & Graf, 2003.

Furuya, Keiji. *Chiang Kai-shek: His Life and Times*. Abridged English edition by Chun-ming Chang. New York: St. John's University, 1981.

Gage, Berkeley. *It's Been a Marvelous Party!* 1989. Courtesy Gage family.

Gannett, Lewis S. *Young China*. New York: The Nation, 1927.

Gellhorn, Martha. *Travels with Myself and Another*. New York: Dodd Mead, 1978.

Gopal, S., ed. *Selected Works of Jawaharlal Nehru*. New Delhi: Orient Longman, 1972–82.

Gunther, John. *Inside Asia*. New York: Harper, 1939.

Hackett, Alice Payne. *Wellesley: Part of the American Story*. New York: E. P. Dutton, 1949.

Hahn, Emily. *Chiang Kai-shek: An Unauthorized Biography*. New York: Doubleday, 1955.

————. *China to Me*. New York: Doubleday, Doran, 1944.

————. *The Soong Sisters*. New York: Doubleday, Doran, 1943.

Han, Suyin. *Eldest Son*. New York: Kodansha International, 1994.

Haynes, John Earl, and Klehr, Harvey. *Venona: Decoding Soviet Espionage in America*. New Haven, Conn.: Yale University Press, 1999.

Holloway, Betsy. *Heaven for Beginners: Recollections of a Southern Town*. Orlando, Fla.: Persimmon Press, 1986.

Hook, Brian, ed. *The Cambridge Encyclopedia of China*. Cambridge, UK: Cambridge University Press, 1991.

Hsiung, S. I. *The Life of Chiang Kai-shek*. London: Peter Davies, 1948.

Jacobs, Dan N. *Borodin: Stalin's Man in China*. Cambridge, Mass.: Harvard University Press, 1981.

Jespersen, T. Christopher. *American Images of China: 1931–1949*. Palo Alto, Calif.: Stanford University Press, 1996.

Jordan, Donald A. *The Northern Expedition*. Honolulu: University Press of Hawaii, 1976.

Kerr, George. *Formosa Betrayed*. www.formosa.org/~taiwanpg/.

————. *Licensed Revolution and the Home Rule Movement 1895–1945*. Honolulu: University Press of Hawaii, 1974.

Kimball, Warren F., ed. *Churchill and Roosevelt: The Complete Correspondence*, Vol. 1. Princeton, N.J.: Princeton University Press, 1984.

Koen, Ross Y. *The China Lobby in American Politics*. New York: Octagon, 1974.

Koo, Madame Wellington. *No Feast Lasts Forever.* New York: Quadrangle, 1975.

Lai, Tse-han, Myers, Ramon H., and Wu, Wei. *A Tragic Beginning: The Taiwan Uprising of February 28, 1947.* Palo Alto, Calif.: Stanford University Press, 1991.

Lanc, Mary C. *Centennial History of Piedmont College: 1897–1997.* Demorest, Ga.: Piedmont College, 1997.

Lattimore, Owen. *China Memoirs: Chiang Kai-shek and the War Against Japan.* Tokyo: University of Tokyo Press, 1990.

Leonard, Royal. *I Flew for China.* Garden City, N.Y.: Doubleday, Doran, 1942.

Li, Ao. *Chiang Kai-shek: A Critical Biography.* Taipei, 1995.

Lin, Bowen. *Song Meiling: Kua shiji diyi furen.* Taipei: China Times Publishing, 2000.

Lin, Shiluan. *Wenchang Xianzhi.* Nanjing: Fangzhi Chubanshe, 2000.

Lin, Yinting. *Zhuisui Banshiji: Li Huan yu Chiang Jingguo Xiansheng.* Taipei: Tianxia Wenhua Chuban, 1998.

Liu, Jiaquan. *Song Qingling Zhuan.* Beijing: Zhongguo Wenlian Chuban Gongsi, 1995.

Loh, Pinchon P. Y. *The Early Chiang Kai-shek: A Study of His Personality and Politics.* New York and London: Columbia University Press, 1971.

MacArthur, Douglas. *Reminiscences.* New York: McGraw-Hill, 1964.

Mancall, Mark, ed. *Formosa Today.* New York: Frederick A. Praeger, 1964.

Mansergh, Nicholas, ed. *The Transfer of Power, Vol. 1.* London: H.M.S.O., 1970.

Marshall, George C. *George C. Marshall: Interviews and Reminiscences for Forrest C. Pogue.* Lexington, Va.: G. C. Marshall Research Foundation, 1991.

McClellan, Robert. *The Heathen Chinee: A Study of American Attitudes Toward China, 1890–1905.* Columbus: Ohio State University Press, 1971.

McCullough, David. *Truman.* New York: Simon & Schuster, 1992.

Merry, Robert W. *Taking on the World: Joseph and Stewart Alsop.* New York: Viking, 1996.

Miller, Richard Lawrence. *The Encyclopedia of Addictive Drugs.* Westport, Conn.: Greenwood Press, 2002.

Mims, Edwin. *History of Vanderbilt University.* Nashville, Tenn.: Vanderbilt University, 1946.

Moran, Lord. *Winston Churchill: The Struggle for Survival, 1940–65.* London: Constable, 1966.

Neal, Steve. *Dark Horse.* Lawrence: University of Kansas Press, 1989.

Nehru, Jawaharlal. *A Bunch of Old Letters.* New Delhi: Oxford University Press, 1988.

Neils, Patricia. *China Images in the Life and Times of Henry Luce.* Savage, Md.: Rowman & Littlefield, 1990.

Nicolay, Helen. *China's First Lady.* New York and London: D. Appleton-Century, 1944.

Nixon, Richard. *In the Arena: A Memoir of Victory, Defeat, and Renewal.* New York: Simon & Schuster, 1990.

————. *Leaders.* New York: Warner Books, 1982.

Oursler, Fulton. *Behold This Dreamer!* Boston: Little, Brown, 1964.

Parks, Lillian Rogers. *My Thirty Years Backstairs at the White House.* New York: Fleet, 1961.

Pepper, Suzanne. *Civil War in China: The Political Struggle, 1945–1949.* Lanham, Md.: Rowman & Littlefield, 1999.

Pickering, W. A. *Pioneering in Formosa.* Taipei: SMC Publishing, 1993.

Pogue, Forrest C. *George C. Marshall: Statesman 1945–1959.* New York: Viking, 1987.

Powell, William S., ed. *Dictionary of North Carolina Biography.* Chapel Hill: University of North Carolina Press, 1979.

Rand, Peter. *China Hands.* New York: Simon & Schuster, 1995.

Rankin, K. Lott. *China Assignment.* Seattle: University of Washington Press, 1964.

Roberts, Claudia P., et al. *The Durham Architectural and Historic Inventory.* Sponsored by the City of Durham and the Historic Preservation Society of Durham. Raleigh, N.C.: Robert M. Leary and Associates, 1982.

Rollyson, Carl. *Nothing Ever Happens to the Brave.* New York: St. Martin's, 1990.

Roosevelt, Eleanor. *This I Remember.* New York: Harper, 1949.

Rubinstein, Murray A., ed. *Taiwan: A New History.* Armonk, N.Y.: M. E. Sharpe, 1999.

Schiffrin, Harold Z. *Sun Yat-sen and the Origins of the Chinese Revolution.* Berkeley: University of California Press, 1968.

Scott, Robert L. Jr. *God Is My Co-Pilot.* Reynoldsburg, Ohio: [self-published], 1989.

Seagrave, Sterling. *Dragon Lady: The Life and Legend of the Last Empress of China.* New York: Vintage Books, 1992.

————. *The Soong Dynasty.* New York: Harper & Row, 1985.

Selle, Earl Albert. *Donald of China.* New York and London: Harper & Brothers, 1948.

Shaw, Yu-ming. *An American Missionary in China: John Leighton Stuart and Chinese-American Relations.* Cambridge, Mass., and London: Council on East Asian Studies, Harvard University, 1992.

Sherwood, Robert E. *Roosevelt & Hopkins: An Intimate History.* New York: Harper, 1948.

Smith, Jean Edward. *Lucius D. Clay: An American Life.* New York: Henry Holt, 1990.

Smith, Whitey, with C. L. McDermott. *I Didn't Make a Million.* Manila: Philippine Education Co., 1956. www.earnshaw.com/shanghai-ed-india/tales/t-wedding.

Snow, Edgar. *Journey to the Beginning.* New York: Random House, 1958.

————. *Red Star Over China.* New York: Grove Press, 1968.

Soong, Ching Ling. *The Struggle for New China*. Peking: Foreign Languages Press, 1953.

Spence, Jonathan D. *The Search for Modern China*. New York: Norton, 1990.

Steele, A. T. *The American People and China*. New York: McGraw-Hill, 1966.

Stilwell, Joseph W. *The Stilwell Papers*. Ed. by Theodore White. New York: W. Sloane Associates, 1948.

Stoler, Mark A. *George C. Marshall*. Boston: Twayne, 1989.

Stowe, Leland. *They Shall Not Sleep*. New York: Knopf, 1944.

Strong, Anna Louise. *China Fights for Freedom*. London: Lindsay Drummond, 1939.

Sues, Ilona Ralf. *Shark's Fins and Millet*. Boston: Little, Brown, 1944.

Sun, Yat-sen. *The Three Principles of the People*. Taipei: China Cultural Service, 1981.

Terrill, Ross. *Mao: A Biography*. New York: Simon & Schuster, 1993.

Thomson, David. *Showman: The Life of David O. Selznick*. New York: Knopf, 1992.

Thomson, James C., Jr. *While China Faced West: American Reformers in Nationalist China, 1928–1937*. Cambridge, Mass.: Harvard University Press, 1969.

Tong, Hollington K. *Dateline: China*. New York: Rockport Press, 1950.

Truman, Harry S. *Memoirs: Volume One*. New York: Doubleday, 1955.

———. *Memoirs: Volume Two*. New York: Doubleday, 1956.

Tuchman, Barbara W. *Stilwell and the American Experience in China*. New York: Macmillan, 1970.

Tully, Grace. *F.D.R., My Boss*. New York: Charles Scribner's Sons, 1949.

Utley, Freda. *China at War*. New York: John Day, 1939.

———. *Last Chance in China*. New York: Bobbs-Merrill, 1947.

Varg, Paul A. *The Making of a Myth: The United States and China 1897–1912*. East Lansing: Michigan State University Press, 1968.

———. *Missionaries, Chinese, and Diplomats: The American Protestant Missionary Movement in China, 1890–1952*. Princeton, N.J.: Princeton University Press, 1958.

Wakeman, Frederic, Jr. *Spymaster: Dai Li and the Chinese Secret Service*. Berkeley: University of California Press, 2003.

Wang, Fong. *Song Meiling: Meili yu aichou*. Taipei: Shu Hua Chuban, 1994.

———. *Wo zai Jiang Jieshi fuzi shenbian de sishisan nian: Weng Yuan koushu*. Beijing: Huawen Chubanshe, 2003.

Wang, Ke-wen. *Modern China: An Encyclopedia of History, Culture, and Nationalism*. New York and London: Garland Publishing, 1998.

Wang, Suijin, ed. *Jiang Jieshi Jia Shi*. Hong Kong: Jin Shi Chubanshe, 1989.

Webb, Mena. *Jule Carr: General Without an Army*. Chapel Hill: University of North Carolina Press, 1987.

White, Theodore H., and Jacoby, Annalee. *In Search of History*. New York: Harper & Row, 1978.

————. *Thunder Out of China.* New York: William Sloane, 1946.

Willkie, Wendell L. *One World.* New York: Limited Editions Club, 1944.

Wilson, James Harrison. *China: Travels and Investigations in the Middle Kingdom.* New York: D. Appleton, 1901.

Wu, Joseph Jaushieh. *Taiwan's Democratization: Forces Behind the New Momentum.* Hong Kong: Oxford University Press, 1995.

INDEX